Montmartre

0 kilometers 1
0 miles 0.5

Opéra Quarter

Tuileries Quarter

La Seine

Beaubourg and
Les Halles

The Marais

St-Germain-des-Prés

Ile de la Cité

Ile St-Louis

Latin Quarter

Luxembourg
Quarter

Jardin des Plantes
Quarter

asse

W9-AQN-418

Opéra Quarter
Pages 214–221

Montmartre
Pages 222–231

**Beaubourg and
Les Halles**
Pages 106–117

The Marais
Pages 92–105

**Luxembourg
Quarter**
Pages 170–175

Latin Quarter
Pages 150–161

**Jardin des Plantes
Quarter**
Pages 162–169

**Ile de la Cité and Ile
St.-Louis**
Pages 78–91

EYEWITNESS TRAVEL

PARIS

Penguin Random House

Project Editor Heather Jones
Art Editor Janis Utton
Editor Alex Gray
Designer Vanessa Hamilton
Design Assistant Clare Sullivan

Contributors
Chris Boicos, Michael Gibson, Douglas Johnson, Alan Tillier

Photographers
Max Alexander, Neil Lukas, Robert O'Dea

Illustrators
Stephen Conlin, Stephen Gyapay, Maltings Partnership

This book was produced with the assistance of Websters International Publishers.

Printed and bound in China

First American Edition, 1993

16 17 18 19 10 9 8 7 6 5 4 3 2 1

Published in the United States by
DK Publishing, 345 Hudson Street,
New York, New York 10014

**Reprinted with revisions 1994, 1995, 1997 (twice), 1999, 2000,
2001, 2002, 2003, 2004, 2005, 2006, 2007, 2008, 2009, 2010,
2011, 2012, 2013, 2014, 2015, 2016**

Copyright © 1993, 2016 Dorling Kindersley Limited, London
A Penguin Random House Company

Published in the UK by Dorling Kindersley Limited.

A catalog record for this book is available from the Library of Congress.

ISSN 1542-1554

ISBN 978-1-4654-4124-9

Throughout this book, floors are referred to in accordance
with European usage, i.e. the "first floor" is one flight up.

MIX
Paper from
responsible sources
FSC™ C018179
www.fsc.org

**The information in this DK Eyewitness Travel Guide
is checked annually.**
Every effort has been made to ensure that this book is as up-to-date as possible at
the time of going to press. Some details, however, such as telephone numbers,
opening hours, prices, gallery hanging arrangements, and travel information are
liable to change. The publishers cannot accept responsibility for any consequences
arising from the use of this book, nor for any material on third-party websites, and
cannot guarantee that any website address in this book will be a suitable source of
travel information. We value the views and suggestions of our readers very highly.
Please write to: Publisher, DK Eyewitness Travel Guides, Dorling Kindersley,
80 Strand, London, WC2R 0RL, UK, or email: travelguides@dk.com.

Front cover main image: The Eiffel Tower on the Champ de Mars

◀ Architect I. M. Pei's iconic glass pyramid that serves as the main entrance to the Musée du Louvre

Henri II (1547–59)

Introducing Paris

Pont Alexandre III

EYEWITNESS TRAVEL

PARIS

Main Contributor **Alan Tillier**

Opéra National de Paris Bastille

The Kiss by Rodin (1886)

Sacré-Coeur in Montmartre

An island in the Bois de Boulogne

Charles de Gaulle airport RER station

The Panthéon

HOW TO USE THIS GUIDE

This Eyewitness Travel Guide helps you get the most from your stay in Paris with the minimum of practical difficulty. The opening section, *Introducing Paris*, locates the city geographically, sets modern Paris in its historical context and explains how Parisian life changes through the year. *Paris at a Glance* is an overview of the city's specialties. The main sightseeing section of the book is *Paris Area by Area*. It describes all the main sights,

with maps, photographs, and detailed illustrations. In addition, eight planned walks take you to parts of Paris you might otherwise miss.

Carefully researched tips for hotels, stores and markets, restaurants and bars, sports, and entertainment are found in *Travelers' Needs*, and the *Survival Guide* has advice on everything from mailing a letter to riding the Metro.

Paris Area by Area

The city has been divided into 14 sightseeing areas. Each section opens with a portrait of the area, summing up its character and history, with a list of all the sights to be covered.

These are clearly located by numbers on an *Area Map*. This is followed by a largescale *Street by Street Map* focusing on the most interesting part of the area. Finding your way about

the section is made simple by the numbering system used throughout for the sights. This refers to the order in which they are described on the pages that complete the section.

Color-coding on each page makes the area easy to find in the book.

A locator map shows you where you are in relation to surrounding areas. The area of the *Street by Street Map* is highlighted.

Numbered circles pinpoint all the listed sights on the area map.

Recommended restaurants in the area are listed and plotted on the map.

1 Area Map
For easy reference, the sights in each area are numbered and located on an area map. To help the visitor, the map also shows metro and main RER stations and parking lots.

Stars indicate the sights that no visitor should miss.

Numbered sights, such as St.-Séverin ❸, are shown on this map.

A suggested route for a walk takes in the most attractive and interesting streets in the area.

2 Street by Street Map
This gives a bird's-eye view of the heart of each sightseeing area. The most important buildings are picked out in stronger color, to help you spot them as you walk around.

Paris at a Glance

Each map in this section concentrates on a specific theme: *Museums and Galleries; Places of Worship; Gardens, Parks, and Squares.* The top sights are shown on the map; other sights are described on the following two pages.

Each sightseeing area is color-coded.

Practical Information lists all the information you need to visit every sight, including a map reference to the Street Finder at the back of the book.

Numbers refer to each sight's position on the area map and its place in the chapter.

3 Detailed information on each sight

All important sights in each area are described in depth in this section. They are listed in order, following the numbering on the *Area Map.* Practical information on opening hours, telephone numbers, websites, admission charges, and amenities available is given for each sight. The key to the symbols used can be found on the back flap.

The Visitors' Checklist provides the practical information you will need to plan your visit.

The facade of each major sight is shown to help you spot it quickly.

Stars indicate the most interesting architectural details of the building, and the most important works of art or exhibits on view inside.

Numbered circles point out key features of the sight listed in a key.

4 Paris's major sights

These are given two or more full pages in the sightseeing area in which they are found. Historic buildings are dissected to reveal their interiors; and museums and galleries have color-coded floorplans to help you find important exhibits.

INTRODUCING PARIS

GREAT DAYS IN PARIS

Paris is a city packed with treasures and wonderful things to see and do. Here are itineraries for some of the best of the attractions, arranged first under themes and then by length of stay. Sightseers should manage everything on these itineraries, but the selections can also be dipped into for ideas. All sights are reachable by public transportation. Price guides on pages 10–11 are for two adults or for a family of two adults and two children, including admission charges and meals.

Artistic Treasures

Two adults
allow at least €220

- Fabulous art at the Louvre
- Lunch at chic Café Marly
- A visit to the Musée Rodin, the Musée Picasso or the Pompidou Center
- Dine at classy restaurant Mini Palais

Morning
Begin with the **Musée du Louvre** (pp122–9), one of the world's most impressive museums. Beat the crowds by using the little-known entrance at the Carrousel du Louvre (99 Rue de Rivoli). You could easily spend a whole day here, but if time is limited, pick up a floorplan and choose a few choice works to concentrate on.

Lunch
There are many eateries nearby, but the smart **Café Marly** (p299) offers an unbeatable setting in the Louvre courtyard. Revel in the cosy red velvet and gilt of the interior or, on warm days, sit in the outside gallery.

Afternoon
Choose from three destinations for the afternoon. If you're in a contemplative mood, head to the **Musée Rodin** (p191) for a soothing stroll in the sculpture garden and a pensive moment next to The Thinker. For modern masterpieces, visit the superb **Pompidou Center** (pp110–13), an intriguing inside-out building housing works from 1905 to the present day. Fans of Picasso shouldn't miss the superb **Musée Picasso** (pp100–101), set in a gorgeous mansion in the Marais.

Evening
The **Palais de Tokyo** (p205) is one of Paris's most adventurous exhibition spaces, and its multimedia displays are open until midnight. Round off the evening with dinner at **Le Mini Palais** (p301), a classy contemporary brasserie with a superb colonnaded terrace.

The entrance to Fauchon, a gastronomic temple on the Right Bank

Food Lovers' Paris

Two adults
allow at least €260

- Buy gourmet treats at La Grande Epicerie
- Lunch at an inventive modern bistro
- Dine at Frenchie

Morning
One of the best one-stop stores for gourmets is La Grande Epicerie at **Le Bon Marché** (p191), in St.-Germain, stocking a superb range of delicious edibles. Other specialty stores in the area include **Poilâne**, renowned for its bread, chocolatier **Richart**, and **Pierre Hermé** (for all, p327), which makes the best macaroons in Paris. Don't miss one of the local morning markets, such as atmospheric Place Monge (Wed, Fri, & Sun am), or head down Rue Mouffetard for the buzzing street market.

Lunch
St.-Germain-des-Prés has some wonderfully inventive modern bistros, few better than **Kitchen Galerie Bis** (p304).

Pyramide du Louvre, from across the fountain pools

◀ View of the market at Fontaine des Innocents by John James Chalon

Afternoon
Make your way to Place de la Madeleine, on the Right Bank, renowned for fabulous food emporiums **Fauchon** *(p327)* and **Hédiard** *(p327)*, plus other gourmet food stores. Enjoy a wine tasting at **Ô Chateau** *(p311)*, or head to the city's most sumptuous *salon de thé* at the **Musée Jacquemart-André** *(p211)*, in a perfectly preserved Haussmann-era mansion.

Evening
For dinner, try to snag a table at **Frenchie** *(p297)*, which serves contemporary French cuisine. If you can't get in, head over the road to **Frenchie Bar à Vins** *(p311)*.

Reflections in La Géode, a giant sphere at the Parc de la Villette

Paris with Children

Family of four
allow at least €180

- Visit the science museum and Parc de la Villette
- Explore the splendid Jardin des Plantes
- Go up the Eiffel Tower

Morning
La Cité des Enfants, the children's section of the science museum (**Cité des Sciences et de l'Industrie**; *pp240–41*) is great for receptive young minds. The museum's permanent exhibition is excellent, with plenty of hands-on activities, but be sure to reserve online. The **Parc de la Villette** *(pp238–9)* has playgrounds, a dragon slide,

and even a decommissioned submarine to explore. Have lunch at the Cité des Sciences or enjoy a picnic in the park.

Afternoon
Cross the river and explore the beautiful **Jardin des Plantes** *(p169)*, a botanical garden with a playground, hothouses, and a small zoo. Even more exciting than the live animals for some kids are the skeletons and stuffed animals in the **Muséum National d'Histoire Naturelle** *(p168)*. If energy levels are still high, make for the **Eiffel Tower** *(pp196–7)*, an irresistible draw to children. Reserve well in advance to avoid long lines. Or you could wait until nightfall, and time your trip to coincide with the lightshow on the changing of the hour, when thousands of lights twinkle for ten minutes. If you're feeling a little less ambitious, a good alternative is a visit to the **Arc de Triomphe** *(pp212–13)*, which also offers splendid panoramic views.

Riverside Parks and Gardens

Two adults
allow at least €69

- Berges de Seine
- Lunch on the Ile St.-Louis
- A walk to the Jardin du Luxembourg
- Take a balloon ride

From the Pont de l'Alma, stroll along the Berges de Seine, a riverside promenade on the Left Bank, comprising floating

Modern water sculpture and glasshouse, Parc André Citroën

gardens, cafés, and often workshops, food fairs, or open-air concerts. When you get to the Pont de la Concorde, either cross over to the elegant **Jardin des Tuileries** *(p132)* or carry on as far as the **Musée d'Orsay** *(pp146–9)* and hop on the batobus. Stop at **Notre-Dame** *(pp82–5)*, then head over to the tranquil **Ile St.-Louis** *(p79)* with its leafy docks.

Lunch
Have lunch at **Café St.-Régis** *(p296)*, on the Ile St.-Louis.

Afternoon
Strike south to the **Jardin du Luxembourg** *(p174)*, one of the city's loveliest parks. Laze on one of the metal chairs scattered around the central pond, or visit the **Musée du Luxembourg**, which hosts excellent art exhibitions. For some wonderful views over Paris, head west to the **Parc André Citroën** *(p245)* and take a tethered balloon ride.

A floral display in the Jardin des Plantes

The medieval Gothic cathedral of Notre-Dame

2 days in Paris

- Explore Ile St.-Louis and visit majestic Notre-Dame
- Admire Old Masters and antiquities in the Louvre
- Ascend the Eiffel Tower at sunset for fabulous views across the city

Day 1
Morning Explore tranquil Ile St.-Louis (*p79*), with its attractive stores and leafy *quais*, before crossing Pont St.-Louis to take in the glorious cathedral of **Notre-Dame** (*pp82–5*), with its buttresses and gargoyles. Head west across **Ile de la Cité** (*pp80–81*) to the Gothic jewel of **Sainte-Chapelle** (*pp88–9*).

Afternoon Walk over to the Right Bank and make for the **Musée du Louvre** (*pp122–9*), home to Leonardo da Vinci's *Mona Lisa* and countless other treasures. Stroll through the charming **Jardin des Tuileries** (*p132*) to the architectural set piece of **Place de la Concorde** (*p133*). Follow **Avenue des Champs-Elysées** (*p211*) as far as the **Arc de Triomphe** (*pp212–13*), which promises fabulous views from the top. Dine in **Montmartre** (*pp224–5*), where the **Sacré-Coeur** (*pp226–7*) is splendidly illuminated at night.

Day 2
Morning Explore the chic streets of the **Marais** (*pp94–5*), the historic Jewish Quarter around **Rue des Rosiers** (*p99*), and the beautiful **Place des Vosges** (*pp98–9*). Visit the splendid **Musée Picasso** (*pp100–101*), or take in the collection of modern art in the dazzling **Pompidou Center** (*pp110–13*).

Afternoon Cross over into **St.-Germain-des-Prés** (*pp138–9*), with its elegant boutiques and food stores. Take a stroll in the **Jardin du Luxembourg** (*p174*), then head over to Louis XIV's imposing **Hôtel des Invalides** (*pp186–7*). End your day with a visit to the **Eiffel Tower** (*pp196–7*). At sunset, the views from the top are unforgettable.

3 days in Paris

- See the Champs-Elysées and the Arc de Triomphe
- Enjoy the Impressionists in the Musée d'Orsay
- Climb up to Montmartre and Sacré-Coeur

Day 1
Morning Start your day in the charming **Café de Flore** (*p141*) in **St.-Germain-des-Prés** (*pp138–9*), which was at the heart of the city's intellectual life in the 1950s. Take in medieval **St.-Séverin** (*p158*) before crossing to the **Ile de la Cité** (*pp80–81*), site of the Gothic **Notre-Dame** (*pp82–5*) and **Sainte-Chapelle** (*pp88–9*) with its beautiful stained-glass windows. Nearby **Ile St.-Louis** (*p79*) is an oasis of calm and has the best ice-cream parlor in the city, **Maison Berthillon** (*p311*).

Afternoon Visit the huge **Musée du Louvre** (*pp122–9*), making a beeline for the works of the Old Masters in the Denon Wing. Walk through the pretty **Jardin des Tuileries** (*p132*) to the historic **Place de la Concorde** (*p133*), then catch a bus along the **Avenue des Champs-Elysées** (*p211*) to the **Arc de Triomphe** (*pp212–13*).

Day 2
Morning Devote your morning to the **Latin Quarter** (*pp152–3*), home to the stately **Panthéon** (*pp160–61*), the great **Sorbonne** university (*p159*), and the superb **Musée de Cluny – Musée National du Moyen Age** (*pp154–7*), which has the beautiful tapestry series *The Lady and the Unicorn*, and Roman baths beneath it. Peer down ancient **Rue Mouffetard** (*p168*) before taking a rest in the **Jardin du Luxembourg** (*p174*).

Afternoon Immerse yourself in the grandeur of the **Hôtel des Invalides** (*pp186–7*), the final resting place of Napoleon Bonaparte. Next stop is the **Musée d'Orsay** (*pp146–9*) and its collection of Impressionist masterpieces. Wind down with a stroll along the Berges de Seine, then pay a sunset visit to the **Eiffel Tower** (*pp196–7*).

Day 3
Morning Explore the vibrant **Marais** (*pp94–5*) and stop for a coffee in **Place des Vosges** (*pp98–9*), the city's most beautiful square. Head to the extraordinary **Pompidou Center** (*pp110–13*), with its world-class collection of modern art.

Main gallery of the Musée d'Orsay, converted from a train station into a museum

Afternoon Contemplate the **Palais-Royal** *(p130)*, the childhood home of Louis XIV, from the delightful **Jardin du Palais-Royal** *(p131)*. Duck in and out of the 19th-century passages off Rue Vivienne, with their quirky stores and wonderful decor, on your way to **Galeries Lafayette** *(p313)*, the classic Parisian department store. Take in the evening light from **Sacré-Coeur** *(pp226–7)* on top of **Montmartre** *(pp224–5)*.

5 days in Paris

- Visit the hauntingly beautiful Père-Lachaise cemetery

- Marvel at Frank Gehry's stunning Fondation Louis Vuitton

- Take a train to Versailles, Louis XIV's splendid palace

Day 1
Morning View Paris from atop the **Arc de Triomphe** *(pp212–13)* before walking east along the **Avenue des Champs-Elysées** *(p211)*. Cross the grand expanse of **Place de la Concorde** *(p133)* and the **Jardin des Tuileries** *(p132)* to the historic **Palais-Royal** *(p130)*, with its immaculate grounds and elegant arcades sheltering quirky stores.

Afternoon Get to know the islands of the Seine, **Ile St.-Louis** *(p79)* and **Ile de la Cité** *(pp80–81)*, where you'll find the Gothic masterpieces **Notre-Dame** *(pp82–5)* and **Sainte-Chapelle** *(pp88–9)*. While away the rest of the day in the spectacular **Musée du Louvre** *(pp122–9)*.

Day 2
Morning Move east across the vibrant **Marais** *(pp94–5)* district from the **Pompidou Center** *(pp110–13)*, with its fabulous modern art collection. Pause for a coffee in the elegant **Place des Vosges** *(p98–9)*.

Afternoon Visit the city's most famous cemetery, the **Cimetière du Père Lachaise** *(pp242–3)*,

to see the tombs of notable figures such as Chopin, Jim Morrison, and Oscar Wilde. Follow the **Canal St.-Martin** *(p237)* to the futuristic **Parc de la Villette** *(pp238–9)*. Take in the state-of-the-art **science museum** *(pp240–41)* or the fascinating **Musée de la Musique** *(p238)*, then catch a concert at the stunning **Philharmonie de Paris** *(p239)*.

Sunny café terrace in the elegant Marais

Day 3
Morning See the dazzling collection of Impressionist paintings at the **Musée d'Orsay** *(pp146–9)* and enjoy a coffee break in its stylish café. Walk on via the riverside promenade known as the Berges de Seine to the **Musée Rodin** *(p191)*, near the impressive **Hôtel des Invalides** *(pp186–7)*. For a change of scene, seek out **Rue Cler** *(p192)*, with its street market and bistros.

Afternoon Scale the **Eiffel Tower** *(pp196–7)*, then either visit the **Musée de l'Homme** *(p203)* in the **Palais de Chaillot** *(p202)*, or head out to the **Bois de Boulogne** *(p247)*, with its attractive gardens and

lakes, and visit the spectacular Frank Gehry-designed Fondation Louis Vuitton.

Day 4
Morning Spend the day out of the city, at magnificent **Versailles** *(pp250–55)*, Louis XIV's royal palace. Tour the sumptuous apartments on the first floor.

Afternoon Explore the palace's fabulous gardens, landscaped by André Le Nôtre, and the smaller **Grand Trianon** and **Petit Trianon** palaces *(p251)*.

Day 5
Morning Sample intellectual Paris in **Café de Flore** *(p141)* in **St.-Germain-des-Prés** *(pp138–39)*, a long-time haunt of writers and philosophers. Visit the **Latin Quarter** *(pp152–3)*, home of the sublime church of **St.-Séverin** *(p158)*, fine medieval art in the **Musée National du Moyen Age** *(pp154–7)*, the **Panthéon** *(pp160–61)* mausoleum, and the **Sorbonne** university *(p159)*. Step back in time on old **Rue Mouffetard** *(p168)* before having lunch in **Montparnasse** *(pp178–9)*.

Afternoon Relax in the **Jardin du Luxembourg** *(p174)*, then head north to the Right Bank and the opulent **Opéra Garnier** *(pp218–19)*. Treat yourself at **Galeries Lafayette** *(p313)*, then climb **Montmartre** *(p224–5)* to the ethereal **Sacré-Coeur** *(pp226–7)* to watch the sun set.

The beautiful formal gardens at Louis XIV's palace, Versailles

Putting Paris on the Map

Paris, the capital of France, is a city of over two million people covering 40.5 sq miles (105 sq km) of northern France. It is on the River Seine at the center of the Ile-de-France, the region that is home to 11.5 million people, around one-fifth of the French population. An important European business and cultural center, it is the focus of activity in the north of France.

Harwich

North Sea

Sheerness

Ramsgate

Zeebrug

Ostend (Oostende)

Dover

Channel Tunnel

Calais

A16

Dunkirk (Dunkerque)

Folkestone

A16

Boulogne

Rouba
Lille

Le Touquet

A26

D939

Lens

Dou

A16

Arras

Abbeville

A28

Amiens

A29

A29

Western Europe

NORWAY

SWEDEN

North Sea

DENMARK

UNITED KINGDOM

NETHERLANDS

POLAND

REP. OF IRELAND

BELGIUM

GERMANY

CZECH REPUBLIC

Atlantic Ocean

Paris

SLOVAKIA

FRANCE

SWITZ.

AUSTRIA

HUNGARY

SLOV.

CROATIA

BOSNIA HERZ.

SERBIA

ITALY

MONTEN.

KOS.

MAC.

PORTUGAL

SPAIN

ALBANIA

GREECE

Le Havre

Rouen

Beauvais

Compiè

A13

Seine

Chantilly

See inset map above

Caen

A28

A13

PARIS

A88 Argentan

N12

Dreux

Sées

Chartres

Fontainebleau

A6

A5

Key

Greater Paris

Freeway

Highway

Railroad

Country border

Nogent-le-Rotrou

A11

N20

A10

A19

For additional map symbols *see back flap*

0 kilometers   50

0 miles   50

Orléans

A77

Central Paris

This book divides Paris into 14 areas, comprising central Paris and the nearby area of Montmartre. Most of the sights covered in the book lie within these areas, each one of which has its own chapter. Each area contains a range of sights that convey some of its history and distinctive character. The sights of Montmartre, for example, reveal its village charm and its colorful history as a thriving artistic enclave. In contrast, Champs-Elysées is renowned for its wide avenues, expensive fashion houses and opulent mansions. Most of the city's famous sights are within reach of the heart of the city and are easy to get to on foot or by public transportation.

Dôme Church
The gilded Dôme Church (see pp188–9) lies at the heart of the Invalides.

Musée du Louvre
Right in the heart of Paris, adjacent to the River Seine and the Tuileries garden, lies the city's most impressive museum, with an unrivalled collection of artifacts from around the world (see pp122–9).

Eiffel Tower
Named after the engineer who designed and built it in 1889, the Eiffel Tower is the city's best-known landmark (see pp196–7). It towers more than 1,050 ft (320 m) above Champ-de-Mars park.

| 0 meters | 800 |
| 0 yards | 800 |

Sacré-Coeur

Standing majestically above Montmartre is the striking basilica of Sacré-Coeur. Built between 1875 and 1914, it is dedicated to the sacred heart of Jesus (*see pp226–7*).

REPUBLIQUE FRANCAISE
LIBERTE EGALITE · FRATERNITE

THE HISTORY OF PARIS

The Paris conquered by the Romans in 52 BC was a small flood-prone fishing village on the Ile de la Cité, inhabited by the Parisii tribe. A Roman settlement soon flourished and spread to the Left Bank of the Seine. The Franks succeeded the Romans, named the city Paris, and made it the center of their kingdom.

During the Middle Ages, the city flourished as a religious center and architectural masterpieces such as Sainte-Chapelle were erected. It also thrived as a center of learning, enticing European scholars to its great university, the Sorbonne.

Paris emerged during the Renaissance and the Enlightenment as a great center of culture and ideas, and under the rule of Louis XIV it also became a city of immense wealth and power. But rule by the monarch gave way to rule by the people in the bloody Revolution of 1789. By the early years of the new century, revolutionary fervor had faded and the brilliant militarist Napoleon Bonaparte proclaimed himself Emperor of France and pursued his ambition to make Paris the center of the world.

Soon after the Revolution of 1848, a radical transformation of the city began. Baron Haussmann's grand urban design replaced Paris's medieval slums with elegant avenues and boulevards. By the end of the century, the city was the driving force of Western culture. This continued into the 20th century, interrupted only by World War I and II, and the German military occupation. Since then, the city has revived and expanded dramatically, as it strives to be at the heart of a unified Europe.

The following pages illustrate Paris's history by providing snapshots of the significant periods in the city's evolution.

A map of Paris (c. 1845)

◀ *Allegory of the Republic* (1848) by Dominique Louis Papety

Kings and Emperors in Paris

Paris became the power base for the kings of France at the beginning of the Capetian dynasty, when Hugh Capet ascended the throne. Successive kings and emperors have left their mark, and many of the places mentioned in this book have royal associations: Philippe-Auguste's fortress, the Louvre Palace, is now one of the world's great museums; Henri IV's Pont Neuf bridge links the Ile de la Cité with the two banks of the Seine; and Napoleon conceived the Arc de Triomphe to celebrate his military victories. The end of the long line of kings came with the overthrow of the monarchy in 1848, during the reign of Louis-Philippe.

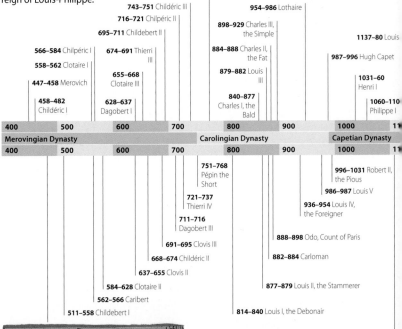

768–814 Charlemagne

743–751 Childéric III
716–721 Chilpéric II
695–711 Childebert II
566–584 Chilpéric I
558–562 Clotaire I
447–458 Merovich
674–691 Thierri III
655–668 Clotaire III
458–482 Childéric I
628–637 Dagobert I

954–986 Lothaire
898–929 Charles III, the Simple
884–888 Charles II, the Fat
879–882 Louis III
840–877 Charles I, the Bald

1137–80 Louis
987–996 Hugh Capet
1031–60 Henri I
1060–110 Philippe I

400	500	600	700	800	900	1000	1
Merovingian Dynasty				**Carolingian Dynasty**		**Capetian Dynasty**	
400	500	600	700	800	900	1000	1

751–768 Pépin the Short
721–737 Thierri IV
711–716 Dagobert III
691–695 Clovis III
668–674 Childéric II
637–655 Clovis II
584–628 Clotaire II
562–566 Caribert
511–558 Childebert I

996–1031 Robert II, the Pious
986–987 Louis V
936–954 Louis IV, the Foreigner
888–898 Odo, Count of Paris
882–884 Carloman
877–879 Louis II, the Stammerer
814–840 Louis I, the Debonair

482–511 Clovis I

1108–37 Louis VI, the Fat

1226–70 Louis IX (St. Louis)

1515–47 François I

1498–1515 Louis XII, Father of His People

1483–98 Charles VIII

1422–61 Charles VII, the Victorious

1270–85 Philippe III, the Bold

1285–1314 Philippe IV, the Fair

1316–22 Philippe V

1328–50 Philippe VI

1547–59 Henri II

1559–60 François II

1610–43 Louis XIII

1643–1715 Louis XIV, the Sun King

1804–14 Napoleon I

1774–93 Louis XVI

| 1200 | 1300 | 1400 | 1500 | 1600 | 1700 | 1800 |

Valois Dynasty **Bourbon Dynasty**

| 1200 | 1300 | 1400 | 1500 | 1600 | 1700 | 1800 |

1314–16 Louis X

1380–1422 Charles VI, the Fool

1560–74 Charles IX

1814–24 Louis XVIII

1824–30 Charles X

1322–28 Charles IV, the Fair

1364–80 Charles V, the Wise

1574–89 Henri III

1830–48 Louis-Philippe I

1852–70 Napoleon III

1350–64 Jean II, the Good

1589–1610 Henri IV

1223–26 Louis VIII, the Lion

1180–1223 Philippe II, Auguste

1461–83 Louis XI, the Spider

1715–74 Louis XV

Gallo-Roman Paris

Paris would not have existed without the Seine. The river provided early peoples with the means to exploit the land, forests, marshes, and islands. Excavations have unearthed canoes dating back to 4500 BC, well before a Celtic tribe, known as the Parisii, settled there in the 3rd century BC, in an area known as Lutetia. From 59 BC, the Romans undertook the conquest of Gaul (France). Seven years later, Lutetia was sacked by the Romans. They fortified and rebuilt it, especially the main island (the Ile de la Cité) and the Left Bank of the Seine.

Extent of the City
200 BC   Today

Bronze-Age Harness
Everyday objects like harnesses continued to be made of bronze well into the Iron Age, which began in Gaul around 900 BC.

Baths

Theater

Forum

Fired-Clay Vase
Pale ceramics with colored decoration were common in Gaul.

Present-day Rue Soufflot

Iron Daggers
From the 2nd century BC, short swords of iron replaced long swords and were sometimes decorated with human and animal shapes.

Glass Beads
Iron-Age glass beads and bracelets have been found on the Ile de la Cité.

Present-day Rue St.-Jacques

4500 BC
Early boatmen operate from the banks of the Seine

Helmet worn by Gaulish warriors

| 4500 | 400 BC | 300 BC | 200 BC | 100 BC |

300 BC
Parisii tribe settle on the Ile de la Cité

52 BC
Labienus, Caesar's lieutenant, defeats the Gauls. Romans rebuild the Ile de la Cité, and create a new town on the Left Bank

Parisii gold coin minted on the Ile de la Cité

Roman Oil Lamp

The inhabitants of the densely populated Ile de la Cité derived comfort during the dark winter months from the warmth of central heating and the light from oil lamps.

Where to See Gallo-Roman Paris

Since the mid-19th century, excavations have yielded evidence of the boundaries of the Roman city which had as its central axes the present-day Rue St.-Jacques and Rue Soufflot (in the 5th arrondissement). Under the Parvis de Notre-Dame (Place Jean-Paul II) in the Crypte Archéologique *(see pp86–7)* the remains of Gallo-Roman houses and Roman ramparts can be seen. Other Roman sites in Paris are the Arènes de Lutèce *(p167)* and the baths at the Musée de Cluny – Musée National du Moyen Age *(pp154–7)*.

Ile de la Cité

Gallo-Roman Goddess

Found in the arena, this head dates from the 2nd century AD.

Temple

The baths *(thermae)* at Cluny had three huge rooms of water with different temperatures.

Stage backdrop

Spectator seats

Arènes de Lutèce

This huge arena, built in the 1st–2nd centuries AD, was used for circuses, theatrical performances, and gladiatorial combat.

Ring Flask

From about 300 AD, this flask was found on the Ile de la Cité.

Lutetia in AD 200

Paris, or Lutetia, was laid out in a grid pattern with bridges linking the Ile de la Cité and the Left Bank.

Roman floor mosaic from the Cluny baths

285 Barbarians advance, Lutetia swept by fire

200 Romans add arena, baths, and villas

360 Julien, prefect of Gaul, is proclaimed Emperor. Lutetia changes its name to Paris after the Parisii

0 BC	100	200	300	400

250 Early Christian martyr, St. Denis, beheaded in Montmartre

451 Sainte Geneviève galvanizes the Parisians to repulse Attila the Hun

485–508 Clovis, leader of the Franks, defeats the Romans. Paris becomes Christian

Medieval Paris

Throughout the Middle Ages, strategically placed towns like Paris, positioned at a river crossing, became important centers of political power and learning. The Church played a crucial part in intellectual and spiritual life. It provided the impetus for education and for technological advances such as the drainage of land and the digging of canals. The population was still confined mainly to the Ile de la Cité and the Left Bank. When the marshes *(marais)* were drained in the 12th century, the city was able to expand.

Extent of the City
☐ 1300 ☐ Today

Sainte-Chapelle
The upper chapel of this medieval masterpiece *(see pp88–9)* was reserved for the royal family.

Octagonal Table
Medieval manor houses had wooden furniture like this trestle table.

The Ile de la Cité,
including the towers of the Conciergerie and Sainte-Chapelle, features in the pages for June.

Drainage
allowed more land to be cultivated.

Weavers' Window
Medieval craftsmen formed guilds, and many church windows were dedicated to their crafts.

A rural life
was led by most Parisians, who worked on the land. The actual city only occupied a tiny area.

512
Death of Sainte Genevieve. She is buried next to Clovis

725–732
Muslims attack Gaul

845–862
Normans attack Paris

| 500 | 600 | 700 | 800 | 900 |

543
Foundation of St-Germain-des-Prés

800
Charlemagne crowned Emperor by the Pope

Golden hand reliquary of Charlemagne

Notre-Dame
The great Gothic cathedrals took many years to build. Work continued on Notre-Dame from 1163 to 1334.

The Monasteries
Monks of many different orders lived in monasteries in Paris, especially on the Left Bank of the Seine.

University Seal
The University of Paris was founded around 1150.

The Louvre of Charles V with its defensive wall is seen here from the Ile de la Cité.

The Nobility
From the mid-14th century, dress was considered to be a mark of class; noble ladies wore high, pointed hats.

A Medieval Romance

It was in the cloisters of Notre-Dame that the romance between the monk Pierre Abélard and the young Héloïse began. Abélard was the most original theologian of the 12th century and was hired as a tutor to the 17-year-old niece of a canon. A love affair soon developed between the teacher and his pupil. In his wrath, Héloïse's uncle had the scholar castrated; Héloïse took refuge in a convent for the rest of her life.

The Months: June and October
This illuminated prayer book and calendar, the Très Riches Heures *(left and above), was made for the Duc de Berri in 1416. It shows many Paris buildings.*

| 1010–22 Christians burn Jews and heretics | 1167 Les Halles food market created on the Right Bank of the Seine | 1245 Work starts on Sainte-Chapelle | 1380 The Bastille fortress completed |
| | | 1253 The Sorbonne opens | |

| 1000 | 1100 | 1200 | 1300 | 1400 |

1079 Birth of Pierre Abélard

1150 Paris University founded

1163 Work starts on Notre-Dame cathedral

1226–70 Reign of Louis IX, St. Louis

Joan of Arc

1430 Henry VI of England crowned King of France after Joan of Arc fails to defend Paris

Renaissance Paris

At the end of the Hundred Years' War with England, Paris was in a terrible state. By the time the occupying English army left in 1453, the city lay in ruins, with many houses burned. Louis XI brought back prosperity and a new interest in art, architecture, and clothes. During the course of the 16th and 17th centuries, French kings came under the spell of the Italian Renaissance. Their architects made the first attempts at town planning, creating elegant, uniform buildings and open urban spaces like the magnificent Place Royale (the present Place des Vosges).

Extent of the City
⬜ 1590 ⬜ Today

Printing Press (1470)
Religious tracts, mainly in Latin, were printed on the first press at the Sorbonne.

A Knight Preparing to Joust
The Place Royale was the setting for jousting displays well into the 17th century.

Jewel-Encrusted Pendant
A sign of the new prosperity, jewels became an important part of dress.

Pont Notre-Dame
This bridge with its row of houses was built at the start of the 15th century. The Pont Neuf (1578–1607) was the first bridge without houses.

Place Royale
Built by Henri IV in 1609, with grand symmetrical houses around an open, central space, this was Paris's first square. Home to the aristocracy, it was renamed Place des Vosges in 1800 (see pp98–9).

1453 End of the Hundred Years' War with England

François I

1516 François I invites Leonardo da Vinci to France. He brings the *Mona Lisa* with him

1450	1460	1470	1480	1490	1500	1510	1520

1469 First French printing works starts operating at the Sorbonne

1528 François I takes residence in the Lou

16th-Century Knife and Fork Set
Ornate knife and fork sets were used in the dining rooms of the wealthy to carve joints of meat. Diners used hands or spoons for eating.

Where to See Renaissance Paris Today

Besides the Place des Vosges, there are many examples of the Renaissance in Paris. Churches include St.-Etienne-du-Mont (p159), St.-Eustache (p116), and the nave of St.-Gervais–St.-Protais (p103). Mansions such as the Hôtel de Sully (p99) and the Hôtel Carnavalet (pp96–7) have been restored. The staircases, courtyard, and turrets of the Hôtel de Cluny (pp154–5) date from 1485–96.

The rood screen of St.-Etienne-du-Mont (about 1520) is of outstanding delicacy.

Queen's Pavilion

Uniform houses with arcades flank the pavilion.

PLACE ROYALE (PLACE DES VOSGES)

Walnut Dresser (about 1545)
Elegant carved wooden furniture decorated the homes of the wealthy.

Nine symmetrical houses line each side of the square.

Hyante and Climente
Toussaint Dubreuil and other artists took up Renaissance mythological themes.

King's Pavilion

Duels were fought in the center of the square in the 17th century.

1534 Ignatius of Loyola founds the Society of Jesus

1546 Work starts on new Louvre palace; first stone quay built along Seine

1559 Primitive street lanterns introduced; Louvre completed

1572 St. Bartholomew's Day massacre of Protestants

1609 Henri IV begins building Place Royale, later renamed Place des Vosges

1589 Henri III assassinated at St.-Cloud, near Paris

|1540|1550|1560|1570|1580|1590|1600|1610|

1534 Founding of the Collège de France

1547 François I dies

1533 Foundation stone of original Hôtel de Ville laid

1559 Henri II killed in a Paris tournament

1589 Henri of Navarre is crowned Henri IV, king of France

1593 Henri IV converts from Protestantism to Catholicism.

1610 Henri IV is assassinated by Ravaillac, a religious fanatic

The Sun King's Paris

The 17th century in France, which became known as *Le Grand Siècle* (the great century), is epitomized by the glittering extravagance of Louis XIV (the Sun King) and his court at Versailles. In Paris, imposing buildings, squares, theaters, and aristocratic *hôtels* (mansions) were built. Beneath this brilliant surface lay the absolute power of the monarch. By the end of Louis' reign, the cost of his extravagance and of waging almost continuous war with France's neighbors led to a decline in the monarchy.

Extent of the City
1657   Today

The mansard roof, with its slopes at both sides and both ends, came to typify French roofs of this period.

An open staircase rose from the internal courtyard.

Cross section of the living quarters

The Gardens of Versailles
Louis XIV devoted a lot of time to the gardens, which were designed by André Le Nôtre.

Louis XIV as Jupiter
On ascending the throne in 1661, Louis, depicted here as Jupiter triumphant, ended the civil wars that had been raging since his childhood.

The ground floor contained the servants' quarters.

Chest of Drawers
This gilded piece was made by André-Charles Boulle for the Grand Trianon at Versailles.

1610 Louis XIII's accession marks the start of *Le Grand Siècle*

Louis XIII

1622 Paris becomes an episcopal see

1624 Completion of Tuileries Palace

1631 Launch of *La Gazette*, Paris's first newspaper

Cardinal Mazarin

1643 Death of Louis XIII. Regency under control of Marie de Médicis and Cardinal Mazarin

1661 Louis XIV becomes absolute monarch. Enlargement of Château de Versailles begins

1610   1620   1630   1640   1650   166

1614 Final meeting of the Estates Council (the main legislative assembly) before the Revolution

1629 Richelieu, Louis XIII's first minister, builds Palais-Royal

1627 Development of the Ile St.-Louis

1638 Birth of Louis XIV

1662 Colbert, Louis XIV's finance minister, founds Gobelins tapestry works

Weaving frame

Ceiling by Charles Le Brun
Court painter to Louis XIV, Le Brun
decorated many ceilings like this one
at the Hôtel Carnavalet *(see p96)*.

Madame de Maintenon
When the queen died
in 1683, Louis married
Madame de
Maintenon, shown
here in a framed
painting by Caspar
Netscher.

Decorated Fan
For special court fêtes, Louis
XIV often stipulated that
women carry fans.

The Galerie d'Hercule
with Le Brun ceiling

Where to See the Sun King's Paris

Many 17th-century mansions
such as the Hôtel Lambert still
exist in Paris, but not all are open
to the public. However, Hôtel des
Invalides *(p191)*, the Dôme
Church *(pp188–9)*, the Palais du
Luxembourg *(p174)*, and Versailles
(pp250–55) give a magnificent
impression of the period.

Dôme Church

Formal Classical Garden

Hôtel Lambert (1640)
In the 17th century, the
aristocracy built luxurious
town houses with grand
staircases, courtyards,
formal gardens, coach
houses, and stables.

Neptune Cup
Made from lapis lazuli with a silver
Neptune on top, this cup was part of
Louis' vast collection of art objects.

1667 Louvre
rebuilt and
observatory
established

1682 Court moves
to Versailles,
where it stays until
the Revolution

1686
Le Procope,
Paris's first café,
is founded

Statue of Louis XIV at
Musée Carnavalet

1715 Louis XIV dies

1670	1680	1690	1700	1710

1670 The decree for
building Hôtel des
Invalides is signed

1692 Great famines
due to bad harvests
and wars

1689 Pont Royal built

1702
Paris first divided into
20 arrondissements (districts)

Paris in the Age of Enlightenment

The Enlightenment, with its emphasis on scientific reason and a critical approach to existing ideas and society, was centered on the city of Paris. In contrast, nepotism and corruption were rife at Louis XV's court at Versailles. Meanwhile the economy thrived, the arts flourished as never before, and intellectuals such as Voltaire and Rousseau were renowned throughout Europe. In Paris, the population rose to about 650,000: town planning was developed, and the first accurate street map of the city appeared in 1787.

Extent of the City
☐ 1720   ☐ Today

Nautical Instruments
As the science of navigation advanced, scientists developed telescopes and trigonometric instruments (used for measuring latitude and longitude).

The auditorium,
with 1,913 seats, was
the largest in Paris.

18th-Century Wigs
These were not only a mark of fashion but also a way of indicating the wearer's class and importance.

Comédie Française
The Age of Enlightenment saw a burst of dramatic activity, and new theaters opened. Among them was the Comédie Française (see p130), still one of the most prestigious theaters in the world.

1734 Fontaine des Quatre Saisons built

1748 Montesquieu's *L'Esprit des Lois* (an influential work about different forms of government) published

1720   **1730**   **1740**   **1750**

1722 City's first fire department founded

Fireman

1733 Voltaire's *Lettres Philosophiques* published

1751 First volume of Diderot's *Encyclopedia* published

Madame de Pompadour
Although generally remembered as the mistress of Louis XV, she was renowned as a patron of the arts and had great political influence.

Chocolate Pot
By the 18th century, bourgeois families could afford tobacco, tea, chocolate, and coffee from Asia and the New World.

Vestibule with painted ceiling

Portico with Doric columns

The Catacombs
These were set up in 1786 as a more hygienic alternative to Paris's cemeteries *(see p181).*

Where to See Enlightenment Paris

The district around the Rue de Lille, the Rue de Varenne, and the Rue de Grenelle *(p191)* has many luxurious town houses, or hôtels, which were built by the aristocracy during the first half of the 18th century. Memorabilia from the lives of the great intellectuals Voltaire and Jean-Jacques Rousseau are in the Musée Carnavalet *(pp96–7),* along with 18th-century interior designs and paintings. The imposing Hôtel des Monnaies (royal mint), which houses the Musée de la Monnaie *(p143),* is a fine example of the rational Neo-Classicism of architecture during the Enlightenment.

Churches were built throughout the Enlightenment. St.-Sulpice *(p174)* was completed in 1776.

Le Procope *(p142)* is the oldest café in Paris. It was frequented by Voltaire and Rousseau.

1757 First oil street lamps

1764 Madame de Pompadour dies

1774 Louis XV, great grandson of Louis XIV, dies

1778 France supports American independence

1785 David paints the *Oath of the Horatii*

1760

1770

1780

c. 1760 Place de la Concorde, Panthéon, and Ecole Militaire built

1762 Rousseau's *Emile* and the *Social Contract* published

Rousseau, philosopher and writer, believed that humans were naturally good and had been corrupted by society.

1782 First sidewalks built, in the Place du Théâtre Français

1783 Montgolfier brothers make the first hot-air balloon ascent

Paris During the Revolution

In 1789 most Parisians were still living in squalor and poverty, as they had since the Middle Ages. Rising inflation and opposition to Louis XVI culminated in the storming of the Bastille, the king's prison; the Republic was founded three years later. However, the Terror soon followed, when those suspected of betraying the Revolution were executed without trial: more than 60,000 people lost their lives. The bloody excesses of Robespierre, the zealous revolutionary, led to his overthrow, and a new government, the Directory, was set up in 1795.

Extent of the City
▧ 1796   ▢ Today

The prison turrets were set alight.

Declaration of the Rights of Man and the Citizen
The Enlightenment ideals of equality and human dignity were enshrined in the Declaration. This illustration is the preface to the 1791 Constitution.

The French guards, who were on the side of the revolutionaries, arrived late in the afternoon with two cannons.

Paper Money
Bonds, called *assignats*, were used to fund the Revolution from 1790–93.

Republican Calendar

The revolutionaries believed that the world was starting again, so they abolished the existing church calendar and took September 22, 1792, the day the Republic was declared, as the first day of the new era. The Republican calendar had 12 equal months, each subdivided into three ten-day periods, with the remaining five days of each year set aside for public holidays. All the months of the year were given poetic names that linked them to nature and the seasons, such as fog, snow, seed-time, flowers, and harvest.

A colored engraving by Tresca showing *Ventôse*, the windy month (Feb 19–Mar 20) from the new Republican calendar

Drawbridge

Aug 4 Abolition of feudalism

Aug 26 Declaration of the Rights of Man and the Citizen

Jul 14 Fall of the Bastille

Sep 17 Law of Suspects passed: the Terror begins

Aug 10 The storming of the Tuileries

| 1789 | 1790 | 1791 | 1792 |

Cartoon on the three Estates: the clergy, the nobility, and the awakening populace

Lafayette, Commander of the National Guard, takes his oath to the Constitution

Jul 17 Champ de Mars massacre

Apr 25 *La Marseillaise* composed

May 5 The Estates council meets

Jul 14 Fête de la Fédération

"Patriotic" Chair
The back of this wooden chair is topped by red bonnets, symbol of revolutionary politics.

The Sans Culottes
By 1792, the wearing of pants instead of breeches (*culottes*) was a political symbol of Paris's artisans and storekeepers.

La Marseillaise
The revolutionaries' marching song is now the national anthem.

The dead and wounded totaled 171 by the end of the day.

Coin tower

Wallpaper
Commemorative wallpaper was produced to celebrate the Revolution.

Great court

Well court

Guillotine
This was used for the first time in France in April 1792.

Storming of the Bastille
The Bastille was overrun on July 14, 1789, and the seven prisoners held there released. The defenders (32 Swiss guards, 82 wounded soldiers, and the governor) were massacred.

n 20 Invasion the Tuileries

Jan 21 Execution of Louis XVI

Oct 16 Execution of Marie-Antoinette

Nov 19 Jacobin Club (a revolutionary pressure group) closed

Aug 22 New constitution: the Directory

Aug 10 Overthrow of Louis XVI

Fall Robespierre in control of Committee of Public Safety

Nov 24 Churches closed

Apr 5 Execution of Danton and supporters

1793	1794	1795

Sep 20 Battle of Valmy

Jul 13 Assassination of Marat, founder of *L'Ami du Peuple*, the revolutionary newspaper

Sep 2–6 September massacres

Jul 27 Execution of Robespierre

Robespierre, revolutionary and architect of the Terror

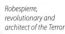

Napoleonic Paris

Napoleon Bonaparte was the most brilliant general in the French army. The instability of the new government after the Revolution gave him the chance to seize power, and in November 1799 he installed himself in the Tuileries Palace as First Consul. He crowned himself Emperor in May 1804. Napoleon established a centralized administration and a code of laws, reformed France's educational system, and set out to make Paris the most beautiful city in the world. The city was endowed with grand monuments and embellished with the spoils of conquest. His power was always fragile and dependent on incessant wars. In March 1814 Prussian, Austrian, and Russian armies invaded Paris and Napoleon fled to Elba. He returned to Paris in 1815 but was defeated at Waterloo and died in exile in 1821.

Extent of the City
1810   Today

Ladies-in-Waiting
hold Josephine's train.

Château de Malmaison
This was the favorite home of Josephine, Napoleon's first wife.

Opaline-Glass Clock
The decoration on this clock echoed the fashion for draperies.

Elephant Project
This monument was planned for the center of the Place de la Bastille.

Eagle's Flight
Napoleon's flight to Elba in 1814 was satirized in this cartoon.

1799 Napoleon seizes power

1797 Battle of Rivoli

1800 Banque de France founded

1802 Legion of Honor established

1809 Napoleon divorces Josephine and marries Marie-Louise

1815 Waterloo; second abdication of Napoleon. Restoration of the monarchy

1800	1805	1810	1815	1820

1804 Napoleon crowned

1800 Napoleon returns from Egypt on his ship *L'Orient*

1806 Arc de Triomphe commissioned

1812 Russian campaign ends in defeat

1814 Napoleon abdicates

Napoleon's death mask

1821 Napoleon dies

Bronze Table Top
Inlaid with Napoleon's portrait, this table marks the victory at Austerlitz.

Josephine kneels before Napoleon.

Napoleon holds the crown for his Empress, Josephine.

Russian Cossacks in the Palais-Royal
After Napoleon's defeat and flight in 1814, Paris suffered the humiliation of being occupied by foreign troops, including Austrians, Prussians, and Russians.

The Pope makes the sign of the cross.

Where to See Napoleonic Paris

Many of the grand monuments Napoleon planned for Paris were never built, but two triumphal arches, the Arc de Triomphe (pp212–13) and Arc de Triomphe du Carrousel (p122), were a major part of his legacy. La Madeleine church (p218) was also inaugurated in his reign and much of the Louvre was rebuilt (pp122–3). Examples of the Empire style can be seen at Malmaison (p248) and at the Carnavalet (pp96–7).

Napoleon's Coronation

Napoleon's rather dramatic crowning took place in 1804. In this recreation by J. L. David, the Pope, summoned to Notre-Dame, looks on as Napoleon crowns his Empress just before crowning himself.

The Empress
Josephine was divorced by Napoleon in 1809.

The Arc de Triomphe du Carrousel was erected in 1806 and crowned with the horses looted from St. Mark's, Venice.

1842 First railroad track between Paris and St.-Germain-en-Laye opens

1825	1830	1835	1840	1845

1830 Revolution in Paris and advent of constitutional monarchy

1831 Victor Hugo's *Notre-Dame de Paris* published. Cholera epidemic hits Paris

1840 Reburial of Napoleon at Les Invalides

Napoleon's tomb

The Grand Transformation

In 1848 Paris saw a second revolution that brought down the recently restored monarchy. In the uncertainties that followed, Napoleon's nephew assumed power in the same way as his uncle before him – by a *coup d'état*. He proclaimed himself Napoleon III in 1851. Under his rule, Paris was transformed into the most magnificent city in Europe. He entrusted the task of modernization to Baron Haussmann. Haussmann demolished the crowded, unsanitary streets of the medieval city and created a well-ordered capital within a geometrical grid of avenues and boulevards. Neighboring districts such as Auteuil were annexed, creating the suburbs.

Extent of the City

  1859   Today

Boulevard des Italiens
This tree-lined avenue, painted by Edmond Georges Grandjean (1889), was one of the most fashionable of the new boulevards.

AVE DE FRIEDLAN

AVE HOCHE

Twelve avenues
formed a star *(étoile)*

AVE DE WAGRAM

PL

Laying the Sewers
This engraving from 1861 shows the early work for laying the sewer system *(see p192)* from La Villette to Les Halles. Most of the system was the work of the engineer Belgrand.

AVE MAC-MAHON

AVE CARNOT

Circular Billboard
Distinctive billboards advertised opera and theater performances.

Grand mansions
were built around the Arc de Triomphe between 1860 and 1868.

1851 Napoleon III declares the Second Empire

1852 Haussmann begins massive town-planning program

Viewing the exhibits at the World Exhibition

1855 World Exhibition

| 1850 | 1852 | 1854 | 1856 | 1858 |

1853 Baltard starts work on new Les Halles buildings

20-centime stamp showing Napoleon III

1857 The poet Baudelaire prosecuted for obscenity for *The Flowers of Evil*

Place de l'Etoile

The new plan for the center of Paris included redesigning the area at one end of the Champs-Elysées (Elysian Fields). Haussmann created a star of 12 broad avenues around the new Arc de Triomphe. (The inset map shows the area as it was in 1790.)

Arc de Triomphe

Site of Arc de Triomphe

Fields

Avenue des Champs-Elysées

Drinking Fountain
In the 1870s, 50 fountains were erected in poor areas of Paris through the generosity of English francophile Richard Wallace.

Bois de Boulogne
Given to the city in 1852 by Napoleon III, this park became a popular place for walking and riding (*see pp247*).

Baron Haussmann

Lawyer by training and civil servant by profession, Georges-Eugène Haussmann (1809–91) was appointed Prefect of the Seine by Napoleon III. For 17 years he was in charge of urban planning. With the best architects and engineers of the day, he planned a new city, improved the water supply and sewerage, and created beautiful parks.

Some avenues were named after French generals.

1861 Garnier designs new Opera House

1863 The nudity in Manet's *Le Déjeuner sur l'Herbe* causes a scandal and is rejected by the Academy (*see p147*)

1867 World Exhibition

1870 Napoleon's wife, Eugénie, flees Paris at threat of war

1862 1864 1866 1868

1863 Crédit Lyonnais bank established

1862 Victor Hugo's epic novel of Paris's poor, *Les Misérables*, published

1868 Press censorship relaxed

1870 Start of Franco-Prussian War

The Belle Epoque

The Franco-Prussian War culminated in the terrible Siege of Paris. When peace came in 1871, it fell to the new government, the Third Republic, to bring about economic recovery. From about 1890 life was transformed: the auto-mobile, airplane, movie theater, telephone, and gramophone all contributed to the enjoyment of life, and the *Belle Epoque* (beautiful age) was born. Paris became a glittering city where the new style, Art Nouveau, decorated buildings and objects. The paintings of the Impressionists, such as Renoir, reflected the *joie de vivre* of the times, while later those of Matisse, Braque, and Picasso heralded the modern movement in art.

Extent of the City
▨ 1895   ▨ Today

The interior was arranged as tiers of galleries around a central grand staircase.

Electricity illuminated the window displays.

Cabaret Poster
Toulouse-Lautrec's posters immor-talized the singers and dancers of the cafés and cabaret clubs of Montmartre, where artists and writers congregated in the 1890s.

Windows facing onto the Boulevard Haussmann displayed goods for sale.

Central Hall of the Grand Palais
The Grand Palais *(p210)* was built to house two huge exhibitions of French painting and sculpture at the Universal Exhibition of 1900.

The Naughty Nineties
The Lumière brothers captured the daring negligée fashions of the 1890s in the first moving images of the cinematograph.

1871 Third Republic established

1872 Monet paints first Impressionist picture: *Impression: Sunrise*

1885 Louis Pasteur discovers rabies vaccine

1891 First metro station opens

1889 Eiffel Tower built

| 1870 | 1875 | 1880 | 1885 | 1890 |

Zoo animals were shot to feed the hungry (see p227)

Entrance ticket to the exhibition

1870 Siege of Paris

Louis Pasteur

1889 Great Exhibition

Citroën 5CV
France led the world in the early development of the automobile. By 1900 the Citroën began to be seen on the streets of Paris, and long-distance auto racing was popular.

The glass dome could be seen from all parts of the store.

Moulin Rouge (1890)
The old, obsolete windmills of Montmartre became nightclubs, like the world-famous Moulin Rouge (red windmill) *(see p230)*.

Galeries Lafayette (1906)
This beautiful department store, with its dome a riot of colored glass and wrought ironwork, was a sign of the new prosperity.

Art Nouveau Cash Register
Even ordinary objects like this cash register were beautified by the new style.

Where to See the Belle Epoque

Art Nouveau can be seen in monumental buildings like the Grand Palais and Petit Palais *(p210)*, while the Galeries Lafayette *(p313)* has beautiful belle époque interiors. The Musée d'Orsay *(pp146–9)* has many objects from this period.

The entrance to the metro at Porte Dauphine was the work of leading Art Nouveau designer Hector Guimard *(p148)*.

The doorway of No. 29 Avenue Rapp *(p193)*, in the Eiffel Tower quarter, is a fine example of Art Nouveau.

Captain Dreyfus was publicly humiliated for selling secrets to the Prussians. He was later found innocent.

1894–1906 Dreyfus affair

1907 Picasso paints *Les Demoiselles d'Avignon*

1913 Proust publishes first volume of *Remembrance of Things Past*

1895	1900	1905	1910

1898 Pierre and Marie Curie discover radium

1909 Blériot flies across the English Channel

1895 Lumière brothers introduce cinematography

1911 Diaghilev brings the Russian ballet to Paris

Avant-Garde Paris

From the 1920s to the 1940s, Paris became a mecca for artists, musicians, writers, and movie-makers. The city was alive with new movements such as Cubism and Surrealism, represented by Cézanne, Picasso, Braque, Man Ray, and Duchamp. Many new trends came from the USA, as writers and musicians, including Ernest Hemingway, Gertrude Stein, and Sidney Bechet, took up residence in Paris. In architecture, the geometric shapes created by Le Corbusier changed the face of the modern building.

Extent of the City
☐ 1940   ☐ Today

The old Trocadéro was changed to the Palais de Chaillot *(see p202)* for the World Exhibition of 1937.

Napoleon by Abel Gance
Paris has always been a city for movie-makers. In 1927, Abel Gance made an innovative movie about Napoleon, using triple screens and wide-angle lenses.

Josephine Baker
Arriving in Paris in 1925, the outlandish dancer catapulted to fame in "La Revue Nègre" wearing nothing but feathers.

Living space was made into a picture gallery.

Stilts supported the concrete shell.

Sidney Bechet
In the 1930s and 1940s, the jazz clubs of Paris resounded to the swing music of black musicians such as the saxophonist Sidney Bechet.

La Roche Villa by Le Corbusier
Made from concrete and steel, with straight lines, horizontal windows, and a flat roof, this house (1923–5) epitomized the new style (see pp246–7).

1919 Treaty of Versailles signed in the Hall of Mirrors

1924 Olympic Games held in Paris

1924 André Breton publishes Surrealist Manifesto

1925 Art Deco style first seen at the Exposition des Arts Décoratifs

1914	1916	1918	1920	1922	1924	1926	1928

1914–18 World War I. Paris is under threat of German attack, saved by the Battle of the Marne. A shell hits St-Gervais-St-Protais.

World War I soldier in uniform

1920 Interment of the Unknown Soldier

An eternal flame for the Unknown Soldier burns under the Arc de Triomphe

Fashion in the 1940s
After World War II, the classic look for men and women was reminiscent of military uniforms.

Airmail Poster
Airmail routes developed during the 1930s, especially to French North Africa.

The roof was designed as a garden terrace.

The bedroom was above the dining room.

The kitchen was built at the back with a sloping glass roof.

The garage was built into the ground floor.

Windows were arranged in a horizontal strip.

Occupied Paris

Paris was under occupation for most of World War II. The Eiffel Tower was a favorite spot for German soldiers, and many of the bourgeois mansions were seized for German officers. The beautiful hotel Le Meurice (p284) served as the headquarters for General von Choltitz, the last commander of Nazi-occupied Paris. The Musée de l'Armée (p190), in the Hôtel des Invalides, has a good display of wartime items, while the Musée de l'Ordre de la Libération (p190) has two galleries devoted to the Free French and their fearless leader, Charles de Gaulle. For places of quiet contemplation, visit the Paris Mémorial des Martyrs de la Déportation behind Notre-Dame (p86), dedicated to the 200,000 people deported from France to the Nazi concentration camps, or the Mémorial de la Shoah (p103), with its eternal flame dedicated to the unknown Jewish martyr.

Claudine in Paris by Colette
The Claudine series of novels, written by Colette Willy, known simply as "Colette," were extremely popular in the 1930s.

1931 Colonial Exhibition

A visitor to the exhibition in colonial dress

1937 Picasso paints *Guernica* in protest at the Spanish Civil War

1940 World War II: Paris bombed and occupied by Nazis

| 1930 | 1932 | 1934 | 1936 | 1938 | 1940 | 1942 |

1934 Riots and strikes in response to the Depression

1935 The talented Edith Piaf discovered singing in the Paris streets

1937 Palais de Chaillot built

Symbol of Free French superimposed on the victory sign

Aug 1944 Liberation of Paris

The Modern City

In 1962, a renovation program began, and run-down districts like the Marais were restored. This project continued with François Mitterrand's *Grands Travaux* (great works) scheme. Access was improved to historical monuments and art collections, such as the Musée du Louvre and Musée d'Orsay. The scheme produced modern monuments such as the Opéra National de Paris Bastille *(p102)*, the Cité des Sciences *(pp240–41)*, and the Bibliothèque Nationale de France *(p244)*. These, and the boldly modern La Défense *(p248)*, Stade de France, Musée du quai Branly *(pp194–5)*, Promenade des Berges de la Seine *(p69)*, Philarmonie de Paris *(p239)*, and Fondation Louis Vuitton *(p247)*, have enriched Paris with truly innovative architecture.

Extent of the City
⬜ 1959   ⬜ Today

La Grande Arche is taller and wider than Notre-Dame and forms part of an axis linking the Arc de Triomphe and the Louvre Pyramid.

Christo's Pont Neuf
To create a work of art, the Bulgarian-born artist Christo wrapped Paris's oldest bridge, the Pont Neuf, in fabric in 1985.

Simone de Beauvoir
Influential philosopher and life-long companion of J.-P. Sartre, de Beauvoir fought for the liberation of women in the 1950s.

Shopping mall

Louvre Pyramid (1989)
I. M. Pei's futuristic glass pyramid forms the entrance to the Louvre, providing a striking contrast to the classical facade of the museum.

1962 André Malraux, Minister of Culture, begins renovation program of run-down districts and monuments

Ducting at the Pompidou Center

1977 Pompidou Center opens. Jacques Chirac is installed as first elected Mayor of Paris since 1871

1980 Thousands greet Pope John-Paul II on his official visit

1950	1955	1960	1965	1970	1975	1980	1985

1958 Establishment of Fifth Republic with de Gaulle as President

President de Gaulle

1964 Reorganization of the Île de France

1968 Student riots and workers strikes in the Latin Quarter

1969 Les Halles market transfers to Rungis

1973 Construction of Montparnasse Tower and the Périphérique (beltway)

1985 Christo wraps Pont Neuf

19 Bicenten celebratic to mark Frer Revolut

Marne La Vallée
Like a gigantic loudspeaker, this residential complex is in one of Paris's dormitory towns near Disneyland® Paris.

Chanel Designs
Paris is the center of the fashion world, with important shows each year.

The Pompidou Center
The nation's collection of modern art is housed here in this popular building *(see pp110–13)*.

The Tour Areva
is one of the iconic skyscrapers in La Défense.

Opéra National de Paris Bastille (1989)
Its opening marked the bicentenary of the fall of the Bastille.

Students at the Barricades

In May 1968, Paris saw a revolution of a kind. The Latin Quarter was taken over by students and workers. What began as a protest against the war in Vietnam spread to other issues and became an expression of discontent with the government. President de Gaulle rode out the storm, but his prestige was severely damaged.

Rioting students clash with police

The Défense Palace, housing the center for industry, is the oldest tower.

La Défense
This enormous business center was started on the edge of Paris in 1958. In excess of 150,000 people work here.

1994 Eurostar inaugurated: Paris to London in 3 hours

2001 Bertrand Delanoe elected first socialist mayor

2002 The Euro replaces the Franc as exclusive legal tender

2007 The Vélib' public bike rental scheme, is launched

2012 Socialist François Hollande elected President

2015 In January, Islamist gunmen shoot dead 17 people, most of them staff at the satirical magazine *Charlie Hebdo*. In September, France launches air strikes against Islamic State Group targets in Syria

| 90 | 1995 | 2000 | 2005 | 2010 | 2015 | 2020 | 2025 |

1998 France hosts – and wins – the 1998 soccer World Cup tournament

Victorious French soccer team holding aloft the World Cup trophy in Paris

2007 Center-right Nicolas Sarkozy elected president

2015 In November, a series of terror attacks launched by Islamic State leaves 130 dead

2014 Anne Hidalgo elected first female mayor

PARIS AT A GLANCE

There are nearly 300 places of interest described in the *Area by Area* section of this book. A broad range of sights is covered from the ancient Conciergerie and its grisly associations with the guillotine *(see p87)*, to the modern Opéra National de Paris Bastille *(see p102)*; and from the oldest house in Paris, No. 51 Rue de Montmorency *(see p116)* to the exotic Musée du quai Branly *(see pp194–5)*.

To help make the most of your stay, the following 20 pages are a time-saving guide to the best Paris has to offer. Museums and galleries, historic churches, spacious parks, gardens and squares are all described. There is also a guide to Paris's famous personalities. Each sight has a cross reference to its own full entry. Below are the top tourist attractions to start you off.

Paris's Top Tourist Attractions

Sacré-Coeur
See pp226–7.

Sainte-Chapelle
See pp88–9.

Palace of Versailles
See pp250–55.

Pompidou Center
See pp110–13.

Jardin du Luxembourg
See p174.

Musée du Louvre
See pp122–9.

Musée d'Orsay
See pp146–9.

Eiffel Tower
See pp196–7.

Bois de Boulogne
See pp247.

Notre-Dame
See pp82–5.

Arc de Triomphe
See pp212–13.

◄ Interior of Notre-Dame Cathedral

Remarkable Parisians

By virtue of its strategic position on the Seine, Paris has always been the economic, political, and artistic hub of France. Over the centuries, many prominent and influential figures from other parts of the country and abroad have come to the city to absorb her unique spirit. In return, they have left their mark: artists have brought new movements; politicians new schools of thought; musicians, movie-makers and fashion designers new trends; and architects a new environment.

Artists

In the early 18th century, Jean-Antoine Watteau (1684–1721) took the inspiration for his paintings from the Paris theater. Half a century later, Jean-Honoré Fragonard (1732–1806), popular painter of the Rococo, lived and died here, financially ruined by the Revolution. Later, Paris became the cradle of Impressionism. Its founders Claude Monet (1840–1926), Pierre-Auguste Renoir (1841–1919), and Alfred Sisley (1839–99) met in a Paris studio. Henri de Toulouse-Lautrec (1864–1901) drank and painted in Montmartre, where Maurice Utrillo (1883–1955) was born and lived all his life. Utrillo painted many local scenes and was one of the 20th century's greatest painters of cityscapes. In 1907, Pablo Picasso (1881–1973) painted the seminal work *Les Demoiselles d'Avignon* at the Bateau-Lavoir *(see p230)*, where Georges Braque (1882–1963), Amedeo Modigliani (1884–1920), and Marc Chagall (1887–1985) also lived.

Sacré-Coeur by Utrillo (1934)

The Paris School eventually moved to Montparnasse, home to sculptors Auguste Rodin (1840–1917), Constantin Brancusi (1876–1957), and Ossip Zadkine (1890–1967).

Contemporary artists who have developed international reputations include Christian Boltanski (b.1944), known for his large *mise en scène* installations, video artist Pierre Huyghe (b.1962), and Sophie Calle (b.1953), renowned for her photographic and film installations.

Political Leaders

Hugh Capet, first King of the Franks, made Paris his capital in 987. Philippe Auguste (1165–1223) built the Louvre fortress and encircled the city with an impressive wall. Henri IV (1553–1610) was the first king to set about making Paris a worthy capital, building the Pont Neuf and Place des Vosges. Cardinal Richelieu (1585–1642), the power behind Louis XIII, created the Académie Française and the Palais-Royal *(see p130)*. Louis XIV (1638–1715) continued the process. Napoleon modernized Paris, building bridges and canals, though it was his nephew Napoleon III who gave Paris its distinctive *grands boulevards*. Général Charles de Gaulle (1890–1970), founder of the Fifth Republic, gave France back the prestige it had lost in the war. The current direction of Paris is largely in the hands of its first female mayor, Anne Hidalgo (b.1959).

Movies and Movie-Makers

Paris has always been at the heart of French cinema. The prewar and immediate post-war classics were usually made on the sets of the Boulogne and Joinville studios, where whole areas of the city were reconstructed. Jean-Luc Godard and other New Wave directors preferred to shoot outdoors. Godard's *A Bout de Souffle* (1960), with Jean-Paul Belmondo and Jean Seberg, was filmed in and around the Champs-Elysées. Catherine Deneuve (b.1943) made her name in Luis Buñuel's *Belle du Jour* (1967).

In the 1980s came the *cinéma du look*, epitomized by visually stylish movies such as *Les Amants du Pont Neuf* (1991), starring Juliette Binoche. A number of recent directors have dwelt on darker, grittier themes. Mathieu Kassovitz's *La Haine* (1995), for example, deals with racism and violence in the *banlieues*, while Céline Sciamma's *Bande de Filles* (2014) focuses on black teenagers coming of age in a deprived Paris suburb.

Portrait of Cardinal Richelieu by Philippe de Champaigne (about 1635)

Musicians

Jean-Philippe Rameau (1683–1764), organist and pioneer of harmony, is associated with St.-Eustache *(see p116)*. Hector Berlioz (1803–69) had his *Te Deum* first performed there in 1855. A great dynasty of organists, the Couperins, gave recitals in St.-Gervais–St.-Protais *(see p103)*.

The stage of the Opéra *(see p219)* has seen many talents, but audiences have not always been appreciative. *Carmen* by George Bizet (1838–75) was booed, as was *Pelléas et Mélisande* by Claude Debussy (1862–1918).

Olivier Messiaen (1908–91) was organist at the Eglise de la Sainte Trinité for 60 years. The composer and conductor Pierre Boulez (1925–2016) founded the experimental music institute IRCAM *(see p114)*.

The diminutive *chanteuse* Edith Piaf (1915–63) began singing in the streets of Paris and then went on to tour the world. During the 1920s, jazz violinist Stéphane Grapelli and guitarist Django Reinhardt pioneered gypsy jazz. Later, Serge Gainsbourg influenced a generation of pop musicians, and rock singer Johnny Halliday made his mark as the "French Elvis." France's strong connections with francophone West Africa mean that many internationally known West African artists, such as Salif Keita, Baaba Maal, Rokia Traoré, and Angélique Kidjo, first made their name in Paris and still attract a big following.

Architects

Gothic, Classical, Baroque, and Modernist – all styles co-exist in Paris. The most brilliant medieval architect was Pierre de Montreuil, who built Notre-Dame and Sainte-Chapelle. Louis Le Vau (1612–70) and Jules Hardouin-Mansart (1646–1708) designed Versailles *(see pp250–55)*. Jacques-Ange Gabriel (1698–1782) built the Petit Trianon *(see p251)* and Place de la Concorde *(see p133)*.

The Grand Trianon at Versailles, built by Jules Hardouin-Mansart in 1687

Haussmann (1809–91) gave the city its boulevards *(see pp36–7)*. Gustave Eiffel (1832–1923) built his tower in 1889. A century later, I. M. Pei added the Louvre's glass pyramid *(see p129)*; Jean Nouvel created the Institut du Monde Arabe *(see pp166–7)*, the Musée du quai Branly *(see pp194–5)*, and the Philharmonie de Paris *(see p239)*; while Dominique Perrault was behind the Bibliothèque Nationale de France *(see p244)*.

Proust by J.-E. Blanche (about 1910)

Writers

French has been dubbed "the language of Molière," after playwright Jean-Baptiste Poquelin, alias Molière (1622–73), who helped create the Comédie-Française, now located near his home in Rue Richelieu. On the Left Bank, the Odéon Théâtre de l'Europe was home to playwright Jean Racine (1639–99). It is near the statue of Denis Diderot (1713–84), who published his *L'Encyclopédie* between 1751 and 1776. Marcel Proust (1871–1922), author of the 13-volume *Remembrance of Things Past*, lived on the Boulevard Haussmann. To the existentialists, the district of St.-Germain was the only place to be *(see pp138–9)*. Here, Sylvia

Beach welcomed James Joyce (1882–1941) to her bookshop on Rue de l'Odéon. Ernest Hemingway (1899–1961) and F. Scott Fitzgerald (1896–1940) wrote novels in Montparnasse. Paris, especially at the time of the Nazi occupation during World War II, is the setting of a number of novels by Patrick Modiano, who was awarded the Nobel Prize for Literature in 2014.

Scientists

Antoine Lavoisier (1743–94), "the father of modern chemistry," first showed that water is a combination of oxygen and hydrogen; his instruments can be seen at the Musée des Arts et Metiers *(see p105)*.

Paris has a Quartier Pasteur, a Boulevard Pasteur, a Pasteur Metro and the world-famous Institut Pasteur *(see pp180–81)*, all in honor of Louis Pasteur (1822–95), the great French chemist and biologist. Discoverers of radium Pierre (1859–1906) and Marie Curie (1867–1934) also worked in Paris.

Fashion Designers

The world capital of fashion boasts many famous designers. The iconic Coco Chanel (1883–1971) revolutionized women's fashion in the 1920s, creating more casual clothes for women. Jeanne Lanvin (1867–1946), founder of Lanvin, the oldest haute couture house still in existence, created fabulous designs and the legendary perfume Arpège. Christian Dior (1905–57) turned fashion upside down with his postwar "New Look," while Yves Saint-Laurent (1936–2008) was equally influential and made *prêt-à-porter*, or ready-to-wear, fashion popular.

Paris's Best: Places of Worship

The Catholic Church has long been the bastion of Parisian society and many of the city's fine churches are worth visiting. Architectural styles vary and the interiors are often spectacular. Most churches are open during the day and many have services at regular intervals. Paris's tradition of church music is still evident. You can spend an evening enjoying the interiors while listening to an organ recital or classical concert *(see p338)*. A more detailed overview of Paris's places of worship is on pages 50–51.

La Madeleine
Built in the style of a Greco-Roman temple, this church is known for its fine sculptures.

0 kilometers 1

0 miles 0.5

Champs-Elysées

Chaillot Quarter

River Seine

Invalides and Eiffel Tower Quarter

Dôme Church
This memorial to the military engineer Vauban lies in the Dôme Church, where Napoleon's remains were buried in 1840.

Sainte-Chapelle
With its fine stained glass, this chapel is a medieval jewel.

Panthéon
The Neo-Classical Sainte-Geneviève, now the Panthéon, was inspired by Wren's St. Paul's Cathedral in London.

Sacré-Coeur
Above the altar in this massive basilica, the chancel vault is decorated with a vast mosaic of Christ by Luc-Olivier Merson.

Montmartre

St.-Eustache
With its mixture of Gothic and Renaissance styles, this is one of the finest churches in Paris.

St.-Paul–St.-Louis
This Christ figure is one of the many rich furnishings in this Jesuit church, built in 1641 for Cardinal Richelieu.

Opéra Quarter

leries arter

Beaubourg and Les Halles

ermain-
s-Prés

The Marais

Ile de la Cité

Ile St-Louis

Notre-Dame
The great cathedral was left to rot after the Revolution, until Victor Hugo led a restoration campaign.

Latin Quarter

Luxembourg Quarter

Jardin des Plantes Quarter

parnasse

Grande Mosquée de Paris
The minaret of this 1920s mosque is nearly 100 ft (33 m) tall.

St.-Séverin
The west door leads into one of the finest medieval churches in the city.

Exploring Paris's Places of Worship

Some of Paris's finest architecture is reflected in the places of worship. The great era of church building was the medieval period but examples survive from all ages. During the Revolution *(see pp32–3)* churches were used as grain or weapons stores but were later restored to their former glory. Many have superb interiors with fine paintings and sculptures.

Facade of Chapelle de la Sorbonne

Tower of St.-Germain-des-Prés

Medieval

Both the pointed arch and the rose window were born in a suburb north of Paris at the Basilique-Cathédrale de St.-Denis, where most of the French kings and queens are buried. This was the first Gothic building, and it was from here that the Gothic style spread. The finest Gothic church in Paris is the city cathedral, **Notre-Dame**, tallest and most impressive of the early French cathedrals. Begun in 1163 by Bishop Maurice de Sully, it was completed over the next century by architects Jean de Chelles and Pierre de Montreuil,

who added the transepts with their fine translucent rose windows. Montreuil's masterpiece is Louis IX's medieval palace chapel, **Sainte-Chapelle**, with its two-tier structure. It was built to house Christ's Crown of Thorns. Other surviving churches in Paris are **St.-Germain-des-Prés**, the oldest surviving abbey church in Paris (1050); the tiny, rustic Romanesque **St.-Julien-le-Pauvre**; and the Flamboyant Gothic **St.-Séverin, St.-Germain l'Auxerrois**, and **St.-Merry**.

Renaissance

The effect of the Italian Renaissance swept through Paris in the 16th century. It led to a unique architectural style in which fine Classical detail and immense Gothic proportions resulted in the attractive "French Renaissance" style. The best example in Paris is **St.-Etienne-du-Mont**, whose interior has the feel of a wide and light basilica. Another is **St.-Eustache**, the massive market church in Les Halles, and the nave of **St.-Gervais–St.-Protais** with its stained glass and carved choir stalls.

St.-Gervais–St.-Protais

Baroque and Classical

Churches and convents flourished in Paris during the 17th century, as the city expanded under Louis XIII and his son Louis XIV. The Italian Baroque style was first seen on the majestic front of **St.-Gervais–St.-Protais**, built by Salomon de Brosse in 1616. The style was toned down to suit French tastes and the rational temperament of the Age of Enlightenment *(see pp30–31)*. The result was a harmonious and monumental Classicism in the form of columns and domes. One example is the distinctive **Chapelle de la Sorbonne**, completed by Jacques Lemercier in 1642 for Cardinal Richelieu. Grander and more richly decorated, with a painted dome, is the church built by François Mansart to honor the birth of the Sun King at the **Val-de-Grâce** convent. The true gem of the period is Jules Hardouin-Mansart's **Dôme des**

Towers, Domes, and Spires

Paris's many churches have dominated her skyline since early Christian times. The Gothic Tour St.-Jacques, the only element still extant from a long-gone church, reflects the medieval love of the defensive tower. St.-Etienne-du-Mont, with its pointed gable and rounded pediment, shows the transition from Gothic to Renaissance. The dome, a much-used feature of the French Baroque, was used to perfection in the Val-de-Grâce, while St.-Sulpice, with its severe arrangement of towers and portico, is typically Neo-Classical. With its ornate spires, Sainte-Clotilde is a Gothic Revival church. Modern landmarks include the mosque, with its minaret.

Tour St.-Jacques

St.-Etienne-du-Mont

Gothic

Renaissance

Invalides, with its enormous gilded dome. An example of Jesuit extravagance can be seen in **St.-Paul–St.-Louis**, built in the style of Il Gesú in Rome. In contrast is Libéral Bruand's chapel **St.-Louis-des-Invalides**, with its severe geometry and unadorned simplicity. Other fine Classical churches are **St.-Joseph-des-Carmes** and the 18th-century **St.-Roch**, with its Baroque Chapelle de la Vierge.

Interior of the Panthéon

Neo-Classical

An obsession with all things Greek and Roman swept France in the mid-18th century and well into the 19th century. The excavations at Pompeii (1738) and the influence of the Italian architect Andrea Palladio produced a generation of architects fascinated by the column, geometry, and engineering. The best example of such churches is Jacques-Germain Soufflot's Sainte-Geneviève, now the **Panthéon**. Begun in 1757, its colonnaded dome was also inspired by Christopher Wren's

St. Paul's in London. The dome is supported by four pillars, built by Guillaume Rondelet, linking four great arches. The first colonnaded facade was Giovanni Niccolo Servandoni's **St.-Sulpice**. Construction of this church began in 1646 and consisted of a two-story portico, topped by a triangular pediment. **La Madeleine**, Napoleon's grand temple to his victorious army, was constructed on the ground plan of a Greco-Roman temple.

Second Empire and Modern

Franz Christian Gau's **Sainte-Clotilde** of the 1840s is the first and best example in Paris of the Gothic Revival or *style religieux*. Showy churches were built in the new districts created by Haussmann in the Second Empire (pp36–7). One of the most lovely is Victor Baltard's St.-Augustin, at the intersection of the Boulevard Malesherbes and the Boulevard de la Madeleine. Here, historic detail combines with modern iron columns and girders in a soaring interior space. The great basilica of the late 19th century, **Sacré-Coeur**, was built as a gesture of religious defiance. **St.-Jean l'Evangéliste** by Anatole de Baudot is an interesting modern church combining the Art Nouveau style with Islamic arches. The modern gem of Islamic architecture, the **Grande Mosquée de Paris**, is an attractive 1920s building in the Hispanic-Moorish style. It has a grand patio, inspired by the Alhambra, woodwork in cedar and eucalyptus, and a fountain.

The arches of St.-Jean L'Evangéliste, reminiscent of Islamic architecture

Finding the Places of Worship

Val-de-Grâce

St.-Sulpice

Sainte-Clotilde

Grande Mosquée de Paris

Baroque and Classical

Neo-Classical

Gothic Revival

Modern

Paris's Best: Gardens, Parks, and Squares

Few cities can boast the infinite variety of styles found in Parisian gardens, parks, and squares today. They date from many different periods and have been central to Parisian life for the past 300 years. The Bois de Boulogne and the Bois de Vincennes enclose the city with their lush, green open spaces, while elegant squares and landscaped gardens, such as the Jardin du Luxembourg, brighten the inner city and provide a retreat for those craving a few moments' peace from the bustling city.

Parc Monceau
This English-style park features many follies, grottoes, magnificent trees, and rare plants.

Champs-Elysées

Tuiler
Quart

Chaillot
Quarter

River Seine

Invalides and Eiffel
Tower Quarter

Montparna

Bois de Boulogne
The Bagatelle gardens, set in this wooded park, have an amazing array of flowers, including the spectacular rose garden.

Esplanade des Invalides
From this huge square, lined with lime trees, are some stunning views over the quays.

Jardin des Tuileries
These gardens are renowned for ornamental ponds, terraces, and the collection of bronze figures by Aristide Maillol.

Parc des Buttes-Chaumont
Once a scraggy hilltop, this park was transformed to provide open spaces for the growing city. It is now beautifully landscaped with huge cliffs revealing caves.

Square du Vert-Galant
The square, named after Henri IV's nickname, forms the west point of the Ile de la Cité.

Place des Vosges
Considered one of the most beautiful squares in the world, it was finished in 1612 and is the oldest square in Paris.

Jardin des Plantes
The botanical garden has a vast collection of plants and flowers from around the world.

éra
rter

Beaubourg
and Les
Halles

The Marais

Germain-
es-Prés

Ile de la
Cité

Ile St-Louis

Latin
Quarter

Luxembourg
Quarter

Jardin des Plantes
Quarter

Bois de Vincennes
The flower garden in this charming park is the perfect place to relax.

Jardin du Luxembourg
This park is a favorite with Parisians wanting to escape the bustle of the Latin Quarter.

0 kilometers   1
0 miles   0.5

Exploring Gardens, Parks, and Squares

Paris is dotted with many areas of parkland, intimate gardens, and attractive tree-lined squares. Each is a reminder of the French capital's illustrious past. Many squares were formed during Napoleon III's transformation of the city, creating a pleasant environment for Parisians to live in *(see pp36–7)*. This aim has been preserved right up to the present day. Paris's parks and gardens have their own character: some are ideal for a stroll, others for romance, while some provide space for sports activities such as a game of *boules*.

Engraving of the Jardin du Palais-Royal (1645)

Historic Gardens

The oldest public gardens in Paris were made for queens of France – the **Jardin des Tuileries** for Catherine de Médicis in the 16th century, and the **Jardin du Luxembourg** for Marie de Médicis in the 17th century. The Tuileries form the beginning of the axis running from the Arc de Triomphe du Carrousel through the Arc de Triomphe *(pp212–13)* to La Défense *(p248)*. These gardens retain the formality devised by landscape architect André Le Nôtre, originally for the **Palace of Versailles**. Many of the Jardin des Tuileries's original sculptures survive, as well as modern pieces, notably the bronze nudes by Aristide Maillol (1861–1944).

The Jardin du Luxembourg also has the traditional formal plan – straight paths, clipped lawns, Classical sculpture, and a superb 17th-century fountain. It is shadier and more intimate than the Tuileries, with lots of seats, pony rides, and puppet shows to amuse the children.

The **Jardins des Champs-Elysées**, also by Le Nôtre, were reshaped in the English style during the 19th century. The gardens have belle époque pavilions, three theaters (L'Espace Pierre Cardin, Théâtre Marigny, and Théâtre du Rond Point), smart restaurants – and the ghost of the novelist Marcel Proust, who once played here as a child.

A haven of peace in a busy district is the **Jardin du Palais Royal**, built by Cardinal Richelieu in the 17th century. An elegant arcade encloses the garden. The 19th-century **Parc Monceau**, in the English picturesque style, has follies and grottoes. The flat **Jardins des Invalides** and the landscaped **Champ-de-Mars** were the grounds of the Hôtel des Invalides and the Ecole Militaire. They were the site of the Paris Universal Exhibition, whose legacy is the Eiffel Tower *(pp196–7)*.

An attractive public garden is attached to the lovely Hôtel Biron, home of the **Musée Rodin**. The 17th-century botanical garden **Jardin des Plantes** is famous for its ancient trees, flowers, alpine garden, hothouses, and small zoo.

Aquatic Garden, Bois de Vincennes

19th-Century Parks and Squares

The great 19th-century parks and squares owe much to Napoleon III's long exile in London before he came to power. The unregimented planting and rolling lawns of Hyde Park and the leafy squares of Mayfair inspired him to bring

Follies and Rotundas

Dramatic features of Paris's parks and gardens are the many follies and rotundas. Every age of garden design has produced these ornaments. The huge Gloriette de Buffon in the Jardin des Plantes was erected as a memorial to the great naturalist *(p168)*. It is the oldest metal structure in Paris. The pyramid in the Parc Monceau, the oriental temple in the Bois de Boulogne, and the 19th-century temple of love in the Bois de Vincennes reflect a more sentimental age. In contrast are the stark, painted-concrete follies that grace the Parc de la Villette.

Relaxing in Jardin du Luxembourg

Egyptian pyramid

Parc Monceau

trees, fresh air, and park benches to what was then Europe's most congested and dirty capital. Under his direction, landscape gardener Adolphe Alphand turned two woods at opposite ends of the city, the **Bois de Boulogne** (known as the "Bois") and the **Bois de Vincennes**, into English-style parks with duck ponds, lakes, and flower gardens. He also added a race track to the "Bois." Its most attractive feature is the Bagatelle rose garden and the Jardin d'Acclimatation, a small theme park for families. The "Bois" is best avoided at night.

The two smaller Alphand parks, **Parc Montsouris** in the south and **Parc des Buttes-Chaumont** in the northeast, are also pleasant. The "Buttes" (hills), a favorite with the Surrealists, was a quarry transformed into two craggy mini-mountains with overhanging vegetation, a suspended bridge, a temple of love, and a lake.

Part of the town-planning programs for the old city included squares and avenues with fountains, sculptures, benches, and greenery. One of the best is Ile de la Cité's **Square du Vert-Galant**. The Avenue de l'Observatoire in the **Jardin du Luxembourg** is rich in sculptures created by Jean-Baptiste Carpeaux.

Fountains and sculpture in the Jardins du Trocadéro

Modern Parks and Gardens

The shady **Jardins du Trocadéro**, sloping down to the river from the Palais de Chaillot, were planted after the 1937 Universal Exhibition. Here is the largest fountain in Paris and fine views of the river and the Eiffel Tower.

More recent Paris gardens eschew formality in favor of wilder planting, multiple levels, mazelike paths, children's gardens, and modern sculpture. Typical are the **Parc André Citroën**, the **Parc de la Villette,** and the Jardins Atlantique, next to the Gare Montparnasse.

Pleasant strolls may be taken in Paris's waterside gardens: in the modern sculpture park behind Notre-Dame, at the Bassin de l'Arsenal at the Bastille, and along the quays of the Seine between the Louvre and the Place de la Concorde, or on the elegantly residential Ile St.-Louis. The planted walkway

above the **Viaduc des Arts** is a peaceful way to observe eastern Paris.

Finding the Gardens, Parks, and Squares

Parc Montsouris

Gloriette de Buffon

Oriental temple

Temple of love

Modern folly

Jardin des Plantes | Bois de Boulogne | Bois de Vincennes | Parc de la Villette

Paris's Best: Museums and Galleries

Some of the oldest, the newest, and certainly some of the finest museums and galleries are to be found in Paris – many are superb works of art in their own right. They house some of the greatest and strangest collections in the world. Some of the buildings complement their themes, such as the Roman baths and Gothic mansion which form the Musée National du Moyen Age, or the Pompidou Center, a modern masterpiece. Elsewhere there is pleasing contrast, such as the Picassos in their gracious 17th-century museum, and the Musée d'Orsay, housed in its grand old train station. Together, they make an unrivalled feast for visitors.

Musée des Arts Décoratifs
Decorative and ornamental art, like this Paris bathroom by Jeanne Lanvin, is displayed here.

Chaillot Quarter

Champs-Elysées

River Seine

Invalides and Eiffel Tower Quarter

Petit Palais
A collection of works by the 19th-century sculptor Jean-Baptiste Carpeaux is housed here, including *The Fisherman and Shell*.

Musée du quai Branly
This wooden sculpture from Papua New Guinea is one of 3,500 artifacts housed in this striking anthropological museum.

Montparn.

Musée Rodin
The museum brings together works bequeathed to the nation by sculptor Auguste Rodin, like the magnificent *Gates of Hell* doors.

Musée d'Orsay
Carpeaux's *Four Quarters of the World* (1867–72) can be found among this collection of 19th-century art.

Musée du Louvre
The museum boasts one of the world's great collections of paintings and sculpture, from the ancient civilizations to the 19th century. This Babylonian monument, the *Code of Hammurabi*, is the oldest set of laws in existence.

Pompidou Center
Paris's modern art collection from 1905 to the present day is housed here. The center also has art libraries and an industrial design center.

Opéra Quarter

Tuileries Quarter

Beaubourg and Les Halles

The Marais

Germain-les-Prés

Ile de la Cité

Ile St-Louis

Latin Quarter

Luxembourg Quarter

Jardin des Plantes Quarter

Musée Picasso Paris
Sculptor and Model (1931) is one of many paintings on display in Picasso's private collection, "inherited" in lieu of tax by the French government after his death in 1973.

Musée Carnavalet
The museum is devoted to the history of Paris. Its historic buildings surround attractive garden courtyards.

Musée de Cluny – Musée National du Moyen Age
The remains of the Gallo-Roman baths are part of this museum of ancient and medieval art.

0 kilometers   1
0 miles   0.5

Exploring Paris's Museums and Galleries

Paris holds great treasures in its museums and art galleries. The major national art collection is to be found at the Musée du Louvre, which began collecting over 400 years ago and is still growing. Other important museums, such as the Musée d'Orsay, the Musée du quai Branly, and the Pompidou Center, have their own treasures, but there are scores of smaller, specialized museums, each with its own interest.

Altar, Musée National du Moyen Age

Dead Poet in Musée Gustave Moreau

Old Masters

The *Mona Lisa* was one of the **Musée du Louvre's** first paintings, acquired over 400 years ago. It also has other fine Leonardos. They are to be found along with superb Titians, Raphaels, and other Italian masters. Other works include Rembrandt's *Pilgrims at Emmäus*, Watteau's *Gilles*, and Fragonard's *The Bathers*. The **Musée Cognacq-Jay** has a small, but exquisite, collection of paintings and drawings by 18th-century French painters. The **Musée Jacquemart-André** has works by such masters as Mantegna, Uccello, Canaletto, Rembrandt, and Chardin.

Greek, Roman, and Medieval Art

The **Musée du Louvre** has a fine collection of sculptures from Greek and Roman times, along with medieval sculptures and vestiges of the medieval Louvre under the Sully wing. The **Musée de Cluny – Musée National du Moyen Age**, a superb 15th-century mansion, houses a major medieval collection. Highlights are the Unicorn Tapestries, the Kings' Heads from Notre-Dame, and Basel Cathedral's golden altar. Late first-century Roman baths adjoin the museum. Remains of houses from Roman and medieval Paris can be seen in the **Crypte Archéologique** near Notre-Dame cathedral.

Impressionist and Post-Impressionist Art

Installed in a converted 19th-century train station, the **Musée d'Orsay** boasts the world's largest collection of art from the period 1848–1904. Admired for its fine Impressionist and Post-Impressionist collections,

it also devotes a lot of space to the earlier Realists and the formerly reviled 19th-century academic and "Salon" masters. There are superb works by Degas, Manet, Courbet (including his controversial *L'Origine du Monde*), Monet, Renoir, Millet, Cézanne, Bonnard, and Vuillard, and some fine Gauguins, Van Goghs, and Seurats.

A great ensemble of late Monets is to be found at the **Musée Marmottan Monet** and another at the **Musée de l'Orangerie**, including Monet's last great waterlily murals (1920–25). Here also is a good collection of Cézannes and late Renoirs.

Three artists' studios and homes are now museums of their life and work. The **Musée Rodin**, in an attractive 18th-century mansion and garden, offers a complete survey of the master's sculptures, drawings, and paintings. The **Musée Delacroix**, set in a garden near St.-Germain-des-Prés, has sketches, prints, and oils by the Romantic artist. The **Musée Gustave Moreau**, in an atmospheric 19th-century town house, has an extraordinary collection of intricately painted canvases of legendary *femmes fatales* and dying youths. The **Petit Palais** has an interesting collection of 19th-century paintings with four major Courbets, including *The Sleep*.

Dante and Virgil in the Underworld (1822) by Delacroix, Musée du Louvre

Modern and Contemporary Art

The Pompidou Center houses the **Musée National d'Art Moderne**, covering 1905 to the present. It has a good selection of Fauvist and Cubist works, particularly by Matisse, Rouault, Braque, Leger, and Delaunay, as well as works by the 1960s' *Nouveaux Réalistes*.

The **Musée d'Art Moderne de la Ville de Paris**, in the elegant 1930s Palais de Tokyo, also has an excellent collection, including Delaunays, Bonnards, and Fauvist paintings. The highlight is Matisse's 1932 mural *The Dance*. In the opposite wing of the same building, the **Palais de Tokyo** showcases some of today's most avant-garde artists.

Penelope by Bourdelle

The **Musée Picasso Paris,** in a lovely 17th-century mansion, has the world's largest Picasso collection, including paintings, drawings, and sculptures. Picasso, Matisse, Modigliani, Utrillo, and late Derains make up the collection on display at the **Musée de l'Orangerie**. For modern sculpture, the small **Musée Zadkine** has Cubist work by a minor school whose leading light was Ossip Zadkine. The **Musée Antoine Bourdelle** and the **Musée Maillol** house work by these two sculptors. The Frank Gehry-designed **Fondation Louis Vuitton** houses contemporary works by the likes of Gilbert & George, Jeff Koons, and Jean-Michel Basquiat.

Furniture, Decorative Arts, and Objets d'Art

Paris's art treasures are not limited to paintings. Furniture and the decorative arts are well represented in a plethora of museums. Fine ensembles of French furnishings and decoration are in the **Louvre** (medieval to Napoleonic) and at the **Palace of Versailles** (17th–18th century). Furniture and *objets d'art* from the Middle Ages to the present century are arranged in period rooms at the **Musée des Arts Décoratifs**. The **Musée d'Orsay** has a large collection of 19th-century furniture, notably Art Nouveau. Louis XV (1715–74) and Louis XVI (1774–93) furniture and decoration can be found in the **Musée Nissim de Camondo**, a mansion from 1912 facing the Parc Monceau. Other notable collections are the **Musée Cognacq-Jay**; the **Musée Carnavalet** (18th-century); the **Musée Jacquemart-André** (French furniture and earthenware); the **Musée Marmottan-Monet** (Empire); and the **Musée d'Art Moderne de la Ville de Paris** (Art Deco).

Cabinet, Musée des Arts Décoratifs

Jeweler's store in the Carnavalet

Specialty Museums

Devotees of antique sporting guns, muskets, and hounds of the chase should make for the attractive Marais **Hôtel de Guénégaud** (Musée de la Chasse et de la Nature). This museum also has some fine 18th-century animal paintings by Jean-Baptiste Oudry and Alexandre-François Desportes, as well as others by Rubens and Brueghel. **The Musée de la Contrefaçon** gives a fascinating insight into the world of counterfeit with examples from every luxury trade, including perfume, wines and spirits, and clothing. Numismatists will find an extensive coin and medallion collection housed in luxurious surroundings at the 18th-century Paris Mint at the **Musée de la Monnaie**. French coins are no longer minted here, but the old Mint still makes medals that are available for sale. Stamps on display are at the **Musée de la Poste**. The history of postal services is also covered, as are all aspects of philately old and new, with temporary shows on current philatelic design. Visitors can marvel at the vast national collection of minerals on display at the **Musée de Minéralogie**, which is housed in the Ecole Nationale Supérieure des Mines. The collection includes 100,000 samples of minerals, rocks, meteorites, gems, ores, and artifical minerals from 72 different countries.

Fashion and Costume

The two rival fashion museums in Paris are the **Musée Galliera** at the Palais Galliera and the **Musée de la Mode** within the **Musée des Arts Décoratifs**. Neither has a permanent collection, but both hold regular shows devoted to the great Paris couturiers, such as Saint Laurent and Givenchy. They sometimes display fashion accessories as well and, more rarely but always fascinatingly, historical costumes.

Poster for the Musée Galliera

Asian, African, and Oceanian Art

The major collection of Asian art in France is housed at the **Musée National des Arts Asiatiques Guimet**, covering China, Tibet, Japan, Korea, Indochina, Indonesia, India, and Central Asia. It includes Chinese bronzes and lacquerware and some of the best Khmer art outside Cambodia. The **Musée Cernuschi** has a smaller but well-chosen Chinese collection, noted for its ancient bronzes and reliefs. France's premier showcase for African, Asian, Native American, and Oceanian arts and cultures is the **Musée du quai Branly**, which displays 3,500 objects in truly breathtaking surroundings. The **Musée Dapper** also houses African art and is part of an important ethnographic research center, housed in an elegant 1901 *hôtel particulier* with an "African" garden. Its collection of tribal masks is particularly dazzling.

Sri Lankan theatrical mask

Café in Musée de Montmartre

History and Social History

Covering the entire history of the city of Paris, the **Musée Carnavalet** is housed in two historic Marais *hôtels*. It has period interiors, paintings of the city and old store signs, a fascinating section covering events and artifacts from the French Revolution, and even Marcel Proust's bedroom. Also in the Marais, the **Musée d'Art et d'Histoire du Judaïsme** explores the culture of French Jewry. The **Musée de l'Armée**, in the Hôtel des Invalides, recounts French military history, and the Musée de l'Histoire de France, in the Rococo **Hôtel de Soubise**, has historical documents from the national archives on display. Famous *tableaux vivants* and characters, both current and historical, await the visitor at the **Grévin** wax museum. The intriguing **Musée de Montmartre**, overlooking Paris's last surviving vineyard, holds exhibitions on the history of Montmartre.

Architecture and Design

The **Cité de l'Architecture et du Patrimoine** charts the history of French architecture with scale models of its most iconic buildings. Superb scale models of fortresses built for Louis XIV and later are on display at the **Musée des Plans-Reliefs**. The work of the celebrated Franco-Swiss architect forms the basis of the **Fondation Le Corbusier**. The showpiece is his 1920s villa for his friend, art collector Raoul La Roche. Some of his furniture is also on display.

The French Impressionists

Impression: Sunrise by Monet

Impressionism, the great art revolution of the 19th century, began in Paris in the 1860s, when young painters, influenced in part by the new art of photography, started to break with the academic values of the past. They aimed to capture the "impression" of what the eye sees at a given moment and used brushwork designed to capture the fleeting effects of light falling on a scene. Their favorite subjects were landscapes and scenes from contemporary urban life.

The movement had no founder, though Edouard Manet (1832–83) and the radical Realist painter Gustave Courbet (1819–77) both inspired many of the younger artists. Paintings of scenes of everyday life by Manet and Courbet often offended the academicians who legislated artistic taste. In 1863, Manet's *Le Déjeuner sur l'Herbe (see p147)* was exhibited at the Salon des Refusés, an exhibition set up for paintings rejected by the official Paris Salon of that year. The first time the term "Impressionist" was used to describe this new artistic movement was at another unofficial exhibition, in 1874. The name came from a painting by Claude Monet, *Impression: Sunrise*, a view of Le Havre in the mist from 1872. Monet was almost exclusively a landscape artist, influenced by the works of the English artists Constable and Turner. He always liked to paint

Monet's sketchbooks

Harvesting (1876) by Pissarro

The living room of La Roche Villa by Le Corbusier (1923)

Science and Technology

In the Jardin des Plantes, the **Muséum National d'Histoire Naturelle** has sections on paleontology, mineralogy, entomology, anatomy, and botany, plus a zoo and a botanical garden. In the Palais de Chaillot, the **Musée de l'Homme** is a museum of anthropology and prehistory.

Next door, the **Musée National de la Marine** covers French naval history from the 17th century onward, with interesting 18th-century models of ships and sculpted figure-heads. The **Musée des Arts et Métiers** displays the world of science and industry, invention and manufacturing. The **Palais de la Découverte** covers the history of science and has a good planetarium, somewhat overshadowed by the specta-cular one at the **Cité des Sciences** in the Parc de la Villette. This museum is on several levels, with an IMAX 3-D movie screen, the Géode.

Finding the Museums

Gabrielle (1910) by Renoir

outdoors and encouraged others to follow his example.

At the 1874 exhibition, a critic wrote that one should stand well back to see these "impressions" – the farther back the better – and that members of the establishment should retreat altogether. Other exhibitors at the show were Pierre-Auguste Renoir, Edgar Degas, Camille Pissarro, Alfred Sisley, and Paul Cézanne.

There were seven more Impressionist shows up to 1886. By then the power of the Salon had waned and the whole direction of art had changed. From then on, new movements were defined in terms of their relation to Impressionism. The leading Neo-Impressionist was Georges Seurat, who used thousands of minute dots of color to build up his paintings. It took later generations to fully appreciate the work of the Impressionists. Cézanne was

rejected all his life, Degas sold only one painting to a museum, and Sisley died unknown. Of the great artists whose genius is now universally recognized, only Renoir and Monet were ever acclaimed in their lifetimes.

Profile of a Model (1887) by Seurat

Artists in Paris

The city first attracted artists during the reign of Louis XIV (1643–1715), and Paris soon became the most sophisticated artistic center in Europe; the magnetism has persisted. During the 18th century, all major French artists lived and worked in Paris. In the latter half of the 19th century and early part of the 20th century, the French capital was the European center of modern and progressive art, and movements such as Impressionism, Post-Impressionism, Divisionism, Fauvism, and Cubism were founded and blossomed in the city. Many artists from all around the world came to Paris to display their works in the many exhibitions and salons.

Boucher's *Diana Bathing* (1742), typical of the Rococo style (Louvre)

1793 Louvre opens as first national public gallery

1667 First Salon, France's official art exhibition; originally held annually, later every two years

1600	1650	1700	1750	1800
Baroque			Neo-Classicism	Romanti
1600	1650	1700	1750	1800

1627 Vouet returns from Italy and is made court painter by Louis XIII. Vouet revived a dismal period in the fortunes of French painting

Philippe de Champaigne's *Last Supper* (about 1652). His style slowly became more Classical in his later years (Louvre)

1819 Géricault paints *The Raft of the Medusa*, one of the greatest works of French Romanticism *(see p124)*

1648 Foundation of the Académie Royale de Peinture et de Sculpture, which had a virtual monopoly on art teaching

Vouet's *The Presentation in the Temple* (1641) with typically Baroque contrasts of light and shade (Louvre)

David's *The Oath of the Horatii* (1784), in the Neo-Classical style (Louvre)

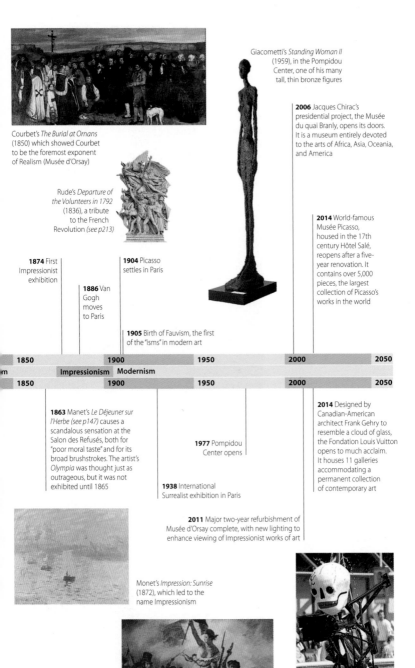

Courbet's *The Burial at Ornans* (1850) which showed Courbet to be the foremost exponent of Realism (Musée d'Orsay)

Rude's *Departure of the Volunteers in 1792* (1836), a tribute to the French Revolution (see p213)

Giacometti's *Standing Woman II* (1959), in the Pompidou Center, one of his many tall, thin bronze figures

2006 Jacques Chirac's presidential project, the Musée du quai Branly, opens its doors. It is a museum entirely devoted to the arts of Africa, Asia, Oceania, and America

2014 World-famous Musée Picasso, housed in the 17th century Hôtel Salé, reopens after a five-year renovation. It contains over 5,000 pieces, the largest collection of Picasso's works in the world

1874 First Impressionist exhibition

1886 Van Gogh moves to Paris

1904 Picasso settles in Paris

1905 Birth of Fauvism, the first of the "isms" in modern art

| 1850 | 1900 | 1950 | 2000 | 2050 |

Impressionism Modernism

| 1850 | 1900 | 1950 | 2000 | 2050 |

1863 Manet's *Le Déjeuner sur l'Herbe* (see p147) causes a scandalous sensation at the Salon des Refusés, both for "poor moral taste" and for its broad brushstrokes. The artist's *Olympia* was thought just as outrageous, but it was not exhibited until 1865

1977 Pompidou Center opens

1938 International Surrealist exhibition in Paris

2011 Major two-year refurbishment of Musée d'Orsay complete, with new lighting to enhance viewing of Impressionist works of art

2014 Designed by Canadian-American architect Frank Gehry to resemble a cloud of glass, the Fondation Louis Vuitton opens to much acclaim. It houses 11 galleries accommodating a permanent collection of contemporary art

Monet's *Impression: Sunrise* (1872), which led to the name Impressionism

Delacroix's *Liberty Leading the People* (1830) romantically celebrates victory in war (Louvre)

Tinguely and Saint Phalle's *Fontaine Igor Stravinsky* (1980), a modern kinetic sculpture (Pompidou Center)

PARIS THROUGH THE YEAR

Paris's pulling power is strongest in spring – the season for sitting at tables under trees. From June, Paris is slowly turned over to tourists; the city almost comes to a standstill for the French Tennis Open at Roland Garros, and the major race tracks stage the big summer horse races. Next comes the July 14 Bastille Day parade down the Champs-Elysées; toward the end of July, the Tour de France usually ends here.

The end of July also sees the end of Paris's month-long Jazz Festival, after which most Parisians abandon the city to visitors until *la rentrée*, the return to school and work in September. Dates of events listed on the following pages may vary. For details, consult the listings magazines. The Office du Tourisme et des Congrès de Paris *(see p359)* also produces an annual calendar of events.

Spring

A good many of the city's annual 20 million visitors arrive in the spring. It is the season for fairs and concerts, when the marathon street race is held and the outdoor temperature is pleasant. Spring is also the time when hoteliers offer weekend packages, often with tickets for jazz concerts and museum passes included.

March

Spring flower shows at Parc Floral (Bois de Vincennes, *p249*) and Bagatelle Gardens (Bois de Boulogne, *pp247*).
Salon International d'Agriculture *(end Feb–early Mar)*, Paris-Expo, Porte de Versailles. Vast farming fair.
Banlieues Bleues Festival *(mid-Mar–early Apr)*, Paris suburbs. Jazz, blues, soul, and funk.
Printemps du Cinema *(3 days late Mar)*. Movies can be seen for a very reasonable price at theaters across Paris and throughout France.

French Tennis Open, Stade Roland Garros

Foire du Trône *(late Mar– May)*, Bois de Vincennes *(p249)*. Large fair with amusements.

April

Paris International Marathon From Place de la Concorde to Avenue Foch.
Chemin de la Croix *(Good Friday)*. Beautiful Stations of the Cross procession, from Montmartre to Sacré-Coeur.
Paris Ceramics Festival *(mid-Apr)*. Renowned artists display their wares related to various themes.
Foire de Paris *(end Apr–1st week May)*, Paris Expo, Porte de Versailles. Food, wine, house and garden, and tourism show.

May

Shakespeare Garden Festival *(until Oct)*, Bois de Boulogne *(pp247)*. Classic plays performed outdoors.
Carré Rive Gauche *(one week, mid-month)*. Exhibits at antiques dealers in and around St.-Germain-des-Prés *(p137)*.

Grandes Concerts de Versailles *(Sep–May)*, Versailles *(p250–55)*. Open-air concerts and pyrotechnic displays on Versailles lake.
French Tennis Open *(last week May –1st week Jun)*, Stade Roland Garros *(p350)*. Parisian society meets sports.
Le Printemps des Rues *(3rd w/end)*. Concerts and free street theater are held in the Bastille/ République area.

Paris International Marathon

Spring color, Jardin du Luxembourg

Average Daily Hours of Sunshine

Sunshine Hours
The northerly position of Paris gives it long and light summer evenings, but in winter the daylight recedes with few truly bright days.

Summer

Summer begins with the French Tennis Open, and there are many events and festivities until July. Thereafter, the French begin thinking of their own annual vacation, but there are big celebrations on Bastille Day (July 14), with military displays for the president and his guests.

Final lap of the Champs-Elysées during the Tour de France

Jardin du Luxembourg in summer

June

Festival St.-Denis, Basilique-Cathédrale de St.-Denis. Concerts emphasize large-scale choral works (p338).
Prix de Diane-Longines (mid-Jun), Chantilly. French equivalent of the US Kentucky Derby high-society horse-racing event.

Fête de la Musique (Jun 21), all over Paris. Nightlong summer solstice musical celebrations.
Fête du Cinéma (late Jun–early Jul). Movies shown all over Paris for a nominal fee (p348).
Fête des Jardins à Bagatelle, Bois de Boulogne (pp247). Celebrating rose season
Paris Jazz Festival (Jun–Jul), Parc Floral de Paris. Jazz musicians come to play in Paris (pp341–2).
Les Grandes Eaux Nocturnes (mid-Jun–mid-Sep), Versailles (pp250–55). Lights and fountains in the gardens with music, dance, and theater.
Gay Pride (end Jun). Lively parade around the Bastille.

Paris Air and Space Technology Show (Jun, alternate years, next show 2017), Le Bourget Airport.

July

Festival du Cinéma en Plein Air (mid-Jul–Aug), Parc de la Villette (pp238–9).
Paris Quartier d'Eté (mid- Jul–mid-Aug). Dance, music, theater, ballet.
Paris Plages (mid-Jul–mid-Aug). Sand and palm trees deposited on the Right Bank of the Seine create a beach.
Tour de France (late Jul). The world's greatest cycle race ends on the Champs-Elysées.

March past of troops on Bastille Day (July 14)

Average Monthly Temperature

Temperature
The chart shows the average temperatures for each month. It is hottest in July and August and coolest between December and February, though Paris is rarely freezing cold. Temperatures are pleasant in the spring when the number of visitors peaks, and also in the fall.

Fall

September sees the start of the social season, with gala showing of new movies, and parties in big houses on the Ile St-Louis. Paris is the world's largest congress center and there is a rush of shows in September, ranging from gifts to leisure and music. The pace barely slackens in October and November when Parisians begin to indulge their great love of movies. French and Hollywood stars often make appearances at premieres staged on the Champs-Elysées.

The Prix de l'Arc de Triomphe (October)

September

Festival d'Automne à Paris (mid-Sep – end Dec), throughout Paris. Music, dance, theater (pp338–9).
La Villette Jazz Festival (mid-Sep). Jazz artists come and blow their horns with gusto throughout the Cité de la Musique (p238).
Journées du Patrimoine (2nd or 3rd week Sep). Historic buildings, monuments, and museums are open free to the public for two days, following an all-night party to kick off proceedings.

October

Nuit Blanche (one Sat in Oct). Museums stay open all night and there are art installations around the city.
Prix de l'Arc de Triomphe (1st week), Longchamp. An international field competes for the richest prize in European horse-racing.
Salon de l'Automobile (1st 2 weeks, alternate years), Paris-Expo, Porte de Versailles. Commercial auto show,

Jazz fusion guitarist Al di Meola playing in Paris

alternated annually in even years with a motorcycle show.
Foire Internationale d'Art Contemporain (FIAC) (last week), Paris-Expo, Porte de Versailles. Paris's biggest international modern and contemporary art fair.

November

BNP Paribas Masters (usually early Nov), Palais Omnisports de Paris-Bercy. Prestigious indoor men's tennis tournament (pp350–51.)
Mois de la Photo (Oct–Nov, every two years, in even years). Numerous photography shows, film screenings, and public discussions.
Beaujolais Nouveau (3rd Thursday Nov). Bars and cafés are crowded on this day, in a race to taste the new vintage.

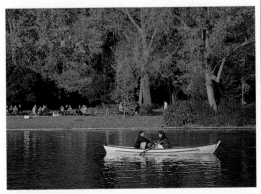

Fall in the Bois de Vincennes

Average Monthly Rainfall

Rainfall
August is the wettest month in Paris. In August and September you may get caught in storms. Sudden showers, sometimes with hail, can occur between January and April – notoriously in March. There is occasional snow in winter.

Winter

Paris rarely sees snow; winter days tend to be invigorating rather than chilly. There are festivals, candlelit Christmas church services, and much celebrating in the streets over the New Year. After New Year, the streets become slightly less congested, and on bright days the quays are a rendezvous for strollers and lovers.

December

Christmas illuminations *(until Jan)* in the department store windows of the Grands Boulevards, Avenue Montaigne, Opéra, Champs-Elysées, and Rue du Faubourg St.-Honoré.
Crèche *(early Dec–early Jan)*, under a canopy in Place de l'Hôtel de Ville, Marais *(p104)*. Life-size Nativity from a different country each year.
Salon du Cheval *(1st 2 weeks)*. Equestrian trade show, exhibitions, and competitions.

January fashion show

Snow in the Tuileries, a rare occurrence

Paris International Boat Show *(1st 2 weeks)*, Paris-Expo, Porte de Versailles.

January

Fête des Rois (Epiphany). *(Jan 6)*. The *boulangeries* are full of *galettes des rois*.
Prix d'Amérique *(end Jan)*. Europe's most famous harness race, Hippodrome de Vincennes.
Fashion shows, summer collections. *(See Couture and High-End Designer Fashion p317.)*

February

Carnaval *(weekend before Mardi Gras)*, Quartier de St.-Fargeau.
Floraisons *(all month)*, Parc Floral de Paris, Bois de Vincennes *(p249)*, and Parc de Bagatelle, Bois de Boulogne *(pp247)*. Say farewell to winter with these colorful and impressive displays of crocuses and snowdrops.

Public Holidays

New Year's Day (Jan 1)
Easter Monday varies
Labor Day (May 1)
VE Day (May 8)
Ascension Day (6th Thu after Easter)
Bastille Day (Jul 14)
Assumption (Aug 15)
All Saints' Day (Nov 1)
Remembrance Day (Nov 11)
Christmas (Dec 25)

Eiffel Tower Christmas decorations

A RIVER VIEW OF PARIS

Historically, the River Seine has been a mode of transportation, a muse for artists and an inspiration for romantics. Flowing through Paris, the Seine has a profound relationship with the city, and it is even a designated UNESCO World Heritage site, protected as an important natural and cultural location. It is also an essential point of reference for the city: distances are measured from it, and street numbers determined by it. The Seine divides the French capital into the Left Bank, on the south side of the river, and the Right Bank, on the north.

Paris's urban development and history can be admired from the banks of this iconic river. The Seine borders ten of the city's 20 arrondissements, its two banks are connected by 32 bridges, and most of Paris's buildings and monuments are either alongside it or within a stone's throw of it. From Notre-Dame to the Grand Palais, from the Eiffel Tower to the Louvre, the river is like a busy floating avenue, its banks providing Parisians and tourists alike with an interesting and dynamic walkway.

Paris's riverbanks are well worth exploring on foot. There are benches and playgrounds, floating cafés and discos, houseboats and *bouquinistes* – bookstands selling second-hand books and prints. From the Musée d'Orsay to the Pont de l'Alma, about 2 miles (3 km) of the Left Bank are part of a regeneration project dedicated to pedestrians, Les Berges de la Seine. This public park and promenade offers gorgeous views, free fitness programs, picnic spots, and playgrounds. Farther down the river, another popular initiative, Paris Plages, takes place during the summer, when the Right Bank, from the Louvre to the Bassin de la Villette, is turned into a giant beach, with everything you need to feel like you are in the South of France, from deckchairs to parasols to beach volleyball.

However, the star of this flowing boulevard remains the Seine itself. It is busy with commercial barges and sightseeing boats, the most famous being the *bateaux mouches*. The best way to start your visit to Paris is with a cruise down the Seine, where you can take in some of the city's most illustrious sights.

This map shows the sections of the river depicted on the following pages.

0 kilometers 2

0 miles 1

◀ View of the Seine from Notre-Dame

For keys to symbols *see back flap*

From Pont de Grenelle to Pont de la Concorde

The soaring monuments and grand exhibition halls along this stretch of the river are remnants of the Napoleonic era and the Industrial Revolution with its great exhibitions. The exhilarating self-confidence of the Eiffel Tower, the Petit Palais, and the Grand Palais is matched by more recent buildings, such as the Palais de Chaillot, the Maison de Radio-France, and the skyscrapers of the Left Bank.

Palais de Chaillot
The curved wings and arching fountains make this a spectacular setting for three museums and a theater *(p202)*.

Palais de Tokyo
Figures by Bourdelle adorn this museum *(p205)*.

Trocadéro Ⓜ

Bateaux Parisiens
Tour Eiffel
Vedettes de Paris Ile de France

Passe
Deb

The Statue of Liberty was given to the city in 1885. It faces west, toward the original Liberty in New York.

Pont d'Iéna

Musée d
quai Bran
(pp 194–

Maison de Radio-France
Studios and a radio museum are housed in this circular building *(p204)*.

Ⓜ Passy

Champ de Mars 🚈

Pont de Bir-Hakeim

Ave du Prés. Kennedy 🚈

Ⓜ Bir-Hakeim

Eiffel Tower
The tower is the symbol of Paris *(pp196–7)*.

Pont de Bir-Hakeim
has a dynamic statue by Wederkinch rising at its north end.

Pont de Grenelle

Ile aux Cignes

Grand Palais
Major exhibitions and a science museum are based here *(p210)*.

Petit Palais
Now the Paris museum of fine arts, this was first designed as a companion to the Grand Palais *(p210)*.

Champs-Elysées Clemenceau

Alma Marceau

Pont de l'Alma

RER Pont de l'Alma

Pont des Invalides

Pont Alexandre III

Pont de la Concorde

Invalides

Bateaux Mouches

The Zouave is a statue of a soldier on a central pier of the bridge. It is used by Parisians to measure the level of the Seine when it is in flood.

The Liberty Flame, commemorating French Resistance fighters, is also an unofficial memorial to Diana, Princess of Wales.

Pont Alexandre III
Flamboyant statuary decorates Paris's most ornate bridge *(p210)*.

Assemblée Nationale Palais-Bourbon
Louis XIV's daughter once owned this palace, which is now used by the Chambre des Députés as the national forum for political debate *(p192)*.

Dôme des Invalides
The majestic gilded dome *(pp188–9)* is here seen from Pont Alexandre III.

For keys to symbols *see back flap*

From Pont de la Concorde to Pont de Sully

The historic heart of Paris lies on the banks and islands of the east river. At its center is the Ile de la Cité, a natural stepping stone across the Seine and the cultural core of medieval Paris. Today, it is still vital to Parisian life.

Jardin des Tuileries
These gardens are in the formal style *(p132)*.

Musée du Louvre
Before becoming the world's greatest museum and home to the *Mona Lisa*, this was Europe's largest royal palace *(pp122–9)*.

Pont de la Concorde

Assemblée Nationale Ⓜ

Passerelle Solférino

RER Quai d'Orsay

Pont Royal

Pont du Carrousel

Passerelle des Arts

Musée de l'Orangerie
An important collection of 19th-century paintings is on display here *(p133)*.

Passerelle des Arts
This steel reconstruction of Paris's first cast-iron bridge (1804) was inaugurated in 1984.

Bâteaux Vedettes du Pont Neuf

Musée d'Orsay
Paris's most important collection of Impressionist art is housed in this converted train station *(pp146–9)*.

Hôtel des Monnaies
Built in 1771–75, this former Mint has a fine coin collection in its old milling halls *(p143)*.

For keys to symbols *see back flap*

Ile de la Cité
The medieval identity of this small island was almost wiped out in the 19th century by Baron Haussmann's grand scheme. Sainte-Chapelle and parts of the Conciergerie are the only buildings of the period that remain. The Square du Vert-Galant, a park at the island's western tip, has views of the Louvre and the Right Bank *(pp78–91)*.

Conciergerie
During the Revolution, this building, with its distinctive towers, became notorious as a prison *(p87)*.

Pont Neuf
Paris's oldest standing bridge, the Pont Neuf links the Right and Left banks to the Ile de la Cité *(p90)*.

St.-Gervais–St.-Protais
One of the oldest organs in Paris, dating from the early 17th century, is in this church *(p103)*.

Jardin Tino Rossi
Created in 1975, this is an open-air sculpture garden dedicated to the Corsican singer.

M Pont Neuf
Neuf

M Châtelet

Pont au Change

Hôtel de Ville
M

Pont Notre-Dame

Cité
M

Pont d'Arcole

RER M
St-Michel

Petit Pont

Pont au Double

Pont Louis-Philippe

Pont St-Louis

M Pont Marie
Pont Marie

Pont de l'Archevêché

Pont de la Tournelle

Sully Morland
M

Pont de Sully

Notre-Dame
This towering cathedral surveys the river *(pp82–5)*.

Bâteaux Parisiens

How to Take a River or Canal Trip

River Seine cruises on a variety of pleasure boats operate along the main sightseeing reaches of the river, taking in many of the city's famous monuments. The Batobus river service operates as a shuttle or bus service, allowing passengers to get on and off anywhere along the route. The main city canal trips operate along the old industrial St.-Martin canal in the east of the city, passing through areas of Paris steeped in history.

Pleasure-cruise boat on the River Seine

Types of Boats

Bateaux mouches, *the largest of the pleasure-cruise boats, are a spectacular sight with their passenger areas enclosed in glass for excellent all round viewing. At night floodlights are used to pick out river bank buildings. A more luxurious version of these is used on the Bateaux Parisien cruises. The vedettes are smaller and more intimate boats, with viewing through glass walls. The Canauxrama canal boats are flat-bottomed.*

Seine Cruises and Shuttle Services

The Seine cruises and shuttle services information below includes the boarding points, the nearest metro and RER stations, and the nearest bus routes. Meal cruises must be reserved in advance, and passengers must board 30 minutes before departure. Timings may vary – visitors are advised to check ahead.

Vedettes de Paris Seine Cruise

These superb cruises cover major sights along the river. Some tickets include a snack or champagne. The boarding point is:

Port de Suffren
Map 10 D3. **Tel** 01 44 18 19 50. Ⓜ Bir Hakeim. Champs de Mars. 22, 30, 32, 44, 63, 69, 72, 82, 87. **Departures** mid-Feb–Oct: 10:30am–11pm (mid-Feb–

Mar: to 9pm); Nov–mid-Feb: 11:15am–9pm Mon–Fri, 10:30am–10pm Sat & Sun, 10:30am–9pm Christmas hols. Every 30–45 mins. **Duration** 1 hr.
Ⓦ vedettesdeparis.com

Croisière Dégustation Champagne

Enjoy champagne while a sommelier provides tasting notes. The boarding point is:

Port de Suffren
Map 10 D3. **Tel** 01 44 18 19 50. Ⓜ Bir Hakeim. **Departures** May–Aug: 6:30pm Mon–Sat. **Duration** 1 hr. Ⓦ vedettesdeparis.com

Bateaux Parisiens Tour Eiffel Cruise

This company offers sightseeing and meal cruises with a commentary in 13 languages. The boarding point is:

Port de la Bourdonnais
Map 10 D2. **Tel** 08 25 01 01 01. Ⓜ Bir Hakeim. Champs de Mars. 42, 82. **Departures** every 30 mins. Apr–May & Sep: 10am–10pm; Jun–Aug: 10am–11pm; Oct–Mar: 10:30am–9pm (hourly). **Duration** 1 hr. **Lunch cruise** 12:45pm. **Duration** 2 hr. **Dinner cruise** 6pm, 8:30pm, 9pm. **Duration** 2.5 hr.
Ⓦ bateauxparisiens.com

Bateaux Parisiens Notre-Dame Cruise

Same route as the Tour Eiffel Cruise, but in the opposite direction. The boarding point is:

Quai de Montebello
Map 13 B4. **Tel** 08 25 01 01 01. Ⓜ Maubert-Mutualité, St.-Michel. St.-Michel. 24, 27, 47. **Departures** Mar 28–Apr 10: 2:20–8:15pm; Apr 11–Jul 4: 12:20–10pm Mon–Thu, 11am–10:45pm Fri–Sun; Jul 5–Aug 23: 11am–11pm; Aug 24–Sep 21: 12:20–10pm; Sep 22–Oct 17: 2:20–6:20pm Sun–Thu; Oct 18–Nov 2: 2:20–8:15pm. **Duration** 1 hr.

Boarding Points

The boarding points for the river cruises and the Batobus services are easy to find along the river. Here you can

buy tickets, and there are amenities such as snack bars. Major cruise companies also have foreign exchange booths. There is limited parking around the points, but none near the Pont Neuf.

River boarding point

Batobus Cruises

Shuttle service. 1- and 2-day as well as annual passes available. **Tel** 08 25 05 01 01. **Departures** daily every 20–45 min (depending on the time of year); check website for latest times. Board at: Eiffel Tower: **Map** 10 D3. Ⓜ Bir Hakeim. Champs-Elysées: **Map** 11 B1. Ⓜ Champs-Elysées-Clemenceau. Musée d'Orsay: **Map** 12 D2. Ⓜ Assemblée Nationale. Louvre: **Map** 12 E2. Ⓜ Louvre. St.-Germain-des-Prés: **Map** 12 E3. Ⓜ St-Germain-des-Prés. Notre-Dame: **Map** 13 B4. Ⓜ St-Michel. Hôtel de Ville: **Map** 13 B4. Ⓜ Hôtel de Ville. ⓦ **batobus.com**

Bateaux Mouches Seine Cruise

One of Paris's best known pleasure boat companies, with a fleet of 14 boats. The boarding point is:

Pont de l'Alma
Map 10 F1.
Tel 01 42 25 96 10.
Ⓜ Alma-Marceau. ⓇⒺⓇ Pont de l'Alma. 🚌 28, 42, 49, 63, 72, 80, 83, 92.
Departure Apr–Sep: 10:15am–10:30pm daily (every 20–45 min); Oct–Mar: 11am–9.20pm (from 10:15am Sat & Sun; every 30 min–1 hr; 50 passengers min). **Duration** 1 hr 10 min.
Lunch cruise 1pm Sat, Sun and bank hols (embark from 12:15pm). **Duration** 1hr 45 min. Under-12s half price. **Dinner cruise** 8:30pm daily (embark from 7:30pm). **Duration** 2 hr 15 min. Formal dress required.
ⓦ **bateaux-mouches.fr**

Bateaux Vedettes Pont Neuf Cruise

This company runs a fleet of six small boats. The boats are of an older style, for a quainter cruise. Price reductions can be obtained when reserving tickets online. The boarding point is:

Square du Vert-Galant (Pont Neuf)
Map 12 F3. **Tel** 01 46 33 98 38.
Ⓜ Pont Neuf. ⓇⒺⓇ Châtelet. 🚌 27, 58, 67, 70, 72, 74, 75.
Departures 10:30am, 11:15am, noon; 1:30–10:30pm daily (every 30 min); Nov–mid-Mar: 10:30am, 11:15am, noon, 2–6:30pm (every 45 min), 8pm, 10pm Mon–Thu; 10:30am, 11:15am, noon, 2–6:30pm, 8pm, 9–10pm (every 45 min) Fri–Sun (Dec 24 & 31: last departure 5:45 pm). **Duration** 1 hr. ⓦ **vedettesdupontneuf.com**

Canal Trips

The Canauxrama company operates boat cruises along the city's Canal St.-Martin and along the banks of the river Marne. The St.-Martin journey passes along the tree-lined canal, which has nine locks, two swing bridges, and eight romantic footbridges. The Bords de Marne cruise travels well into the suburbs, as far as Bry-sur-Marne. The **Paris Canal Company** (01 42 40 96 97; www.pariscanal.com) also has a St.-Martin canal trip, from Parc de la Villette and extending beyond the canal, passing into the River Seine and as far as the Musée d'Orsay.

Canal St.-Martin

The Canauxrama company offers many different trips along this canal, but it has two 125-passenger boats that operate regularly between the Bassin de la Villette and the Port de l'Arsenal. The boarding points are:
Bassin de la Villette: **Map** 8 E1. Ⓜ Jaurès. Port de l'Arsenal: **Map** 14 E4. Ⓜ Bastille. **Tel** 01 42 39 15 00.
Departures Apr–Nov, times may vary so phone to check and to make a reservation: Bassin de la Villette 9:45am and 2:45pm; Port de l'Arsenal 9:45am and 2:30pm daily. On weekday mornings there are concessions for students, seniors, and children under 12. Children under four travel free (although trip is not recommended for this age). Concert cruises are available on chartered trips on the Canal St.-Martin and the Seine. **Duration** 2 hr 30 min. ⓦ **canauxrama.fr**

Bords de Marne Croisière

This all-day cruise extends westward out of Paris down the Marne. The trip includes a commentary, stories, and dancing. Bring a picnic or eat lunch in a *guinguette* (open-air café). The boarding point is: Port de l'Arsenal: **Map** 14 E4. Ⓜ Bastille. **Tel** 01 42 39 15 00. **Departures** Apr–Oct: 9am (reservations only), Jul–Aug: Thu–Sun (arrive 20 min before). Reservations recommended. **Duration** 8 hr.

Canal-cruise boat in the Bassin de la Villette

View of the cityscape of Paris ▶

PARIS AREA BY AREA

ILE DE LA CITE AND ILE ST.-LOUIS

The history of Paris started on the Ile de la Cité, an island formed by two meanders of the Seine. Inhabited by the Parisii Gauls from the 3rd century BC and taken over in 52 BC by Caesar's Romans, the Ile de la Cité was the birthplace of river commerce and a center of political and religious power. Some imposing evidence of this power can still be seen in the Conciergerie, a medieval palace turned prison; in Sainte-Chapelle, a small church with sparkling stained-glass windows; and in Notre-Dame, the island's world-famous Gothic cathedral.

There are also charming snippets of another time amid the tiny stone houses and narrow streets in the Ancien Cloître Quartier, and around the picturesque Square du Vert-Galant and the ancient Place Dauphine. However, most of the island's historic heritage has been wiped away by the modernization of the last few centuries.

Crossing the St.-Louis bridge onto the smaller Ile St.-Louis, you enter a charming 17th-century oasis with tree-lined quays, elegant mansions and the legendary Maison Berthillon ice-cream parlor *(see p311)*.

Sights at a Glance

Historic Buildings and Streets
- **2** Ancien Cloître Quartier
- **6** Hôtel Dieu
- **8** Conciergerie
- **10** Palais de Justice
- **16** Hôtel de Lauzun

Churches and Cathedrals
- **1** Notre-Dame pp82–5
- **9** Sainte-Chapelle pp88–9
- **15** St.-Louis-en-l'Ile

Monuments
- **4** Paris Mémorial des Martyrs de la Déportation

Markets
- **7** Marché aux Fleurs Reine Elizabeth II

Squares and Gardens
- **3** Square Jean XXIII
- **11** Place Dauphine
- **13** Square du Vert-Galant

Museums and Galleries
- **5** Crypte Archéologique
- **14** Société Historique et Littéraire Polonaise

Bridges
- **12** Pont Neuf

☐ **Restaurants** see p296
1 Au Bougnat
2 Café St.-Régis

See also Street Finder map 12–13

0 meters   400
0 yards   400

◀ Statues of apostles that look over the main entrance to Notre-Dame

For keys to symbols *see back flap*

Street by Street: Ile de la Cité

The origins of Paris are here on the Ile de la Cité, the boat-shaped island on the Seine first inhabited over 2,000 years ago by Celtic tribes. One tribe, the Parisii, eventually gave its name to the city. The island offered a convenient river crossing on the route between northern and southern Gaul and was easily defended. In later centuries, the settlement was expanded by the Romans, the Franks, and the Capetian kings to form the nucleus of today's city.

There is no older place in Paris, and remains of the first buildings can still be seen today in the archaeological crypt under the square in front of Notre-Dame, the great medieval cathedral and place of pilgrimage for millions of visitors each year. At the other end of the island is another Gothic masterpiece, Sainte-Chapelle – a miracle of light.

❼ ★ Marché aux Fleurs Reine Elizabeth II
This colorful, lively market is one of Paris's few remaining flower markets. Birds are sold at the Sunday market.

The Cour du Mai is the impressive main courtyard of the Palais de Justice.

To Pont Neuf

❽ ★ Conciergerie
A grisly antechamber to the guillotine, this prison was much used in the Revolution.

The Quai des Orfèvres owes its name to the goldsmiths (orfèvres) who frequented the area from medieval times onward.

❿ Palais de Justice
With its ancient towers lining the quays, the old royal palace is today a massive complex of law courts. Its history extends back over 16 centuries.

The Préfecture de Police is the headquarters of the police and was the scene of intense battles during World War II.

❾ ★ Sainte-Chapelle
A jewel of Gothic architecture and one of the most magical sights in Paris, Sainte-Chapelle is noted for the magnificence of its stained glass.

CRYPTE DU PARVIS

❺ ★ Crypte Archéologique
Deep under the square lie the remains of houses from 2,000 years ago.

The Statue of Charlemagne commemorates the King of the Franks, who was crowned emperor in 800. He united all the Christian peoples of the West.

Locator Map
See Central Paris Map pp16–17

Key
— Suggested route

The Rue Chanoinesse has many charming old restaurants, cafés, and stores.

6 Hôtel Dieu
Once an orphanage, this is now a city hospital.

Point Zéro is the point from which all distances are measured in France.

2 Ancien Cloître Quartier
These quaint streets were once home to medieval clergymen and students.

1 ★ Notre-Dame
This cathedral is a superb example of French medieval architecture.

To Latin Quarter

3 The Square Jean XXIII
is a peaceful square close to the river.

❶ Notre-Dame

No other building is more associated with the history of Paris than Notre-Dame. It stands majestically on the Ile de la Cité, cradle of the city. Pope Alexander III laid the first stone in 1163, marking the start of 170 years of toil by armies of Gothic architects and medieval craftsmen. Ever since, a procession of the famous has passed through the three main doors below the massive towers.

The cathedral is a Gothic masterpiece, standing on the site of a Roman temple. At the time it was finished, in about 1334, it was 430 ft (130 m) long and featured flying buttresses, a large transept, a deep choir, and 228-ft (69-m) high towers.

★ **West Front**
Three main doors with superb statuary, a central rose window, and an openwork gallery are important details here.

★ **Galerie des Chimères**
The cathedral's legendary gargoyles (chimères) hide behind a large upper gallery between the towers.

KEY

① **Portal of the Virgin** The Virgin surrounded by saints and kings is a fine composition of 13th-century statues.

② **The south tower** houses the cathedral's famous Emmanuel bell.

③ **The spire**, designed by Viollet-le-Duc, soars to a height of 295 ft (90 m).

④ **The treasury** houses the cathedral's religious treasures, including Christ's purported Crown of Thorns.

⑤ **The transept** was built at the start of Philippe-Auguste's reign, in the 13th century.

⑥ **The King's Gallery** features 28 Kings of Judah gazing down on the crowds.

★ **West Rose Window**
This window depicts the Virgin in a medallion of rich reds and blues.

★ **Flying Buttresses**
Jean Ravy's spectacular flying buttresses at the east end of the cathedral have a span of 50 ft (15 m).

VISITORS' CHECKLIST

Practical Information
6 Pl du Parvis Notre-Dame. **Map**
13 B4. **Tel** 01 42 34 56 10. **Open**
8am–6:30pm daily (to 7:15pm Sat
& Sun). 🕇 8am, 9am (ex Jul, Aug),
noon, 5:45pm, 6:15pm (6:30pm
Sat) Mon–Sat; 8:30am, 9:30am,
10am, 11:30am, 12:45pm, 5:45 pm,
6:30pm Sun. 🗓 2pm Wed, Thu;
2:30pm Sat (English). 🔲 Towers:
Rue du Cloître. **Tel** 01 53 40 60 80.
Open 10am–6:30pm (Oct–Mar:
to 5:30pm; Jul & Aug: to 11pm Fri
& Sat). **Closed** Jan 1, May 1 &
Dec 25. 🔁 🔲 **notre-dame-de-
paris.monuments-nationauxfr**

Transportation
Ⓜ Cité. 🚌 21, 38, 47, 85, 96.
Ⓡ Notre-Dame. 🅿 Pl du Parvis.

★ **South Rose Window**
This south facade window,
with its central
depiction of
Christ, is an
impressive
43 ft (13m)
high.

1163 Foundation stone laid by Pope Alexander III	**1572** Marguerite de Valois marries Henri of Navarre (later Henri IV)	**1793** Revolutionaries loot the cathedral and rename it Temple of Reason		
			1944 Liberation of Paris Thanksgiving ceremony	
1150	**1550**	**1750**	**1900**	**2015**
1708 Choir remodeled by Louis XIV, fulfilling his father's promise to honor the Virgin	**1795–1802** Cathedral closed			**2013** The cathedral celebrates its 850th anniversary
1804 Napoleon crowns himself Emperor of France			**1970** State funeral of General de Gaulle	

Napoleon I

A Guided Tour of Notre-Dame

Notre-Dame's interior grandeur is instantly apparent on seeing the high-vaulted central nave. This is bisected by a huge transept, at either end of which are medieval rose windows, 43 ft (13 m) in diameter. Works by major sculptors adorn the cathedral. Among them are Jean Ravy's old choir screen carvings, Nicolas Coustou's *Pietà*, and Antoine Coysevox's Louis XIV statue. In this majestic setting, kings and emperors were crowned and royal Crusaders were blessed. But Notre-Dame was also the scene of turmoil. Revolutionaries ransacked it, banished religion, changed it into a temple to the Cult of Reason, and then used it as a wine store. Napoleon restored religion in 1804 and architect Viollet-le-Duc later restored the buildings, replacing missing statues, as well as raising the spire and fixing the gargoyles.

⑨ **North Rose Window**
This 13th-century stained-glass window depicts the Virgin encircled by figures from the Old Testament.

⑩ **View and Gargoyles**
The 387 steps up the north tower lead to sights of the famous gargoyles and magnificent views of Paris.

Entrance to the tower

Entrance

① **View of Interior**
From the main entrance, the view takes in the high-vaulted central nave looking down toward the huge transept, the choir, and the high altar.

Key

━ Suggested route

② **Le Brun's "May" Paintings**
These religious paintings by Charles Le Brun hang in the side chapels. In the 17th and 18th centuries, the Paris guilds presented a painting to the cathedral on May Day each year.

⑦ **Louis XIII Statue**
After many years of childless marriage, Louis XIII pledged to erect a high altar and to redecorate the east chancel to honor the Virgin if an heir was born to him. The future Louis XIV was born in 1638, but it took 60 years before the pledges were fulfilled. One of the surviving features from that time is the carved choir stalls.

⑧ **Carved Choir Stalls**
Noted for their early 18th-century carved woodwork, the choir stalls were commissioned by Louis XIII, whose statue stands behind the high altar. Among the details carved in bas-relief on the back of the high stalls are scenes from the life of the Virgin.

Entrance to Treasury

Entrance to Sacristy

⑥ **Pietà**
Behind the high altar is Nicolas Coustou's *Pietà*, standing on a gilded base sculpted by François Girardon.

⑤ **Chancel Screen**
A 14th-century high stone screen enclosed the chancel and provided canons at prayer with peace and solitude from noisy congregations. Some of it has survived to screen the first three north and south bays.

③ **South Rose Window**
Located at the south end of the transept, this window retains some of its original 13th-century stained glass. The window depicts Christ in the center, surrounded by virgins, saints, and the 12 Apostles.

④ **Statue of the Virgin and Child**
Against the southeast pillar of the transept stands the 14th-century statue of the Virgin and Child. It was brought to the cathedral from the chapel of St. Aignan, and is known as Notre-Dame de Paris (Our Lady of Paris).

The Square Jean XXIII behind Notre-Dame

❷ Ancien Cloître Quartier

Rue du Cloître-Notre-Dame north to Quai aux Fleurs 75004. **Map** 13 B4. Ⓜ Cité. ᴿᴱᴿ St.-Michel.

To the north of Notre-Dame lies a warren of little-explored streets known as the "Old Cloister" quarter. They are all that remains of a once-bustling medieval hub frequented by cathedral seminary students. Today, the narrow streets with well-preserved medieval mansions make for an interesting stroll. The mansions in Rue des Chantres and Rue des Ursins in particular have pretty gardens and cobblestone courtyards.

❸ Square Jean XXIII

Rue du Cloître-Notre-Dame 75004. **Map** 13 B4. Ⓜ Cité.

Notre-Dame's St. Stephen's door (porte St.-Etienne) opens onto this pleasant garden square, dedicated to Pope John XXIII. The garden runs alongside the river and is an excellent place for enjoying the sculptures, rose windows, and flying buttresses of the east end of the cathedral.

From the 17th century, the square was occupied by the archbishop's palace, which was ransacked by rioters in 1831 and later demolished. A square was conceived as a replacement by the Prefect of Paris, Rambuteau. The Gothic-style fountain of the Virgin in the square dates to 1845.

❹ Paris Mémorial des Martyrs de la Déportation

Sq de l'Ile de France 75004. **Map** 13 B4. **Tel** 01 46 33 87 56. Ⓜ St.-Paul, Maubert-Mutualité. ᴿᴱᴿ St.-Michel. **Open** 10am–noon, 2–5pm Tue–Sun (until 7pm Apr–Sep). **Closed** Jan 1, May 1, Jul 14, Aug 15 & Dec 25.

The memorial to the 200,000 French men, women, and children deported to Nazi concentration camps in World War II is covered with the names of the camps. Earth from these camps has been used to form tombs, and the interior walls are inscribed with poetry. At the far end is a tomb dedicated to the Unknown Deportee.

❺ Crypte Archéologique

7 Pl du Parvis Notre-Dame 75004. **Map** 13 A4. **Tel** 01 55 42 50 10. Ⓜ Cité. **Open** 10am–6pm Tue–Sun (last adm: 30 min before closing). **Closed** Jan 1, May 1, May 8, Jul 14, Aug 15, Nov 1 & 11, Dec 25 & religious hols. 🎟 free for children under 14. 📷 📷 🖥 crypte.paris.fr

Located on the main square (the *parvis*) in front of

Gallo-Roman ruins in the Crypte Archéologique

Notre-Dame and stretching 393 ft (120 m) underground, this crypt exhibits the remains of foundations and walls that predate the cathedral by several hundred years. The foundations of Paris's oldest rampart, dating from the third century BC, are displayed as are the medieval foundations of the Hôtel Dieu. Within the crypt are also traces of a sophisticated underground heating system used for Ancient Roman thermal baths.

Huge variety of colorful flowers for sale at the Marché aux Fleurs Reine Elizabeth II

Arched entrance of Hôtel Dieu, Paris's central hospital

❻ Hôtel Dieu

1 Pl du Parvis Notre-Dame 75004. **Map** 13 A4. **Tel** 01 42 34 82 34. **Closed** to the public for visits. Ⓜ Cité.

On the north side of the Place du Parvis Notre-Dame is the Hôtel Dieu, the city's oldest hospital serving central Paris. It was built on the site of an orphanage between 1866 and 1878. The original Hôtel Dieu, built in the 12th century and stretching across the island to both banks of the river, was demolished in the 19th century to make way for one of Baron Haussmann's urban-planning programs. It was here in 1944 that the Paris police courageously resisted the Germans; the battle is commemorated by a monument in Cour de 19-Août.

❼ Marché aux Fleurs Reine Elizabeth II

Pl Louis-Lépine 75004. **Map** 13 A3. Ⓜ Cité. **Open** 8am–7pm Mon–Sat; Marché aux Oiseaux: Sun.

The year-round flower market adds color and scent to an area otherwise dominated by administrative buildings. It is the most famous and unfortunately one of the last remaining flower markets in the city of Paris, offering a wide range of specialties such as orchids. Each Sunday it makes way for an animal market, which is best avoided by sensitive animal lovers.

❽ Conciergerie

2 Blvd du Palais 75001. **Map** 13 A3. **Tel** 01 53 40 60 80. Ⓜ Cité. **Open** 9:30am–6pm daily (last adm: 30 min before closing). **Closed** Jan 1, May 1, Dec 25. 🅰 (combined ticket with Sainte-Chapelle, *pp88–9*, available.) 🅲 phone to check. 🅷 🆆 **conciergerie. monuments-nationaux.fr**

The Conciergerie was under the administration of the palace "concierge," the keeper of the King's mansion. When the King moved to the Marais (in 1417), the palace remained the seat of royal administration and law, and the Conciergerie became a prison, with the "concierge" as its chief jailer. Henry IV's assassin, Ravaillac, was imprisoned and tortured here.

During the Revolution it housed over 4,000 prisoners, including Marie Antoinette, who was held in a tiny cell, and Charlotte Corday, who stabbed Revolutionary leader Marat as he lay in his bath. Ironically, the Revolutionary judges Danton and Robespierre also became "tenants" before being sent to the guillotine.

The Conciergerie has a superb four-aisled Gothic Salle des Gens d'Armes (Hall of the Men-at-Arms), the dining hall for the castle's 2,000 members of staff. The building, renovated in the 19th century, retains the 14th-century public clock tower on the Tour de l'Horloge (Palais de Justice). It is the city's oldest and is still operating.

The Conciergerie forms part of the larger Palais du Justice, which is still used by the judicial system.

The Gothic Salle des Gens d'Armes (Hall of the Men-at-Arms) in the Conciergerie

❾ Sainte-Chapelle

Ethereal and magical, Sainte-Chapelle has been hailed as one of the greatest architectural master-pieces of the Western world. In the Middle Ages the devout likened this church to "a gateway to heaven." Today no visitor can fail to be transported by the blaze of light created by the 15 magnificent stained-glass windows, separated by the narrowest of columns that soar 50 ft (15 m) to the star-studded, vaulted roof. The windows portray over 1,000 religious scenes in a kaleidoscope of red, gold, green, blue, and mauve. The chapel was built in 1248 by Louis IX to house Christ's purported Crown of Thorns (now housed in the Notre-Dame treasury).

★ Rose Window
Best seen at sunset, the religious story of the Apocalypse is told in 86 panels of stained glass. The window was a gift from Charles VIII in 1485.

Lower Chapel Servants and commoners worshipped here, while the chapel above was reserved for the use of the king and the royal family.

Main Portal
The two-tier structure of the portal, the lower half of which is shown here, echoes that of the chapel.

KEY

① **The Crown of Thorns** decorates the pinnacle as a symbol of the first relic bought by Louis IX.

② **The spire** rises 245 ft (75 m) into the air. It was erected in 1853 after four previous spires burned down.

③ **The angel** once revolved so that its cross could be seen from anywhere in Paris.

St. Louis' Relics

Louis IX was extremely devout, and was canonized in 1297, not long after his death. In 1239 he acquired the Crown of Thorns from the Emperor of Constantinople and, in 1241, a fragment of Christ's Cross. He built this chapel as a shrine to house them. Louis paid nearly three times more for the relics than for the construction of Sainte-Chapelle. The Crown of Thorns is now kept at Notre-Dame.

LOUIS IX.

VISITORS' CHECKLIST

Practical Information
8 Blvd du Palais, 75001. **Map** 13
A3. **Tel** 01 53 40 60 80. **Open**
daily. Mar–Oct: 9:30am–6pm
(May–Sep: 9am–9pm Wed);
Nov–Feb: 9am–5pm. Last adm
30 min before closing.
Closed Jan 1, May 1, Dec 25.
🎫 (combined ticket with
Conciergerie, p87, is available.)
📷 🏛 🌐 sainte-chapelle.
monuments-nationaux.fr

Transportation
Ⓜ Cité. 🚌 21, 27, 38, 85, 96 to
Ile de la Cité. 🚆 St.-Michel. 🅿
Notre-Dame. 🅿 Palais de Justice.

Upper Chapel The windows are a pictorial Bible, showing scenes from the Old and New Testaments.

Upper Chapel Windows

1 Genesis

2 Exodus

3 Numbers

4 Deuteronomy: Joshua

5 Judges

6 *left* Isaiah *right* Rod of Jesse

7 *left* St. John the Evangelist *right* Childhood of Christ

8 Christ's Passion

9 *left* St. John the Baptist *right* Story of Daniel

10 Ezekiel

11 *left* Jeremiah *right* Tobiah

12 Judith and Job

13 Esther

14 Book of Kings

15 Story of the Relics

16 Rose Window: The Apocalypse

★ Apostle Statues
These magnificent examples of medieval stone carving adorn the 12 pillars of the upper chapel.

★ Window of Christ's Passion
The Last Supper is shown here in one of the most beautiful windows in the upper chapel.

A sculptured relief on the Palais de Justice

⑩ Palais de Justice

4–10 Blvd du Palais (entrance by the Cour de Mai, 10 Blvd du Palais) 75001. **Map** 13 A3. **Tel** 01 44 32 52 52. Ⓜ Cité. **Open** 9am–6pm Mon–Fri. ✉ Ⓦ ca-paris.justice.fr

The monumental block of buildings making up the law courts stretches the entire width of the Ile de la Cité. It is a splendid sight with its old towers lining the quays. The site has been occupied since Roman times and was the seat of royal power until Charles V moved the court to the Hôtel St.-Paul in the Marais during the 14th century. In April 1793, the Revolutionary Tribunal began dispensing justice from

the Première Chambre (gilded chamber), but this court eventually degenerated into Robespierre's Reign of Terror. Today, the site embodies Napoleon's great legacy – the French judicial system.

⑪ Place Dauphine

75001 (enter by Rue Henri-Robert). **Map** 12 F3. Ⓜ Pont Neuf, Cité.

East of Pont Neuf is this ancient square, laid out in 1607 by Henri IV and named after the Dauphin, the future Louis XIII. It is actually triangular in shape and lined with cafés, wine bars, and restaurants. In the middle is a park with trees and benches.

No. 14 is one of the few buildings to have avoided any subsequent restoration. This haven of 17th-century charm is popular with *pétanque* (boules) players and employees of the adjoining Palais de Justice.

⑫ Pont Neuf

Quai de la Mégisserie and Quai des Grands Augustins 75001. **Map** 12 F3. Ⓜ Pont Neuf, Cité.

Despite its name (New Bridge), this is the oldest of the existing bridges in Paris and has been immortalized by major literary and artistic figures since it was built. The first stone was laid by Henri III in 1578, but it was Henri IV who inaugurated it and gave it its name in 1607. His statue stands in the central section.

The bridge, which was the widest of its kind in Paris, has 12 arches and spans 912 ft (275 m). The first stone bridge to be built without houses and with sidewalks for pedestrians, it heralded a new era in the relationship between the Cité and the river.

From its very beginning, the Pont Neuf has had heavy traffic. It has undergone many renovations and repairs over the centuries.

The Pont Neuf, extending to the north and south of the Ile de la Cité

Henri IV in Square du Vert-Galant

⑬ Square du Vert-Galant

Ile de la Cité 75001. **Map** 12 F3.
M Pont Neuf, Cité.

One of the magical spots of Paris, this square bears the nickname of Henri IV. This amorous and colorful monarch did much to beautify Paris in the early 17th century, and his popularity has lasted to this day. From here, there are splendid views of the Louvre and the Right Bank of the river, where Henri was assassinated in 1610. This is also the point from which the Vedettes du Pont Neuf pleasure boats depart *(see pp74–5)*.

⑭ Société Historique et Littéraire Polonaise

6 Quai d'Orléans 75004. **Map** 13 C4.
Tel 01 55 42 83 83. M Pont Marie.
Open 2.15–6pm Tue–Fri. 🎫 📷
call on 01 55 42 83 85 for reservation.
W bibliotheque-polonaise-paris-shlp.fr

The Polish Romantic poet Adam Mickiewicz, who lived in Paris in the 19th century, was a major force in Polish cultural and political life, devoting his writing to helping his countrymen who were oppressed at home and abroad. The museum, founded in 1903, has exhibition galleries dedicated to not only Mickewicz but also Frédéric Chopin and

Boleslas Biegas. The Society's library, founded in 1838, preserves documents and mementos relating to Polish history and culture, develops historical and literary studies, and organizes cultural events.

⑮ St.-Louis-en-l'Ile

19 Rue St.-Louis-en-l'Ile 75004.
Map 13 C4. **Tel** 01 46 34 11 60.
M Pont Marie. **Open** 9.30am–1pm &
2–7.30pm daily (to 7pm Sun & public hols). Mass: 6.45pm Mon–Fri, 6.30pm Sat, 11am Sun.

The construction of this church began in 1664 from plans by the royal architect Louis Le Vau, who lived on the island. It was completed and consecrated in 1726. Among its outstanding exterior features are the 1741 iron clock at the entrance and the pierced iron spire.

The interior, in the Baroque style, is richly decorated with gilding and marble. There is a statue of St. Louis holding a crusader's sword. A plaque in the north aisle bears the inscription "in grateful memory of St. Louis in whose honor the City of St. Louis, Missouri, USA is named". The church is also twinned with Carthage cathedral in Tunisia, where St. Louis is buried.

A bust of Adam Mickiewicz

The interior of St.-Louis-en-l'Ile

⑯ Hôtel de Lauzun

17 Quai d'Anjou 75004. **Map** 13 C4.
Tel 01 42 76 54 04. M Pont Marie.
Closed to the public. W paris.fr

This splendid mansion, also known as Hôtel Pimodan, was built by Louis Le Vau in the mid-1650s for Charles Gruyn des Bordes, an arms dealer. It was sold in 1682 to the French military commander Duc de Lauzun, who was a favorite of Louis XIV. It later became a focus for Paris's Bohemian literary and artistic life. It now belongs to the city of Paris, and an establishment dedicated to scientific research is housed here. For those lucky enough to see inside, it offers an unsurpassed insight into wealthy lifestyles in the 17th century. Charles Le Brun worked on the decoration of its magnificent paneling and painted ceilings before moving on to Versailles.

The poet Charles Baudelaire (1821–67) lived on the third floor and wrote most of his controversial masterpiece *Les Fleurs du Mal* in a room packed with antiques and bric-a-brac. The celebrated French Romantic poet, traveler and critic, Théophile Gautier (1811–72), had apartments here in 1848. Meetings of the Club des Haschischines (the Hashish-Eaters' Club) took place here too.

Other famous residents were the Austrian poet Rainer Maria Rilke, the English artist Walter Sickert, and the German composer Richard Wagner.

ES PAINS

Pains
au
cumin

Pains
au
pavot

Łazowy

ogalik

Bagels

•letzels

Halès

LES DOUCEURS

VATROUCHKA
AU
FROMAGE

Traditionnelle
Light
au Citron
aux Griottes
Cannelle-Orange

STRUDELS

Viennois
Roumain
Mame Strudel
au Pavot

AU CHOCOLAT

Reine de Saba
Sacher torte

A Jewish pâtisserie on Rue des Rosiers

Sights at a Glance

Historic Buildings and Streets

Churches

Monuments

Squares

Opera Houses

Museums and Galleries

THE MARAIS

The Marais went from royal enclave in the 17th and 18th centuries to a wasteland during the Revolution. Eventually taken over by artists and storekeepers, this area has now climbed its way out of dilapidation, with trendy restaurants, bars, and chic boutiques, while rising real-estate prices have driven many locals away. Its elegant mansions, world-class museums and art galleries such

as Musée Picasso, Musée Carnavalet, and Maison de Victor Hugo, as well as the beautiful Place des Vosges, make it a must on every visitor's list. Some of its old-world charm can still be found in Rue des Rosiers, Paris's Jewish quarter, with its small cafés and cobblestone passageways. A hot spot for eclectic art galleries, the Marais is also the heart of the Parisian gay community.

See also Street Finder maps 13–14

0 meters 400
0 yards 400

For keys to symbols *see back flap*

Street by Street: The Marais

Once an area of marshland as its name suggests (*marais* means swamp), the Marais grew steadily in importance from the 14th century, by virtue of its proximity to the Louvre, the preferred residence of Charles V. Its heyday was in the 17th century, when it became the fashionable area for the monied classes. They built many grand and sumptuous mansions (*hôtels*) that still dot the Marais today. Many of these *hôtels* have been restored and turned into museums. Once again fashionable with the monied classes, designer boutiques, trendy restaurants, art galleries, and cafés now line the streets.

To the
Pompidou
Center

RUE BARBETTE

RUE ELZEVIR

RUE DES HOSPITALIÈRES ST GERVAIS

RUE DES F

RUE DES ROSIERS

RUE PAVEE

RUE MALHER

❸ Rue des Francs-Bourgeois
This ancient street is lined with intriguing buildings and trendy stores.

❽ Rue des Rosiers
The smell of hot pastrami and borscht wafts from restaurants and stores in the heart of the Jewish area.

❹ Musée Cognacq-Jay
An exquisite collection of 18th-century paintings and furniture is shown in perfect period setting.

0 meters	100
0 yards	100

Key

— Suggested route

❷ Hôtel de Lamoignon
Behind the ornate doorway of this fine mansion is Paris's historical library.

🔟 ★ Musée Picasso Paris
The renovated Hôtel Salé is the setting for the largest collection of Picassos in the world, the result of a family bequest to the state *(see pp100–101).*

Locator Map
See Central Paris Map pp16–17

The Hôtel Le Peletier de St.-Fargeau adjoins the Hôtel Carnavalet to form a museum of Paris's history.

❶ ★ Musée Carnavalet
The statue of Louis XIV in Roman dress by Coysevox is in the courtyard of the Hôtel Carnavalet.

❻ Maison de Victor Hugo
Author of *Les Misérables*, Victor Hugo lived at No. 6 Place des Vosges, where his house is now a museum of his life and work.

To Metro
Sully Morland

❼ Hôtel de Bethune-Sully
This *hôtel* was built for a notorious gambler.

❺ ★ Place des Vosges
Once the site of jousting and tournaments, the historic Place des Vosges, in the very heart of the Marais, is a square of perfect symmetry.

❶ Musée Carnavalet

Devoted to the history of Paris, this vast museum occupies two adjoining mansions, with entire rooms decorated with paneling, furniture, and *objets d'art*; many works of art such as paintings and sculptures of prominent personalities; and engravings showing Paris being built. The main building is the Hôtel Carnavalet, built as a town house in 1548 and transformed in the mid-17th century by François Mansart. The neighboring 17th-century mansion, Hôtel Le Peletier de St.-Fargeau, features superb early 20th-century interiors, and the restored Orangery is devoted to Prehistory and Gallo-Roman Paris.

Louis XV Room
This delightful room contains art from the Bouvier collection and paneling from the Hôtel de Broglie.

Memorabilia in this room is dedicated to 18th-century philosophers, in particular Jean-Jacques Rousseau and Voltaire.

★ **Charles Le Brun Ceiling**
Magnificent works by the 17th-century artist, originally in the Hôtel de la Rivière, decorate the former study and great hall.

Entrance

★ **Mme de Sévigné's Gallery**
The gallery includes this portrait of Mme de Sévigné, the celebrated letter-writer, whose beloved home this was for the 20 years up to her death.

★ **Hôtel d'Uzès Reception Room**
The room was created in 1761 by Claude Nicolas Ledoux. The gold-and-white paneling is from a Rue Montmartre mansion.

Exit

Second floor

Convention Room
Georges Danton's
portrait is among
the memorabilia
of the Revolution.

First floor

VISITORS' CHECKLIST

Practical Information
16 Rue des Francs-Bourgeois
75003. **Map** 14 D3. **Tel** 01 44 59
58 58. **Open** 10am–6pm Tue–Sun
(last adm: 5pm for temporary,
5:30pm for permanent exhibits.
Due to renovations, rooms open
in rota; call to check). **Closed**
Mon, public hols. 📞 phone for
times. 🆆 carnavalet.paris.fr 📷

Transportation
Ⓜ St.-Paul, Chemin Vert. 🚌 29,
69, 76, 96 to St.-Paul, Pl des Vosges.
🅿 Hôtel de Ville, Rue St.-Antoine.

**Marie-Antoinette in
Mourning** (1793)
Alexandre Kucharski painted her
at the Temple prison after the
execution of Louis XVI.

**Fouquet Jewelry
Boutique** (1900)
The Art Nouveau
decor of this store
from Rue Royale
is by A. Mucha.

Hôtel Le Peletier de
St.-Fargeau

Key to Floorplan

- 🔲 Prehistory to Gallo-Roman
- 🔲 Medieval Paris
- 🔲 Renaissance Paris
- 🔲 17th-century Paris
- 🔲 Louis XV's Paris
- 🔲 Louis XVI's Paris
- 🔲 Revolutionary Paris
- 🔲 19th Century
- 🔲 20th Century
- 🔲 Temporary exhibitions
- 🔲 Nonexhibition space
- 🔲 18th-century Paris

★ Ballroom of the Hôtel de Wendel
The early 20th-century ballroom interior has been
reconstructed. This immense mural depicts the retinue
of the Queen of Sheba and is by the Catalan designer
and painter José María Sert y Badia.

Gallery Guide

*The collection is mainly arranged chronologically. Hôtel Carnavalet
covers the history of Paris up to 1789. The exhibits covering the 17th
century to the Revolution are on the first floor. In the Hôtel Le Peletier
de St.-Fargeau, the ground floor covers the First–Second Empires,
with the Prehistory–Gallo-Roman departments in the Orangery;
from the Second Empire to the present day is on the first floor; and
the second floor is devoted to the Revolution. Some of the rooms are
closed due to renovation and are expected to reopen in 2019.*

❷ Hôtel de Lamoignon

24 Rue Pavée 75004. **Map** 14 D3.
Tel 01 44 59 29 40. Ⓜ St-Paul.
Open 10am–6pm Mon–Sat.
Closed public hols. Ⓐ Ⓦ **paris.fr**

The imposing Hôtel de Lamoignon, one of the oldest mansions in Paris, is home to the Historical Library of the city (BHVP). It was built in 1585 for Diane de France, also known as the Duchesse d'Angoulême, daughter of Henri II. The building is noted for six high Corinthian pilasters topped by a triangular pediment and flourishes of dogs' heads, bows, arrows, and quivers – recalling Diane's passion for hunting. The collection includes documents from the French Revolution and 80,000 prints covering the history of Paris.

❸ Rue des Francs-Bourgeois

75003, 75004. **Map** 14 D3.
Ⓜ Rambuteau, Chemin-Vert.

This street is an important thoroughfare in the heart of the Marais, linking the Rue des Archives and the Place des Vosges, with the imposing Hôtel de Soubise at one end and the Musée Carnavalet at the other. The street got its name from the *francs* (free from taxes) –

The exquisite 18th-century works of art and furniture in the Musée Cognacq-Jay

poorhouses built for the needy in 1334 at Nos. 34 and 36. These were later closed because of illegal financial activities, although the state kept the pawnshop nearby, still there today.

❹ Musée Cognacq-Jay

Hôtel Donon, 8 Rue Elzévir 75003. **Map** 14 D3. **Tel** 01 40 27 07 21. Ⓜ St-Paul, Chemin Vert. **Open** 10am–6pm Tue–Sun. **Closed** public hols. Ⓒ by appt. Ⓐ Ⓦ **museecognacqjay.paris.fr**

This fine small collection of French 18th-century works of art and furniture was formed by Ernest Cognacq and his wife, Louise Jay, founder of the Art Deco La Samaritaine, which was once Paris's largest department store *(see p117)*. The private collection was bequeathed to the city and

is now housed in the heart of the Marais at the Hôtel Donon – an elegant building dating from 1575 with an 18th-century facade.

❺ Place des Vosges

75003, 75004. **Map** 14 D3.
Ⓜ Bastille, St-Paul.

This square is considered among the most beautiful in the world by Parisians and visitors alike *(see pp26–7)*. Its impressive symmetry – 36 houses, 9 on each side, of brick and stone, with deep slate roofs and dormer windows over arcades – is still intact after 400 years. It has been the scene of many historic events over the centuries. A three-day tournament was held here to celebrate the marriage of Louis XIII to Anne of Austria in

The beautiful Place des Vosges with fountains in the central courtyard

1615. The famous literary hostess, Madame de Sévigné, was born here in 1626; Cardinal Richelieu, pillar of the monarchy, stayed here in 1615; and Victor Hugo, the writer, lived here for 16 years.

❻ Maison de Victor Hugo

6 Pl des Vosges 75004. **Map** 14 D3. **Tel** 01 42 72 10 16. Ⓜ Bastille, Chemin Vert. **Open** 10am–6pm Tue–Sun. **Closed** public hols. 🖼 exhibitions only. 📷 by appt. 🌐 **maisonvictorhugo.paris.fr**

The French poet, dramatist, and novelist lived on the second floor of the former Hôtel Rohan-Guéménée from 1832 to 1848. It was here that he wrote most of *Les Misérables* and completed many other famous works. On display are some reconstructions of the rooms in which he lived, pen-and-ink drawings, books, and mementos from the crucially important periods in his life, from his childhood to his exile between 1852 and 1870. Temporary exhibitions on Hugo take place regularly.

Marble bust of Victor Hugo by Auguste Rodin

❼ Hôtel de Bethune-Sully

62 Rue St.-Antoine 75004. **Map** 14 D4. **Tel** 01 44 61 21 50. Ⓜ Bastille, St.-Paul. **Closed** to the public, but the gardens are open 9am–7pm & the bookstore 10am–7pm, except public hols. 🖼 by reservations; 16 people max. 📷 🌐 **sully.monuments-nationales.fr**

This fine 17th-century mansion on one of Paris's oldest streets has been extensively restored, using old engravings and drawings as reference. It was built in 1624 for a notorious gambler, Petit Thomas, who lost his whole fortune in one night. The Duc de Sully, Henri IV's chief minister, purchased the house in 1634 and added some of the interior

Late-Renaissance facade of the Hôtel de Bethune-Sully

decoration as well as the Petit Sully orangery in the gardens. The Hôtel de Bethune-Sully is now the headquarters for the Centre des Monuments Nationaux.

❽ Rue des Rosiers

75004. **Map** 13 C3. Ⓜ St.-Paul.

The Jewish quarter in and around this street is one of the most colorful areas of Paris. The street's name refers to the rosebushes within the old city wall. Jews first settled here in the 13th century, with a second significant wave of immigration occurring in the 19th century from Russia, Poland, and central Europe. Sephardic Jews arrived from Algeria, Tunisia, Morocco, and Egypt in the 1950s and

A bakery on Rue des Rosiers

1960s. Some 165 students were rounded up and deported from the Jewish Boys' school nearby at 10 rue de Hospitalières-St.-Gervais in World War II. *N'Oubliez pas* (Lest we forget) is engraved on the wall. Today this area contains synagogues, bakeries, and kosher restaurants.

❾ Hôtel de Coulanges

35 Rue des Francs-Bourgeois, 75004. **Map** 13 C3. **Tel** 01 44 61 85 85. Ⓜ St.-Paul, Rambuteau. **Open** 2–6pm Mon–Fri (until 7pm Apr–Sep). **Closed** public hols. 🌐 **paris-europe.eu**

This *hôtel* is a magnificent example of the architecture of the early 18th century. The right wing of the building, separating the courtyard from the garden, dates from the early 17th century. The *hôtel* was given in 1640 to Philippe II de Coulanges, the King's counselor. Renamed the Petit Hôtel Le Tellier in 1662 by its new owner Le Tellier, this is where the children of Louis XIV and Madame de Montespan were raised in secrecy. It is home to the Maison de l'Europe, with exhibitions on themes relating to Europe.

⓾ Musée Picasso Paris

On the death of the Spanish-born artist Pablo Picasso (1881–1973), who lived most of his life in France, the French State inherited many of his works in lieu of death duties. It used them to establish the Musée Picasso Paris, which opened in 1985. The museum is housed in a large 17th-century mansion, the Hôtel Salé, in the Marais. The original character of the *Hôtel*, which was built in 1656 for Aubert de Fontenay, a salt-tax collector (*salé* means "salty"), has been preserved. The museum holds the world's largest collection of Picasso's works – paintings, sculptures, ceramics, drawings, and etchings – covering all his creative periods.

★ Self-Portrait
Poverty, loneliness, and the onset of winter all made the end of 1901, when this picture was painted, a particularly difficult time for Picasso.

Violin and Sheet Music
This collage (1912) is from the artist's Synthetic Cubist period.

Second floor

★ The Two Brothers (1906)
During the summer of 1906, Picasso returned to Catalonia in Spain, where he painted this picture.

★ The Kiss (1969)
Picasso married Jacqueline Roque in 1961, and at around the same time, he returned to the familiar themes of the couple and of the artist and model.

Basement

Gallery Guide

The basement reconstructs Picasso's studios using his prints, photographs, and personal items. The next three levels follow his work chronologically, from 1895 up to his death in 1973. Some rooms follow a theme, such as his Blue and Pink periods, self-portraits, and subjects like bull-fighting, family, and war. The top floor holds Picasso's private art collection, with works by the likes of Renoir, Cezanne, Braque, and Matisse.

Woman with a Mantilla (1949)
Picasso extended his range when he began working in ceramics in 1948.

Painter with Palette and Easel (1928)

This Post-Cubist portrait in oils was painted at a time when Picasso's work was verging on Surrealism.

Third floor

VISITORS' CHECKLIST

Practical Information
Hôtel Salé, 5 Rue de Thorigny 75003. **Map** 14 D2. **Tel** 01 85 56 00 36. **Open** 9.30am–6pm Tue–Sun. **Closed** Jan 1, May 1, Dec 25. 🅿 🛗 📷 groups by appt only, reserve online. 🖥 📷 Concerts, conferences, and performances. 🆆 **museepicassoparis.fr**

Transportation
Ⓜ St.-Sébastien Froissart, St.-Paul, Chemin Vert. 🚌 29, 69, 75, 96 to St.-Paul, Bastille, Pl des Vosges. 🆁🅴🆁 Châtelet-Les-Halles. 🅿 Rue St.-Antoine, Bastille.

Picasso and Spain

After 1934, Picasso never returned to his homeland due to his rejection of Franco's regime. However, throughout his life in France he used Spanish themes in his art, such as the bull (often in the form of a minotaur) and the guitar, which he associated with his Andalusian childhood.

Woman Reading (1932)

Purples and yellows were often used by Picasso when painting his model Marie-Thérèse Walter.

First floor

Entrance

★ **Two Women Running on the Beach** (1922)
In 1924, this was used for the stage curtain design for Diaghilev's ballet *The Blue Train*. It proved to be his last major design work for any theater.

Ground floor

Key to Floorplan

- ☐ Cubism
- ☐ Male Portraits
- ☐ Picasso's Private Collection
- ☐ Early Works: 1895–1931
- ☐ Modern Classicism: 1918–43
- ☐ Second World War Years
- ☐ Bull/Minotaur Works
- ☐ Later Years 1950–73
- ☐ Studios

Entrance

⓫ Pavillon de l'Arsenal

21 Blvd Morland 75004. **Map** 14 D5. **Tel** 01 42 76 33 97. Ⓜ Sully Morland, Bastille. **Open** 10.30am–6.30pm Tue–Sat, 11am–7pm Sun. **Closed** Jan 1. 🖥 📷 🎧 by appointment only. 🌐 pavillon-arsenal.com

The Pavillon de l'Arsenal houses a small but fascinating exhibition illustrating the architectural evolution of Paris. Using movies, models and panoramic images, this permanent exhibition explores how Paris was built over the centuries, as well as looking at future plans for the city. Up to three temporary exhibitions are also programmed each year.

⓬ Opéra National de Paris Bastille

120 Rue de Lyon 75012. **Map** 14 E4. **Tel** 01 40 01 19 70 or 08 92 89 90 90. Ⓜ Bastille. **Open** for guided tours only. Performance times are published online. **Closed** certain public hols. 📷 ♿ 🎧 compulsory; reserve in advance. *See Entertainment pp337, 339.* 🌐 operadeparis.fr

The controversial "people's opera" was officially opened on 14 July 1989 to coincide with the bicentennial celebrations of the Storming of the Bastille. Carlos Ott's imposing building is a notable break with 19th-century opera-house design, epitomized by Garnier's opulent Opéra in the heart of the city *(see pp218–19)*. It is a massive, modern, curved, glass building.

The "genius of liberty" on top of the Colonne de Juillet

The main auditorium seats an audience of 2,700; its design is functional and modern with black upholstered seats contrasting with the granite of the walls and the impressive glass ceiling. With its five moveable stages, this opera house is certainly a masterpiece of technological wizardry.

⓭ Colonne de Juillet

Pl de la Bastille 75004. **Map** 14 E4. Ⓜ Bastille. **Closed** to the public.

Topped by the elegant, gilded statue of the winged "genius of liberty," this column of hollow bronze reaches 166 ft (50.5 m) into the sky. It is a memorial to those who died in the street battles of July 1830 that led to the overthrow of the monarch *(see pp34–5)*. The crypt contains the remains of 504 victims of the violent fighting and others who died in the 1848 revolution.

⓮ Place de la Bastille

75004. **Map** 14 E4. Ⓜ Bastille.

Nothing is left of the prison stormed by the revolutionary mob on July 14, 1789 *(see pp32–3)* – an event celebrated annually by the French – although the stones were used for the construction of the Pont de la Concorde. The large, traffic-clogged square that marks the site was once the border between central Paris and the eastern working-class areas *(faubourgs)*. Gentrification, however, is well under way: the lively marina known as Bassin de l'Arsenal welcomes 180 pleasure boats and plays host to the small Jardin de l'Arsenal garden, a terraced café, and a playground. This project has re-energized the northern end of the marina with trendy bars, cafés, seafood restaurants, and art galleries.

Just east of the Opéra Bastille is the starting point of the Promenade Plantée, also known as the Coulée Verte René Dumont, a 2.8-mile (4.5-km) elevated walking trail built on the former tracks of a disused railroad that ends up at the Bois de Vincennes.

⓯ St.-Paul–St.-Louis

99 Rue St.-Antoine 75004. **Map** 14 D4. **Tel** 01 42 72 30 32. Ⓜ St.-Paul. **Open** 8am–8pm daily. Mass: 6pm Sat, 9.30am, 11am, 7pm Sun. Concerts.

A Jesuit church, St.-Paul–St.-Louis was an important symbol of the influence that the Jesuits held from 1627, when Louis XIII laid the first stone, to 1762 when they were expelled from France. The Gesù church in

The glass facade of the Opéra National de Paris Bastille

Rome served as the model for the nave, while the 180-ft (60-m) high dome was the forerunner of those of the Invalides and the Sorbonne. Most of the church's treasures were removed during periods of turmoil, but Delacroix's masterpiece, *Christ in the Garden of Olives*, can still be seen. The church is on one of the main streets of the Marais, but can also be approached by the ancient Passage St.-Paul.

The Hôtel des Archevêques de Sens, now home to a fine arts library

⑯ Hôtel des Archevêques de Sens

1 Rue du Figuier 75004. **Map** 13 C4.
Tel 01 42 78 14 60. Ⓜ Pont-Marie.
Open 1pm–7.30pm Tue, Fri, Sat; 10am–7.30pm Wed, Thu. Call ahead of your visit. 🖼 🎦 by appt only.

The former residence of the influential archbishop of Sens was built in the late 15th century and is one of the few medieval buildings left in Paris. Today, it houses the Forney fine arts library. In the 16th century, at the time of the Catholic League, it was occupied by the Bourbons, the Guises and Cardinal de Pellevé, whose religious fervor led him to die of rage in 1594 on hearing that the Protestant Henri IV had entered Paris. Marguerite de Valois, lodged here by her ex-husband, Henri IV, led a life of breathtaking debauchery and scandal, beheading an ex-lover who had assassinated her current favorite. The gardens are open to the public.

⑰ Maison Européenne de la Photographie

5–7 Rue de Fourcy 75004. **Map** 13 C3.
Tel 01 44 78 75 00. Ⓜ St.-Paul, Pont-Marie. **Open** 11am–8pm Wed–Sun.
Closed public hols. 🖼 🎦 🎥
🌐 **mep-fr.org**

Located in the heart of the Marais, in the elegant 18th-century Hotel Henault de Cantobre, the Maison Européenne de la Photographie (MEP) puts on some of the best exhibitions of contemporary photography in Europe. It organizes cutting-edge shows alongside retrospectives on major photographers, and since opening its doors in 1996, it has hosted displays by such celebrated photographers as Elliott Erwitt, Don McCullin, Annie Leibovitz, and Henri Cartier-Bresson. The MEP's huge permanent collection on the history of photography is a must-see for anyone interested in exploring this medium.

⑱ Mémorial de la Shoah

17 Rue Geoffroy-l'Asnier 75004. **Map** 13 C4. **Tel** 01 42 77 44 72. Ⓜ Pont-Marie, St.-Paul. **Open** 10am–6pm Sun–Fri (10am–10pm Thu). Multimedia & reading rooms: 10am–5.30pm Sun–Fri (to 7.30pm Thu). **Closed** public & Jewish hols. 🎦 exhibitions. 🎥🎦
🎦 🌐 **memorialdelashoah.org**

The eternal flame burning in the crypt here is the memorial

to the unknown Jewish martyr of the Holocaust. Its striking feature is a large cylinder that bears the names of the concentration camps where Jewish victims of the Holocaust died. In 2005, a stone wall, engraved with the names of 76,000 Jews – 11,000 of them children – who were deported from France to the Nazi death camps, was erected here. Artifacts from the camps are also on display.

⑲ St.-Gervais–St.-Protais

Pl St.-Gervais 75004. **Map** 13 B3.
Tel 01 48 87 32 02. Ⓜ Hôtel de Ville. **Open** 5.30am–9pm daily.

Named after Gervase and Protase, two Roman soldiers who were martyred by Nero in the 1st century AD, St.-Gervais–St.-Protais is on the site of a 6th-century church. The current church was built in 1494–1660. It has splendid stained-glass windows and the oldest Classical facade in Paris, which is formed of a three-tiered arrangement of columns: Doric, Ionic, and Corinthian. Behind its facade lies a beautiful Gothic church renowned for its association with religious music. It was for the church's fine organ that François Couperin (1668–1733) composed his two masses. The church currently has a Roman Catholic monastic community whose liturgy attracts people from all over the world.

The facade of St.-Gervais–St.-Protais, with its Classical columns

The elaborate facade of the town hall (Hôtel de Ville), rebuilt in the 19th century according to its original Neo-Renaissance design

⑳ Hôtel de Ville

Pl de l'Hôtel de Ville (entrance 29 Rue de Rivoli) 75004. **Map** 13 B3. **Tel** 01 42 76 40 40. **M** Hôtel-de-Ville. **Open** 10am–7pm Mon–Sat for temporary exhibitions; groups: by appt, **Tel** 01 42 76 43 43 or 01 42 76 54 04. **Closed** public hols, official functions. ♿ 🏠 **w** paris.fr/municipalite

Home of the city council, the town hall is a 19th-century reconstruction of the original building, erected between 1533 and 1628, that was burned down in 1871. It is highly ornate, with elaborate stonework, turrets, and statues overlooking a pedestrian-only square whose fountains are illuminated at night.

The square was once the main site for hangings, burnings, and other executions. It was here that Ravaillac, Henri IV's assassin, was quartered alive, his body ripped to pieces by four strong horses.

Inside, a notable feature is the long Salle des Fêtes (ballroom), with adjoining salons devoted to science, literature, and the arts. The impressive staircase, the decorated ceilings with their chandeliers, and the statues and caryatids all add to the air of ceremony and pomp. While these parts are mostly closed to the public (except during some of the Journées du Patrimoine (see p66) and group visits), certain annexes are used for temporary exhibitions on themes related to France (see www.paris.fr for more info).

㉑ Cloître des Billettes

24 Rue des Archives 75004. **Map** 13 B3. **Tel** 06 63 22 91 73 **M** Hôtel-de-Ville. **Open** Cloister 2–7pm daily; church 6:30–8pm Thu, 9:30am–4pm Sun. 🎵 Concerts, **Tel** 06 62 45 91 29.

This is the only remaining medieval cloister in Paris. It was built in 1427 for the Brothers of Charity, or *Billettes*, and three of its four original galleries are still standing. The adjoining church is a simple Classical building, which replaced the monastic original in 1756.

Cloître des Billettes, Paris's oldest cloister

㉒ Notre-Dame-des-Blancs-Manteaux

1 Rue de l'Abbé Migne 75004. **Map** 13 C3. **Tel** 01 42 72 09 37. **M** Rambuteau. **Open** 5–7:30pm Mon, 8am–noon & 4–5:30pm Tue–Fri, 9am–noon & 4–7:30pm Sat, 10am–noon Sun . 🕐 6:15pm Sat, 11am Sun, other times during wk. 🎵 on request. Concerts. **w** ndbm.fr

The name of this church, built in 1685, derives from the white habits worn by the Augustinian

friars who founded a convent here in 1258. It has an interesting 18th-century Rococo Flemish pulpit, and its famous organ can be heard at one of the concerts.

㉓ Hôtel de Rohan

87 Rue Vieille-du-Temple 75003. **Map** 13 C2. **Tel** 01 40 27 60 29. **M** Rambuteau. **Closed** for renovations; call for up-to-date information.

The Hôtel de Rohan, forming a pair with the Hôtel de Soubise, was built by the same architect, Delamair, for Armand de Rohan-Soubise, Bishop of Strasbourg. The *hôtel* has been home to a part of the national archives (one of the largest in the world) since 1927. In the courtyard over the doorway of the stables is the 18th-century sculpture *Horses of Apollo* by Robert Le Lorrain.

Horses of Apollo by Le Lorrain

The Hôtel de Soubise

㉔ Hôtel de Soubise

60 Rue des Francs-Bourgeois 75003.
Map 13 C2. **Tel** 01 40 27 60 96.
Ⓜ Rambuteau. Musée de l'Histoire
de France **Open** 10am–5:30pm Mon,
Wed–Fri, 2–5:30pm Sat & Sun. ☑
Tel 06 10 12 62 72. ☒ ☒ **archives
nationales.culture.gouv.fr**

This imposing mansion, built
from 1705 to 1709 for the
Princesse de Rohan, is one of
two main buildings housing the
national archives. (The other is
the Hôtel de Rohan). The Hôtel
de Soubise displays a majestic
courtyard and a magnificent
interior decoration dating from
1735 to 1740 by some of the
most gifted painters and
craftsmen of the day: Carl Van
Loo, Jean Restout, Charles
Natoire, and François Boucher.
    Natoire's *rocaille* work on the
Princess's bedroom, the Oval
Salon, forms part of the Musée de
l'Histoire de France. Other exhibits
include Napoleon's will, in which
he asks for his remains to be
returned to France, and letters by
Joan of Arc and Voltaire.

㉕ Hôtel de Guénégaud (Musée de la Chasse et de la Nature)

62 Rue des Archives 75003. **Map** 13
C2. **Tel** 01 53 01 92 40. Ⓜ Hôtel de
Ville Museum. **Open** 11am–6pm Tue–
Sun (to 9:30pm Thu). **Closed** public
hols. ☒ ☒ ☒ **chassenature.org**

The celebrated architect François
Mansart built this superb mansion in the mid-17th century for
Henri de Guénégaud des Brosses,
Secretary of State and Keeper of
the Seals. It contains the Musée
de la Chasse et de la Nature
(Hunting Museum) inaugurated
by André Malraux in 1967, where
the collections of François and
Jacqueline Sommer include a fine
collection of hunting weapons,
plus drawings and paintings by
Oudry, Rubens (including *Diane
and her Nymphs Preparing to
Hunt*), and Rembrandt.

㉖ Musée des Arts et Métiers

60 Rue Réaumur 75003. **Map** 13 B1-C1.
Tel 01 53 01 82 00. Ⓜ Arts et Métiers.
Open 10am–6pm Tue–Sun (to 9:30pm
Thu). **Closed** May 1 & Dec 25. ☒ ☒
☒ ☒ ☒ **arts-et-metiers.net**

Housed within the old Abbey
of St.-Martin-des-Champs, the
Arts and Crafts museum was
founded in 1794. After major
renovations in the 1990s, it
reopened in 2000 as a high-
quality museum of science and
industry displaying 5,000 items
(it has 75,000 other artifacts in
storage available to academics
and researchers). The theme is
man's ingenuity and the world
of invention and manufacturing,
covering such topics as textiles,
photography, and machines.
Among the most entertaining
displays are ones of musical
clocks, mechanical musical
instruments, and automata
(mechanical figures), one
of which, the Joueuse de
Tympanon, is said to represent
Marie-Antoinette.

㉗ Square du Temple

75003. **Map** 13 C1. Ⓜ Temple.

A quiet and pleasant square
today, this was once a fortified
center of the medieval Knights
Templar. A state within a state,
the area contained a palace, a
church, and stores behind high
walls and a drawbridge, making
it a haven for those who were
seeking to escape from royal
jurisdiction. Louis XVI and Marie-
Antoinette were held here after
their arrest in 1792 *(see pp32–3)*.
The king left from here for his
execution by the guillotine.

The exterior of the Musée d'Art et d'Histoire
du Judaïsme

㉘ Musée d'Art et d'Histoire du Judaïsme

Hôtel de St-Aignan, 71 rue du Temple
75003. **Map** 13 C2. **Tel** 01 53 01 86 60.
Ⓜ Rambuteau. **Open** 11am–6pm
Mon–Fri, 10am–6pm Sun (last adm:
5:15pm). **Closed** Jan 1, May 1, Rosh
Hashanah & Yom Kippur. ☒ ☒ ☒
☒ ☒ ☒ **mahj.org**

Housed in an elegant Marais
mansion, the museum unites
collections formerly scattered
around the city, and commemorates the culture of French
Jewry from medieval times to
the present. There has been a
sizable Jewish community in
France since Roman times, and
some of the world's greatest
Jewish scholars were French.
Much exquisite craftsmanship is
displayed, with elaborate silverware and Torah covers. There are
also historical documents, photographs, paintings, and cartoons.

BEAUBOURG AND LES HALLES

Sandwiched between the Tuileries and the Marais, Beaubourg and Les Halles are busy centers for shopping, eating, and sightseeing. The area mixes the modern and the old – one minute you could be facing the Pompidou Center, an architectural wonder of inside-out industrial design with scaffolds, pipes, and steel ducts; the next, be strolling by the Renaissance Fontaine des Innocents.

Les Halles, also known as the "Belly of Paris," was an 800-year-old food market that once provided the city's sustenance. It has since

been transformed into a huge underground mall called the Forum des Halles, with stores, movie theaters and even a swimming pool. Above ground, there are gardens, cafés, bars, and vintage stores, but after dark the area can be quite seedy. A massive renovation is scheduled for completion by early 2017.

Sights in the area include the Eglise St.-Eustache, modeled after Notre-Dame, and Vieux Rue Montorgueil, a cobblestone pedestrian-only district with produce stores, terraced cafés and trendy bars.

Sights at a Glance

Historic Buildings and Streets
10 No. 51 Rue de Montmorency
11 Tour Jean Sans Peur
13 Bourse du Commerce
15 La Samaritaine
16 Tour St.-Jacques

Churches
3 St.-Merry
12 St.-Eustache
14 St.-Germain l'Auxerrois

Modern Architecture
2 Place Igor Stravinsky
8 Forum des Halles

Historic Cafés
6 Café Beaubourg

Fountains
4 Fontaine des Innocents

Museums and Galleries
1 *Pompidou Center pp110–13*
5 Galerie Marian Goodman
7 Forum des Images
9 Musée de la Poupée

Restaurants *see pp296–8*
1 L'Ambassade d'Auvergne
2 L'Ange 20
3 Auberge Nicolas Flamel
4 Benoît
5 Blend
6 Filakia
7 Frenchie
8 Le Garde Robe
9 Le Hangar
10 Le Pharamond
11 La Régalade St.-Honoré
12 Spring
13 Le Tir Bouchon
14 Yam'Tcha

See also Street Finder map 12, 13

0 meters 400
0 yards 400

◀ Large air vents on the exterior of the Pompidou Center

For keys to symbols *see back flap*

Street by Street: Beaubourg and Les Halles

When Emile Zola described Les Halles as the "belly of Paris," he was referring to the meat, vegetable, and fruit market that had thrived here since 1183. Traffic congestion in the 1960s forced the market to move to the suburbs and Baltard's giant umbrella-like market pavilions were pulled down, despite howls of protest, and replaced by a shopping and leisure complex, the Forum. The conversion worked: today, Les Halles and the Pompidou Center, which lies in the Beaubourg quarter and has been one of Paris's main tourist attractions ever since it opened in 1977, draw the most mixed crowds in Paris.

The Rue Quincampoix is lined by 18th-century *hôtels* that have been beautifully restored and totally refurbished.

8 ★ **Forum des Halles**
Beneath the stores, restaurants, movie theaters and swimming pool is the world's busiest subway station.

7 Forum des Images
Visitors can enjoy watching movies on one of the five screens here.

Rue de la Ferronnerie was where, in 1610, the religious fanatic Ravaillac assassinated Henri IV while his carriage was caught in the traffic.

4 ★ **Fontaine des Innocents**
This is the last Renaissance fountain left in Paris. It was designed by the sculptor and architect Jean Goujon.

Key

— Suggested route

Le Défenseur du Temps
This impressive brass-and-steel mechanical clock and sculpture was designed by Jacques Monastier in 1979. It portrays a soldier defending the passage of time against savage beasts that represent the elements.

Locator Map
See Central Paris Map pp16–17

0 meters 100
0 yards 100

❶ ★ Pompidou Center
Paris's museum of modern art is housed here, along with extensive art libraries and an industrial design center.

RAMBATEAU

QUINCAMPOIX

ST MARTIN

PL GEORGES POMPIDOU

Metro Rambuteau

RUE BEAUBOURG

UCHER

RUE ST MERRI

RUE

RUE BRISMICHE

RUE DU RENARD

RUE DE LA VERRERIE

❷ ★ Place Igor Stravinsky
is dominated by the first contemporary Parisian fountain, created by Niki de Saint Phalle and Jean Tinguely.

❸ St.-Merry
The pulpit of this beautiful church was designed by the Stodtz brothers in the mid-18th century and is supported by a pair of carved palm trees, one on either side.

IRCAM is a research center dedicated to pioneering new ways of making music.

❶ Pompidou Center

The Pompidou Center is like a building turned inside out: escalators, elevators, air and water ducts, and even the massive steel struts that are the building's skeleton have all been placed on the outside. This allowed architects Richard Rogers, Renzo Piano, and Gianfranco Franchini to create an uncluttered, flexible space within it for the Musée National d'Art Moderne, the world's largest collection of modern art, and for other activities. Schools represented in the museum include Fauvism, Cubism, and Surrealism. Outside in the piazza, the street performers attract crowds. The Pompidou Center also hosts temporary exhibitions that thrust it into the heart of the international art scene.

The escalator that rises step by step up the facade overlooking the piazza runs through a glass conduit. From the top there is a spectacular view over Paris that includes Montmartre, La Défense, and the Eiffel Tower.

Key to Floor Plan

▢ Exhibition space

▨ Nonexhibition space

Gallery Guide

The permanent collections are on Levels 4, 5 & 6: Level 4 shows contemporary art from the 1960s onward, while works from 1905 to 1960 are on Levels 5 and 6. Levels 1 & 6 are for major exhibitions, while Levels 1, 2 & 3 house an information library. The lower levels make up "The Forum," the focal public area, which includes a performance center for dance, theater, and music, a movie theater, and a children's workshop.

Portrait of the Journalist Sylvia von Harden *(1926)*
The surgical precision of Dix's style makes this a harsh caricature.

Le Cheval Majeur
This bronze horse (1914–16) by Duchamp-Villon is one of the finest examples of Cubist sculpture.

To Russia, the Asses and the Others (1911)
Throughout his life Chagall drew inspiration from the small Russian town of Vitebsk, where he was born.

VISITORS' CHECKLIST

Practical Information
Pl Georges Pompidou.
Map 13 B2. **Tel** 01 44 78 12 33.
☑ **centrepompidou.fr**
Open MNAM & temp exhibs:
11am–9pm Wed–Mon (to 11pm
Thu); Library: noon–10pm Wed–
Mon (from 11am Sat, Sun &
public hols); Atelier Brancusi:
2–6pm Wed–Mon.
🎫 ♿ 🎫 (free for under 18s on
1st Sun of month). 📷 ✏️ 💻 🏛️

Transportation
Ⓜ Rambuteau, Châtelet, Hôtel
de Ville. 🚌 21, 29, 38, 47, 58, 69,
70, 72, 74, 75, 76, 81, 85, 96.
🚆 Châtelet-Les-Halles.

Basin and Sculpture Terrace

The Breakfast Table (1915)
Juan Gris' fragmented objects with sharp edges represent the synthetic Cubism style of art.

Le Duo (1937)
Georges Braque, like Picasso, developed the Cubist technique of representing different views of a subject in a single picture.

Basin and Sculpture Terrace

Color-Coding

The colored pipes that are the most striking feature of the back of the Pompidou, on the rue du Renard, moved one critic to compare the building to an oil refinery. Far from being merely decorative, the colors serve to distinguish the pipes' various functions: air-conditioning ducts are blue, water pipes are green, and electrical lines are painted yellow. The areas through which people move vertically (such as escalators) are red. The white funnels are ventilation shafts for the underground areas, and structural beams are clad in stainless steel. The architects' idea was to help the public understand the dynamics of how the building functions.

Exploring the Pompidou's Modern Art Collection

With over 60,000 works of art from over 5,000 artists, the Pompidou holds Europe's largest collection of modern and contemporary art. Classic disciplines – painting, sculpture, drawing, and photography – are integrated with cinema, architecture, design, and audio-visual archives, to form a complete, chronological overview of modern and contemporary art. The collections, however, keep changing. Works are often loaned out, so some pieces may not be on display.

The Two Barges (1906) by André Derain

From 1905 to 1960

The "historical" collections bring together the great artistic movements of the first half of the 20th century, from Fauvism to Abstract Expressionism, to the changing currents of the 1950s. The rich collection of Cubist sculptures, of which the *Cheval Majeur* by Duchamp-Villon (1914–1916) is a fine example, is displayed, as well as examples of the great masters of the 20th century. Matisse, Picasso, Braque, Duchamp, Kandinsky, Léger, Miró, Giacometti, and Dubuffet command large areas at the heart of the collection.

Toward the end of his life, Matisse made several collages from cut-up large sheets of gouache-painted paper. Among others, the museum possesses *Jazz* (1943–7). With *Homme à la Guitare* (Man with a Guitar), Braque demonstrates his command of the Cubist technique that he pioneered along with Picasso. Considered as one of the first, if not the first, Abstract painter, Kandinsky transformed works inspired by nature into constructions of color and form. The museum has a large collection of the Russian painter's works, of which the Impressions (*Impressions V, Parc, 1911*) mark the end of his Expressionist period before his plunge into Abstract art with *Improvisations XIV* or *Avec l'Arc Noir* (With the Black Arc) both dating from 1912 compositions.

The collection also shows the groups and the movements on which the history of modern art is based, or by which it has been affected, including Dada, Abstract Art, and Informal. A pioneer of Informal art, Jean Fautrier is represented in the collections with *Otages* (Hostages), a commemoration of the suffering of the resistance fighters.

At the heart of this chronological progression, various thematic displays are a revelation. One set shows non-figurative art from "Groupe Espace and the Magazine," a collaboration between painters, sculptors, architects, and engineers. Another room recreates the atmosphere of André Breton's workshop in which the works of his Surrealist friends are also shown. Silent pauses have also been allowed for; the room reserved for Miró has vast, moody canvases such as *La Sieste* that give visitors reason to meditate on the explosion and revolutions of modern art.

Brancusi's Studio

The Atelier Brancusi, on the rue Rambuteau side of the piazza, is a reconstruction of the workshop of the Romanian-born artist Constantin Brancusi (1876–1957), who lived and worked in Paris from 1904. He bequeathed his entire collection of works to the French state on condition that his workshop be rebuilt as it was on the day he died. The collection includes sculptures and plinths, photographs, and a selection of his tools. Also featured are some of his more personal items such as documents, pieces of furniture, and his book collection.

With the Black Arc (1912) by Vassily Kandinsky

Miss Pogany (1919–20) by Constantin Brancusi

The Good-bye Door (1980) by Joan Mitchell

Art Since 1960

The contemporary art section occupies the fourth floor of the Pompidou Center and consists of approximately 500 works. Jean-Michel Alberola's exceptional, boldly colored mural, *Vous avez le bonjour de Marcel* (2002), welcomes visitors and sets the tone for the contemporary collection.

The collection starts with works by leading French artists of the second half of the 20th century: artist and sculptor Louise Bourgeois, whose work is strongly influenced by the Surrealists, Abstract Expressionism, and Minimalism; Pierre Soulages; Jean-Pierre Raynaud; François Morellet; and Bertrand Lavier.

Yayoï Kusama's restored masterpiece *My Flower Bed* (1965–6), made of painted mattress springs and stuffed gloves, is also on view.

The display is organized around a central aisle from which the rooms holding the museum's collections lead off. The central aisle is dotted with sculptures including works by Toni Grand, John Chamberlain, and Xavier Veilhan. This hall is, however, dedicated principally to painting, with works by Gerhard Richter, Brice Marden, Jean-Michel Basquiat, Philip

Mobile on Two Planes (1955) by Alexander Calder

Guston, Bernard Piffaretti, and Katharina Grosse.

Room 3 is an homage to artist, philosopher, and art critic Pontus Hulten who was chosen by George Pompidou to plan and run the national museum of modern art as its founding director from 1973 to 1981. This was to be one of the four departments of the Pompidou Center.

Homogenous Infiltration (1966) by Joseph Beuys

Pontus Hulten was responsible for making the Musée d'art Moderne the open and cross-disciplinary museum that its founder had intended. Works by Jean Tinguely, Andy Warhol, and Niki de Saint Phalle are to be found in this room.

Certain areas in the Pompidou Center have been designated to bring together different disciplines around a theme such as minimalist painting or conceptual art, rather than a school or movement. Other rooms, however, are artist-specific, with rooms dedicated to New Realist Martial Raysse, Robert Filliou, Christian Botanski, Sarkis, Joseph Beuys, and Marcel Broodthaers. These rooms explore installation and photography as well as painting.

The fourth floor allows different aspects of the museum's collections to be

discovered, often reflecting a preference for the more ironic and conceptual forms. German artist Joseph Beuys's *Plight* (1985), for example, consists of a grand piano in a room where the walls are covered from floor to ceiling with about seven tons of thick felt arranged in rolls.

With regard to design and architecture, inflatable structures are explored in an unprecedented way with acidically colored inflatable pieces on display.

A room is dedicated to French designer Philippe Starck's work, with items from the 1960s through to the present day on display.

Another room focuses on leading young international architects and designers of the moment, along with a space dedicated to Japanese artists, including Shigeru Ban, the architect behind the construction of the Pompidou Center's sister gallery in Metz.

Lastly, there is a "global" room bringing together major contemporary pieces by African, Chinese, Japanese, and American artists. *Denkifuku* (1956), a dress made from light-bulbs, is a key work by Atsuko Tanaka of Japan.

The museum gallery allows temporary exhibitons to be mounted from works held in reserve. A graphic arts exhibition room and a video area complete the arrange-ment. A screening room gives access to the museum's entire collection of videos of a wide range of modern artists.

Le Rhinocéros (1999) by Xavier Veilhan

❷ Place Igor Stravinsky

75004. **Map** 13 B2. Ⓜ Rambuteau.

This lively square on the south side of the Pompidou Center is filled with modern sculptures and street performers. Since 1983 it has contained the Stravinsky Fountain, which features 16 moving, water-spraying sculptures of skeletons, dragons, and a large pair of red lips. The black iron and colorful polyester mechanical sculptures were created by husband-and-wife team Jean Tinguely and Niki de Saint Phalle and pay homage to Igor Stravinsky. Each sculpture represents one of his compositions, including *The Firebird* and *The Rite of Spring*.

Stravinsky's music paved the way for the pioneering work of IRCAM (Institut de la Researche et de la Coordination Acoustique/Musique), which has an entrance on the west side of the square. Founded by the composer Pierre Boulez, it is a research center dedicated to creating new technologies for contemporary music, as well as a venue for concerts. Much of the Institute is underground, with an overground extension by Renzo Piano, one of the Pompidou Center's architects. IRCAM runs an annual festival, which usually takes place for up to two weeks in June.

❸ St.-Merry

76 Rue de la Verrerie 75004. **Map** 13 B3. **Tel** 01 42 71 93 93. Ⓜ Hôtel-de-Ville. **Open** Apr–Oct: 3–7pm Mon–Sat; Nov–Mar: 2–6pm Mon–Sat. 🎵 8pm Sat & 4pm Sun. ✝ 12.15pm Mon–Fri, 6.30pm Sat, 10 & 11.15am Sun. Concerts. 🖵 saintmerry.org

The site of this church dates back to the 7th century. St. Médéric, abbot of St.-Martin d'Autun, was buried here at the beginning of the 8th century after he died while on pilgrimage in Paris. The construction of the church, in the Flamboyant Gothic style, took place between 1500 and 1550. The west front is particularly rich in

A Nativity scene from the stained-glass windows in St.-Merry

decoration, and the northwest turret contains the oldest bell in Paris, dating from 1331. St.-Merry was the wealthy parish church of the Lombard money-lenders, who gave their name to the nearby Rue des Lombards.

❹ Fontaine des Innocents

Pl Joachim-du-Bellay 75001. **Map** 13 A2. Ⓜ Les Halles. 🚇 Châtelet-Les-Halles.

This carefully restored Renaissance fountain stands in the Place Joachim-du-Bellay, the area's main crossroads. Erected in 1549 on the Rue St.-Denis, it was moved to its present location in the 18th century, when the square was constructed on the site of a former graveyard. Originally set into a wall, the fountain had only three sides, so a fourth had to be constructed. The fountain is a popular meeting place and one of the landmarks of Les Halles.

❺ Galerie Marian Goodman

79 Rue du Temple 75003. **Map** 13 C2. **Tel** 01 48 04 70 52. Ⓜ Rambuteau. 🚇 Châtelet-Les-Halles. **Open** 11am–7pm Tue–Sat. **Closed** between exhibitions. 🖵 mariangoodman.com

This cutting-edge gallery is the sister of two Marian Goodman exhibition spaces – one in New York, the other in London – that have played an important role in presenting European artists to international audiences since the 1970s. Many important contemporary artists, from the continent and the US, have been exhibited in the Paris gallery, including Gerhard Richter, Jeff Wall, Tacita Dean, William Kentridge, Chantal Akerman, and Cristina Iglesias.

Housed in a beautiful 17th-century mansion, the contemporary works on display and the Manhattan-style interior contrast in an appealing, if strikingly anachronistic way with the period facade.

❻ Café Beaubourg

43 Rue St.-Merry, Esplanade du Centre Georges Pompidou 75004. **Map** 13 B2. **Tel** 01 48 87 63 96. Ⓜ Les Halles, Rambuteau, Hôtel-de-Ville. 🚇 Châtelet-Les-Halles. **Open** 8am–2am daily. 🖵 cafebeaubourg.com

Opened by Gilbert Costes in 1987, this stylish café was designed by one of France's

Decoration on the Fontaine des Innocents

The terrace of the Café Beaubourg

star architects, Christian de Portzamparc, who created the impressive Cité de la Musique in the Parc de la Villette (see p238). Its vast terrace is lined with comfortable wicker chairs. The spacious and coolly elegant interior is decorated with rows of books, which soften its severely Art Deco ambience. A favorite meeting point for art dealers from the surrounding galleries and Pompidou Center staff, it serves light meals and brunch. If the crowds get over-whelming around Les Halles, the Café Beaubourg is the ideal place to soothe the nerves.

❼ Forum des Images

2 Rue du Cinéma, Forum des Halles 75001. **Map** 13 A2. **Tel** 01 44 76 63 00. Ⓜ Les Halles. ⓇⒺⓡ Châtelet-Les-Halles. **Open** Collections: 1–9pm Tue–Fri, 2–9pm Sat & Sun. Information & Café: 12:30–9pm Tue–Fri, 2–9pm Sat & Sun. ⬛ ⬛ ⬛ Ⓦ **forumdesimages.fr**

At the forum you can choose from thousands of movies, television shows, and amateur films. Many feature the city of Paris. There is footage on the history of Paris since 1895, including a remarkable newsreel of General de Gaulle avoiding sniper fire during the Liberation of Paris in 1944. There are countless movies such as Truffaut's *Baisers Volés*. On Friday evenings, the forum also hosts "Cours de Cinéma," when classic films are analyzed. There are also regular film festivals, "midnight movie" screenings, and short film evenings.

❽ Forum des Halles

101 Porte Berger 75001. **Map** 13 A2. **Tel** 01 44 76 95 56. Ⓜ Les Halles. ⓇⒺⓡ Châtelet-Les-Halles. **Open** 10am–8pm Mon–Sat.

The present Forum des Halles, known simply as Les Halles, was built in 1979, amid much controversy, on the site of the famous old fruit and vegetable market. Emile Zola named the area *Le Ventre de Paris* (The Belly of Paris). The complex is currently being rebuilt, and hence is partially closed. Some of the amenities, such as the multi-screen movie theater, swimming pool, as well as the fantastic Forum des Images film archive, continue to remain open. Beneath this complex is a

Metro station and major urban rail (RER) hub. Above ground, there is the Nelson Mandela Garden with fountains, ponds, and a terraced flower garden.

Sadly, Les Halles can be rather sketchy, and is not recommended at night. However, under the direction of architect David Mangin, the major and much-needed remodeling project will hopefully transform the area as well as bring back a food market. Redevelopment is expected to continue until 2017. Remember to explore the surrounding streets, including the trendy Rue Montorgueil to the north.

Pygmalion by Julio Silva in the Forum des Halles

A collection of handmade dolls in the Musée de la Poupée

❾ Musée de la Poupée

Impasse Berthaud 75003. **Map** 13 B2. **Tel** 01 42 72 73 11. Ⓜ Rambuteau. **Open** 1–6pm Tue–Sat. **Closed** public hols. 🅿 🎫 🌐 **museedela poupeeparis.com**

An impressive collection of hand-made dolls, from the mid-19th century to the present day, is on show in this charming museum. Thirty-six of the displays contain French dolls with porcelain heads ranging from 1850 to 1950. Another 24 display windows are devoted to themed exhibitions of dolls from around the world.

Father and son, Guido and Samy Odin, who own the museum, are at your service. The museum store stocks every-thing needed to preserve and maintain these unique works of art, and the "doll hospital" will repair dolls or stuffed animals. There are also workshops for kids on Wednesdays based on themes connected to the current exhibition.

❿ No. 51 Rue de Montmorency

75003. **Map** 13 B1. Ⓜ Réaumur-Sébastopol. **Open** to the public.

This house is considered to be the oldest in Paris. No. 51 was built in 1407 by Nicolas Flamel, a bookkeeper and alchemist. His house was always open to the poor, from whom he asked nothing more than that they should pray for those who were dead. Today, the house is a French restaurant.

⓫ Tour Jean Sans Peur

20 Rue Etienne-Marcel 75002. **Map** 13 A1. **Tel** 01 40 26 20 28. Ⓜ Etienne-Marcel. **Open** 1.30–6pm Wed–Sun. 🎫 🌐 **tourjeansanspeur.com**

The Duc de Bourgogne feared reprisals after the Duc d'Orléans was assassinated on his orders in 1408. To protect himself, he had this 88-ft (27-m) tower built onto his home, the Hôtel de Bourgogne, and moved his bedroom up to the fourth floor (reached by a flight of 140 steps).

⓬ St.-Eustache

2 Impasse St.-Eustache, Pl du Jour 75001. **Map** 13 A1. **Tel** 01 42 36 31 05. Ⓜ Les Halles. ⓇⒺⓇ Châtelet-Les-Halles. **Open** 9.30am–7pm Mon–Fri, 9am–7pm Sat & Sun. 🅿 📷 🎫 12.30pm Mon–Fri, 6pm Sat, 11am, & 6pm Sun. Organ recitals and concerts. 🌐 **saint-eustache.org**

With its Gothic plan and Renaissance decoration, St.-Eustache is one of the most beautiful churches in Paris. Its interior plan is modeled on Notre-Dame, with five naves and side and radial chapels. The 105 years (1532–1637) it took to complete the church saw the flowering of the Renaissance style, which is evident in the arches, pillars, and columns. The stained-glass windows in the chancel are created from cartoons by Philippe de Champaigne.

The church has associations with many famous figures: Molière was buried here; the Marquise de Pompadour, official mistress of Louis XV, was baptized here, as was Cardinal Richelieu.

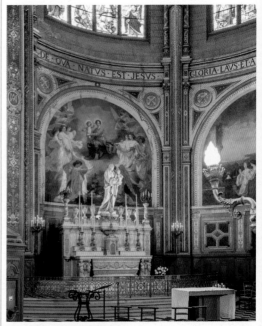

The ornate Renaissance interior of St.-Eustache

Entrance to the Bourse du Commerce, the old corn exchange

⑬ Bourse du Commerce

2 Rue de Viarmes 75001. **Map** 12 F2. **Tel** 08 20 01 21 12 or 01 42 33 06 67. Ⓜ Les Halles. ⓇⒺⓇ Châtelet-Les-Halles. **Open** 8.30am–6.30pm Mon–Fri (ID required). 🔲 groups of up to 10 people by appt. ♿ 🌐 sgbcp.fr

Compared dismissively by Victor Hugo to a jockey's cap without a peak, the old grain exchange building was France's first iron structure. It was constructed in the 18th century and remodeled in 1889. Today, its huge, domed hall is filled with the hustle and bustle of the Chambre de Commerce et d'Industrie de Paris. It is still worth entering to marvel at the architecture, in particular the beautifully restored cupola and its decor. Also worth a look are the murals depicting French trade and industry through the ages, which were painted in 1889 and have since been restored.

⑭ St.-Germain l'Auxerrois

2 Pl du Louvre 75001. **Map** 12 F2. **Tel** 01 42 60 13 96. Ⓜ Louvre, Pont-Neuf. **Open** 9am–7pm Tue–Sat, 9.30am–8.30pm Sun (Jul & Aug: 9.30am–7pm Tue–Sun). 🔔 various times. Concerts. 🌐 saintgermainauxerrois.cef.fr

This church has been built in a combination of Renaissance and Gothic styles. The first church on the site was constructed in the 12th century, of which only the foundations of the bell tower remain. The splendid rose stained-glass windows date from the Renaissance period.

After the Valois Court decamped to the Louvre from the Ile de la Cité in the 14th century, this became the favored church of kings.

The church's many historical associations include the horrific St. Bartholomew's Day Massacre on 24 August 1572, the eve of the royal wedding of Henri of Navarre and Marguerite de Valois. Thousands of Huguenots who had been lured to Paris for the wedding were murdered as the church bell tolled. Later, after the Revolution, the church was used as a barn and as a police station. Despite many restorations, it is a jewel of Gothic architecture.

⑮ La Samaritaine

83 Rue de Rivoli 75001. **Map** 12 F2. Ⓜ Pont-Neuf. **Tel** 01 56 81 28 40. **Closed** to the public. 🌐 projet. samaritaine.com

This former department store was founded in 1900 by Ernest Cognacq. Built in 1926 with a framework of iron and wide expanses of glass, La Samaritaine is an outstanding example of the Art Deco style. Cognacq was also a collector of 18th-century art, and his collection is now on display in the Musée Cognacq-Jay in the Marais quarter *(see p98)*.

The building is being redeveloped to create housing, a hotel, and a shopping complex due for completion in 2018.

The Tour St.-Jacques, with its ornate decoration

⑯ Tour St.-Jacques

Square de la Tour St.-Jacques, corner of Rue de Rivoli and Sebastopol 75004. **Map** 13 A3. Ⓜ Châtelet or Hôtel de Ville. **Open** Gardens: year-round. Tower: early Jul–early Sep: 10am–5pm Fri–Sun, visits by appt, call 01 83 96 15 05. 🔲 Gardens: Fri–Sun.

This imposing late Gothic tower, dating from 1523, is all that remains of an ancient church that was a rendezvous for pilgrims setting out on long journeys. The church was destroyed after the Revolution. Earlier, Blaise Pascal, the 17th-century mathematician, physicist, philosopher, and writer, used the tower for experiments. Queen Victoria passed by on her state visit in 1854, giving her name to the nearby Avenue Victoria.

The St. Bartholomew's Day Massacre (c.1572–84) by François Dubois

TUILERIES QUARTER

Located in the 1st arrondissement, the Tuileries area is classic Paris, with grand squares, iconic buildings, and fine-dining restaurants. Taking its name from the tile factories that stood on the site when Queen Catherine de Médici had her palace built, the Tuileries is now known for the beautiful sculpted gardens that line the Seine from Place de la Concorde to the Louvre. Grab a chair and watch the children float sailboats in one of the ponds. Stop at the Musée de l'Orangerie, or walk along the area's main streets, such as Rue St.-Honoré, full of designer boutiques, and Rue de Rivoli, with its bookstores, luxury hotels, and fabulous views across the gardens. The Palais-Royal is worth a visit for its splendid architecture and famous courtyard, or catch a theater production at the Comédie Française.

Sights at a Glance

Historic Buildings and Streets
3 Palais-Royal
18 Banque de France

Churches
7 St.-Roch

Theaters
4 Comédie Française

Stores
2 Louvre des Antiquaires
11 Rue de Rivoli

Squares, Parks, and Gardens
5 Jardin du Palais-Royal
8 Place des Pyramides
12 Jardin des Tuileries
15 Place de la Concorde
17 Place Vendôme
19 Place des Victoires

Monuments and Fountains
6 Fontaine Molière
10 Arc de Triomphe du Carrousel

Museums and Galleries
1 Musée du Louvre pp122–9
9 Musée des Arts Décoratifs
13 Galerie Nationale du
    Jeu de Paume
14 Musée de l'Orangerie
16 Village Royal

▢ Restaurants see pp298–300
1 Bistrot Victoires
2 Café Marly
3 Carré des Feuillants
4 La Cordonnerie
5 Les Fines Gueules
6 Le Grand Véfour
7 Kei
8 Le Meurice
9 Verjus

See also Street Finder
map 5–6, 11–12

0 meters 400
0 yards 400

◀ La Fontaine des Fleuves in Place de la Concorde

Street by Street: Tuileries Quarter

Elegant squares, formal gardens, street arcades, and courtyards give this part of Paris its special character. Monuments to monarchy and the arts coexist with contemporary luxury: sumptuous hotels, world-famous restaurants, fashion emporiums, and jewelers of international renown. Sandblasting and washing have given a fresh glow to the facades of the Louvre and the Palais-Royal square, where Cardinal Richelieu's creation, the Royal Palace, is now occupied by government offices. From here, the Ministry of Culture surveys the cleaning and restoration of the city's great buildings. The other former royal palace, the Louvre, is one of the great museums of the world.

❼ St.-Roch
The papal statue stands in this remarkably long 17th-century church, unusually set on a north-south axis. St.-Roch is a treasure house of religious art.

The Paris Convention and Visitors' Bureau

Metro Pyramides

The Normandy is an elegant hotel in the Belle Epoque style, a form of graceful living that prevailed in Paris at the turn of the 20th century.

❽ Place des Pyramides
Frémet's gilded statue of Joan of Arc is the focus of pilgrimage for royalists.

↓ To the Quai du Louvre

⓬ ★ Jardin des Tuileries
Pony rides are a popular attraction in these formal gardens, which were designed by the royal gardener André Le Nôtre in the 17th century.

❾ Musée des Arts Décoratifs
A highlight of the museum's displays of art and design is the Art Nouveau collection.

6 Fontaine Molière
Louis Visconti's fountain is of the famous playwright, who lived nearby.

Le Grand Véfour
The 18th-century decor makes this one of the most beautiful restaurants in Paris. Napoleon and Victor Hugo were two of the many famous people who dined here. *(See p300.)*

Locator Map
See Central Paris Map pp16–17

5 ★ Jardin du Palais-Royal
With a fountain pool and benches, the garden is a city haven, bordered by arcades housing restaurants, art galleries, and stores.

4 Comédie Française
France's national theater is the setting for the works of great dramatists, such as Molière.

3 ★ Palais-Royal
In the 18th century, this former royal palace was a setting for brilliant gatherings, debauchery, and gambling. Today, modern sculptures grace the square.

Metro Palais-Royal,
Musée du Louvre

Key

— Suggested route

2 Louvre des Antiquaires
Three floors of a former department store house this chic art and antiques supermarket for the rich collector.

1 ★ Musée du Louvre
Home to French kings for almost four centuries, the Louvre is now a museum with one of the world's great art collections.

RUE DE RICHELIEU
RUE DE MONTPENSIER
RUE DE VALOIS
PL DU PALAIS-ROYAL

| 0 meters | | 100 |
| 0 yards | | 100 |

❶ Musée du Louvre

The Musée du Louvre, containing one of the most important art collections in the world, has a history extending back to medieval times. First constructed as a fortress in 1190 by King Philippe-Auguste to protect Paris against Viking raids, it lost its imposing keep in the reign of François I, who replaced it with a Renaissance-style building. Thereafter, four centuries of French kings and emperors improved and enlarged it. A glass pyramid designed by I. M. Pei was added to the main courtyard in 1989. All the galleries can be reached from here.

The east facade, facing St.-Germain l'Auxerrois

KEY

① **Pavillon des Session**

② **The Jardin du Carrousel**, now part of the Jardin des Tuileries, was once the grand approach to the Tuileries Palace, which was burned down in 1871 by the Communards.

③ **The Carrousel du Louvre** underground visitors' complex lies beneath the Arc de Triomphe du Carrousel.

④ **The inverted glass pyramid** brings light to the subterranean complex, echoing the museum's main entrance in the Cour Napoléon.

⑤ **Cour Marly** is the glass-roofed courtyard that now houses the Marly Horses (see p125).

⑥ **The Petite Galerie du Louvre**, in the Richelieu Wing, has educational exhibitions for children.

⑦ **Cour Puget**

⑧ **Cour Khorsabad**

⑨ **Cour Carrée**

⑩ **The Louvre of Charles V** was transformed from Philippe-Auguste's robust old fortress into a royal residence in about 1360.

⑪ **The Salle des Caryatides** takes its name from the statues of women created by Jean Goujon in 1550 to support the upper gallery.

⑫ **Sully Wing**

⑬ **Cour Napoléon**

⑭ **Cour Visconti-Islamic Art**

⑮ **Denon Wing**

★ **Arc de Triomphe du Carrousel**
This triumphal arch was built to celebrate Napoleon's victories in 1805.

Building the Louvre

Over many centuries the Louvre was enlarged by a succession of French rulers, shown below with their dates.

Major Alterations

▨	Reign of François I (1515–47)
▨	Catherine de Médici (about 1560)
▨	Reign of Henri IV (1589–1610)
▨	Reign of Louis XIII (1610–43)
▨	Reign of Louis XIV (1643–1715)
▨	Reign of Napoleon I (1804–14)
▨	Reign of Napoleon III (1852–70)
▨	I.M. Pei (1989) (architect)

Pavillon Richelieu
This imposing 19th-century pavilion is part of the Richelieu Wing, once home to the Ministry of Finance but now converted into magnificent galleries.

★ **Pyramid Entrance**
The main entrance, designed by the architect I. M. Pei, was opened in 1989.

★ **Perrault's Colonnade**
The east facade with its majestic rows of columns was built by Claude Perrault, who worked on the Louvre with Louis Le Vau in the mid-17th century.

⑤ ⑥ ⑦ ⑧ ⑬ ⑫ ⑨ ⑪ ⑩ ⑭

★ **Medieval Moats**
The base of the twin towers and the drawbridge support of Philippe-Auguste's fortress can be seen in the excavated area.

The Louvre's Collection

The Louvre's treasures can be traced back to the collection of François I (1515–47), who purchased many Italian paintings including the *Mona Lisa* (*La Gioconda*). In Louis XIV's reign (1643–1715) there were a mere 200 works, but donations and purchases augmented the collection. The Louvre was first opened to the public in 1793 after the Revolution, and has been continually enriched ever since.

The Raft of the Medusa (1819)
Théodore Géricault derived his inspiration for this gigantic and moving work from the shipwreck of a French frigate in 1816. The painting shows the moment when the few survivors sight a sail on the horizon.

The Dying Slave
Michelangelo sculpted this work between 1513 and 1520 as part of a group of statues for the base of the tomb of Pope Julius II in Rome.

Cour Marly

Richelieu Wing

Main entrance

Underground visitors' complex

Pavillon des Sessions

Cour Visconti-Islamic Arts

★ Mona Lisa
Leonardo da Vinci painted this small portrait of a Florentine noblewoman, known as *La Gioconda*, in about 1504. It was soon regarded as the prototype of the Renaissance portrait. The sitter's engaging smile has prompted endless commentary ever since. The painting has its own wall in the Salle des Etats (Denon Wing).

Gallery Guide
The main entrance is beneath the glass pyramid. The works are displayed on four floors: the painting and sculpture collections are arranged by country of origin. There are eight departments: Near Eastern antiquities; Egyptian antiquities; Greek, Etruscan, and Roman antiquities; Islamic art; sculptures; decorative arts; paintings; and prints and drawings.

The Lacemaker
In this exquisite picture from about 1665, Jan Vermeer gives us a glimpse into everyday domestic life in Holland. The painting came to the Louvre in 1870.

Second floor

★ **Marly Horses**
Since the 19th century, these wild horses by Guillaume Coustou have stood near the Place de la Concorde. Replicas have replaced them – the originals are now in a glass-covered courtyard in the Louvre.

First floor

Cour Puget

Cour Khorsabad

Cour Napoléon

★ **Venus de Milo**
Found in 1820 on the island of Milos in Greece, this ideal of feminine beauty was made in the Hellenistic Age at the end of the 2nd century BC.

Sully Wing

Key to Floor Plan

- Painting
- *Objets d'art* (Decorative Arts)
- Sculpture
- Antiquities
- Nonexhibition space

Cour Carrée

Ground floor

Exploring the Louvre's Collections

It is important not to underestimate the size of these vast collections, and useful to set a few viewing priorities before starting. The collection of European paintings (1200–1850) is comprehensive, and 40 per cent of the works are by French artists, while the selection of sculptures is less complete. The museum's antiquities – Oriental, Islamic, Egyptian, Greek, Etruscan, and Roman – are of world renown and offer the visitor an unrivaled range of objects. The *objets d'art* on display are very varied and include furniture and jewelry.

The Fortune Teller (c. 1594) by Caravaggio

European Painting: 1200 to 1850

Painting from northern Europe is well covered. One of the earliest Flemish works is Jan van Eyck's *Madonna of Chancellor Rolin* (about 1435), which shows the Chancellor of Burgundy kneeling in prayer before the Virgin and Child. Hieronymus Bosch's *Ship of Fools* (1500) is a fine, satirical account of the

Portrait of Erasmus (1523) by Hans Holbein

futility of human existence. In the Dutch collection, Van Dyck's portrait *King Charles out Hunting* (1635) shows Charles I of England in all his refined elegance. Jacob Jordaens, best known for scenes of gluttony and lust, reveals unusual sensitivity in his *Four Evangelists*. The saucy smile of the *Gipsy Girl* (1628) displays Frans Hals' effortless virtuosity, in sharp contrast to Vermeer's highly-finished *Lacemaker*. Rembrandt's Self-portraits, *Disciples at Emmaus* (1648), and *Bathsheba* (1654) are fine examples of his genius.

There is relatively little German painting, but the three major German painters of the 15th and 16th centuries are represented by important works. There is a *Self-portrait* by Albrecht Dürer as a young artist of 22 (1493), a *Venus* by Lucas Cranach (1529), and a portrait of the great humanist scholar Erasmus by Hans Holbein. Works by English artists include Thomas Gainsborough's

Conversation in a Park (around 1746), Sir Joshua Reynolds' *Master Hare* (1788), and France's only painting by J. M. W. Turner, *Landscape with a River and a Distant Bay* (around 1840).

Many of the masterworks in the Spanish collection depict the tragic side of life: El Greco's *Christ on the Cross Adored by Donors* (1576) and Francisco de Zurbarán's *Lying-in-State of St. Bonaventura* (about 1629) with its dark-faced corpse are two of the Louvre's prize pieces. The subject of José de Ribera's *Club-Footed Boy* (1642) is a beggar boy, who carries a scrap of paper requesting alms. Portraits by Goya from the late 18th and early 19th century are in a lighter vein.

The museum's large collection of Italian paintings covers the period 1200 to 1800. The father figures of the early Renaissance, Cimabue and Giotto, are here, as is Fra Angelico, with his *Coronation of the Virgin* (around 1430–1432), and Raphael, with his stately *Portrait of Baldassare Castiglione* (around 1514). There is also a fine portrait in profile of *Sigismondo Malatesta* by Piero della Francesca (around 1450) and an action-packed battle scene by Paolo Uccello. Several paintings by Leonardo da Vinci – for instance, the *Virgin with the Infant Jesus* and *St. Anne* – are as enchanting as his *Mona Lisa*.

The collection of French painting ranges from the 14th century to 1848. Paintings after this date are housed in the

Gilles or Pierrot (c. 1717) by Jean-Antoine Watteau

Leonardo da Vinci in France

Leonardo, artist, engineer, and scientist, was born in 1452 and became a leading figure in the Italian Renaissance. François I met Leonardo in 1515 and invited him to live and work in France. The painter brought the *Mona Lisa* with him. Already in poor health, he died three years later in the arms of the king.

Self-portrait (early 16th century)

Musée d'Orsay *(see pp146–9)*. Outstanding early works are Jean Fouquet's *Portrait of Charles VIII* (around 1450) and *Gabrielle d'Estrée*, mistress of Henri IV, in her bathtub with her sister (1594). From the 16th and 17th centuries there are several splendid works by Georges de la Tour.

That great 18th-century painter of melancholy, Jean Watteau, is represented, as is J. H.Fragonard, master of the Rococo. His delightfully frivolous subjects are evident in *The Bathers* from 1770. In stark contrast is the Classicism of Nicolas Poussin and the history painting of J. L. David. Most of J. D. Ingres' work is in the Musée d'Orsay, but the Louvre kept the erotic *Turkish Bath* of 1862.

European Sculpture: 1100 to 1850

Early Flemish and German sculpture in the collection has many masterpieces, such as Tilman Riemenschneider's *Virgin of the Annunciation* from the end of the 15th century and an unusual life-size, nude figure of the penitent *Mary Magdalen* by Gregor Erhart (early 16th century). An ornate gilded-wood altarpiece of the same period exemplifies Flemish church art. Another important work of Flemish sculpture is Adrian de Vries's long-limbed *Mercury and Psyche* from 1593, which was originally made for the court of Rudolph II in Prague. The French section opens with early Romanesque works, such as a *figure of Christ* by a 12th-century Burgundian sculptor and a *head of St. Peter*. With its eight black-hooded mourners, the *tomb of Philippe Pot* (a high-ranking official in Burgundy) is one of the more unusual pieces. Diane de Poitiers, mistress of Henri II, had a large figure of her namesake Diana, goddess of the hunt, installed in the courtyard of her castle west of Paris. It is now in the Louvre.

The works of Pierre Puget (1620–94), the great sculptor from Marseille, have been assembled inside a glass-covered courtyard, Cour Puget. They include a figure of *Milo of Crotona*, the Greek athlete who got his hands caught in the cleft of a tree stump and was eaten by a lion. The wild horses of Marly now stand in the glass-roofed Cour Marly, surrounded by other masterpieces of French sculpture, including Houdon's early 19th-century busts of Diderot and Voltaire, and two equestrian pieces by Coysevox.

The Italian sculpture collection includes pre-Renaissance work by Duccio and Donatello, and later masterpieces such as Michelangelo's *Slaves* and Cellini's Fontainebleau *Nymph*.

Tomb of Philippe Pot (late 15th century) by Antoine le Moiturier

Near Eastern, Egyptian, Greek, Etruscan, and Roman Antiquities

The range of antiquities in the Louvre is impressive. There are objects from the Neolithic period (about 6000 BC) to the fall of the Roman Empire. Important works of Mesopotamian art include the seated figure of Ebih-il, from 2400 BC, and several portraits of Gudea, Prince of Lagash, from about 2255 BC. A black basalt block bearing the code of the Babylonian King Hammurabi, from about 1700 BC, is one of the world's oldest legal documents.

The warlike Assyrians are represented by delicate carvings and a spectacular reconstruction of part of Sargon II's (722–705 BC) palace with its huge winged bulls. A fine example of Persian art is the enameled brickwork depicting the king of Persia's personal guard of archers (5th century BC). It decorated his palace at Susa.

Most Egyptian art was made for the dead, who were provided with the things that they needed for the afterlife. It often included vivid images of daily life in ancient Egypt. One example is the tiny funeral chapel built for a high official in about 2500 BC. It is covered with exquisite carvings: men in sailing ships, catching fish, and tending cattle and fowl.

It is also possible to gain insights into family life in ancient Egypt through a number of lifelike funeral portraits, like the squatting scribe, and several sculptures of married couples. The earliest sculpture dates from 2500 BC, the latest from 1400 BC.

From the New Kingdom (1555–1080 BC) a special crypt dedicated to the god Osiris contains some colossal sarcophagi and a large number of mummified animals.

Some smaller objects of considerable charm include an 11-inch (29-cm) headless body of a woman, sensually outlined by the transparent veil of her dress and thought to be Queen Nefertiti (about 1365–1349 BC).

The department of Greek, Roman, and Etruscan antiquities contains a vast array of fragments, among them some exceptional pieces. There is a large, geometric head from the Cyclades (2700 BC) and an elegant, swan-necked bowl, quite modern in its unadorned simplicity. It is hammered out of a single gold sheet and dates from about 2500 BC. The Archaic Greek period, from the 7th to the 5th century BC, is represented by the *Auxerre Goddess*, one of the earliest known pieces of Greek sculpture, and the *Hera of Samos* from the Ionian Islands. From the height of the Classical Greek period (about the 5th century BC) there are several fine male torsos and heads, such as the *Laborde Head*. This head has been identified as part of the sculpture that once decorated the west pediment of the Parthenon in Athens.

The two most famous Greek statues in the Louvre, the *Winged Victory of Samothrace* and the *Venus de Milo* (see p 125), belong to the Hellenistic period (late 3rd to 2nd century BC) when more natural-looking human forms were beginning to be produced.

The undisputed star of the Etruscan collection is the terracotta *Sarcophagus of the*

Winged Bull with Human Head from 8th century BC, found in Khorsabad, Assyria

Winged Victory of Samothrace (Greece, late 3rd–early 2nd century BC)

Etruscan sarcophagus (6th century BC)

Cenestian Couple, who appear as though they are attending an eternal banquet.

The sculptures in the Roman section demonstrate the great debt owed to the art of ancient Greece. There are also fine pieces: a bust of Agrippa, a basalt head of Livia, the wife of Augustus, and a splendid, powerful bronze head of Emperor Hadrian from the 2nd century AD. This has the look of a true portrait, unlike so many Imperial heads that are uninspired and impersonal.

Squatting Scribe (Egyptian, about 2500 BC)

Decorative Arts

The term *objets d'art* (art objects) covers a vast range of "decorative art" objects: from jewelry, silver, and glassware, to French and Italian bronzes, porcelain, snuffboxes, and armor. The Louvre has well over 8,000 items, from many eras and regions.

Many of these precious objects were in the Abbey of St.-Denis, where the kings of France were crowned. Long before the Revolution, a regular flow of visitors had made it something of a museum. After the Revolution, all the objects were removed and presented to the nation. Much was lost or stolen during the move, but what remains is still outstanding.

The treasures include a serpentine stone plate from the 1st century AD with a 9th-century border of gold and precious stones. (The plate itself is inlaid with eight golden dolphins.) There is also a porphyry vase which Suger, Abbot of St.-Denis, had mounted in gold in the shape of an eagle, and the golden scepter made for King Charles V in about 1380.

The French crown jewels include the coronation crowns of Louis XV and Napoleon, scepters, swords, and other accessories of the coronation ceremonies. Also on view is the Regent, one of the purest diamonds in the world. It was bought in 1717 and worn by Louis XV at his coronation in 1722.

One whole room is taken up with a series of tapestries called the *Hunts of Maximilian*, which were originally executed for Emperor Charles V in 1530 after drawings by Bernard Van Orley.

The large collection of French furniture ranges from the 16th to the 19th centuries and is assembled by period, or in rooms devoted to donations by distinguished collectors such as

The Eagle of Suger (mid-12th century)

Isaac de Camondo. On display are important pieces by exceptionally prominent furniture-makers such as André-Charles Boulle, cabinet-maker to Louis XIV, who worked at the Louvre in the late 17th to mid-18th centuries. He is noted for his technique of inlaying copper and tortoiseshell. From a later date, the curious inlaid steel and bronze writing desk created by Adam Weisweiler for Queen Marie-Antoinette in 1784 is one of the more unusual pieces in the museum's collection.

In 2012 the Islamic Art Department opened in the Cour Visconti I with around 18,000 objects on display, covering 3,000 years of history from three continents. The museum also recently installed decorative art galleries dedicated to art objects from the reign of Louis XIV and the 18th century.

The Glass Pyramid

Plans for the modernization and expansion of the Louvre were first conceived in 1981. They included the transfer of the Ministry of Finance from the Richelieu wing of the Louvre to offices elsewhere, and a new main entrance to the museum. A Chinese-American architect, I. M. Pei, was chosen to design the changes. He designed the pyramid as both the focal point and entrance to the Louvre. Made out of glass, it enables the visitor to see the historic buildings that surround it while allowing light down into the underground visitors' reception area.

❷ Louvre des Antiquaires

2 Pl du Palais-Royal 75001. **Map** 12 F2.
Tel 01 42 97 27 27. Ⓜ Palais-Royal.
Open 11am–7pm Tue–Sun. ⊘ ▣
See Shopping pp328–9.
🆆 louvre-antiquaires.com

A large department store – the
Grands Magasins du Louvre –
was converted at the end of
the 1970s into this three-floor
collection of art galleries and
antiques shops. Few bargains
are found here, but the 250
shops of this chic market
provide clues about what
nouveaux riches collectors
are seeking.

❸ Palais-Royal

Pl du Palais-Royal 75001. **Map** 12 E1.
Ⓜ Palais-Royal. **Closed** to the public.
🆆 palais-royal.monuments.
nationaux.fr

This former royal palace has had
a turbulent history. Starting out
in the early 17th century as
Richelieu's Palais Cardinale, it
passed to the Crown on his
death and was the childhood
home of Louis XIV. Under the
control of the 18th-century
royal dukes of Orléans it saw
brilliant gatherings, as well as
periods of debauchery and
gambling. The cardinal's theater,
where Molière had performed,
burned down in 1763, but was
replaced by the Comédie
Française. After the Revolution,
the palace became a gambling
house. It was reclaimed in

Colonnaded facade of the Comédie Française

1815 by the future King Louis-
Philippe, one of whose librarians
was Alexandre Dumas. The
building escaped the flames
of the 1871 uprising.

After being restored again,
between 1872 and 1876, the
palace reverted to the state, and
it now houses both the Council
of State, the supreme legal body
for administrative matters, and
its more recent "partner," the
Constitutional Council. Another
wing of the palace is occupied
by the Ministry of Culture.

❹ Comédie Française

1 Pl Colette 75001. **Map** 12 E1.
Tel 0825 101 680 (tickets) or 01 44
58 15 15 (info). Ⓜ Palais-Royal.
Open for performances. ♿ ☷
🚻 ✉ *See Entertainment p334.*
🆆 comedie-francaise.fr

Overlooking two charming, if
traffic-choked, squares named

after the writers Colette and
André Malraux, sits France's
national theater. The company
has its roots partly in Molière's
17th-century players. In the
lobby is the armchair in which
Molière collapsed, dying, on
stage in 1673
(ironically,
while he was
performing
*Le Malade
Imaginaire –
The Hypochon-
driac*). Since
the company's
founding in
1680 by Louis
XIV, the theater

A stone plaque to
Pierre Corneille

has enjoyed state patronage as a
center of national culture, and it
has been based in the present
building since 1799. The
repertoire includes works of
Racine, Molière, Corneille, and
Shakespeare, as well as those
of modern playwrights.

Palais Royal courtyard lined with columns

❺ Jardin du Palais-Royal

6 Rue de Montpensier, Place du Palais-Royal 75001. **Map** 12 F1. **Tel** 01 47 03 92 16. Ⓜ Palais-Royal. **Open** daily. Apr–May: 7am–10.15pm; June–Sep: 7am–11pm (Sep: to 9:30pm); Oct–Mar: 7:30am–8:30pm.

The present garden is about a third smaller than the original one, laid out by the royal gardener for Cardinal Richelieu in the 1630s. This is due to the construction, between 1781 and 1784, of 60 uniform houses bordering three sides of the square. Today, restaurants, art galleries, and specialty stores line the square, which has numbered Jean Cocteau, Colette, and Jean Marais among its famous former residents.

The courtyard contains the controversial black-and-white striped stone columns that form conceptual artist Daniel Buren's *Les Deux Plateaux*. Installed in the pedestrian-only Palais-Royal courtyard in 1986, despite strong opposition, the columns are now loved by children and skateboarders alike.

Statue in the Jardin du Palais-Royal

❻ Fontaine Molière

Rue de Richelieu 75001. **Map** 12 E1. Ⓜ Palais-Royal.

France's most famous play-wright lived near here, in a house on the site of No. 40 Rue de Richelieu. The 19th-century fountain is by Louis Visconti, who also designed Napoleon's tomb at Les Invalides *(see pp188–9)*.

Vien's *St. Denis Preaching to the Gauls* (1767) in St-Roch

❼ St.-Roch

296 Rue St.-Honoré 75001. **Map** 12 E1. **Tel** 01 42 44 13 20. Ⓜ Tuileries, Pyramides. **Open** 8.30am–7pm daily. **Closed** non-religious public hols. 🖼 3pm 2nd Thu of month. ✝ 6:30pm daily, plus other times. Concerts.

This huge church was designed by Lemercier, architect of the Louvre, and its foundation stone was laid by Louis XIV in

Seated statue of Molière

1653. Jules Hardouin-Mansart added the large Chapelle de la Vierge, with its richly decorated dome and ceiling, in the 18th century and two further chapels extended the church to 413 ft (126 m), just short of Notre-Dame. It is a treasure-house of religious art, much of it from now-vanished churches and monasteries. It also contains the tombs of the playwright Pierre Corneille, the royal gardener André Le Nôtre, and the philosopher Denis Diderot. The facades reveal marks of Napoleon's attack, in 1795, on royalist troops who were defending the church steps.

❽ Place des Pyramides

75001. **Map** 12 E1. Ⓜ Tuileries, Pyramides.

Joan of Arc, wounded nearby fighting the English in 1429, is honored by a 19th-century equestrian statue by the sculptor Emmanuel Frémiet. The statue is a rallying point for royalists.

❾ Musée des Arts Décoratifs

Palais du Louvre, 107–111 Rue de Rivoli 75001. **Map** 12 E2. **Tel** 01 44 55 57 50. Ⓜ Palais-Royal, Tuileries. **Open** 11am–6pm Tue–Sun (until 9pm Thu for temporary exhibitions); last adm 30 min before closing. Library: **Tel** 01 44 55 59 36. **Open** 10am– 6pm Mon–Fri (from 1pm Mon & Thu). **Closed** public hols. 🅿 ♿ 📷 ⌀ 🎞 Ⓦ **lesartsdecoratifs.fr**

Lemot's Restoration group of statues with the gilded figure of Victory

Spread out over five floors and 100 rooms, this museum is in the Palais du Louvre's western wing, the Pavillon de Marsan. It offers an eclectic display of decorative and ornamental art and design from the Middle Ages to the present. Among the highlights are the Art Nouveau and Art Deco rooms, jewelry, and Gallé glass. The doll collection is remarkable.

The Galerie des Bijoux is particularly interesting, with a huge collection of more than 1,300 pieces, from medieval brooches to Cartier designs.

The Fashion and Textiles department houses more than 150,000 pieces – costumes, accessories, and textiles – spanning from the 3rd century to the present day. Past exhibitions have included a tribute to Christian Lacroix, with a retrospective of his couture creations.

With a catalog featuring more than 40,000 historic posters dating from the 18th century to 1949, the museum's Advertising and Graphic Design department brings together thousands of objects linked to advertising as well as movies. The museum's restaurant offers lovely views over the Jardin des Tuileries. Dual tickets can be purchased that allow access to the Musée Nissim de Camondo too *(see pp234–5)*.

❿ Arc de Triomphe du Carrousel

Pl du Carrousel 75001. **Map** 12 E2. Ⓜ Palais-Royal.

Built by Napoleon in 1806–8 as an entrance to the former Palais des Tuileries, this vast arch's marble columns are topped by Grande Armée soldiers. They replaced the Horses of St. Mark's, which were returned to Venice in 1815.

⓫ Rue de Rivoli

75001. **Map** 11 C1 & 13 A2. Ⓜ Louvre, Palais-Royal, Tuileries, Concorde.

The long arcades with their stores, topped by Neo-Classical apartments, date back to the early 18th century, though they were only finished in the 1850s. Commissioned by Napoleon after his victory at Rivoli, in 1797, this majestic street completed the link between the Louvre and the Champs-Elysées, and became an important artery as well as an elegant center for commerce. The Tuileries walls were replaced by railings and the whole area opened up.

Today, along the Rue de Rivoli, there are makers of expensive men's shirts and bookstores toward the Place de la Concorde, and popular department stores near Châtelet and Hôtel de Ville. Angélina's, at No. 226, is said to serve the best hot chocolate in Paris *(see p311)*.

⓬ Jardin des Tuileries

Pl de la Concorde 75001. **Map** 12 D1. **Tel** 01 40 20 90 43. Ⓜ Tuileries, Concorde. **Open** Apr–May & Sep: 7am– 9pm; Jun–Aug: 7am–11pm; Oct–Mar: 7.30am–7.30pm.

These formal gardens were once the gardens of the old Palais des Tuileries. They are an integral part of the landscaped area running parallel to the Seine from the Louvre to the Champs-Elysées and the Arc de Triomphe.

The gardens were laid out in the 17th century by André Le Nôtre, royal gardener to Louis XIV. Restoration created an additional garden as well as filling the entire gardens with striking sculptures. A staggering 125,000 plants are replanted annually.

The formal gardens of Jardin des Tuileries

⓭ Galerie Nationale du Jeu de Paume

Jardin des Tuileries, 1 Pl de la Concorde 75008. **Map** 11 C1. **Tel** 01 47 03 12 50. Ⓜ Concorde. **Open** 11am–7pm Tue–Sun (to 9pm Tue). **Closed** Jan 1, May 1, & Dec 25 as well as in between exhibitions. 🎨 ✉ ♿ 🏛 📷 🏠 ꟽ **jeudepaume.org**

The Jeu de Paume – or *réal* tennis court – was built by Napoleon III in 1851. When *réal* (royal) tennis was replaced in popularity by lawn tennis, the court was used to exhibit art. Eventually, an Impressionist museum was founded here. In 1986, the collection moved to the Musée d'Orsay *(see pp146–9)*. The Jeu de Paume now houses the Centre National de la Photographie, and shows exhibitions of contemporary art.

⓮ Musée de l'Orangerie

Jardin des Tuileries, Pl de la Concorde 75001. **Map** 11 C1. **Tel** 01 44 77 80 07. Ⓜ Concorde. **Open** 9am–6pm Wed–Mon (last adm: 5.15pm). **Closed** May 1, Jul 14 morning, & Dec 15. 🎨 ♿ 📷 by appt. 🏛 🏠 ꟽ **musee-orangerie.fr**

Claude Monet's crowning work, the water lily series, or *Nymphéas*, can be found here. The series was painted in his garden at Giverny, near Paris, and presented to the public in 1927. This superb work is complemented well by the outstanding Walter-Guillaume collection of artists of the Ecole de Paris, from the late Impressionist era to the inter-war period. This is a remarkable concentration of masterpieces, including a room of dramatic works by Soutine and some 14 works by Cézanne – still lifes, portraits *(Madame Cézanne)*, and landscapes, such as *Dans le Parc du Château Noir*.

Pierre-Auguste Renoir is represented by 27 canvases, including *Les Fillettes au Piano (Young Girls at the Piano)*. There are early Picassos, works by Henri Rousseau – notably *La Carriole du Père Junier (Old Junier's Cart)* – Matisse, and a portrait of Paul Guillaume by Modigliani. All are bathed in the natural light that flows through the window. Temporary exhibitions are shown on the lower ground floor.

Place de la Concorde, dominated by the 3,200-year-old obelisk from Luxor

⓯ Place de la Concorde

75008. **Map** 11 C1. Ⓜ Concorde.

One of the most magnificent and historic squares in the whole of Europe, Place de la Concorde covers more than 20 acres (8 ha) in the middle of Paris. Starting out as Place Louis XV, for displaying a statue of the king, it was built in the mid-18th century by architect Jacques-Ange Gabriel, who chose to make it an open octagon with only the north side containing mansions. In the square's next incarnation, as the Place de la Révolution, the statue was replaced by the guillotine. The death toll in the square in two and a half years was 1,119, including Louis XVI, Marie-Antoinette (who died in view of the secret apartment she kept at No. 2 Rue Royale), and the revolutionary leaders Danton and Robespierre.

In the spirit of reconciliation, the square was then renamed Concorde (originally by chastened Revolutionaries). Its grandeur was enhanced in the 19th century by the 3,200-year-old Luxor obelisk, two fountains, and eight statues personifying French cities. It has become the culminating point of triumphal parades down the Champs-Elysées each July 14, most notably on the memorable Bastille Day of 1989 when the Revolution's bicentenary was celebrated by a million people, and many world leaders.

Monet's water lilies, on display in the Musée de l'Orangerie

Colonnaded entrance to the Village Royale

🔟 Village Royal

75008. **Map** 5 C5. Ⓜ Madeleine.
Galerie Royale: **Open** 8am–8:30pm,
boutiques 10am–7pm Mon–Sat.
Closed public hols.

This delightful enclave of
18th-century town houses sits
discreetly between the Rue
Royale and the Rue Boissy
d'Anglas. The Galerie Royale is
the former home of the
Duchess d'Abrantès. It was
converted in 1994 by architect
Laurent Bourgois who has
combined both classical and
modern elements in superb
style. The village was formerly
the home of glassworkers and
silversmiths, and for a while

examples of antique glass and
silverware were on display.
Nowadays, chic shoppers flock in
droves to the designer boutiques
that are here, such as Chanel, Dior,
and Eric Bompard Cashmere, or
they stop by for a coffee break
in the upscale café, Le Village.

🔟 Place Vendôme

75001. **Map** 6 D5. Ⓜ Tuileries.

Perhaps the best example of
18th-century elegance in the
city, the architect Jules
Hardouin-Mansart's royal
square was begun in 1698. The
original plan was to house
academies and embassies
behind the arcaded facades.
However, bankers moved in
and created opulent homes.
Miraculously the square has
remained virtually intact, and is
home to jewelers and bankers.
Among the famous, Frédéric
Chopin died here in 1848 at
No. 12 and César Ritz
established his famous hotel
at the turn of the 20th century
at No. 15.

🔟 Banque de France

31 Rue Croix des Petits Champs 75001.
Map 12 F1. Ⓜ Palais Royal.
Open by appt only; reserve at least a
year in advance. Call 01 42 92 26 33 or
01 42 92 21 71. Open to the public
10am–7pm for Heritage Days in Sep.

Founded by Napoleon in 1800,
France's central bank is housed
in a building intended for quite
different purposes. The 17th-
century architect François
Mansart designed this mansion

Napoleon's statue in
Place Vendôme

Formal Gardens in Paris

The South Parterre at Versailles *(see pp250–51)*

For the past 300 years the main
formal gardens in Paris have been
open to the public and are a firm
fixture in the city's life. The Jardin
des Tuileries *(see p132)* is a beautiful
extension of the Louvre, with
ongoing replanting; the Jardin du
Luxembourg *(see p174)*, the private
garden of the French Senate, is still
beloved of Left Bankers; and the
Jardin du Palais-Royal *(see p131)* is
enjoyed by those who seek peace
and privacy.
   French landscaping was raised to
an art form in the 17th century,
thanks to Louis XIV's talented
landscaper André Le Nôtre, who
created the gardens of Versailles
(see pp250–51). He achieved a
brilliant marriage between the
traditional Italian Renaissance
garden and the French love of
rational design.
   The role of the French garden
architect was not to tend nature
but to transform it, pruning and
planting to create leafy sculptures
out of trees, bushes, and hedges.
Complicated geometrical designs
that were created in beds and
paths were interspersed with

The long Galerie Dorée in the Banque de France

for Louis XIII's Secretary of State, Louis de la Vrillière, with the splendid 164-ft (50-m) long Galerie Dorée specially created for hanging his great collection of historical paintings. The house was later sold to the Comte de Toulouse, son of Louis XIV and Madame de Montespan. It was reconstructed in the 19th century after the Revolution. The bank's most famous alumnus is Jacques Delors, president of the European Commission 1985–1994.

⑲ Place des Victoires

75002. **Map** 12 F1. **M** Palais-Royal.

This circle of elegant mansions was built in 1685 solely to offset the statue of Louis XIV by Desjardins, which was placed in the middle, with torches burning day and night. The proportions of the buildings and even the arrangement of the surrounding streets were all designed by the architect and courtier

Jules Hardouin-Mansart to display the statue to its best advantage.

Unfortunately, the 1792 mobs were less sycophantic and tore down the statue. A replacement, of a different style, was erected in 1822, to the detriment of the whole system of proportions of buildings to statue. Yet the square retains much of the original design, and today it is the address of major names in the fashion business, most notably Thierry Mugler and Kenzo.

Louis XIV on Place des Victoires

A Bagatelle garden with floral color *(see p247)*

pebbles and carefully thought-out splashes of floral color. Symmetry and harmony were the landscaper's watchwords, a sense of grandeur and magnificence his ultimate goal. In the 17th century, as now, French formal gardens served two purposes: as a setting or backdrop for a château or palace, and for enjoyment. The best view

of a formal garden was from the first floor of the château, from which the combination of boxwood hedges, flowers, and gravel came together in an intricate, abstract pattern, a blossoming tapestry that complemented the château's interior. Paths of trees drew the eye into infinity, reminding the onlooker of how

much land belonged to his host, and therefore establishing his undoubted wealth. So, early on the formal garden became a status symbol, and it still is. This is obvious in both private gardens and in grand public projects. Napoleon Bonaparte completed his vista from the Jardin des Tuileries with a triumphal arch. The late President Mitterrand applied the principle in building his Grand Arche de la Défense *(see pp42–3, 248)* along the same axis as the Tuileries and Arc de Triomphe.

But formal gardens were also made to be enjoyed. People in the 17th century believed that walking in the fresh air kept them in good health. What more perfect spot than a formal garden bedecked with statues and fountains for additional entertainment. The old and infirm could be carried around in sedan chairs, and people could meet one another around a boxwood hedge or on a stone bench under the marble gaze of the goddess Diana.

ST.-GERMAIN-DES-PRES

The intellectuals of the 1950s may have left, but this area is still renowned for its youthful student atmosphere and literary traditions. The bookstores, museums, art galleries, and historic cafés – such as Café de Flore, Les Deux Magots, and Le Procope – are now thronged by tourists, fashionistas, and publishing executives.

The Musée d'Orsay, housed in a former train station, is the neighborhood's most celebrated museum. On Rue Bonaparte is the prestigious Ecole Nationale Supérieure des Beaux-Arts, where many famous artists studied. Rue de Seine is lined with charming restaurants and contains many high-end galleries where the smart set purchase their art. Window displays of grand couturiers compete against one another on Boulevard St.-Germain and adjacent streets, where shoppers go looking for sales, or *soldes*.

Sights at a Glance

Historic Buildings and Streets
- ❷ Palais Abbatial
- ❼ Boulevard St.-Germain
- ❽ Rue du Dragon
- ❿ Rue de l'Odéon
- ⓬ Cour de Rohan
- ⓭ Cour du Commerce St.-André
- ⓯ Académie Française
- ⓰ Ecole Nationale Supérieure des Beaux-Arts
- ⓱ Hôtel Feydeau de Brou
- ⓲ Quai Voltaire

Churches
- ❶ St.-Germain-des-Prés

Theaters
- ⓫ Odéon Théâtre de l'Europe

Historic Cafés and Restaurants
- ❹ Les Deux Magots
- ❺ Café de Flore
- ❻ Brasserie Lipp
- ❾ Le Procope

Museums and Galleries
- ❸ Musée Eugène Delacroix
- ⓮ Musée de la Monnaie
- ⓳ *Musée d'Orsay pp146–9*
- ⓴ Musée Nationale de la Légion d'Honneur

☐ Restaurants *see pp303–5*
- 1 Alcazar
- 2 Le Balto
- 3 Bistrot de Paris
- 4 Les Bouquinistes
- 5 Le Comptoir du Relais
- 6 L'Epigramme
- 7 Kitchen Galerie Bis
- 8 Restaurant AG
- 9 Shu
- 10 Ze Kitchen Galerie

See also Street Finder map 11–12

◀ The clock in the main hall of the Musée d'Orsay

For additional keys to symbols *see back flap*

Street by Street: St.-Germain-des-Prés

After World War II, St.-Germain-des-Prés became synonymous with intellectual life centered on bars and cafés. Philosophers, writers, actors, and musicians mingled in the cellar nightspots and brasseries, where existentialist philosophy co-existed with American jazz. The area is now smarter than in the heyday of Jean-Paul Sartre and Simone de Beauvoir, the haunting singer Juliette Greco and the New Wave movie-makers. The writers are still around, enjoying the pleasures of sitting in Les Deux Magots, Café de Flore, and other haunts. The 17th-century buildings have survived, but signs of change are evident in the plethora of affluent stores dealing in antiques, books, and fashion.

❹ **Les Deux Magots**
The café is famous for the patronage of celebrities such as Earnest Hemingway.

❺ **Café de Flore**
In the 1950s, French intellectuals wrestled with new philosophical ideas in the Art Deco interior of the café.

RUE DU DRAGON
RUE DU SABOT
RUE DE RENNES
RUE BONAPARTE
RUE DU FOUR

❻ **Brasserie Lipp**
Colorful ceramics decorate this famous brasserie once frequented by politicians.

❶ ★ **St.-Germain-des-Prés**
Descartes and Casimir, king of Poland, who became abbot of St.-Germain in 1669, are among the notables buried here in Paris's oldest church.

❼ ★ **Boulevard St.-Germain**
Café terraces, boutiques, movie theaters, restaurants, and bookstores characterize the central section of the Left Bank's main street.

Picasso's sculpture Homage to Apollinaire is a tribute to the artist's friend, the poet Guillaume Apollinaire. It was erected in 1959, near the Café de Flore, where the poet held court.

Locator Map
See Central Paris Map pp16–17

❸ ★ **Musée Eugène Delacroix**
Here, Delacroix created the splendid mural, *Jacob Wrestling*, for St.-Sulpice *(see p174).*

Key

— Suggested route

0 meters   100
0 yards   100

Rue de Fürstenberg is a tiny square with old-fashioned street lamps and shady trees. It is often used as a movie location.

Rue de Buci was for centuries an important Left Bank street and the site of some *réal* tennis courts. It now holds a lively market every day.

❷ **Palais Abbatial**
This was the residence of abbots from 1586 till the 1789 Revolution.

Marché St.-Germain is an old covered food market which opened in 1818, taking over the site of a former fairground *(see p331).*

Danton's statue (1889), by Auguste Paris, is a tribute to the Revolutionary leader.

❶ St.-Germain-des-Prés

3 Pl St.-Germain-des-Prés 75006. **Map** 12 E4. **Tel** 01 55 42 81 10. Ⓜ St.-Germain-des-Prés. **Open** 8am–7.45pm daily. Concerts (call ahead for times). 🕀 7pm Mon–Fri; 12.15pm, 7pm Sat; 11am, 5pm (in Spanish), 7pm Sun. 🖼 3pm Tue, Thu, & 3rd Sun of month. Call 01 55 42 81 18. 🖼 🇼 **eglise-sgp.org**

This is the oldest church in Paris, originating in 543 when King Childebert built a basilica to house holy relics. This became a powerful Benedictine abbey, which was suppressed during the French Revolution, when most of the buildings were destroyed by a fire in 1794. One of the Revolution's most horrific episodes took place in a nearby monastery when 318 priests were hacked to death by the mob on September 3, 1792. The present church dates from about the 11th century and was restored in the 19th century. One of the three original towers survives, housing one of the oldest belfries in France. The interior is an interesting mix of architectural styles, with some 6th-century marble columns, Gothic vaulting, and Romanesque arches. Famous tombs include those of René Descartes, the poet Nicolas Boileau, and John Casimir, king of Poland, who later became abbot of St.-Germain-des-Prés in 1669.

Our Lady of Consolation statue in St.-Germain-des-Prés

❷ Palais Abbatial

1–5 Rue de l'Abbaye 75006. **Map** 12 E4. Ⓜ St.-Germain-des-Prés. **Closed** to the public.

This brick and stone palace was built in 1586 for Charles of Bourbon who was cardinal-abbot of St.-Germain and, very briefly, king of France. Ten more abbots lived here until the Revolution, when the building

An ironwork detail from the facade of the Palais Abbatial

was sold. James Pradier, the 19th-century sculptor who was famous for his female figures, established a studio here. The palace is now noted for its mixture of building materials and its vertical windows.

Eugène Delacroix

❸ Musée Eugène Delacroix

6 Rue de Fürstenberg 75006. **Map** 12 E4. **Tel** 01 44 41 86 50. Ⓜ St.-Germain-des-Prés, Mabillon. **Open** 9.30am–5.30pm Wed–Mon (last adm: 4.30pm). **Closed** Jan 1, May 1, Dec 25. 🖼 (free 1st Sun of month). 🖼 🖼 🇼 **musee-delacroix.fr**

The leading non-conformist Romantic painter, Eugène Delacroix, known for his passionate and highly colored canvases, lived and worked here from 1857 to his death in 1863. Here, he painted *The Entombment of Christ* and *The Way to Calvary* (which now hang in the museum). He also created superb murals for the Chapel of the Holy Angels in the nearby St.-Sulpice church, which is part of the reason why he moved to

this area. The first-floor apartment and garden studio now form a national museum, where regular exhibitions of Delacroix's work are held. The apartment has a portrait of George Sand, self-portraits, studies for future works, and artistic memorabilia.

The charm of Delacroix's garden is reflected in the tiny Fürstenberg square. With its pair of rare catalpa trees and old-fashioned street lamps, the square is one of Paris's most romantic corners.

❹ Les Deux Magots

6 Pl St.-Germain-des-Prés 75006. **Map** 12 E4. **Tel** 01 45 48 55 25. Ⓜ St.-Germain-des-Prés. **Open** 7.30am–1am daily. **Closed** for one week in Jan. 🇼 **lesdeuxmagots.com**

The café still trades on its reputation as the meeting place of the city's literary and intellectual elite. This derives from the patronage of Surrealist artists and writers including Ernest Hemingway in the 1920s and 1930s, and existentialist philosophers and writers in the 1950s.

The present clientele is more likely to be publishers or people-watchers than the new Hemingway. The café's name comes from the two wooden statues of Chinese commercial agents (*magots*) that adorn one of the pillars. This is a good place for enjoying an old-fashioned hot chocolate and watching the world go by.

The interior of Les Deux Magots

Facade of the Café de Flore, former meeting place of artists, writers, and philosophers

❺ Café de Flore

172 Blvd St.-Germain 75006. **Map** 12 E4. **Tel** 01 45 48 55 26. Ⓜ St.-Germain-des-Prés. **Open** 7.30am–1.30am daily. ♿ restricted. ⓦ **cafedeflore.fr**

The classic Art Deco interior of this café, all-red seating, mahogany and mirrors, has changed little since the war. Like its rival Les Deux Magots, Café de Flore has hosted most of the French intellectuals during the post-war years. Jean-Paul Sartre and Simone de Beauvoir developed their philosophy of existentialism here.

Exterior of the Brasserie Lipp

❻ Brasserie Lipp

151 Blvd St.-Germain 75006. **Map** 12 E4. **Tel** 01 45 48 53 91. Ⓜ St.-Germain-des-Prés. **Open** 8.30am–1am daily. ⓦ **brasserielipp.fr**

This Left Bank fixture – once popular with French politicians and fashion gurus – combines Alsatian beer, sauerkraut and sausages (it was founded by a refugee from Alsace) with excellent coffee. Originally opened in the late 19th century, it is regarded by many as the quintessential Parisian brasserie,

although the experience is more atmospheric than culinary these days. The interior is bright with ceramic tiles of parrots and cranes. The café sponsors a prestigious literary competition, the Prix Cazes, for writers under the age of 40 who have never received a literary award.

❼ Boulevard St.-Germain

75006, 75007. **Map** 11 C2 & 12 D4. Ⓜ Solférino, Rue du Bac, St.-Germain-des-Prés, Mabillon, Odéon.

The Left Bank's most celebrated thoroughfare, over 2 miles (3 km) long, curves across three districts from the Ile St.-Louis to the Pont de la Concorde. The architecture is homogeneous because the boulevard was another of Baron Haussmann's bold strokes of 19th-century urban planning, but it encompasses a wide range of different lifestyles as well as a number of religious and cultural institutions. From the east (the low street numbers), the boulevard

passes the late François Mitterrand's private town residence in the Rue de Bièvre, as well as the Maubert-Mutualité market square, the Musée de Cluny and the Sorbonne university, before crossing the lively Boulevard St.-Michel.

It continues past the Ecole de Médecine and the Place de l'Odéon to St.-Germain-des-Prés, with its historic church and café terraces. Fashion boutiques, movie theaters, restaurants, and bookstores give this central portion its distinctive character. It is also here that one is most likely to see a celebrity. The area is active from midday to the early morning hours.

Continuing farther, beyond this section the boulevard becomes more exclusively residential and then distinctly political with the Ministry of Defence and the National Assembly buildings.

❽ Rue du Dragon

75006. **Map** 12 D4. Ⓜ St.-Germain-des-Prés.

This short street, between the Boulevard St.-Germain and the Carrefour de la Croix Rouge, dates back to the Middle Ages and still has houses from the 17th and 18th centuries. Notice their large doors, tall windows and ironwork balconies. A group of Flemish painters lived at No. 37 before the Revolution. The novelist Victor Hugo rented a garret at No. 30 when he was a 19-year-old bachelor.

A plaque at No. 30 Rue du Dragon commemorating Victor Hugo's house

❾ Le Procope

13 Rue de l'Ancienne-Comédie 75006.
Map12 F4. **Tel** 01 40 46 79 00.
Ⓜ Odéon. **Open** 11:30am–midnight
daily (to 1am Thu–Sat).
Ⓦ procope.com

Founded in 1686 by the Sicilian
Francesco Procopio dei Coltelli,
this claims to be the world's first
coffee house. It quickly became
popular with the city's political
and cultural elite.

Its patrons have included the
philosopher Voltaire – who
supposedly drank 40 cups of his
favorite mixture of coffee and
chocolate every day – and the
young Napoleon, who would
leave his hat as security while he
went searching for the money
to pay the bill. Le Procope is
now an 18th-century-style
restaurant run by the famous
Frères Blanc group.

Odéon Théâtre de l'Europe, former home
of the Comédie Française

❿ Rue de l'Odéon

75006. **Map** 12 F5. Ⓜ Odéon.

Sylvia Beach's bookshop
Shakespeare & Co. (see pp323–4)
stood at No. 12 from 1921 to
1940. She befriended many
struggling American and British
writers, such as Ezra Pound,
T. S. Eliot, F. Scott Fitzgerald,
and Ernest Hemingway. It was
largely due to her support – as
secretary, editor, agent, and
banker – that James Joyce's
Ulysses was first published in
English. Adrienne Monnier's
French bookstore at No. 7
opposite, Les Amis des Livres,
was frequented by André Gide
and Paul Valéry.

Opened in 1779 to improve
access to the Odéon theater,
this was the first street in
Paris to have sidewalks with
gutters, and it still has many
attractive houses and stores,
most of them dating from the
18th century.

The rear facade of Le Procope restaurant

⓫ Odéon Théâtre de l'Europe

Pl de l'Odéon 75006. **Map** 12 F5.
Tel 01 44 85 40 40. Ⓜ Odéon,
Luxembourg. **Open** for performances
only: 8pm Tue–Sat, 3pm Sun. Visits on
request; check website for details. 🚫
♿ 📷 See Entertainment pp334, 336.
Ⓦ theatre-odeon.eu

This Neo-Classical theater was
built in 1779 on the grounds of
the former Hôtel de Condé. The
site had been purchased by the
king and given to the city to
house the Comédie Française.
The premiere of The Marriage of
Figaro, by Beaumarchais, took
place here in 1784. With the
arrival of a new company in
1797, the name of the theater
was changed to Odéon. In 1807
it was consumed by fire, and
rebuilt later the same year by
architect Jean-François Chalgrin.

Following World War II, the
theater specialized in modern
drama. Today, plays are often
performed in foreign languages,
including English. The auditorium is very impressive, not least
for its ceiling, painted by André
Masson in 1965.

A young Hemingway in the 1920s

The unusual middle courtyard in the
Cour de Rohan

⓬ Cour de Rohan

75006. **Map** 12 F4. Ⓜ Odéon. Access
from the Rue du Jardinet until 8pm;
8pm–8am access from the Boulevard
St.-Germain.

This picturesque series of three
courtyards was originally part
of the 15th-century pied-à-
terre of the archbishops of
Rouen (corrupted to "Rohan").
The middle courtyard is the
most unusual. Its three-legged
wrought-iron mounting block,
known as a pas-de-mule, was
used at one time by elderly
women and overweight
prelates to mount their mules.
It is probably the last
mounting block left in Paris.
Overlooking the yard is the
facade of a fine Renaissance
building, dating from the
beginning of the 17th century.
One of its important former
residents was Henri II's
mistress, Diane de Poitiers.

The third courtyard opens
on to the tiny Rue du Jardinet,
where the composer Saint-
Saëns was born in 1835.

⑬ Cour du Commerce St.-André

75006. **Map** 12 F4. Ⓜ Odéon.

No. 9 has a particularly grisly past, because it was here that Dr. Guillotin is supposed to have perfected his "philanthropic decapitating machine." In fact, although the idea was Guillotin's, it was Dr. Louis, a Parisian surgeon, who was responsible for putting the "humane" plan into action. When the guillotine was first used for execution in 1792, it was known as a *Louisette*.

A print of a Revolutionary mob at a guillotine execution

⑭ Musée de la Monnaie

11 Quai de Conti 75006. **Map** 12 F3. **Tel** 01 40 46 56 66. Ⓜ Pont-Neuf, Odéon. **Open** Temporary exhibitions: 11am–7pm daily. Permanent exhibition & gardens: **Closed** until 2017. 🎦 Movies. Ⓦ **monnaiedeparis.fr**

In the late 18th century, when Louis XV decided to rehouse the Mint, he launched a design competition for the new building. The Hôtel des Monnaies is

the result. It was completed in 1775, and the architect, Jacques Antoine, lived here until his death.

Coins were minted in the mansion until 1973, when the process was moved to Pessac in the Gironde. The minting and milling halls now contain the coin and medallion museum.

Centered around a tranquil public space and surrounded by artist workshops, the permanent gallery focuses on the history of coins and minting. There are also shops selling work by resident artisans, a gastronomic restaurant run by Chef Guy Savoy, and a more casual café.

⑮ Académie Française

23 Quai de Conti 75006. **Map** 12 E3. **Tel** 01 44 41 43 00. Ⓜ Pont-Neuf, St.-Germain-des-Prés. **Open** 2nd Sun of the month. 🎦 Reserve in advance at www.institut-de-france.fr 🗓 entry by guided tours only for 30 people or more as part of a conference. Ⓦ **academie-francaise.fr**

This striking Baroque edifice was built as a school for young noblemen in 1688 and given over to the Institut de France in 1805. Its cupola was designed by architect Louis Le Vau to harmonize with the Palais du Louvre.

The Académie Française is the oldest of the five academies of the institute. Founded in 1635 by Cardinal Richelieu, it is charged with regulating the French language by deciding acceptable grammar and vocabulary, and with the compilation of an official dictionary of the French

A sign to the former Mint, which is now a museum

language. From the beginning, membership has been limited to 40, who are entrusted with a lifelong commitment of working on the dictionary.

⑯ Ecole Nationale Supérieure des Beaux-Arts

13 Quai Malaquais & 14 Rue Bonaparte 75006. **Map** 12 E3. **Tel** 01 47 03 50 00. Ⓜ St.-Germain-des-Prés. **Open** times vary; groups by appt only (01 47 03 50 00). 🎦 Temporary exhibitions: Tue–Fri (check website for times.) 🗓 10am Mon–Fri. Reserve ahead. 📖 Library. Ⓦ **beauxartsparis.com**

The main French school of fine arts occupies an enviable position at the corner of the Rue Bonaparte and the riverside Quai Malaquais. The school is housed in several buildings, the most imposing being the 19th-century Palais des Etudes.

A host of budding French and foreign painters and architects have crossed the large courtyard to study in the ateliers of the school. Young American architects, in particular, have studied there since the late 19th century.

The facade of the Ecole Nationale Supérieure des Beaux-Arts

The Celebrated Cafés of Paris

Outdoor seating at the busy Café de Flore

One of the most enduring images of Paris is the café scene. For the visitor, it is the romantic vision of great artists, writers, or eminent intellectuals consorting in one of the Left Bank's celebrated cafés. For the Parisian, the café is one of life's constants, an everyday experience, providing people with a place to tryst, drink, and meet friends, or to conclude business deals, or to simply watch the world go by.

The first café anywhere can be traced back to 1686, when the café Le Procope (see p142) was opened. In the following century, cafés became a vital part of Paris's social life. And with the widening of the city's streets, particularly during the 19th century and the building of Haussmann's Grands Boulevards, the cafés spread out onto the sidewalks, evoking Emile Zola's comment as to the "great silent crowds watching the street live."

The nature of a café was sometimes determined by the interests of its patrons. Some were the gathering places for those interested in playing chess, dominoes, or billiards. Literary gents gathered in Le Procope

⑰ Hôtel Feydeau de Brou

13 Rue de l'Université 75007. **Map** 12 D3. Ⓜ Rue du Bac. **Closed** to the public.

This fine 18th-century mansion was originally built as two houses in 1643 by Briçonnet. In 1713 they were replaced by a *hôtel*, built by Thomas Gobert for the widow of Denis Feydeau de Brou. It was passed on to her son, Paul-Espirit Feydeau de Brou, until his death in 1767. The *hôtel* then became the residence of the Venetian ambassador. It was occupied by Belzunce in 1787 and became a munitions depot during the Revolution until the restoration of the monarchy in 1815.

It once housed the Ecole Nationale d'Administration (now in Strasbourg), where many of the elite in politics, economics, and science were once students. Today the building is used by France's famous Science Po University.

⑱ Quai Voltaire

75006 and 75007. **Map** 12 D3. Ⓜ Rue du Bac.

Formerly part of the Quai Malaquais, then later known as the Quai des Théatins, the Quai Voltaire is now home to some of the most important antiques dealers in Paris. It is also noted for its attractive 18th-century

Plaque marking the house in Quai Voltaire where Voltaire died

houses and for the famous people who lived in many of them, making it an especially interesting and pleasant street to walk along.

The 18th-century Swedish ambassador Count Tessin lived at No. 1, as did the sculptor James Pradier, famed for his statues and for his wife, who swam naked across the Seine. Louise de Kéroualle, spy of Louis XIV and created Duchess of Portsmouth by the infatuated Charles II of England, lived at Nos. 3–5.

Famous past residents of No. 19 included the composers Richard Wagner and Jean Sibelius, the novelist Charles Baudelaire, and the exiled Irish writer and wit Oscar Wilde.

The French philosopher Voltaire died at No. 27, the Hôtel de la Villette. St.-Sulpice, the local church, refused to accept his corpse (on the grounds of his atheism) and his body was rushed into the countryside to avoid a pauper's grave.

Entertainment in the Claude Alain café in the Rue de Seine during the 1950s

and Montparnasse, where the literati of old used to gather and where the glitterati of today love to be seen. Before World War I, Montparnasse was haunted by hordes of Russian revolutionaries, most eminently Lenin and Trotsky, who whiled away their days in the cafés, grappling with the problems of Russia and the world over a *petit café*. Cultural life flourished in the 1920s, when Surrealists, like Salvador Dalí and Jean Cocteau, dominated café life, and later when American writers led by Ernest Hemingway and F. Scott Fitzgerald talked, drank, and worked in various cafés, among them La Coupole *(see p180)*, Le Sélect, and La Closerie des Lilas *(see p181)*.

become the dominant creed and Jean-Paul Sartre its tiny charismatic leader. Sartre and his intellectual peers and followers, among them the writers Simone de Beauvoir and Albert Camus, the poet Boris Vian, and the enigmatic singer Juliette Greco, gathered to work and discuss their ideas in Les Deux Magots *(see p140)* and the nearby rival Café de Flore *(see p141)*. The traditional habitué of these cafés is still to be seen, albeit mixing with the international jet set and with self-publicizing intellectuals hunched over their notebooks.

during Molière's time in the 17th century. In the 19th century, First Empire Imperial guards officers were drawn to the Café d'Orsay, and Second Empire financiers gathered in the cafés along the Rue de la Chaussée d'Antin. The chic patronized the Café de Paris and Café Tortini, and theater-goers met at the cafés around the Opéra, including the Café de la Paix *(see p217)*. The most famous cafés are on the Left Bank, in St.-Germain

After the end of World War II, the cultural scene shifted northward to St.-Germain. Existentialism had

Works by one of St.-Germain's elite, Albert Camus (1913–60)

⑲ Musée d'Orsay

See pp146–9.

⑳ Musée Nationale de la Légion d'Honneur

2 Rue de la Légion d'Honneur (Parvis du Musée d'Orsay) 75007. **Map** 11 C2. **Tel** 01 40 62 84 25. Ⓜ Solférino. ⒭⒠⒭ Musée d'Orsay. **Open** 1–6pm Wed–Sun. Group visits by appt on Tue. **Closed** Jan 1, May 1, Aug 15, Nov 1, Dec 25. ♿ ⬜ ⬜ ⬜ **musee-legiondhonneur.fr**

Next to the Musée d'Orsay is the truly massive Hôtel de Salm. It

Napoleon III's Great Cross of the Legion of Honor

The Musée d'Orsay, converted from a train station into a museum

was one of the last great mansions to be built in the area (1782). The first owner was a German count, Prince de Salm-Kyrbourg, who was guillotined in 1794.

Today the building contains a museum where one can learn all about the Legion of Honor, a decoration launched by Napoleon I. Those awarded the

honor wear a small red rosette in their buttonhole. The impressive displays of medals and insignia are complemented by paintings. In one of the rooms, Napoleon's Legion of Honor is on display with his sword and breastplate.

The museum also covers decorations from most parts of the world, among them the American Purple Heart and the British Victoria Cross.

⑲ Musée d'Orsay

In 1986, 47 years after it had closed as a main train station, Victor Laloux's superb late 19th-century building was reopened as the Musée d'Orsay. Commissioned by the Orléans railroad company to be its Paris terminal, it avoided demolition in the 1970s. During the conversion much of the original architecture was retained. The museum was set up to present each of the arts of the period from 1848 to 1914 in the context of contemporary society and the other forms of creative activity happening at the time. Renovations to the upper levels have expanded exhibition spaces to improve the display of works.

The Museum, from the Right Bank
Victor Laloux designed the building as a train station for the Universal Exhibition in 1900.

Chair by Charles Rennie Mackintosh
The style developed by Mackintosh was an attempt to express ideas in a framework of vertical and horizontal forms, as in this tearoom chair (1900).

★ **The Gates of Hell** (1880–1917)
Rodin included figures that he had already created, such as *The Thinker* and *The Kiss*, in this famous gateway.

Key to Floorplan

- Architecture & Decorative Arts
- Sculpture
- Painting before 1880
- Impressionism
- Neo- and Post-Impressionism
- Naturalism and Symbolism
- Art Nouveau
- Symbolism (small formats)
- Temporary exhibitions
- Nonexhibition space

Gallery Guide

The collection occupies three levels. On the ground floor there are works from the mid- to late 19th century. The middle level features Art Nouveau decorative art and a range of paintings and sculptures from the second half of the 19th century to the early 20th century, as well as Neo-Impressionist art. The upper level has an outstanding collection of Impressionist art.

The Dance (1867–8)
Carpeaux's sculpture caused a scandal when first exhibited.

★ **Le Déjeuner sur l'Herbe**
(1863)
Manet's painting, first exhibited in Napoleon III's Salon des Refusés, is presently on display in the first area of the upper level.

VISITORS' CHECKLIST

Practical Information
1 Rue de la Légion d'Honneur.
Map 12 D2. **Tel** 01 40 49 48 14 (groups 01 53 63 04 50).
Open 9:30am–6pm Tue–Sun (9:45pm Thu) (last ticket sold 1 hour before closing; tickets available online, combined ticket with Musée de l'Orangerie also available).
Closed Jan 1, May 1, Dec 25.
w musee-orsay.fr

Transportation
M Solférino. 24, 68, 69, 84 to Quai A. France; 73 to Rue Solférino; 63, 83, 84, 94 to Bd St.-Germain. RER Musée d'Orsay. P Rue du Bac, Bd St.-Germain.

Upper level

Middle level

★ **Dancing at the Moulin de la Galette**
To capture the dappled light filtering through the trees, Renoir painted this colorful picture (1876) out in the open in Montmartre.

★ **La Belle Angèle**
This portrait (1889) by Paul Gauguin shows the sitter in traditional Breton costume.

Entrance

Ground floor

Store

The Tiger Hunt by Eugène Delacroix
Painted in 1854 for a dealer named Weill, this was described by Baudelaire as profound, sensual, and terrible.

Exploring the Musée d'Orsay

The Musée d'Orsay picks up where the Louvre ends, showing a variety of art forms from 1848 to 1914. Its star attraction is a superb collection of Impressionist art, which includes famous works by Monet, Renoir, Manet, and Degas as well as Neo-Impressionist works by pointillist Georges Seurat and Post-Impressionist works by Gauguin and Van Gogh. The museum also holds world-class temporary exhibitions and excellent lunchtime and evening concerts.

Ceiling design (1911) by the artist and designer Maurice Denis

Art Nouveau

The Belgian architect and designer Victor Horta was among the first to give free rein to the sinuous line that gave Art Nouveau its French sobriquet of *Style Nouille* (noodle style). Taking its name from a gallery of modern design that opened in Paris in 1895, Art Nouveau flourished throughout Europe until World War I.

In Vienna, Otto Wagner, Koloman Moser and Josef Hoffmann combined high craft with the new design, while the School of Glasgow, under the impetus of Charles Rennie Mackintosh, developed a more rectilinear approach which anticipated the work of Frank Lloyd Wright in the United States.

René Lalique introduced the aesthetics of Art Nouveau into jewelry and glassware, while Hector Guimard, inspired by Horta, is most famous today for his once-ubiquitous Art Nouveau entrances to the Paris Metro.

One exhibit not to be missed is the carved wooden bookcase by Rupert Carabin (1890), with its proliferation of allegorical seated female nudes, bronze palm fronds, and severed bearded heads.

Sculpture

The museum's central aisle overflows with an oddly assorted selection of sculptures. These illustrate the eclectic mood around the middle of the 19th century when the Classicism of Eugène Guillaume's *Cenotaph of the Gracchi* (1848–53) co-existed with the Romanticism of François Rude. Rude created the relief on the Arc de Triomphe (1836), often referred to as *La Marseillaise* (see p213).

There is a wonderful series of 36 busts of members of parliament (1832) – bloated, ugly, unscrupulous, and self-important – by the satirist Honoré Daumier, and work by the vital but short-lived genius Jean-Baptiste Carpeaux, whose first major bronze, *Count Ugolino* (1862), was a character from Dante. In 1868, he produced his Dionysian delight, *The Dance*, which caused a storm of protest: it was "an insult to public morals." This contrasts with the derivative and mannered work of such sculptors as Alexandre Falguière and Hyppolyte Moulin.

Edgar Degas' famous *Young Dancer of Fourteen* (1881) was displayed during his lifetime, but the many bronzes on show were made from wax sculptures found in his studio after his death. In contrast, the sculpture of Auguste Rodin was very much in the public eye, and his sensuous and forceful work makes him pre-eminent among 19th-century sculptors. The museum contains many of his works, including the original plaster of *Balzac* (1897). Rodin's talented companion, Camille Claudel, who spent much of her life in an asylum, is represented by a grim allegory of mortality, *Maturity* (1899–1903).

The turn of the 20th century is marked by the work of Emile-Antoine Bourdelle and Aristide Maillol.

Painting Before 1880

The surprising diversity of styles in 19th-century painting is emphasized by the close juxtaposition on the ground floor of all paintings prior to 1870 – the crucial year in which Impressionism first made a name for itself. The raging color and almost Expressionistic vigour of Eugène Delacroix's *Lion Hunt* (1854) stands next to Jean-Dominique Ingres' cool Classical *The Spring* (1820–56). As a reminder of the academic manner that dominated the century up to that point, the uninspired waxwork style of Thomas Couture's monumental *The Romans in the Age of Decadence* (1847) dominates the central aisle. In a class of their own are Edouard Manet's provocative *Olympia* and *Le Déjeuner sur l'Herbe* (1863), while works painted around the same time by his friends, Claude Monet, Pierre-Auguste Renoir, Frédéric Bazille, and Alfred Sisley, give a glimpse of the Impressionists before the Impressionist movement began.

Young Dancer of Fourteen (1881) by Edgar Degas

Olympia (1863) by Edouard Manet

Impressionism

Rouen Cathedral caught at various moments of the day (1892–3) is one of the many works on show by Claude Monet, the leading figure of the Impressionist movement. Pierre-Auguste Renoir's plump nudes and his young people *Dancing at the Moulin de la Galette* (1876) were painted at the high point of his Impressionist period. Other artists on display include Camille Pissarro, Alfred Sisley, and Mary Cassatt.

Edgar Degas and Paul Cézanne are included here, although their techniques differed from those of the Impressionists. Degas often favored crisp Realism, though he was quite capable of using the sketchy manner of the Impressionists, as, for instance, in *L'Absinthe* (1876). Cézanne was more concerned with substance than light, as can be seen in his *Apples and Oranges*

Blue Water Lilies (1919)
by Claude Monet

(1895–1900). Van Gogh was momentarily influenced by the movement but then went his own way, illustrated here by works from the collection of Dr. Gachet.

Breton Peasant Women (1894)
by Paul Gauguin

Neo-Impressionism

Although labeled Neo-Impressionism, the work of Georges Seurat (which includes *The Circus* from 1891) was quite unrelated to the older movement. He, along with Maximilien Luce and Paul Signac, painted by applying small dots of color that blended together when viewed from a distance. *Jane Avril Dancing* (1892) is just one of many pictures by Henri de Toulouse-Lautrec on display. The work Paul Gauguin made at Pont-Aven in Brittany is shown next to that of younger artists who knew him at the

time, such as Emile Bernard and the Nabis group. There are also a number of paintings from his Tahitian period. Works by Vincent Van Gogh are also included here.

The Nabis (which included Pierre Bonnard) tended to treat the canvas as a flat surface out of which a sense of depth emerged as the viewer gazed upon it.

The dream-like visions of Odilon Redon are in the Symbolist vein, while the naïve art of Henri (Douanier) Rousseau is represented by *War* (1894) and *The Snake Charmer* (1907).

Naturalism and Symbolism

Three large rooms are devoted to paintings that filled the Salons from 1880 to 1900. The work of the Naturalists was sanctioned by the Third Republic and widely reproduced at the time. Fernand Cormon's figure of *Cain* was highly acclaimed when it first appeared in the 1880 Salon. Jules Bastien-Lepage's interest lay in illustrating peasant life, and in 1877 he painted *Haymaking*, which established him as one of the leading Naturalists. His fairly free handling of paint was influenced by what he had learned from Manet and his friends. More sombrely (and effectively) naturalistic is Lionel Walden's view of *The Docks of Cardiff* (1894).

Symbolism developed as a reaction against Realism and Impressionism and tended to be dominated by images of dreams and thoughts. This resulted in a wide variety of subjects and modes of expression. There is the over-sweet vision of levitating harpists, *Serenity* by Henri Martin (1899), Edward Burne-Jones' monumental work *Wheel of Fortune* (1883), and Jean Delville's *School of Plato* (1898). One of the most evocative paintings in this section is Winslow Homer's lyrical *Summer Night* (1890).

LATIN QUARTER

Located on the Left Bank, the Latin Quarter spreads over the 5th and 6th arrondissements. One of the oldest and best-known areas of Paris, this lively neighborhood exudes a Bohemian charm. It emerged in the Middle Ages as a student quarter, with the celebrated Sorbonne University attracting scholars from all over Europe, and it continues to have a significant student presence today.

Bisected by Boulevards St.-Germain and St.-Michel, most of the area is a maze of tiny cobblestone streets leading to a medieval garden or an ancient church. Many of these charming streets, like Rue du Chat qui Pêche (Cat who Fishes) and Rue St.-Jacques, which is probably the oldest in Paris, are now pedestrian-only and filled with small cafés, ethnic boutiques, and second-hand bookstores. Meet up with friends at the tree-lined Place St.-André des Arts, an old gathering place for French artists, or wander to the fascinating Musée de Cluny, set inside old Roman baths and filled with colorful artifacts and works of art.

Sights at a Glance

Historic Buildings and Streets
❷ Boulevard St.-Michel
❼ La Sorbonne
❽ Collège de France

Churches
❸ St.-Séverin
❹ St.-Julien-le-Pauvre
❾ Chapelle de la Sorbonne
❿ St.-Etienne-du-Mont
⓫ Panthéon pp160–61

Squares
❺ Place Maubert

Museums and Galleries
❶ Musée de Cluny – Musée National du Moyen Age pp154–7
❻ Musée de la Préfecture de Police

☐ Restaurants see pp303–5
1 Anahuacalli
2 L'Atlas
3 Brasserie Balzar
4 Breakfast in America
5 Café de la Nouvelle Mairie
6 Itinéraires
7 El Loubnane
8 Perraudin
9 Le Petit Châtelet
10 Le Petit Pontoise
11 Le Pré Verre
12 Shakespeare & Co. Café
13 Sola
14 Terroir Parisien
15 La Tour d'Argent

0 meters 200
0 yards 200

See also Street Finder map 12, 13, 17

◀ Interior view of the Panthéon's dome

For keys to symbols see back flap

Street by Street: Latin Quarter

Since the Middle Ages, this riverside quarter has been dominated by the Sorbonne, and acquired its name from the early Latin-speaking students. It dates back to the Roman town across from the Ile de la Cité; at that time, the Rue St.-Jacques was one of the main roads out of Paris. The area is generally associated with artists, intellectuals, and the bohemian way of life; it also has a history of political unrest. In 1871, the Place St.-Michel became the center of the Paris Commune, and in May 1968, it was the site of the student uprisings. Today, the eastern half has become sufficiently chic, however, to contain the homes of some of the establishment.

Place St.-Michel contains a fountain by Davioud. The bronze statue by Duret shows St. Michael killing the dragon.

Metro St.-Michel

Metro Cluny La Sorbonne

BLVD ST MICHEL

RUE DE LA HARPE

RUE ST.-JACQUES

RUE DES ECOLES

❷ ★ **Boulevard St.-Michel**
The northern end of the Boul'Mich, as it is affectionately known, is a lively mélange of cafés and book- and clothes stores, with bars and experimental movie theaters nearby.

❶ ★ **Musée National du Moyen Age**
One of the finest collections of medieval art in the world is kept here in a superb late 15th-century building.

No. 22 Rue St.-Séverin is the narrowest house in Paris and used to be the residence of Abbé Prévost, author of *Manon Lescaut*.

3 ★ St.-Séverin
Begun in the 13th century, this beautiful church took three centuries to build and is a fine example of the Flamboyant Gothic style.

Rue du Chat qui Pêche (meaning "street of the fishing cat") is the narrowest street in Paris at just 6 ft (1.8 m) wide.

Little Athens is a lively place in the evening, especially on the weekend, when the Greek restaurants located in the touristy streets around St.-Séverin are at their busiest.

Locator Map
See Central Paris Map pp16–17

Shakespeare & Co. *(see pp323–4)* at No. 37 Rue de la Bûcherie is a delightful, if chaotic, bookstore. Any books purchased here are stamped with *Shakespeare & Co. Kilomètre Zéro Paris*.

4 ★ St.-Julien-le-Pauvre
One of the oldest churches in Paris, St.-Julien-le-Pauvre has 13th-century Romaneque architecture. The vault was added in the 17th century.

Rue du Fouarre used to host lectures in the Middle Ages. The students sat on straw *(fouarre)* in the street.

Metro Maubert Mutualité

Rue Galande was home to the rich and chic in the 17th century, but subsequently became notorious for its taverns.

0 meters 100
0 yards 100

Key
— Suggested route

● Musée de Cluny – Musée National du Moyen Â

The museum is housed in the former town house of the Abbots of Cluny, l'Hotel de Cluny. Surrounded by imaginatively recreated medieval gardens, the museum is a unique combination of Gallo-Roman ruins, incorporated into a medieval mansion, and one of the world's finest collections of medieval art including paintings, sculptures, tapestries, stained glass, and silver and ivory objects.

Medieval Mansion
The museum building was completed in 1500 during the abbacy of Jacques d'Amboise, Abbot of Cluny.

★ **Golden Rose** (1330)
The goldsmith Minucchio da Siena made this rose for the Avignon Pope John XXII.

★ **Lady with the Unicorn**
This outstanding series of six tapestries is a fine example of the *millefleurs* style, which was developed in the 15th and early 16th centuries. The style is noted for its graceful depiction of plants, animals, and people.

Gallo-Roman Baths
Built in AD 100, the baths lasted for about 200 years before being abandoned.

Caldarium
(hot bath room)

Gallo-Roman Frigidarium
The arches of this cold bath room date from the 1st and 2nd centuries. They have been decorated with pairs of carved ship's prows, thought to refer to the association of Paris boatmen.

Books of Hours
The museum possesses Books of Hours from the 15th century. The illuminated pages include scenes showing the Labors of the Months, accompanied by the relevant sign of the zodiac.

Medieval chapel

Octagonal tower

Entrance

Key to Floorplan
- Gallo-Roman ruins
- Medieval mansion
- 19th- and 20th-century section

Courtyard entrance

★ **Gallery of the Kings**
In 1977, 22 of the 27 stone heads of the Kings of Judah (carved around 1220 during the reign of Philippe Auguste and removed from Notre-Dame in the 18th century) were unearthed during excavations behind the Opéra.

Gallery Guide

The collection is spread throughout the two floors of the building. It is mainly medieval and covers a wide range of items, including illuminated manuscripts, tapestries, textiles, precious metals, alabaster, ceramics, sculpture, and church furnishings. A number of Gallo-Roman artifacts are displayed around the sides of the frigidarium, and the small circular room nearby contains some capitals.

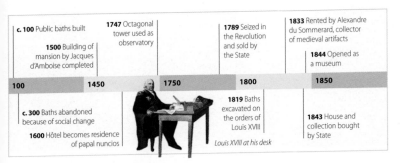

100		1450		1750		1800		1850

c. 100 Public baths built

1747 Octagonal tower used as observatory

1500 Building of mansion by Jacques d'Amboise completed

1789 Seized in the Revolution and sold by the State

1833 Rented by Alexandre du Sommerard, collector of medieval artifacts

1844 Opened as a museum

c. 300 Baths abandoned because of social change

1819 Baths excavated on the orders of Louis XVIII

1600 Hôtel becomes residence of papal nuncios

1843 House and collection bought by State

Louis XVIII at his desk

Exploring the Musée de Cluny's Collection

Alexandre du Sommerard settled in the Hôtel de Cluny in 1833 and installed his art collection with great sensitivity to the surroundings and a strong sense of the dramatic. After his death the Hôtel and its contents were sold to the State and turned into a museum.

The Arithmetic tapestry

Tapestries

The tapestries are remarkable for their quality, age, and state of preservation. In *The Arithmetic*, arithmetic – one of the liberal arts of the Quadrivium alongside geometry, astronomy, and music – is personified by an elegant female figure who is counting tokens while consulting the book given as a present by one of the surrounding men. More everyday scenes are shown in the magnificent series *The Noble Life* (about 1500). Upstairs is the *Lady with the Unicorn* series.

Carvings

The diverse techniques of medieval European wood-carvers are well represented. From the Nottingham work-shops in England, there are wood as well as alabaster works which were widely used as altarpieces all over Europe. Among the smaller works of this genre are *The School*, which is touchingly realistic and dates from the early 16th century.

Upstairs there are some fine Flemish and south German woodcarvings. The multi-colored figure of St. John is typical. Two notable altar-pieces on display are the intricately carved and painted *Lamentation of Christ* (about 1485) from the Duchy of Clèves, and the Averbode altarpiece, which was made in 1523 in Antwerp, and depicts three scenes including the Last Supper. Not to be missed is a beautiful full-length figure of Mary Magdalene.

Stained Glass

Most of the Cluny's glass from the 12th and 13th centuries is French. The oldest examples were originally installed in the Basilique-Cathédrale de St.-Denis in 1144. There are also three fragments from the Troyes Cathedral, destroyed by fire, two of which illustrate the life of St. Nicholas while the third depicts that of Christ.

Numerous panels came to the Cluny from Sainte-Chapelle *(see pp88–9)*, during its mid-19th-century restoration, and were never returned, including five scenes from the story of Samson dating from 1248.

The technique of contrasting colored glass with surrounding grisaille (grey-and-white panels) developed in the latter half of the 13th century. Four panels from the royal château at Rouen illustrate this.

Stained-glass scene from Brittany (1400)

The School woodcarving (English, early 16th century)

La Reine de Saba, the head of a queen from St.-Denis c.1140

Sculpture

The highlight here is the Gallery of the Kings, a display of heads and decapitated figures, originally from Notre-Dame. There is also a graceful statue of Adam, sculpted in the 1260s.

In the vaulted room opposite are displays of fine Romanesque sculpture retrieved from French churches. Among the earliest are the 12 capitals from the nave of St.-Germain-des-Prés, from the early 11th century. Retrieved from the portal of St.-Denis is a boldly sculpted head of a queen, *Le Reine de Saba* (c.1140) which, though badly mutilated, is still compelling.

Other Romanesque and early Gothic capitals include three finely sculpted works from Catalonia and four of the museum's most famous statues, early 13th-century apostles made for Sainte-Chapelle.

Everyday Objects

Household goods show another side to medieval life, and this large collection is grouped in a sensitive way to illustrate their use – from wallhangings and caskets to kitchenware and clothing. Children's toys bring a very human aspect to the display, while travel cases and religious emblems evoke journeys of exploration and pilgrimage.

Precious Metalwork

The museum has a fine collection of jewelry, coins, metal, and enamelwork from Gallic times to the Middle Ages. The showcase of Gallic jewelry includes gold torques, bracelets, and rings, all of a simple design. In between these is one of the Cluny's most precious exhibits, the Golden Rose, a delicately wrought piece commissioned by Pope John XXII in 1330 and the oldest known of its kind.

The earliest enamelwork on display is the late Roman and Byzantine *cloisonné* pieces, culminating in the remarkable Limoges enamels, which flourished in the late 12th century. There are also two exceptional altarpieces, the Golden Altar of Basel and the Stavelot altarpiece.

Cross from Italy (late 15th century)

The Pillar of the Nautes

Gallo-Roman Ruins

One of the main reasons for visiting the Musée de Cluny – Musée National du Moyen Age is to see the scale and layout of its earliest function, the Gallo-Roman baths. The vaulted *frigidarium* (cold bath room) was the largest of its kind in France. Here there is another of the museum's highlights, the restored Pillar of the Nautes (boatmen), unearthed during excavations beneath Notre-Dame in 1711. Composed of five carved stone blocks representing Gallic and Roman divinities, its crowning element is presumed to depict the Seine's boatmen. There are also the ruins of the *caldarium* and *tepidarium* (hot and tepid baths), and visitors can tour the underground vaults.

Lady with the Unicorn Tapestries

This series of six tapestries was woven in the late 15th century. They are valued for their fresh harmonious colors and the poetic elegance of the central figure. Allegories of the senses are illustrated in the first five tapestries: sight (gazing into a mirror), hearing (playing a portable organ), taste (sampling candies), smell (sniffing carnations), and touch (the lady holding the unicorn's horn). The enigmatic sixth tapestry (showing jewels being placed in a box) includes the words "to my only desire" and is thought to represent a sixth sense "Heart" and the principle of free choice..

Unicorn on the sixth tapestry

❷ Boulevard St.-Michel

75005 & 75006. **Map** 12 F5 & 16 F1.
Ⓜ St.-Michel, Cluny-La Sorbonne.
🚉 Luxembourg.

Cut through the area in 1869, the boulevard initially gained fame from its many literary cafés, but nowadays many have been replaced by clothing shops. Nos. 60–64 house the Ecole Nationale Supérieure des Mines, one of France's leading engineering schools *(see p175)*. In the Place St.-Michel, marble plaques commemorate the many students who died here in 1944 fighting the Nazis.

Door of St.-Séverin church decorated with carved stone arches

❸ St.-Séverin

3 Rue-des-Prêtres-St.-Séverin 75005.
Map 13 A4. **Tel** 01 42 34 93 50.
Ⓜ St.-Michel. **Open** 11am–7:30pm Mon–Sat, 9am–8:30pm Sun. 🕊 daily.
Concerts. 🏧 saint-severin.com

One of the most beautiful churches in Paris, St.-Séverin is a perfect example of the Flamboyant Gothic style. It is named after a 6th-century hermit who lived in the area and persuaded the future St.. Cloud, grandson of King Clovis, to take holy orders. Construction finished in the early 16th century and included a remarkable double

Inside St.-Julien-le-Pauvre

ambulatory circling the chancel. In 1684 the Grande Mademoiselle, cousin to Louis XIV, adopted St.-Séverin after breaking with St.-Sulpice and had the chancel modernized.

The burial ground here, which is now a garden, was the site of the first operation for gallstones in 1474. An archer who had been condemned to death was offered his freedom by Louis XI if he consented to the operation and lived. (It was a success, and the archer went free.) In the garden stands the church's medieval gable-roofed charnel house.

❹ St.-Julien-le-Pauvre

79 Rue Galande 75005. **Map** 13 A4.
Tel 01 43 54 52 16. Ⓜ St.- Michel.
🚉 St. Michel-Notre-Dame.
Open 9:30am–1:30pm & 3–6:30pm daily. 🕊 12:15pm Tue & Thu, 11am Sun. Concerts. *See Entertainment p338.*
🏧 sjlpmelkites.fr.

At least three saints can claim to be patron of this church, but the most likely is St. Julian the Hospitaler. The church, together with St.-Germain-des-Prés, is one of the oldest in Paris, dating from between 1165 and 1220. The university held official meetings in the church until 1524, when a student protest created so much damage that university meetings were barred from the church by parliament. Since 1889 it has belonged to the Melchite sect of the Greek Orthodox Church, and it is now the setting for chamber and religious music concerts.

❺ Place Maubert

75005. **Map** 13 A5.
Ⓜ Maubert-Mutualité.

From the 12th to the middle of the 13th century, "La Maub" was one of Paris's scholastic centers, with lectures given in the open air. After the scholars moved to the new colleges of the Montagne Sainte-Geneviève, the square became a place of torture and execution, including that of the philosopher Etienne Dolet, who was burned at the stake in 1546.

So many Protestants were burned here in the 16th century that it became a place of pilgrimage for the followers of the new faith. Its dark reputation has been replaced by respectability and a notable street market.

❻ Musée de la Préfecture de Police

4 Rue de la Montagne Sainte-Geneviève 75005. **Map** 13 A5. **Tel** 01 44 41 52 50. Ⓜ Maubert-Mutualité.
Open 9:30am–5pm Mon–Fri, 10:30am–5:30pm 3rd Sat of month.
Closed Sun & public hols. 🎟 by appt.

A darker side to Paris's history is illustrated in this small, rather old-fashioned museum. Created in 1909, the collection traces the development of the police in Paris from the Middle Ages to the 20th century. Curiosities on show include arrest warrants for figures such as the famous revolutionary Danton, and a rather sobering display of weapons and tools used by famous criminals. There is also a section on the part the police played in the Resistance and subsequent liberation of Paris.

Weapons in the police museum

❼ La Sorbonne

1 Rue Victor Cousin 75005. **Map** 13 A5. **Tel** 01 40 46 22 11. Ⓜ Cluny-La Sorbonne, Maubert-Mutualité. **Open** by appt only. Ⓒ Mon–Fri, plus one Sat a month, by appt only: write to visites.sorbonne@ac-paris.fr. Ⓦ **english.paris-sorbonne.fr**

The Sorbonne, seat of the University of Paris, was established in 1253 by Robert de Sorbon, confessor to Louis IX, for 16 poor students to study theology. The college soon became the center of scholastic theology. In 1469 the rector had three printing machines brought over from Mainz, thereby founding the first printing house in France. The college's opposition to liberal 18th-century philosophy led to its suppression during the Revolution. It was reestablished by Napoleon in 1806. The buildings built by Richelieu in the early 17th century were replaced by the ones seen today, with the exception of the chapel.

Statues outside the Collège de France

❽ Collège de France

11 Pl Marcelin-Berthelot 75005. **Map** 13 A5. **Tel** 01 44 27 12 11 or 01 44 27 11 47. Ⓜ Maubert-Mutualité. **Open** Oct–Jun: 9am–6pm Mon–Fri. Ⓦ **college-de-france.fr**

One of Paris's great institutes of research and learning, the college was established in 1530 by François I. Guided by the great humanist Guillaume Budé, the king aimed to counteract the intolerance and dogmatism of the Sorbonne. A statue of Budé stands in the west courtyard, and the unbiased approach to learning is reflected in the inscription on the old college entrance: *docet omnia* (all are taught here). Lectures are free and open to the public, depending on availability.

❾ Chapelle de la Sorbonne

Pl de la Sorbonne 75005. **Map** 13 A5. **Tel** 01 40 46 22 11. Ⓜ Cluny-La Sorbonne, Maubert-Mutualité. ⓇⒺⓇ Luxembourg. **Open** for guided tours only (one Sat every month), by appt. 🅿

Designed by Lemercier and built between 1635 and 1642, this chapel is, in effect, a monument to Richelieu, with his coat of arms on the dome supports and his white marble tomb, carved by Girardon in 1694, in the chancel. The chapel's attractive lateral facade looks onto the main courtyard of the Sorbonne.

Chapelle de la Sorbonne clock

❿ St.-Etienne-du-Mont

30 Rue Descartes, Pl Sainte-Geneviève 75005. **Map** 17 A1. **Tel** 01 43 54 11 79. Ⓜ Cardinal Lemoine. **Open** 8:45am–7:45pm Tue–Fri, 8:45am–noon & 2–7:45pm Sat, 8:45am–12:15pm & 2:30–7pm Sun (school holidays: 10am–noon & 4–7:45pm Tue–Sat). Ⓒ 🅃 daily. 🅿 Ⓦ **saintetiennedumont.fr**

This remarkable church houses the shrine of Sainte Geneviève, patron saint of Paris, and the remains of the great literary figures Racine and Pascal. Some parts are in the Gothic style and others date from the Renaissance, including a magnificent rood screen that bridges the nave. The stained-glass windows are also notable.

St.-Etienne-du-Mont

16th-century belfry tower

Medieval window

Rood screen

⑪ Panthéon

When Louis XV recovered from desperate illness in 1744, he was so grateful to be alive that he conceived a magnificent church to honor Sainte Geneviève. The design was entrusted to the French architect Jacques-Germain Soufflot, who planned the church in Neo-Classical style. Work began in 1757 and was completed in 1790, ten years after Soufflot's death, under the control of Guillaume Rondelet. But with the Revolution underway the church was soon turned into a pantheon – a location for the tombs of France's great and good. Napoleon returned it to the Church in 1806, but it was secularized and then desecularized once more before finally being made a civic building in 1885.

The Facade
Inspired by the Rome Pantheon, the temple portico has 22 Corinthian columns.

Pediment Relief
David d'Angers' pediment bas-relief depicts the mother country (France) granting laurels to her great men.

The Panthéon Interior
The interior has four aisles arranged in the shape of a Greek cross, from the center of which the great dome rises.

KEY

① **The arches of the dome** show a renewed interest in the lightness of Gothic architecture and were designed by Rondelet. They link four pillars supporting the dome, which weighs 11,000 tons and is 272 ft (83 m) high.

② **The dome galleries** afford a magnificent panoramic view of France's capital.

③ **The dome lantern** allows only a little light to filter into the church's center. Intense light was thought inappropriate for the place where France's heroes rested.

Entrance

★ **Frescoes of Sainte Geneviève**
Murals along the south wall of the nave depict the life of Sainte Geneviève. They are by Pierre Puvis de Chavannes, the 19th-century fresco painter.

★ **Iron-Framed Dome**
The tall dome, with its stone cupolas and three layers of shells, was inspired by St. Paul's in London and the Dôme des Invalides *(see pp188–9)*.

Colonnade
The colonnade encircling the dome is both decorative and part of an ingenious supporting system.

Monument to Diderot
This is Alphonse Terroir's statue (1925) to the political writer Denis Diderot.

The Panthéon's Enshrined

The first of France's great men to be entombed was the popular orator Honoré Mirabeau. (Later, under the revolutionary leadership of Maximilien Robespierre, he fell from grace and his body was removed.) Voltaire followed. A statue of Voltaire by Jean-Antoine Houdon stands in front of his tomb. In the 1970s the remains of the wartime Resistance leader Jean Moulin were reburied here. Pierre and Marie Curie's remains were transferred here in 1995, followed by Alexandre Dumas in 2002. Others here include Jean-Jacques Rousseau, Victor Hugo, and Emile Zola.

★ **Crypt**
Covering the entire area under the building, the crypt divides into galleries flanked by Doric columns. Many French notables rest here.

JARDIN DES PLANTES QUARTER

Founded in 1626 as the royal medicinal plant gardens, this tranquil area soon became a scientific laboratory and botanical research center. It is dominated by the Jardin des Plantes, but it also contains three galleries of the Natural History Museum, a small zoo, and a botanical school. Head to the daily market on Rue Mouffetard to buy cheese and wine, then enjoy a picnic lunch in the gardens. Another calm respite from the busy city is the Institut du Monde Arabe, with panoramic views across the Seine to Notre-Dame.

Sights at a Glance

Historic Buildings and Streets
4 Arènes de Lutèce
6 Rue Mouffetard

Churches
7 St.-Médard
8 Grande Mosquée de Paris

Modern Architecture
1 Institut du Monde Arabe

Squares, Parks, and Gardens
3 Ménagerie
5 Place de la Contrescarpe
10 Jardin des Plantes

Museums and Galleries
2 Musée de la Sculpture en Plein Air
9 Muséum National d'Histoire Naturelle
11 Fondation Jérôme Seydoux-Pathé
12 Mobilier National et La Manufacture des Gobelins

☐ Restaurants see pp303–5
1 L'Agrume
2 Chez Gladines
3 Dans les Landes
4 Marty
5 Mavrommatis

0 meters 400
0 yards 400

See also Street Finder map 13, 17–18

◀ Pedestrians strolling in the Jardin des Plantes

For keys to symbols *see back flap*

Street by Street: Jardin des Plantes Quarter

Two physicians to Louis XIII, Jean Hérouard and Guy de la Brosse, obtained permission to establish the royal medicinal herb garden in the sparsely populated St.-Victor suburb in 1626. The herb garden and gardens of various religious houses gave the region a rural character. In the 19th century, the population and thus the area expanded and it became more built up, until it gradually assumed the character it has today: a well-to-do residential patchwork of 19th- and early 20th-century buildings interspersed with much older and some more recent buildings.

Metro Cardinal Lemoine

⑤ Place de la Contrescarpe
This village-like square filled with restaurants and cafés buzzes with student life after dusk.

⑥ ★ Rue Mouffetard
Locals flock to the daily open-air market here which is one of the oldest Paris street markets. A hoard of *louis d'or gold* coins from the 18th century was found at No. 53 during its demolition in 1938.

Pot de Fer fountain is one of 14 that Marie de Médici had built on the Left Bank in 1624 as a source of water for her palace in the Jardin du Luxembourg. The fountain was rebuilt in 1671.

Metro Place Monge

Passage des Postes is an ancient alley which was opened in 1830. Its entrance is in the Rue Mouffetard.

⑦ St.-Médard
This church was started in the mid-15th century and completed by 1655. In 1784, the choir was made Classical in style, and the nave's 16th-century windows were replaced with contemporary stained glass.

RUE DU CARDINAL LEMOINE

RUE ROLL

RUE ST MEDARD

RUE ORTOLAN

RUE MOUFFETARD

RUE DE L'EPEE DE

RUE DES PATRIARCHES

RUE DE L'ARBALETE

RUE DE CANDOLLE

❹ ★ Arènes de Lutèce
The Roman amphitheater of Lutetia was used for burials in the 4th century.

Locator Map
See Central Paris Map pp16–17

Rue des Arènes is round the corner from the Arènes de Lutèce. No. 5 is an interesting Gothic Revival house in which the writer Jean Paulhan lived from 1940.

Cuvier Fountain is a memorial to naturalist Georges Cuvier. It was erected in 1840 by P Vigouroux, with figure carving by Jean-Jacques Feuchère.

Metro Censier-Daubenton

❽ ★ Grande Mosquée de Paris
This Hispano-Moorish mosque, the center of Paris's Muslim community, includes within its walls a Turkish bath, a Moorish café and restaurant, and an oriental bazaar.

Key

— Suggested route

0 meters   100
0 yards   100

❶ Institut du Monde Arabe

1 Rue des Fossées St.-Bernard, Pl Mohammed V 75005. **Map** 13 C5.
Tel 01 40 51 38 38. Ⓜ Jussieu, Cardinal-Lemoine. **Open** Museum & temp exhibs: 10am–6pm Tue–Thu (until 9.30pm Fri, 7pm Sat & Sun and public hols). Library: call for opening hours. 🅿 ♿ 🎫 Lectures. 🖊 📺
Ⓦ **imarabe.org**

This cultural institute was founded in 1980 by France and 20 Arab countries with the intention of fostering cultural links between the Arab world and the West. It is housed in a magnificent building designed by Jean Nouvel (also responsible for the Musée du quai Branly, *see pp194–5*), combining modern materials with the spirit of traditional Arab architecture. The white marble book tower, which can be seen through the glass of the west wall, spirals upward bringing to mind the minaret of a mosque. The emphasis that is traditionally placed on interior space in Arab architecture has been used here to create an enclosed courtyard reached by a narrow gap splitting the building in two.

From floors four to seven, there's a fascinating display of Islamic works of art from the 9th to the 19th centuries, including ceramics, sculpture, carpets, and astrolabes. There is also a library and media archive.

❷ Musée de la Sculpture en Plein Air

Quai St.-Bernard, Square Tino Rossi 75005. **Map** 13 C5. Ⓜ Gare d'Austerlitz, Sully-Morland.

Butting up to the left-hand corner of the Institut du Monde Arabe, the Pont de Sully links the Ile St. Louis with both banks of the Seine. Opened in 1877 and built of cast iron, the Pont de Sully is not an especially beautiful structure. Despite this, it is well worth pausing for a moment on the bridge for a fabulous view of Notre-Dame rising dramatically behind the graceful Pont de la Tournelle.

Running along the river from the Pont de Sully as far as the Pont d'Austerlitz is the peaceful Quai St.-Bernard. Not always so sedate, Quai St.-Bernard was famous during the 17th century as a spot for nude bathing, until scandalized public opinion made it illegal. The grassy slopes adjoining the *quai* make a perfect spot to enjoy a picnic. Opened in 1975, they are known as the Jardin Tino Rossi in honor of the celebrated Corsican singer. The garden has a display of open-air sculpture known as the Musée de la Sculpture en Plein Air. Vandalism and other problems have unfortunately necessitated the removal of some of the exhibits.

❸ Ménagerie

57 Rue Cuvier/Rue Buffon 75005.
Map 17 C1. **Tel** 01 40 79 37 94.
Ⓜ Jussieu, Austerlitz. **Open** summer: 9am–6pm daily (to 6.30pm Sun & public hols); winter: 9am–5/5.30pm daily. Last adm 30 min before closing.
🅿 🖊 📺 🅿 📷 🎫 for groups, by appt. Ⓦ **zoodujardindesplantes.fr**

France's oldest public zoo is located in the pleasant surroundings of the Jardin des Plantes. The Ménagerie was set up during the Revolution to house the survivors from the Royal menagerie at Versailles – all four of them. The state then rounded up animals from circuses, and a number of exotic creatures were sent from abroad. Unfortunately, during the Prussian siege of Paris (1870–1871), most of these animals were slaughtered in order to feed the hungry citizens (*see p227*).

Today, the zoo specializes in small mammals, insects, birds, primates, and reptiles. It is a great favorite with children as it allows them to get quite close to the animals, either in the petting enclosure, or during feeding times. The lion house contains panthers from China and other attractions include a large monkey house, a waterfowl aviary, and wild sheep and goats.

Child playing at the zoo

Light Screens
The south elevation is made up of 1,600 high-tech metal screens that filter the light entering the building. Their design is based on *moucharabiyahs* (carved wooden screens found on the outsides of buildings from Morocco to Southeast Asia).

Each screen contains 21 irises which are controlled electronically, opening and closing in response to the amount of sunlight falling on photosensitive screens.

The central iris is made up of interlocking metal blades which move to adjust the size of the central opening.

The peripheral irises are linked to one another and to the central iris. They open and close in unison forming a delicate pattern of light and shade inside the institute.

The displays in the vivarium (enclosures of live animals in their natural habitat) are changed at regular intervals, and there is a permanent exhibition of micro-arthropods (also known as creepy-crawlies!)

④ Arènes de Lutèce

49–59 Rue Monge/4 Rue des Arènes 75005. **Map** 17 B1. **Tel** 01 45 35 02 56. **M** Jussieu, Cardinal Lemoine. **Open** hours vary, but usually 8/9am–6pm, depending on the time of year.

The remains of this vast Roman arena (Lutetia was the Roman name for Paris) date from the late 1st century (*see p23*). Its destruction began toward the end of the 3rd century at the hands of the Barbarians, and later, parts of it were used to build the walls of the Ile de la Cité. The arena was then gradually buried and its exact location preserved only in old documents and the local name Clos des Arènes. It was rediscovered in 1869 during the construction of the Rue Monge and the allocation of building lots nearby.

Action toward its restoration began with the campaigning of Victor Hugo (among others) in the 19th century but work did not get really underway until 1918.

With a seating capacity of 15,000, arranged in 35 tiers, the original arena was used both for theatrical performances and as an amphitheater for gladiator fights. This type of combined use was peculiar to Gaul (France), and the arena is similar to the other ones in Nîmes and Arles.

⑤ Place de la Contrescarpe

75005. **Map** 17 B1. **M** Place Monge.

At one time, this site lay outside the city walls. It gets its name from the backfilling of the moat that ran along Philippe-Auguste's wall. The present square was laid out in 1852, but the small fountain was added in 1994. At No. 1, there is a memorial plaque to the old "pine-cone club" immortalized in the writings of Rabelais; here, a group of writers known as *La Pléiade* (named after the constellation of The Pleiades) used to meet in the 16th century. Four hundred years later, authors such as Ernest Hemingway, James Joyce, and George Orwell also found the streets of this historically working-class neighborhood a great source of inspiration.

The area has always been used for meetings and festivals. Today, it still embodies old Paris, with its narrow cobblestone streets and charming cafés, and is very lively on weekends.

Part of the medieval city wall near Place de la Contrescarpe

Buffon and the Jardin des Plantes

At the age of 32, Georges Louis Leclerc, Comte de Buffon (1707–88), became the curator of the Jardin des Plantes at a time when the study of natural history was at the forefront of contemporary thought – Charles Darwin's *On the Origin of Species* was to be published 120 years later. Buffon masterminded the reorganization of the Jardin, propelling it to a pre-eminent position within the scientific world. He was elected to the Académie Française in 1752 following the publication of his two main works, *Natural History* and *The Epoques of Nature*. He died in his house in the Jardin.

Illustration of a primate from Buffon's *Natural History*

6 Rue Mouffetard

75005. **Map** 17 B2. **M** Censier-Daubenton, Place Monge. **Open** Market Place Maubert: 7am–2.30pm Tue, Thu, Sat (to 3pm Sat); Place Monge: 7am–2.30pm Wed, Fri, Sun (to 3pm Sun). *See Stores and Markets p331.*

A major thoroughfare since Roman times, when it linked Lutetia (Paris) and Rome, this street is one of the oldest in the city. In the 17th and 18th centuries, it was known as the Grande Rue du Faubourg St.-Marcel, and many of its buildings date from that time. Some of the small stores still have ancient painted signs, and some houses have mansard roofs. No. 125 has an attractive, restored Louis XIII facade, and the entire front of No. 134 has beautiful decoration of wild beasts, flowers, and plants. At No. 60, the *Fontaine de Pot-de-Fer* is a small fountain dating from Roman times. Later on, it was connected to an aqueduct used by Marie de Médicis to take water to the Palais du Luxembourg and its gardens.

The area is known for its open-air markets, especially those in Place Maubert, Place Monge, and Rue Daubenton, a side street where a lively African market takes place.

At night, the street bustles with people enjoying the Greek, Italian, Argentinian, and other cuisines on offer at the many small restaurants.

7 St.-Médard

141 Rue Mouffetard 75005. **Map** 17 B2. **Tel** 01 44 08 87 00. **M** Censier-Daubenton. **Open** 8am–12.30pm & 2.30–7.30pm Tue–Sat; 9am–noon & 4–8.30pm Sun. ✝ various times. ♿ **W** saintmedard.org

The origins of this church go back to the 9th century. St, Médard, counsellor to the Merovingian kings, was known for giving a wreath of white roses to young girls noted for their virtue. The churchyard became notorious in the 18th century as the center of the cult of the Convulsionnaires, whose hysterical fits were brought on by the contemplation of miracle cures. The interior has many fine paintings, including the 17th-century *St. Joseph Walking with the Christ Child* by Francisco de Zurbarán.

8 Grande Mosquée de Paris

2 bis Pl du Puits de l'Ermite 75005 (Turkish baths/tearoom: 39 Rue Geoffrey St.-Hilaire). **Map** 17 C2. **Tel** 01 45 35 97 33; 01 43 31 14 32 (baths, tearoom). **M** Place Monge. **Open** 9am–noon, 2–6pm. Baths: 10am–9pm Wed–Mon; tearoom: 9am–midnight daily. **Closed** Muslim hols. ✎ ▣ ▨ Library. **W** mosqueede paris.net Café & baths: **W** la-mosquee.com

Built in the 1920s in the Hispano-Moorish style, this complex is the spiritual center for Paris's Muslim community and the home of the Grand Imam. It has religious, educational, and commercial sections; at its heart is a mosque. Each of the mosque's domes is decorated differently, and the minaret stands nearly 100 ft (33 m) high. Inside is a grand patio with mosaics on the walls and tracery on the arches.

Once used only by scholars, the mosque's place in Parisian life has grown over the years. The Turkish baths are strictly for women only. A tearoom and restaurant serve Moorish specialties.

Tiles inside the Grande Mosquée de Paris

9 Muséum National d'Histoire Naturelle

2 Rue Buffon 75005. **Map** 17 C2. **Tel** 01 40 79 54 79 or 01 40 79 54 56 01. **M** Jussieu, Austerlitz. **Open** Grande Galerie: 10am–6pm Wed–Mon. **Closed** May 1. ▨ ♿ restricted. ▣ ▧ Library. **W** mnhn.fr

Originally a botany research center in the 17th century, the museum was founded in 1793 to include the study of animals. It was the stomping ground of naturalists Buffon *(see above left)* and Lamarck, whose research eventually influenced Charles Darwin and his *On the Origin of Species*.

The museum has three galleries in the surroundings of the Jardin des Plantes: the Galerie de Minéralogie et de Géologie, with its crystals, gems, and meteorites; the Galeries d'Anatomie Comparée et de Paléontologie, housing dinosaur skeletons and fossils; and the Grande Galerie de l'Evolution, featuring stuffed tigers and elephants. With more than

62 million specimens, the museum has the third-largest research collection in the world.

Built in 1838 for the Universal Exposition, the Galeries d'Anatomie Comparée et de Paléontologie mesmerize young visitors with their collection of dinosaur skeletons, including a Triceratops and a Tyrannosaurus rex. Children will also be entranced by the Grande Galerie de l'Evolution, with its vast display illustrating the evolution and subsequent extinction of various organisms. Climate change and sustainability also play a large part in this exhibit. Created for children aged 6–12 and their families in mind, the Children's Gallery, also in the Grande Galerie de l'Evolution, is a hands-on exhibition focusing on biodiversity and man's impact on the environment.

The bookstore is located in the house where Buffon lived until his death in 1788.

Skull of a dimetrodon, in the Muséum National d'Histoire Naturelle

❿ Jardin des Plantes

57 Rue Cuvier/2 Rue Buffon 75005. **Map** 17 C1. **Tel** 01 40 79 56 01. Ⓜ Jussieu, Austerlitz. **Open** 7.30am–8pm (8am–5.30pm winter) daily. 🅿️ 🅾️

A treasure to locals in the 5th arrondissement, the Jardin des Plantes comprises a museum, a zoo, botanical gardens, a science lab, and a university research center. Previously known as Jardin de Roi, it started as a medicinal herb garden created by Guy de la Brosse and Jean Hérouard, King Louis XIII's physicians in 1626. After opening to the public in 1640 and offering a free school of botany, chemistry, and

The cedar of Lebanon, Jardin des Plantes

anatomy, it quickly attracted renowned scientists, such as the Comte de Buffon (*see opposite*), whose studies were to shape Darwin's views on evolution.

Today, this popular botanical garden is home to three galleries of the Muséum National d'Histoire Naturelle, and it includes a small zoo, a gorgeous rose garden, and a labyrinth that kids adore. As well as beautiful vistas and walkways flanked by ancient trees and punctuated with statues, the park features a remarkable alpine garden with plants from the Alps, the Himalayas, Corsica, and Morocco, and an unrivalled display of wild and herbaceous plants. It also has the first cedar of Lebanon to be planted in France, originally from Britain's Kew Gardens.

⓫ Fondation Jérôme Seydoux-Pathé

73 Ave des Gobelins 75013. **Map** 17 B4. **Tel** 01 83 79 18 96. Ⓜ Place d'Italie, Les Gobelins. **Open** Salle Charles Pathé & Exhibitions: 1–7pm Tue–Fri, 10am–7pm Sat. Research Center: by appt only. Ciné-Spectacle: 2.30pm Wed (01 83 79 18 96). 🅿️ 🅾️ Ⓦ **fondation-jeromeseydoux-pathe.com**

The headquarters of the Fondation Jérôme Seydoux-Pathé sits on the site of a mid-19th-century theater that was transformed into one of Paris's first movie theaters in the mid-1900s. Pathé, a major French

movie production and distribution company, is the second-oldest operating film company in the world. The foundation is dedicated to the preservation of Pathé's legacy and to promoting cinematography. The building has a 68-seat screening room for silent movies, plus temporary and permanent collections of films, cameras, projectors, programs, and posters dating back to 1896. It is a treasure trove for movie enthusiasts and researchers.

⓬ Mobilier National et La Manufacture des Gobelins

42 Ave des Gobelins 75013. **Map** 17 B3. **Tel** 01 44 08 53 49. Ⓜ Gobelins. **Open** 11am–6pm Tue–Sun (for temp exhibitions only). Groups by appt. 🅿️ **Closed** Jan 1, May 1, Dec 25. Ⓦ **mobiliernational.culture. gouv.fr**

Originally a dyeing workshop set up in about 1440 by the Gobelin brothers, the building became a tapestry factory early in the 17th century. Louis XIV took it over in 1662 and gathered together the greatest craftsmen of the day – carpet weavers, cabinet-makers, and silversmiths – to furnish his new palace at Versailles (*see pp250–55*). Working under the direction of court painter Charles Le Brun, 250 Flemish weavers laid the foundations for the factory's international reputation. Today, weavers continue to work in the traditional way but with modern designs, including those of Picasso and Matisse.

Versailles tapestry by Le Brun, La Mobilier National et La Manufacture des Gobelins

LUXEMBOURG QUARTER

Nestled between St.-Germain-des-Prés and the Latin Quarter, this area has its own unique charm of winding streets, beautiful buildings, bookstores, and art galleries. From the austerity of the Palais du Luxembourg, home of the French Senate, to the calm of the magnificent church of St.-Sulpice, this is a much sought-after part of Paris. However, it is the Jardin de Luxembourg, one of the most beautiful landmarks of the city, that dominates the area. Inspired by the Boboli Gardens in Florence, it was started by Marie de Médici in 1612. The garden beckons with its expansive lawns, charming fountains, and gorgeous sculptures. Breathtaking orchid and rose gardens, outdoor photography exhibitions, and traditional games of *boules* played under chestnut trees add to the serenity of the area.

Sights at a Glance

Historic Buildings and Streets
❸ Palais du Luxembourg
❻ Institut Catholique de Paris

Churches
❷ St.-Sulpice
❼ St.-Joseph-des-Carmes
❿ Val-de-Grâce

Fountains
❹ Fontaine Médicis
❾ Fontaine de l'Observatoire

Squares, Parks, and Gardens
❶ Place St.-Sulpice
❺ Jardin du Luxembourg

Museums and Galleries
❽ Musée du Luxembourg
⓫ Ecole Nationale Supérieure des Mines

☐ **Restaurants** *see pp305–6*
1 L'Auberge du 15
2 L'Ourcine
3 Les Papilles

See also Street Finder maps 12, 16

| 0 meters | 400 |
| 0 yards | 400 |

◀ Fontaine Médicis, Jardin du Luxembourg

For keys to symbols *see back flap*

Street by Street: Luxembourg Quarter

Located only a few steps from the bustle of St.-Germain-des-Prés, this graceful and historic area offers a peaceful haven in the heart of a modern city. The Jardin du Luxembourg and Palais du Luxembourg dominate the quarter. The gardens became fully open to the public in the 19th century under the ownership of the Comte de Provence (later Louis XVIII), when, for a small fee, visitors could come in and feast on fruit from the orchard. Today, the gardens, palace, and old houses on the streets to the north remain unspoiled and attract many visitors.

To St.-Germain-des-Prés

❶ Place St.-Sulpice
The Fontaine des Quatre Points Cardinaux depicts four church leaders at the cardinal points of the compass. Point also means "never": the leaders were never made cardinals.

❷ ★ St.-Sulpice
This Classical church was built over 134 years to Daniel Gittard's plans. It has a facade by the Italian architect Giovanni Servandoni.

RUE HENRI DE JOUVENEL

RUE SERVANDONI

RUE FEROU

RUE DE VAUGIRARD

The Monument to Delacroix
(1890) by Jules Dalou is located near the private gardens of the French Senate. Beneath the bust of the leading Romantic painter Eugène Delacroix are the allegorical figures of Art, Time and Glory.

❺ ★ Jardin du Luxembourg
Many fine statues were erected in the Luxembourg gardens in the 19th century during the reign of Louis-Philippe.

The Rue de Tournon is full of elegant architecture, boutiques, and old bookstores. At No. 12 is the Grand Hôtel d'Entragues, reconstructed by Neveu in the 18th century during Louis XVI's reign.

Locator Map
See Central Paris Map pp16–17

Key

— Suggested route

| 0 meters | 100 |
| 0 yards | 100 |

❸ ★ Palais du Luxembourg
In 1794, during the Revolution, the painter Jacques-Louis David was imprisoned here and made sketches for the *Intervention of the Sabine Women*.

RUE DE TOURNON

RUE DE MÉDICIS

❹ ★ Fontaine Médicis
The 17th-century fountain is in the style of an Italian grotto and is thought to have been designed by Salomon de Brosse.

Sainte Geneviève, the patron saint of Paris, was a wealthy 5th-century Gallo-Roman landowner. When Paris was invaded by the Huns in AD 451, she prayed with women friends that the city would be spared – their prayers were answered. This statue by Michel-Louis Victor (1845) pays homage to her.

The Octagonal Lake (Grand Bassin), attributed to Jean-François Chalgrin, is surrounded by formal terraces where visitors to the gardens often sunbathe.

...ce

...name, was
...t in the last half of the
18th century.

Two main features of the square are the Fountain of the Four Bishops by Joachim Visconti (1844) and the pink-flowering chestnut trees. There is also the Café de la Mairie, a rendezvous of writers and students, which is often featured in French movies.

Stained-glass window of St.-Sulpice

❷ St.-Sulpice

2 Rue Palatine, Pl St-Sulpice 75006. **Map** 12 E5. **Tel** 01 42 34 59 98. Ⓜ St.-Sulpice. **Open** 7.30am–7.30pm daily. 🔔 daily. 📷 Crypt: 3.30pm 2nd & 4th Sun of month (Tel 01 43 25 03 10). Concerts. 🖥 paroisse-saint-sulpice-paris.org

It took over a century, from 1646, for this imposing church to be built. The result is a simple two-

story west front with two tiers of elegant columns. The overall harmony of the building is marred only by the towers, one at each end, which do not match.

Large arched windows fill the interior with light. By the front door are two huge shells given to François I by the Venetian Republic – they rest on bases sculpted by Jean-Baptiste Pigalle.

In the side chapel to the right of the main door are three magnificent murals by Eugène Delacroix: *Jacob Wrestling with the Angel (see p139)*, *Heliodorus Driven from the Temple* and *St.-Michael Killing the Dragon*. If you are lucky, you can catch an organ recital.

❸ Palais du Luxembourg

19 Rue de Vaugirard 75006. **Map** 12 E5. **Tel** 01 42 34 20 60 (groups, apply three months in advance); 01 44 54 19 30 (individuals, email visites@senat.fr). Ⓜ Odéon. 🚈 Luxembourg. **Open** 10am–7pm daily (to 10pm Mon during exhibitions). 📷 one Sat each month. 📷 🖥 senat.fr/visite

Now the home of the French Senate, this palace was designed by Salomon de Brosse in the style of Florence's Pitti Palace to remind Marie de Médicis, widow of Henri IV, of her native town. By the time it was finished (1631), Marie had been banished, but it remained a royal palace until the Revolution, when it temporarily served as a prison. In World War II, it was the headquarters of the Luftwaffe. The Musée du Luxembourg, in the east gallery, hosts art exhibitions *(see p175)*.

❹ Fontaine Médicis

Jardin du Luxembourg, Rue de Vaugirard 75006. **Map** 12 F5. 🚈 Luxembourg.

Built in 1624 for Marie de Médici by an unknown architect, this vigorous Baroque fountain stands at the end of a long pond filled with goldfish. The mythological figures were added much later by Auguste Ottin (1866).

❺ Jardin du Luxembourg

Blvd St.-Michel/Rue de Vaugirard/Rue Guynemer 75006. **Map** 12 E5. **Tel** 01 42 34 23 89 or 01 42 34 20 00. Ⓜ Odéon. 🚈 Luxembourg. **Open** dawn–dusk daily. 📷 Wed (Apr–Oct). 📷 🖥 senat.fr/visite

A green oasis covering 60 acres (25 ha) in the heart of the Left Bank, this is one of the most popular parks in Paris. The beautifully sculpted gardens are centered around the Palais du Luxembourg and feature an octagonal basin that is often surrounded by children sailing their toy boats.

The Jardin du Luxembourg was created at the request of Marie de Médici between 1612 and 1631. Homesick for her hometown of Florence, she had it designed to remind her of the Boboli Gardens. The original garden measured 20 acres (8 ha), and remaining today are the large pond, the Fontaine Médicis, and 2,000 elm trees.

Statues were placed around the park around 1848, and they include those of the queens of France, famous French women – *Sainte Genevieve*, patron of Paris, is an impressive example – and, later, famous writers and artists, too, totalling 106 statues.

The garden is a great space for children, with activities such as a puppet theater starring the famous character Guignol, a fenced-in playground, a carousel, and tennis courts. Adults can play chess or bridge, wander through the open-air photography exhibitions, or grab a seat and enjoy a free concert.

Sculptures on the Palais du Luxembourg

❻ Institut Catholique de Paris

21 Rue d'Assas 75006. **Map** 12 D5.
Tel 01 44 39 52 00. Ⓜ St.-Placide,
Rennes. Musée Bible et Terre Sainte
Open Call to check times. **Tel** 01 45
44 09 55. Ⓦ icp.fr

Founded in 1875, this is
one of the most distinguished
teaching institutions in
France with some 23,000
students. It also houses a
small museum, the Musée
Bible et Terre Sainte, which
displays numerous objects
excavated in the Holy Land.
They give an interesting insight
into daily life in Palestine
throughout the ages.

❼ St.-Joseph-des-Carmes

70 Rue de Vaugirard 75006. **Map** 12
D5. **Tel** 01 45 44 89 77. Ⓜ St.-Placide.
Open 9.30am–1.30pm Mon, Tue, &
Fri, 11am–6pm Wed, 9.30am–7pm
Thu. **Closed** Easter Mon, Pentecost.
✝ various times. ♿ restricted. 📷
3pm Sat. Ⓦ sjdc.fr

Completed in 1620, this church
was built as the chapel for a
Carmelite convent but was
used as a prison during the
Revolution. In 1792, more than
a hundred priests met a grisly
end in the church's courtyard
as part of the September
Massacres (see pp32–3). Their
remains are now in the crypt.

Facade of St.-Joseph-des-Carmes, a site of
the September Massacres in 1792

Carpeaux's fountain sculpture

❽ Musée du Luxembourg

19 Rue de Vaugirard 75006. **Map** 12 E5.
Tel 01 40 13 62 00. Ⓜ St.-Sulpice. RER
Luxembourg. **Open** 10am–7.30pm
daily (to 10pm Mon & Fri). Times
vary depending on exhibitions;
check website ahead of visit. **Closed**
May 1 & Dec 25. ♿ 🅿 📷 🖥 ✉
📷 Ⓦ museeduluxembourg.fr

In 1615, under the orders of
Marie de Médicis, architect
Salomon de Brosse built the
Palais du Luxembourg. The two
adjoining galleries were created
to hang the Queen's collection of
paintings by Rubens. In 1750, the
east wing became France's first
public gallery, housing works
by artists such as Leonardo da
Vinci, Van Dyck, and Rembrandt.
Following extensive renovations,
today it hosts impressive
temporary exhibitions.

❾ Fontaine de l'Observatoire

Ave de l'Observatoire/Rue d'Assas.
Map 16 E2. RER Port Royal.

Located at the southern tip of
the Jardin du Luxembourg, this
is one of the liveliest fountains in
Paris. Made of bronze, it has four
women holding aloft a globe
representing four continents –

a fifth, Oceania, was left out for
reasons of symmetry. There are
some subsidiary figures, including
dolphins, horses, and a turtle.
The sculpture was erected in
1873 by Jean-Baptiste Carpeaux.

❿ Val-de-Grâce

1 Pl Alphonse-Laveran 75005. **Map** 16
F2. **Tel** 01 40 51 51 92. Ⓜ Gobelins.
RER Port Royal. **Open** noon–6pm Tue–
Thu, Sat–Sun. 🅿 ✝ frequent, pm;
11am Sun (except Aug). 📷 by appt
noon–6pm Tue, Wed, Sat & Sun
(01 40 51 51 92). Museum: **Open** as
church. **Closed** Jan 1, May 1, Dec 25.
Concerts. Ⓦ valdegrace.org

One of France's most beautiful
churches, Val-de-Grâce was built
for Anne of Austria (wife of Louis
XIII) in thanks for the birth of her
son. Young Louis XIV laid the first
stone in 1645. François Mansart
is the great architect behind it.

The church is noted for its
imposing lead-and-gilt dome,
which stands at an impressive
135 ft (41 m). In the cupola is
Pierre Mignard's fresco, with over
200 triple-life-size figures. The six
huge marble columns that frame
the altar are similar to those at
St. Peter's in Rome. Henrietta of
France (wife of Charles I) is buried
here, along with 26 members of
the French royal family.

Today, the church is part of
a military hospital complex,
which also houses a museum
of military medicine.

⓫ Ecole Nationale Supérieure des Mines

60 Blvd St.-Michel. **Map** 16 F1. **Tel** 01 40
51 91 39. RER Luxembourg. Museum:
Open 1.30–6pm Tue–Fri, 10am–
12.30pm & 2–5pm Sat. Times vary in
Jul & Aug. **Closed** public hols. 🅿 📷
call 01 40 51 92 90 to request a visit.
Ⓦ musee.mines-paristech.fr

Louis XIV set up the School of
Mines in 1783 to train mining
engineers. Today, it is one of the
most prestigious *grandes écoles*
– schools that provide the elite
for the civil service and
professions. It also houses the
national Musée de Minéralogie.

MONTPARNASSE

This historic area takes its name from the Mount Parnassus of Ancient Greece, the home of Apollo, god of poetry and music. After 1910, Paris's artistic community moved from Montmartre to Montparnasse, where they would frequent cafés such as La Closerie des Lilas and La Coupole. These days, Montparnasse has gone upscale, but the intellectual and artsy crowd still congregates

in these legendary cafés, and in art galleries such as the Fondation Cartier, where the building is as much a work of art as the exhibitions themselves. The Tour de Montparnasse offers panoramic views of the city, and Montparnasse Cemetery is the final resting place for some of the famous artists and writers who gathered here, such as Jean-Paul Sartre, Simone de Beauvoir, and Man Ray.

Sights at a Glance

Historic Buildings and Streets
- ③ Rue Campagne-Première
- ⑨ Notre-Dame du Travail
- ⑪ Catacombes de Paris
- ⑫ Observatoire de Paris

Museums and Galleries
- ② Musée Zadkine
- ⑥ Musée Antoine Bourdelle
- ⑦ Musée de la Poste
- ⑧ Institut Pasteur
- ⑩ Fondation Cartier

Modern Architecture
- ⑤ Tour Montparnasse

Historic Cafés and Restaurants
- ① La Coupole
- ⑬ La Closerie des Lilas

Cemeteries
- ④ Cimetière du Montparnasse pp182–3

Restaurants see pp305–6
1. L'Arbre de Sel
2. L'Assiette
3. La Cantine du Troquet
4. La Cerisaie
5. Chez Marcel
6. Le Dôme
7. L'Epicuriste
8. Le Jeu de Quilles
9. Moustache
10. Le Parc aux Cerfs
11. Le Sélect
12. Tavola di Gio
13. Le Timbre
14. Les Zazous

See also Street Finder maps 15–16

Street by Street: Montparnasse

Renowned for its mix of art and high living, Montparnasse continues to live up to its name: Mount Parnassus was the mountain dedicated by the ancient Greeks to Apollo, god of poetry, music, and beauty. That mix was especially potent in the 1920s and 1930s, when such artists and writers as Picasso, Hemingway, Cocteau, Giacometti, Matisse, and Modigliani were to be seen in the local bars, cafés, and cabarets.

❺ ★ Tour Montparnasse
One of Europe's tallest tower blocks rests on 56 piles that extend 203 ft (62 m) below the surface.

Metro Edgar Quinet

❹ ★ Cimetière du Montparnasse
This fine sculpture, *The Separation of a Couple* by De Max, stands in the smallest of the city's major cemeteries.

RUE DU DEPART

RUE D'ODESSA

RUE DU MONTPARNASSE

BLVD. EDGAR QUIN

RUE DE LA GAITE

The Théâtre Montparnasse
at No. 31, has fully restored original 1880s decor.

Académie de la Grande-Chaumière at No. 14 offers tuition in painting and sculpture. Former students of note include Alberto Giacometti and Amedeo Modigliani.

Locator Map
See Central Paris Map pp16–17

Rue Bréa has a variety of stores, restaurants and hotels, all within 300 ft (90 m).

The statue of Balzac by Auguste Rodin was erected in 1939, and stands 10 ft (3 m) tall.

❶ ★ **La Coupole**
This traditional brasserie-style café, with its large enclosed terrace, opened in 1927 and became a famous meeting place for artists and writers.

❸ ★ **Rue Campagne-Première**
The block of artists' studios at No. 31 was built in 1911, and the facade was decorated by the ceramicist Paul Bigot.

Metro Vavin

RUE BRÉA

RUE NOTRE DAME DES CHAMPS

RUE J. CHAPLAIN

RUE DE LA GDE CHAUMIERE

PARNASSE

RUE DELAMBRE

RUE HUYGHENS

BLVD RASPAIL

RUE LÉOPOLD ROBERT

Metro Raspail

| 0 meters | 100 |
| 0 yards | 100 |

Key

— Suggested route

❶ La Coupole

102 Blvd du Montparnasse 75014.
Map 16 D2. **Tel** 01 43 20 14 20.
Ⓜ Vavin, Montparnasse. **Open**
8am–11pm daily (to midnight Sat &
Sun). *See Where to Eat and Drink p305.*

Established in 1927, this historic
café-restaurant and dance hall
underwent a face-lift in the
1980s. Its red velvet seats and
famous columns, decorated by
various artists, have survived.
Among its clientele have been
Jean-Paul Sartre, Josephine
Baker, and Roman Polanski.

❷ Musée Zadkine

100 bis Rue d'Assas 75116. **Map** 16 E1.
Tel 01 55 42 77 20. Ⓜ Notre-Dame-
des-Champs. **Open** 10am–6pm Tue–
Sun. **Closed** public hols. 🅿 🅲 by
appt, Tel 01 49 54 75 92. ♿ limited.
Ⓦ **zadkine.paris.fr**

The Russian-born sculptor
Ossip Zadkine lived here from
1928 until his death in 1967.
The small house, studio, and
garden contain his works.
Here he produced his great
commemorative sculpture,
Ville Détruite, commissioned by
Rotterdam after World War II,
and two monuments to Vincent
Van Gogh, one for Holland and
one for Auvers-sur-Oise, where
Van Gogh died. The museum's
works span the development of
Zadkine's style, from his Cubist
beginnings to Expressionism
and Abstractionism.

❸ Rue Campagne-Première

75014. **Map** 16 E2. Ⓜ Raspail.

This street has some interesting
Art Deco buildings and a long
artistic tradition. Modigliani,
ravaged by opium and
tuberculosis, lived at No. 3 during
his last years. Between the wars
many artists resided here, such as
Picasso, Joan Miró, and Kandinsky.

❹ Cimetière du Montparnasse

See pp182–3.

❺ Tour Montparnasse

33 Ave du Maine 75014. **Map** 15 C2.
Ⓜ Montparnasse-Bienvenüe. **Tel** 01
45 38 52 56. **Open** Apr–Sep: 9.30am–
11.30pm daily; Oct–Mar: 9.30am–
10.30pm daily (to 11pm Fri & Sat); last
elevator 30 min before closing). 🅿 🅲
🖥 🅲 Ⓦ **tourmontparnasse56.com**

This was Europe's largest office
block when it was built in 1973
as the focal point of a new
business sector. At 690 ft (210 m)
high, it dominates the area's
skyline. The views from the 56th
floor are spectacular – up to
25 miles (40 km) on a clear day.
The tower also has Europe's
fastest elevator (56 floors in
38 seconds) and a panoramic bar.

❻ Musée Antoine Bourdelle

18 Rue Antoine Bourdelle 75015.
Map 15 B1. **Tel** 01 49 54 73 73.
Ⓜ Montparnasse-Bienvenüe.
Open 10am–6pm Tue–Sun.
Closed public hols. 🅿 ♿ limited.
Ⓦ **bourdelle.paris.fr**

The prolific sculptor Antoine
Bourdelle lived and worked in
the studio here from 1884 until
his death in 1929. The house,
studio, and garden are now a
museum devoted to his life and
work. Among the 900 sculptures
on display are the original plaster
casts of his monumental works
planned for wide public squares.
They are housed in the Great

Sculptures in the Great Hall of the
Musée Antoine Bourdelle

Panoramic view of Paris from the
56th floor of Tour Montparnasse

Hall in an extension and include
the group of sculptures for the
relief decoration of the Théâtre
des Champs-Elysées.

❼ Musée de la Poste

34 Blvd de Vaugirard 75015. **Map** 15 B2.
Tel 01 42 79 24 24 or 01 53 71 98 49.
Ⓜ Montparnasse-Bienvenüe.
Closed for renovations until 2017;
temporary exhibitions take place at
various venues in Paris until 2017.
🅿 🅲 by appt. Library.
Ⓦ **ladressemusee delaposte.fr**

Every conceivable aspect of the
history of the French postal
service and its transportation is
covered in this well laid-out
collection. There is even a room
devoted to mail delivery in times
of war – carrier pigeons were
used during the Franco-Prussian
War with postmarks stamped
on their wings. Postage stamp
art is displayed in the gallery.

❽ Institut Pasteur

25–28 Rue du Docteur Roux 75015.
Map 15 A2. **Tel** 01 45 68 80 00.
Ⓜ Pasteur. **Open** 2–5.30pm Mon–Fri.
Closed Aug, public hols. 🅿 🅲
compulsory (2, 3, & 4pm); ID required.
Tours of 10+ people: apply 3 months
in advance (01 45 68 82 83 or musee@
pasteur.fr). 🌐 🅿 Ⓦ **pasteur.fr**

The Institut Pasteur, France's
leading medical research center,
was founded by the scientist

Louis Pasteur in 1888–9. He discovered the process of milk pasteurization, as well as vaccines against rabies and anthrax. The center houses a museum that includes a reconstruction of Pasteur's apartment and laboratory. It was designed by his grandchildren (also scientists) and is faithful to the original down to the last detail. Pasteur's tomb is in a basement crypt built in the style of a small Byzantine chapel. The tomb of Dr. Emile Roux, who discovered the treatment for diphtheria, is in the garden. The institute has laboratories for pure and applied research, lecture theaters, a reference section, and a hospital established to apply Pasteur's theories. There is also a library – the institute's original building from 1888 – where research into AIDS is carried out, led by pioneering Professor Luc Montagnier, who discovered the HIV virus in 1983.

❾ Notre-Dame du Travail

36 Rue Guilleminot 75014. **Map** 15 B3. **Tel** 01 44 10 72 92. Ⓜ Pernety. **Open** 7.30am–7.45pm Mon–Fri, 9am–7.30pm Sat, 8.30am–7.30pm Sun. ⬆ 9am, 12.15pm, 7pm Mon–Fri (only at 7pm on Wed during school hols); 6.30pm Sat; 9am (in Portuguese), 10.45am, 6pm Sun (in Latin). Ⓦ **notredame dutravail.net**

This church dates from 1901 and is made of an unusual mix of materials: stone, rubble, and bricks over a riveted steel and iron framework. It was the creation of Father Soulange-Boudin, a priest who organized cooperatives and sought to reconcile labor and capitalism. Local parishioners raised the money for its construction, but lack of funds meant that many features, such as the bell towers, were never built. On the facade hangs the Sebastopol Bell, a trophy from the Crimean War given to the people of the Plaisance district by Napoleon III. The Art Nouveau interior has been completely restored and features paintings of saints.

❿ Fondation Cartier

261 Blvd Raspail 75014. **Map** 16 E3. **Tel** 01 42 18 56 50. Ⓜ Raspail. **Open** 11am–8pm Tue–Sun (to 10pm Tue). **Closed** Jan 1, Dec 25. 🅿 ♿ ✉ 📷 Ⓦ **fondation.cartier.com**

This foundation for contemporary art is housed in a building designed by architect Jean Nouvel. He has created an air of transparency and light, as well as incorporating a cedar of Lebanon planted in 1823 by François-René de Chateaubriand. The structure complements the nature of the exhibitions of progressive art, which showcase personal, group, or thematic displays, often including works by young unknowns.

⓫ Catacombes de Paris

1 Ave du Colonel Henri Rol-Tanguy 75014. **Map** 16 E4. **Tel** 01 43 22 47 63. Ⓜ Denfert-Rochereau. **Open** 10am–5pm Tue–Sun (last adm: 4pm). **Closed** public hols. 🅿 Ⓦ **catacombes.paris.fr**

In 1786 a monumental project began here: the removal of the millions of skulls and bones from the unsanitary city cemetery in Les Halles to the quarries at the base of the three "mountains": Montparnasse, Montrouge, and Montsouris.

During World War II, the French Resistance set up its headquarters here. Above the door outside are the words "Stop! This is the empire of death."

Skulls and bones stored in the Catacombes de Paris

⓬ Observatoire de Paris

77 Ave Denfert-Rochereau 75014. **Map** 16 E3. **Tel** 01 40 51 22 21 (2–4pm Mon–Fri). Ⓜ Denfert-Rochereau. **Closed** to the public for renovations; call for latest details. 🅿 📷 visite. paris@obspm.fr Ⓦ **obspm.fr**

In 1667 Louis XIV was persuaded by his scientists and astronomers that France needed a royal observatory. Building began on June 21, the day of the summer solstice, and took five years to complete.

One of the leading astronomy centers in the world, research undertaken here included the calculation of the exact dimensions of the solar system in 1672, calculations of the dimensions of longitude, the mapping of the moon in 1679 and the discovery of the planet Neptune in 1846.

The facade of the Observatoire

⓭ La Closerie des Lilas

171 Blvd du Montparnasse 75014. **Map** 16 E2. **Tel** 01 40 51 34 50. Ⓜ Vavin. Ⓡ Port Royal. **Open** Piano bar: 11–1.30am, restaurant: noon–2.30pm & 7–10.30pm, brasserie: noon–12.30am. Ⓦ **closeriedeslilas.fr**

Lenin, Trotsky, Hemingway, and F. Scott Fitzgerald all frequented the Montparnasse bars, but the Closerie was their favorite. Much of Hemingway's novel *The Sun Also Rises* takes place here– he wrote it on the terrace in just six weeks. Today the terrace is ringed with trees and the area is more elegant than in the 1920s, but much of the original decor remains.

❹ Cimetière du Montparnasse

The Montparnasse Cemetery was planned by
Napoleon outside the city walls to replace the
numerous, congested small cemeteries within
the old city, viewed as a health hazard at the
turn of the 19th century. It was opened in 1824
and became the resting place of many
illustrious Parisians, particularly Left Bank
personalities. Like all French cemeteries, it is
divided into rigidly aligned paths forming
blocks or divisions. The Rue Emile Richard cuts
it into two parts, the Grand Cimetière and the
Petit Cimetière.

★ Charles Baudelaire Cenotaph
This is a monument
to the great poet and
critic (1821–67),
author of *The Flowers
of Evil*.

AVE   DU   MID

AVE THIERRY

RUE EMILE RICHARD

★ Charles Pigeon Family Tomb
This wonderfully pompous belle époque tomb
depicts the French industrialist and inventor in
bed with his wife.

KEY

① **Charles-Augustin Sainte-Beuve**
was a critic of the French Romantic
generation, and is generally
described as the "father of
modern criticism."

② **André Citroën**, an engineer and
industrialist who died in 1935,
founded the famous auto company.

③ **Frédéric Auguste Bartholdi** was
the sculptor of the Statue of Liberty
(1886) in New York.

④ **Alfred Dreyfus** was a Jewish
army officer whose unjust trial for
treason in 1894 provoked a political
and social scandal.

⑤ **The Pétain tomb** contains
the family of the marshal who
collaborated with the Germans
during World War II. Pétain himself
is buried on Ile d'Yeu, where he
was imprisoned.

⑥ **Guy de Maupassant** was a
19th-century novelist.

⑦ **Samuel Beckett**, the great Irish
playwright renowned for *Waiting for
Godot*, spent most of his life in Paris.
He died in 1989.

⑧ **The Tower** is all that remains of
a 17th-century windmill. It was part
of the old property of the Brothers
of Charity on which the cemetery
was built.

⑨ **Tristen Tzara,** the Romanian
writer, was leader of the literary and
artistic Dada movement in Paris
in the 1920s.

⑩ **Man Ray** was an American
photographer who immortalized the
Montparnasse artistic and café scene
in the 1920s and 1930s.

⑪ **Charles Baudelaire,** the
19th-century poet, is buried here in
his detested stepfather's family tomb,
along with his beloved mother.

⑫ **Chaïm Soutine**, a poor Jewish
Lithuanian, was a Montparnasse
Bohemian painter of the 1920s.
He was a friend of the Italian
artist Modigliani.

⑬ **Camille Saint-Saëns**, the pianist,
organist, and composer who died in
1921, was one of France's great post-
Romantic musicians.

The Kiss by Brancusi
This is the famous
Primitivo-Cubist
sculpture (a response
to Rodin's *Kiss*) by the
great Romanian artist,
who died in 1957 and
is buried just off the
Rue Emile Richard.

★ **Serge Gainsbourg**
The French singer, composer, and pop icon of the 1970s and 1980s is best known for his wistful and irreverent songs. He was married to the actress Jane Birkin.

VISITORS' CHECKLIST

Practical Information
3 Blvd Edgar Quinet.
Map 16 D3.
Tel 01 44 10 86 50.
Open Mid-Mar–mid-Nov: 8am–6pm Mon–Fri, 8:30am–6pm Sat, 9am–6pm Sun; mid-Nov–mid-Mar closes 5:30pm. 🅿 ♿

Transportation
Ⓜ Edgar Quinet. 🚌 28, 58, 68, 82, 83, 88, 91 to Port Royal. RER Port Royal. 🅿 Rue Campagne-Première, Blvd St.-Jacques.

Génie du Sommeil Eternel
Horace Daillion's wistful bronze angel of Eternal Sleep (1902) is the cemetery's centerpiece.

Henri Laurens
The French sculptor (1885–1954) was a leading figure in the Cubist movement.

Jean Seberg
The Hollywood actress, chosen by Jean-Luc Godard as the star of his film *A Bout de Souffle*, was the epitome of American blonde beauty, youth, and candor.

JEAN PAUL SARTRE
1905 – 1980
SIMONE DE BEAUVOIR
1908 – 1986

★ **Jean-Paul Sartre and Simone de Beauvoir**
The famous existentialist couple, undisputed leaders of the postwar literary scene, lie here close to their Left Bank haunts.

INVALIDES AND EIFFEL TOWER QUARTER

Running along the Seine, this quarter in the 7th arrondissement is full of splendid government buildings: members of Parliament make laws in the Assemblée Nationale Palais-Bourbon, modeled on the Grand Trianon de Versailles, while the Prime Minister lives in the elegant Hôtel Matignon. The government theme continues with the Hôtel des Invalides, with its stunning golden dome, a major landmark. Built as a military hospital and home for French war veterans, it now houses Napoleon's tomb and several military history museums. But the reason most people visit the area is to ascend the Eiffel Tower, which also provides a spectacular light show every night.

Sights at a Glance

Historic Buildings and Streets
6 Hôtel des Invalides
8 Hôtel Matignon
9 Le Bon Marché
12 Assemblée Nationale
Palais-Bourbon
13 Rue Cler
16 Champ-de-Mars
18 No. 29 Avenue Rapp
19 Ecole Militaire

Church and Temples
1 Dôme des Invalides pp188–9
2 St.-Louis-des-Invalides
11 Sainte-Clotilde

Modern Architecture
20 UNESCO

Monuments and Fountains
17 Eiffel Tower pp196–7

Museums and Galleries
3 Musée de l'Ordre de la Libération
4 Musée de l'Armée
5 Musée des Plans-Reliefs
7 Musée Rodin
10 Musée Maillol
14 Musée des Egouts
15 Musée du quai Branly pp194–5

Restaurants see pp302–3
1 L'Affable
2 L'Affriolé
3 L'Ami Jean
4 L'Arpège
5 La Billebaude
6 Au Bon Accueil
7 Café Constant
8 Les Cocottes de Christian Constant
9 Coutume
10 Le Florimond
11 La Fontaine de Mars
12 Giallo Oro
13 Le Jules Verne
14 Pasco
15 Au Petit Sud Ouest
16 Le Troquet
17 La Villa Corse

See also Street Finder
maps 10, 11

The Eiffel Tower in the Champs-de-Mars

For keys to symbols see back flap

Street by Street: Invalides

The imposing Hôtel des Invalides, from which the area takes its name, was built from 1671 to 1676 by Louis XIV for his wounded and homeless veterans and as a monument to his own glory. At its center, the glittering golden roof of the Sun King's Dôme des Invalides marks the final resting place of Napoleon Bonaparte. The emperor's body was brought here from St. Helena in 1840, 19 years after he died, and placed inside the majestic sarcophagus, designed by Joachim Visconti, that lies at the center of the Dôme's circular glass-topped crypt. Just to the east of the *Hôtel* on the corner of the Boulevard des Invalides, the superb Musée Rodin offers artistic relief from the pomp and circumstance of the surrounding area.

General de Gaulle's Liberation Order and compass

Metro La Tour Maubourg

The facade of the Hôtel is 645 ft (196 m) long and is topped by dormer windows, each decorated in the shape of a different trophy. A head of Hercules sits above the central entrance.

❹ ★ **Musée de l'Armée**
This vast museum covers military history from the Stone Age to World War II. It contains the third-largest collection of armory in the world.

❸ **Musée de l'Ordre de la Libération**
The Order was set up to honor feats of heroism during World War II.

❷ ★ **St.-Louis-des-Invalides**
From St.-Louis, the soldier's chapel, it is possible to see into the Dôme, which was built as Louis XIV's private chapel.

AVE DE TOURVILLE

AVE DE SEGOR

0 meters 100
0 yards 100

❻ Hôtel des Invalides
After the two World Wars, Louis XIV's *Hôtel*
was returned to its original use
as a hospital for veterans.

Locator Map
See Central Paris Map pp16–17

Key

— Suggested route

Metro Varenne

The Invalides gardens were designed by
de Cotte in 1704 and are lined by bronze
cannons from the 17th and 18th centuries.

❺ Musées des Plans-Reliefs
This museum contains military models
of forts and towns, as well as a display
on model-making.

❼ ★ Musée Rodin
By the time he died
in 1917, Auguste
Rodin had revolu-
tionized the art of
sculpture. All his
key works, including
The Thinker (c.1880),
are on display.

The Cour d'Honneur is still used
for military parades. Seurre's statue
of Napoleon, known as the Little
Corporal, stands above the south side.

❶ ★ Dôme des Invalides and Napoleon's Tomb
The Dôme took 27 years to build. In the crypt lies
Napoleon, whose final wish was to have his ashes
"rest on the banks of the Seine."

❶ Dôme des Invalides

Jules Hardouin-Mansart was asked in 1676 by the Sun King, Louis XIV, to build the Dôme des Invalides among the existing buildings of the Invalides military complex. A soldiers' church had already been built, but the Dôme was to be reserved for the exclusive use of the Sun King and for the location of royal tombs. The resulting masterpiece complements the surrounding buildings and is one of the greatest examples of 17th-century French architecture.

After Louis XIV's death, plans to bury the royal family in the church were abandoned, and it became a monument to Bourbon glory. In 1840, Louis-Philippe decided to install Napoleon's remains in the crypt, and the addition of the tombs of Vauban, Marshal Foch, and other figures of military prominence has since turned this church into a French military memorial.

Gilded Dome
The cupola was first gilded in 1706.

① Tomb of Joseph Bonaparte
The sarcophagus of Napoleon's older brother, the King of Naples and later of Spain, is in the side chapel to the right as visitors enter.

Key

— Tour route

Main entrance

② Memorial to Vauban
Commissioned by Napoleon I in 1808, this contains an urn with Sébastien le Prestre de Vauban's heart. He was Louis XIV's great military architect and engineer who died in 1707. His long military career culminated in his appointment as Marshal of France in 1703. He revolutionized siege warfare when he introduced his ricochet-batteries. His reclining figure by Antoine Etex lies on top of the memorial, mourned by Science and War.

⑥ Glass Gallery
Access to the glass-topped crypt containing Napoleon's tomb is by the curved stairs in front of the ltar. The glass partition behind the altar separates the Dôme from the older Invalides chapel beyond.

VISITORS' CHECKLIST

Practical Information

6 Blvd des Invalides, Esplanade des Invalides. **Map** 11 A4. **Tel** 08 10 11 33 99. Hôtel National des Invalides: **Open** Apr–Oct: 10am–6pm (Jul & Aug: to 7pm; Apr–Sep: to 9pm Tue); Nov–Mar: 10am–5pm. **Closed** 1st Mon of month, Jan 1, May 1, Dec 25. 🅿️ 🚹 limited (01 47 05 36 47). 📷 groups. 💻 📷 W **musee-armee.fr**

Transportation

Ⓜ La Tour- Maubourg, Varenne. 🚌 28, 63, 69, 80, 82, 83, 87, 92, 93 to Les Invalides. 🚇 Invalides. ⬛ Tour Eiffel. 🅿️ Rue de Constantine.

⑤ St-Jérôme's Chapel
Passing across the center of the church, the side chapel to the left of the main entrance contains the tomb of Napoleon's younger brother, Jérôme, King of Westphalia, presenting his sword to Christ.

Stairs to crypt

④ Dôme Ceiling
Looking upward, Charles de la Fosse's circular painting (1692) on the ceiling shows the Glory of Paradise, with St. Louis presenting his sword to Christ.

Napoleon's Return

King Louis-Philippe decided to bring the Emperor Napoleon's body back from St. Helena *(see pp34–5)* as a gesture of reconciliation to the Republican and Bonapartist parties contesting his regime. The Dôme des Invalides, with its historical and military associations, was an obvious choice for Napoleon's final resting place. His body was encased in six coffins and finally placed in the crypt in 1861, in the culmination of a grand ceremony that was attended by Napoleon III.

③ Tomb of Marshal Foch
Ferdinand Foch's imposing bronze tomb was built by Paul Landowski in 1937.

The impressive altar of St.-Louis-des-Invalides

❷ St.-Louis-des-Invalides

Hôtel des Invalides, 129 Rue de Grenelle/6 Blvd des Invalides 75007. **Map** 11 A3. Ⓜ La Tour-Maubourg, Varenne. **Tel** 08 10 11 33 99/01 44 42 38 77. **Open** 10am–6pm daily (Nov–Mar: to 5pm). **Closed** Jan 1, May 1, Dec 25. Ⓦ **musee-armee.fr**

The "soldiers' church" was built 1679–1708 by Jules Hardouin-Mansart from the original designs by Libéral Bruand. The imposing, but stark, interior is decorated with banners seized in battle. The first performance of Berlioz's *Requiem* was given on the fine 17th-century organ in 1837, with an orchestra accompanied by a battery of outside artillery.

❸ Musée de l'Ordre de la Libération

Hôtel des Invalides, 129 Rue de Grenelle/Place Vauban 75007. **Map** 11 A3. **Tel** 01 47 05 04 10. Ⓜ La Tour-Maubourg. **Open** Apr–Sep: 10am–6pm daily (to 6.30pm Sun); Oct–Mar: 10am–5pm daily (to 5.30pm Sun). **Closed** 1st Mon of month, public hols. Ⓐ Ⓒ Ⓦ **ordredelaliberation.fr**

This museum is devoted to the wartime Free French and their

leader, General Charles de Gaulle. The Order of Liberation was created by de Gaulle in 1940. It is France's highest honor and was bestowed on those who made an outstanding contribution to the final victory in World War II.

Among the recipients of the honor are French civilians and members of the armed forces, plus some overseas leaders such as Dwight Eisenhower, King George VI, and Winston Churchill.

❹ Musée de l'Armée

Hôtel des Invalides, 129 Rue de Grenelle/6 Bd des Invalides 75007. **Map** 11 A3. **Tel** 08 10 11 33 99. Ⓜ La Tour-Maubourg, Varenne. Ⓡ Invalides. **Open** 10am–6pm (to 9pm Tue) daily (Nov–Mar: to 5pm; last adm: 30 min before closing time). Times may vary; check website ahead of visit. **Closed** 1st Mon of month (except Jul, Aug, Sep), Jan 1, May 1, Dec 25. Ⓐ (Ticket includes entry to the Musée de l'Ordre de la Libération and the Musée des Plans-Reliefs.) Ⓖ ground floor only. Ⓒ Ⓓ Ⓕ Film. Ⓦ **musee-armee.fr**

This is one of the most comprehensive museums of military history in the world, with exhibits ranging from the Stone Age to the final days of World War II.

Located in the northeast refectory, the Ancient Armory department is worth visiting for the collection on display, one of the largest in the world, as much as for the 17th-century murals by Joseph Parrocel adorning the walls. These celebrate Louis XIV's military conquests.

The life of Charles de Gaulle and his role in World War II are documented in the *Historial de Gaulle*, a movie and multimedia attraction (closed on Mondays).

The Département Moderne is in two parts: the first (1648–1792) covers the reign of Louis XIV, while the second (1792–1871) displays a collection of Napoleon's mementos. Items include his famous frock coat and felt hats, as well as his stuffed dog.

A map of Alessandria, Italy (1813)

❺ Musée des Plans-Reliefs

Hôtel des Invalides 75007. **Map** 11 A3. **Tel** 01 45 51 95 05 or 01 45 51 92 45. Ⓡ Invalides. **Open** 10am–6pm (Nov–Mar: 5pm) daily. **Closed** 1st Mon of month (except Jul, Aug, Sep), Jan 1, May 1, Nov 1, Dec 25. Ⓐ Ⓒ Ⓦ **museedesplansreliefs.culture.fr**

The detailed models of French forts and fortified towns, some dating back to Louis XIV's reign, were considered top secret until the 1950s, when they were put on public display. The oldest model is that of Perpignan, dating to 1686. It shows the fortifications drawn up by the legendary 17th-century military architect Vauban, who built the defences around several French towns, including Briançon.

The facade of the Musée de l'Ordre de la Libération

The Invalides main entrance

❻ Hôtel des Invalides

6 Blvd des Invalides, Esplanade des Invalides 75007. **Map** 11 A3. **Tel** 08 10 11 33 99. Ⓜ La Tour-Maubourg, Varenne. **Open** 7.30am–7pm daily (Apr–Sep: to 9pm Tue). Last adm: 15 min before closing. **Closed** Jan 1, May 1, Dec 25. 🅿 📷 🆆 **musee-armee.fr**

Founded by Louis XIV, this was the first military hospital and home for French war veterans and disabled soldiers who had hitherto been reduced to begging. The decree for building this vast complex was signed in 1670, and construction, following the designs of Libéral Bruand, was finished five years later.

Today, the Classical facade is one of the most impressive sights in Paris, with its four stories, cannon in the forecourt, garden, and tree-lined esplanade stretching to the Seine. The south side leads to St.-Louis-des-Invalides, the soldiers' church, which backs on to the magnificent Dôme des Invalides of Jules Hardouin-Mansart. The dome was regilded in 1989.

❼ Musée Rodin

79 Rue de Varenne 75007. **Map** 11 B3. **Tel** 01 44 18 61 10. Ⓜ Varenne. **Open** 10am–5.45pm Tue–Sun (to 8.45pm Wed). **Closed** Jan 1, May 1, Dec 25. 🅿 ♿ restricted. 📷 🎦 occas. 🆆 **musee-rodin.fr**

Auguste Rodin, widely regarded as one of the greatest French sculptors of the 19th century, lived and worked in the elegant Hôtel Biron from 1908 until his death in 1917. In return for a state-owned apartment and studio, Rodin agreed to leave his work to the nation. Nearly 300 works from Rodin's collection can now be seen in the museum. The garden consists of a rose garden, an ornamental garden, and a relaxation area with benches and contains some of Rodin's most celebrated sculptures: *The Thinker*, *The Burghers of Calais*, *The Gates of Hell*, and *Balzac*. Spread across 18 rooms, the museum combines a chronology of Rodin's creative development with a thematic exploration of his workshop. It has even re-created a space exactly as it was when Rodin lived and worked here.

❽ Hôtel Matignon

57 Rue de Varenne 75007. **Map** 11 C4. **Tel** 01 42 75 80 00. Ⓜ Solférino, Rue du Bac. **Closed** to the public, but garden open to public 1st Sat of each month.

One of the most beautiful mansions in the Faubourg area, this was built by Jean Courtonne in 1721 and has been substantially remodeled since. Former owners include Talleyrand, the statesman and diplomat who held legendary parties here, and several members of the nobility. It has been the official residence of the French Prime Minister since 1958 and has the largest private garden in Paris.

❾ Le Bon Marché

24 Rue de Sèvres 75007. **Map** 11 C5. **Tel** 01 44 39 80 00. Ⓜ Sèvres-Babylone. **Open** 10am–8pm Mon–Sat (to 9pm Thu & Fri). 🆆 **lebonmarche.com**

Welcoming as many as 15,000 customers per day, "The Good Market" (or "The Good Deal") is the swankiest department store in Paris, selling luxury goods and gourmet foods. It is also the world's oldest department store, founded in 1852 by Aristide Boucicaut and his wife. The Boucicauts used their keen sense of commerce to introduce innovative practices – fixed prices, sales, home delivery, advertising, and guarantees – that became the standard for other *grands magasins*. Designed by Louis-Charles Boileau and Gustave Eiffel, the Bon Marché is also an architectural landmark.

❿ Musée Maillol

59/61 Rue de Grenelle 75007. **Map** 11 C4. **Tel** 01 42 22 59 58. Ⓜ Sèvres-Babylone, Rue du Bac. **Open** 10am–7pm Tue–Sun, but call ahead for more information. **Closed** lunchtime; Jan 1, Dec 25. ♿ 🖥 📷 🎦 🆆 **museemaillol.com**

Once the home of novelist Alfred de Musset, this museum was created by Dina Vierny, former model of Aristide Maillol. All aspects of the artist's work are here: drawings, engravings, paintings, sculpture, and decorative objects. Also displayed is Vierny's private collection, including works by Matisse, Picasso, and Rodin.

Large allegorical figures of the city of Paris and the four seasons decorate Bouchardon's fountain in front of the house.

Rodin's *The Kiss* (1886) at the Musée Rodin

⓫ Sainte-Clotilde

12 Rue de Martignac 75007. **Map** 11 B3. **Tel** 01 44 18 62 60. Ⓜ Solférino, Varenne, Invalides. **Open** 9am–7.30pm Mon–Fri, 10am–8pm Sat & Sun. Times vary for Jul & Aug; check website. **Closed** non-religious public hols.
🕇 📷 🌐 sainte-clotilde.com

Designed by the German-born architect François-Christian Gau and the first of its kind to be built in Paris, this Neo-Gothic church was inspired by the mid-19th-century enthusiasm for the Middle Ages, made fashionable by such writers as Victor Hugo. The church is noted for its imposing twin towers, visible from across the Seine. The interior includes sculpted stations of the cross by James Pradier and stained-glass windows. The composer César Franck was the organist here for 32 years.

Sculptured figures at Sainte-Clotilde

⓬ Assemblée Nationale Palais-Bourbon

126 Rue de l'Université 75007. **Map** 11 B2. **Tel** 01 40 63 60 00. Ⓜ Assemblée-Nationale. 🚉 Invalides. **Closed** Individual guided visits are suspended indefinitely; call 01 40 63 56 00 for further details. 📷 📷
🌐 assemblee-nationale.fr

Built in 1722 for the Duchesse de Bourbon, daughter of Louis XIV, the Palais-Bourbon was confiscated during the Revolution. It has been home to the lower house of the French Parliament since 1830.
During World War II, the palace became the Nazi administration's seat of government. The grand Neo-Classical facade with its fine columns was added in 1806,

Neo-Classical facade of the Assemblée Nationale Palais-Bourbon

partly to mirror the facade of La Madeleine church facing it across the Seine. The adjacent Hôtel de Lassay is the residence of the president of the National Assembly. Group tours can be organized for a maximum of 50 people on the invitation of a member of parliament, with several months' prior notice.

⓭ Rue Cler

75007. **Map** 10 F3. Ⓜ Ecole-Militaire, La Tour-Maubourg. Market: **Open** all day Tue–Sat & Sun am. *See Stores and Markets p330*

This is the street market of the 7th arrondissement, the richest in Paris. The bulk of senior civil servants, wealthy expatriates, business leaders, and many diplomats live in this residential neighborhood. The market area occupies a cobblestone pedestrian-only precinct stretching south from the Rue de Grenelle. Popular with locals, the colorful market is frequented by the best-dressed shoppers in town. The produce is excellent, especially the pâtisseries and cheese stores.

⓮ Musée des Egouts

Pont Alma, Right Bank, opposite 93 Quai d'Orsay 75007. **Map** 10 F2. **Tel** 01 53 68 27 81. Ⓜ Alma-Marceau. 🚉 Pont de l'Alma. **Open** Oct–Apr: 11am–5pm Sat–Wed (until 6pm from May–Sep). Last adm 1 hour before closing. **Closed** Jan 1, 2 wks Jan, Dec 25. 📷 📷

One of Baron Haussmann's finest achievements, the majority of Paris's sewers (*égouts*) date from the Second Empire (*see pp36–7*). If laid end to end, the 1,300 miles (2,100 km) of sewers would stretch from Paris to Istanbul. In the 20th century, the sewers became a popular attraction. All tours explain the history of the sewers. They are limited to a small area around the Quai d'Orsay entrance and are on foot (the sewers may close after heavy rain). Be aware that they can be dangerous to explore on your own.

⓯ Musée du quai Branly

See pp194–5.

The fruit and vegetable market in the Rue Cler

oorway at No. 29 Avenue Rapp

❾ Champ-de-Mars

5007. **Map** 10 E3. Ⓜ Ecole-Militaire.
🚇 Champ-de-Mars–Tour-Eiffel.

he gardens stretching from
he Eiffel Tower to the Ecole
Militaire were originally a
parade ground for the officer
cadets of the Ecole Militaire.
The area has since been used
or horse-racing, balloon ascents,
nd the mass celebrations for
uly 14, the anniversary of the
Revolution. The first ceremony
was held in 1790 in the
presence of a glum, captive
Louis XVI. Vast exhibitions were
eld here in the late 19th
entury, including the 1889
World Fair for which the Eiffel
ower was erected. *Le Mur de
a Paix*, Jean-Michel Wilmotte's
monument to world peace,
stands at one end.

These days, the park is
popular with Parisian families
nd tourists, who come here
o relax, walk their dogs
Champ-de-Mars is one of
he few parks in Paris where
ogs are allowed), and to
articipate in the numerous
ctivities for children, which
clude playgrounds, pony rides,
uppet shows, and a carousel.
here is also an outdoor café.

Eiffel Tower

ee pp196–7.

⓲ No. 29 Avenue Rapp

75007. **Map** 10 E2. Ⓜ Pont-de-l'Alma.

A superb example of Art
Nouveau architecture can
be found at No. 29 Avenue
Rapp. This building won its
designer, architect Jules
Lavirotte, the first prize at the
Concours des Façades de la
Ville de Paris in 1901. Its
ceramics and brickwork are
elaborately decorated with
animal and flower motifs
intermingling with female
figures. These are super-
imposed on a multicolored
sandstone base to produce a
facade that is deliberately
erotic, and was certainly
subversive in its day.

Also worth visiting is another
of Lavirotte's buildings, which
can be found at No. 3 Square
Rapp – this is more restrained
but has a lovely watchtower
and wrought iron balconies.

⓳ Ecole Militaire

1 Pl Joffre 75007. **Map** 10 F4. **Tel** 01 80
50 14 00. Ⓜ Ecole-Militaire. **Closed**
Visits are suspended indefinitely; call
for up-to-date information.

Founded in 1751 to educate 500
sons of impoverished officers,
the Royal Military Academy was
designed by architect Jacques-
Ange Gabriel. The central
pavilion, a magnificent example
of the French Classical style,
has eight Corinthian pillars
and a quadrangular dome.
The interior is decorated in
Louis XVI style; of main interest
are the chapel and a Gabriel-
designed wrought-iron banister
on the main staircase.

An early cadet was Napoleon,
whose passing-out report
stated that "he could go far
if the circumstances are right."
Today, the academy is used
as a cavalry training ground.

⓴ UNESCO

7 Pl de Fontenoy 75007. **Map** 10 F5.
Tel 01 45 68 10 00, 01 45 68 10 60 (in
English). Ⓜ Ségur, Cambronne. **Open**
by 30-minute guided visits only: 10am
& 3pm Tue–Fri. 📷 **Closed** public hols;
Sat & Sun. ♿ 🎦 Booking essential:
visits@unesco.org 🔗 by reservation.
📷 Exhibitions, films. 🌐 **unesco.org**

This modern building completed
in 1958 is the headquarters of
the United Nations Educational,
Scientific, and Cultural
Organization (UNESCO). The
organization's stated aim is to
contribute to international
peace and security through
education, science, and culture.

It is a trove of modern art,
notably a huge mural by Picasso
and sculptures by Henry Moore.

Moore's *Reclining
Figure* at UNESCO
(erected 1958)

⓯ Musée du quai Branly

Widely regarded as former President Jacques Chirac's legacy to Paris's cultural scene, quai Branly has proved a major tourist pull since it opened in 2006. The stylish Jean Nouvel building displays 3,500 exhibits from the French state's vast nonwestern art collection, one of the world's most prolific. Outside, the grounds offer visitors breathing space and in summer, the museum's 500-seat auditorium opens onto an outdoor theater for music and dance. The rooftop restaurant boasts breathtaking views.

Interior
Subdued natural light creates intimacy, while an undulating open-plan design reflects the diversity and convergence of different cultures.

Scarecrow (Vietnam)
This bamboo scarecrow is used by hill minorities in South East Asia to protect the rice fields. It is adorned with powerful and protective designs like the central "solar" symbol.

Musical instrument tower

Collection of slit drums (Vanuatu, mid-20th century)
Used for dance and transmitting messages, these vertical drums produce different sounds depending on the thickness of the slit cut into them.

Ramp to main collection

Ticket desks and entrance

Sculpted hook (Papua New Guinea, early 20th century)
Tribal men would hang ritual offerings on the hook protruding from this sculpted female figure.

Head Trophy
(Nigeria, 20th century)
Ekoi tribes transformed their enemies' heads into war trophies, decorating them with wooden horns and antelope skins.

Mezzanine level

Different-sized display boxes jut out of the building facade, lending it a unique shape.

VISITORS' CHECKLIST

Practical Information
37 Quai Branly. **Map** 10 E2.
Tel 01 56 61 70 00.
W www.quaibranly.fr
Open 11am–7pm Tue, Wed, Sun, (to 9pm Thu–Sat) **Closed** Mon (except during all school vacations except summer vacation), Jan 1, Dec 25. 🚗 🅿 📷 📹 📁 💻 🎭
Exhibitions, film, library, theater.

Transportation
Ⓜ Alma-Marceau, Bir-Hakeim, Iéna. 🚌 42, 63, 72, 80, 82, 92.
🚆 Pont de l'Alma.

★ Androgynous statue (Mali, 10–11th century)
This 6.3 ft (1.91 m) wooden statue combines a regal male head with the breasts of a fertile woman. The bracelets worn around the wrist total seven, the number of perfect union.

Main collection level

Ramp from entrance level

Gallery Guide

Tickets are bought outside the main building. Once inside, visitors take a 590-ft (180-m) ramp that spirals up around a large glass tower displaying the museum's reserve of musical instruments. This leads to the main collection level, where a suggested route passes through four color-coded zones of Oceania, Asia, Africa, and the Americas. There are stairs from the main collection level to the three mezzanine galleries, all of which house temporary exhibitions.

Yup'ik mask (Alaska)
This shaman mask represents the spirit of the Moon and is used in dances performed inside the communal men's house.

Key to Floorplan

- ⬜ Asia
- ⬜ Africa
- ⬜ The Americas
- ⬜ Oceania
- ⬜ Temporary exhibition space
- ⬜ Musical instrument tower
- ⬜ Nonexhibition space

★ Museum architecture
Set on pillars above the verdant museum gardens, architect Jean Nouvel's elegant building resembles the elongated shadow of the nearby Eiffel Tower. An exterior glass wall and thickets of trees help shield the museum from the outside world.

⓱ Eiffel Tower

Originally built to impress visitors to the 1889 Universal Exhibition, the Eiffel Tower (Tour Eiffel) was meant to be a temporary addition to the Paris skyline. Built by the engineer Gustave Eiffel, it was fiercely decried by 19th-century esthetes. The author Guy de Maupassant lunched there to avoid seeing it. The world's tallest structure until 1931, when New York's Empire State Building was completed, the tower is now the symbol of Paris and attracts 7 million visitors a year. The glass floored first level houses a modern visitors' center and an interactive museum on the history of the tower.

Ironwork Pattern
According to Eiffel, the complex pattern of wrought-iron girders came from the need to stabilize the tower in strong winds. But Eiffel's design quickly won admirers for its pleasing symmetry.

Elevator Engine Room
Eiffel emphasized safety over speed when choosing the elavators for the tower.

The Daring and the Deluded

The tower has inspired many crazy stunts. It has been climbed by mountaineers, cycled down by a journalist, and used by trapeze artists and as a launch pad by parachutists. In 1912, an Austrian tailor, Franz Reichelt, attempted to fly from the parapet with only a modified cape for wings. He plunged to his death in front of a large crowd. According to the autopsy, he died of a heart attack before even touching the ground.

Birdman Reichelt

★ **Hydraulic Elevator Mechanism**
Still in working order, this part of the original 1900 mechanism was automated in 1986.

KEY

① **The third level**, 905 ft (276 m) above the ground, can hold 400 people at a time. A champagne bar and Gustave Eiffel's offices are here

② **Le Jules Verne Restaurant**, one of the best in Paris, offers superb food and panoramic views *(see p303)*.

③ **The second level** is at 376 ft (115 m), reached from the first level by 359 steps, or a short elevator ride. Souvenirs can be bought here.

④ **The first level**, at 187 ft (57 m) high, with its high-tech visitors' center, can be reached by elevator or by 345 steps.

Champ-de-Mars
The gardens of this former parade ground stretch from the base of the tower to the Ecole Militaire.

★ Viewing Gallery
On a clear day it is possible to see for
45 miles (72 km), including a distant
view of Chartres Cathedral.

Double-Decker Elevators
The limited capacity of the elevators
means it can take up to a couple of hours
to reach the top. Tickets can be reserved
ahead online. Standing in line requires
patience and a good head for heights.

The Tower in Figures

- The top (including the antennae) is 1,063 ft
  (324 m) high
- The top can move in a curve of 7 in (18 cm)
  under the effect of heat
- 1,665 steps to the third level
- 2.5 million rivets hold the tower together
- Never sways more than 2.5 in (7 cm)
- 11,000 tons in weight
- 65 tons of paint are used every
  seven years

A workman building the tower

★ Eiffel Bust
Eiffel (1832–1923) was awarded
the Légion d'Honneur in 1889.
Another honor was the bust
by Antoine Bourdelle,
placed beneath the
tower in 1929.

CHAILLOT QUARTER

The Chaillot Quarter was just a village before becoming absorbed into the city of Paris in the 19th century. This exclusive neighborhood now contains wide avenues, grand mansions and embassies, and elegant stores. The fall of his empire put a stop to Napoleon's plans to build a palace for his son on Chaillot Hill, but the site was later used for the palace of the Trocadéro, erected for the 1878 Universal Exhibition. With gorgeous views across the Seine to the Eiffel Tower, the Palais de Chaillot contains three museums, including the Musée de l'Homme, an aquarium, and the National Theater of Chaillot. Close by is the Musée d'Art Moderne, in the vast Palais de Tokyo.

Sights at a Glance

Gardens
6 Jardins du Trocadéro

Modern Architecture
1 Palais de Chaillot

Aquarium
2 Aquarium de Paris – Cinéaqua

Cemeteries
10 Cimetière de Passy

Museums and Galleries
3 Cité de l'Architecture et du Patrimoine
4 Musée de l'Homme
5 Musée National de la Marine
7 Musée du Vin
8 Maison de Balzac
9 Maison de Radio-France
11 Musée de la Contrefaçon
12 Musée Dapper

13 Galerie-Musée Baccarat
14 Musée National des Arts Asiatiques Guimet
15 Palais Galliera
16 Musée d'Art Moderne de la Ville de Paris
17 Palais de Tokyo

See also Street Finder maps 3–4, 9–10

☐ **Restaurants** see pp300–302
1 6 New York
2 Antoine
3 L'Astrance
4 Chez Géraud
5 Hiramatsu
6 Paul Chêne
7 Prunier

0 meters 500
0 yards 500

◀ Gilded bronze statues outside the Palais de Chaillot, with the Eiffel Tower in the background **For keys to symbols** see back flap

Street by Street: Chaillot

The Chaillot hill, with its superb position overlooking the Seine, was the site chosen by Napoleon for "the biggest and most extraordinary" palace that was to be built for his son – but by the time of his downfall, only a few ramparts had been completed. Today, the monumental Palais de Chaillot, with its two massive curved wings, stands on the site. From the terrace in front of the Palais there is a magnificent view over the Trocadéro gardens and the Seine to the Eiffel Tower.

The statue of Marshal Ferdinand Foch, who led the Allies to victory in 1918, was unveiled on November 11, 1951. The monument was built by Robert Wlérick and Raymond Martin to commemorate the centennial of Foch's birth and the 33rd anniversary of the 1918 Armistice.

Metro Trocadéro

The Place du Trocadéro was created for the Universal Exhibition of 1878. Initially it was known as the Place du Roi-de-Rome, in honor of Napoleon's son.

❺ Musée National de la Marine
With a focus on France's maritime history, this museum includes exhibits of navigational instruments.

PL DU TROC ADERO

PL J MARTI

AVE PAUL DOUMER

RUE FRANKLIN

BLVD DELESSERT

RUE LE

0 meters   100
0 yards   100

❶ Palais de Chaillot
This Neo-Classical building was created for the World's Fair of 1937. It replaced the Palais du Trocadéro, which was originally built in 1878.

❹ Musée de l'Homme
The vast collection of items on display here focuses on evolution and cultures of the world throughout the ages.

The Théâtre National de Chaillot, beneath the terrace, includes a multi-purpose cultural center and a modern 1,200-seat theater. *(See pp334, 336).*

Locator Map
See Central Paris Map pp16–17

❸ Cité de l'Architecture et du Patrimoine
This vast complex houses an architecture museum, a school, library, and archive, and various heritage organizations.

❻ Jardins du Trocadéro
The present layout of the gardens was created by R. Lardat after the World's Fair of 1937.

❷ Aquarium de Paris – Cinéaqua
Built to blend in with the Chaillot hillside, this aquarium also has a movie theater complex.

The Pont d'Iéna was built by Napoleon to celebrate his victory in 1806 over the Prussians at Jena (Iéna) in Prussia. It was widened in 1937 to complement the building of the Palais de Chaillot.

The Trocadéro fountains are operated in sequence, culminating in the massive water cannons in the center firing toward the Eiffel Tower. They are illuminated at night.

DU PRESIDENT WILSON

AVE ALBERT DE MUN

AVE DES NATIONS UNIES

NEW YORK

PL DE VARSOVIE

NS UNIES

PONT D'IENA

AVE DE

Key
— Suggested route

Trocadéro fountains in front of the Palais de Chaillot

❶ Palais de Chaillot

17 Place du Trocadéro 75016. **Map** 9
C2. **Tel** 01 53 65 30 00. **M** Trocadéro.

The Palais, with its huge, curved
colonnaded wings each
culminating in an immense
pavilion, was designed in Neo-
Classical style for the 1937 Paris
Exhibition by Léon Azéma,
Louis-Hippolyte Boileau, and
Jacques Carlu. It is adorned with
sculptures and bas-reliefs. On
the walls of the pavilions there
are gold inscriptions by the
poet and essayist Paul Valéry.

The *parvis*, or square, located
between the two pavilions is
decorated with large bronze
sculptures and ornamental pools.
On the terrace in front of the
parvis stand two bronzes, *Apollo*
by Henri Bouchard and *Hercules*
by Albert Pommier. Stairways
lead from the terrace to the

Théâtre National de Chaillot *(see
pp334, 336)*, which, since World
War II, has enjoyed huge fame for
its avant-garde productions.

❷ Aquarium de Paris – Cinéaqua

5 Ave Albert de Mun 75016.
Map 10 D2. **Tel** 01 40 69 23 23.
M Trocadéro, Iéna. **Open** 10am–7pm
daily; (last adm: 6pm). **Closed** Jul 14.
W cineaqua.com

Originally built in 1878 for the
Universal Exhibition, this is now
a state-of-the-art aquarium
that is home to over 500 species
of sea creatures, including
seahorses, clownfish, stonefish,
and some spectacular sharks
and rays.

The building is located in a
former quarry and has been
designed to blend in entirely
with the Chaillot hillside.

Movie screens showing
cartoons and animal documentaries are interspersed with the
aquariums. There are also art
exhibitions and shows for
children in the theater.

Church model from Bagneux, Cité de
l'Architecture et du Patrimoine

❸ Cité de l'Architecture et du Patrimoine

Palais de Chaillot, Pl du Trocadéro
75016. **Map** 9 C2. **Tel** 01 58 51 52 00.
M Trocadéro. **Open** 11am–7pm
Wed–Mon (to 9pm Thu).
W citechaillot.fr

In the east wing of the Palais
de Chaillot, this museum charts
the development of French
architecture through the ages.
Among the unmissable
displays is the Galerie des
Moulages, which covers the
period from the Middle Ages to
the Renaissance. Here you will
find three-dimensional models
of great French cathedrals,
such as Chartres. Also worth
a look is the Galerie Moderne
et Contemporaine, with
a reconstruction of a Le
Corbusier-designed apartment.

Shark basin, one of the 43 tanks at the Aquarium de Paris – Cinéaqua

❹ Musée de l'Homme

Palais de Chaillot, 17 Pl du Trocadéro 75016. **Map** 9 C2. **Tel** 01 44 05 72 72. Ⓜ Trocadéro. **Open** 10am–6pm Wed–Mon (to 9pm Wed). **Closed** Jan 1, Dec 25. 🖼 Exhibitions, films. 🖼 📷 🌐 **museedehomme.fr**

Located in the west wing of the Chaillot palace, this museum traces the process of human evolution, from prehistoric times to the present, through anthropological exhibits from around the world. It houses one of the world's most comprehensive prehistoric collections. Displays show how humans have adapted to the environment, and there is also a focus on the development of language and culture.

Gabon mask at Musée de l'Homme

Relief outside the Musée de la Marine

❺ Musée National de la Marine

Palais de Chaillot, 17 Pl du Trocadéro 75016. **Map** 9 C2. **Tel** 01 53 65 69 69. Ⓜ Trocadéro. **Open** 10am–6pm Wed–Mon. **Closed** Jan 1, May 1, Dec 25. 🖼 📷 🎫 by appt; 01 53 65 69 53. 📷 Films, videos. 🌐 **musee-marine.fr**

French maritime history from the days of the royal wooden warships to today's aircraft carriers and nuclear submarines is told through wonderfully exact scale models (most of them two centuries old), mementos of naval heroes, paintings, and navigational instruments. The museum was set up by Charles X in 1827, and was then moved to the Chaillot palace in 1943. Exhibits include Napoleon's barge, models of the fleet he assembled at Boulogne-sur-Mer in 1805 for his planned invasion of Britain, and displays on underwater exploration and fishing vessels.

❻ Jardins du Trocadéro

75016. **Map** 10 D2. Ⓜ Trocadéro.

The centerpiece of these lovely gardens is a long rectangular ornamental pool, bordered by stone and bronze-gilt statues, which look spectacular at night when the fountains are illuminated. The statues include *Man* by P. Traverse and *Woman* by G. Braque, *Bull* by P. Jouve, and *Horse* by G. Guyot. On either side of the pool, the slopes of the Chaillot hill lead down to the Seine and the Pont d'Iéna. There is an aquarium in the northeast corner of the gardens, which are laid out with trees, small streams, and bridges. There is also a lovely Christmas market in December.

❼ Musée du Vin

5 Sq Charles Dickens 75016. **Map** 9 B3. **Tel** 01 45 25 70 89. Ⓜ Passy. **Open** 10am–6pm Tue–Sat. **Closed** Jan 1, Dec 25. 🖼 🎫 ♿ 🍷 tours with wine tasting available for groups. Reserve in advance. 🍴 noon–3pm Tue–Sat. **Tel** 01 45 25 63 26. 🌐 **museeduvinparis.com**

Waxwork figures and cardboard cutouts graphically illustrate the history of wine making in these atmospheric vaulted medieval cellars, which were once used by the monks of Passy. The exhibits include a collection of old wine bottles, glasses, and corkscrews, as well as an array of scientific instruments that were used in the winemaking and bottling processes. There is also an atmospheric restaurant, wine for sale, and tours that include a wine-tasting session.

Wax figure on display in the vaulted cellar of Musée du Vin

Balzac's modest house

❽ Maison de Balzac

47 Rue Raynouard 75016. **Map** 9 B3. **Tel** 01 55 74 41 80. Ⓜ Passy, La Muette. **Open** 10am–6pm Tue–Sun (last adm: 5:30pm). **Closed** public hols. Reference library: Tue & Thu. 🖼 for temporary exhibitions. 📷 📷 📷

The novelist Honoré de Balzac lived here from 1840 to 1847 under a false name, Monsieur de Brugnol, to avoid his numerous creditors. During this time he wrote many of his most famous novels, among them *La Cousine Bette* (1846).

The house now contains a reference library, with first editions and manuscripts, and a museum with memorabilia from his life. Many of the rooms have drawings and paintings portraying Balzac's family and close friends. The Madame Hanska room is devoted to the memory of the Russian woman who corresponded with Balzac for 18 years and was his wife for the five months before his death in 1850.

The house has a back entrance leading into Rue Berton, which was used to evade unwelcome callers. Rue Berton, with its ivy-covered walls, has retained much of its old, rustic charm.

Debussy's grave in the Cimetière de Passy, in the shadow of the Eiffel Tower

❾ Maison de Radio-France

116 Ave du Président-Kennedy 75016. **Map** 9 B4. **Tel** 01 56 40 22 22. Ⓜ Ranelagh. **Open** for concerts, check website for details; Sat for visits, reserve online or **Tel** 01 56 40 15 16. ♿ Ⓦ **maisondelaradio.fr**

Maison de Radio-France is an impressive building designed by Henri Bernard in 1963 as the headquarters of France's public radio network. The largest single structure in France, it is made up of three concentric circular buildings with a rectangular tower and covers 5 acres (2 ha).

The 70-some studios and main public auditorium are the home of French national public radio. Radio France sponsors more than 100 concerts each year, including performances by the Orchestre National de France – several of these concerts are held at the Maison de Radio-France.

❿ Cimetière de Passy

2 Rue du Commandant-Shloesing 75016. **Map** 9 C2. Ⓜ Trocadéro. **Open** 8am–5:30pm Mon–Sat, 9am–5:30pm Sun (to 6pm Mar 16–Nov 5).

This small cemetery, opened in 1820, is packed with the graves of eminent Parisians, including the composers Claude Debussy and Gabriel Fauré and painter Edouard Manet. Politicians and aristocrats include Ghislaine Dommanget, Princess of Monaco, Leila Pahlavi, daughter of the Shah of Iran, and Michel Droit, writer and journalist.

⓫ Musée de la Contrefaçon

16 Rue de la Faisanderie 75016. **Map** 3 A5. **Tel** 01 56 26 14 03. Ⓜ Porte Dauphine. **Open** 2–5:30pm Tue–Sun (ring doorbell). Morning visits by appt. **Closed** public hols, 2 weeks and weekends in Aug. 📷 🎧 📱 Ⓦ **musee-contrefacon.com**

French cognac and perfume producers, and the luxury trade in general, have been plagued for years by counterfeiters operating around the world. This museum was set up by the manufacturers' union and illustrates the history of this type of fraud, which has been going on since Roman times. Among the impressive forgeries are fake wine, copies of Louis Vuitton luggage and Cartier watches.

⓬ Musée Dapper

35 bis Rue Paul-Valéry, 75116. **Map** 3 C4. **Tel** 01 45 00 91 75. Ⓜ Victor-Hugo. **Open** Temporary exhibitions: 11am–7pm Wed, Fri– Mon (to 10pm Fri & Sat). **Closed** Jan 1, Dec 25. 📷 🎧 by appt. 📱 🖥 Ⓦ **dapper.fr**

Not just a museum, but a world-class ethnographic research center called the Dapper Foundation, this lively center showcases African and Caribbean art and culture. Located in an attractive building with an "African" garden, it is a treasure-house of vibrant color and powerful, evocative work from sub-Saharan Africa. The emphasis is on precolonial folk arts, with sculpture, carvings, and tribal work, but there is later art too.

Displays include a collection of tribal masks, with a dazzling array of richly carved religious, ritual, and funerary masks, as well as theatrical masks used for comic, magical, or symbolic performances, some dating back to the 12th century.

⓭ Galerie-Musée Baccarat

11 Pl des Etats-Unis 75016. **Map** 4 D5. **Tel** 01 40 22 11 00. Ⓜ Boissière, Iéna. **Open** 10:30am–7pm Mon–Sat. **Closed** public hols. 📷 🎧 by appt. 📱 Ⓦ **baccarat.fr**

The Galerie-Musée Baccarat shows off some 1,200 articles made by the Baccarat crystal glass company, which was founded in Lorraine. These include services created for the royal and imperial courts of Europe and one-of-a-kind pieces created in the workshops.

Khmer art in the Musée National des Arts Asiatiques Guimet

⓮ Musée National des Arts Asiatiques Guimet

6 Pl d'Iéna 75116. **Map** 10 D1. **Tel** 01 56 52 53 00. Ⓜ Iéna. **Open** 10am–6pm Wed–Mon (last adm: 5:15pm). **Closed** Jan 1, May 1, Dec 25. 📷 📹 ♿ 📱 🖥 📷 Panthéon Bouddhique: (additional galleries) at 19 Ave d'Iéna **Tel** 01 40 73 88 00. **Open** Call ahead; 10am–5:45pm Wed–Mon (garden open to 5pm). Ⓦ **guimet.fr**

The Musée Guimet has the finest collection of Khmer (Cambodian) art in the West. It was originally set up in Lyon in 1879 by the industrialist and orientalist Emile Guimet.

Moved to Paris in 1884, it meticulously represents every artistic tradition from Afghanistan to India, China, Japan, and the rest of southeast Asia. With over 45,000 artworks, the museum is acclaimed for some especially unusual collections, including the Cambodian Angkor Wat sculptures and 1,600 artworks from the Himalayas. Other highlights include Chinese bronzes and lacquerware, and many statues of Buddha. Seasonal tea ceremonies are held in the Panthéon Bouddhique. Call for details.

⓯ Palais Galliera

10 Ave Pierre 1er de Serbie 75116. **Map** 10 E1. **Tel** 01 56 52 86 00. Ⓜ léna, Alma Marceau. Museum: **Open** for exhibitions only. 10am–6pm Tue-Sun (to 9pm Thu). Library & documentation center: by appt, call 01 56 52 86 46. **Closed** public hols and in between expos. 🎨 ♿ Children's workshops. Ⓦ **palaisgalliera.paris.fr**

Devoted to the evolution of fashion, this museum, also known as the Musée de la Mode de la Ville de Paris, is housed in the Renaissance-style palace built for the Duchesse Maria de Ferrari Galliera in 1892. It comprises more than 100,000 outfits, from the 18th century to the present, some donated by such fashion icons as Baronne Hélène de Rothschild and Princess Grace of Monaco. The various garments are displayed in rotation twice per year. The museum holds around three temporary exhibitions every year.

Gabriel Forestier's sculpted doors, Musée d'Art Moderne

⓰ Musée d'Art Moderne de la Ville de Paris

11 Ave du Président-Wilson 75116. **Map** 10 E1. **Tel** 01 53 67 40 00. Ⓜ léna, Alma Marceau. **Open** 10am–6pm Tue–Sun (to 10pm Thu). **Closed** public hols. 🎨 temporary exhibitions. 🅿 📷 📖 🔍 🎬 Films. Ⓦ **mam.paris.fr**

This large, lively museum houses Paris's own renowned collection of modern art. It has about 10,000 works representing major 20th-century and 21st-century artistic movements and artists. Established in 1961, the museum occupies the vast east wing of the Palais de Tokyo, which was built for the 1937 World's Fair.

One of the museum's highlights is Raoul Dufy's gigantic mural *La Fée Electricité (The Spirit of Electricity)*, which traces the history of electricity through the ages. One of the largest paintings in the world at 6,500 sq ft (600 sq meters), this curved mural takes up a whole room. Also notable are the Cubists, Amedeo Modigliani, Georges Rouault, and the Fauves. This group of avant-garde artists was dominated by Henri Matisse, whose celebrated mural *La Danse*, is on display here in both versions. There are also frequent temporary exhibitions.

Bas-relief on the walls of Palais de Tokyo

⓱ Palais de Tokyo

Palais de Tokyo, 13 Ave du Président-Wilson 75116. **Map** 10 E1. **Tel** 01 81 97 35 88. Ⓜ léna, Alma Marceau. **Open** noon–midnight Wed–Mon. **Closed** Jan 1, May 1, Dec 25, 2 wks in Dec. 🎨 🅿 📷 📖 🎬 Ⓦ **palaisdetokyo.com**

This open-space modern art museum is in an adjacent wing of the Musée d'Art Moderne de la Ville de Paris, within the imposing 1937 Palais de Tokyo building. It hosts an innovative, changing program of contemporary art exhibitions, fashion shows, and avant-garde performances. Installations by artists such as Pierre Joseph, Wang Du, and Frank Scurti have earned the Palais de Tokyo a reputation as one of the most cutting-edge art houses in Europe. Parts of the building are closed for renovation.

Garden and rear facade of the Palais Galliera

CHAMPS-ELYSEES

There are several main reasons to explore this former marshland – shopping, dining, and entertainment. The broad Avenue des Champs-Elysées, starting from the Jardin des Tuileries, is one of the most ostentatious and famous thoroughfares in the world. While this celebrated avenue dominates this part of the city, other streets of note are Rue St.-Honoré, home to the presidential Palais de l'Elysée, huge mansions, and many embassies, and Avenue Montaigne, a hub for high-end luxury boutiques. However, the area is of equal interest for its historical and cultural landmarks, such as the monumental Arc de Triomphe, the Art Nouveau Grand Palais, which hosts exhibitions, and the Petit Palais, housing the Musée des Beaux Arts de la Ville de Paris.

Sights at a Glance

Historic Buildings and Streets
5 Palais de l'Elysée
6 Avenue Montaigne
8 Avenue des Champs-Elysées
9 Place Charles de Gaulle (l'Etoile)

Monuments
10 Arc de Triomphe pp212–13

Bridges
1 Pont Alexandre III

Museums and Galleries
2 Grand Palais
3 Palais de la Découverte
4 Petit Palais
7 Musée Jacquemart-André

☐ Restaurants see pp300–302
1 Apicius
2 Café Lenôtre
3 Chez Diep
4 Le Cinq (Four Seasons George V)
5 Copenhague
6 L'Epicure (Hotel Bristol)
7 Graindorge
8 Le Hide
9 L'Huîtrier
10 Korean Barbecue Champs-Elysées
11 Lasserre
12 Mini Palais
13 Pierre Gagnaire
14 Relais de l'Entrecôte
15 Relais Plaza
16 Taillevent
17 Le Timgad

0 meters 500
0 yards 500

See also Street Finder maps 3–4, 5, 10–11

◄ Detail of a sculpture on the main facade of the Arc de Triomphe

For keys to symbols see back flap

Street by Street: Champs-Elysées

The formal gardens that line the Champs-Elysées from the Place de la Concorde to the Rond-Point have changed little since they were laid out by the architect Jacques Hittorff in 1838. They were used as the setting for the World's Fair of 1855, which included the Palais de l'Industrie, Paris's answer to London's Crystal Palace. The Palais was later replaced by the Grand Palais and Petit Palais, which were created as a showpiece of the Third Republic for the Universal Exhibition of 1900. They sit on either side of an impressive vista that stretches from Place Clémenceau across the elegant curve of the Pont Alexandre III to the Invalides.

The Théâtre du Rond-Point was the home of the Renaud-Barrault Company. There are plaques on the back door of the theater representing Napoleon's campaigns.

Metro Franklin D Roosevelt Ⓜ

❻ Avenue Montaigne
Christian Dior and other *haute couture* houses are based on this chic avenue.

❷ ★ Grand Palais
Designed by Charles Girault, this grand 19th-century building is still used for major exhibitions.

The Lasserre restaurant is decorated in the style of a luxurious ocean liner from the 1930s.

❸ Palais de la Découverte
Outside this museum of scientific discoveries is a pair of equestrian statues.

AVE DES

AVE G. EISENHOWER

AVE FRANKLIN D ROOSEVELT

RUE JEAN GOUJON

RUE FRANÇOIS PREMIER

PL DU CANADA

COURS LA REIN

PONT DES INVALIDES

LASSERRE

❽ ★ Avenue des Champs-Elysées
This was the setting for the victory parades following the two world wars, and for the bicentennial parade in 1989.

Locator Map
See Central Paris Map pp16–17

Key

— Suggested route

| 0 meters | 100 |
| 0 yards | 100 |

Metro Champs-Elysées-Clemenceau

AVE GABRIEL

AVE DE MARIGNY

Ⓜ

AVE DES CHAMPS ELYSEES

PL CLEMENCEAU

AVE WINSTON CHURCHILL

PONT ALEXANDRE III

To the Place de la Concorde →

The Jardins des Champs-Elysées, with their fountains, flower beds, paths, and pleasure pavilions, became very popular toward the end of the 19th century. Fashionable Parisians, including Marcel Proust, often came here.

❹ ★ Petit Palais
Lit by natural light, this palace is as much a work of art as the wide-ranging collections it contains, from antiquity to the belle époque.

the ↓
alides

❶ ★ Pont Alexandre III
The bridge's four columns help to anchor the piers that absorb the immense forces generated by such a large single-span structure.

Pont Alexandre III

● Pont Alexandre III

75008. **Map** 11 A1. Ⓜ Champs-Elysées-Clemenceau.

This is Paris's prettiest bridge with its exuberant Art Nouveau decoration of lamps, cherubs, nymphs, and winged horses at either end. It was built between 1896 and 1900, in time for the Universal Exhibition, and it was named after Czar Alexander III, whose son Nicholas II laid the foundation stone in October 1896.

The style of the bridge reflects that of the Grand Palais, to which it leads on the Right Bank. The construction of the bridge is a marvel of 19th-century engineering, consisting of an 18-ft (6-m) high single-span steel arch across the Seine. The design was subject to strict controls that prevented the bridge from obscuring the view of the Champs-Elysées or the Invalides, so today you can still enjoy magnificent views from here.

● Grand Palais

Porte A, Ave Général Eisenhower 75008. **Map** 11 A1. **Tel** 01 44 13 17 17. Ⓜ Champs-Elysées-Clemenceau. **Open** for temporary exhibitions (check website for opening hours). **Closed** May 1, Dec 25. 🎨 ✉ ♿ 🎦 usually 6pm Wed–Fri, 11am & 4:45pm Sat but call to check. 🎧 ⬛ 🎭 Ⓦ **grandpalais.fr**

Built at the same time as the Petit Palais and the Pont Alexandre III, the exterior of this massive palace combines an imposing Classical stone facade

with a riot of Art Nouveau ironwork. The enormous glass roof (160,000 sq ft/15,000 sq m) has Récipon's colossal bronze statues of flying horses and chariots at its four corners. The metal structure supporting the glass weighs 9,300 tons, some 550 tons more than the Eiffel Tower. Today, the restored Grand Palais hosts contemporary art exhibitions and other events; major temporary and touring exhibitions are held at the Galeries Nationales in the same building.

● Palais de la Découverte

Ave Franklin D. Roosevelt 75008. **Map** 11 A1. **Tel** 01 44 43 20 20. Ⓜ Franklin D. Roosevelt. **Open** 9:30am– 6pm Tue–Sat (to 7pm Sat), 10am–7pm Sun. **Closed** Jan 1, May 1, Jul 14, Aug 15, Dec 25. 🎨 by permission. 🎫 ⬛ Ⓦ **palais-decouverte.fr**

Opened in a wing of the Grand Palais for the World's Fair of 1937, this science museum is a much-loved Paris institution. Demonstrations and displays, including a planetarium, cover many subjects and explain such phenomena as electromagnetism.

Palais de la Découverte

Grand Palais

Entrance to the Petit Palais

● Petit Palais

Ave Winston Churchill 75008. **Map** 11 B1. **Tel** 01 53 43 40 00. Ⓜ Champs-Elysées-Clemenceau. **Open** 10am–6pm Tue–Sun (to 7pm Thu). **Closed** public hols. 🎨 🎦 for exhibitions. ⬛ Ⓦ **petitpalais.paris.fr**

Built for the Universal Exhibition in 1900, to stage a major display of French art, this jewel of a building now houses the Musée des Beaux-Arts de la Ville de Paris. Arranged around a pretty semicircular courtyard and garden café, the palace is similar in style to the Grand Palais, and has Ionic columns, a grand porch, and a dome, which echoes that of the Invalides *(see p188–9)*.

The Cours de la Reine wing, closest to the river, is used for temporary exhibitions, while the Champs-Elysées side of the palace houses the permanent collections. These are divided into sections: Greek and Roman; medieval and Renaissance ivories and sculptures; Renaissance clocks and jewelry; and 17th-,

Exhibition space   Iron supports

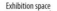

8th-, and 19th- century art and furniture. There are also many works by the Impressionists.

❺ Palais de l'Elysée

55 Rue du Faubourg-St.-Honoré 75008. **Map** 5 B5. Ⓜ St.-Philippe-du-Roule. **Closed** to the public.

Backing onto splendid English-style gardens, the Elysée Palace was built in 1718 for the Comte d'Evreux and has been official residence of the President of the Republic since 1873. From 1805 to 1808 it was home to Napoleon's sister, Caroline, and her husband, Murat. Two charming rooms have been preserved from this period: the Salon Murat and the Salon d'Argent. General de Gaulle gave press conferences in the Hall of Mirrors. Today, the President's modernized apartments are on the first floor opposite the Rue de l'Elysée.

❻ Avenue Montaigne

75008. **Map** 10 F1. Ⓜ Franklin D Roosevelt.

In the 19th century this avenue was famous for its dance halls and its Winter Garden, where Parisians went to hear Adolphe Sax play his newly invented saxophone. Today it is still one of Paris's most fashionable streets, bustling with cafés, restaurants, hotels, and designer boutiques. At one end lies the beautiful Art Deco Théâtre de Champs-Elysées, built in 1913.

The Second Empire Smoking Room in the Musée Jacquemart-André

❼ Musée Jacquemart-André

158 Blvd Haussmann 75008. **Map** 5 A4. **Tel** 01 45 62 11 59. Ⓜ Miromesnil, St.-Philippe-du-Roule. **Open** 10am–6pm daily (to 8:30pm Mon & Sat). 🚫🛇📷📷💻♿ restricted. 🔽 **musee-jacquemart-andre.com**

This museum is known for its Italian Renaissance and French 18th-century works of art, as well as its beautiful frescoes by Tiepolo. Highlights include works by Mantegna, Uccello's masterpiece *St. George and the Dragon* (circa 1435), paintings by Boucher and Fragonard, and 18th-century tapestries.

❽ Avenue des Champs-Elysées

75008. **Map** 5 A5. Ⓜ Franklin D. Roosevelt, George V.

Paris's most famous and popular thoroughfare was laid out in about 1667, when landscape garden designer, André Le Nôtre, extended the royal view from the Tuileries by creating a tree-lined avenue that became known as the Champs-Elysées (Elysian Fields). It has been France's national "triumphal way" ever since the homecoming of Napoleon's body from St. Helena in 1840. With the addition of cafés and restaurants in the second half of the 19th century, the Champs-Elysées became the place to be seen. In December it hosts a huge Christmas market and holiday light show.

❾ Place Charles de Gaulle (l'Etoile)

75008. **Map** 4 D4. Ⓜ Charles de Gaulle-Etoile.

Known as the Place de l'Etoile until the death of Charles de Gaulle in 1969, the area is still referred to simply as l'Etoile, the star. The present *place* was laid out in accordance with Baron Haussmann's plans of 1854 *(see pp36–7)*. For drivers, it is the ultimate challenge.

Glass cupola

Quadriga (chariot and four horses) by Récipon

❿ Arc de Triomphe

After his greatest victory, the Battle of Austerlitz in 1805, Napoleon promised his men, "You shall go home beneath triumphal arches." The first stone of what was to become the world's most famous triumphal arch was laid the following year. But disruptions to architect Jean Chalgrin's plans and the demise of Napoleonic power delayed the completion of this monumental building until 1836. Standing 164 ft (50 m) high, the Arc is now the customary starting point for victory celebrations and parades.

★ **Tomb of the Unknown Soldier**
An unknown French soldier from World War I is buried here.

KEY

① **The Battle of Aboukir**, a bas-relief by Seurre the Elder, depicts a scene of Napoleon's victory over the Turkish army in 1799.

② **The frieze** was executed by Rude, Brun, Jacquet, Laitié, Caillouette, and Seurre the Elder. This east facade shows the departure of the French armies for new campaigns. The west side shows their return.

③ **Thirty shields** just below the Arc's roof each bear the name of a victorious Napoleonic battle fought in either Europe or Africa.

④ **East facade**

⑤ **The viewing platform** affords one of the best views in Paris, overlooking the Champs-Elysées on one side, and the Grande Arche de la Défense on the other.

⑥ **The Battle of Austerlitz** by Gechter shows Napoleon's army breaking up the ice on the Satschan lake in order to drown thousands of enemy troops.

⑦ **Officers** of the Imperial Army are listed on the walls of the smaller arches.

⑧ **Entrance to museum**

Triumph of Napoleon
J. P. Cortot's high-relief celebrates the Treaty of Vienna peace agreement of 1810.

1806 Napoleon commissions Chalgrin to build triumphal Arc

1836 Louis-Philippe completes the Arc

1885 Victor Hugo's body lies in state under the Arc

1944 Liberation of Paris. De Gaulle leads the crowd from the Arc

1800

1850

1900

1840 Napoleon's cortège passes under the Arc

1919 Victory parade of Allied armies through the Arc

1815 Downfall of Napoleon. Work on Arc ceases

Napoleon's Nuptial Parade

Napoleon divorced Josephine in 1809 because she was unable to bear him children. A diplomatic marriage was arranged in 1810 with Marie-Louise, daughter of the Austrian emperor. Napoleon was determined to impress his bride by going through the Arc on their way to the wedding at the Louvre, but work had barely been started. So Chalgrin built a full-scale mock-up of the arch on the site for the couple to pass beneath.

VISITORS' CHECKLIST

Practical Information
Pl Charles de Gaulle. **Map** 4 D4.
Tel 01 55 37 73 77. **Open** Apr–
Sep: 10am–11pm daily; Oct–Mar:
10am–10:30pm daily (last adm:
30 min earlier). **Closed** am only
May 8, Jul 14, & Nov 11; all day Jan
1, May 1, Dec 25. 🎟 🚻 🏛 ♿
W arc-de-triomphe.
monuments-nationaux.fr

Transportation
M RER Charles de Gaulle–Etoile.
🚌 22, 30, 31, 52, 73, 92 to
Pl C. de Gaulle. **P** off Pl
C. de Gaulle.

General Marceau's Funeral
Marceau defeated the Austrians in 1795, only to be killed the following year, still fighting them.

★ **Departure of
the Volunteers
in 1792**
François Rude's
work shows citizens
leaving to defend
the nation.

Place Charles de Gaulle
Twelve avenues radiate from the Arc at the center. Some bear the names of important French military leaders, such as avenues Marceau and Foch. *(See pp36–7).*

OPERA QUARTER

Known for its Grands Boulevards and the Opéra Garnier, this area has a 19th-century grandeur to it, exemplified in Baron Haussmann's city planning and architecture. Cutting through the district, the boulevards Madeleine, Capucines, Italien, and Montmartre host a range of high-end businesses, restaurants, and stores, from the *grands magasins* to characterful shopping arcades. During the day, the area is more of a business hub, its streets bustling with bankers, publishers, editors, and, of course, shoppers. The heart of the quarter is the world-famous opera house, with its belle époque interior and Chagall's magnificent ceiling. Clustered around the Grands Boulevards are the historic covered passageways, with their steel-and-glass roofs. The most opulent of these is the 1823 Galerie Vivienne, containing high-end boutiques and interior design stores. More traditional are the Passages Verdeau, Panoramas, and Jouffroy, known for their antiques dealers, specialty crafts, and collectors' stores. Night-time revelers will also find a host of clubs and theaters in this area; the historic Olympia concert hall has hosted many musicians and singers over the years, including Edith Piaf, Johnny Halliday, The Beatles, Judy Garland, The Supremes, and Madonna.

Sights at a Glance

Historic Buildings and Streets
- ❷ Place de la Madeleine
- ❸ Les Grands Boulevards
- ❾ Le Grand Rex
- ⓫ Palais Brongniart
- ⓭ Avenue de l'Opéra

Churches
- ❶ La Madeleine

Stores
- ❼ Drouot (Hôtel des Ventes)
- ❿ Les Passages

Opera Houses
- ❹ Opéra National de Paris Garnier

Museums and Galleries
- ❺ Bibliothèque-Musée de l'Opéra
- ❻ Paris Story
- ❽ Musée Grévin
- ⓬ Bibliothèque Nationale Richelieu

Restaurants *see pp298–300*
1. L'Adjugé
2. Café de la Paix
3. Le Cap Bourbon
4. Caviar Kaspia
5. Chartier
6. Chez Georges
7. Fauchon Le Café
8. Les Noces de Jeannette
9. Racines
10. Le Vaudeville

| 0 meters | 500 |
| 0 yards | 500 |

See also Street Finder maps 5–6

◀ The ceiling of the lobby of the Opéra National de Paris Garnier

For keys to symbols *see back flap*

Street by Street: Opéra Quarter

It has been said that if you sit for long enough at the Café de la Paix (opposite the Opéra National de Paris Garnier) the whole world will pass by. During the day, the area is a mixture of commerce – France's top three banks are based here – and tourism. A profusion of stores, ranging from the chic, exclusive, and expensive to popular department stores, draws the crowds. In the evening, the theaters and movie theaters attract a totally different clientele, and the cafés along the Boulevard des Capucines throb with life.

Statue by Gumery on the Opéra

2 Place de la Madeleine
On the north side of the square, the windows of the Fauchon store are filled with exquisite delicacies.

RUE AUB

RUE TRONCHET

RUE VIGNON

RUE GODOT DE MAUROY

RUE CAUMARTIN

RUE FDC

PL DE LA MADELEINE

BLVD DE

BLVD DE LA MADELEINE

Metro Madeleine Ⓜ

0 meters 100
0 yards 100

Key

— Suggested route

1 ★ La Madeleine
The final design of this church, which is dedicated to Mary Magdalene, differs from this original model, now in the Musée Carnavalet (see pp96–7).

❹ ★ Opéra National de Paris Garnier
With a mixture of styles ranging from Classical to
Baroque, this building from 1875 has come to
symbolize the opulence of the Second Empire.

Locator Map
See Central Paris Map pp16–17

**❺ Bibliothèque-Musée
de l'Opéra**
The world of opera is
celebrated here.

The Place de l'Opéra
was designed by
Baron Haussmann and
is one of Paris's busiest
intersections.

PL DIAGHILEV

RUE GLUCK

RUE HALEVY

PL J
ROUCHE

RUE SCRIBE

PL CH
GARNIER

RUE

Metro Chaussée
d'Antin Ⓜ

PL DE
L'OPÉRA

Ⓜ Metro Opéra

CINES

RUE DAUNOU

AVE DE
L'OPÉRA

The Café de la Paix maintains its
old-fashioned ways and still has
its 19th-century decor, designed by
Garnier. Their vanilla slices are
legendary *(see p310)*.

Harry's Bar was named
after Harry MacElhone, a
bartender who bought the bar
in 1913. Past regulars have
included F. Scott Fitzgerald and
Ernest Hemingway.

**❸ ★ Les Grands
Boulevards**
At No. 14 Boulevard des
Capucines, a plaque tells
of the world's first public
screening of a movie, by
the Lumière brothers in
1895; it took place in the
Salon Indien, a room in
the Grand Café.

Charles Marochetti's *Mary Magdalene Ascending to Heaven* (1837) behind the high altar of La Madeleine

❶ La Madeleine

Pl de la Madeleine 75008. **Map** 5 C5. **Tel** 01 44 51 69 00. Ⓜ Madeleine. **Open** 9:30am–7pm daily. 🚇 frequent. Concerts. 🎭 *See Entertainment pp338–9* 🌐 **eglise-lamadeleine.com**.

This church, which is dedicated to Mary Magdalene, is one of the best-known buildings in Paris because of its prominent location and great size. It stands facing south to Place de la Concorde and is the architectural counterpoint of the Palais-Bourbon (home of the Assemblée Nationale, the French parliament) across the river. It was started in 1764 but not consecrated until 1845. There were proposals to convert it into a parliament, a stock exchange, or the city's first train station.

Napoleon decided to build a temple dedicated to military glory and he commissioned Pierre Vignon to design it, after the battle of Jena (Iéna) in 1806. A colonnade of 64 ft high (20 m) Corinthian columns encircles the building and supports a sculptured frieze. The bas-reliefs on the bronze doors are by Henri de Triqueti and show the Ten Commandments. The inside is decorated with marble and gilt, and has some fine sculpture, notably François Rude's *Baptism of Christ*.

❷ Place de la Madeleine

75008. **Map** 5 C5. Ⓜ Madeleine. Flower market **Open** 8am–7:30pm Mon–Sat.

The place de la Madeleine was created at the same time as the Madeleine church. It is a food lover's paradise, with many stores specializing in luxuries such as truffles, champagne, caviar, and handmade chocolates. Fauchon, the millionaires' supermarket, is located at No. 26 and stocks more than 20,000 items *(see pp325, 327)*. The large house at No. 9 is where Marcel Proust spent his childhood. To the east of La Madeleine is a small flower market *(see p330)* and some excellently preserved 19th-century public restrooms.

Fauchon tin

Opéra National de Paris Garnier

Scenery backdrop operated by pulley

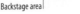

Backstage area

Stag

❸ Les Grands Boulevards

75002 & 75009. **Map** 6 D5–7 C5.
Ⓜ Madeleine, Opéra, Richelieu-Drouot, Grands Boulevards.

A broad thoroughfare divided into eight boulevards – Madeleine, Capucines, Italiens, Montmartre, Poissonnière, Bonne Nouvelle, St.-Denis, and St.-Martin – runs from La Madeleine to the Place de la République. The route was constructed in the 17th century to turn obsolete city fortifications into fashionable promenades – *boulevard* came from the Middle Dutch *bulwerc*, meaning bulwark or rampart. The boulevards became so famous in the 19th century that the name *boulevardier* was coined for someone who cuts a figure on the boulevards.

Around the Madeleine church and the Opéra it is still possible to gain an impression of what the Grands Boulevards looked like in their heyday, lined with cafés and chic stores. Elsewhere, most of the cafés and restaurants have long since gone, and the old facades are now hidden by neon advertising. However, the Grands Boulevards and the

Boulevard de la Madeleine

nearby department stores on Boulevard Haussmann still attract large crowds.

❹ Opéra National de Paris Garnier

Pl de l'Opéra 75009. **Map** 6 D4–E4.
Tel 08 92 89 90 90. Ⓜ Opéra.
Open 10am–4:30pm daily (1pm on matinée days); mid-Jul–late Aug: 10am–5:30pm. Reservations for guided tours 01 42 46 92 04 (from abroad: +33 1 71 25 24 23. **Closed** Jan 1, May 1. 🅿️ 🅲 📷 *See Entertainment pp337, 339.* 🆆 **operadeparis.fr**

Sometimes compared to a giant wedding cake, this building was designed by Charles Garnier for Napoleon III; construction started in 1862. Its unique appearance is due to a mixture of materials (including stone, marble, and bronze) and styles, ranging from

Classical to Baroque, with a number of columns, friezes, and sculptures on the exterior. The building was not completed until 1875; work was interrupted by the Prussian War and 1871 uprising.

In 1858 Count Orsini had attempted to assassinate the emperor outside the old opera house. This prompted Garnier to include a pavilion on the east side of the building, with a curved ramp leading up to it so that the sovereign could safely step out of his carriage into the suite of rooms adjoining the royal box.

Behind the flat-topped lobby, the cupola sits above the auditorium, while the triangular pediment that rises up behind the cupola marks the front of the stage. Underneath the building is a small lake, which provided inspiration for the phantom's hiding place in Paul Leroux's *Phantom of the Opera*, and is used by firemen for water rescue safety training.

Don't miss the magnificent Grand Staircase, made of white marble with a balustrade of red and green marble, and the Grand Foyer, with its domed ceiling covered with mosaics. The five-tiered auditorium is a riot of red velvet, plaster cherubs, and gold leaf, which contrast with the false ceiling painted by Marc Chagall in 1964.

Most operas are performed at the Opéra Nationale de Paris Bastille (*see p102*), but the ballet remains here.

Statue by Millet

Green copper roofed cupola

Emperor's pavilion

Grand Foyer with mosaic ceiling

Auditorium with seating for about 2,000

Grand Staircase

Model of a set for *Les Huguenots* (1875) in the Musée de l'Opéra

❺ Bibliothèque-Musée de l'Opéra

Palais Garnier, corner of Rue Scribe & Rue Auber, Pl de l'Opéra 75009. **Map** 6 E5. **Tel** 01 53 79 37 40. 🚇 Opéra. **Open** 10am–5pm Mon–Sat. **Closed** 1 week in Sep, public hols. 🖼 📷 📷

The way into this small, charming museum was once the emperor's private entrance to the Opéra. The museum tells the history of opera and ballet through a large collection of scores, manuscripts, photographs, and artists' memorabilia. Other exhibits include paintings, models of stage sets, and busts of major composers. There is also a superb library, containing books and manuscripts on theater, dance, and music. The museum organizes two special exhibitions every year.

❻ Paris Story

11 bis Rue Scribe 75009. **Map** 6 D4. **Tel** 01 42 66 62 06. 🚇 Opéra. **Open** 10am–6pm daily; show every hour. 📷 📷 📷 🌐 **paris-story.com**

Especially useful for the first-time visitor, this small museum covers everything you need to know about the history and architecture of Paris in an hour-long movie and interactive display. The movie covers 2,000 years of history from Lutetia (the Roman name for Paris) to the Paris of today. The show is narrated by a holographic figure of Victor Hugo and

visitors can listen to it in English via headphones. A 3-D model of the city allows you to pinpoint and learn about various monuments with a description of the 156 most important and interesting sites. Plasma screens show a sequence shot by the Lumière Brothers in 1898.

❼ Drouot (Hôtel des Ventes)

9 Rue Drouot 75009. **Map** 6 F4. **Tel** 01 48 00 20 20. 🚇 Richelieu Drouot. **Open** 11am–6pm Mon–Fri (to 9pm Thu), sales from 2pm. Also open some Sat & Sun, call in advance. 📷 📷 📷 📷 *See Stores and Markets pp328–9.* 🌐 **drouot.com**

This is the leading French auction house (Hôtel des Ventes) and it takes its name from the Comte de Drouot who was Napoleon's aide-de-camp. There has been an auction house on the site since 1858, and in 1860, Napoleon III visited the Hôtel and purchased a couple of earthenware pots. It has been known as the Nouveau Drouot ever since the 1970s, when the original building was demolished and replaced with today's rather dull structure.

Although overshadowed internationally by Christie's and Sotheby's, auctions at the Nouveau Drouot nevertheless provide a lively spectacle and involve a fascinating range of rare objects. Its presence in the area has attracted many antiques and stamp shops.

❽ Musée Grévin

10 Boulevard Montmartre 75009. **Map** 6 F4. **Tel** 01 47 70 85 05. 🚇 Grands Boulevards. **Open** 9am–7pm daily (times can vary, call ahead to check). 🖼 📷 📷 📷 🌐 **grevin.com**

This waxwork museum was founded in 1882 and is now a Paris landmark, on a par with Madame Tussauds in London. It contains tableaux of vivid historical scenes (such as Louis XIV at Versailles and the arrest of Louis XVI), the Palais des Mirages (a giant walk-in kaleidoscope), and the Cabinet Fantastique, which includes regular conjuring shows given by a live magician. Famous figures from the worlds of art, sport, and politics are also on show, with new celebrities replacing faded and forgotten stars.

Le Grand Rex Art Deco tower

❾ Le Grand Rex

1 Blvd Poissonnière 75002. **Map** 7 A5. **Tel** 01 45 08 93 89. 🚇 Bonne Nouvelle. 🌐 **legrandrex.com**

Considered a national monument, as well as an innovative example of Art Deco architecture, Le Grand Rex, built in 1932, was long touted as Europe's most opulent movie theater, hosting many red-carpet events. Still one of the largest of its kind in Europe, the Grand Rex is a fading but beautiful symbol of the history of cinema. The large auditorium has a starred ceiling, 2,800 seats, and an enormous screen, the largest in Paris. Every December, the movie theater hosts the Féerie des Eaux, a family-film event featuring an on-stage water show.

The elegant Galerie Vivienne, one of Paris's covered shopping arcades

⑩ Les Passages

75002. **Map** 6 F5. Ⓜ Bourse.

These 19th-century shopping arcades are located between Boulevard Montmartre and Rue St.-Marc, and between Rue du Quatre Septembre and Rue des Petits Champs. At the time of their construction, around the 1820s and 1830s, the *passages* represented a traffic-free area for commerce, workshops, and apartments. They targeted the new bourgeoisie with amenities such as gas lighting, shelter from the rain and mud, eating establishments, and shopping all under one roof. They were the models for the future *grand magasins*, or department stores, but eventually fell into disuse. In the 1970s, they were revamped and now house an eclectic mixture of small stores selling anything from rare books to designer jewelry. They have high, vaulted roofs of iron and glass. Many have seen better days, but one of the most fashionable and high-end is the Galerie Vivienne (off Rue Vivienne and Rue des Petits Champs), with its designer boutiques, mosaic floor, excellent tearoom, and Legrand Filles et Fils, one of the best wine *caves* (cellars) in Paris.

⑪ Palais Brongniart

(Bourse des Valeurs) 4 Pl de la Bourse 75002. **Map** 6 F5. **Tel** 01 83 92 20 20. Ⓜ Bourse. **Closed** to the public. Ⓦ palaisbrongniart.com

This Neo-Classical temple of commerce was commissioned by Napoleon and was home to the French Stock Exchange from 1826 to 1987. It earlier housed the trading floor of the Palais de la Bourse.

Today, the French stock market is located at 29 Rue Cambon (not open to visits). This building is now used as a conference center.

⑫ Bibliothèque Nationale Richelieu

58 Rue de Richelieu and 5 Rue Vivienne 75002. **Map** 6 F5. **Tel** 01 53 79 59 59. Ⓜ Bourse. **Open** 10am–6pm Mon–Fri, 9am–5pm Sat. **Closed** public hols, 2 weeks in Sep. Ⓒ by appt; 01 53 79 49 49. Ⓦ **bnf.fr**

The Bibliotheque Nationale (National Library) originated with the manuscript collections of medieval kings, to which, by law, a copy of every French book printed since 1537 has been added. The collection, which includes two Gutenberg Bibles, is partially housed in this complex. Despite the removal of the printed books, periodicals, and CD-Roms to the Bibliothèque Nationale François-Mitterrand *(see p244)* at Tolbiac, the Rue Richelieu buildings still contain a huge variety of items, including original manuscripts by Victor Hugo and Marcel Proust. The library also has the richest collection of engravings and photographs in the world. Sadly, the 19th-century reading room is not open to the public.

The library is undergoing renovation until 2019, however it is still open to the public.

⑬ Avenue de l'Opéra

75001 & 75002. **Map** 6 E5. Ⓜ Opéra, Pyramides.

This broad avenue is a notable example of Baron Haussmann's dramatic modernization of Paris in the 1860s and 1870s *(see pp36–7)*, and is the city's only tree-less avenue. Much of the medieval city (including a mound from which Joan of Arc began her crusade against the English) was cleared to make way for the wide thoroughfares. The Avenue de l'Opéra, running from the Palais-Royal to the Opéra National de Paris Garnier, was completed in 1876. The uniformity of the five-story buildings that line it contrasts with those found in nearby streets, which date from the 17th and 18th centuries. Nearby, in Place Gaillon, is the bar and restaurant Drouant where the Goncourt Prize for literature is decided. The avenue is dominated by travel and luxury stores. The Institut d'Etudes Supérieures des Arts is at No. 5.

Avenue de l'Opéra

MONTMARTRE

Once a separate village outside Paris, Montmartre still retains its charm, with narrow winding streets, cafés, a tiny vineyard, and stunning views of the city. At the end of the 19th century, this bohemian area had a reputation for decadence and free living, as well as low-cost housing, which made it into a magnet for artists, writers, and intellectuals. The still-standing Bateau-Lavoir was a shared studio and home to artists like Matisse, Picasso, Modigliani, and Cocteau. Nowadays, that creative spirit lives on in Place du Tertre

and around the massive Sacré-Coeur, where street artists hoping to be discovered paint tourists' portraits and art galleries flourish.

As the home of the Moulin Rouge, said to have been the birthplace of the cancan dance, Montmartre still has its fair share of cabarets, which continue to draw visitors to the area. While Upper Montmartre (Haut Montmartre) tends to be calmer and more residential, it is Lower Montmartre (Bas Montmartre), filled with lively bars and restaurants, that is famous for its nightlife and entertainment.

Sights at a Glance

Historic Buildings and Streets
- ⑪ Bateau-Lavoir
- ⑭ Moulin de la Galette
- ⑮ Avenue Junot

Churches
- ① Sacré-Coeur pp226–7
- ② St.-Pierre de Montmartre
- ⑧ Chapelle du Martyre
- ⑩ St.-Jean l'Evangéliste de Montmartre

Cemeteries
- ⑬ Cimetière de Montmartre

Squares
- ③ Place du Tertre
- ⑨ Place des Abbesses

Theaters and Nightclubs
- ⑥ Au Lapin Agile
- ⑫ Moulin Rouge

Museums and Galleries
- ④ Espace Dalí Montmartre
- ⑤ Musée de Montmartre
- ⑦ Halle Saint Pierre

☐ Restaurants see pp298–300
1. Babalou
2. La Balançoire
3. Le Chamarré de Montmartre
4. Chez Toinette
5. Crêperie Broceliande
6. La Famille
7. Le Grand 8
8. Guilo Guilo
9. Le Lamarck
10. Le Miroir
11. Le Pantruche
12. Le Progrès
13. Rouge Bis
14. Tentazioni
15. La Tiborna
16. Un Zèbre à Montmartre

See also Street Finder maps 2, 6, 7

| 0 meters | 400 |
| 0 yards | 400 |

◀ Display of vintage posters in Montmartre

For map symbols see back flap

Street by Street: Montmartre

The steep *butte* (hill) of Montmartre has been associated with artists for over 200 years. Théodore Géricault and Camille Corot came here at the start of the 19th century, and in the 20th century, Maurice Utrillo immortalized the streets in his works. Today, street painters thrive on a lively tourist trade as visitors flock to this picturesque district that in places still preserves the atmosphere of pre-war Paris. The name of the area is ascribed to local martyrs tortured in Paris around AD 250, hence *mons martyrium*.

Clos Montmartre is o of the last surviving vineyards in Paris. The grape harvest is celebrated on the first Saturday in October.

Metro Lamarck
Caulaincourt

RUE ST-V
RUE DE L'ABREUVOIR
RUE DES SAULES
CO
RUE
RUE ST-
NOR
RUE LEPIC
PL J B CLEMENT
RUE POULBOT
RUE DE LA MIRE
RUE GABRI
PL RAVIGNAN
PL E GOUDEAU
RUE
RUE BER
RUE DES TROIS FRERES

⑥ ★ Au Lapin Agile
This rustic café and cabaret was a popular meeting point for artists including Picasso.

⑤ ★ Musée de Montmartre
The museum features the work of artists who lived in the area: this *Portrait of a Woman* (1918) is by the Italian painter and sculptor Amedeo Modigliani.

④ Espace Dalí Montmartre
This is France's only permanent collection of the Surrealist master's sculptures, paintings, and graphic works.

③ ★ Place du Tertre
The bustling square is the tourist center of Montmartre and is full of portraitists and other easel artists. Cafés and bars surround the square.

A La Mère Catherine was a favorite eating place of Russian Cossacks in 1814. They would bang on the table and shout *"Bistro!"* (Russian for "quick") – hence the Paris bistro was born.

| 0 meters | 100 |
| 0 yards | 100 |

Locator Map
See Central Paris Map pp16–17

Key

— Suggested route

❶ ★ **Sacré-Coeur**
This Romano-Byzantine church, started in the 1870s and completed in 1914, has many treasures, such as this figure of Christ by Eugène Benet (1911).

RUE DU CHEVALIER

RUE DU CARDINAL GUIBERT

RUE LAMARCK

RUE PAUL ALBERT

PL DU PARVAIS DU SACRÉ-COEUR

RUE AZAIS

T-ELEUTHERE

RUE DU CARDINAL DUBOIS

RUE CH NODIER

SQ WILLETTE

RUE CHAPPE

PL ST-PIERRE

RUE TARDIEU

RUE DE STEINKERQUE

❷ **St.-Pierre de Montmartre**
This church became the Temple of Reason during the Revolution.

❼ **Halle Saint Pierre**
The museum hosts exhibitions of Art Brut and Naïve Art. This oil painting, *L'Opéra de Paris* (1986), is by L. Milinkov.

Square Willette lies below the parvis (forecourt) of Sacré-Coeur. It is laid out on the side of the hill in a series of descending terraces with lawns, shrubs, trees, and flowerbeds.

The funiculaire, or cable railroad, at the end of Rue Foyatier takes you to the foot of the basilica of Sacré-Coeur. Metro tickets are valid on it.

❶ Sacré-Coeur

At the outbreak of the Franco-Prussian War in 1870, two Catholic businessmen made a private religious vow to build a church dedicated to the Sacred Heart of Christ, should France be spared the impending Prussian onslaught. The two men, Alexandre Legentil and Hubert Rohault de Fleury, lived to see Paris saved from invasion despite the war and a lengthy siege – and the start of work on the Sacré-Coeur basilica. The project was taken up by Archbishop Guibert of Paris. Work began in 1875 to Paul Abadie's designs. They were inspired by the Romano-Byzantine church of St.-Front in Périgueux. The basilica was completed in 1914, but its consecration was forestalled by World War I until 1919, when France was victorious.

The Principal Facade
The best view of the domed and turreted Sacré-Coeur is from the gardens below.

★ **Great Mosaic of Christ**
The colossal mosaic (1912–22) dominating the chancel vault was designed by Luc Olivier Merson and Marcel Magne.

Virgin Mary and Child (1896)
This Renaissance-style silver statue is one of two in the ambulatory by P. Brunet.

KEY

① **The bell tower** (1895) is 252 ft (83 m) high and contains one of the heaviest bells in the world. The bell itself weighs 20 tons and the clapper 1,900 lb (850 kg).

② **Spiral staircase**

③ **The inner structure** supporting the dome is made from stone.

④ **The stained-glass gallery** affords a view of the whole of the interior.

★ **Crypt Vaults**
A chapel in the basilica's crypt contains Legentil's heart in a stone urn.

The Siege of Paris

Prussia invaded France in 1870. During the four-month siege of Paris, instigated by the Prusso-German statesman Otto von Bismarck, hungry Parisians were forced to eat the city's horses and other animals.

★ **Ovoid Dome**
This is the second-highest point in Paris, after the Eiffel Tower.

Statue of Christ
The basilica's most important statue is symbolically placed above the two bronze saints.

Equestrian Statues
The statue of Joan of Arc is one of a pair by H. Lefèbvre. The other is of St. Louis.

★ **Bronze Doors**
Relief sculptures on the doors in the portico entrance illustrate scenes from the life of Christ, such as the Last Supper.

Main entrance

Paintings for sale and a restaurant on Place du Tertre, in Montmartre

❷ St.-Pierre de Montmartre

2 Rue du Mont-Cenis 75018.
Map 6 F1. **Tel** 01 46 06 57 63.
M Abbesses. **Open** 9am–7.30pm daily (to 6pm Fri). 🕇 various times. 🛇 Concerts. **W** saintpierrede montmartre.net

Situated in the shadow of the Sacré-Coeur basilica, St.-Pierre de Montmartre is one of the oldest churches in Paris. It is all that remains of the great Benedictine Abbey of Montmartre, which was founded in 1133 by Louis VI and his wife, Adelaide of Savoy, who, as its first abbess, is buried here.

Inside the church are four marble columns supposedly from a Roman temple which once stood on the site. The vaulted choir dates from the 12th century, the nave was remodelled in the 15th century and the west front in the 18th. During the Revolution, the abbess was executed by guillotine, and the church fell into disuse. St.-Pierre was reconsecrated in 1908. Gothic-style stained-glass windows replace those destroyed by a bomb in World War II. The tiny cemetery opens to the public only once a year, on November 1.

Doors to St.-Pierre church

❸ Place du Tertre

75018. **Map** 6 F1. **M** Abbesses.

Tertre means "hillock", or mound, and this picturesque square is the highest point in Paris at some 430 ft (130 m). It was once the site of the abbey gallows but is associated with artists, who began exhibiting paintings here in the 19th century. It is lined with colorful restaurants – La Mère Catherine dates back to 1793. The house at No. 21 was formerly the home of the irreverent "Free Commune", founded in 1920 to perpetuate the Bohemian spirit of the area. The Old Montmartre information office is now here.

Surrealist artist Salvador Dalí

❹ Espace Dalí Montmartre

11 Rue Poulbot 75018. **Map** 6 F1.
Tel 01 42 64 40 10. **M** Abbesses.
Open 10am–6pm daily (to 8pm Jul–Aug). 🈁 🛇 🈶 🈚 **W** daliparis.com

A permanent exhibition of 330 works by the prolific painter and sculptor Salvador Dalí is displayed here at the heart of Montmartre. Inside, the vast, dark setting reflects the dramatic character of this 20th-century genius as moving lights grace first one, then another, of his Surrealist works to a soundtrack of Dalí's recorded voice. This fascinating museum also houses a commercial art gallery, a library, and a shop selling books, prints and postcards.

❺ Musée de Montmartre

12 Rue Cortot 75018. **Map** 2 F5.
Tel 01 49 25 89 37. **M** Abbesses, Anvers, Blanche, Lamarck-Caulaincourt.
Open 10am–6pm daily (Jun–Sep: to 7pm). **Closed** 1 Jan, 25 Dec. 🈁 🈚 🈁 **W** museedemontmartre.fr

During the 17th century, this charming home belonged to the actor Roze de Rosimond (Claude de la Rose), a member of Molière's theatre company who, like his mentor Molière, died during a performance of Molière's play *Le Malade Imaginaire*. From 1875, the big white house, undoubtedly the finest in Montmartre, provided living and studio space for artists, including Maurice Utrillo and his mother, Suzanne Valadon, a former acrobat and model who became a talented painter, as well as Raoul Dufy and Auguste Renoir.

The museum recounts the history of Montmartre from the days of the abbesses to the present, through artifacts, drawings and photographs. It is particularly rich in memorabilia of Bohemian life, and has a reconstruction of the Café de l'Abreuvoir, Utrillo's favourite watering hole.

Café de l'Abreuvoir reconstructed

The deceptively rustic exterior of Au Lapin Agile, in the heart of Montmartre

❻ Au Lapin Agile

22 Rue des Saules 75018. **Map** 2 F5.
Tel 01 46 06 85 87. **M** Lamarck-Caulaincourt. **Open** 9pm–1am
Tue–Sun. *See Entertainment pp334, 336.*
W au-lapin-agile.com

The former Cabaret des Assassins derived its current name from a sign painted by the humorist André Gill. His picture of a rabbit escaping from a cooking pot *(Le Lapin à Gill)* is a pun on his own name. The club enjoyed popularity with intellectuals and artists at the start of the 20th century. Here in 1911, the novelist Roland Dorgelès and a group of other regulars staged one of the modern art world's most celebrated hoaxes, with the help of the café owner's donkey, Lolo. A paintbrush was tied to Lolo's tail, and the resulting daub was shown to critical acclaim at the Salon des Indépendants, under the enlightening title *Sunset over the Adriatic*, before the joke was revealed.

In 1903, the premises were bought by the cabaret entrepreneur Aristide Bruand (painted in a series of posters by Toulouse-Lautrec). The venue was depicted by Pablo Picasso in an oil painting which was sold for $20 by the cabaret's owner in 1912. In 1989, the painting was sold at auction for $67.5 million.

Today, the cabaret venue manages to retain much of its original atmosphere.

❼ Halle Saint Pierre

Halle St.-Pierre, 2 Rue Ronsard 75018.
Map 7 A1. **Tel** 01 42 58 72 89.
M Anvers. **Open** 10am–6pm Mon–Fri, 11am–7pm Sat, noon–6pm Sun
(Aug: noon–6pm Mon–Fri). **Closed**
some public hols. 🏛️ ✉️ ♿ 🖥️ 📷
W hallesaintpierre.org

In 1945, the French painter Jean Dubuffet developed the concept of *Art Brut* (Outsider or Marginal Art) to describe works created outside the boundaries of "official" culture, often by psychiatric patients, prisoners, and children. The Halle Saint Pierre, at the foot of the Butte, is

Art Brut at Halle Saint Pierre

a museum and gallery devoted to these "raw" art forms. It also hosts avant-garde theatre and musical productions, holds regular literary evenings and debates and runs children's workshops. The permanent collection includes more than 500 works of Naïve art collected by the publisher Max Fourny in the 1970s. There is also a specialist bookshop and café.

❽ Chapelle du Martyre

9 Rue Yvonne-Le-Tac 75018. **Map** 6 F1.
M Pigalle. **Open** 3–5pm Fri, 1st Sat &
Sun of each month.

This 19th-century chapel stands on the site of a medieval convent chapel, which was said to mark the place where the early Christian martyr and first bishop of Paris, Saint Denis, was beheaded by the Romans in AD 250. It remained a major pilgrimage site throughout the Middle Ages. In 1534, in the crypt of the original chapel, Ignatius de Loyola, founder of the Society of Jesus (the mighty Jesuit order designed to save the Catholic Church from the onslaught of the Protestant Reformation), took his Jesuit vows with six companions.

The famous silhouette of the Moulin Rouge nightclub

⓿ Place des Abbesses

75018. **Map** 6 F1. Ⓜ Abbesses.

This is one of Paris's most picturesque squares. It is sandwiched between the rather dubious attractions of Place Pigalle with its strip clubs and Place du Tertre, mobbed by tourists. Be sure not to miss the Abbesses metro station with its unusual green wrought-iron arches and amber lights. Designed by the architect Hector

Entrance to the Abbesses metro

Guimard, it is one of the few original Art Nouveau stations.

❿ St.-Jean l'Evangéliste de Montmartre

19 Rue des Abbesses 75018. **Map** 6 F1. **Tel** 01 46 06 43 96. Ⓜ Abbesses. **Open** 9am–7pm Mon–Sat; 9:30am–6pm Sun (to 7pm summer). 🕑 12:15pm Tue & Thu, 6:30pm Sat, 10:30am Sun. 📷 Ⓦ **saintjean demontmartre.com**

Designed by Anatole de Baudot and completed in 1904, this church was the first to be built from reinforced concrete. The flower motifs on the interior are typical of Art Nouveau, while its interlocking arches suggest Islamic architecture. The red-brick facing has earned it the nickname St.-Jean-des-Briques.

Detail of St.-Jean l'Evangéliste facade

⓫ Bateau-Lavoir

13 Pl Emile-Goudeau 75018. **Map** 6 F1. Ⓜ Abbesses. **Closed** to public.

This ramshackle tenement building took its name from its resemblance to the laundry boats that used to operate along the River Seine. Between 1890 and 1920 it was home to some of the most talented artists and poets of the day. They lived in squalid conditions with only one faucet and took turns sleeping in the beds. Picasso, Raoul Dufy, Van Dongen, Marie Laurencin, Juan Gris, Modigliani, and Jean Cocteau were just a few of the residents. It was here that Picasso painted *Les Demoiselles d'Avignon* in 1907, usually regarded as the painting that inspired Cubism. The original building burned down in 1970, but a concrete replica has been built – with studio space for up-and-coming artists.

⓬ Moulin Rouge

82 Blvd de Clichy 75018. **Map** 6 E1. **Tel** 01 53 09 82 82. Ⓜ Blanche. **Open** Dinner: 7pm; shows: 9pm and 11pm daily. 🎭 🎭 *See Entertainment pp335–6.* Ⓦ **moulinrouge.fr**

Built in 1885, the Moulin Rouge was turned into a dance hall as early as 1900. The cancan originated in Montparnasse, in the polka gardens of the Rue de la Grande-Chaumière, but it will always be associated with the Moulin Rouge where the wild and colorful dance shows were immortalized in the posters and drawings of Henri de Toulouse-Lautrec. The high-kicking routines of famous "Dorriss girls" such as Yvette Guilbert and Jane Avril continue today in a glittering, Las Vegas-style revue that includes sophisticated light shows and displays of magic.

⑬ Cimetière de Montmartre

20 Ave Rachel 75018. **Map** 2 D5.
Tel 01 53 42 36 30. Ⓜ Place de
Clichy, Blanche. **Open** 8am–6pm
daily (opens 8:30am Sat, 9am Sun).
♿ 🅟 call 01 53 42 36 30.

This has been the resting place
for many artistic luminaries
since the beginning of the
19th century. The composers
Hector Berlioz and Jacques
Offenbach (who wrote the
famous cancan tune) are
buried here, alongside many
other celebrities such as La
Goulue (stage name of Louise
Weber, the high-kicking
danseuse who was the cancan's
first star performer and
Toulouse-Lautrec's model), the
painter Edgar Degas, writer
Alexandre Dumas *fils*, German
poet Heinrich Heine, Russian
dancer Vaslav Nijinsky, and film
director François Truffaut. It's an
evocative, atmospheric place,
conveying some of the heated
energy and artistic creativity of
Montmartre a century ago.

Nearby, close to Square
Roland Dorgelès, is another,
smaller, often overlooked
Montmartre cemetery –
Cimetière St.-Vincent. Here lie
more of the great artistic
names of the district, including
the Swiss composer Arthur
Honegger and the writer
Marcel Aymé. Most notable of
all at St.-Vincent is the grave
of the great French painter
Maurice Utrillo, the quintessential Montmartre artist, many

Moulin de la Galette

of whose works are now some
of the most enduring images
of the area.

⑭ Moulin de la Galette

T-junction at Rue Tholozé and Rue
Lepic 75018. **Map** 2 E5. Ⓜ Lamarck-
Caulaincourt, Abbesses.

Once some 14 windmills dotted
the Montmartre skyline and
were used for grinding wheat
and pressing grapes. Today only
two remain, both on Rue Lepic:
the Radet, now above a
restaurant confusingly named
Moulin de la Galette, and the
reconstructed Moulin de la
Galette, originally built in 1622
and formerly known as the
Blute-fin. One of its mill owners,
Debray, was supposedly crucified
on the windmill's sails during the
1814 Siege of Paris. He had been
trying to repulse the invading
Cossacks. At the end of the

19th century both mills became
famous dance halls providing
inspiration for many artists,
notably Pierre-Auguste Renoir
and Vincent Van Gogh.

The steep Rue Lepic is a
busy shopping area. The
Impressionist painter Armand
Guillaumin once lived on the
first floor of No. 54. Van Gogh
inhabited its third floor, and
painted the view from there.

⑮ Avenue Junot

75018. **Map** 2 E5. Ⓜ Lamarck-
Caulaincourt.

Opened in 1910, this broad,
peaceful street includes many
painters' studios and beautiful Art
Deco houses. No. 13 has mosaics
designed by its former resident,
illustrator Francisque Poulbot,
who was famous for his drawings
of children and street urchins. At
No. 15 is Maison Tristan Tzara,
named after its previous owner,
the Romanian Dadaist poet. Its
eccentric design by the Austrian
architect Adolf Loos aimed to
complement the poet's
character. No. 23 is Villa Léandre,
with its quaint Anglo-Norman
style houses.

Just off the Avenue Junot up
the steps of the Allée des
Brouillards is an 18th-century
architectural folly, the Château
des Brouillards. In the 19th
century it was the home of the
French Symbolist writer Gérard
de Nerval, who took his pet
lobster for walks in the Palais-
Royal gardens.

Cimetière de Montmartre, the final resting place of many famous artists and writers

FARTHER AFIELD

Away from the center, but still within the *périphérique* beltway circling Paris, the city becomes greener. Former working-class areas like Belleville, Ménilmontant, and Batignolles are turning into *bobo* (bourgeois bohemian) villages, with hip bars, vintage markets, and

Internet start-ups. Beyond the *périphérique*, the Bois de Boulogne and Bois de Vincennes are two of the city's largest public parks, with ponds, flower gardens, and children's activities. Beautiful cathedrals and chateaux also beckon, such as Versailles, evoking royal grandeur.

Sights at a Glance

Historic Buildings and Streets

7 Portes St.-Denis et St.-Martin
16 Bibliothèque Nationale
    François Mitterrand
19 Cité Universitaire
22 Rue la Fontaine
23 Fondation Le Corbusier
27 *Versailles pp250–55*
28 Château de Malmaison
29 La Défense

Churches

1 Cathédrale St.-Alexandre-Nevsky
31 Basilique-Cathédrale de
    St.-Denis

Markets

13 Marché d'Aligre
30 Marché aux Puces de St.-Ouen

Leisure Parks

9 *Parc de la Villette pp238–41*
33 *Disneyland® Paris pp256–9*

Parks, Gardens, and Canals

2 Parc Monceau
8 Parc des Buttes-Chaumont
12 Canal St.-Martin
18 Parc Montsouris
20 Parc André Citroën
25 Bois de Boulogne
32 Château et Bois de Vincennes

Museums and Galleries

3 Musée Nissim de Camondo
4 Musée Cernuschi
6 Musée Gustave Moreau
14 Musée de l'Histoire
    de l'Immigration

24 Musée Marmottan-Monet
26 Musée des Années 30

Neighborhoods

5 Batignolles
10 Belleville and Ménilmontant
15 Bercy
17 13th Arrondissement
21 Front de Seine (Beaugrenelle)

Cemeteries

11 *Cimetière du Père Lachaise
    pp242–3*

Key

▨ Main sightseeing areas
═══ Freeways
▬▬ Major Highways

0 km — 5
0 miles — 3

Sights Outside the Centre

◀ Formal garden at Versailles   For additional keys to symbols *see back flap*

Farther Afield within the Périphérique

The gilded domes of the 19th-century Cathédrale St.-Alexandre-Nevsky

❶ Cathédrale St.-Alexandre-Nevsky

12 Rue Daru 75008. **Map** 4 F3. **Tel** 01 42 27 37 34. M Courcelles. **Open** 3pm–5pm Tue, Fri, Sun. ✝ 6pm Sat, 10am Sun. ⬛ ☐ by appt (reserve at visites.cathedrale.daru@gmail.com).

This imposing Russian Orthodox cathedral with its five golden-copper domes was designed by members of the St. Petersburg Fine Arts Academy and financed jointly by Tzar Alexander II and the local Russian community. The cathedral was completed in 1861. Inside, a wall of icons divides the church in two. The

Greek-cross plan and the rich interior mosaics and frescoes are Neo-Byzantine in style, while the exterior and gilt domes are traditional Russian Orthodox.

Paris's Russian population increased dramatically following the Bolshevik Revolution of 1917, when thousands of Russians fled to France for safety. Rue Daru, in which the cathedral stands, and the surrounding area form "Little Russia," with its Russian schools and the many dance academies, tea shops and bookstores.

❷ Parc Monceau

35 Blvd de Courcelles 75017. **Map** 5 A3. **Tel** 01 42 27 39 56. M Monceau. **Open** 7am–8pm daily (to 10pm summer). *See Eight Guided Walks pp262–3.*

This green haven dates back to 1778 when the Duc de Chartres (later Duc d'Orléans) commissioned the painter-writer and amateur landscape designer Louis Carmontelle to create a magnificent garden. Also a theater designer, Carmontelle created a "garden of dreams," an exotic landscape full of the architectural follies in imitation of English and German fashions of the time. In 1783, the Scottish landscape gardener Thomas Blaikie laid out an area of the garden in English style. The park was the scene of the first recorded parachute landing, made by André-Jacques Garnerin on October 22, 1797. Over the years, the park changed hands and in 1852 it was acquired by

the state and half the land sold off for real estate development. The remaining land was made into public gardens. These were restored and new buildings erected by Adolphe Alphand, architect of the Bois de Boulogne and the Bois de Vincennes.

The park, one of the most chic in Paris, has lost many of its early features. A *naumachia* basin – an ornamental version of a Roman pool used for simulating naval battles – remains, flanked by Corinthian columns. There are also a Renaissance arcade, pyramids, a river, and the Pavillon de Chartres, a charming rotunda designed by Nicolas Ledoux which was once used as a tollhouse. Just south of here is a huge red pagoda, which now houses a gallery devoted to Asian art.

Musée Nissim de Camondo, housing a collection of decorative arts

❸ Musée Nissim de Camondo

63 Rue de Monceau 75008. **Map** 5 A3. **Tel** 01 53 89 06 40, 01 53 89 06 50. M Monceau, Villiers. **Open** 10am–5.30pm Wed–Sun (last adm: 4.30pm). **Closed** public hols. ⬛ ♿ restricted. Ⓦ lesartsdecoratifs.fr

Comte Moïse de Camondo, a leading Jewish financier during the Belle Epoque, commissioned this mansion in 1914. It was built in the style of the Petit Trianon, at Versailles *(see pp250–55)*, to house a rare collection of

Colonnade beside the *naumachia* basin in the Parc Monceau

18th-century furniture, tapestries, paintings, and other precious objects. The museum has been faithfully and lovingly restored to recreate an aristocratic town house of the Louis XV and Louis XVI eras. In the museum, there are Savonnerie carpets, Beauvais tapestries, and the Buffon service (Sèvres porcelain). The very latest gadgets, for the period, are now displayed in the restored kitchen and service quarters, equipped with the utmost efficiency, taste, and forethought by their owner.

❹ Musée Cernuschi

7 Ave Vélasquez 75008. **Map** 5 A3. **Tel** 01 53 96 21 50. Ⓜ Villiers, Monceau. **Open** 10am–6pm Tue–Sun (last adm: 5.30pm). **Closed** public hols. 🔲 📷 🏠 🌐 **cernuschi.paris.fr**

One of the oldest museums in Paris, the Cernuschi is housed in a splendid, light-filled mansion near Parc Monceau and contains an intriguing private collection of late East Asian art, which was amassed by the Milanese-born politician and banker Enrico Cernuschi (1821–96). The original bequest of 5,000 lacquered, ceramic, bronze and ivory items has been augmented by a number of donations and acquisitions over the years. The wide-ranging collection, now about 10,000 items, includes a 5th-century seated Bodhisattva (Buddhist divine being) from Yunkang; *La Tigresse* (a heavily decorated Shang Dynasty bronze vase dating from the 12th century BC); and *Horses and Grooms*, an 8th-century T'ang painting on silk attributed to the era's greatest horse painter, court artist Han Kan.

The magnificent carved altarpiece in the church of Sainte-Marie des Batignolles

Bodhisattva in the Musée Cernuschi

❺ Batignolles

Batignolles, 75007. Ⓜ Porte de Clichy, Place de Clichy.

Formerly used as a royal hunting ground, this neighborhood in the 17th arrondissement of northwestern Paris later grew into a small hamlet. Although it officially became part of the city in the second half of the 19th century, it still feels like a small French village inside cosmopolitan Paris. In the 19th century, it had a lively cultural vibe and counted among its residents the painter Edouard Manet and his fellow artists, who became known as the Groupe des Batignolles, the writer Emile Zola, and, later, the Belgian singer Jacques Brel.

The lovely Church of Sainte-Marie des Batignolles sits in the heart of the neighborhood. While Batignolles has a calm, community feel, it also has a slightly urban atmosphere, with a good mix of lively bars, stylish boutiques, and restaurants. It was one of the first areas in Paris to label their new class of residents *bobos*, or bourgeois bohemians.

Two markets are held in the area: the organic Marché Biologique des Batignolles

and the covered market on Rue Lemercier, which dates back to 1846. On weekends, families converge on the area's several parks, the two largest being the Square des Batignolles and the Parc Clichy – Martin Luther King, which features playgrounds, duck ponds, a skate park, and running trails. The area had been earmarked to be the Olympic Village during the bid for the 2012 Games, which Paris lost to London. The district has undergone substantial development since then, and there are new apartments, stores, and office buildings.

❻ Musée Gustave Moreau

14 Rue de la Rochefoucauld 75009. **Map** 6 E3. **Tel** 01 48 74 38 50. Ⓜ Trinité. **Open** 10am–12.45pm, 2–5.15pm Mon, Wed, Thu, 10am–5.15pm Fri–Sun. **Closed** Jan 1, May 1, Dec 25. 🔲 🏠 🌐 **musee-moreau.fr**

The Symbolist painter Gustave Moreau (1825–98), known for his vivid, imaginative works depicting biblical and mythological fantasies, left to the French state a vast collection of more than 1,000 oils, watercolors and some 4,000 drawings in his town house. One of Moreau's best-known and most outstanding works, *Jupiter and Semele*, can be seen here. There is also a superb collection of his unfinished sketches.

Angel Traveller by Gustave Moreau, in the Musée Gustave Moreau

❼ Portes St.-Denis et St.-Martin

Blvds St.-Denis & St.-Martin 75010.
Map 7 B5, C5. Ⓜ Strasbourg-St.-Denis.

These imposing gates give access to the two ancient and important thoroughfares whose names they bear, running across Paris in a north–south direction. They once marked the entrance to the city. The Porte St.-Denis is 76 ft (23 m) high and was built in 1672 by François Blondel. It is decorated with figures by Louis XIV's sculptor, François Girardon. The gates commemorate victories of the king's armies in Flanders and the Rhine that year. Porte St.-Martin is 56 ft (17 m) tall and was built in 1674 by Pierre Bullet. It celebrates Besançon's capture and the defeat of the Triple Alliance of Spain, Holland, and Germany.

❽ Parc des Buttes-Chaumont

Rue Manin 75019 (main access from Rue Armand Carrel). Ⓜ Botzaris, Buttes-Chaumont. **Open** 7am–8pm daily (until 10pm in summer). 📷 📝 *See pp272–3.*

For many, this is the most pleasant and unexpected park in the city. The panoramic hilly site was formerly a gallows for the execution of criminals, a lime quarry and a garbage dump. It was converted in the mid-1860s, one of

Western arch of the Porte St.-Denis, once the entrance to the city

Napoleon III's many projects to renovate the city *(see pp36–7)*. Baron Haussmann worked with the landscape architect/designer Adolphe Alphand, who organized a vast program to furnish the new sidewalk-lined avenues with benches and lampposts. Others involved in the creation of this large park were the engineer Darcel and the landscape gardener Barillet-Deschamps. They created a lake, made an island with real and artificial rocks, gave it a Roman-style temple (the Temple de la Sibylle, modeled after the Temple of Sybil in Tivoli, Italy) and added a waterfall, streams, two foot-bridges leading to the island, and beaches. Today, visitors will also find boating amenities and donkey rides.

❾ Parc de la Villette

See pp238–41.

The Temple de la Sibylle, high above the Parc des Buttes-Chaumont

❿ Belleville and Ménilmontant

75011, 75012, 75019, 75020.
Le Food Market: Blvd de Belleville.
Ⓜ Couronnes, Ménilmontant.
Open 6pm–10.30pm one Thu per month. 🌐 lefoodmarket.fr
Edith Piaf Museum: 5 Rue Crespin-du-Gast. **Tel** 01 43 55 52 72.
Ⓜ Ménilmontant. **Open** by appointment only, 1–6pm Mon–Wed.

Originally two separate villages on the outskirts of the capital, the neighborhoods of Belleville and Ménilmontant now share four different arrondissements in Paris: the 11th, 12th, 19th, and 20th. In the past, the local population tended to be mainly working class and multi-ethnic – a combination of Chinese, North African, and Jewish. Nowadays, although both quarters remain diverse, they have proved popular with young professionals, who have moved in looking for affordable rents, a lively night-life, organic markets, and a dynamic arts scene. This delightful mix of inexpensive and sophisticated has contributed to creating a modern but charming neighborhood. Food-wise, Belleville is known as the second Chinatown, rivaling the one in the 13th arrondissement, with many authentic restaurants and a Chinese New Year's parade. The hip monthly Le Food Market has sprung up in Ménilmontant, featuring up-and-coming chefs and innovative cuisine. Be sure to put your name on their mailing list to be informed of their next event.

The two largest pockets of green in these neighborhoods are the Parc de Belleville and the cemetery at Père Lachaise *(see pp242–3)*, where the likes of Jim Morrison, Edith Piaf, and Oscar Wilde are buried. The Parc de Belleville has something for everyone, from a skate park and children's playgrounds to lush picnic areas. Toward the top of the park, there is even a small vineyard, covered with Pinot Meunier and Chardonnay vines that produce a handful of kilos of grapes each year. An annual neighborhood festival celebrates the wine. At the top of the vineyard, Belleville has stunning panoramic views over Paris that compare to those from Montmartre.

Near Père Lachaise, in the apartment where she lived when she was 18, is the tiny Edith Piaf Museum, which consists of two red-painted rooms crammed with the singer's personal items, letters, books, and records. Don't miss the remarkable street art of ever-changing colorful murals on Rue Dénoyez.

⓫ Cimetière du Père Lachaise

See pp242–3.

⓬ Canal St.-Martin

Map 8 E2. Ⓜ Jaurès, J. Bonsergent, Goncourt. *See pp264–5.*

The 3-mile (5-km) canal, opened in 1825, provides a shortcut for river traffic between loops of the Seine. It has long been loved by novelists, movie directors and tourists alike. It is dotted with barges and pleasure boats that leave from the Port de l'Arsenal. At the north end of the canal is the Bassin de la Villette waterway and the elegant Neo-Classical Rotonde de la Villette, spectacularly floodlit at night.

Views over Paris from the top of the Parc de Belleville

⓭ Marché d'Aligre

Place d'Aligre 75012. **Map** 14 F5. Ⓜ Ledru-Rollin. **Open** 9am–1pm Mon–Sat (outdoor market closed Mon), 9am–1.30pm Sun.

On Sunday mornings, this lively market offers one of the most colorful sights in Paris. French, Arab, and African traders hawk fruit, vegetables, flowers, and clothing on the streets, while the adjoining covered market, the Beauveau St. Antoine, offers fruit, vegetables, and many intriguing international delicacies.

Aligre is where old and new Paris meet. Here, the established community of this old artisan quarter coexists with a more recently established group of hip urban professionals, lured here by the transformation of the nearby Bastille area *(see p102)*. The indoor market is being renovated following a fire in 2015, but some parts are open.

⓮ Musée de l'Histoire de l'Immigration

293 Ave Daumesnil 75012. **Tel** 01 53 59 58 60. Ⓜ Porte Dorée. **Open** 10am–5.30pm Tue–Fri, 10am–7pm Sat, Sun. **Closed** Jan 1, May 1, Dec 25. 🖼 📷 🎥 ♿ restricted. 📷 🔲 histoire-immigration.fr

This museum and aquarium is housed in a beautiful Art Deco building that was designed especially for the 1931 Colonial Exhibition. The impressive facade has a vast frieze by

A. Janniot, depicting the contributions of France's overseas territories.

Formerly the home of the Musée National des Arts d'Afrique et d'Océanie (whose collection was moved to the Musée du quai Branly in 2003, *see pp194–5*), the Palais de la Porte Dorée now houses the Cité Nationale de l'Histoire de l'Immigration. This acts as both a museum and a cultural center, with regular live performances and movies on the history of immigration in France.

The magnificent 1930s Hall d'Honneur and the Salle des Fêtes (ballroom) are also open to the public. In the basement, there is a magnificent tropical aquarium filled with colorful fish, as well as several terrariums containing tortoises and crocodiles.

Exterior relief on the Musée de l'Histoire de l'Immigration

❾ Parc de la Villette

The old slaughterhouses and livestock market of Paris have been transformed into this Bernard Tschumi-designed urban park. Its vast amenities stretch across 136 acres (55 ha) of a previously run-down part of the city. The plan was to revive the tradition of parks for meetings and activities and to stimulate interest in the arts and sciences. Work began in 1984, and the park has grown to include a science museum, a concert hall, an exhibition pavilion, a spherical movie theater, a circus, and a music center. Linking them all is the park itself, Paris's third largest, with its *folies*, walkways, gardens, and playgrounds. In the summer, the park holds an open-air film festival.

The Folies
These red cubes punctuate the park and provide a variety of services, such as a café and a children's workshop.

Children's Playground
The maze-like setting, complete with sand pits and colorful play equipment, makes this playground a paradise for young children.

★ Grande Halle
The old cattle hall has been transformed into a flexible exhibition space with mobile floors and auditorium.

Entrance

★ Cité de la Musique
This complex holds the music conservatory, library, studios, and the Musée de la Musique, housing over 4,500 objects.

WIP Villette regularly holds shows and exhibitions.

Entrance

★ **Cité des Sciences et de l'Industrie**
This huge science museum boasts the latest in futuristic equipment and has dazzling hands-on displays *(see pp240–41)*.

VISITORS' CHECKLIST

Practical Information
211 Ave Jean Jaurès 75019.
Tel 01 40 03 75 75. **Open** Public spaces: 6am–1am daily. Gardens: May–Sep: 3–7pm Sat & Sun; Oct–Mar: by reservation only.
Le Jardin des Vents et des Dunes: 10am–8pm daily (Nov–Mar: only Wed, Sat & Sun, plus holidays and school vacations). Info Desk: 9.30am–6.30pm daily.
w lavillette.com
Philharmonie de Paris: **Tel** 01 44 84 44 84. **Open** noon–6pm Tue–Sun (from 10am Sun).
Closed May 1.

Transportation
M Porte de Patin, Porte de la Villette. 🚌 75, 139, 150, 152, 375. 🚊 T3b.

★ **Zénith Theater**
This vast polyester tent was built as a venue for pop concerts with a capacity to seat more than 6,000 spectators.

Philharmonie de Paris

This €390-million cultural center encompasses many spaces dedicated to music, including concert and exhibition halls and rehearsal and educational rooms. Architect Jean Nouvel's stunning cutting-edge design for this symphonic concert hall features moving panels to redirect sound, sound-absorbing walls to increase acoustics, and 2,400 seats where the farthest spectator is never more than 105 ft (32 m) away from the conductor.

L'Argonaute
The exhibit consists of a 1950s submarine and a nearby navigation museum.

Cité des Sciences et de l'Industrie

This hugely popular science and technology museum occupies the largest of the old Villette slaughterhouses, which now form part of a massive urban park, Parc de la Villette. Architect Adrien Fainsilber has created an imaginative interplay of light, vegetation, and water in the high-tech, five-story building, which soars 133 ft (40 m) high, stretching over 7 acres (3 ha). At the museum's heart is the Explora exhibit, a fascinating guide to the worlds of science and technology. Visitors can take part in computerized games on space, the earth, transportation, energy, design, and sound. On other levels, there is a children's science city, a planetarium, a library, and stores.

The Main Hall
With a soaring network of shafts, bridges, escalators, and balconies, the vast Main Hall has a cathedral-like atmosphere.

★ The Story of the Universe
An exploration of the birth of the universe, this exhibit takes you back 13.7 billion years to the creation of the first atom.

400-seat auditorium

Hemispheric screen

Main lobby

La Géode

This vast sphere houses a hemispherical screen, 11,000 sq ft (1,000 sq m), showing IMAX and 3D movies. The Géode is prohibited for women more than six-months pregnant.

KEY

① **The moat** was designed by Fainsilber so that natural light could penetrate into the lower levels of the building.

② **The Globalo-Scope** is a 3D projection on a globe, which shows climate change and several other phenomena on a global scale.

③ **The greenhouse** is a square hothouse, 105 ft (32 m) high and wide, linking the park to the building.

Planetarium
Explore our solar system in immersive movies and sessions with astronomy specialists.

Cupolas
The two glazed domes, 56 ft (17 m) in diameter, filter the flow of natural light into the main hall.

VISITORS' CHECKLIST

Practical Information
30 Ave Corentin-Cariou 75019.
Tel 01 40 05 70 00/80 00. **Open**
10am–6pm Tue–Sat, 10am–7pm
Sun. **Closed** Jan 1, May 1, Dec 25.
🖼 ♿ ⬛ ⬛ ⬛ ⬛ Shows,
movies, videos, library, conference
center. **W** cite-sciences.fr

Transportation
Ⓜ Porte de la Villette. 🚌 75,
139, 150, 152, 375, Tramway T3b.
Ⓟ Quai de la Charente.

③

To La Géode

The Round About
Part of the Transportation and Mankind exhibition, this interactive exhibit features several screens that illustrate many different types of transportation.

Walkways
The walkways cross the encircling moat to link the various floors of the museum to the Géode and the park.

★ Children's City
In this lively, extensive area, children can experiment and play with machines that show how scientific principles work.

⓫ Cimetière du Père Lachaise

Paris's most prestigious cemetery is set on a wooded hill overlooking the city. The land was once owned by Père de la Chaise, Louis XIV's confessor, but it was bought in 1803 by order of Napoleon to create a new cemetery. Père Lachaise, the first cemetery in France with a crematorium, became so popular that it was expanded six times during the century. It now contains over 70,000 graves, including those of the writer Honoré de Balzac, the composer Frédéric Chopin, the singer Jim Morrison, and the actor Yves Montand. These, along with striking funerary sculpture, make Père Lachaise a pleasant place for a stroll.

The Columbarium was built at the end of the 19th century. The American dancer Isadora Duncan is one of the many celebrities whose ashes are housed here

★ **Simone Signoret and Yves Montand**
France's most famous post-war cinema couple were renowned for their left-wing views and long turbulent relationship.

KEY

① **Marcel Proust** brilliantly chronicled the *Belle Époque* in his novel *Remembrance of Things Past*.

② **Allan Kardec** was the founder of a 19th-century spiritual cult, which still has a strong following. His tomb is forever covered in pilgrims' flowers.

③ **Mur des Fédérés** is the wall against which the last Communard rebels were shot by government forces in 1871. It is now a place of pilgrimage for left-wing sympathizers.

④ **George Rodenbach**, the 19th-century poet, is depicted as rising out of his tomb with a rose in the hand of his outstretched arm.

⑤ **Elizabeth Demidoff**, a Russian princess who died in 1818, is honored by a three-story Classical temple by Quaglia.

⑥ **The remains of Molière**, the great 17th-century actor and dramatist, were transferred here in 1817 to add historic glamor to the new cemetery.

⑦ **Frédéric Chopin**, the great Polish composer, belonged to the French Romantic generation.

⑧ **Monument aux Morts** by Paul Albert Bartholomé is one of the best monumental sculptures in the cemetery. It dominates the central avenue.

Théodore Géricault
The French Romantic painter's masterpiece, *The Raft of the Medusa* (*see p124*), is depicted on his tomb.

Entrance

★ Oscar Wilde
The Irish dramatist, aesthete, and great wit was cast away from virtuous Britain to die of drink and dissipation in Paris in 1900. Jacob Epstein sculpted the monument.

★ Edith Piaf
Known as "the little sparrow" because of her size, Piaf was the 20th century's greatest French popular singer. In her tragic voice, she sang of the sorrows and love woes of the Paris working class.

Victor Noir
The life-size statue of this 19th-century journalist shot by Pierre Bonaparte, a cousin of Napoleon III, is said to have fertility powers.

Sarah Bernhardt
The great French tragedienne, who died in 1923 aged 78, was famous for her portrayal of Racine heroines.

François Raspail
The tomb of this much-imprisoned partisan of the 1830 and 1840 revolutions is in the form of a prison.

★ Jim Morrison
The death of *The Doors'* lead singer in Paris in 1971 is still a mystery.

⑮ Bercy

75012. **Map** 18 F3. Ⓜ Bercy, Cour St.-Emilion.

This former wine-trading quarter east of the city center, with its once-grim warehouses, pavilions and slum housing, has been transformed into a modern district. An automatic Metro line (Line 14) links it to the heart of the city.

The centerpiece of Bercy is the Palais Omnisports de Paris-Bercy, now the city center's principal venue. The vast pyramidal structure has become a contemporary landmark. Many sports events are held here, as well as classical operas and rock concerts *(see pp337 and 341–2)*.

Other architecturally adventurous buildings dominate Bercy, notably Chemetov's building for the Ministry of Finance, and Frank Gehry's American Center. This houses the Cinematheque Française, a wonderful cinema museum that hosts frequent retrospectives on famous directors.

At the foot of these structures, the imaginatively designed 173-acre (70-ha) Parc de Bercy provides a welcome green space for this part of the city. The park's attractions for children include a traditional carousel.

Former wine stores and cellars along Cours St.-Emilion have been restored as bars, restaurants, and stores, and one of the warehouses now

Bibliothèque Nationale François Mitterrand

contains the Musée des Arts Forains (Fairground Museum), open only for private tours. There is also a multiscreen movie theater and numerous hotels.

⑯ Bibliothèque Nationale François Mitterrand

Quai François-Mauriac 75013. **Map** 18 F4. **Tel** 01 53 79 59 59. Ⓜ Bibliothèque F. Mitterrand, Quai de la Gare. **Open** 9am–7pm daily (from 2pm Mon, from 1pm Sun). Exhibitions: 10am–8pm Tue–Sat, 1–7pm Sun. **Closed** public hols & 2 wks Sep. ♿ 📷 📷 for groups by appt. ♿ 📷 📷 Ⓦ **bnf.fr**

Dominique Perrault's 1996 landmark national library is the most striking of all the *Grands Projets* with which President Mitterrand revitalized this area. Four towers house 12,000,000

volumes, with reference and research libraries in the central podium. Resources include 50,000 digitized illustrations, sound archives, and CD-ROMs. Exhibitions on its hidden collections are often held.

⑰ 13th Arrondissement

Zac Paris Rive Gauche, 75013. **Map** 1 F5. Ⓜ Bibliotheque F. Mitterrand.

Following a ten-year redevelopment project, the Zac Paris Rive Gauche, Paris's 13th arrondissement, has become an area of startling urban regeneration. The once-disused area of land between Gare d'Austerlitz and Ivry-sur-Seine has now been revived to house a university with some 30,000 students. The area also boasts the MK2 Bibliothèque, a vast movie complex with 14 screens, cafés, and exhibition areas. Connected to Bercy by a bridge, the area also offers new housing, schools, and business opportunities.

⑱ Parc Montsouris

2 Rue Gazan, Blvd Jourdan 75014. Ⓜ Porte d'Orléans. 🚊 Cité Universitaire, Glaciere. **Open** 8am–5.30pm Mon–Fr (to 9:30pm in summer), 9am–dusk weekends. Times may vary. 📷

Created in response to Napoleon III's desire for English-style parks, Parc Montsouris was laid out between 1865 and 187 by the landscape architect

Bercy's striking American Center, designed by Frank Gehry

dolphe Alphand on the site of a former granite quarry and cemetery. Montsouris is one of the largest parks in Paris. It has mall hills, clumps of trees, a arge lake, small bridges, grottoes, a waterfall, numerous bronze and stone sculptures, and a restaurant. The park draws a number of migratory birds and is a great place for birding. Children will enjoy the playgrounds, pony rides, carousel, and Guignol puppet theater. Students from the nearby Cité Universitaire come here to jog, relax, or listen to concerts on the expansive lawns. The renowned Montsouris weather station, the oldest continual weather observation post in Paris, is also located in the park.

Relaxing by the lake in the Parc Montsouris

⑲ Cité Universitaire

17–21 Blvd Jourdan 75014. **Tel** 01 44 16 64 00. **M** Porte d'Orléans. **RER** Cité Universitaire. **W** ciup.fr

This is an international city in miniature for more than 5,000 foreign students attending university in Paris. Created in the 1920s, it now contains 40 houses and, fascinatingly, each is in an architectural style linked to different countries. The Swiss House and the Franco-Brazilian House were designed by the Modernist architect Le Corbusier. The International House, donated by John D. Rockefeller in 1936, has a library, restaurant, swimming pool, and theater. The student community makes this a lively and stimulating area of the city to visit.

⑳ Parc André Citroën

Rue Balard 75015. **Tel** 01 56 56 11 56. **M** Javel, Balard. **Open** 8am–dusk daily (9am Sat, Sun & public hols). **♿ 🎫** reservation 01 40 71 75 60.

Opened in 1992, this park offers the city's third large-scale vista on the Seine,

Hot-air balloon, Parc André Citroën

along with Les Invalides and the Champ-de-Mars. Designed by both landscape gardeners and architects, it is a blend of styles, ranging from a wildflower meadow in the north to the sophisticated monochrome mineral and sculpture gardens of the southern section. Water sculptures dot the park, and glasshouses nurture a range of environments. During the summer, there is a tethered hot-air balloon from which visitors can enjoy great views of the city.

International House at the Cité Universitaire

The high-rise buildings of the Front de Seine neighborhood

㉑ Front de Seine (Beaugrenelle)

Bordering the Seine at Quai André Citroën, Quai Grenelle, between Rue de Javel & Rue Emeriau & Place de Brazzaville 75015. Ⓜ Charles Michel. Beaugrenelle shopping and leisure complex: 12 Rue Linois. **Tel** 01 53 95 24 00. **Open** 10am–9pm daily (to 8pm Sun). Ⓦ **beaugrenelle-paris.com**

A few blocks southwest of the Eiffel Tower, along the Seine, in the 15th arrondissement, is the Front de Seine, also known as Beaugrenelle. An innovative urban planning project started in the1970s, this is one of the few areas within the city featuring high-rise towers – most such buildings have been erected outside Paris. The urban design of the Front de Seine was ambitious and creative, and it developed with a vision of the future in mind. Today it is a young, fashionable neighborhood.

Twenty towers surround a connected esplanade painted with murals that can be seen only from the towers them-selves. Different from other high-rises, which are purely residential, and from those at La Défense, which are predominantly commercial, Beaugrenelle's buildings combine "living, working, and leisure," as its motto describes. There are apartments on the upper floors, businesses on the lower floors, and street-level stores and hotels. In order to create a complete neighborhood, the Front de Seine also includes a large supermarket, a gym, a bowling alley, a park, and even a laser-tag venue. The latest addition to the mix is the Beaugrenelle shopping and leisure complex, with more than 120 stores, numerous restaurants, a swimming pool, a post office, a large multiplex movie theater, and a rooftop garden.

An Art Nouveau window in the Rue la Fontaine

㉒ Rue la Fontaine

75016. **Map** 9 A4. Ⓜ Jasmin, Michel-Ange Auteuil.

The Rue la Fontaine and surrounding streets act as a showcase for some of the most exciting architecture of the early 20th century. At No. 14 stands the Castel Béranger, a stunning apartment block made from cheap building materials to keep costs low, yet featuring stained glass, convoluted ironwork, balconies, and mosaics. It established the reputation of Art Nouveau architect Hector Guimard, who went on to design the entrances for the Paris Metro. Several more examples of his work can be seen farther along the street, such as the Hôtel Mezzara at No. 60.

㉓ Fondation Le Corbusier

10 Square du Docteur Blanche 75016. **Tel** 01 42 88 75 72. Ⓜ Jasmin. **Open** Villa La Roche only: 1.30–6pm Mon, 10am–6pm Tue–Sat. Library open by appt, 1.30–6pm Mon–Thu, to 5pm Fri, **Tel** 01 42 88 41 53. **Closed** public hols, 1 week in Aug, Dec 24–Jan 2. 🎦 Movies. 🎦 Tue at 2pm (Tue & Fri in summer). 🏛 *See History of Paris pp40–41.* Ⓦ **fondationlecorbusier.asso.fr**

In a quiet corner of Auteuil are the villas La Roche *(see p269)* and Jeanneret, the first two Parisian houses designed by the architect Charles-Edouard Jeanneret, known as Le Corbusier. Built in the 1920s, they show his revolutionary use of white concrete in Cubist forms. Rooms flow into each other allowing maximum light, and the houses stand on stilts with windows along their entire

:ngth. Villa La Roche was
wned by the art patron Raoul
a Roche and today serves as
documentation center on
e Corbusier. Villa Jeanneret
ouses a library and archives
nd is open only to
esearchers and students
y prior appointment.

Musée Marmottan-Monet

Rue Louis Boilly 75016. **Tel** 01 44 96
0 33. M Muette. **Open** 10am–6pm
ue–Sun (to 9pm Thu). **Closed** Jan 1,
May 1, Dec 25. 🔊 🔊 🔊
marmottan.fr

he museum was created in
934 in the 19th-century
nansion of the art historian
aul Marmottan. In 1932, he
bequeathed his house and his
Renaissance, Consular, and First
Empire collections of paintings
and furniture to the Institut de
France. The focus of the
museum changed after the
bequest by Michel Monet of
65 paintings by his father, the
Impressionist Claude Monet.
Some of his most famous
paintings are here, including
Impression – Sunrise, a beautiful
canvas from the Rouen
Cathedral series, and several
Water Lilies.

Part of Monet's personal art
collection also passed to the
museum, including paintings
by Camille Pissarro and the
Impressionists Pierre Auguste
Renoir and Alfred Sisley. The
museum also displays medieval
illuminated manuscripts.

Villa La Roche, home of the Fondation Le Corbusier

Beyond the Périphérique

🌐 Bois de Boulogne

75016. M Porte Maillot, Porte Dauphine, Porte d'Auteuil, Sablons. **Open**
24 hrs daily. 🔊 to specialty gardens
& museum. 🔊 Shakespeare garden:
Open 9.30am–dusk daily. 🔊 Open-air
theater: **Open** May–Sep. Bagatelle &
Rose gardens: **Open** 9.30am. Closing
times vary according to season (from
4.30pm to 8pm). Jardin d'Acclimatation:
Tel 01 40 67 90 82. **Open** 10am–7pm
daily (Oct–Mar: 6pm). 🔊 🔊 🔊
Fondation Louis Vuitton: 8 Ave du
Mahatma Gandhi 75116. **Tel** 01 40 69
96 00. M Sablons. **Open** 10am–8pm
daily (to 11pm Fri). 🔊 🔊 🔊
fondationlouisvuitton.fr

Between the western edges of
Paris and the Seine, this 2,137-
acre (865-ha) park offers greenery
for strolling and a boating lake,
plus opportunities for horseback
riding, picnicking, or a day at the
races. The Bois de Boulogne is
all that remains of the royal
hunting grounds of the Forêt du
Rouvre. In the mid-19th century,
Napoleon III had it redesigned
and landscaped by Haussmann
along the lines of London's
Hyde Park and Regent's Park.

There are many beautiful
areas within and around the
Bois, including the famous
Hippodrome de Longchamp
race track, the Jardin
d'Acclimatation amusement
park, with traditional rides and
a puppet theater, and Roland
Garros, home to the French
Tennis Open championships.
The Pré Catelan is a self-
contained park with the widest
beech tree in Paris. Hidden
within its borders is the Théâtre
de Verdure, an open-air play-
house that puts on Shakespeare,
dance, and musical performances
in summer. The charming
Bagatelle Gardens feature
architectural follies and an
18th-century orangery famous
for its rose garden, where an
international rose competition
takes place in June. The orangery
was built in 64 days as a bet
between the Comte d'Artois and
Marie-Antoinette. Opened in
2014, Frank Gehry's stunning
Fondation Louis Vuitton is a
cultural center dedicated to
modern art.

The Bois de Boulogne has a
reputation as a seedy area after
dark, so it is best avoided at night.

The orangery, Bagatelle Gardens in the Bois de Boulogne

㉖ Musée des Années 30

28 Ave André Morizet, Boulogne-Billancourt 92100. **Tel** 01 55 18 53 00/ 01 55 18 46 42. **M** Marcel Sembat. **Open** 11am–6pm Tue–Sun. **Closed** Jan 1, May 1, Dec 25. & 🖼 🖼 🖨 🖼 **W** annees30.com

Inaugurated in 1998, this museum of the 1930s forms part of an arts complex, the Espace Landowski, named after Paul Landowski, a sculptor who lived in Boulogne-Billancourt from 1905 until his death in 1961, and his musician brother, Marcel. Several of Paul's works are on show here among the collection of some 800 sculptures, 2,000 paintings, furniture, and ceramics.

The museum gives a vivid impression of the aesthetic mood of the era and its decorative arts through the work of artists such as Juan Gris and Robert Mallet-Stevens, classics of industrial design, and movie-makers such as Renoir and Pagnol. The museum organizes temporary exhibitions, as well as themed tours of the architectural and industrial heritage of Boulogne-Billancourt.

㉗ Versailles

See pp250–55.

㉘ Château de Malmaison

Ave du Château de Malmaison 92500 Rueil-Malmaison. **Tel** 01 41 29 05 55. **RER** La Défense then bus 258. **Open** Apr–Sep: 10am–12.30pm & 1.30–5.45pm Wed–Mon (6.15pm Sat, Sun); Oct–Mar: 10am–12.30pm & 1.30–5.15pm Wed–Mon (5.45pm Sat, Sun). Park: 10am–6.30pm daily (Oct–Mar: to 6pm). **Closed** Jan 1, Dec 25. 🖼 🖼 See History of Paris pp34–5. **W** chateau-malmaison.fr

This 17th-century château was bought in 1799 by Josephine de Beauharnais, wife of Napoleon I. A magnificent veranda, Classical statues, and a small theater were added. After his campaigns,

The vast Grande Arche in La Défense

Napoleon and his entourage would come here to relax. The château became Josephine's main residence after their divorce. Today, it is an important Napoleonic museum, together with the nearby Château de Bois-Préau. Furniture, portraits, artifacts, and mementos of the imperial family are displayed in rooms reconstructed in the style of the First Empire.

Part of the original grounds still exist, including Josephine's famous pretty rose garden.

㉙ La Défense

1 Parvis de la Défense. **M** **RER** La Défense. La Grande Arche: **Closed** to the public. 🛈 See History of Paris pp42–3. **W** grandearche.com

This skyscraper business district on the western edge of Paris is one of Europe's largest modern office developments and covers 80 ha (198 acres). It was launched in 1958 to create a new home for leading French and multinational companies. Since then, a major artistic scheme has transformed many

of the squares into fascinating open-air museums.

In 1989, one of Paris's most striking landmarks La Grande Arche was added to the complex – an enormous hollow cube large enough to contain Notre-Dame cathedral. This was designed by Danish architect Otto von Spreckelsen as part of major construction works, or Grands Travaux, which were initiated by (and are now a memorial to) the late President François Mitterrand. The sides of the cube contain offices. The arch is closed to the public.

㉚ Marché aux Puces de St.-Ouen

Rue des Rosiers, St.-Ouen 75018. **Map** 2 F2. **M** Porte-de-Clignancourt, Garibaldi. **Open** 9am–6pm Sat, 10am–6pm Sun, 11am–5pm Mon; reduced hours during summer. 🖼 call 01 40 11 77 36. See Markets p331. **W** marcheaux puces-saintouen.com

This is the oldest, most expensive and largest of the Paris flea markets, covering

First Empire decor at the Château de Malmaison

Marché aux Puces de St.-Ouen, an antiques and bric-a-brac market

15 acres (6 ha). In the 19th century, rag merchants and hobos would gather outside the city limits and offer their wares for sale. By the 1920s, there was a proper market here, where masterpieces could sometimes be purchased cheaply from the often uninformed sellers. Today, it is divided into specialty markets. Known especially for its profusion of furniture and ornaments from the Second Empire (1852–70), few bargains are to be found these days, yet some 150,000 bargain-hunters, tourists, and dealers still flock here to browse among more than 2,000 stands (*see p331*).

③ Basilique-Cathédrale de St.-Denis

1 Rue de la Légion D'Honneur, 93200 St.-Denis. **Tel** 01 48 09 83 54. **M** St.-Denis-Basilique. **RER** St.-Denis. **Open** Apr–Sep: 10am–6.15pm Mon–Sat, noon–6.15pm Sun; Oct–Mar: 10am–5.15pm Mon–Sat, noon–5.15pm Sun (last adm: 30 min before closing). **Closed** Jan 1, May 1, Dec 25. ✝ 8.30am, 10am Sun. 🅿🅐🅒🅑

Constructed between 1137 and 1281, the cathedral is on the site of the tomb of St. Denis, the first bishop of Paris, who was beheaded in AD 250. The building was the original influence for Gothic art. From Merovingian times, it was a burial place for rulers of France. During the Revolution, many tombs were desecrated and scattered, but the best were stored, and now represent a collection of funerary art. Memorials include those of Dagobert (died 638), Henri II (died 1559), Catherine de Medici (died 1589), and Louis XVI and Marie-Antoinette (died 1793).

③ Château et Bois de Vincennes

M Château de Vincennes. **RER** Vincennes. Château: Ave de Paris 94300 Vincennes. **Tel** 01 43 28 15 48. **Open** Mid-May–mid-Sep: 10am–6pm daily; mid-Sep–mid-May: 10am–5pm daily; options available for guided visits, last adm: 45 min before closing. **Closed** public hols. 🅐🅒🅑 Bois de Vincennes: **Open** dawn to dusk daily. 🅦 **chateau-vincennes.fr**

The Château de Vincennes, enclosed by a defensive wall and a moat, was once a royal residence. It was here that Henry V of England died of dysentery, after suffering agonizing pain, in 1422. His body was boiled in the château's kitchen to prepare it for shipping back to England. Abandoned when the palace of Versailles was completed, the château was subsequently converted into an arsenal by Napoleon.

The 14th-century *donjon*, or keep, is the tallest such structure in Europe and is a fine example of medieval military architecture. It houses the château's museum. Building work on the Gothic chapel started in 1380, but was not finished until around 1550. The chapel features beautiful stone rose windows and a single aisle. Two 17th-century pavilions house a fascinating museum of army insignia.

Once a royal hunting ground, the Bois de Vincennes was given to the City of Paris by Napoleon III in 1860. Baron Haussmann's landscape architect added a number of ornamental lakes and cascades. Among the forest's main attractions is the largest amusement park in France (open from Palm Sunday to end of May) and the renovated Parc Zoologique de Paris. This zoo makes a special effort to preserve, protect and promote animal species and raise awareness of the importance of protecting our environment.

The imposing Château de Vincennes

㉗ The Palace and Gardens of Versailles

Visitors passing through the rich interior of this colossal palace, or strolling in its vast gardens, will understand why it was the glory of the Sun King's reign. Starting in 1668 with his father's modest hunting lodge, Louis XIV built the largest palace in Europe, housing 20,000 people at a time. Architects Louis Le Vau and Jules Hardouin-Mansart designed the buildings, Charles Le Brun did the interiors, and André Le Nôtre, the great landscaper, redesigned the gardens. The gardens are formally styled into regular patterns of paths and groves, hedges and flowerbeds, pools of water, and fountains.

★ **Formal Gardens**
Geometric paths and shrubberies are features of the formal gardens.

★ **The Château**
Louis XIV made the château into the center of political power in France (see pp252–5).

KEY

① **The Water Parterre's** vast pools of water are decorated with superb bronze statues.

② **The Fountain of Latona** features marble basins topped with Balthazar Marsy's statue of the goddess Latona.

③ **The South Parterre's** shrubbery and ornate flowerbeds overlook the Swiss pond.

④ **The Orangery** was built beneath the Parterre du Midi to house exotic plants in winter.

⑤ **The King's Garden with Mirror Pool** is a 19th-century English garden and pool created by Louis XVIII.

⑥ **The Grand Canal** was the setting for Louis XIV's many boating parties.

Fountain of Neptune

Dragon Fountain
The fountain's centerpiece is a winged monster.

Colonnade
Mansart designed this circle of marble arches in 1685.

VISITORS' CHECKLIST

Practical Information
Place d'Armes, Versailles. **Tel** 01 30 83 78 00. **Open** Château: 9am–6.30pm Tue–Sun (Nov–Mar: to 5.30pm). Grand & Petit Trianons: noon–6.30pm Tue–Sun (Nov–Mar: to 5.30pm daily). Gardens: 8am–8.30pm daily (winter: to 6pm). Park: from 7am daily. 🚻♿🎁🎧🍴📷🎫 Les Grandes Eaux Musicales: Apr–Oct: Sat & Sun, Tue in Jun; La Serenade Royale de la Galerie des Glaces: mid-Jun–mid-Sep: daily; Les Grandes Eaux Nocturnes: mid-Jun–mid-Sep: Sat. **W** chateauversailles.fr

Transportation
🚌 Versailles Express from Eiffel Tower. **RER** Versailles Rive Gauche, Versailles Chantier.

⑥

Petit Trianon
Built in 1762 as a retreat for Louis XV, this small palace became a favorite of Marie-Antoinette.

Fountain of Neptune
Groups of sculptures spray spectacular jets of water in Le Nôtre and Mansart's 17th-century fountain.

★ Grand Trianon
Louis XIV built this small palace of stone and pink marble in 1687 to escape the rigors of court life, and to enjoy the company of his mistress, Madame de Maintenon.

The Main Palace Buildings of Versailles

The present palace grew as a series of "envelopes" enfolding the original hunting lodge, whose low brick front is still visible in the center. In the 1660s, Louis Le Vau built the first envelope, a series of wings that expanded into an enlarged courtyard. It was decorated with marble busts, antique trophies, and gilded roofs. On the garden side, columns were added to the west facade and a great terrace was created on the first floor. Mansart took over in 1678 and added the two immense north and south wings and filled Le Vau's terrace to form the Hall of Mirrors. He designed the chapel, which was finished in 1710. The Opera House (L'Opéra) was added by Louis XV in 1770.

Main Gate

South Wing
The wing's original apartments for great nobles were replaced by Louis-Philippe's museum of French history.

KEY

① **The Main Gate of Honor**, Mansart's original gateway grille is surmounted by the royal arms, and is the entrance to the Courtyard of Honor.

② **Courtyard of Honor**

③ **The Royal Courtyard** was separated from the Courtyard of Honor by elaborate grillwork during Louis XIV's reign. It was accessible only to royal carriages.

④ **The Clock** overlooking the Marble Courtyard is flanked by Hercules and Mars.

⑤ **Versailles History Gallery** has a permanent exhibition detailing the construction of Versailles from Louis XIII's hunting lodge to modern times.

1661 Louis XIV enlarges château

1667 Grand Canal begins

1668 Construction of new château by Le Vau

1722 12-year-old Louis XV occupies Versailles

Louis XV

1793 Louis XVI and Marie-Antoinette executed

1837 Inauguration of the Museum of the History of France

1682 Louis XIV and Marie-Thérèse move to Versailles

1671 Interior decoration by Le Brun begins

1715 Death of Louis XIV. Versailles abandoned by court

1789 King and queen forced to leave Versailles for Paris

1774 Louis XVI and Marie-Antoinette live at Versailles

1919 Treaty of Versailles signed on June 28

1650 1700 1750 1800 1850 1900

★ Marble Courtyard
The courtyard is decorated with marble paving, urns, busts and a gilded balcony.

North Wing
The chapel, Opéra, and picture galleries occupy this wing, which originally housed royal apartments.

★ L'Opéra
Built for the 1770 marriage of the future Louis XVI and Marie-Antoinette, the Opéra is now used as a theater.

★ Chapelle Royale
Mansart's last great work, this two-story Baroque chapel was Louis XIV's last addition to Versailles.

Inside the Château of Versailles

The sumptuous main apartments are on the first floor of the vast château complex. Around the Marble Courtyard are the private apartments of the king and the queen. On the garden side are the state apartments where official court life took place. These were richly decorated by Charles Le Brun with colored marbles, stone and wood carvings, murals, velvet, silver, and gilded furniture. Beginning with the Salon d'Hercule, each state room is dedicated to an Olympian deity. The climax is the Hall of Mirrors, where 357 great mirrors face 17 tall arched windows.

★ Queen's Bedroom
In this room, the queens of France gave birth to the royal children in full public view.

Key to Floorplan

- South wing
- Coronation room
- Madame de Maintenon's apartments
- Queen's apartments and private suite
- State apartments
- King's apartments and private suite
- North wing
- Non-exhibition space

The Salon du Sacre is adorned with huge paintings of Napoleon by Jacques-Louis David.

Cour des Princes; access to gardens

Exit to gardens

Entrance

Stairs to ground floor reception area

Dufour Pavillion Entrance

Pursuit of the Queen

On October 6, 1789, a Parisian mob invaded the palace seeking the despised Marie-Antoinette. The queen, roused in alarm from her bed, fled toward the king's rooms through the anteroom known as the Oeil-de-Boeuf. As the mob tried to break into the room, the queen beat on the door of the king's bedroom. Once admitted, she was safe, at least until morning, when she and the king were removed to Paris by the cheering and triumphant mob.

★ Chapelle Royale
The chapel's first floor was reserved for the royal family and the ground floor for the court. The interior is richly decorated in white marble, gilding and Baroque murals.

★ **Hall of Mirrors**
Great state occasions were held in this multi-mirrored room stretching 240 ft (73 m) along the west facade. The Treaty of Versailles was ratified here in 1919, ending World War I.

Oeil-de-Boeuf

The King's Bedroom is where Louis XIV died in 1715, aged 77.

Salon de la Guerre
The room's theme of war is dramatically reinforced by Antoine Coysevox's stuccoed relief of Louis XIV riding to victory.

Salon d'Apollon
Designed by Le Brun and dedicated to the god Apollo, this was Louis XIV's throne room. A copy of Hyacinthe Rigaud's famous portrait of the king (1701) hangs here.

The Cabinet du Conseil is where the king received his ministers and his family.

Louis XVI's library features Neo-Classical paneling and the king's terrestrial globe.

★ **Salon de Vénus**
A Louis XIV statue stands amid the rich marble decor of this room.

㉝ Disneyland® Paris

Disneyland® Paris is built on a massive scale – the 5,510-acre (2,230-ha) site encompasses two theme parks; seven hotels (several with swimming pools); a shopping, dining, and entertainment village; an ice-skating rink; a lake; two convention centers; and a golf course. One stop down the line from its very own train station lies Val d'Europe, a huge shopping mall with more than 180 shopping outlets, including 60 discount stores, and a SEA LIFE Aquarium.

Unbeatable for complete escapism, combined with vibrant excitement and sheer energy, the parks offer extreme rides and gentle experiences accompanied by phenomenal visual effects.

The Queen of Hearts' Castle, in Alice's Curious Labyrinth

The Parks

Disneyland® Paris consists of Disneyland® Park and Walt Disney Studios® Park. Disneyland® Park is based on the Magic Kingdom of California and has more than 60 rides or attractions. The most recent is Walt Disney Studios® Park, where interactive exhibits and live shows bring alive the wizardry of the movie and television industry. Find out more at: www.disneylandparis.com or call 0844 800 8898 (UK), 0825 30 60 30 or 30 05 00 (France).

Getting There

By Car

Disneyland® Paris lies 20 miles (32 km) east of Paris, and has its own link (exit 14) from the A4 eastbound from Paris and the A4 westbound, from Strasbourg. Follow the signs to Marne la Vallée (Val d'Europe) until you see the Disneyland signs. (Disney's Davy Crockett Ranch is exit 13.)

By Air

Both Orly and Charles de Gaulle Airports have a shuttle bus (VEA) which runs every 30 minutes (45 in low season). No reservations are necessary. The fare is about €13–17 per person.

By Train

The Paris RER A runs directly to the parks at Marne la Vallée, as does the TGV with connections throughout Europe, including with the Eurostar.

Parking

There is space for over 12,000 vehicles, and an efficient moving sidewalk conveys you to the exit. Parking costs €15 per day for cars, and €20 for RVs and buses. Parking at Disneyland® Paris hotels is free to guests, and the Disneyland® Hotel and Disney's Hotel New York® offer valet parking.

Opening Hours

The Parks tend to open at 10am year round. Disneyland® Park closes at 11pm in high season and earlier in low season. The Walt Disney Studios® Park closes at 8pm in high season and 6pm in low season. Special events, such as Hallowe'en and New Year's Eve, can mean extended hours; check the website for details.

When to Visit

The busiest times are Christmas and New Year, mid-February to early April and July to early September, and mid-October. Busiest days are Saturday–Monday; Tuesday and Wednesday are quietest.

Length of Visit

To experience everything Disneyland® Paris has to offer, you really need to spend three or four days at the resort. Although it is possible to tour the Parks in one day each, to enjoy them at less than break-neck pace you need at least two days for Disneyland® Park alone, and if you want to include Buffalo Bill's Wild West show or

Eating and Drinking

There's no need to leave the park to eat during the day. **Au Chalet de la Marionnette** (Fantasyland®) is excellent for kids (and almost deserted at 3pm), as is the **Cowboy Cook-out Barbecue** (Frontierland®), which tends to be rather more crowded. **Colonel Hathi's Pizza Outpost** (Adventureland®) is worth a visit just to see the authentic colonial gear, while **Café Hyperion – Videopolis** (Discoveryland) offers good food plus excellent entertainment, but service is very slow.

You pay a premium for full-service restaurants but the experience of eating at **Blue Lagoon Restaurant** (Adventureland®) is one you will remember. You dine on the "shore" of a Caribbean Pirate hideaway while the ships from *Pirates of the Caribbean* glide past. **Walt's**, on Main Street, USA®, is also a good but pricey restaurant offering American fare. If you're lucky, they'll seat you so that you can watch the afternoon Main Street parade in comfort from an upstairs window.

In Disney Village® **Annette's Diner** is staffed by roller-skating waitresses against a background of 1950s records. **Planet Hollywood®** is another good option, and the **Rainforest Café®** provides an interestingly animated meal. Bavarian specialties are on the menu in **King Ludwig's Castle**, while a giant **McDonald's®** serves the usual fare. The hotel restaurants are more expensive the nearer they are located to the park.

visit all of the attractions in Disney Village®, then you'll be pushed to manage it all in under four days. Locals turn up on a daily basis from Paris, which is only 35 minutes away on the RER, but most guests from farther afield will stay in hotels. Disney offers several packages for those who wish to stay on site. These include passes for the Parks, and accommodations with continental breakfast included. All-inclusive packages are also available.

Tickets

Tickets can be bought online, as part of a package, or from any Disney Store before you leave home, or at the Park upon arrival – though this means standing in line. One-, two-, or three-day tickets are available. Hopper tickets allow same-day entry to both Parks. The Paris transportation system RATP also sells tickets combining RER travel and entry to the Parks. Once inside, you can use your ticket to get a fast pass for certain rides, with a specific time slot, to avoid the lines.

Getting Around

Disney provides an efficient transportation system between the Parks and the hotels (except Disney's Davy Crockett Ranch), with buses on the half hour. In summer, a fleet of little open-top buses drives slowly around Lake Disney, ferrying guests between the three lakeside hotels and Disney Village®. If you're staying at any of the

Sleeping Beauty Castle, the centerpiece of the Park

Which Hotel?

There are six hotels on site, and one in woodland 3 miles (2 km) away. The best hotels are the closest to the Parks.

Hotel Santa Fe®: basic, small, and reasonably inexpensive. The only hotel offering parking immediately outside your room.
Hotel Cheyenne®: a Wild West theme hotel, about 17 minutes' walk from the Park. Small rooms (with bunks for the kids); a Native American village play area. Inexpensive and a great experience. Kids love this hotel.
Sequoia Lodge®: a lakeside "hunter's lodge," moderately priced with more than 1,000 rooms. Ask for a room in the main building. Rooms at the front have great views.
Newport Bay Club®: a huge, nautically themed hotel on the lakeside. Moderately priced, this massive hotel has a huge convention center, magnificent swimming pool, and three floors offering extra services for a supplement.
Disney's Hotel New York®: expensive and business-oriented with a large convention center. An ice-skating rink is available Oct–Mar.
Disneyland® Hotel: the jewel in the crown. Expensive, but right at the entrance to the Disneyland® Park. Full of delightful touches, such as grandfather clocks and ever-present Disney characters. The Castle Club is a 50-room hotel-within-a-hotel. If you can afford it, a week of decadent fawning and unrestrained hedonism can be yours!
Disney's Davy Crockett Ranch: log cabins sleeping 4–6 are grouped around a woodland trail, as well as traditional camping amenities. The best choice for family activities with some excellent amenities: the pool ranks as one of the best in Disneyland® Paris.

on-site hotels it's only a short walk (20 minutes at most) to the Park gates.

Money

Credit cards are accepted everywhere within the resort. ATMs and commission-free foreign exchange are available immediately inside the Park entrances and at reception in all the hotels.

Disabled Travellers

City Hall (immediately within Disneyland® Park) has a brochure outlining the facilities for the disabled, and a Disabled Guest Guide can be pre-ordered (free) from the website. The complex is designed very much with the disabled in mind and wheelchairs can be hired, but note that cast members are not allowed to assist with lifting people or moving wheelchairs.

Staying in a Disney Hotel

The on-site hotels offer rooms at a wide range of prices; generally, those closest to the Parks are the most expensive.

The runaway mine-train track of Big Thunder Mountain

Advantages include virtually no traveling to reach the Parks, fast passes (ask at reception about restrictions), and "early bird" entry to the parks on selected dates (usually at peak times).

If you stay at a Disney hotel, you will be given a hotel ID card which is very important. As well as being used to charge anything you buy back to your hotel room (and have it delivered there), it also allows you entry to the Disneyland hotel grounds early in the morning while they're still closed to day trippers (the grounds also act as an entrance to the Park).

For children (of any age), one of the most exciting bonuses of staying in an on-site hotel is the chance to dine with Disney characters.

Exploring Disneyland® Paris

The resort consists of two large entertainment areas, Disneyland® Park and the Walt Disney Studios® Park. The former celebrates Hollywood folklore and fantasies, while the latter highlights the ingenuity involved in cinema, animation, and television production. In the run-up to the resort's 25th anniversary, in 2017, many attractions are being enhanced. As a result, some rides may be closed during this time.

Disneyland® Park

Main Street, USA®

Main Street represents a fantasy small-town America, right down to the traffic, which includes horse-drawn rail cars, a paddy wagon, and other vintage transportation in a system that runs between Town Square and Central Plaza. The Victorian facades offer a wealth of detail, and front interesting stores. The Emporium is the place for gifts. Farther along, you can snack at Casey's Corner or succumb to the aromas from Cookie Kitchen or the Cable Car Bake Shop. Either side of the stores are the Discovery and Liberty Arcades, offering a covered route to the Central Plaza and hosting displays and small stands.

On certain nights, thousands of lights set Main Street's paving aglow. Disney's Fantillusion, a fantasy of music, live action, and illuminated floats, begins at Town Square. From Main Street you can ride a 19th-century "steam" engine. Do note that boarding elsewhere than Main Street is not always possible before noon.

Frontierland®

This homage to America's Wild West hosts some of the Park's most popular attractions. Big Thunder Mountain, a rollercoaster ride, is circled by the Thunder Mesa riverboat that takes a musical cruise around America's finest natural monuments. Phantom Manor is an excellent ghost ride with realistic special effects. Pocahontas Indian Village and Legends of the Wild West are both popular with younger children.

Adventureland®

Enjoy the wild rides and Audio-Animatronics of Adventureland®. Indiana Jones™ and the Temple of Peril hurtles you through a derelict mine. The ride has torches, steep drops, and tight 360° loops.

Pirates of the Caribbean is a great boat ride through underground prisons and past fighting galleons. La Cabane des Robinson, based on Jonathan Wyss's *Swiss Family Robinson*, starts with a shaky climb up an 88-ft (27-m) Banyan Tree. From here, you explore the rest of the island, including the caves of Ben Gunn from *Treasure Island* and the awe-inspiring suspension bridge near Spyglass Hill. The children's playground, Pirates' Beach, and Aladdin's Enchanted Passage are also well worth a visit.

Fantasyland®

The buildings here are modeled on those in animated movies. Many attractions are for younger children, such as Snow White and the Seven Dwarfs, and Pinocchio's Fantastic Journey. The very young will love Dumbo the Flying Elephant. Peter Pan's Flight is a triumph of imagination and technology, flying you high over the streets of London. A popular diversion is Alice's Curious Labyrinth.

Hourly, there's a musical parade of clockwork figures at "It's a small world." Aboard a boat, you meander through lands of animated models to the strains of the eponymous song. Le Pays des Contes de Fées (Storybook Land) is another boat ride. Next, hop aboard Casey Jr. for a train ride circling the boats.

Discoveryland

Science fiction and the future are the themes here. The multi-loop ride Space Mountain®: Mission 2 draws crowds from the outset, but at the end of the day, you can often walk straight on. Les Mystères du Nautilus takes you right into the submarine from *20,000 Leagues Under the Sea*. At Autopia, kids can drive a real car, while Orbitron® features spaceships. Star Tours takes you on a breathtaking journey in a star shuttle. Buzz Lightyear Laser Blast takes you into the world of toys.

Videopolis has the best shows. Captain EO is a masterpiece of total sensory stimulation. The Jedi Training Academy welcomes aspiring Padawans to learn to use the Force. Register early.

Walt Disney Studios® Park

Front lot

Inside the giant studio gates, you can't miss Mickey Mouse as he appears in *The Sorcerer's Apprentice*. Also hard to miss is the "Earful Tower," a massive studio icon based on the water tower at the Disney Studios in California. Disney Studio 1 houses a film set boulevard, complete with stylised street facades and venues such as the 1930s-style Club Swankedero, the Liki Tiki tropical bar, and the ultra cool rat-packesque Hep Cat Club. Also behind the facades is the Legends of Hollywood store.

Toon Studio®

A huge *Sorcerer's Apprentice* hat marks the entrance to the Art of Disney Animation®, an interactive attraction tracing the history of moving imagery. Animagique® brings together some of the greatest moments from the Disney corpus. In Flying Carpets over Agrabah®, the genie from *Aladdin* invites spectators to take part in an astonishing magic carpet ride. Crush's Coaster® takes you into the underwater animated world of Nemo where you face sharks. Toy Story Playland takes visitors to "Andy's Backyard" for a simulated parachute drop.

Production Courtyard®

At the interactive attraction Stitch Live!, an animated Stitch talks to the audience. CinéMagique is a must for movie buffs, as it covers the history of both American and European cinema. Must-dos include the

Studio Tram Tour and a ride on the Twilight Zone Tower of Terror™ where you plunge 13 floors inside a haunted hotel.

Backlot

This area focuses on special effects, movie music recording, and dare-devil stunts. Armageddon Special Effects presents a tour of film trickery, while Rock 'n' Roller Coaster is a high-speed attraction (in fact, it is the fastest ride in any Disney theme park)

that combines a once-in-a-lifetime ride with neon lights and pulsating Aerosmith music.

La Place de Rémy

This themed area plays host to the park's 60th attraction, Ratatouille : L'Aventure Totalement Toquée de Rémy. The six-seater "ratmobile" whisks visitors off on a culinary adventure through the cold storage and dining room of Chef Gusteau's famous Paris restaurant.

Rides and Attractions — This chart is designed to help you make the best use of your time at Disneyland.	Lines	Height / Age Restriction	Best Time to Ride or Visit	Fastpass®	Scary Rating	May Cause Motion Sickness	Rating Overall
Phantom Manor	◗		Any		❷		★
Big Thunder Mountain	●	1.2m	FT	✔	❷		★
Pocahontas Indian Village	○		Any		❶		▼
Indiana Jones™ & the Temple of Peril	●	1.4m	LT	✔	❸	✔	★
Adventure Isle	○		Any		❶		▼
La Cabane des Robinson	○		Any		❶		▼
Pirates of the Caribbean	○		Any		❶		★
Peter Pan's Flight	●		FT	✔	❶		◆
Snow White & the Seven Dwarfs	●		>11		❶		◆
Pinocchio's Fantastic Journey	●		>11		❶		▼
Dumbo the Flying Elephant	●		FT		❶		▼
Mad Hatter's Teacups	◗		>12		❶		▼
Alice's Curious Labyrinth	○		Any		❶		▼
"It's a Small World"	○		Any		❶		◆
Casey Jr. – Le Petit Train du Cirque	○		>11		❶		◆
Le Pays des Contes de Fées	○		Any		❶		◆
Buzz Lightyear Laser Blast	◗		Any	✔	❶	✔	◆
Star Tours	○	1.32m	Any	✔	❶		★
Space Mountain®: Mission 2	●	1.32m	LT	✔	❸	✔	★
Captain EO	○		Any		❶		★
Autopia	●	1.2m	FT		❶		▼
Orbitron®	●		FT		❶		▼
Jedi Training Academy	◗	7–12 yrs	FT		❶		◆
Disney Studio 1	◗		Any		❶		◆
Art of Disney Animation®	◗		Any		❶		▼
Animagique®	●		Any		❶		◆
Crush's Coaster®	○	1.07m	Any		❶	✔	★
Flying Carpets Over Agrabah®	●	1.2m	FT		❶	✔	◆
Playhouse Disney Live on Stage!	○		Any		❶		★
CinéMagique	◗		Any		❶		◆
Stitch Live!	◗		FT		❶		◆
Studio Tram Tour®	●		FT		❶		★
Twilight Zone Tower of Terror™	●	1.02m	Any	✔	❸	✔	★
Armageddon Special Effects	●		Any		❶		▼
Rock 'n' Roller Coaster	●	1.2m	Any	✔	❸	✔	★
L'Aventure Totalement Toquée de Rémy	●	1.07m	Any	✔	❶		▼

Short - ○ Medium - ◗ Long - ● Anytime - Any Before 11- >11 First thing - FT Last thing - LT
Not Scary - ❶ Slightly - ❷ Very - ❸ Quite good - ▼ Very good - ◆ Outstanding - ★

EIGHT GUIDED WALKS

Paris is a city for walking. It is more compact and easier to get around than many other great capitals. Most of its great sights are within walking distance of one another and they are close to the heart of the city, the Ile de la Cité.

There are 14 classic tourist areas described in the *Area by Area* section of this book, each with a short walk marked on its *Street by Street map*, taking you past many of the most interesting sights. Yet Paris offers a wealth of lesser-known but equally remarkable areas, whose special history, architecture, and local customs reveal other facets of the city.

The eight walks around the following neighborhoods take in the main sights and also introduce visitors to their subtle details, such as street markets, quirky churches, canals, gardens, old village streets, and bridges. And the literary, artistic, and historical associations allow the past and present to blend into the changing and vibrant life of the modern city. Auteuil is renowned for its

luxury modern residential architecture, Monceau for its sumptuous Second Empire mansions, and Ile St.-Louis for its *ancien régime* town houses and narrow streets. The old-fashioned charm of the iron footbridges survives along Canal St.-Martin, and steep village streets that were once home to famous artists still enrich Montmartre. A tranquil village atmosphere also pervades two lesser-known hilltop districts – Buttes-Chaumont, with one of Paris's loveliest parks, and Buttes-aux-Cailles, whose quaint, cobble-stone alleys belie its association with the ill-fated Paris Commune of 1871, while the once working-class area of Faubourg St.-Antoine has been given a new lease on life as an arti-sans' quarter with a pleasure-boat harbor.

All the walk areas are readily accessible by public transportation and the nearest Metro stations and bus routes are listed in the *Tips for Walkers* boxes. For each walk, there are suggestions on convenient resting points, such as cafés and squares, along the route.

Montmartre
(pp270–71)

Parc Monceau
(pp262–3)

Buttes-
Chaumont
(pp272–3)

Canal St.-Martin
(pp264–5)

Opéra
Quarter

Champs-
Elysées

Chaillot
Quarter

Tuileries
Quarter

Beaubourg
and
Les Halles

The
Marais

Faubourg
St.-Antoine
(pp274–5)

Seine

Invalides
and
Eiffel Tower
Quarter

St-Germain-
des-Prés

Ile St-Louis

Ile de La
Cité (pp266–7)

Auteuil
(pp268–9)

Latin
Quarter

Luxembourg
Quarter

Jardin des
Plantes
Quarter

Montparnasse

Buttes-aux-Cailles
(pp276–7)

Key

0 kilometers 2

0 miles 1

••• Walk route

◀ Paintings for sale at the bustling Place du Tertre

A 90-Minute Walk around Parc Monceau

This leisurely walk passes through the exquisite late-18th-century Parc Monceau, the centerpiece of a smart Second Empire district. It then follows a route along surrounding streets, where groups of opulent mansions stunningly convey the magnificence in which some Parisians live, before ending at Place St.-Augustin. For details on Monceau sights, see page 234.

Ruysdaël gate

Parc Monceau to Avenue Velasquez

The walk starts at the Monceau Metro station ① on the Boulevard de Courcelles. Enter the park where Nicolas Ledoux's 18th-century tollhouse ② stands. On either side are sumptuously gilded 19th-century wrought-iron gates that support ornate lampposts.

Parc Monceau's tollhouse ②

19th-century Neo-Classical mansions. At No. 7 is the splendid Cernuschi museum ⑥, which houses a collection of Far Eastern art (see p235).

Take the second path on the left past the monument to Guy de Maupassant ③ (1897). This is only one of a series of six Belle Epoque monuments of prominent French writers and musicians that are picturesquely scattered throughout the park. Most of them feature a solemn bust of a great man who is accompanied by a swooning muse.

Straight ahead is the most important remaining folly, a moss-covered Corinthian colonnade ④ running around the edge of a tiny lake with the requisite island in the center. Walk around the colonnade and under a 16th- century arch ⑤ transplanted from the old Paris Hôtel de Ville (see p104), which burned down in 1871.

Turn left on the Allée de la Comtesse de Ségur and go onto Avenue Velasquez, a wide tree-lined street with

Ambroise Thomas statue ⑧

Colonnade in Parc Monceau ④

Avenue Velasquez to Avenue Van Dyck

Re-enter the park and turn left onto the second small winding path, which is bordered by an 18th-century mossy pyramid ⑦, antique tombs, a stone arcade, an obelisk, and a small Chinese stone pagoda. The romantically melancholy tone of these follies suits the spirit of the late 18th century.

Turn right on the first path past the pyramid and walk back to the central avenue. Straight ahead, a Renaissance bridge fords the little stream running from the lake. Turn left and walk

past the monument (1902) to the musician Ambroise Thomas ⑧. Immediately behind, there is a lovely artificial mountain with cascade. Turn left on the next avenue and walk to the monument to the composer Charles Gounod ⑨ (1897) on the left. From here, follow the first winding path to the right toward the Avenue Van Dyck exit. Ahead to the right, in the corner of the park, is the Chopin monument ⑩ (1906), and looking along the Allée de la Comtesse de Ségur, the monument to the 19th-century French poet Alfred de Musset.

Avenue Van Dyck to Rue de Monceau

Leave the park and pass onto Avenue Van Dyck. No. 5 on the right is an impressive Parc Monceau mansion ⑪, a Neo-Baroque structure built by chocolate manufacturer Emile Menier; No. 6 is in the French Renaissance style that came back into favor in the 1860s. Straight ahead, beyond the ornate grille, there is a fine view of Avenue Hoche and in the distance, the Arc de Triomphe.

The mountain cascade ⑧

Walk past the gate and turn left onto Rue de Courcelles and left again onto Rue Murillo, bordered by more elaborate town houses in 18th-century and French Renaissance styles ⑫. At the crossing of Rue Rembrandt, on the left, is another gate into the park and on the right, a massive apartment building from 1900 (No. 7) and an elegant French Renaissance house with an elaborately carved wooden front door (No. 1). At the corner of the Rue Rembrandt and the Rue de Courcelles is the oddest of all the neighbor-hood buildings, a striking five-story red Chinese pagoda ⑬. It is an exclusive emporium of Chinese art.

Turn left onto the Rue de Monceau, walk past Avenue Ruysdaël, and continue to the Musée Nissim de Camondo at No. 63 Rue de Monceau ⑭ *(see pp234–5)*. Some nearby buildings worth having a look at are Nos. 52, 60, and 61 ⑮.

Boulevard Malesherbes

At the intersection of Rue de Monceau and Boulevard Malesherbes, turn right. This long boulevard with dignified six-story apartment buildings is typical of the great avenues cut through Paris by Baron Haussmann, Prefect of the Seine during the Second Empire *(see pp36–7)*. They greatly pleased the Industrial Age bourgeoisie, but horrified sensitive souls and writers who compared them with the buildings of New York.

No. 75 is the elegant marble front of Benneton, the most fashionable Paris card and stationery engraver ⑯. On the left, approaching the Boulevard Haussmann, looms the greatest 19th-century Paris church, St.-Augustin ⑰, built by Victor-Louis Baltard. Enter the church through the back door on Rue de la Bienfaisance. Walk through the church and leave by the main door. On the left is the massive stone building of the French Officers' club, the Cercle Militaire ⑱. Ahead is a bronze statue of Joan of Arc ⑲. Continue to Place St.-Augustin to St.-Augustin Metro station.

Joan of Arc statue ⑲

Tips for Walkers

Starting point: Blvd de Courcelles.
Length: 2 miles (3 km).
Getting there: The nearest Metro is Monceau, reached by bus No. 30; No. 84 goes to Metro Courcelles and No. 94 stops between Monceau & Villiers Metros.
St. Augustin church: Open 8.30am–7pm Mon–Fri, 8.30am–noon & 2.30–7.30pm Sat, 8.30am–12.30pm & 4–7.30pm Sun.
Stopping off points: Near the Renaissance bridge in the Parc Monceau, a kiosk serves coffee and sandwiches (summer only). There is a brasserie on Place de Rio de Janeiro and several cafés around Place St.-Augustin. The Square M Pagnol off Avenue C Claire is a pleasant place to take in the beauty of the park.

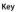 Villiers M

Key

••• Walk route

0 meters 250
0 yards 250

Five-story Chinese pagoda ⑬

For additional keys to symbols *see back flap*

A 90-Minute Walk along the Canal St.-Martin

The walk along the quays on either side of the Canal St.-Martin is an experience of Paris very different from that of smarter districts. Here, the older surviving landmarks of the neighborhood – the factories, warehouses, dwellings, taverns, and cafés – hint at life in a thriving 19th-century industrial, working-class world. But there are also the gentler charms of the old iron footbridges, the tree-lined quays, the inevitable fishermen, the river barges, and the still waters of the broad canal basins. A walk along the canal, which connects the Bassin de la Villette with the Seine, will evoke images of the Pernod-drinking, working-class Paris of Jean Gabin and Edith Piaf.

The 18th-century
Rotonde de la Villette ②

Bassin de la Villette looking north ③

Place de Stalingrad to Avenue Jean-Jaurès

From the Stalingrad Metro station ①, follow Boulevard de la Villette to the square in front of the Rotonde de la Villette ②. This is one of the few remaining 18th-century tollhouses in Paris, designed by the celebrated Neo-Classical architect Nicolas Ledoux in the 1780s. The fountains, square, and terraces were designed in the 1980s to provide an attractive setting and fine views of the Bassin de la Villette ③ to the north.

Walk toward Avenue Jean-Jaurès. On the left is the first lock ④ leading down to the canal, as well as the art-house movie theater chain MK2's landmark complexes, which are linked together by a boat.

Tips for Walkers

Starting point: Place de Stalingrad.
Length: 2 miles (3.5 km).
Getting there: The nearest Metro is Stalingrad; bus No. 54 stops there, and No. 26 at Metro Jaurès.
Hôpital St.-Louis: Chapel open 2–5pm Fri–Sun; the courtyard is open daily.
Stopping off points: International food stores and restaurants abound in lively Rue du Faubourg du Temple and nearby streets. The Quai de Valmy and Rue Beaupaire offer plenty of modish restaurants and bars (Le Point Ephémère, The Hôtel Du Nord, Chez Prune). There is a shady public garden on Boulevard Jules Ferry.

View from Rue E. Varlin bridge ⑦

Key

••• Walk route

0 meters   500
0 yards   500

Courtyard garden of Hôpital St.-Louis ⑭

first Bourbon king, to care for the victims of the plague. Leave the courtyard from the central gate on the wing on your left. Here, you pass by the 17th-century hospital chapel ⑮ and out onto the Rue de la Grange aux Belles.

Turn left and walk back to the canal. At the intersection of Rue de la Grange aux Belles and the Quai de Jemmapes stood, until 1627, the Montfaucon gallows ⑯, one of the chief public execution spots of medieval Paris. Turn onto the Quai de Jemmapes. At No. 101 ⑰ is the original front of the Hôtel du Nord, made famous in the eponymous 1930s movie. In front is another iron footbridge and a drawbridge ⑱ for traffic, providing a charming setting with views of the canal on either side. Cross over and continue down the Quai de Valmy until the last footbridge ⑲ at the corner of the Rue Léon-Jouhaux. From here, the canal can be seen disappearing under the surface of Paris, to continue its journey through a great stone arch.

Nearby is the French Communist Party headquarters ⑨ on Place du Colonel Fabien, with its curving glazed tower.

Return to the Quai de Jemmapes, where at No. 134 ⑩ stands one of the few surviving brick-and-iron industrial buildings that used to line the canal in the 19th century. At No. 126 ⑪ is another notable modern building, a residence for the elderly, with monumental concrete arches and glazed bay windows. Farther along, at No. 112 ⑫, is an Art Deco apartment building with bay windows, decorative iron balconies, and tiles. On the ground floor is a modernized former 1930s proletarian café. Here, the canal curves gracefully into the third lock, spanned by a charming iron footbridge ⑬.

Hôpital St.-Louis to Rue Léon-Jouhaux

Turn left onto Rue Bichat, which leads to the remarkable 17th-century Hôpital St.-Louis ⑭. Enter through the hospital's old main gate with its high-pitched roof and massive stone arch. Pass into the courtyard. The hospital was founded in 1607 by Henri IV, the

Square Frédéric Lemaître to Place de la République

Walk along Square Frédéric Lemaître ⑳ to the start of Boulevard Jules Ferry, which has a public garden stretching down its center. The garden was built over the canal in the 1860s. At its head stands a charmingly nostalgic statue of a flower girl of the 1830s, *La Grisette* ㉑. This is the intersection of busy, working-class Rue du Faubourg du Temple ㉒, with flourishing international stores and restaurants. Follow the street to the right and on to the Metro station in the Place de la République.

Store, Rue du Faubourg du Temple ㉒

iron footbridges over the canal ⑤

Quai de Valmy to Rue Bichat

Cross over to the Quai de Jemmapes, which runs the length of the east side of the canal and down to the first bridge on Rue Louis Blanc ⑤. Cross the bridge to the Quai de Valmy. From the corner, there is a glimpse of the oblique granite and glass front of the Paris Industrial Tribunal ⑥ on the Rue Louis Blanc.

Continue along Quai de Valmy. At Rue E Varlin, cross the bridge ⑦, from where there is an attractive view of the second canal lock, the lock-keeper's house, public gardens, and old lampposts. At the other side of the bridge and slightly to the left, go along the pedestrian-only Rue Haendel, which provides a good view of the towering buildings of a social housing project ⑧.

For additional keys to symbols *see back flap*

A 90-Minute Walk around the Ile St.-Louis

The walk around this tiny island passes along the picturesque tree-lined quays from Pont Louis-Philippe to Quai d'Anjou, taking in the 17th-century *hôtels* that infuse the area with such a powerful sense of period. It then penetrates into the heart of the island along the main street, Rue St.-Louis-en-l'Ile, enlivened by chic restaurants, cafés, art galleries, and boutiques, before returning to the north side of the island and back to Pont Marie. For more information on the main sights, see pages 79 and 91.

Left Bank view of the Ile St.-Louis

Fishing on a St.-Louis quayside

Metro Pont Marie to Rue Jean-du-Bellay

From the Pont Marie Metro station ①, walk down Quai des Celestins and Quai de l'Hôtel de Ville, lined with bookstands, with views of Ile St.-Louis. Turn left at Pont Louis-Philippe ② and, having crossed it, take the steps down to the lower quay immediately to the right. Walk around the tree-shaded west point of the island ③, then up the other side to the Pont St.-Louis ④. Opposite the bridge, on the corner of Rue Jean-du-Bellay, is Le Flore en l'Ile ⑤, the smartest café-cum-tea salon on the island.

Quai d'Orléans

From the corner of the Quai d'Orléans and the Rue Jean-du-Bellay, there are fine views of the Panthéon's dome and Notre-Dame. Along the quay, Nos. 18–20, the Hôtel Rolland, has unusual Hispano-Moorish windows ⑥. No. 12 is one of several stately 17th-century houses with handsome wrought-iron

balconies. At No. 6, the former Polish library, founded in 1838, now houses the Société Historique et Littéraire Polonaise *(see p91)*, focusing on the life of Polish poet Adam Mickiewicz ⑦; it also contains some Chopin scores and autographs by George Sand and Victor Hugo. On the right, the Pont de la Tournelle ⑧ links the island to the Left Bank.

Windows of the Hôtel Rolland ⑥

Key

••• Walk route

| 0 meters | 250 |
| 0 yards | 250 |

Quai de Béthune to Pont Marie

Continue beyond the bridge and onto Quai de Béthune, where the Nobel-laureate Marie Curie lived at No. 36 ⑨, and where beautiful wrought-iron balconies gracefully decorate Nos. 34 and 30. The Hôtel

St.-Louis church door ⑰

a late 19th-century bridge joining the riverbanks. Ahead is the charming 19th-century Square Barye ⑬, a shady public garden at the east point of the island, from where there are fine river views.

From here, travel toward the Quai d'Anjou as far as the corner of Rue St.-Louis-en-l'Ile to see the most famous house on the island, the Hôtel Lambert ⑭ *(see pp28–9)*. Continue onto the Quai d'Anjou, where Hôtel de Lauzun ⑮ at No. 17 has a severe Classical front and a beautiful gilded balcony. Now turn left onto Rue Poulletier and note the convent of the Daughters of Charity ⑯ at No. 5 bis. Farther on, at the corner of Rue Poulletier and Rue St.-Louis-en-l'Ile, is the island church, St.-Louis ⑰, with its unusual tower, projecting clock, and carved main door.

Proceed along Rue St.-Louis-en-l'Ile, which abounds in small, chic, bistro-style restaurants with pleasantly old-fashioned interiors. No. 31 is the original Berthillon ice cream parlor ⑱, No. 60 an art gallery ⑲ with an original 19th-century window front, and at No. 51 is one of the few 18th-century *hôtels* on the island, Hôtel Chernizot ⑳, with a superb Rococo balcony resting on leering gargoyles. Turn right onto Rue Jean-du-Bellay and along to Pont Louis-Philippe. Turn right again onto the Quai de Bourbon, lined by

Gargoyle at No. 51 Rue St.-Louis-en-l'Ile ⑳

one of the island's finest rows of *hôtels*, the most notable being Hôtel Jassaud at No. 19 ㉑. Continue to the 17th-century Pont Marie ㉒ and cross it to the Pont Marie Metro on the other side.

Tips for Walkers

Starting point: Pont Marie Metro.
Length: 1.6 miles (2.6 km).
Getting there: The walk starts from the Pont Marie Metro. However, bus route 67 takes you to Rue du Pont Louis-Philippe and also crosses the island along Rue des Deux Ponts and Boulevard Pont de Sully; routes 86 and 87 also cross the island along Boulevard Pont de Sully.
Stopping off points: There are cafés, such as Flore en l'Ile and the Berthillon parlors for ice cream *(see p310)*. Restaurants on the Rue St.-Louis-en-l'Ile include Auberge de la Reine Blanche (No. 30) and Le Fin Gourmet (No. 42), as well as a pâtisserie and a cheese store. Good resting points are the tree-shaded quays and Square Barye to the eastern end of the island.

Richelieu ⑩ at No. 18 is one of the island's most beautiful houses. It features a fine garden where it has retained its original Classical blind arcades.

If you turn left down Rue Bretonvilliers, there is an imposing 17th-century house ⑪, with a high-pitched roof resting on a great Classical arch spanning the street. Back on the Quai de Béthune, proceed to the Pont de Sully ⑫,

The 17th-century Pont Marie ㉒

A 90-Minute Walk in Auteuil

Part of the fascination of the walk around this bastion of bourgeois life in westernmost Paris lies in the contrasting nature of the area's streets. The old village provincialism of Rue d'Auteuil, where the walk begins, leads on to masterpieces of luxurious modern architecture along Rue La Fontaine and Rue du Docteur Blanche. The walk ends at the Jasmin Metro station. For more on the sights of Auteuil, see page 246.

Rue d'Auteuil

The walk begins at Place d'Auteuil ①, a leafy village square with a striking Guimard-designed Metro station entrance, an 18th-century funerary obelisk, and the 19th-century Neo-Romanesque Notre-Dame d'Auteuil. Walk down Rue d'Auteuil, the main street of the old village, and take in the sense of a past provincial world. The Auberge du Mouton Blanc brasserie at No. 40 ② now occupies the premises of the area's oldest tavern, favored by Molière and his actors in the 1600s. The house at Nos. 45–47 ③ was the residence of American presidents John Adams and his son John Quincy Adams. Move on to the pleasantly shaded Place Jean Lorrain ④, the site of the local market. Here, there is a Wallace drinking fountain, donated by the English millionaire Richard Wallace in the 19th century. Turn left down Rue Poussin and right onto Rue Donizetti to see the Villa Montmorency ⑤, a private enclave of luxury villas, built on the former country estate of the Comtesse de Boufflers.

Wallace fountain ④

Rue La Fontaine

Return to Rue La Fontaine, renowned for its many Hector Guimard buildings. Marcel Proust was born at No. 96. Henri Sauvage's ensemble of artists' studios at No. 65 ⑥ is one of the most original Art Deco buildings in Paris. No. 60 is a Guimard Art Nouveau house ⑦ with elegant cast-iron balconies. Farther along, there is a small Neo-Gothic chapel at No. 40 ⑧ and Art Nouveau apartment buildings at Nos. 19 and 21 ⑨. No. 14 is Guimard's most spectacular building, the Castel Béranger ⑩, with a superb iron gate.

Tips for Walkers

Starting point: Place d'Auteuil.
Length: 2 miles (3 km).
Getting there: The nearest Metro station to the starting point is Eglise d'Auteuil, and buses that take you there are Nos. 22, 52, and 62.
Stopping off points: At No. 40 Rue d'Auteuil is the inexpensive trendy brasserie L'Auberge du Mouton Blanc, with 1930s decor. At No. 35 bis Rue La Fontaine is Acajou, serving innovative cuisine and owned by a young chef. Place Jean Lorrain is a pleasantly shaded square where walkers can rest, and on Rue La Fontaine, there is a small park in front of the Neo-Gothic chapel at No. 40. Farther on at Place Rodin, there is a pleasant public garden.

Obelisk, Place d'Auteuil ①

RUE DU DOCTEUR BLANCHE ⑯

RUE D

RUE H. HEINE ⑰ ⑱

RUE

RUE RAFFET

RUE DE LA SO

Villa Montmorency

RUE POUSSIN ⑤

RUE LA F

RUE D'AUTEUIL PLACE J. LORRAIN ④ RUE ② D

Ⓜ Michel Ange Auteuil ③

RUE MICHEL ANGE

RUE BOILEAU

Key

••• Walk route

0 meters   250
0 yards   250

Doorway of No. 28 Rue d'Auteuil

Rue de l'Assomption to Rue Mallet-Stevens

At the corner of Rue de l'Assomption, there is a view of the massive Maison de Radio-France ⑪, built in 1963 to house French radio and television (see p204). It was one of the first modern postwar buildings in the city. Turn left onto Rue de l'Assomption and walk to the fine 1920s apartment building at No. 18 ⑫. Turn left onto Rue du Général Dubail and follow the street to Place Rodin, where the great sculptor's bronze

Notre-Dame de l'Assomption, pietà ⑮

nude, *The Age of Bronze* (1877) ⑬, occupies the center of the traffic circle.

Take the Avenue Théodore Rousseau back to Rue de l'Assomption and turn left toward Avenue Mozart. Cut through in the 1880s, this is the principal artery of the 16th arrondissement, linking north and south and lined with typical bourgeois apartment buildings of the late 19th century. Cross the avenue and continue to the Avenue des Chalets where there is a typical collection of weekend villas ⑭ recalling the quieter suburban Auteuil of the mid-19th century. Farther along Rue de l'Assomption, Notre-Dame de l'Assomption ⑮ is a Neo-Renaissance 19th-century church. Turn left onto Rue du Docteur Blanche. At No. 9 and down the adjoining Rue Mallet-Stevens ⑯, there is a row of celebrated modern houses in the International Modern style by the architect Robert Mallet-Stevens. In this expensive, once avant-garde enclave lived

No. 18 Rue de l'Assomption, detail ⑫

architects, designers, artists, and their modern-minded clients. The original proportions, however, were altered dramatically by the addition of an extra three stories in the 1960s.

Continue on Rue du Docteur Blanche until coming to Villa du Docteur Blanche on the left. At the end of this small cul-de-sac is the most celebrated modern house in Auteuil, Le Corbusier's Villa Roche ⑰. Together with the adjoining Villa Jeanneret, it is now part of the Corbusier Foundation (see pp40–41, 246). Built for an art collector in 1923–5 using the new technique of reinforced concrete, the house, with its geometric forms and lack of ornamentation, is a model of early Modernism.

Shuttered bay window at No. 3 Square Jasmin ⑲

Rue du Docteur Blanche to Rue Jasmin

Walk back to Rue du Docteur Blanche and turn right onto Rue Henri Heine. No. 18 bis ⑱ is a very elegant Neo-Classical 1920s apartment building offering a good contrast to one of Guimard's last creations from 1926 next door – an Art Nouveau facade much tamer than that at Castel Béranger but still employing brick, and with projecting bay windows and a terraced roof. Turn left on Rue Jasmin. In the second cul-de-sac on the left, there is another Guimard house at No. 3 Square Jasmin ⑲. Toward the end of Rue Jasmin is the Metro station.   The Age of Bronze ⑬

For additional keys to symbols see back flap

A 90-Minute Walk in Montmartre

The walk begins at the base of the sandstone *butte* (hill), where old theaters and dance halls, once frequented and depicted by painters from Renoir to Picasso, have now been taken over by rock clubs. It continues steeply uphill to the original village, along streets that still retain the atmosphere caught by artists like Van Gogh, before winding downhill to end at Place Blanche. For more on the main sights of Montmartre and Sacré-Coeur, see pages 222–31.

Montmartre seen from a distance

St.-Jean l'Evangéliste, detail ⑨

Place Pigalle to Rue Ravignan

The walk starts at the lively Place Pigalle ① and follows Rue Frochot to the Rue Victor Massé. At the corner is the ornate entrance to an exclusive private street bordered by late 19th-century chalets ②. Opposite, at No. 27 Rue Victor Massé, is an ornate mid-19th-century

Tips for Walkers

Starting point: Place Pigalle.
Length: 1.4 miles (2.3 km). The walk goes up some very steep streets to the top; if you do not feel like the climb, consider taking the Montmartrobus, which covers most of the walk and starts at Place Pigalle.
Getting there: The nearest Metro is Pigalle; buses that take you there are Nos. 30, 54, and 67.
Stopping off points: There are many cafés and stores on Rue Lepic and the Rue des Abbesses. Le Saint Jean (16 Place des Abbesses) remains a locals' haunt and serves well-priced brasserie food. For shade and a rest, Place Jean-Baptiste Clément and Square S. Buisson at Avenue Junot are charming public squares.

apartment building, and No. 25 is where Vincent Van Gogh and his brother Theo lived in 1886 ③. The famous Chat Noir ④, Montmartre's most renowned artistic cabaret in the 1890s, flourished at No. 12. At the end of the street begins the wide tree-lined Avenue Trudaine. Take Rue Lallier on the left to Boulevard de Rochechouart. Continue east. No. 84 is the first address of the Chat Noir and No. 80 was the Grand Trianon ⑤, Paris's oldest-surviving movie theater (early 1890s), now a regular theater. Farther along, No. 72 is the original front of Montmartre's first great cancan dance hall, the Elysée-Montmartre ⑥. Following a fire, it is currently closed.

Turn left onto Rue du Steinkerque, which leads to Sacré-Coeur gardens, and then left onto Rue d'Orsel, which leads to the leafy square, Place Charles Dullin, where the small early 19th-century Théâtre de l'Atelier ⑦ stands. Continue up the hill on Rue des Trois Frères and turn left on Rue Yvonne le Tac, which leads to Place des Abbesses ⑧. This is one of the most pleasant and liveliest squares in the area. It has conserved its entire canopied Art Nouveau Metro entrance by Hector Guimard. Opposite is St.-Jean l'Evangéliste ⑨, an unusual brick and mosaic Art Nouveau church. To the right of the church a flight of steep steps leads to the tiny Rue André Antoine, where

Rue André Antoine ⑩

he Pointillist painter Georges
eurat lived at No. 39 ⑩. Return
o Rue des Abbesses and turn
ight at Rue Ravignan.

Rue Ravignan
rom here, there is a sweeping
iew of Paris. Climb the steps
traight ahead to the deeply
haded Place Emile Goudeau
⑪. To the left, at No. 13, is the
riginal entrance to the Bateau-
Lavoir, the most important
cluster of artists' studios in
Montmartre. Here, Picasso lived
and worked in the early 1900s.

Walking past Montmartre Vineyard ⑱

Farther up, at the corner of Rue
Orchampt and Rue Ravignan,
there is a row of picturesque
19th-century artists' studios ⑫.

Rue Ravignan to Rue Lepic
Continue up the hill along the
small public garden, Place Jean-
Baptiste Clément ⑬. At the top,
cross Rue Norvins. Opposite is
an old restaurant, Auberge de la
Bonne Franquette ⑭, which used
to be a favorite gathering place
for 19th-century artists.
Continue along the narrow Rue
St.-Rustique, from where Sacré-
Coeur can be seen. At the end
and to the right is Place du
Tertre ⑮, the main village
square. From here, go north on
Rue du Mont Cenis and turn left
to Rue Cortot. Erik Satie, the
eccentric composer, lived in
No. 6 ⑯, and at No. 12 is the
Musée de Montmartre ⑰. Turn
right on Rue des Saules and
walk past the very pretty
Montmartre vineyard ⑱ to the
Au Lapin Agile ⑲ at the corner of
Rue St.-Vincent. Go back down
Rue des Saules and right on Rue

de l'Abreuvoir, an attractive
street of late 19th-century
villas and gardens. Continue
onto l'Allée des Brouillards, a
leafy pedestrian-only alley.
No. 6 ⑳ was Renoir's last house
in Montmartre. Take the steps
down into the Rue Simon
Dereure, immediately turn left
into a small park and cross it to
reach Avenue Junot. Here, No.
15 ㉑ was the house of Dadaist
Tristan Tzara in the early 1920s.
Continue up Avenue Junot, turn
right on Rue Girardon and right
again on Rue Lepic.

Au Lapin Agile cabaret ⑲

Rue Lepic to Place Blanche
On the corner is one of the
area's few surviving windmills,
the Moulin du Radet ㉒, now a
restaurant confusingly called
Moulin de la Galette. Continue
along Rue Lepic: to the right at
the top of a slope is another
windmill, the original Moulin
de la Galette ㉓, now a private
home. Turn left on Rue de
l'Armée d'Orient, with its quaint
artists' studios ㉔, and left again
onto Rue Lepic. Van Gogh lived
at No. 54 ㉕ in June 1886.
Continue to Place Blanche, and
on Boulevard de Clichy to the
right is the Moulin Rouge ㉖.

RUE SAINT VINCENT

⑰ ⑯
CORTOT

⑮
PLACE DU
TERTRE

Sacré
Coeur

GABRIELLE

SQUARE
LOUISE
MICHEL

ÈRES

SQUARE
WILLETTE

Y LE TAC

RUE D'ORSEL

RUE DE STEINKERQUE

D'ORSEL

PLACE
C DULLIN ⑦

⑤ ⑥

RUE
DANCOURT

BD DE ROCHECHOUART

Ⓜ
Anvers

SQUARE
D'ANVERS

RUE BOCHART DE SARON

RUE LALLIER

AVENUE TRUDAINE

Key

••• Walk route

0 meters _____ 250
0 yards _____ 250

Moulin Rouge cabaret near the Place Blanche ㉖

For additional keys to symbols *see back flap*

A 90-Minute Walk in Buttes-Chaumont

This area in the east of the city is little known to many visitors, yet it contains one of Paris's biggest and most beautiful parks and some fascinating architecture. The walk is quite strenuous with many steps, and takes in a charming micro-village, the Butte Bergeyre, which is perched high above the city and has unusual houses in contrasting styles. After descending from the village, the walk continues in Buttes-Chaumont park, a vast hill complete with a lake with a huge island and folly, rocky outcrops, and a wonderful variety of trees and plants.

garden ⑩. This is owned by the city but tended by local residents who can often be found working here.

Head back down the Rue Georges Lardennois to the Rue Michel Tagrine and take the ivy-draped steps back down to the main road ⑪. Continue straight and then turn right onto the Avenue Mathurin-Moreau, noting the fine Art Deco building at No. 42 ⑫ with its glittering gold-colored tile detail. At the end of the road, cross Rue Manin to the entrance to the park.

View across the city toward Sacré-Coeur ⑧

The Butte Bergeyre

From the Metro Buttes-Chaumont ①, take the Rue Botzaris, turning right onto the Avenue Simon Bolivar until you reach the stairs at No. 54 ②, which lead up into the Butte Bergeyre. At the top of the stairs, pause to absorb the enchanting atmosphere of this micro-village of five little streets. Construction started in the 1920s, but there are also some modern buildings. Carry on into the Rue Barrelet de Ricou ③ to admire the ivy-covered house at No. 13 ④, then continue to the end of the road to make a left into the Rue Philippe Hecht ⑤, where the chalet-style house at No. 7 ⑥ is an interesting contrast to the creeper-covered Art Deco gem at No. 13 ⑦. At the end of the street, turn left up to the corner of the Rue Georges Lardennois and the Rue Rémy-de-Gourmont for a wonderful view across the city ⑧ of Montmartre with its wedding-cake Sacré-Coeur on top. Be sure to admire the tiny patch of grapevines ⑨ in the residents' garden below. Close to this mini-vineyard is a small

Some of the lovely mature trees in the park

The suspension bridge, for the best view of the park ⑱

Key

••• Walk route

```
0 meters        200
0 yards         200
```

PARC DES BUTTES CHAUMONT

⑳ Ⓜ **Botzaris**

RUE DE CRIMÉE
RUE DE LA CASCADE
RUE BOTZARIS
RUE MANIN

Clifftop folly, the park's summit ⑰

The Buttes-Chaumont Park

Commissioned by Napoleon III and Baron Haussmann in 1864, the park covers 61 acres (25 ha) and took four years to complete. It was built by the engineer Adolphe Alphand and the architect Gabriel Davioud. It is packed with mature trees including planes, poplars, ash, maples, chestnuts, sequoias, and beautiful magnolias. At the entrance to the park there is a man-made rock structure ⑬ with steps carved out of the facade; climb them to the top. Go on along a tree-lined path to join the Avenue du General Puebla Liniers and follow this until reaching the Carrefour de la Colonne ⑭, where there is a red-brick mansion house. With your back to this go forward to a little bridge lined with terracotta tiles. Cross the bridge ⑮. Take the right branch of steps and head up to the top of the cliff. Cross a tiny bridge ⑯ and turn left up some steps to the folly ⑰, a copy of the Temple of Sibyl near Rome. This is the highest point in the park, providing views across the city all the way to Sacré-Coeur. Now take the path on the right back to the first bridge. Then branch right down the steps within man-made rock to an impressive 206-ft (63-m) long bridge ⑱. Towering over the lake, this provides wonderful views of the park. The bridge may be closed for repairs, so in that instance use the terracotta-tiled bridge as before. Cross the bridge and follow the path down to the lake. The lake ⑲ is encircled by weeping willows and benches from which to admire the 164-ft (50-m) high man-made island ⑳. Follow the lakeshore round until you hear rushing water. One of the park's most impressive features is the 105-ft (32-m) high waterfall ㉑ hidden inside a grotto. Walk right up to the waterfall looking up to see a patch of sky and some glorious man-made stalactites. Take a stepping-stone to the other side of the cave and then exit and rejoin the path round the lake, heading left. Ascend the few steps, then veer to the left and up the hill ㉒. Follow the path around to the Carrefour de la Colonne and continue along the Avenue de la Cascade to the exit ㉓. From here, you can take the Metro from Botzaris.

Tips for Walkers

Starting point: Metro b... Chaumont.
Length: 1.5 miles (2.5 km). Note: This is a very steep walk in parts, with many steps.
Getting there: Go to Buttes-Chaumont Metro station, on line 7 bis. Or take bus Nos. 26, 60, or 75 to the stop for Buttes-Chaumont park.
Stopping off points: The park is full of lovely spots to rest, and the benches near the lake are good if bringing your own refreshments. La Kaskad café opposite the park (at 2 Place Armand-Carrel) is a fashionable spot for snacks and drinks, with a terrace that is ideal on a sunny day.

Man-made waterfall, inside the grotto ㉑

For additional keys to symbols *see back flap*

A 90-Minute Walk in Faubourg St.-Antoine

In the east of the city, a few steps away from the bustle of the Bastille, lies the Faubourg St.-Antoine district, traditionally a working-class neighborhood full of furniture designers, carpenters, and artisans whose legacy can still be seen today. From the Place de la Bastille, the walk takes in Paris's pleasure-boat port, the artisan area around the Viaduc des Arts – a former viaduct with arts and crafts studios nestling in the arches – and on to the Promenade Plantée for a fascinating tree-filled stroll.

Les Grandes Marches, Place de la Bastille

The Port de Plaisance, with many pleasure boats ②

Port de Plaisance

Tucked away near the traffic of Place de la Bastille ① lies an area of tranquility that's of interest to boat-lovers and landlubbers alike. The Port de Plaisance and Paris-Arsenal garden ② was inaugurated in 1983 to provide a harbor for pleasure craft. Linking the Seine to the Canal St.-Martin, the harbor was previously where commercial barges loaded and unloaded cargo. Today, it's a pretty spot full of yachts, dinghies, and Parisians out for a stroll. The cobblestones on the quayside and old-fashioned lampposts add to the port's atmosphere. The lawns are perfect for a picnic and the children's play areas, while small, are well stocked with rocking chairs, slides, and climbing apparatus ③. Continue to the end of the marina to the lock ④. Cross over the lock bridge, observing the pedestrian crosswalk sign, and head down on the other quayside, turning back toward the Place de la Bastille. Just before the grey steel bridge ⑤, take the stairs up and

then the bridge over to the Boulevard de la Bastille ⑥. Cross the boulevard and make a right and then left onto the Rue Jules César ⑦ all the way to the end of the street, go left and then cross the Rue de Lyon turning right onto the Avenue Daumesnil and the start of the Viaduc des Arts ⑧.

Viaduc des Arts

In 1859, the Paris Viaduct was built to take a railroad track linking the Faubourg St.-Antoine district with the suburbs. In 1994, the restored and revamped Viaduc des Arts opened with 50 stores and studios nestling in the bridge's rose stone archways.

In keeping with the tradition of the area, the ateliers are all linked to the arts, and some of the city's master craftsmen call the arches home. The superb window displays at the first studio,

Place de la Bastille, with the impressive Opéra National de Paris Bastille ①

Maison Guillet ⑨, give a hint of the quality of craftsmanship to come. Guillet specializes in providing silk flowers for Paris's top theaters and fashion houses. The Ateliers du Temps Passé ⑩ at No. 5 is a restorer of paintings, while Lorenove at No. 11 restores period glass. No. 13 is the base for fashionable interior designer Cherif, and the whimsical Le Bonheur des Dames ⑪ at No. 17 provides all sorts of materials for embroidery fans. For refreshment, stop at the Viaduc Café at No. 43 ⑫, which serves simple meals and hearty salads to the area's hip creatives. Vertical at No. 63 ⑬ mixes art and nature with twisting "botanical

One of the arts and crafts storefronts under the Viaduc des Arts ⑧

sculptures." Moving on past the metal furniture-maker Baguès at 73, the antique lace restorer Marie Lavande at No. 83, and the Atelier Le Tallec at Nos. 93/95, which specializes in hand-painted porcelain, it is clear that the spirit of the old artisans' area is alive and well. For those of a musical bent, Allain Cadinot repairs and sells Boehm flutes at No. 99, and luthier Roger Lanne makes cellos and violins at No. 103 ⑭. With a coppersmith at No. 111, a terracotta tile specialist at No. 113, and a frame-maker at No. 117, you are close to the end of the viaduct, where the last atelier, Jean-Charles

woods. For a longer walk, turn right along the Promenade and follow it to the city's edge and the woods. Or turn left and head back toward the Bastille. This narrow walkway offers wonderful views of the rooftops and apartments. With roses, lavender, and maples, the walkway is a delight. At the Bastille end ⑰, take the steps down to the Rue de Lyon ⑱ leading to the Bastille Metro, pausing to ponder the modern architecture of the Opéra National de Paris Bastille ⑲ (see p102).

Promenade Plantée, a lovely rooftop-level walkway ⑯

Tips for Walkers

Starting point: Bastille Metro.
Length: 1.6 miles (2.6 km).
Getting there: Bastille Metro is served by lines 1, 8, and 5. Bus Nos. 29, 65, 69, 76, 86, 87, 91 and more. Get off at "Place de la Bastille" stop.
Stopping off points: The area is full of great cafés, bars, and restaurants. Les Grandes Marches (Place de la Bastille) is a chic place for lunch, dinner, or just coffee before you start or afterward. Nearby Rue de Charonne is lined with some fun bars. During the walk, take a break at the Viaduc Café (43 Viaduc des Arts).

Brosseau ⑮, perhaps sums up the street's diversity, specializing in making hats, scent, and cutlery.

Promenade Plantée

Turn left, follow the signs and take the steps up to the Promenade Plantée ⑯, a walkway on top of the viaduct. It is 2.8 miles (4.5km) long and goes all the way to the Vincennes

Key

••• Walk route
••• Detour route

0 meters 200
0 yards 200

Montgallet 300 metres / 330 yards
Bois de Vincennes 3 km / 2 miles
Dugommier 450 metres / 500 yards

For additional keys to symbols see back flap

A 90-Minute Walk in Butte-aux-Cailles

This walk takes place in and around the Butte-aux-Cailles, a lovely "village" set on a hill that is all quiet streets, leafy squares, and buzzy local bistros. The area made history in 1783 when the first manned balloon flight touched down here. In the 1800s, it was home to many workers from the small factories in the area and was one of the first areas to fight during the Paris Commune. However, it only really developed after 1910 and the architecture reflects the social ideals of the day – that individual houses and green spaces aid health.

a major street battle in May 1871. Continue up the Rue de la Butte-aux-Cailles. Les Abeilles at No. 21 ⑬ is a curious store dedicated to bee-keeping and a delight for honey lovers. Pancakes in the old-fashioned crêperie Des Crêpes et des Cailles at No. 13 may satisfy if you are just peckish, but farther down at No. 18 is the area's best-known restaurant, Le Temps de Cerises ⑭. Fittingly, as it's only a few minutes' walk from the Place de la Commune, it's run as a co-operative and is also the unofficial neighborhood HQ. At the end of the road

Quiet, cobblestone streets typify the Butte-aux-Cailles ⑪

Buttes-aux-Cailles

Take the "Auguste Blanqui" exit out of the Place d'Italie Metro station ①, noting the Guimard decoration. Follow the bustling Rue Bobillot until you reach the Rue Paulin-Méry ② and take your first steps into the peace of the Butte-aux-Cailles. The contrast is surprising as you walk the quiet, narrow, cobblestone streets with their old-fashioned street lamps. Note the painted shutters on No. 5 ③ and the trees in the small garden in front of the house opposite. Continue straight ahead, cross over the Rue du Moulin-des-Prés and turn left onto the Rue Gérard past the red-brick row houses and plant-decked villas ④. Keep on onto Rue Samson and turn right onto Rue Jonas then left onto the Rue des Cinq Diamants ⑤. At No. 43 ⑥ there is a hip Franco-Thai restaurant, Le 43. Those interested in history may appreciate the Association des Amis de la Commune de Paris at No. 46 ⑦, which sells T-shirts, books, and pamphlets on that

Road sign in the Butte-aux-Cailles area

bloody episode in Parisian history. Turn right into the Passage Barrault, a cobblestone alleyway with ivy-covered walls and a countryside feel ⑧. At the end of the passage, turn left onto the Rue Barrault and continue up the street until the right turn onto the Rue Daviel. At 10 Rue Daviel, the row of cottages known as "Little Alsace" ⑨ because of their chalet style is, in fact, one of the first public housing schemes in Paris. The public can visit their intimate courtyards during the day. Opposite, walk down the Villa Daviel ⑩, a tiny street of terraces with small front gardens overflowing with greenery. Retrace your steps back up to the Rue Barrault, turn left and then right onto the artery of the area, the Rue de la Butte-aux-Cailles ⑪. Head up the street to the Place de la Commune de Paris ⑫, which today looks unremarkable yet was the site of

Les Abeilles, for honey enthusiasts ⑬

Le Temps des Cerises, full of bohemian atmosphere ⑭

Tips for Walkers

Starting point: Place d'Italie Metro.
Length: 1.6 miles (2.6 km).
Getting there: Start from the Place d'Italie Metro via line 5, 6, or 7. Or take bus No. 27, 47, 57, 67 or 83 and get off at the stop "Place d'Italie".
Stopping off points: The Rue de la Butte-aux-Cailles is full of great cafés and restaurants. Le Temps des Cerises (No. 18) is very atmospheric, while Fusion (No. 12) is devoted to fusion cuisine. On Rue des Cinq Diamants, Chez Gladines (No. 30) is a great bet for a good lunch, while Les Cailloux (No. 58) is a chic option.

is the Place Paul Verlaine ⑮. On the other side of the square is the red-brick Art Nouveau swimming pool ⑯. Built in 1924, it houses one indoor pool and two lovely outdoor swimming areas. Take the steps in front of the building to find the modern fountain on the square ⑰. This is supplied by Le Puits Artésian, a local well 1,902 ft (580 m) deep, dating from 1863. You may see locals lining up to fill plastic bottles here. Exit the square, make a right and then another right past the chic restaurant Chez Nathalie with its flowery terrace, which is always packed in summer, onto the Rue Vandrezanne, continuing down this pedestrian-only street into the passage Vandrezanne, a steep cobble-stone alleyway with antiquated lampposts ⑱. Cross over the Rue du Moulinet and take the Rue du Moulin des Prés until you come to the Rue de Tolbiac. Cross this busy road, then make a right, stepping back into another time at the Square des Peupliers ⑲. Built in 1926, each house is different, reflecting the ideals of the time. All have pretty little gardens, most have lovely Art Nouveau porches, and the ornate gilded lampposts are very special. Leave the Square des Peupliers and make a right back onto the Rue du Moulin-des-Prés. Head down

Crêpes from Des Crêpes et des Cailles

the street, noting the interesting rough stone houses ⑳, and go straight, past an unusual purple Art Nouveau-style house at No. 104 ㉑. Make a right onto the Rue Damesme, turn right onto the Rue du Docteur Leray and then right again onto Rue Dieulafoy ㉒. Here are several unique, colorful cottages with flower-filled front gardens behind railings. At the end of the row, make a right onto the Rue Henri Pape, a left onto the Rue Damesme, walk up to the Rue de Tolbiac and back out into modern, busy, Paris. Turn right and walk up to the Metro Tolbiac ㉓.

Square des Peupliers, with its unique houses ⑲

Key

••• Walk route

| 0 meters | 200 |
| 0 yards | 200 |

For additional keys to symbols *see back flap*

TRAVELERS' NEEDS

WHERE TO STAY

Paris has more guest rooms than almost any other city in Europe. Its hotels vary from magnificent luxury operations like Le Meurice and Four Seasons George V (the French call them *palaces*) to much simpler hotels that are nevertheless full of charm. It is worth noting that *hôtel* does not always mean "hotel." It can also mean a town hall *(hôtel de ville)*, hospital *(Hôtel-Dieu)* or mansion. A wide range of hotels, listed under five themes – luxury, charming *(hôtels de charme)*, design, romantic, and vacation rentals and bed-and-breakfasts – and in three price brackets, are reviewed on pages 284–7. All offer good value for money.

Where to Look

Hotels in Paris tend to cluster by type in particular areas. As a very broad generalization, luxury and big-business hotels tend to be on the Right Bank and *hôtels de charme* are on the Left Bank.

In the fashionable districts near the Champs-Elysées and the Opéra Garnier lie many of the city's grandest hotels, including Le Bristol, the Four Seasons George V and Le Meurice *(see p284)*. Several less well known but elegant hotels can be found in the residential and ambassadorial quarter near the Palais de Chaillot.

To the east, still on the Right Bank, in the Marais, a number of old mansions have been converted into exceptionally attractive boutique hotels, such as Le Pavillon de la Reine *(see p284)*. The nearby areas around Les Halles and Rue St.-Denis, however, tend to be seedy and attract prostitutes and drug addicts. Just south of the Marais, across the Seine, the Ile St.-Louis has several lovely hotels.

The Left Bank covers some of the most popular tourist areas and has an excellent range of small hotels of great character. The atmosphere subtly changes from the much-upgraded Latin Quarter and the chic and arty areas north and south of Boulevard St.-Germain to the rather run-down Boulevard itself and the staid institutional area toward Les Invalides and the Eiffel Tower. The hotels tend to reflect this.

Farther from the center, Montparnasse has several large business hotels in high-rise blocks, and the Porte de Versailles area to the south is usually packed with trade fair participants. The station areas around Gare du Nord and Gare de Lyon offer a number of basic hotels (choose carefully). Montmartre has some pleasant hotels if you don't mind the hilly location, and a number of hip designer hotels have opened in rapidly gentrifying South Pigalle.

If you are looking for a hotel in person, the best times for inspecting are late morning

Bathroom with charming murals in Les Degrés de Notre Dame *(see p285)*

or mid-afternoon. If the hotels are fully booked, try again after 6pm, when unclaimed provisional bookings become free. Don't rely on the impression of a hotel given by the reception desk; ask to see the room offered. For airport hotels, see p369.

Hotel Prices

Hotel prices aren't always lower in the off season (mid-November through March; July and August), because fashion shows and other major events throughout the year can pack rooms, raising prices. However, in the older hotels, differences in the size and position of rooms can have a marked effect on cost.

Rooms with two single beds are slightly more expensive than those with one double bed; single occupancy rates are as high or nearly as high as for two people sharing (tariffs are almost always quoted per room, not per person).

Facade of the chic Hôtel D'Aubusson *(see p284)*

◀ Le Consulat restaurant on Rue Norvins, Montmartre

Rooms without a bathroom tend to be about 20 per cent cheaper than those with.

It is always worth trying to negotiate a discount. In some hotels, special deals are offered, especially for students, families, and seniors. Discounts are often available online or when booking a package trip.

Hidden Extras

By law, tax and service must be included in the price quoted or displayed at the reception desk or in the rooms. Tips are unnecessary other than for exceptional service, such as if the concierge reserves tickets for a show for you, or if the maid does some laundry for you. Before you make a reservation, establish whether breakfast is included in the price. Beware of extras such as drinks or snacks in your room, especially from a mini-bar, which will probably be pricey, as will laundry services, garage parking, and telephone calls from your room. Some hotels charge extra for Wi-Fi.

Check the hotel's cancellation policy – some hotels charge a fee for cancellation less than 24 or 48 hours before the start of the reservation.

Hotel Gradings

French hotels are classified by the tourist authorities into five broad categories: one to five stars. Some very simple types

Four Seasons George V (see p284)

A suite at the historic Lancaster (see p287)

of accommodations are unclassified. Star ratings provide an indication of the level of amenities you can expect – for example, any hotel with more than three stars should have an elevator. Increasingly, the rating system also tries to take account of such factors as room size, service, attentiveness of the staff, cleanliness, dining options, and decor.

Amenities

Few Parisian hotels below a four-star rating have a restaurant, although there is nearly always a breakfast room. Many hotel restaurants close in August. Older hotels may also lack a public lounge area. More modern or expensive hotels have correspondingly better amenities and usually some kind of bar.

Inexpensive hotels may not have an elevator – this can be a big drawback when you are dragging suitcases upstairs. Usually, only the more expensive hotels have parking. If you are driving, you may prefer to stay in one of the peripheral motel-style chains (see pp282 & 283).

All but the very simplest of city hotels will have a telephone in the bedroom; most also have a television. Business amenities such as conference rooms and equipment are available in grander hotels, and Wi-Fi is standard. Two people who are sharing can specify whether they want a double bed (grand lit) or two single beds (lits jumeaux).

Traveling with Children

Families with young children will often find they can share a room at no or very little extra cost. Few hotels refuse to accept children, though amenities specifically for children are not universal. Some hotels will arrange babysitting.

Apartments

Staying in an apartment is an increasingly popular alternative to staying in a hotel, especially if you are in Paris for more than a few days or traveling with children, and it can often work out cheaper too. With the advent of websites such as **airbnb**, which allows home owners to rent out rooms in their houses or apartments, the choice of accommodations has grown enormously.

Le Meurice in the Tuileries Quarter *(see p284)*

Campanile, Ibis, and Choice Hotels. These establishments are practical, relatively inexpensive, and useful if you have a car, but they lack any real Parisian atmosphere or character. Many are in drab locations on busy highways and may suffer from traffic noise. The newer motels of these chains are smarter and better equipped than the older ones.

Several chains – Sofitel, Novotel, and Mercure – are more geared to business travelers, providing better amenities at higher prices; indeed, some of the more central ones are positively luxurious. Reductions can make these hotels good value on weekends. Many of them have restaurants attached.

Airbnb is a good place to start – you'll find anything from studio garrets to luxurious five-bedroom houses. **Housetrip** is another good bet, with around 1,600 apartments listed. There are also a number of more traditional lettings agencies, including **At Home in Paris**, **Haven in Paris**, and **Holiday France Rentals**.

Also worth considering is the **Citadines Apart'hotel** chain, which offers fully furnished studios and apartments with kitchens in several central Paris locations. Some hotel-type amenities are available, such as laundry services, breakfast and babysitting, for an extra fee.

Bed-and-Breakfast

The bed-and-breakfast is known as *chambre d'hôte* or *café-couette* ("coffee and a quilt") in France. B&B accommodations are generally available at moderate prices, between €65 and €110 for a double room per night. **Alcôve & Agapes** offers rooms in some enviable districts of Paris, all within walking distance of a Metro station. It is worth enquiring about suites and rooms with a private lounge, kitchen, or terrace. All homes are routinely inspected. **Good Morning Paris** offers

more than 100 guest rooms, many in central locations. A two-night minimum stay is required when making a reservation. **France-Lodge** is a good-value agency specializing in bed-and-breakfasts as well as long-stay room rentals and apartments.

Chain Hotels

A mushroom crop of motel-style establishments on the outskirts of Paris accommodates large numbers of both business and leisure visitors. The budget chains – such as Formule 1, Première Classe and Fasthôtel – really have nothing except price to recommend them. Higher up the ladder are

Hostels

There are several hostel organizations in Paris. **Maisons Internationales de la Jeunesse et des Etudiants (MIJE)** provides dormitory rooms for ages 18 to early 30s in three splendid 17th-century mansions in the Marais. Online reservations are offered.

The **Bureau Voyage Jeunesse (BVJ)** has two hostels with double rooms and dormitory accommodations, breakfast, and luggage room amenities. **Ethic Etapes** has five centers in and around Paris with individual, shared, and dormitory rooms.

The **Fédération Unie des Auberges de Jeunesse (FUAJ)** is a member of the International Youth Hostels Federation.

The wooden-beamed dining area inside Jeu de Paume *(see p284)*

The courtyard of the Relais Christine *(see p284)*

There is no age limit at their three Paris area hostels.

St Christopher's Paris, on the Canal St.-Martin, provides excellent amenities and also offers tours of Paris. Prices at most of the hostels start at around €30 per night.

How to Book

Paris is busiest at Christmas and New Year, and during France's school breaks, around Easter and October. Tourists pour in from May to September, but Parisians pour out en masse in August, when many stores and restaurants close.

If you have decided on a hotel, it is vital to reserve at least a month ahead. The hotels listed on pages 284–7 are among the best in their category and will fill particularly quickly. The best way is to make a reservation directly with the hotel. Some hotels offer special deals for visitors who book online. If you reserve by phone, you will be asked for either your credit card number (from which any cancellation fee may be deducted) or a deposit *(arrhes)*, which can be as much as the price of a night's stay.

If you prefer to use an agency, **Ely 12 12** can reserve hotels and other kinds of accommodations, as well as excursions such as boat trips along the Seine.

If you aren't too fussy about where you stay, or if all the hotels are full, you can book via the tourist office's airport or train station information desks *(see p358)*, but only in person and for the same day.

Recommended Hotels

The hotels on pages 284–7 of this guide book are a selection of the best luxury, *de charme*, design, and romantic hotels in Paris. They are first listed according to type, and then by area and by price. Most of the hotels are spread across the main tourist areas, although some that are farther afield have been included if they offer particularly good value for money, amenities, service, or charm. The selection also includes bed-and-breakfasts and vacation rental apartments. What they all have in common is that they are more than just a bed for the night – they have something extra that makes it worth seeking them out. Throughout the listings, certain hotels have been marked DK Choice – these offer an exceptional experience, such as beautiful rooms, a historic setting, superlative service, spectacular views, a fabulous spa, family-friendly amenities, or a combination of these.

DIRECTORY

Apartments

Airbnb
w airbnb.com

At Home in Paris
Tel 01 42 12 40 40.
w athomeinparis.fr

Citadines Apart'hotel
Tel 01 41 05 79 05.
w citadines.com

Haven In Paris
Tel 617 395 42 43 (US).
w haveninparis.com

Holiday France Rentals
Tel 01 55 37 97 36
or 06 08 07 46 98.
w holidays-france-rentals.com

Housetrip
w housetrip.com

Bed & Breakfast

Alcôve & Agapes
Tel 07 64 08 42 77.
w bed-and-breakfast-in-paris.com

France-Lodge
2 Rue Meissonier 75017.
Tel 01 56 33 85 85/80.
w francelodge.fr

Good Morning Paris
43 Rue Lacépède 75005.
Tel 01 47 07 28 29.
w goodmorningparis.fr

Hostels

Bureau Voyage Jeuness (BVJ)
20 Rue Jean-Jacques Rousseau 75001.
Tel 01 53 00 90 90.
w bvj-hotel.com

Ethic Etapes – FIAP Jean Monnet
3 Rue Cabanis 75014.
Tel 01 43 13 17 00.
w ethic-etapes.fr

FUAJ – Le d'Artagnan
80 Rue Vitruve 75020.
Tel 01 40 32 34 56.
w fuaj.org

Maisons Internationales de la Jeunesse et des Etudiants (MIJE)
13 Boulevard Beaumarchais 75004.
Tel 01 42 74 23 45.
w mije.com

St Christopher's Paris
159 Rue de Crimée 75019.
Tel 01 40 34 34 40.
w st-christophers.co.uk

Reservations Agencies

Ely 12 12
182 Rue du Faubourg St.-Honoré 75008. **Tel** 01 43 59 12 12. **w** ely1212.com

Where to Stay

Luxury

Ile de la Cité and Ile St-Louis

Jeu de Paume €€€
54 Rue St.-Louis-en-l'Ile, 75004
Tel *01 43 26 14 18*   **Map** 13 C4
W jeudepaumehotel.com
A beamed building dating from the early 17th century has been transformed into a rustic-chic hotel with luxurious rooms.

Beaubourg and The Marais

DK Choice

Le Pavillon de la Reine €€€
28 Place des Vosges, 75003
Tel *01 40 29 19 19*   **Map** 14 D3
W pavillon-de-la-reine.com
Overlooking the city's most beautiful square, this hotel has an unrivaled setting. The 17th-century mansion, once home to Anne of Austria, has been modernized in elegant country-house style, with plush, romantic bedrooms and a pampering spa. It also has a peaceful small garden.

Tuileries, Opéra, and Montmartre

Mandarin Oriental €€€
251 Rue St.-Honoré, 75001
Tel *01 70 98 78 88*   **Map** 12 D1
W mandarinoriental.com/Paris
The rooms here are very comfortable, with Art Deco and Oriental details. Eastern service and Parisian style provide a winning combination.

Le Meurice €€€
228 Rue de Rivoli, 75001
Tel *01 44 58 10 10*   **Map** 12 D1
W dorchester.collection.com
The last word in Empire-style luxury, this is the most stylish of the city's *grande dame* hotels: a palace with glitzy rooms, glorious views, and a luxurious spa.

W Paris – Opéra €€€
4 Rue Meyerbeer, 75009
Tel *01 77 48 94 94*   **Map** 6 E4
W wparisopera.com
France's first W has a cool, young vibe. It's a combination of 1870s features and witty modern furnishings, with comfortable beds and excellent cocktails.

Champs-Elysées and Chaillot Quarter

Keppler €€
10 Rue Keppler, 75116
Tel *01 47 20 65 05*   **Map** 4 E5
W keppler.fr
A super-chic hotel, with bold black-and-white decor, offering classic comfort. The rooms contain beautiful antiques.

Le Bristol €€€
112 Rue du Faubourg St.-Honoré, 75008
Tel *01 53 43 43 00*   **Map** 5 A4
W lebristolparis.com
Antiques, Flemish tapestries, and chandeliers fill this elegant hotel. Don't miss a dip in the pool.

Four Seasons George V €€€
31 Avenue George V, 75008
Tel *01 49 52 71 00*   **Map** 4 E5
W fourseasons.com/paris
An icon. The glamor and glitz of the original George V is enhanced by modern Four Seasons luxury.

St.-Germain and Latin Quarter

Hôtel d'Aubusson €€€
33 Rue Dauphine, 75006
Tel *01 43 29 43 43*   **Map** 12 F4
W hoteldaubusson.com
Four-star comfort in a 17th-century stone house with a courtyard.

Relais Christine €€€
3 Rue Christine, 75006
Tel *01 40 51 60 80*   **Map** 12 F4
W relais-christine.com
A luxurious and intimate haven of calm with a paneled salon and a private garden.

The Caron de Beaumarchais, with its delightful 18th-century decor

Price Guide

Prices are based on one night's stay in high season for a standard double room, inclusive of service charges and taxes.

€	under €150
€€	€150–€300
€€€	over €300

Hôtels de Charme

Beaubourg and The Marais

Hôtel du 7e Art €
20 Rue St.-Paul, 75004
Tel *01 44 54 85 00*   **Map** 14 D4
W paris-hotel-7art.com
An homage to old movies, with framed film posters everywhere. Snug bar and modest bedrooms.

Britannique €€
20 Avenue Victoria, 75001
Tel *01 42 33 74 59*   **Map** 13 A3
W hotel-britannique.fr
Seascapes and other naval details adorn this hotel with a British feel.

Caron de Beaumarchais €€
12 Rue Vieille du Temple, 75004
Tel *01 42 72 34 12*   **Map** 13 C3
W carondebeaumarchais.com
The 18th-century theme here comes alive with colorful fabrics and dainty upholstered furniture.

Tuileries, Opéra, and Montmartre

L'Ermitage Sacre-Coeur €
24 Rue Lamarck, 75018
Tel *01 42 64 79 22*   **Map** 7 A1
W ermitagesacrecoeur.fr
Murals by the artist Roland Dubuc decorate this delightful hotel.

Hôtel Chopin €
46 Passage Jouffroy, 75009
Tel *01 47 70 58 10*   **Map** 6 F4
W hotelchopin.fr
A popular hotel, located in a 19th-century glass-roofed arcade.

Brighton €€
218 Rue de Rivoli, 75001
Tel *01 47 03 61 61*   **Map** 12 D1
W paris-hotel-brighton.com
Enjoy views of the Tuileries amid faux marble columns and chandeliers. Family-friendly.

Mansart €€
5 Rue des Capucines, 75001
Tel *01 42 61 50 28*   **Map** 6 D5
W paris-hotel-mansart.com
The antiques-filled bedrooms here have plenty of character.

The tranquil summer garden at Le Bristol

Champs-Elysées and Chaillot Quarter

Nicolo €€
3 Rue Nicolo, 75116
Tel *01 42 88 83 40* **Map** 9 A2
W hotel-nicolo.fr
A blissfully quiet hotel crammed with antique furniture, Oriental rugs, and huge wildlife prints.

St.-Germain and Latin Quarter

Les Degrés de Notre Dame €€
10 Rue des Grands Degrés, 75005
Tel *01 55 42 88 88* **Map** 13 B4
W lesdegreshotel.com
A vintage charmer: attractive beamed bedrooms lead off a frescoed staircase.

Hôtel de Fleurie €€
32–34 Rue Grégoire de Tours, 75006
Tel *01 53 73 70 00* **Map** 12 F4
W hoteldefleurieparis.com
The statue-adorned facade draws you into this hotel, and its modern comforts keep you there.

Hôtel des Grandes Ecoles €€
75 Rue Cardinal Lemoine, 75005
Tel *01 43 26 79 23* **Map** 17 B1
W hotel-grandes-ecoles.com
A hotel that exudes old-fashioned charm. The garden is perfect for summer breakfasts.

Hôtel St-Paul Rive Gauche €€
43 Rue Monsieur le Prince, 75006
Tel *01 43 26 98 64* **Map** 12 F5
W hotelsaintpaulparis.com
Stone walls and beams at this hotel offer a country vibe. Stylish rooms, some with four-poster beds.

Verneuil €€
8 Rue de Verneuil, 75007
Tel *01 42 60 82 14* **Map** 12 D3
W hotel-verneuil-saint-germain.com
Cosy rooms, antiques, books, and *objets d'art*, at this homey hotel.

Luxembourg and Montparnasse

Lenox Montparnasse €
15 Rue Delambre, 75014
Tel *01 43 35 34 50* **Map** 16 D2
W paris-hotel-lenox.com
This intimate hotel near the Montparnasse brasseries has an Old World charm. Guests enjoy an honesty bar in the lounge.

DK Choice

Hôtel des Académies et des Arts €€
15 Rue de la Grande Chaumière, 75006
Tel *01 43 26 66 44* **Map** 16 D2
W hotel-des-academies.com
Two artists have created an original look for this captivating hotel. Jerôme Mesnager's joyful painted silhouettes of dancers and acrobats decorate the walls, while sculptor Sophie de Watrigant's equally charming figures adorn the hotel staircase. The bedrooms, tearoom, and spa have a refined feel.

Hotel Sainte-Beuve €€
9 Rue Sainte-Beuve, 75006
Tel *01 45 48 20 07* **Map** 16 D1
W hotelsaintebeuve.com
Low-key but with an inherent sense of style, the Sainte-Beuve has colorful bedrooms with free Wi-Fi. A log fire burns in the lovely salon in winter.

Récamier €€€
3 bis Place St.-Sulpice, 75006
Tel *01 43 26 04 89* **Map** 12 E5
W hotelrecamier.com
This small but perfectly formed hotel in a quiet location offers neat rooms with iPod docks and LCD TVs, plus impeccable service. Modern artworks are scattered throughout the building.

Farther Afield

Hôtel du Nord €
47 Rue Albert Thomas, 75010
Tel *01 42 01 66 00* **Map** 8 D5
W hoteldunord-leparivelo.com
A cosy, modest hotel with pretty, distinctive rooms and bicycles for guests to use.

Hôtel de la Porte Dorée €
273 Avenue Daumesnil, 75012
Tel *01 43 07 56 97*
W hoteldelaportedoree.com
Traditional elegance: cosy rooms with beautiful furniture, antiques, and *trompe-l'oeil* murals.

Langlois €€
63 Rue St.-Lazare, 75009
Tel *01 48 74 78 24* **Map** 6 D3
W hotel-langlois.com
Housed in a former 19th-century bank, this traditional hotel offers bags of character and Belle Epoque and Art Nouveau decor.

Manoir de Beauregard €€
43 Rue des Lilas, 75019
Tel *01 42 03 10 20*
W manoir-de-beauregard-paris.com
A B&B in a fine 18th-century manor with a formal garden.

La Manufacture €€
8 Rue Philippe de Champagne, 75013
Tel *01 45 35 45 25* **Map** 17 C4
W hotel-la-manufacture.com
A smart, modern hotel in a 19th-century building, with warm wood floors and attractive decor.

Résidence Foch €€
10 Rue Marbeau, 75116
Tel *01 45 00 46 50* **Map** 3 B4
W foch-paris-hotel.com
Historical prints decorate the walls and fabrics at this intimate hotel.

La Villa Paris €€
33 Rue de la Fontaine à Mulard, 75013
Tel *01 43 47 15 66*
W la-villa-paris.com
Enjoy all the comforts of home at this B&B in a 1920s house. Rooms are luxurious with refined decor.

Design

Champs-Elysées and Chaillot Quarter

Le A €€
4 Rue d'Artois, 75008
Tel *01 42 56 99 99* **Map** 5 A4
W hotel-le-a.com
Bold murals and a monochromatic theme feature in this stylish, cutting-edge hotel.

For more information on types of hotels *see pages 280–83*

Refined elegance at the Duc de Saint Simon

Hotel Fouquet's Barrière €€€
46 Avenue George V, 75008
Tel *09 70 80 91 11*　　**Map** 4 E5
🅦 lucienbarriere.com
A very hip, modern hotel with
Surrealist design touches.

Invalides and
Eiffel Tower Quarter

Mayet €€
3 Rue Mayet, 75006
Tel *01 47 83 21 35*　　**Map** 15 B1
🅦 mayet.com
Colorful painted tables and
abstract murals jazz up the decor
at this smart hotel.

Valadon Colors €€
16 Rue Valadon, 75007
Tel *01 47 53 89 85*　　**Map** 10 F3
🅦 hotelvaladon.com
Superb beds, bold colors and
funky furniture – a three-star hotel
that stands out from the crowd.

7 Eiffel €€€
17 bis Rue Amélie, 75007
Tel *01 45 55 10 01*　　**Map** 10 F3
🅦 hotel-7eiffel-paris.com
Subdued, stylish decoration with
dashes of color make up this
elegant hotel. Great roof terrace.

St.-Germain and
Latin Quarter

Bel Ami €€
7–11 Rue St.-Benoît, 75006
Tel *01 42 61 53 53*　　**Map** 12 E3
🅦 hotel-bel-ami.com
In a former 19th-century printing
works, this hip, minimalist hotel is
where the media crowd hangs out.

Le Bellechasse €€
8 Rue de Bellechasse, 75007
Tel *01 45 50 22 31*　　**Map** 11 C3
🅦 lebellechasse.com
Vibrant frescoes, zany patterns
and brilliant colors fill this fun,
Christian Lacroix-designed gem.

Seven €€
20 Rue Berthollet, 75005
Tel *01 43 31 47 52*　　**Map** 17 A2
🅦 sevenhotelparis.com
With a space-age design, this
chic hotel has fibre-optic lighting
and themed rooms.

Luxembourg and
Montparnasse

Apostrophe €€
3 Rue de Chevreuse, 75006
Tel *01 56 54 31 31*　　**Map** 16 E2
🅦 apostrophe-hotel.com
A quirky, family-run hotel that will
appeal to people with an artistic
or literary bent. Rooms have
been decorated by local artists.

Le Six €€€
14 Rue Stanislas, 75006
Tel *01 42 22 00 75*　　**Map** 16 D1
🅦 hotel-le-six.com
Decorated in understated coffee
and cream, this is a chic, modern
hotel. The spa and hammam are
an added luxury.

Farther Afield

Mama Shelter €
109 Rue de Bagnolet, 75020
Tel *01 43 48 48 48*
🅦 mamashelter.com/en/paris
Classy and hip. The Philippe
Starck-designed rooms have
iMacs and mood lighting.

Romantic

Ile de la Cité and
Ile St.-Louis

Saint Louis en l'Isle €€
75 Rue St.-Louis-en-l'Ile, 75004
Tel *01 46 34 04 80*　　**Map** 13 C4
🅦 saintlouisenlisle.com
A superb location without sky-high
prices. Stylish and intimate, with
rooms in neutral shades.

Beaubourg and
The Marais

DK Choice

Le Petit Moulin €€
29–31 Rue du Poitou, 75003
Tel *01 42 74 10 10*　　**Map** 14 D2
🅦 hotelpetitmoulinparis.com
The oldest *boulangerie* in Paris
now houses a tiny, eccentric
hotel designed by Christian
Lacroix. The 17 distinctive
rooms display the same love
of color and opulence that
shapes his fashion designs.
All are wildly romantic, with
audacious murals.

Tuileries, Opéra, and
Montmartre

Le Relais Montmartre €€
6 Rue Constance, 75018
Tel *01 70 64 25 25*　　**Map** 6 E1
🅦 hotel-relais-montmartre.com
Arranged around a diminutive
courtyard, this welcoming hotel's
rooms have dainty period
furniture and painted beams.

Hotel Particulier Montmartre €€€
23 Avenue Junot, Pavillon D, 75018
Tel *01 53 41 81 40*　　**Map** 2 E5
🅦 hotel-particulier-montmartre.com
The five intimate suites here
feature cutting-edge design and
are the size of small apartments.
There is also a pretty garden.

DK Choice

Terrass €€€
*12–14 Rue Joseph de Maistre,
75018*
Tel *01 46 06 72 85*　　**Map** 6 E1
🅦 terrass-hotel.com
A relaxed four-star hotel with
elegant rooms, Terrass has the
seasons covered. In winter,
there's a cosy piano bar with an
open fire and armchairs to sink
into. In summer, the roof terrace
comes into its own. The top
floor affords spectacular views
across the rooftops to the Eiffel
Tower and beyond.

Champs-Elysées and
Chaillot Quarter

Daniel €€€
8 Rue Frédéric Bastiat, 75008
Tel *01 42 56 17 00*　　**Map** 4 F4
🅦 hoteldanielparis.com
A Chinese jewel box, this hotel
is filled with Oriental fabrics,
wallpapers, carpets, and objects.
Flamboyant and uplifting.

Lancaster €€€
7 Rue de Berri, 75008
Tel 01 40 76 40 76 **Map** 4 F4
W hotel-lancaster.com
Marlene Dietrich's favorite hotel
exudes understated luxury.

Shangri-La €€€
10 Avenue d'Iéna, 75116
Tel 01 53 67 19 98 **Map** 10 D1
W shangri-la.com/paris/shangrila
A madly romantic hotel in a Belle
Epoque palace, the former home
of Napoleon's grandnephew.

Invalides and Eiffel Tower Quarter

Hôtel de la Tour Maubourg €€
150 Rue de Grenelle, 75007
Tel 01 47 05 16 16 **Map** 11 A3
W hoteltourmaubourgparis.com
A gracious and homey hotel with
harmonious bedrooms.

Hôtel de Varenne €€
44 Rue de Bourgogne, 75007
Tel 01 45 51 45 55 **Map** 11 B3
W varenne-hotel-paris.com
A lovely garden is the main asset
of this hotel, which offers Louis
XVI- and Empire-style bedrooms.

DK Choice

Duc de Saint Simon €€€
14 Rue de St.-Simon, 75007
Tel 01 44 39 20 20 **Map** 11 C3
W hotelducdesaintsimon.com
In an 18th-century town house,
this alluring, quiet hotel has
traditional decor. Upholstered
furniture, antiques, skilful paint
effects, and bedrooms in
sumptuous colors lend it a
smart but homey feel. Relax in
the cellar bar, so glorious you'll
never want to leave. Since
standard rooms are on the
small side, it's worth upgrading.

St.-Germain and Latin Quarter

Hôtel de Buci €€
22 Rue de Buci, 75006
Tel 01 55 42 74 74 **Map** 12 E4
W buci-hotel.com
Travel back to the 18th century
at this hotel with antiques, rich
colors, and luxurious fabrics.

Relais St.-Germain €€
9 Carrefour de l'Odéon, 75006
Tel 01 44 27 07 97 **Map** 12 F4
W hotel-paris-relais-saint-
germain.com
Irresistible and typically Parisian,
this hotel has an upscale bistro
and large, luxurious bedrooms.

Hôtel des Grands Hommes €€€
17 Place du Panthéon, 75005
Tel 01 46 34 19 60 **Map** 17 A1
W hoteldesgrandshommes.com
Enjoy views of the Panthéon at
this glossy hotel. Housed in an
18th-century building, it has
sumptuous Baroque-style decor.

Villa d'Estrées €€€
17 Rue Gît le Cœur, 75006
Tel 01 55 42 71 11 **Map** 12 F4
W villadestrees.com
An elegant hideaway, this family-
run establishment offers rooms,
suites, and apartments.

Luxembourg and Montparnasse

Hotel Louis 2 €€
2 Rue St.-Sulpice, 75006
Tel 01 46 33 13 80 **Map** 12 E4
W hotel-louis2.com
The rooms in this friendly hotel are
full of character, with handmade
mattresses and pretty fabrics.

Hôtel de L'Abbaye €€€
10 Rue Cassette, 75006
Tel 01 45 44 38 11 **Map** 12 D5
W hotelabbayeparis.com
Fresh flowers, deep sofas, and
picture-covered walls set the
scene at this elegant hotel.

Farther Afield

Hôtel de Banville €€
166 Boulevard Berthier, 75017
Tel 01 42 67 70 16 **Map** 4 D1
W hotelbanville.fr
Comfort and refinement are key
at this Art Deco hotel.

Vacation Rentals and B&B

Ile de la Cité and Ile St.-Louis

Hospitel €
1 Place du Parvis Notre-Dame, 75004
Tel 01 44 32 01 00 **Map** 13 A4
W hotel-hospitel.fr
A bright, comfortable B&B with
welcoming staff above a hospital.

Tuileries, Opéra, and Montmartre

Loft Paris €
7 Cité Véron, 75018
Tel 06 14 48 47 48 **Map** 6 E1
W loft-paris.fr
Five homey apartments offer
plenty of character. There are
great views from the top-
floor apartment.

Champs-Elysées and Chaillot Quarter

Hotel Palais de Chaillot €
35 Avenue Raymond Poincaré, 75116
Tel 01 53 70 09 09 **Map** 9 C1
W hotelpalaisdechaillot.com
A simple, modern B&B decorated
in bright colors.

St.-Germain and Latin Quarter

Marignan €
13 Rue du Sommerard, 75005
Tel 01 43 54 63 81 **Map** 13 A5
W hotel-marignan.com
Pristine bedrooms and a quaint
breakfast room are a feature of
this family-run B&B.

Farther Afield

DK Choice

Arvor Saint Georges €€
8 Rue Laferrière, 75009
Tel 01 48 78 60 92 **Map** 6 F3
W hotelarvor.com
Behind a subdued facade,
this welcoming, family-friendly
B&B offers retro-modern style.
The open-plan reception, which
includes a bar and breakfast
area, is decorated with
conceptual artist Daniel Buren's
striped posters. A single wall
of bold color enlivens the
otherwise white and minimalist,
though comfortable, bedrooms.

HotelHome Paris 16 €€€
36 Rue George Sand, 75016
Tel 01 45 20 61 38
W hotelhome.fr
Seventeen cheerfully decorated
apartments of various sizes make
up this apartment-hotel
complex. Good for families.

The colorful Christian Lacroix-designed
Le Petit Moulin

For more information on types of hotels *see pages 280–83*

WHERE TO EAT AND DRINK

The French national passion for good cuisine makes eating out one of the greatest pleasures of a visit to Paris. Everywhere in the city you see people eating – in restaurants, bistros, tearooms, cafés, and wine bars.

Most restaurants serve French food, but there is a range of Chinese, Vietnamese, Thai, Korean, and North African eateries in many areas, as well as Italian, Greek, Middle Eastern, and Indian ones. Most places serve lunch from noon to about 2pm, and the menu often includes fixed-price meals. Parisians usually start to fill restaurants for dinner around 8pm and most places serve from around 7pm until 11pm. Many restaurants are closed on Mondays and in August. *(See also Bars, Tearooms and Street Food pp309–11.)*

What to Eat

A tremendous range of food is available in Paris, from the rich meat dishes and perfect pâtisserie for which France is most famous to simpler French regional cuisines *(see pp292–3)*. The latter are available in brasseries and bistros – the type usually depends on the birthplace of the chef. Simple, small meals can be enjoyed in cafés, wine bars, and pâtisseries, while more substantial meals can be had in the numerous brasseries and bistros.

The best international food comes from France's former colonies: Vietnam and North Africa. North African eateries are known as couscous restaurants and serve filling, somewhat spicy, inexpensive food that varies in quality. Vietnamese restaurants are also a good deal and provide a light alternative to rich French food. Paris has some good Japanese restaurants, notably around Rue Monsieur le Prince (6th arrondissement), as well as Rue Sainte-Anne (2nd) and Avenue de Choisy (13th).

Where to find good Restaurants and Cafés

You can eat well in almost any part of Paris. Wherever you are, as a rule of thumb you will find that the most outstanding restaurants and cafés are those that cater predominantly to a French clientele.

The Left Bank probably has the greatest concentration of restaurants, especially in tourist areas like St.-Germain-des-Prés and the Latin Quarter. The quality of food varies, but there are some commendable bistros, outdoor cafés, and wine bars – see pages 309–11 for a selection of the best places to go in Paris for light meals and snacks. The Latin Quarter also has a high concentration of Greek and Turkish restaurants centered chiefly around Rue de la Huchette.

Le Pré Verre restaurant *(see p304)*

In the Marais and Bastille areas, small bistros, tearooms, and cafés are plentiful, some modern and fashionable. These areas also have many traditional long-established bistros and brasseries that are good.

The Champs-Elysées and Madeleine area offer everything from chic, traditional cafés to fast-food outlets and a scattering of delectable tearooms. There are some very good expensive restaurants here too.

Montparnasse still has some great cafés and restaurants from the 1920s, such as La Coupole and Le Sélect on the Boulevard du Montparnasse *(see p305 & 306)*. Sensitive renovation has recaptured much of their old splendor. This area is also well known for its many pancake restaurants *(crêperies)*. Rue de Montparnasse, for example, is lined with *crêperies* serving *galettes*, sweet *crêpes*, and Normandy cider.

Le Verre Volé bistrot and wine store *(see p308)*

There are many noteworthy restaurants, bistros, and cafés in the Louvre-Rivoli area, competing with tourist-oriented, overpriced cafés. Just to the east, Les Halles is packed with fast food joints and mediocre restaurants, but there are a few places of note.

Good Japanese food can be found near the Opéra, along with some fine brasseries, but otherwise the area around the Opéra and Grands Boulevards is not the best for restaurants. Near the Bourse are some reputable restaurants and bistros, often frequented by stockbrokers.

Montmartre has a predictable number of tourist restaurants, but it also has a few very pleasant small bistros. One traditional bistro, complete with a zinc bar, is Un Zèbre à Montmartre (see p298), which serves delicious, inexpensive food.

Quiet neighborhoods in the evening, the Invalides, Eiffel Tower, and Palais de Chaillot tend to have less noisy, more serious restaurants than areas with lively nightlife. Prices can be high.

Two Chinatowns, one in the area south of the Place d'Italie, the other in the traditionally working-class, hill-top area of Belleville, have Asian food but few French restaurants of note. Ménilmontant and Belleville are going through a regeneration, and becoming celebrated for their culinary scene, with gourmet restaurants, hip bars, and brunch venues.

Le Grand Véfour next to the Palais-Royal gardens (see p300)

Types of Restaurants and Cafés

One of the most enjoyable aspects of eating in Paris is the diversity of places to eat. Bistros are small, often moderately priced restaurants with a limited selection of dishes. Those from the belle époque era are particularly beautiful, with zinc bars, mirrors, and attractive tiles. The food is generally, but not always, regional and traditional. Many chefs from the finest restaurants have also opened bistros, and these can be very good deals.

A typical bistro menu

Brasseries are mostly large, bustling eateries, many with an Alsatian character, serving carafes of Alsatian wine and platters of sauerkraut and sausage. They have immense menus, and most serve food throughout the day and are open late. Outside you may see impressive sidewalk displays of shellfish, with apron-clad oyster shuckers working late into the night.

Cafés open early in the morning, and aside from the large tourist cafés, most close by around 10pm. They serve drinks and food all day long from a short menu of salads, sandwiches, omelets, and grills. At lunch most also offer a small choice of hot daily specials. Café prices vary from area to area, in direct proportion to the number of tourists. More stylish cafés, like Café de Flore and Les Deux Magots, serve food until late at night. Those cafés specializing in beer almost always include onion tarts, French fries, and hearty bowls of steamed mussels on the menu. Brunch is served in many places on weekends, from around €17.

Wine bars are informal. They usually have a moderately priced, simple lunch menu and serve wine by the glass. Some serve snacks at any time of day – such as marvelous open sandwiches (tartines) made with sourdough Poilâne bread topped with cheese, sausage, or pâté. A few stay open for dinner.

Tearooms open for breakfast or mid-morning until the early evening. Many offer lunch, as well as a selection of sweet pastries for afternoon tea. They are best visited in the middle of the afternoon and offer coffee and hot chocolate as well as fine teas. Some, like Le Loir dans la Théière, are casual with sofas, while Mariage Frères is more formal. Angélina on the Rue de Rivoli is famous for its hot chocolate, and Ladurée has excellent macaroons. (For addresses see p311.)

La Tour d'Argent decoration (see p305)

Bofinger, a traditional brasserie in Bastille *(see p297)*

Vegetarian Food

Wholly vegetarian restaurants in Paris are still relatively few, and standard restaurant menus typically offer only a few vegetarian options. You can often fare well by ordering two courses from the list of *entrées* (main courses). North African restaurants will serve couscous with vegetables only, but these may have come out of the meat pot.

Never be timid about asking for a change in a dish. If you see a salad with ham, bacon, or foie gras, ask the waiter for it without the meat. If you are going to a smart restaurant, telephone ahead and ask the manager if it is possible to prepare a special meal for you. Most restaurants will be happy to oblige.

Organic produce is increasingly used in French cuisine – look out for *biologique* or *bio* on the menu. Some places can also provide gluten-free dishes.

How Much to Pay

Prices for meals in Paris range from the extremely economic to the astronomical. You can still enjoy a hearty restaurant or café lunch for €25, but a typical good bistro, brasserie, or restaurant meal in central Paris will average €40–€55 with wine. Remember that selecting one of the better French wines will increase the size of your check significantly.

More expensive restaurants begin at about €60 with wine and go up to €210 for the top establishments. Many places offer a *formule* or *prix-fixe* (fixed price) menu, especially at lunch, and this will almost always offer the best value. Some restaurants feature two course menus for under €20 – a few at this price include wine. Coffee usually carries an extra charge.

All French restaurants are obliged by law to display their menu outside. The posted rates include service but a tip for particularly good service will always be appreciated (any amount from one Euro to five per cent of the total).

The most widely accepted credit card is Visa. Few restaurants accept American Express, and some bistros do not accept credit cards at all, so it is wise to inquire when you book. Travelers' checks are not accepted either.

The Menu

Menu boards in small restaurants and bistros, and even in big brasseries, are often handwritten and can be difficult to decipher, so ask for help if necessary. The first course generally includes a choice of seasonal salads or vegetables, pâté, and small hot or cold vegetable dishes or tarts. Small fish dishes like smoked salmon, grilled sardines, herring, fish salads, and tartares are also often on the menu. Brasseries have shellfish such as oysters, which can also be eaten as a main course.

Main dishes usually include a selection of meat, poultry, and fish. Game often features in the autumn. Most restaurants also offer fresh, good-value daily specials *(plats du jour)*.

Eating at the classy Benoît, run by Alain Ducasse *(see p298)*

Cheese is eaten either as a dessert or as a pre-dessert course. Coffee is served after, not with, dessert. You will need to ask specifically if you want it *au lait* (with milk). Decaffeinated coffee *(décaféiné)* and herbal teas *(tisanes)* are also popular.

In most restaurants you will be asked if you would like a drink before ordering food. A typical apéritif is kir (white wine with a drop of *crème de cassis*, a black currant liqueur) or *kir royal* (champagne with *crème de cassis*). Beer is rarely drunk before a meal in France *(see What to Drink in Paris pp294–5)*.

Bistros and brasseries usually include the wine list with the menu. The more expensive restaurants have separate wine lists, which are generally brought to the table by the wine waiter *(sommelier)*, who can help with choosing the wine.

Qui Plume La Lune, a chic modern restaurant *(see p298)*

The lavish interior of Le Train Bleu restaurant in the Gare de Lyon *(see p308)*

Service

The lunchtime service in popular Paris eateries is generally very brisk, if sometimes a little brusque, due to the sheer pressure of numbers. Evening meals can usually be enjoyed at a more leisurely pace.

Children

French children are introduced early to eating in restaurants and as a rule are well-behaved. Consequently, children are usually very welcome. However, there may be little room inside a busy restaurant to bring in a cumbersome stroller, and relatively few restaurants provide special amenities such as high-chairs or booster seats.

Terminus Nord brasserie *(see p308)*, opposite the Gare du Nord

Smoking

There are strict anti-tobacco laws in France. It is illegal to smoke inside bars and restaurants. Smoking is permitted, however, on restaurant, café, and pub patios provided they are not enclosed.

Wheelchair Access

Parisian restaurants are generally accommodating, and a word when you book should ensure that you are given a more conveniently located table. It is always worth checking that restrooms can also be used by wheelchair users, since access can be restricted.

Picnics

Picnicking is the best way to enjoy the wonderful fresh produce, local bread, cheeses, charcuterie, and pastries from the markets and enticing stores to be found all over the city. For more details see pages 325–7. It is also a good way of enjoying the many parks that Paris has to offer.

Recommended Restaurants

The restaurants on pages 296–308 of this guide cover a spectrum of cuisine styles and prices, and are the best of their kind in Paris. They are listed by area, mostly in the main tourist districts, although there are a number slightly farther afield that merit a special trip.

Many Paris restaurants are still firmly rooted in the past, serving traditional French bistro and brasserie specialties such as *steak-frites*, snails, and seafood, as well as regional dishes such as cassoulet and *confit* of duck. However, there are also those that embrace new trends in a modern bistro style of high-caliber cooking – *"cuisine bistronomique"*. These bistros offer an inventive, market-driven reworking of classic recipes, served in casual surroundings at reasonable prices. Another development in the Paris restaurant scene, especially at haute cuisine establishments, is the influx of foreign chefs. Many of them come from Japan, and they are refreshing and invigorating Parisian dining.

Throughout the listings, certain restaurants have been highlighted as DK Choice. These offer a particularly special quality, such as outstanding food, excellent value, a romantic ambience, a uniquely Parisian dining experience, or a combination of these.

The Flavors of Paris

From the glittering temples of haute cuisine to the humblest neighborhood bistro, Paris is a paradise for food lovers, whether you dine on foie gras and truffles or steak-frites, a seafood platter or a perfumed Moroccan couscous. France is immensely proud of its food, from classic haute cuisine to the most rustic of regional dishes. All are available in the capital and, though the French themselves will debate endlessly about the ideal sauce to complement meat or fish, or the right wine to accompany them, they will always be in total agreement that theirs is the best food in the world.

Girolles (chanterelles) on a stand in rue Mouffetard market

prize ingredients of the season. Even if you are not shopping for food to cook, the markets are worth browsing and, after an hour or so in the crowded, narrow streets of the rue de Buci or rue Mouffetard, you will be more than ready for lunch.

The food of the French provinces, once despised for its rusticity, is now celebrated, and almost every region is

represented in the capital, from the rich, bourgeois cuisines of Burgundy and Lyon to the celebrated healthy Mediterranean diet of Provence. Paris itself is surrounded by top-quality market gardens that supply young peas, carrots, and potatoes. Salmon, asparagus, and wild mushrooms come from the Loire; Normandy brings

What all French chefs agree on is the importance of using the finest-quality ingredients, and there is no better place to appreciate the quality of French produce than in the markets of Paris. Here, top chefs may be spied early in the morning, alongside local shoppers, seeking inspiration and the

Selection of fine French cheeses in perfect condition

Comté, Brie, Tomme de chèvre, Ami du Chambertin, Roquefort

Classic French Cuisine

What is usually thought of as classic French cuisine was developed in royal palaces and noble châteaux, with the emphasis on luxury and display, not frugality or health. Dishes are often bathed in rich sauces of butter or cream, enhanced with luxurious ingredients like truffles, foie gras, rare mushrooms, and alcohol. Meat is treated with reverence, and you will usually be asked how you want your beef, lamb, or duck cooked; the French tend to like their beef rare or medium rare (*bleu* or *saignant*) and their lamb and duck pink (*rose*). For well-cooked meat, ask for "*bien cuit*" but still expect at least a tinge of pinkness. The most famous country classics include slowly cooked casseroles like *coq au vin* and *boeuf bourguignon*, as well as the bean, sausage, and baked duck dish *cassoulet*, from the southwest.

Escargots à la Bourguignon are plump Burgundy snails served in their shells with garlic, butter, and parsley.

...lt-marsh lamb, apples, and ...amembert. Salers beef ...nd lentils come from the ...uvergne; beef and Bresse ...hickens from Burgundy; and ...on't forget Basque ham, ...ollioure anchovies, lamb from ...e Pyrenees, or fragrant ...rovençal melons.

...he New Style

...n recent years, innovative ...hefs have developed new ...yles of cooking, reacting ...gainst the richness of trad-...onal cooking, and using fresh ...ngredients, lightly cooked to ...etain their flavor. Sauces are ...ade of light reductions to ...nhance, not obscure, the ...ain ingredient of a dish. ...wave of invention and ...riginality has resulted in ...plethora of unusual ...ngredients, fresh twists on ...e classics, and sometimes

Mouthwatering display in a Parisian patisserie

wonderful new combinations and flavors, such as sea bass with bean purée and red wine sauce, or with fermented grape juice; sole with quince juice and tarragon; tempura of langoustines with cinnamon beurre blanc; rabbit with Indian spices and tomato polenta; and rosemary ice cream or lavender sorbet.

Foreign Food

Paris can also offer diners an amazing selection of world flavors, especially those of France's former colonies – for example, Moroccan tajines and Cambodian fish with coconut milk. Most fascinating of all is to observe how these cuisines are developing, as young chefs adapt and combine traditional ingredients and culinary styles with those of France.

On the Menu

Andouillettes Sausages made from pork intestines

Blanquette de veau Veal stew with a creamy sauce

Confit de canard Cured duck leg with garlic and herbs

Crottin chaud en salade Goat's cheese on toast with salad

Cuisses de grenouille Frogs' legs in garlic butter

Iles flottantes Meringues floating in a custard sauce

Plateau de fruits de mer Platter of raw and cooked seafood

Ris de veau Veal sweetbreads

Rognons à la moutarde Kidneys in mustard sauce

Salade frisée aux lardons Endive salad with fried bacon

Sole meunière Fried sole with melted butter

...ealed jars of whole duck-liver foie ...ras, a luxury item

Moules marinière are mussels steamed in a fragrant sauce of white wine, garlic, parsley, and sometimes cream.

Coq au vin is a male chicken braised with red wine, herbs, garlic, baby onions, and button mushrooms.

Tarte tatin is a caramelized upside-down buttery apple tart, created at the Hôtel Tatin in the Loire Valley.

What to Drink in Paris

Paris is the best place in France to sample a wide range of the country's many different wines. It's cheapest to order wine by the carafe, normally referred to by size: 25cl *(quart)*, 33cl *(fillette)*, 50cl *(demi)* or 75cl *(pichet*, equivalent to a bottle*)*. Cafés and wine bars usually offer wine by the glass – *un petit blanc* is a small glass of white, a larger glass of red is *un ballon de rouge*. House wine is nearly always reliable.

Paris's last vineyard, near Sacré-Coeur *(see p224)*

Red Wine

Some of the world's finest red wines come from the Bordeaux and Burgundy regions, but for everyday drinking choose from the vast range of basic southern French or Côtes du Rhône wines. Or try one of the Beaujolais *crus*, such as Morgon or Fleurie from southern Burgundy, or lighter reds from the Loire, such as Chinon or Saumur-Champigny.

Distinctive bottle shapes for Bordeaux and Burgundy

Bordeaux châteaux include Margaux, which makes some of the world's most elegant red wines.

Burgundy includes some big, strong red wines from the village of Gevrey-Chambertin in the Côte de Nuits.

Beaujolais Nouveau, the fruity first taste of the year's new wine, is released on the third Thursday of November.

The Loire has very good red wines from the area around Chinon. They are usually quite light and very dry.

Southern Rhône is famous for its dark, rich red wines from Châteauneuf-du-Pape, north of Avignon.

Northern Rhône has some dark, spicy red wines, best aged for at least ten years, from Côte-Rôtie near Vienne.

Fine Wine Vintage Chart	2009	2008	2007	2006	2005	2004	2003	2002	2001
Bordeaux									
Margaux, St.-Julien, Pauillac, St.-Estèphe	10	8	7	8	9	7	8	6	7
Graves, Pessac-Léognan (red)	9	8	7	8	9	7	6	6	7
Graves, Pessac-Léognan (white)	7	8	7	8	9	8	7	6	7
St.-Emilion, Pomerol	9	8	7	8	9	7	6	5	8
Burgundy									
Chablis	9	8	9	8	9	8	7	8	8
Côte de Nuits (red)	9	7	6	7	9	7	7	6	7
Côte de Beaune (white)	9	7	7	8	9	8	7	8	8
Loire									
Bourgueil, Chinon	9	8	8	7	9	7	7	8	7
Sancerre (white)	9	8	7	8	9	8	7	7	8
Rhone									
Hermitage (red)	9	7	10	7	9	7	7	4	7
Hermitage (white)	9	8	10	7	9	7	6	4	8
Côte-Rôtie	8	7	8	7	9	7	6	4	7
Châteauneuf-du-Pape	9	8	9	8	9	7	6	3	7

The quality scale from 1 to 10 represents an overall rating for the year and is only a guideline

White Wine

The finest white Bordeaux and Burgundies are best with food, but for everyday drinking try a light dry wine such as Entre-Deux-Mers from Bordeaux, or Anjou Blanc or Sauvignon de Touraine from the Loire. Alsace makes some reliable white wines. Sweet wines such as Sauternes, Barsac, or Coteaux du Layon are delicious with foie gras.

Alsace Riesling and Burgundy

Sparkling Wine

In France champagne is the first choice for a celebration drink, and styles range from nonvintage to deluxe. Many other wine regions make sparkling wines by the champagne method which tend to be a lot cheaper. Look out for Crémant de Loire, Crémant de Bourgogne, Vouvray Mousseux, Saumur Mousseux, and Blanquette de Limoux.

Champagne

Aperitifs and Digestifs

Kir, white wine mixed with a small amount of black currant liqueur or *crème de cassis*, is the ubiquitous *apéritif*. Also common is aniseed-flavored *pastis* which is served with ice and a pitcher of water and can be very refreshing. Vermouths, especially Noilly-Prat, are also common apéritifs. *Digestifs*, or after-dinner drinks, are often ordered with coffee and include *eaux-de-vie*, the strong colorless spirits infused with fruit, and brandies such as Cognac, Armagnac, and Calvados.

Kir: white wine with *cassis*

Beers

Beer in France is sold either by the bottle or, more cheaply, on tap by the glass – *un demi*. The cheapest is lager-style *bière française*, and the best brands are Meteor and Mutzig, followed by "33," "1664," and Kronenbourg. Pelforth makes very good dark beer and lager. Some bars and cafés specialize in foreign beers, especially from Belgium, and these are very malty and strong – Leffe, for example, comes as *brune* (dark, fully flavored) or as a lighter *blonde* (lager). There are bars that brew their own beer. (For beer bars see *p309*).

Alsace wines are usually labeled by grape variety. Gewürztraminer is one of the most distinctive.

Loire wines include Puilly-Fumé. It is very dry, often with a slightly smoky perfume.

Burgundy wines include Chablis, a fresh, full-flavored dry wine from the northernmost vineyards.

The Loire has the perfect partner to seafood dishes in Muscadet, a dry white wine from the Atlantic Coast.

Champagne vineyards east of Paris produce the famous sparkling wine. Billecart-Salmon is a light, pink Champagne.

Sweet Bordeaux are luscious, golden-colored dessert wines, the most famous being Barsac and Sauternes.

Other Drinks

The brightly colored drinks consumed in cafés all over Paris are mixtures of flavored syrups and mineral waters, called *sirops à l'eau*. The emerald-green drinks use mint syrup, the red ones grenadine. Fruit juices and tomato juice are sold in bottles unless you specify *citron pressé* or *orange pressée* (freshly squeezed lemon or orange), served with a pitcher of water and with sugar or sugar syrup for you to dilute and sweeten to taste. If you ask for water, you will be served mineral water, sparkling *(gazeuse)* or still *(naturelle)*; if you don't want to be charged, ask for tap water *(eau de robinet)* or a pitcher of water *(carafe d'eau)*.

Fresh lemon juice is served with water and sugar

Where to Eat and Drink

Ile de la Cité and Ile St.-Louis

Café St Régis €
Traditional French **Map** 13 B4
6 Rue Jean du Bellay, 75004
Tel *01 43 54 59 41*
This popular, friendly café with a traditional bistro decor serves food all day – from classic *croques-monsieur* to hamburgers. The interesting Sunday brunch menu features oysters and waffles. Good breakfasts, too.

Au Bougnat €€
Traditional French **Map** 13 B4
26 Rue Chanoinesse, 75004
Tel *01 43 54 50 74*
The modest decor at this bistro echoes its simple, traditional cuisine – delicious frogs' legs, veal stew, *entrecôte*, and pear tart.

Beaubourg and The Marais

Amici Miei €
Sardinian **Map** 14 E3
44 Rue St.-Sabin, 75011
Tel *01 42 71 82 62* **Closed** *Mon & Sun*
Fans claim that this rustic, unpretentious trattoria makes the best thin-crust pizzas in Paris. Follow a pizza with the strawberry and basil panna cotta.

Blend €
American **Map** 13 A1
44 Rue d'Argout, 75002
Tel *01 40 26 84 57*
A no-nonsense restaurant where the chef blends different cuts of top-quality beef and fresh produce to make the perfect gourmet burger. There are four branches in Paris.

Café Charlot €
International **Map** 14 D2
38 Rue de Bretagne, 75003
Tel *01 44 54 03 30*
Grab a seat on the popular terrace or enjoy the handsome interior of this cool café set in a former *boulangerie*. The daily specials are usually excellent, or you can just hang out with a coffee or a cocktail.

Café de l'Industrie €
Traditional French **Map** 14 E3
19 Rue St.-Sabin, 75011
Tel *01 47 00 13 53*
You could while away hours at this relaxed favorite in the Bastille, with its attractive Neo-Colonial decor and old movie posters. There is also an annexe across the road.

Chez Hanna €
Moroccan and Israeli **Map** 13 C3
54 Rue des Rosiers, 75004
Tel *01 42 74 74 99/01 73 20 23 71*
Closed *Mon*
This is a firm favorite among locals, who come here for the famous hummus and falafel sandwiches: golden outside, moist within, and crammed with crisp vegetables, juicy aubergine and chilli, and creamy tahini sauce.

Le Dindon en Laisse €
Traditional French **Map** 14 D4
18 Rue Beautreillis, 75004
Tel *01 48 04 06 24*
"The Turkey on a Leash" is a cheerful eatery with stellar food: risottos, flavorsome meat and game dishes, as well as good wines. In summer, it is possible to dine alfresco.

Filakia €
Greek **Map** 13 A
9 Rue Mandar, 75002
Tel *01 42 21 42 88*
This cosy venue serves delicious and authentic souvlaki wraps filled with succulent grilled marinated chicken, lamb, steak, or vegetables – all accompanied by French fries or salad.

Le Garde Robe €
French tapas **Map** 12 F.
41 Rue de l'Arbre Sec, 75001
Tel *01 49 26 90 60* **Closed** *Su*
This narrow space serves a wide range of tapas – oysters, cheeses and charcuterie – accompanied by wonderful wines.

L'Ambassade d'Auvergne €€
Auvergnat **Map** 13 B.
22 Rue du Grenier St-Lazare, 75003
Tel *01 42 72 31 22*
With the atmosphere of a rustic inn, this restaurant transports you to rural Auvergne. A menu highlight is *aligot* (potatoes with cheese and garlic).

L'Ange 20 €€
Traditional French **Map** 14 E3
44 Rue des Tournelles, 75003
Tel *01 49 96 58 39* **Closed** *Mon & Tue*
Choose between seven-hour cooked lamb and duck with orange at this snug bistro. Both are deliciously tender.

The bustling interior of Café St Régis with retro vintage decor

The belle époque decor at Bofinger

DK Choice

Auberge Nicolas Flamel €€
Traditional French **Map** 13 C2
51 Rue de Montmorency, 75003
Tel 01 42 71 77 78   **Closed** Sun
Nicolas Flamel, said to have been an alchemist, built this house, the oldest in Paris, in 1407. The interior, set over two floors, is charmingly haphazard, and candlelit dinners among the stone walls and beams have a romantic ambience. The traditional dishes are well executed.

Bofinger €€
Alsatian **Map** 14 E4
5–7 Rue de la Bastille, 75004
Tel 01 42 72 87 82
A perfectly preserved Belle Epoque interior – with a stained-glass cupola and an elegant staircase with a polished brass handrail – makes this one of the city's most beautiful brasseries. The menu of classic dishes includes great shellfish.

Les Bonnes Soeurs €€
Modern French **Map** 14 D3
8 Rue du Pas de la Mule, 75003
Tel 01 42 74 55 80
This small modern bistro, close to the fashionable Place des Vosges, is known for good-value brunches (reservations are recommended).

Café Beaubourg €€
Modern French **Map** 13 B2
43 Rue St.-Merri, Esplanade du Centre Georges Pompidou, 75004
Tel 01 48 87 63 96
The ample, sunny terrace of this stylish café on the piazza of the Pompidou Center is the perfect spot for a relaxing drink and some people-watching. The food is decent (if a little overpriced).

Le Chemise €€
Modern French **Map** 14 E1
42 Rue de Malte, 75011
Tel 01 49 29 98 77 **Closed** Sat, Sun & Mon lunch
A sleek, chic neo-bistro: wooden floors, super-comfortable leather chairs, and cooking that puts a creative spin on the traditional.

Claude Colliot €€
Modern French **Map** 13 B2
40 Rue des Blancs Manteaux, 75004
Tel 01 42 71 55 45 **Closed** Sun & Mon
Innovative seasonal cooking by this self-taught chef in a sleek setting, frequented by the stars.

Le Colimaçon €€
Modern French **Map** 13 C3
44 Rue Vieille du Temple, 75004
Tel 06 27 18 08 07 **Closed** lunch Mon–Sat
Traditional recipes are interpreted in a modern way, and prepared with seasonal ingredients, at this restaurant with rustic-style decor. The signature dish is melt-in-the-mouth snails.

Frenchie €€
Modern French **Map** 7 A5
5–6 Rue du Nil, 75002
Tel 01 40 39 96 19 **Closed** lunch daily; Sat & Sun
One of Paris's hottest bistros. The intensely flavored dishes, on fixed-price menus, are an irresistible draw. Book months ahead, or try your luck at the wine bar opposite, which also serves food.

Le Hangar €€
Traditional French **Map** 13 B2
12 Impasse Berthaud, 75003
Tel 01 42 74 55 44 **Closed** Mon & Sun
Dishes here include pan-fried foie gras on puréed potatoes, and creamy risotto, as well as great desserts. No credit cards are accepted.

L'Ilot €€
Seafood **Map** 14 D1
4 Rue de la Corderie, 75003
Tel 06 95 12 86 61
The trendy inhabitants of the Marais come here to savor fish and shellfish brought in daily from the French coast. A selective wine list accompanies their seafood dishes.

Le Petit Marché €€
Modern French **Map** 14 D3
9 Rue de Béarn, 75003
Tel 01 42 72 06 67
Highlights of the short Asian-inspired menu here include succulent beef, enticing sesame-seared tuna, and decadent chocolate fondant with praline crème anglaise.

Le Pharamond €€
Traditional French **Map** 13 A2
24 Rue de la Grande Truanderie, 75001
Tel 01 40 28 45 18 **Closed** Mon & Sun
Norman specialties, including tripe cooked in cider and Calvados, feature strongly on the menu at this restaurant inside a Belle Epoque building.

Les Philosophes €€
Traditional French **Map** 13 C3
28 Rue Vieille du Temple, 75004
Tel 01 48 87 49 64
Try this popular all-day café for first-rate onion soup, steak-frites, omelettes, and the house specialty: tomato tarte tatin. The desserts are truly memorable.

La Régalade St-Honoré €€
Traditional French **Map** 12 F2
123 Rue St.-Honoré, 75001
Tel 01 45 45 68 58 **Closed** Mon lunch; Sat & Sun
Make sure you're hungry when you get here: Bruno Doucet's glorious, complex country cooking is served in generous portions.

Le Tir Bouchon €€
Traditional French **Map** 13 A1
22 Rue Tiquetonne, 75002
Tel 01 42 21 95 51
An endearingly old-fashioned restaurant where the chef adds a gourmet touch to classic regional dishes. The honey-roasted duck is very popular.

Le Trumilou €€
Traditional French **Map** 13 B4
84 Quai de l'Hôtel de Ville, 75004
Tel 01 42 77 63 98
Sit out in summer and enjoy the river views at this legendary bistro. With few frills, the fare is as traditional as the decor. House specialties include canard aux pruneaux (duck with prunes).

For more information on types of restaurants see pages 288–91

Le Villaret   €€
Traditional French   **Map** 14 E2
13 Rue Ternaux, 75011
Tel *01 43 57 89 76 or 01 43 57 75 56*
Closed *Sat lunch & Sun*
This snug eatery, all exposed
brick walls and beams, is
renowned for using ingredients
fresh from the morning market.
There is also a great cheeseboard.

Benoît   €€€
Lyonnaise   **Map** 13 B2
20 Rue St-Martin, 75004
Tel *01 42 72 25 76*
A Paris institution, the Benoît
is run by renowned chef Alain
Ducasse. Choose from a menu
of hearty standards such as
veal sweetbreads and cassoulet.
Outstanding wine list.

Qui Plume La Lune   €€€
Modern French   **Map** 14 D1
50 Rue Amelot, 75011
Tel *01 48 07 45 48*   **Closed** *Mon, Tue & Sun*
At this Michelin-starred
establishment, diners splash
out on the five-course menu:
each dish is a sparkling fusion
of Breton and Japanese cuisines.
The minimalist, stylish decor
includes an illuminated tree.

DK Choice

Spring   €€€
Modern French   **Map** 12 F2
6 Rue Bailleul, 75001
Tel *01 45 96 05 72*   **Closed** *Mon & Sun*
A magician in the kitchen,
Chicago-born Daniel Rose
produces a fixed-price tasting
menu that is created around
what's fresh in the market.
There's no choice, but his
unique versions of French
classics, paired with outstanding
wines, are inspired. If you can't
get a table, try his wine bar,
Buvette, in the basement.

Yam'Tcha   €€€
Asian fusion   **Map** 12 F2
4 Rue Sauval, 75001
Tel *01 40 26 08 07*   **Closed** *Mon & Sun; Tue lunch*
The name means "drink tea," and
tea pairings are recommended
with Adeline Grattard's Chinese-
influenced dishes with subtle
French notes. Reserve in advance.

Tuileries, Opéra, and Montmartre

Babalou   €
Italian   **Map** 7 A1
4 Rue Lamarck, 75018
Tel *01 42 51 37 32*   **Closed** *mid-Jan–mid-Feb*
A restaurant with a big heart and
smiling staff. Home-made pasta,
pizza, risotto, and other Italian
staples are all perfectly cooked.

Bistrot Victoires   €
Traditional French   **Map** 12 F1
6 Rue la Vrillière, 75001
Tel *01 42 61 43 78*
Entrecôte, roast chicken, and other
classics are served at this bistro.
The vintage interior features a
zinc bar and banquette seating.

Le Cap Bourban   €
Traditional French   **Map** 6 E5
1 Rue Louis Le Grand, 75002
Tel *01 42 61 81 05*   **Closed** *Sat & Sun*
This is the place for Creole
specialties from Réunion Island,
like *boeuf massalé* (beef curry),
samosas, and shrimp curry.

Chartier   €
Traditional French   **Map** 6 F4
7 Rue du Faubourg Montmartre, 75009
Tel *01 47 70 86 29*
Leap back to the 1890s at this
iconic brasserie. Traditionally
dressed waiters deliver simple,
inexpensive food in glorious
Belle Epoque surroundings.

Crêperie Broceliande   €
Crêperie   **Map** 6 F1
15 Rue des Trois Frères, 75018
Tel *01 42 23 31 34*   **Closed** *Mon & Tue lunch; 3 wks in summer*
A little slice of Brittany, complete
with a carved dresser and
checked tablecloths. The crêpes
are utter perfection: paper-thin
and with a range of delicious
fillings, both savory and sweet.

Le Progrès   €
Traditional French   **Map** 6 F1
7 Rue des Trois Frères, 75018
Tel *01 42 64 07 37*
This traditional, charming café
with huge bay windows is the
ideal spot for relaxing and
watching the world go by over
a morning coffee or an evening
aperitif. On the menu is simple,
reasonably priced food.

Tentazioni   €
Sicilian   **Map** 6 E1
26 Rue Tholozé, 75018
Tel *01 53 28 45 20*   **Closed** *Mon*
All the traditional dishes are
tempting at this cosy, rustic
trattoria run by the welcoming
Leopardi family. However, be
sure to leave some room for
the rich, decadent tiramisu.

La Tiborna   €
Portuguese   **Map** 6 E1
19 Rue Durantin, 75018
Tel *01 46 06 19 46*
This warm and convivial café
serves up specialties from the
Iberian Peninsula. Locals come
here for the excellent brunch,
prepared with organic produce.

Un Zèbre à Montmartre   €
Lyonnaise   **Map** 6 E1
38 Rue Lepic, 75018
Tel *01 42 23 97 80*
Enjoy a bargain set-price meal
at this colorful, bustling bistro.
Highlights include slow-cooked
beef, and chocolate fondant.

L'Adjugé   €€
Modern French   **Map** 6 F4
9 Rue Drouot, 75009
Tel *01 47 70 72 04*   **Closed** *Sun*
Culinary treasures abound at the
in-house restaurant of the Drouot
auction house. Those needing a
break from the bidding come to
dine on classic French dishes in
intimate and quiet surroundings.

La Balançoire   €€
Traditional French   **Map** 6 E1
6 Rue Aristide Bruant, 75018
Tel *01 42 23 70 83*
"The Swing" is a child-friendly
restaurant dotted with jars of
candies. The menu is seasonal
and imaginative.

Chartier, a Belle Epoque brasserie in Montmartre

The elegant interior of Qui Plume La Lune

Café Marly €€
Traditional French **Map** 12 E2
93 Rue de Rivoli, 75001
Tel *01 49 26 06 60*
This elegant café is set in an arcaded terrace overlooking the glass pyramid of the Louvre. The menu offers a range of French and international dishes. Prices tend to reflect the location, but you can always just have a drink.

Chez Georges €€
Traditional French **Map** 12 F1
1 Rue du Mail, 75002
Tel *01 42 60 07 11* **Closed** *Sat & Sun*
A vintage treasure, beloved of cookery writer Julia Child. The traditional bistro fare is sublime, and includes *steak au poivre.*

Chez Toinette €€
Traditional French **Map** 6 E1
20 Rue Germain Pilon, 75018
Tel *01 42 54 44 36* **Closed** *Mon & Sun; Aug*
Behind an unprepossessing facade, this small restaurant bursts with charm. Among the best dishes are the delicious duck foie gras, roast pigeon (in winter), snails, lamb shank, and sea bass.

DK Choice

La Cordonnerie €€
Traditional French **Map** 12 E1
20 Rue St.-Roch, 75001
Tel *01 42 60 17 42*
For a typical French bistro experience, try this friendly eatery decorated with shiny copper pans and a grandfather clock. The owner/chef, who was taught to cook by his father, uses market-fresh produce, prepared in an open kitchen, and discusses the menu with every customer. An experience not to be missed.

La Famille €€
Modern French **Map** 6 F1
41 Rue des Trois Frères, 75018
Tel *01 42 52 11 12* **Closed** *Mon & Sun; Aug*
Chef Iñaki Aizpitarte first drew attention to this hotspot. He has gone, but his fusion menu remains, as do the fashionistas.

Fauchon Le Café €€
Traditional French **Map** 5 C5
24–30 Place de la Madeleine, 75008
Tel *01 70 39 38 39* **Closed** *Sun*
Part of an upscale delicatessen, this eatery serves food that is as elegant as the surroundings. For lower prices, try La Cantine, the informal basement eatery.

Les Fines Gueules €€
Traditional French **Map** 12 F1
43 Rue Croix des Petits Champs, 75001
Tel *01 42 61 35 41*
Part wine bar, part bistro, this spot is renowned for its platters of excellent charcuterie, and for its steak tartare with sautéed potatoes. There is also a large wine list.

Le Grand 8 €€
Traditional French **Map** 7 A1
8 Rue Lamarck, 75018
Tel *01 42 55 04 55* **Closed** *Mon & Tue*
A tiny restaurant with a touch of class, often frequented by locals. The perfect beef, lamb, and vegetable risottos are a highlight, not to mention the terrific caramelized apple *millefeuille.*

Guilo Guilo €€
Asian **Map** 6 E1
8 Rue Garreau, 75018
Tel *01 42 54 23 92* **Closed** *Mon & Sun*
Palate-popping "New Wave" Japanese cuisine. Watching chef Eichi Edakuni at work in his open kitchen is not unlike witnessing a theatrical performance.

Le Lamarck €€
Corsican **Map** 7 A1
8 Rue Lamarck, 75018
Tel *01 53 41 01 60* **Closed** *Sun–Tue*
Owner François Grimaldi plays guitar and sings while diners enjoy his tasty traditional dishes. A restaurant full of real warmth and charm.

Le Miroir €€
Traditional French **Map** 6 F3
94 Rue des Martyrs, 75018
Tel *01 46 06 50 73* **Closed** *Sun & Mon*
Bistro-style comfort food is served here, cooked by an haute cuisine-trained trio of chefs. This airy restaurant with a cosy wine bar, red banquettes, and large mirrors is a magnet for locals.

Le Nansouty €€
Traditional French **Map** 7 A1
35 Rue Ramey, 75018
Tel *01 42 52 58 87* **Closed** *lunch Sat & Mon*
This cosy restaurant-bar, off the beaten track in Montmartre, serves traditional, hearty French fare. There is an excellent wine list.

Les Noces de Jeannette €€
Traditional French **Map** 6 F5
Corner of Rue Favart & Rue d'Amboise, 75002
Tel *01 42 96 36 89*
Named after an opera by Victor Massé, this restaurant has two intimate rooms, superbly decorated with opera and movie posters. It serves excellent brasserie-style cuisine.

Le Pantruche €€
Modern French **Map** 6 E2
3 Rue Victor Massé, 75009
Tel *01 48 78 55 60* **Closed** *Sat & Sun; 3 wks Aug*
Chef Franck Baranger wows the crowds with seasonal specialties such as celery root soup at this retro-chic 1930s bistro. The fixed-price menu offers great value.

DK Choice

Racines €€
Bistro/Wine bar **Map** 6 F5
8 Passage des Panoramas, 75002
Tel *01 40 13 06 41* **Closed** *Sat & Sun; 3 wks Aug*
Its setting in a gorgeous 19th-century shopping arcade makes this charming *bistrot à vins* a favorite with shoppers and locals alike. The short menu features French and Italian dishes, excellent charcuterie, ratatouille, lamb, and pork, and seductive desserts. Serious wines, many from biodynamic producers, are a bonus.

For more information on types of restaurants *see pages 288–91*

The dining room of Le Meurice

Rouge Bis €€
Traditional French Map 6 E1
7 Place Blanche, 75009
Tel *01 40 16 45 36*
Exceptionally personable staff
make this restaurant-bar across
from the Moulin Rouge a top
spot for locals and theater-goers.
The classic dishes served in
generous portions are delicious
and good value.

Le Vaudeville €€
Traditional French Map 6 F5
29 Rue Vivienne, 75002
Tel *01 40 20 04 62*
A boisterous, marble-clad
brasserie with a delightful Art
Deco interior. You can't go wrong
by ordering the seafood platter
or smoked salmon. Sit outside on
the terrace in summer and watch
the world go by.

Café de la Paix €€€
Traditional French Map 6 D4
*InterContinental Paris Le Grand,
5 Place de l'Opéra, 75009*
Tel *01 40 07 36 36*
This grand old café, once
frequented by the likes of Zola,
Maupassant, and Tchaikovsky,
boasts a beautiful frescoed
interior and a lovely *terrasse*
fronting the Opéra Garnier.
Although it's not cheap, it's
well worth it.

Carré des Feuillants €€€
French fine dining Map 12 D1
14 Rue de Castiglione, 75001
Tel *01 42 86 82 82* **Closed** *Sun*
Legendary chef Alain Dutournier
prepares exquisite dishes from
his native Gascony with sheer
genius at this elegant, friendly
restaurant hung with modern
art. Accompany them with a
wine from an extensive and
interesting list.

Caviar Kaspia €€€
Russian Map 5 C5
*17 Place de la Madeleine,
75008*
Tel *01 42 65 33 32* **Closed** *Sun*
Enjoy traditional dishes from
Russia, including caviar and
smoked salmon, accompanied
by the obligatory chilled vodka,
in plush surroundings with
honey-colored paneling, heavy
curtains, and marvelous views.
Popular with the arty crowd.

**Le Chamarré
de Montmartre** €€€
French–Mauritian
fusion Map 2 F5
52 Rue Lamarck, 75018
Tel *01 42 55 05 42*
The creative fare from Mauritian
chef Antoine Heerah includes
Seychelles-style sea bass at this
elegant restaurant serving
traditional cuisine with exotic
touches. The airy dining room
has striped furnishings and a
flower-filled terrace.

The enchanting Louis XVI decor at the
historic Le Grand Véfour

Le Grand Véfour €€€
Modern French fine dining
Map 12 F1
17 Rue de Beaujolais, 75001
Tel *01 42 96 56 27* **Closed** *Sat & Sun;
Aug*
Savor celebrated chef
Guy Martin's astonishing cuisine
in an 18th-century jewel-like
restaurant next to the Palais-
Royal gardens. This has been
the haunt of many famous
artists, writers, and politicians,
including Napoleon

DK Choice

Kei €€€
Modern French Map 12 F1
5 Rue Coq Héron, 75001
Tel *01 42 33 14 74* **Closed** *Mon
& Sun, Thu lunch*
Fusing French and Japanese
cuisines, Kei Kobayashi is at the
helm of this sophisticated
restaurant. Decorated in
elegant silver and grey, Kei is a
showcase for imaginative and
delicious dishes that skillfully
balance flavors and textures.
A top sommelier advises on the
best wines to pair with the food.

Le Meurice €€€
Modern French fine dining
Map 12 D1
228 Rue de Rivoli, 75001
Tel *01 44 58 10 55* **Closed** *Sat & Sun*
Enjoy Yannick Alléno's subtle,
varied cooking at this Michelin-
starred restaurant in Philippe
Starck's reinterpretation of a
Versailles salon. Service is
formal, but not stiff. Menus
change seasonally.

Verjus €€€
American Map 12 E1
52 Rue de Richelieu, 75001
Tel *01 42 97 54 40* **Closed** *Sat & Sun*
Intensely flavored, tapas-style
dishes are served in this casual,
white-walled dining room. Less
expensive fare is available in the
cellar wine bar and sandwich bar.

Champs-Elysées and
Chaillot Quarter

**Korean Barbecue
Champs-Elysées** €
Korean Map 5 A5
7 Rue de Ponthieu, 75008
Tel *01 42 25 35 41* **Closed** *Sun;
3 wks Aug*
Paper-thin beef from the
barbecue, so tender it melts in
your mouth, and crisp vegetables
are among the highlights at this
friendly, family-run restaurant.

DK Choice

Café Lenôtre €€
Modern French **Map** 5 B5
*Le Pavillon Elysée Lenôtre,
10 Avenue des Champs-Elysées,
75008*
Tel *01 42 65 85 10* **Closed** *Nov–
Mar: Sun & Mon*
An elegant pavilion built for the
1900 Exposition Universelle is
now occupied by an outpost of
the Lenôtre catering company.
The decor is smart and modern,
complementing the creative,
contemporary food; the
desserts, in particular, are show-
stealers. In summer, diners can
enjoy lunch on the terrace. The
food is reasonably priced and
the staff is very attentive.

Chez Diep €€
Asian **Map** 5 A5
22 Rue de Ponthieu, 75008
Tel *01 42 56 23 96* **Closed** *Sun*
Appetizing specialties from
China, Thailand, and Vietnam
pepper the menu at this
modest restaurant with
decor that evokes Thailand.
Attentive service.

Chez Géraud €€
Traditional French **Map** 9 B3
31 Rue Vital, 75016
Tel *01 45 20 33 00* **Closed** *Sat & Sun*
An enduring neighborhood
fixture, where dishes made from
fresh produce are served in an
appealing, traditional setting.

Graindorge €€
Belgian **Map** 4 D3
15 Rue de l'Arc de Triomphe, 75017
Tel *01 47 54 00 28* **Closed** *Sun*
A splendid selection of beers
on tap accompanies Belgian
national treasures such as
waterzooi de homard (lobster
broth) and *potjevleesch*
(meat terrine).

Le Hide €€
Traditional French **Map** 4 D3
*10 Rue du Général Lanrezac,
75017*
Tel *01 45 74 15 81* **Closed** *lunch &
Sun; 1 wk May, 2nd wk Aug*
Japanese chef Hide Kobayashi
prepares generous, no-nonsense
bistro food. Good-value fixed-
price menu.

L'Huîtrier €€
Seafood **Map** 4 E2
16 Rue Saussier-Leroy, 75017
Tel *01 40 54 83 44*
Oysters – ordered by the dozen
or half-dozen – are the
undisputed stars of the show
at this modern restaurant.

Le Mini Palais €€
Modern French **Map** 11 A1
*Grand Palais, 3 Avenue Winston
Churchill, 75008*
Tel *01 42 56 42 42*
A gastronomic treat in an
elegant, fashionable setting with
a lovely colonnaded terrace.

DK Choice

Relais de l'Entrecôte €€
Steakhouse **Map** 4 F5
15 Rue Marbeuf, 75008
Tel *01 49 52 07 17*
Established in 1959, this family-
run restaurant offers a warm
atmosphere and fantastic
steaks. Once you get in – the
lines can be long – your hardest
decision will be how to have
your steak cooked. The high-
quality beef is cut thin, the
frites are done to perfection
and the secret-recipe sauce is
something to write home
about. A great place for a
family outing.

Le Timgad €€
Moroccan **Map** 3 C3
21 Rue Brunel, 75017
Tel *01 45 74 23 70*
Parisians flock to Le Timgad to
enjoy terrific Moroccan food in an
ornate setting. *Briks* (thin pastry
with a deep-fried filling), tagines,
and couscous are imaginatively
spiced and impeccably cooked.

6 New York €€€
Modern French **Map** 10 E1
*6 Avenue de New York,
75016*
Tel *01 40 70 03 30* **Closed** *Sun*
Enjoy fabulous dishes such as
grilled swordfish with chorizo,
green apple, and aubergine
caviar at this modern, welcoming
restaurant. The food is prepared
by talented chef Jérôme
Gangneux with ingredients
fresh from the market.

DK Choice

Antoine €€€
Seafood **Map** 10 E1
10 Avenue de New York, 75116
Tel *01 40 70 19 28* **Closed** *3 wks
Aug*
Enjoy sensational seafood while
admiring the view at this
riverside restaurant – you can
see across the Seine to the Eiffel
Tower. Chef Antoine Vigneron's
cuisine centers on produce
imported from the Basque
country, the Mediterranean,
Brittany, and even Norway. Try
the bouillabaisse or the sea bass,
grilled on fennel wood and
served with steamed vegetables.

Apicius €€€
Modern French fine dining
Map 4 F4
20 Rue d'Artois, 75008
Tel *01 43 80 19 66* **Closed** *Sat & Sun*
Jean-Pierre Vigato produces
culinary fireworks in this 18th-
century mansion set in glorious
gardens. Reserve ahead – and
bring a plump pocketbook.

L'Astrance €€€
Modern French fine dining
Map 9 C3
4 Rue Beethoven, 75016
Tel *01 40 50 84 40* **Closed** *Mon,
Sat & Sun*
Reserve months in advance to
secure a table at this celebrated
three-Michelin-starred 26-seater,
and sample Pascal Barbot's
inspired tasting menu.

Le Cinq €€€
Modern French fine dining
Map 4 E5
*Four Seasons George V, 31 Avenue
George V, 75008*
Tel *01 49 52 71 54*
Hotel dining at its sublime best.
Chef Eric Briffard produces
original cuisine in a sumptuous
grey-and-gold dining room.

The bar at Carré des Feuillants, a temple of haute cuisine

For more information on types of restaurants *see pages 288–91*

Copenhague €€€
Danish   **Map** 4 E4
142 Avenue des Champs-Elysées, 75008
Tel *01 44 13 86 26* **Closed** *3 wks Aug*
If you crave a change from French cooking, this restaurant could be ideal. Fish is the star attraction here, along with the spectacular views over the Champs-Elysées.

L'Epicure €€€
Traditional French fine dining
Map 5 B4
Le Bristol, 112 Rue du Faubourg St.-Honoré, 75008
Tel *01 53 43 43 40*
A lovely room, with windows overlooking the garden, is the ideal backdrop to Eric Fréchon's triple-Michelin-starred cooking at this restaurant.

Hiramatsu €€€
Modern French fine dining
Map 9 C1
52 Rue de Longchamp, 75116
Tel *01 56 81 08 80* **Closed** *Sat & Sun*
Hiroyuki Hiramatsu's cooking is a flawless blend of French and Japanese styles. Splash out on the wonderful nine-course tasting menu.

Lasserre €€€
Traditional French fine dining
Map 11 A1
17 Avenue Franklin D. Roosevelt, 75008
Tel *01 43 59 02 13* **Closed** *Sun & Mon; 3 wks Aug*
The lavish orchid-filled interior is a fitting background for Christophe Moret's refined cooking. A retractable roof opens to the stars. Great selection of desserts.

Paul Chêne €€€
Traditional French fine dining
Map 9 C1
123 Rue Lauriston, 75116
Tel *01 47 27 63 17* **Closed** *Sat lunch; Sun*
Step back in time at this classic restaurant, founded in 1959 by Paul Chêne, linchpin of traditional cuisine, and little changed since. There is a wide choice of superb desserts.

Pierre Gagnaire €€€
Modern French fine dining
Map 4 E4
6 Rue Balzac, 75008
Tel *01 58 36 12 50* **Closed** *Sat & Sun; Aug, Christmas holidays*
Pierre Gagnaire, an advocate of molecular gastronomy, provides groundbreaking cuisine at this three-Michelin-starred restaurant.

Prunier €€€
Seafood   **Map** 4 D4
16 Avenue Victor Hugo, 75116
Tel *01 44 17 35 85* **Closed** *Sun; Aug*
This pretty Art Deco jewel has a seasonal menu, along with an impressive variety of caviars.

Relais Plaza €€€
Modern French   **Map** 10 F1
Le Plaza Athenée, 25 Avenue Montaigne, 75008
Tel *01 53 67 64 00*
This fashionable brasserie with Art Deco touches is to see and be seen in. The imaginative menu is inspired by Alain Ducasse.

Taillevent €€€
Traditional French fine dining
Map 4 F4
15 Rue Lamennais, 75008
Tel *01 44 95 15 01* **Closed** *Sat & Sun; Aug; public hols*
Exquisite haute cuisine in a 19th-century mansion. Alain Solivérès's incomparable cooking is paired with a remarkable wine list.

Invalides and Eiffel Tower Quarter

Café Constant €
Traditional French   **Map** 10 E3
139 Rue St.-Dominique, 75007
Tel *01 47 53 73 34*
Arrive early to be sure of a table at Christian Constant's no-frills café. Brilliantly conceived comfort food, such as beef stew, is on the menu.

Coutume €
Modern French   **Map** 11 B4
47 Rue de Babylone, 75007
Tel *01 45 51 50 47* **Closed** *2 wks Aug*
This bright and airy café serves superb coffee and healthy sandwiches, as well as salads for lunch. A good brunch option.

The rustic and cosy interior of L'Ami Jean, a Basque bistro

Pasco €
Mediterranean   **Map** 11 A3
74 Blvd de la Tour Maubourg, 75007
Tel *01 44 18 33 26*
You will find dishes with simple, seasonal ingredients – such as fish, fresh vegetables, herbs, spices and lashings of olive oil – at this contemporary, rustic restaurant.

L'Affable €€
Modern French   **Map** 11 C3
10 Rue de St.-Simon, 75007
Tel *01 42 22 01 60* **Closed** *Sat & Sun; Aug*
This bistro has an excellent *prix-fixe* lunch and attentive waiters. On the menu are hearty classics such as *ris de veau* (sweetbreads).

L'Affriolé €€
Traditional French   **Map** 10 F2
17 Rue Malar, 75007
Tel *01 44 18 31 33* **Closed** *Sun & Mon; Aug*
A local fixture, this colorful bistro is usually packed. Dishes such as caramelized lamb sweetbreads with aubergine caviar and mustard are cooked with finesse.

L'Ami Jean €€
Basque   **Map** 10 F2
27 Rue Malar, 75007
Tel *01 47 05 86 89* **Closed** *Sun & Mon; Aug*
Stéphane Jego puts an avant-garde spin on Basque cooking, with dishes such as lamb sweet-breads with paper-thin chorizo, at this lively eatery. Reserve ahead.

La Billebaude €€
Burgundian   **Map** 10 F3
29 Rue Exposition, 75007
Tel *01 45 55 20 96* **Closed** *Sun & Mon; Aug*
Melt-in-the-mouth scallops, sea bream with sorrel sauce, wild boar stew and foie gras are just some of this cheerful restaurant's standard regional dishes.

Au Bon Accueil €€
Modern French   **Map** 10 E2
14 Rue de Monttessuy, 75007
Tel *01 47 05 46 11* **Closed** *Sat & Sun; 3 wks Aug*
The good-value *prix-fixe* menus at this upscale bistro never skimp on quality ingredients. Sit at the sidewalk tables for a great view of the Eiffel Tower.

Les Cocottes de Christian Constant €€
Modern French   **Map** 10 E3
135 Rue St.-Dominique, 75007
Tel *01 45 50 10 31*
The clue is in the name – *cocottes* (dishes served in cast-iron casseroles) are the specialty here. Service is very efficient.

The view from Le Jules Verne, on the second level of the Eiffel Tower

Le Florimond €€
Traditional French   Map 10 F3
19 Avenue de la Motte-Picquet, 75007
Tel *01 45 55 40 38* **Closed** *Sun & first Sat of the month; 1 wk Aug*
Pascal Guillaumin's authentic menu includes his grandmother's recipe for stuffed cabbage, and delectable lobster ravioli, plus vanilla *millefeuille*.

La Fontaine de Mars €€
Southwestern French   Map 10 F3
129 Rue St.-Dominique, 75007
Tel *01 47 05 46 44*
Complete with lace curtains, gingham tablecloths, efficient waiters, and fantastic food, this is an archetypcal bistro. Duck *cassoulet* is the signature dish when in season (Sep–May).

Giallo Oro €€
Italian   Map 11 B3
38 Rue de Bourgogne, 75007
Tel *01 45 50 14 57* **Closed** *Sun*
The menu at this tiny, friendly restaurant consists mainly of pasta, but there are also seafood and meat dishes.

Au Petit Sud Ouest €€
Southwestern French   Map 10 E3
46 Avenue de la Bourdonnais, 75007
Tel *01 45 55 59 59* **Closed** *Sun & Mon; Aug*
Enjoy authentic specialties from the Landes, many of them duck-based, at this friendly restaurant. Individual toasters serve piping-hot bread for the foie gras.

Le Troquet €€
Basque   Map 10 F5
21 Rue François Bonvin, 75015
Tel *01 45 66 89 00* **Closed** *Sun & Mon; Aug; 1 wk Christmas; 1st wk May*
A favorite with serious foodies. Chef Marc Mouton's dishes are full of surprises and forthright flavors. The six-course tasting menu is fabulous.

La Villa Corse €€
Corsican   Map 10 E5
164 Boulevard de Grenelle, 75015
Tel *01 53 86 70 81* **Closed** *Sun*
Tastes and aromas transport you to the Mediterranean island of Corsica. Delicious, strongly flavored dishes such as olive veal and wild boar stew are served in warm surroundings.

L'Arpège €€€
Traditional French fine dining
Map 11 B3
84 Rue de Varenne, 75007
Tel *01 47 05 09 06* **Closed** *Sat & Sun*
Alain Passard grows his own produce for this glossy three-Michelin-starred restaurant. Try his superb signature apple tart.

Le Jules Verne €€€
Modern French fine dining
Map 10 D3
5 Avenue Gustave Eiffel, 75007
Tel *01 45 55 61 44*
Alain Ducasse's restaurant on the Eiffel Tower's second platform has a breathtaking 360-degree view and stylish cuisine.

St.-Germain, Latin Quarter, and Jardin des Plantes Quarter

Le Balto €
Traditional French   Map 12 F4
15 Rue Mazarine, 75006
Tel *01 44 07 12 37*
Try the duck confit at this lively bistro, the perfect place for a glass of Sancerre and a warm ambience.

Breakfast in America €
American   Map 13 B5
17 Rue des Ecoles, 75005
Tel *01 43 54 50 28*
All-day breakfast is served at this authentic US diner: crispy bacon, pancakes with maple syrup, burgers, fries, and much more.

Chez Gladines €
Basque   Map 17 B5
30 Rue des Cinq Diamants, 75013
Tel *01 45 80 70 10*
A haven of satisfying, no-frills cooking. The house specialty – gigantic salads, served in earthenware bowls and smothered with sautéed potatoes – is not to be missed.

Shakespeare & Co. Café €
International   Map 13 A4
37 Rue de la Bucherie, 75005
Tel *01 43 25 95 95*
Next door to, and owned by, the legendary bookstore, this café continues the literary theme, with secondhand novels and cookbooks on the shelves. Come for a bagel or sandwich, and enjoy unbeatable views of Notre-Dame from the *terrasse*.

L'Agrume €€
Modern French   Map 17 C2
15 Rue des Fossés St.-Marcel, 75005
Tel *01 43 31 86 48* **Closed** *Sun, Mon & Tue; Aug; 2 wks Dec*
Foodies roll up here to sample the five-course tasting menu. The presentation is simple, but the flavors are fabulous.

Alcazar €€
Modern French   Map 12 F4
62 Rue Mazarine, 75006
Tel *01 53 10 19 99* **Closed** *Aug*
British style-guru Terence Conran's contemporary take on a Parisian brasserie. Seafood, Mediterranean cuisine, and English-inspired dishes are on the menu.

Anahuacalli €€
Mexican   Map 13 B5
30 Rue des Bernardins, 75005
Tel *01 43 26 10 20*
A cheerful cantina serving typical Mexican dishes – guacamole, corn tortillas, and *queso* (melted cheese) with chorizo.

L'Atlas €€
Moroccan   Map 13 B5
12 Boulevard St.-Germain, 75005
Tel *01 44 07 23 66* **Closed** *Mon*
With its Moorish decor and tasty tagines, you will feel like you're in Marrakech in this restaurant. Try the monkfish with cinnamon.

Bistrot de Paris €€
Traditional French   Map 12 D3
33 Rue de Lille, 75007
Tel *01 42 61 16 83* **Closed** *Sun & Mon; 26 & 27 Jul; Christmas; New Year*
Tables are always packed at this Art Nouveau gem, a former haunt of the Left Bank literati. The menu features superior bistro classics.

DK Choice

Brasserie Balzar   €€
Traditional French   **Map** 13 B5
49 Rue des Ecoles, 75005
Tel *01 43 54 13 67*
Highly skilled waiters in long aprons and waistcoats serve solid brasserie fare at this venerable institution. It certainly looks the part, with its smoked mirrors and globe lights. You're likely to rub shoulders with an academic crowd from La Sorbonne. There's a café section as well.

Brasserie Lipp   €€
Traditional French   **Map** 12 E4
151 Boulevard St.-Germain, 75006
Tel *01 45 48 53 91*
Once the haunt of politicians, intellectuals, and artists, this venerable brasserie with a 1920s interior is worth a visit for a light lunch and to soak up the decor and historic atmosphere.

Café de Flore   €€
Traditional French   **Map** 12 E4
172 Boulevard St.-Germain, 75006
Tel *01 45 48 55 26*
A St.-Germain institution, the Flore is renowned for the postwar writers and philosophers who used to come here. The menu ranges from snacks to full meals.

Café de la Nouvelle Mairie   €€
Traditional French   **Map** 17 A1
19 Rue des Fossés St.-Jacques, 75005
Tel *01 44 07 04 41*   **Closed** *Sat & Sun*
Set in a lovely square, this bustling café and wine bar serves good seasonal food and a great choice of natural wines by the glass. Turn up early for lunch, as it gets busy with academics and students from the nearby Sorbonne.

Dans Les Landes   €€
Southwestern French tapas
Map 17 B2
119 bis Rue Monge, 75005
Tel *01 45 87 06 00*
A fun place for sharing dishes. Choose from a long list of tapas-style dishes or try a *plat du jour*.

Les Deux Magots   €€
Traditional French   **Map** 12 E4
6 Place St.-Germain-des-Prés, 75006
Tel *01 45 48 55 25*
Like Café Flore, this café was once the haunt of the postwar literary elite and has preserved much of its original decor. It's a little more touristy than its rival, but still a great spot for a bite to eat. The evening menu includes more substantial fare, like steak and fish.

L'Epigramme   €€
Traditional French   **Map** 12 F4
9 Rue de l'Éperon, 75006
Tel *01 44 41 00 09*   **Closed** *Mon & Sun; Aug; 1 wk Dec*
Impeccable bistro dishes are served at this inviting restaurant with contemporary country-inn-style decor. Try the pork with turnip *choucroute*.

Itinéraires   €€
Modern French   **Map** 13 B5
5 Rue de Pontoise, 75005
Tel *01 46 33 60 11*   **Closed** *Sat lunch; Sun & Mon; 2 wks Aug; 2 wks Dec*
The calm, contemporary decor here is as stylish as Sylvain Sendra's cooking. With a young vibe and a shared-table policy, this is a perfect place for singles.

Kitchen Galerie Bis   €€
Modern French   **Map** 12 F4
25 Rue des Grands Augustins, 75006
Tel *01 46 33 00 85*   **Closed** *Sun & Mon; 2 wks Aug*
Doubling up as a modern art gallery, this restaurant with minimalist decor serves contemporary French cuisine with an Asian twist. Try the fabulous tapas-style dishes.

El Loubnane   €€
Lebanese   **Map** 13 A4
29 Rue Galande, 75005
Tel *01 43 26 70 60*   **Closed** *Mon*
Enjoy delicious meze at this family-run restaurant. Don't miss the *makanik* sausages and the *katayef* – miniature crêpes stuffed with rosewater and pistachio nuts.

Marty   €€
Traditional French   **Map** 17 B3
20 Avenue des Gobelins, 75005
Tel *01 43 31 39 51*   **Closed** *Aug*
The Art Deco interior of this venerable institution is lovely, but it is the robust dishes, such as roast duck and *steak-frites*, that steal the show.

Mavrommatis   €€
Greek   **Map** 17 B2
42 Rue Daubenton, 75005
Tel *01 43 31 17 17*   **Closed** *Sun & Mon*
Take a Greek culinary cruise at this stylish restaurant. Superb food, including grilled octopus and moussaka.

Perraudin   €€
Traditional French   **Map** 16 F1
157 Rue St.-Jacques, 75005
Tel *01 46 33 15 75*
Checked tablecloths and hearty fare characterize this old-fashioned restaurant. Reservations are accepted only 7–8pm.

Le Petit Châtelet   €€
Traditional French   **Map** 13 A4
39 Rue de la Bûcherie, 75005
Tel *01 46 33 53 40* **Closed** *Sun & Mon; Christmas*
This small restaurant is renowned for its pitched roof and a terrace with views of Notre-Dame.

Le Petit Pontoise   €€
Traditional French   **Map** 13 B5
9 Rue de Pontoise, 75005
Tel *01 43 29 25 20*   **Closed** *Christmas*
Blackboards display specials such as duck *parmentier* and pan-fried foie gras at this bistro. Reserve.

Le Pré Verre   €€
Modern French   **Map** 13 A5
8 Rue Thénard, 75005
Tel *01 43 54 59 47*   **Closed** *Mon & Sun*
There are Asian accents in the dishes at this snug eatery. Wines come from small producers.

Le Procope   €€
Traditional French   **Map** 12 F4
13 Rue de l'Ancienne Comédie, 75006
Tel *01 40 46 79 00*
The city's oldest café – a magnet for writers, politicians, and artists since 1686 – still has its original ambience. Specialties include *coq au vin* and shellfish platters.

The 18th-century-style dining room of Le Procope, the oldest café in Paris

For key to prices *see page 296*

The elegant dining room at La Tour d'Argent

Restaurant AG €€
Modern French **Map** 12 E4
6 Rue Clement, 75006
Tel *01 43 25 77 66* **Closed** *Sun*
Chef Alan Geeam runs this cosy neighborhood bistro serving modern French cuisine. The desserts are especially inviting.

Shu €€
Japanese **Map** 12 F4
8 Rue Suger, 75006
Tel *01 46 34 25 88* **Closed** *Sun; 1 wk Easter; 3 wks Aug*
Owner/chef Osamu Ukai constructs ravishing skewers for *omakase* dining, which means leaving the choice up to him. Service is charming and attentive.

Terroir Parisien €€
Traditional French **Map** 13 B5
20 Rue St.-Victor, 75005
Tel *01 44 31 54 54*
The classic dishes here are made from locally grown produce from small farms. This latest venture of Yannick Alléno (of Le Meurice fame, *see p300*) is in a beautiful modern space with a vaulted wooden ceiling.

Les Bouquinistes €€€
Modern French **Map** 12 F3
53 Quai des Grands Augustins, 75006
Tel *01 43 25 45 94* **Closed** *2 wks Aug*
Overlooking the Seine, this is an offshoot of Guy Savoy's gastronomic empire. It serves relatively simple dishes based on exquisite seasonal produce.

Le Comptoir du Relais €€€
Traditional French **Map** 12 F4
9 Carrefour de l'Odéon, 75006
Tel *01 44 27 07 97*
Devotees have been known to wait hours for a table at Yves Camdeborde's celebrated temple to bistro cuisine. Try the signature pig's trotters.

Sola €€€
Japanese fusion **Map** 13 A4
12 Rue de l'Hôtel Colbert, 75005
Tel *09 65 01 73 68 (lunch)/01 43 29 59 04 (dinner)* **Closed** *Sun & Mon; 3 wks Aug*
Hiroki Yoshitake's wonderfully subtle dishes blend the best of Japanese and French cuisines. Well-stocked sake bar.

DK Choice

La Tour d'Argent €€€
Traditional French fine dining
Map 13 B5
15 Quai de la Tournelle, 75005
Tel *01 43 54 23 31* **Closed** *Sun & Mon; 3 wks Aug*
Established in 1582 and showing no signs of age, this famous institution has a romantic sixth-floor dining room complete with spectacular views. The service is formal and elegant. Chef Laurent Delabre has rejuvenated the menu of classic French dishes with great panache.

Ze Kitchen Galerie €€€
International fusion **Map** 12 F4
4 Rue des Grands Augustins, 75006
Tel *01 44 32 00 32* **Closed** *Sat & Sun; 2 wks Aug*
Inventive cooking, informed by chef William Ledeuil's travels in Southeast Asia, is offered in this eatery with displays of modern art.

Luxembourg and Montparnasse

L'Arbre de Sel €€
Korean **Map** 15 B1
138 Rue de Vaugirard, 75015
Tel *01 47 83 29 52* **Closed** *Sun; Aug*
Mouthwatering dishes – spicy, very spicy, and vegetarian – are beautifully presented at this pleasant restaurant with efficient service.

L'Assiette €€
Southwestern French **Map** 15 C4
181 Rue du Château, 75014
Tel *01 43 22 64 86* **Closed** *Mon & Tue; late Jul–late Aug*
David Rathgeber, who trained under Alain Ducasse, brings style to the earthy regional cuisine here.

L'Auberge du 15 €€
Modern French **Map** 16 F3
15 Rue de la Santé, 75013
Tel *01 47 07 07 45* **Closed** *Sun & Mon; Aug*
A contemporary spin on classic bistro fare is served at this eatery with modern rustic decor.

La Cantine du Troquet €€
Basque **Map** 15 B3
101 Rue de l'Ouest, 75014
Tel *01 45 40 04 98* **Closed** *Sat & Sun*
Savor dishes prepared with flair by Christian Etchebest at this lively bistro with long, shared tables. No reservations are taken, so arrive when it opens, at 7pm.

La Cerisaie €€
Southwestern French **Map** 15 C2
70 Boulevard Edgar Quinet, 75014
Tel *01 43 20 98 98* **Closed** *Sat & Sun; mid-Jul–mid-Aug*
Regional specialties come in generous portions at this tiny, friendly bistro. The first-class wine list includes a number of talented small producers.

La Coupole €€
Traditional French **Map** 16 D2
102 Boulevard du Montparnasse, 75014
Tel *01 43 20 14 20*
Visit this historic 600-seat brasserie, dating from 1927, for the bustling ambience and fabulous Art Deco furnishings. Seafood platters top the bill. Great for people-watching.

Adding the finishing touches to a seafood platter at La Coupole

For more information on types of restaurants *see pages 288–91*

L'Epicuriste €€
Traditional French   Map 15 A1
41 Boulevard Pasteur,
75015
Tel *01 47 34 15 50*   **Closed** *Sun*
& Mon; Aug
Enjoy specialties created
with ingredients fresh from
the market in this bistro with
a modern interior. The signature
dish is braised lamb shanks in
red wine sauce with caramelized
fennel with orange and capers.

Le Jeu de Quilles €€
Traditional French   Map 16 D4
45 Rue Boulard, 75014
Tel *01 53 90 76 22*   **Closed** *Mon & Sun;*
Tue lunch; 2 wks Aug
Top-quality ingredients (some
available from the *épicerie* at
the front) make up the timeless
dishes in this eatery with a
simple interior.

Moustache €€
Modern French   Map 16 D1
3 Rue Ste-Beuve, 75006
Tel *01 42 22 56 65*   **Closed** *Mon & Sun;*
1 wk Aug
Exposed brick walls and crisp
tablecloths create a stylish
setting for Fabien Chivot's
sensational dishes, injected
with Asian flavors.

L'Ourcine €€
Southwestern French   Map 17 A3
92 Rue Broca, 75013
Tel *01 47 07 13 65*   **Closed** *Mon & Sun;*
Jul–Aug
Sylvain Danière has lighted
upon a recipe for success at
this simple bistro. The menu
changes all the time, depending
on what is in season. Expect
superb dishes from the Basque
and Béarn regions, such as
piquillo peppers stuffed with
puréed cod and potato.

Les Papilles €€
Traditional French   Map 16 F1
30 Rue Gay Lussac,
75005
Tel *01 43 25 20 79*   **Closed** *Sun*
Les Papilles is a charming multi-
tasker: deli, coffee bar, wine
store, and bistro all rolled into
one. The set, fixed-price dinners
are unforgettable.

Le Parc aux Cerfs €€
Traditional French   Map 16 D2
50 Rue Vavin, 75006
Tel *01 43 54 87 83*   **Closed** *2 wks*
Aug
Good-value prices and a
pleasant courtyard for alfresco
dining make "The Deer Park"
a winner. The menu features
innovative variations on old
French classics.

Le Sélect €€
Traditional French   Map 16 D2
99 Boulevard du Montparnasse, 75006
Tel *01 45 48 38 24*
Once the favorite haunt of expat
authors such as F. Scott Fitzgerald
and Ernest Hemingway, Le Sélect
is one of Montparnasse's great
historic café-brasseries. Drink in
the atmosphere over a cup of
coffee or a relaxed lunch.

Tavola di Gio €€
Italian   Map 16 D2
210 Boulevard Raspail, 75014
Tel *01 43 35 47 17*   **Closed** *Christmas &*
New Year
A genial trattoria with a pristine
modern look, but traditional
specialties. The pasta and
seafood are recommended.

DK Choice

Le Timbre €€
Traditional French   Map 16 D1
3 Rue Ste.-Beuve, 75006
Tel *01 45 49 10 40*   **Closed** *Sun &*
Mon; mid-Jul–mid-Aug
This is what its name says: a
"postage stamp" of a restaurant,
the realm of British chef Chris
Wright. For his short but
considered menu, he chooses
the finest, freshest ingredients
and prepares them in full view
of the diners. Don't miss his
terrine de campagne.

Les Zazous €€
Traditional French   Map 15 C1
46 Boulevard du Montparnasse 75015
Tel *01 45 49 32 88*   **Closed** *Mon*
Classic bistro, with creative menus
and fixed-priced meals, plus a
terrace for alfresco dining in the
warmer months.

Chez Marcel €€€
Traditional French   Map 16 D1
7 Rue Stanislas, 75006
Tel *01 45 48 29 94*   **Closed** *Sat & Sun*
Marcel offers classic dishes and
advises customers. The *coq au*
vin is especially tasty.

DK Choice

La Closerie des Lilas €€€
Traditional French   Map 16 E2
171 Blvd du Montparnasse, 75006
Tel *01 40 51 34 50*
This long-lived, little-changed
establishment has always been
favored by literati and artists.
If you're feeling flush, splash
out on classic cuisine in the
restaurant proper. Prices are
kinder in the brasserie and bar,
where a pianist plays nightly. The
summer terrace is also a treat.

Le Dôme €€€
Seafood   Map 16 D2
108 Blvd du Montparnasse, 75014
Tel *01 43 35 25 81*   **Closed** *mid-Jul–*
mid-Aug
A rendezvous for US intellectuals
in the early 1900s, Le Dôme is
known for its seafood. You can't
go wrong with the oysters or
mixed seafood platters.

Farther Afield

DK Choice

Le Baron Rouge €
Wine bar/tapas & platters
Map 14 F5
1 Rue Théophile Roussel, 75012
Tel *01 43 43 14 32*
Sample divine oysters direct
from the Atlantic coast, or
platters of charcuterie and
cheeses, inside this tiny, lively
bar. At peak times, the crowd
spills out onto the sidewalk.
There is a great selection of
wines by the glass, or fill an
empty bottle from one of the
barrels bulging in the doorways.

L'Encrier €
Traditional French   Map 14 F5
55 Rue Traversière, 75012
Tel *01 44 68 08 16*   **Closed** *Sun; 3 wks*
Aug–Sep
An inviting, homey restaurant,
jam-packed with locals. Try the
Rocquefort, and Jurançon wine.

La Marine €
Seafood   Map 8 D5
55 bis Quai de Valmy, 75010
Tel *01 42 39 69 81*
Unsurprisingly, fish is this buzzing
restaurant's specialty: served in a
stew or in pastry, or as a steak
with nettle sauce. Advance
reservations recommended.

Sign for the cosy Le Baron Rouge bar,
serving tapas and platters

The splendid Art Nouveau interior of the historic Julien brasserie

Rose Bakery €
British vegetarian **Map** 6 F3
46 Rue des Martyrs, 75009
Tel *01 42 82 12 80* **Closed** *2 wks Aug*
The haunt of expat Brits homesick for scones, as well as a growing crowd of Anglophile Parisians, this café serves quiches, salads, soup, and English cakes, plus fabulous coffee and Neal's Yard cheeses.

Albion €€
Mediterranean **Map** 7 A3
80 Rue du Faubourg Poissonnière, 75010
Tel *01 42 46 02 44* **Closed** *Sat & Sun; 3 wks Aug; 2 wks Christmas*
A wine-focused bistro, bar and store in one. Eat simple, delicious fare in the dining area at the back, and soak up the genial ambience.

DK Choice

Auberge Etchegorry €€
Basque **Map** 17 B4
41 Rue de Croulebarbe, 75013
Tel *01 44 08 83 51* **Closed** *Sun & Mon, 3 weeks in Aug*
In the early 19th century, this was the site of a rural tavern frequented by Victor Hugo. Today, the old, rustic interior of this restaurant, with copper pans on the walls and salamis hanging from wooden beams, evokes those days. The food is as comforting as the decor – dishes include *confits* and scallops and black pudding with caramelized apples.

A La Biche au Bois €€
Traditional French **Map** 14 E5
45 Avenue Ledru-Rollin, 75012
Tel *01 43 43 34 38* **Closed** *Sat & Sun; late Jul–end Aug; Christmas; New Year*
Popular for its exemplary home cooking, this bistro comes into its own in the game season, with grouse, venison, and wild boar dishes. The *prix fixe* menu includes a platter of cheeses and desserts.

Le Bistrot Lorette €€
Modern French **Map** 6 E3
43 Rue Notre-Dame de Lorette, 75009
Tel *01 42 81 13 87* **Closed** *Sun & Mon; first 3 wks Aug*
Locals love this restaurant for its fantastic food and cosy, laid-back atmosphere. Specialties include prawns with avocado tartare, tender veal with *chèvre* and basil sauce, and lamb *en croûte* with a Provençal lasagne.

Le Bistrot Paul Bert €€
Traditional French **Map** 2 F2
18 Rue Paul Bert, 75011
Tel *01 43 72 24 01* **Closed** *Sun & Mon; Aug*
Superb food, a great wine list and charming 1930s decor ensure this bistro never falls out of fashion.

DK Choice

Brasserie Flo €€
Alsatian **Map** 7 B4
7 Cour des Petites-Ecuries, 75010
Tel *01 47 70 13 59*
This captivating brasserie features striking decoration dating from the early 1900s: rich wood wall panels, colorful stained-glass windows, leather-covered bench seats, and brass luggage racks. The fare reflects its Alsatian origins, with a straightforward brasserie menu that includes superb shellfish and sauerkraut, and beer drawn from the barrel.

Chatomat €€
Modern French
6 Rue Victor Letalle, 75020
Tel *01 47 97 25 77* **Closed** *Sun & Mon; mid-Aug–early Sep*
Housed in an airy, industrial-looking building with exposed brick walls, this lively restaurant offers a limited menu, but the food is astonishingly original.

La Cicciolina €€
Italian
9–11 Rue Crespin du Gant, 75011
Tel *01 43 55 70 57*
Located in the up-and-coming Ménilmontant area, this light and airy trattoria oozes Italian style. Head for the terrace and enjoy authentic pizzas with generous toppings and specialty pasta while sipping an Italian cocktail.

Les Enfants Perdus €€
European **Map** 7 C4
9 Rue des Récollets, 75010
Tel *01 81 29 48 26*
Hip locals congregate at this spot next to the Canal St.-Martin, where innovation and tradition come together in a range of delightful, hearty dishes. On Sundays, the chef serves up a generous brunch with ingredients delivered fresh from the market.

Julien €€
Alsatian **Map** 7 B5
16 Rue du Faubourg St.-Denis, 75010
Tel *01 47 70 12 06*
Inside a splendid Art Nouveau building dating to the beginning of the 20th century and featuring Alphonse Mucha murals and huge mirrors, this historic brasserie serves appetizing classic dishes, from grilled Chateaubriand to sole meunière.

Khun Akorn €€
Thai
8 Avenue de Taillebourg, 75011
Tel *01 43 56 20 03*
In warm weather, head straight for the pretty roof terrace at Khun Akorn. The interior, decorated in Eastern style, is also attractive. The cuisine is beautifully flavored. Advance reservations are recommended.

For more information on types of restaurants *see pages 289–91*

Mama Shelter €€
Traditional French
109 Rue de Bagnolet, 75020
Tel *01 43 48 48 48*
Philippe Starck's on-trend decor sets the scene for this lively brasserie. The food from chef Alain Senderen's kitchen is firmly rooted in tradition, featuring classics such as duck *parmentier*.

Neva Cuisine €€
Modern French **Map** 5 C2
2 Rue de Berne, 75008
Tel *01 45 22 18 91* **Closed** *Sat & Sun; 3 wks Aug*
A 1930s café is home to Mexican-born Beatriz Gonzalez's stylish restaurant. The innovative cooking includes pea soup and cod steak with aubergine caviar. Don't miss chef Yannick Tranchant's desserts.

Septime €€
Modern French
80 Rue de Charonne, 75011
Tel *01 43 67 38 29* **Closed** *Sat & Sun; Aug*
The elegant, minimalist decor and an open kitchen complement Bertrand Grébaut's avant-garde cooking at this bistro.

Terminus Nord €€
Traditional French **Map** 7 B2
23 Rue de Dunkerque, 75010
Tel *01 42 85 05 15*
A great Parisian institution dating from 1925, this Art Nouveau and Art Deco gem serves delicious classic food. Always bustling and fun for people-watching.

Le Verre Volé €€
Modern French **Map** 8 D4
67 Rue de Lancry, 75010
Tel *01 48 03 17 34* **Closed** *Aug*
Reservations are essential at this tiny, easy-going wine store-cum-bistro, with a kitchen that punches well above its weight. Staff can advise on the best wine pairings

Villa Pereire €€
Modern French **Map** 4 E1
116 Boulevard Pereire, 75017
Tel *01 43 80 88 68* **Closed** *Aug*
Popular with locals, this eatery has plush, Empire-style decor. The fusion menu includes crayfish and vegetable spring rolls.

Le Volant Basque €€
Basque **Map** 10 D5
13 Rue Béatrix Dussane, 75015
Tel *01 45 75 27 67* **Closed** *Sun; last wk Jul; 3 wks Aug*
A cosy restaurant serving traditional cuisine at its best: staples include the signature *boeuf bourguignon*, veal stew, home-made fruit tarts, and chocolate mousse.

Les Zygomates €€
Modern French
7 Rue de Capri, 75012
Tel *01 40 19 93 04* **Closed** *Sun & Mon; Aug*
Wonderfully innovative food is served in this charming former delicatessen. Dishes include turkey in a salted rosemary crust and snail and mushroom ravioli.

Le Grand Venise €€€
Italian
171 Rue de la Convention, 75015
Tel *01 45 32 49 71* **Closed** *Sun & Mon; Aug; Christmas*
As a restaurant, Le Grand Venise is generous in every respect: from the owner's warm hospitality to the enormous portions of pasta, meat, and fish dishes. Be sure to try the caramel ice cream.

Le Pavillon de la Grande Cascade €€€
Traditional French fine dining
Map 3 A3
Bois de Boulogne, Allée de Longchamp, 75016
Tel *01 45 27 33 51*
Savor superb cuisine – sautéed sweetbreads, or macaroni stuffed

with celeriac, foie gras and black truffle – in this crescent-shaped dining room, the epitome of belle époque elegance. This restaurant is located in the middle of the Bois de Boulogne and diners enjoy stunning views from the romantic terrace.

Le Pavillon Montsouris €€€
Modern French
20 Rue Gazan, 75014
Tel *01 43 13 29 00* **Closed** *mid-Feb–mid-Mar*
Enjoy classic dishes with a modern creative twist and fine views in the conservatory or on the terrace of this elegant belle époque pavilion with a magical, tranquil setting on the edge of Park Montsouris. The fixed-price menu is good value.

Le Quinzième €€€
Modern French
14 Rue Cauchy, 75015
Tel *01 45 54 43 43* **Closed** *Sat & Sun; 2 wks Aug*
There is a happy marriage of tradition and innovation in celebrity TV chef Cyril Lignac's exquisite seasonal cuisine at this restaurant near the Parc André Citroën. Dishes might include Brittany scallops with a smoky Lapsang Souchong cream, or roast duck. The service is seamless. Enjoy dining alfresco on the large, tranquil terrace.

DK Choice

Le Train Bleu €€€
Traditional French **Map** 18 F1
Gare de Lyon, 1 Place Louis Armand, 75012
Tel *01 43 43 09 06*
Named after the express train that once whisked the in-crowd to the Riviera, this isn't just a station restaurant. Its early 19th-century decor is ravishing and richly romantic, with flamboyantly gilded ceilings and enchanting frescoes. The menu consists of upscale brasserie classics made from fresh seasonal produce. The pastries are a highlight.

Au Trou Gascon €€€
Southwestern French
40 Rue Taine, 75012
Tel *01 43 44 34 26* **Closed** *Sat & Sun*
Exquisite cuisine is served at Alain Dutournier's restaurant. Try the signature *cassoulet*, or lamb from the Pyrenees. There is an astonishing Armagnac selection, and the wines range from prestigious Bordeaux to little-known *crus*.

Terminus Nord, a historic brasserie near the Eurostar terminal

For key to prices *see page 296*

Bars, Tearooms, and Street Food

There are many wonderful places in Paris where you can enjoy a drink or a snack. Tearooms are perfect for a reviving afternoon stop, perhaps with a decadent cake or two. Wine bars *(bars à vin)* in every quarter offer various wines by the glass and, increasingly, excellent food. Beer bars have astounding selections, and Irish pubs are much-loved spots serving Guinness in a relaxed, sometimes rowdy atmosphere. Alternatively, choose from chic hotel bars or fun late-night venues. Street food is a growing phenomenon in Paris, with food trucks and deli sandwich bars elbowing out the traditional ham-and-cheese baguette sandwich.

Wine Bars

Most Parisian wine bars are small, convivial neighborhood places. The more traditional ones serve inexpensive wine by the glass and platters of cheese or charcuterie. A more recent crop of wine bars, however, focuses on natural and organic wines made by small producers, typically accompanied by tapas-style bites. The cuisine is often innovative and as much of a draw as the wine. You can't usually make reservations at these places.

One of the best of this new wave of wine bars is **L'Avant Comptoir**, a small place run by celebrity chef Yves Camdeborde. It serves a choice selection of natural wines and delicious sharing plates, such as artichoke and ham waffles. **Le Garde Robe** *(see p296)* is a stylish neighborhood favorite, offering natural and biodynamic wines and a good lunchtime menu with vegetarian choices. **Au Passage** (dinner only, open till 1.30am) and **Le Verre Volé** *(see p308)* (reservations advised) are also popular *bars à vins*.

Also increasingly popular is the *cave à manger* – a wine cellar with a dining area. You can eat in, as long as you order one of their wines by the glass or buy a bottle and pay a moderate corkage charge; the advantage is that you can always take away a few bottles of anything you've tried and liked. Usually, these *cavistes* stock a superb range of wines, mostly natural and organic, many inexpensive. **La Quincave** operates on this model, selling some 200 wines; the food, such as terrine and *saucisson*, is simple and tasty. Popular for its great-value lunch, **5e Cru** switches focus in the evening, when the emphasis is more on the wine, with sharing plates of uncooked, but still delicious, food. **Pratz** has a great selection of wine and sharing plates; it also sells a *sac apéro*, a nifty bag containing a bottle of wine, cheese, ham and half a baguette.

A number of top restaurants have opened annexes where you can eat more cheaply, but the food and quality of the wine is still extremely high; **Frenchie Bar à Vins**, for example, is an offshoot of the acclaimed Frenchie restaurant *(see p297)*.

More traditional *bars à vins* include **Le Baron Rouge** *(see p306)*, with its great selection of wines, and **Taverne Henri IV**, where lawyers from the nearby Palais de Justice wind down over a glass of wine and generous platters of cheese or charcuterie.

If you're keen to learn more about French wines, you can also join a tasting session; **Ô Chateau** wine bar runs very popular sessions with English-speaking sommeliers.

Beer Bars and Pubs

Whereas pubs are simply for drinking, beer bars also serve a particular style of food and are larger. *Moules-frites* (a bowl of steamed mussels served with French fries), *tarte aux poireaux* (leek tart) and *tarte aux oignons* (onion tart) are classic examples of the food on offer. The chief reason for going to a beer bar, however, is the beer. Some specialize in Belgian *gueuze* (heavy, malty, very alcoholic beer), while others have beers from all around the world. Either way, the lists are often vast.

Some beer bars open at noon, whereas pubs may open later in the afternoon, and often until 1 or 2am. Some pubs are also microbreweries, serving beer brewed on the premises. The **Frog and Princess** and the **Frog and Rosbif** are good examples of this type of venue. The bar staffers are very friendly and will happily help you choose a beer that's right for you. Aside from traditionally English pubs such as **The Bombardier** in the Latin Quarter, Paris has dozens of Irish pubs and a few Scottish ones, too. The best Irish pubs include **Coolin** and **Corcoran's** in St.-Germain-des-Prés and **O'Sullivans by the Mill** in Montmartre. A Highland fling and good whisky can be found in **Highlander** in St.-Germain-des-Prés and **The Auld Alliance** in the Marais.

Cocktail and Late-Night Bars

Being such an elegant city, it's no surprise that Paris has more than its share of cocktail and late-night bars. Some handsome Paris brasseries, such as **La Coupole** *(see p305)* and **La Closerie des Lilas** *(see p306)*, have long wooden or zinc bars, a glamorous ambience and a sense of distinguished times past. Hotel bars are some of the loveliest places for cocktails in Paris. **Bar 228** at the hotel Le Meurice *(see p284)* has a cosy atmosphere and lavish decor. It serves a wide range of cocktails, and there is live jazz every night. Other hotel bars of note include **Le Bar** at the Four

Seasons George V *(see p284)*, where bartenders will shake your Martini at your table and present it in an individual silver shaker, and the fashionable **Bar du Plaza** at the Plaza Athénée Hotel.

If you are after an inventive cocktail, head to a speakeasy-style bar. One of the best is the **Prescription Cocktail Club**, a glamorous venue serving creative cocktails to a cool young crowd. Also popular is the stylish **Experimental Cocktail Club**, which lives up to its name with cocktails such as Blind Date at Chelsea (sloe gin, cognac, maraschino, and strawberries). **Le China**, an Asian bar/restaurant with chic Neo-Colonial decor, also does great cocktails.

Other cool bars include tiny **Andy Wahloo**, with its Moroccan design; **De LaVille**, popular as a pre-club destination; and **The Lizard Lounge**, which attracts a noisy, young crowd.

Oberkampf, in the east, is one of the best areas to go for some late-night bar action; well established on the scene are **Café Charbon** and **Le Kitch**. **Bespoke** is a speakeasy-style bar specializing in creative cocktails – try, for example, the Capri C'est Fini (tomato, basil, and balsamic vinegar). The Canal St.-Martin area also has some great venues for canalside drinking, such as the energetic **Point Ephémère**, which programs live music and DJ nights. A number of bars bring in DJs on the weekends; the best are listed on *p345*.

Bars that are less trendy but great for a relaxing drink include the tiny, stone-clad **Stolly's** in the Marais and the legendary **Harry's Bar**, which claims to have invented the Bloody Mary.

Tearooms

Tearooms are well-established Paris institutions. They usually serve a tempting array of exquisite cakes and a wide choice of tea. Typical opening

hours are 11.30am–7pm. Some *salons de thé* also offer light lunches, as well as breakfast and afternoon tea; many open on Sunday for brunch.

A long-time favorite, dating from around 1903 and sporting a fabulous belle époque interior, is **Angélina**, renowned for its thick hot chocolate and the Mont Blanc, a rich chestnut, cream, and meringue confection. **Mariage Frères**, in business since 1854, is an elegant *salon de thé* in the Marais, well known for its exhaustive choice of tea; you can also buy loose-leaf tea from an impressive array of caddies lining the walls, plus lovely teapots to take home. Also very classy is **Ladurée**, near Place de la Madeleine; well-heeled ladies sip tea and nibble the house specialties, macaroons, amid the splendor of gilt-edged mirrors and ceiling frescoes. Ladurée has equally grand outlets on the Champs-Elysées and in St.-Germain. Perhaps the city's most sumptuous tea room, though, is the lavishly decorated café in the **Musée Jacquemart-André** *(see also p211)*, where you can enjoy tea and fine pastries while admiring the wall tapestries and Tiepolo's ceiling fresco.

More relaxed options include **Le Loir dans la Théière** in the Marais, where you can sit back in a comfy sofa and feast on the heavenly lemon meringue pie. **A Priori Thé** enjoys a lovely setting in one of the old Passages and serves crumbly home-made scones and cheesecake, as well as a popular brunch on Sunday. Also good for both Sunday brunch and afternoon tea is the charming **L'Heure Gourmande**, hidden away down a *passage* in St.-Germain; on sunny days you can relax on the tranquil terrace, away from the crowds, and enjoy hot chocolate and home-made cakes. Another haven from the city bustle is the lovely, mosaic-tiled **Café de la Mosquée**, where you can get sticky pastries and aromatic mint tea. Nearby, and perfect after a visit to

Notre-Dame, is **La Fourmi Ailée**, a cosy place with books on the shelves and a fire burning away in the colder months; it's also an excellent lunch or dinner stop.

Chocolate-lovers should head to **Chocolaterie Jacques Genin**, which combines a store and a *salon de thé*; you might want to buy a bag of the delicious caramels to take away, too.

Street Food

Street food has really taken off in Paris, and there's a large variety of offerings. Alongside the more traditional crêpes and ham-and-cheese baguettes, you'll also find New York deli-style sandwiches, bagels, burgers, tacos, and *empañadas*. **Frenchie To Go** attracts lines at lunchtime for its pastrami sandwiches and other deli-style fillings. **Chezaline** serves gourmet baguettes in a converted horse butcher's, and **Big Fernand** styles itself as an *atelier du hamburger*, using carefully sourced ingredients to produce burgers with a French twist. At lunchtime, **La Pointe du Groin**, a café/wine bar near the Gare du Nord, does excellent take-out Breton-style rolls and baguettes with fillings such as goat's cheese, pickled peppers, and rosemary honey. For Middle Eastern street food, head to Rue des Rosiers, in the Marais, where you'll find the renowned **L'As du Falafel** *(see p296)*, among many other falafel joints. Montparnasse has the best crêpe stands: the undisputed favorite is **Crêperie Josselin**.

Ice-cream stands open up around noon and stay open late in the summer. It's worth lining up (sometimes around the block) for the city's best ice cream at **Maison Berthillon**; seasoned gourmets come from across the city to sample a scoop or two of their delicious concoctions. **Amorino** makes excellent Italian-style *gelati*. Don't miss the *amaretto gelato*, which comes sprinkled with crushed *amaretti* biscuits.

DIRECTORY

Ile de la Cité and Ile St.-Louis

WINE BARS

Taverne Henri IV
13 Pl du Pont Neuf 75001.
Map 12 F3.

ICE–CREAM PARLORS

Amorino
47 Rue St.-Louis-en-l'Ile
75004. **Map** 13 C4.

Maison Berthillon
29–31 Rue St.-Louis-en-
l'Ile 75004. **Map** 13 C4.

Tuileries Quarter

WINE BARS

Frenchie Bar à Vins
5 Rue du Nil 75002.
Map 7 A5.

Ô Chateau
68 Rue Jean-Jacques
Rousseau 75001.
Map 12 F2.

BARS

Harry's Bar
5 Rue Daunou 75002.
Map 6 E5.

TEAROOMS

Angélina
226 Rue de Rivoli 75001.
Map 12 D1.

A Priori Thé
35–37 Galerie Vivienne
75002. **Map** 12 F1.

Ladurée
16 Rue Royale 75008.
Map 5 C5.

STREET FOOD

Big Fernand
40 Pl du Marché St.-
Honoré 75001. **Map** 12 E1.

Frenchie To Go
9 Rue du Nil 75002.
Map 7 A5.

The Marais

PUBS

The Auld Alliance
80 Rue François Miron
75004. **Map** 13 C3.

BARS

The Lizard Lounge
18 Rue du Bourg-Tibourg
75004. **Map** 13 C3.

Stolly's
16 Rue Cloche Perce
75004. **Map** 13 C3.

TEAROOMS

Chocolaterie Jacques Genin
133 Rue de Turenne
75003. **Map** 14 D1.

Le Loir dans la Théière
3 Rue des Rosiers 75004.
Map 13 C3.

Mariage Frères
30–32 Rue du Bourg-
Tibourg 75004.
Map 13 C3.

STREET FOOD

L'As du Falafel
32 Rue des Rosiers 75004.
Map 13 C3.

Beaubourg and Les Halles

WINE BARS

Le Garde Robe
41 Rue de l'Arbre Sec
75001. **Map** 12 E2.

PUBS

Frog and Rosbif
116 Rue St.-Denis 75002.
Map 13 B1.

BARS

Andy Wahloo
69 Rue des Gravilliers
75003. **Map** 13 B1.

De LaVille
34 Blvd Bonne Nouvelle
75010. **Map** 7 A5.

Experimental Cocktail Club
37 Rue St.-Sauveur 75002.
Map 13 A1.

Latin Quarter

WINE BARS

5e Cru
7 Rue du Cardinal
Lemoine. **Map** 13 B5.

PUBS

The Bombardier
2 Place du Panthéon
75005. **Map** 17 A1.

TEAROOMS

La Fourmi Ailée
8 Rue du Fouarre 75005.
Map 13 A4.

St.-Germain

WINE BARS

L'Avant Comptoir
9 Carrefour de l'Odéon
75006. **Map** 12 F4.

La Quincave
17 Rue Bréa, 75006.
Map 16 D2.

PUBS

Coolin
15 Rue Clément 75006.
Map 12 E4.

Corcoran's
28 Rue St.-André des Arts
75006. **Map** 12 F4.

Frog and Princess
9 Rue Princesse 75006.
Map 12 E4.

Highlander
8 Rue de Nevers 75006.
Map 12 F3.

BARS

Prescription Cocktail Club
23 Rue Mazarine 75006.
Map 12 F4.

TEAROOMS

L'Heure Gourmande
22 Passage Dauphine
75006. **Map** 12 F4.

Jardin des Plantes

TEA ROOMS

Café de la Mosquée
39 Rue Geoffroy St.-Hilaire
75005. **Map** 17 C2.

Montparnasse

STREET FOOD

Crêperie Josselin
67 Rue du Montparnasse
75014. **Map** 16 D2.

Invalides and Eiffel Tower Quarter

BARS

Bar du Plaza
Plaza Athénée Hotel, 25
Ave Montaigne 75008.
Map 10 F1.

TEAROOMS

Café Jacquemart-André
158 Blvd Haussmann
75008. **Map** 5 A4.

Ladurée
75 Avenue des Champs-
Elysées 75008. **Map** 4 F5.

Montmartre

WINE BARS

Pratz
59 Rue Jean Baptiste
Pigalle 75009. **Map** 6 E2.

PUBS

O'Sullivans by the Mill
92 Blvd de Clichy 75018.
Map 6 E2.

STREET FOOD

La Pointe du Groin
8 Rue de Belzunce 75010.
Map 7 B3.

Farther Afield

WINE BARS

Le Baron Rouge
1 Rue Théophile Roussel
75012. **Map** 14 F5.

Au Passage
1 bis Passage St.-Sébastien
75011. **Map** 14 E2.

Le Verre Volé
67 Rue de Lancry 75010.
Map 8 D4.

BARS

Bespoke
3 Rue Oberkampf 75011.
Map 14 E2.

Café Charbon
109 Rue Oberkampf
75011. **Map** 14 E1.

Le China
50 Rue de Charenton
75012. **Map** 14 F5.

Le Kitch
10 Rue Oberkampf 75011.
Map 14 E2.

Point Ephémère
200 Quai de Valmy 75010.
Map 8 E2.

STREET FOOD

Chezaline
85 Rue de la Roquette
75011. **Map** 14 F3.

STORES AND MARKETS

Paris seems to be the very definition of luxury and good living. Beautifully dressed people sip wine by the banks of the Seine against a backdrop of splendid architecture, or hurry down gallery-lined streets carrying parcels from specialty stores. The least expensive way of joining the chic set is to create French style with accessories or costume jewelry. Alternatively, splash out on the fashion, or the wonderful food and related items, from kitchen gadgets to tableware. Remember, too, that Parisian stores and markets are the ideal place to indulge in the French custom of strolling through the streets, seeing and being seen. For high fashion, there are the exquisite couture house window displays on Avenue Montaigne, or you can browse the bookstands selling secondhand books and prints along the Seine. An overview of some of the most famous places to shop follows.

Opening Hours

Stores are usually open 10am–7pm, Monday to Saturday, but hours can vary. Many department stores stay open late on Thursday, while boutiques may shut for an hour or two at midday. Markets and local neighborhood stores close on Mondays. Some smaller stores shut for the summer, usually in August, but they may leave a note on the door suggesting an equivalent store that is open nearby.

How to Pay

Cash is readily available from the ATMs in most banks, which accept both credit and bank debit cards. Visa and MasterCard are the most widely accepted credit cards.

Sales Tax Exemption

A sales tax (TVA) of 5.5–19.6 per cent is imposed on most goods and services in EU countries.

Non-EU residents shopping in France are entitled to a refund of this if they spend a minimum of €175 in one store in one day. You must have been resident in France for less than six months and either carry the goods with you out of the country within three months of purchase or get the store to forward them to you. If shopping in a group, you can usually buy goods together in order to reach the minimum.

Larger stores and department stores will generally supply a form (*bordereau de détaxe* or *bordereau de vente*) and help you to fill it out. When you leave France or the EU, you present the form to Customs, who either permit you to be reimbursed straight away, or forward your claim to the place where you bought the merchandise; the store eventually sends you a refund. If you know someone in Paris, it may be quicker if they can pick up the refund for you at the store. Alternatively, at

Shopping in one of the elegant stores in Avenue Montaigne

large airports such as Orly and Roissy, some banks may have the facilities to refund you on the spot. Though the process involves a lot of paperwork, it can be worth it. There is no refund on food, drink, tobacco, cars, and motorbikes. Bicycles, however, can be reimbursed.

Sales

The best sales (*soldes*) are held in January and July, although increasingly often you can find sale items throughout the year, and especially at Christmas. If you see goods labeled *Stock*, it means that they are stock items. *Dégriffé* means designer labels marked down, frequently from the previous year's collections. A *dépôt-vente* sells high-end secondhand clothes. The sales tend to occupy prime floor space for the first month and are then relegated to the back of the store.

Printemps, the *grande dame* of Parisian department stores

Department Stores

Much of the pleasure of shopping in Paris is derived from going to the small specialty stores. But if time is short, try the *grands magasins* (department stores). Some still operate a ticket system for selling goods. The store clerk writes up a ticket for goods from their own boutique, which you take to one of the cashiers. You then return with your validated ticket to pick up your purchase. This can be time-consuming, so go early in the morning and don't shop on Saturdays. The French don't pay much attention to lines, so be assertive! Because of security issues, guards will ask to check your bags before you enter the store. They may also ask to inspect them as you leave. These are random checks, not an implication of theft.

Department stores vary in style and content, but all have places to eat. **Printemps** is noted for its innovative household goods section and large menswear store. The clothes departments for women and children are well stocked. Visit the lovely domed restaurant in the cupola during shopping hours. **BHV** (Le Bazar de l'Hôtel de Ville) is a DIY enthusiast's paradise. It also sells a host of other items related to home decor. The Left Bank **Le Bon Marché** is considered to be the world's first department store and today is Paris's most chic. The designer clothing section is well-sourced, the high-end accessories are excellent, and the own-brand linen has a good

Kenzo designerwear in the Place des Victoires *(see pp317, 319)*

quality-to-price ratio. The prepared food sections serve restaurant-quality fare to go.

There are also a number of US-style malls *(centres commerciaux)*, such as **Beaugrenelle**, **Passy Plaza** and **Les Quatre Temps** – quick options if you want all your stores in one place. However, clothing and shoe boutiques tend to be smaller, with less choice than their stand-alone or flagship stores. These malls also have large movie theaters.

Galeries Lafayette is perhaps the best-known department store and has a wide range of clothing available at all price levels. Its first-floor trends section plays host to lots of innovative designers. Galeries Lafayette boasts a wonderful food hall, Lafayette Gourmet, which offers a vast array of mouthwatering goodies.

FNAC is the largest retailer in France of books, music, and electronic equipment. There are

numerous stores around Paris, but the branch on the Champs-Elysées specializes in music, DVDs, and concert tickets and is open until 11.45pm daily. All of their products are available online, too, along with tickets for concerts, sporting events, and theatrical events.

The splendid interior of Galeries Lafayette

Paris's Best: Stores and Markets

By turns ultra-conservative and wackily avant-garde, Paris is a treasure trove of quality stores and boutiques. Time-honored emporia mix with modern shopping centers in a city that buzzes with life in its inner quarters, not least in the markets. Here you can buy everything from exotic fruit and vegetables to fine china and vintage treasures. Whether you're shopping for handmade shoes, perfectly cut clothes, or traditionally made cheeses, or simply soaking up the atmosphere, you won't be disappointed.

Place de la Madeleine
Top-class groceries and delicacies are sold on the north side of this square. *(See p218.)*

The Center of Paris Couture

M George V · RUE DE PONTHIEU · St-Philippe-du-Roule · RUE DU FAUBOURG ST HONORE · BLVD MALESHERBES

AVENUE · RUE FRANCOIS 1er · AVENUE GEORGE V · AVE MARCEAU · Franklin D. Roosevelt M · AVE FRANKLIN D ROOSEVELT · Guy Laroche · Chanel · Nina Ricci · AVENUE MONTAIGNE · Christian Dior · Yves Saint Laurent · Givenchy · Alma Marceau M · CHAMPS · AVE DE MARIGNY · ST HONORE · Hermès · RUE ROYALE · AVENUE GABRIEL · Champs Elysees Clemenceau M · ELYSEES · Concorde M · PLACE DE LA CONCORDE

COURS ALBERT 1er · AVE W CHURCHILL · COURS LA REINE

Seine

See inset map

Champs-Elysées

Chanel
Coco Chanel (1883–1971) reigned over the fashion world from No. 31 Rue Cambon. The main boutique is in the Avenue Montaigne. *(See pp317, 319.)*

Rue de Rivoli
Inexpensive mementos like this Paris snow globe can be found in the stores on the Rue de Rivoli. *(See p132.)*

Invalides and Eiffel Tower Quarter

Marché aux Puces de la Porte de Vanves
This charming and relaxed market sells old books, linen, postcards, china, and musical instruments. *(Weekends only – see p331.)*

0 kilometers

0 miles   0.5

Kenzo
The Japanese designer has colorful apparel for men, women, and children in his stores. *(See pp317, 319.)*

Cartier
The early Cartier jewelry designs, with their beautifully cut stones, are still highly sought after. This store in the Rue de la Paix sells all the Cartier lines. *(See p320.)*

Rue de Paradis
Here you can buy porcelain and crystal at reduced prices at the company showrooms. Look out for La Cristallerie Paradis, which stocks Baccarat and Bernardaud. *(See pp322, 324.)*

Galerie Vivienne
This lovely Neo-Classical shopping arcade with mosaics features fashion and home furnishings. *(See p221.)*

Opéra Quarter

Kenzo

Tuileries Quarter

Beaubourg and Les Halles

The Marais

Seine

St-Germain-des-Prés

Ile de la Cité

Ile St-Louis

Latin Quarter

Rue des Francs-Bourgeois
Stylish fashion stores *(see pp316, 319)* line this thoroughfare in the Marais.

Luxembourg Quarter

Jardin des Plantes Quarter

Montparnasse

Marché aux Puces de la Porte de Vanves

Rue Mouffetard
The market sells cheeses and other quality foods. *(See p331.)*

bibliothèque du cinéma

Forum des Halles
This modern glass arcade has many stores. *(See p115.)*

Clothes and Accessories

For many people, Paris is synonymous with fashion, and Parisian style is the ultimate in chic. More than anywhere else in the world, women in Paris seem to be in tune with current trends. Though generally less fashion conscious, Parisian men have a keen sense of style, and mix and match patterns and colors with élan. Top designer boutiques are concentrated around the Champs-Elysées, on streets such as Avenue Montaigne, Rue Francois-1er, and Rue du Faubourg-St.-Honoré, and also in St.-Germain. High-end labels abound on Rue Etienne and around Place Sainte-Victoire. Farther east, in the Marais, Canal St.-Martin, and Bastille areas, as well as in South Pigalle and Montmartre, there are lots of trendy, independent fashion labels. High-street fashion tends to be concentrated in Les Halles and surrounding streets.

Department and Concept Stores

A good place to start a clothes-shopping spree in Paris is one of the city's grand department stores *(see p313)*. **Galeries Lafayette** has an excellent range of high-end fashion, nearly a whole floor of lingerie, and another of shoes, while **Printemps** is particularly strong on men's fashion, with seven floors of clothes and accessories. Less upscale, but carrying a wide range of women's and men's fashion, is **BHV Marais**. At the budget end is the popular discount department store **Tati**, which includes among its customers Catherine Deneuve and Sonia Rykiel.

Also handy for a one-stop shop are the city's ever-growing concept stores. One of the best known is **Colette**, which combines high fashion, design, and hip accessories. **Spree**, in Montmartre, mixes fashion, art, and design, while **Merci**, set in a huge old wallpaper factory, sells an attractive range of women's clothing, alongside homewares, jewelry and secondhand books; the clothes are not especially cheap, but all profits go to charity. The Rue Sévigné branch of **L'Eclaireur** is vaunted as an "interactive installation"; clothes, mostly by top fashion designers such as Balenciaga and Jean Rousseau, are hidden behind screens and sliding panels. Just off the trendy Canal St.-Martin lies pioneering concept store **Centre Commercial**, concerned with the environment and fair trade, and stocking eco-friendly French designers such as Valentine Gauthier, plus a decent selection of lesser-known men's labels.

Parisian Chic

There are many wonderful stores where you can achieve the Parisian look without spending over the odds. Boulevard St.-Germain and Rue du Jour/Rue Etienne Marcel are good hunting grounds for French labels. For many, **Agnès B**, on Rue du Jour, epitomizes Parisian chic – her clothes are understated and timeless, and not overly expensive. Other labels nearby include Paris-based **B&ash**, creating fresh, modern chunky knits, wool dresses, and bold-colored silk tops; and **Claudie Pierlot**, whose designs sport an elegant, slightly gamine look. **Comptoir des Cotonniers** is very popular for its well-cut basics, while a little more daring are the designs by **Paul & Joe** for both men and women; Paul & Joe Sister caters to a younger, more contemporary look. With many branches around the city, **Sandro**, founded by Parisian Evelyne Chétrite, is a good bet for well-cut staples, as well as floaty dresses and casual men's clothes. Other reliable brands to look out for are **Zadig & Voltaire**, which has made its mark with chic casual basics such as everyday T-shirts and cashmere sweaters; and **Vanessa Bruno**, whose clothes are popular with all ages for their classic, high-quality designs.

The northeast of the city, around the Marais and Bastille, is another great area for clothes shopping, with a mix of established and more cutting-edge designers. Rue des Francs-Bourgeois is full of elegant boutiques, such as **Autour du Monde**, selling young, colorful clothes and canvas sneakers by French designer Bensimon, while the quieter roads to the north, such as Rue Charlot and Rue de Poitou, harbor some of the city's most exciting young fashion designers. **Yves Andrieux et Vincent Jalbert** create elegant jackets and skirts from such unlikely fabrics as recycled 1950s army uniforms, while **Swildens** is worth seeking out for feminine clothes with a nod to vintage style. **La Fausse Boutique** stocks young French designers.

Rue Keller, in the Bastille, also has a cluster of independent designers, such as **Gaëlle Barré** and **Anne Willi**, while trendy Rue de Charonne is home to **Sessùn**, where Emma François creates casual-chic clothes from quality fabrics. A few blocks down is **Isabel Marant** (and her more affordable line, Etoile), internationally renowned for her flattering, understated womenswear. The stores along the Canal St.-Martin reflect the bohemian-bourgeois character of its residents; one that stands out above all others is **Antoine et Lili**, with its three candy-colored storefronts. It is known for its bright, cheerful clothes with an ethnic twist for women and children.

Also good for more alternative fashions is the area at the foot of Montmartre and South Pigalle. Streets worth checking out for offbeat designers are rues des Martyrs, des Trois Frères, de la Vieuville, and Houdon.

Couture and High-End Designer Fashion

Paris is the home of *haute couture*. Original couture garments are beautiful one-off creations, and their astronomical prices put them beyond the reach of all but a few people with immensely deep pockets. However, *haute couture* is also the lifeblood of the fashion industry, providing inspiration for the mass market. Most couture houses make *prêt-à-porter* as well – ready-to-wear clothes fitted on a standard model. They're still not cheap, but they give you some of the elegance and creativity of a couture designer at a fraction of the cost.

The highest concentration of couture houses is on the Right Bank. Most flagship stores are on or near Rue du Faubourg-St.-Honoré and the classier Avenue Montaigne: **Christian Dior**, **Pierre Cardin**, **Chanel**, **Gianni Versace**, **Givenchy**, and **Nina Ricci** are all here. **Hermès** offers timeless chic, while **Lanvin**, the oldest fashion house still in existence, embodies Parisian elegance. **Karl Lagerfeld** has a store where the latest creations from his own line, Lagerfeld Gallery, are exhibited. Designers such as **Kenzo** cluster on Place des Victoires and Rue St.-Etienne Marcel.

St.-Germain, especially Rue du Cherche Midi, also has a large concentration of high-end designer stores. Here you'll find **Sonia Rykiel**, famous for her striped skinny ribs, and her less expensive offshoot, **Sonia by Sonia Rykiel**. **Barbara Bui** is popular for her soft, feminine clothes, while **Saint-Laurent** and **Jil Sander** are hard to beat for their exquisite tailoring. For a good collection of designerwear in one store, try **Kabuki Femme** (there's a men's branch down the street).

Menswear

In addition to the outlets mentioned above, Paris has many excellent menswear stores. At the designer end of the scale, on the Right Bank, are **Giorgio Armani**, **Pierre Cardin**, **Kenzo**, **Lanvin** (also good for accessories), and **Saint-Laurent**. On the Left Bank, **Michel Axel** and **Jean-Charles de Castelbajac** are known for their ties and elegant suits. **APC**, **Paul Smith**, and **Sandro** are rather more contemporary, and **Loft Design By** is chic without being overtly trendy.

Independent and cutting-edge men's designers abound in the Marais. **French Trotters** stocks covetable own-brand Breton shirts, as well as more unusual French labels, such as Commune de Paris. A stylishly revamped pharmacy sets the tone for **Christophe Lemaire**'s elegant coats and everyday wear, while **Nodus** has an unbeatable range of classic and fashion shirts and ties. At **Printemps Homme** you'll find all you need to look fashionable.

Vintage, Secondhand, and Discount Stores

There are some wonderful stores to plunder for a retro look. The best of the bunch is **Didier Ludot**, which elegantly displays an Aladdin's cave of vintage *haute couture*. From Courrèges dresses to excellent-condition Chanel suits, this is the place for top-of-the-range retro. The Marais has a good number of less expensive vintage stores; try **Free "P" Star** for 1970s floral dresses and **Mamz'Elle Swing** for 1950s fashions. For great-condition secondhand wear of more recent vintages, **Violette & Léonie** stocks both designer and high-street labels, while **Kiliwatch** specializes in streetwear and jeans.

Another way to get your hands on recent designer fashion is to head for one of the many consignment stores (*dépôt-vente*) in the city. Chic Parisians discard their outfits with the seasons, so it is very easy to pick up some quality items that are normally in top condition from places such as **Réciproque** in Passy or **Dépôt-Vente de Buci-Bourbon**. In addition, a number of dedicated "stock" stores sell end-of-line and last season's collections at substantial reductions; try, for example, **Le Mouton à Cinq Pattes** or **Défilé de Marques**. If you're planning to go to Disneyland, you could also check out **La Vallée** outlet mall, boasting more than 100 luxury brands, both French and international.

Children's Clothes

The city has a delightful range of stores where you can buy all you need to transform your children into little trendy Parisians. A concentration of children's clothes stores can be found on Rue Vavin, in St.-Germain, and the big department stores also stock a wide range. Popular brands such as **Jacadi** and **Du Pareil au Même** sell colorful clothes at reasonable prices. The more upscale **Tartine et Chocolat** offers delectable classics with a contemporary twist, while **Bonpoint** stocks adorably chic clothing for mini-Parisians. **Petit Bateau** is coveted as much by adults as it is by children. Kids even have their own concept store in **Bonton**, which stocks baby toiletries, stylish clothing, toys, and furniture for children's rooms. Parisian teenagers flock to **Citadium**, a department store near Printemps, for its wide range of streetwear and sneakers.

For little feet, **Froment-Leroyer** probably offers the best all-round classics. **Six Pieds Trois Pouces** has a vast choice of styles.

Jewelry

For seriously expensive jewelry, head to Rue de la Paix and Place Vendôme, where top jewelers such as **Boucheron**, **Mauboussin**, **Poiray**, and **Cartier** cluster. Also here are **Dinh Van**, which has some quirky pieces, and **Mikimoto**, a must for pearls. On nearby Rue de Castiglione, **H Stern** has some innovative designs that feature semi-precious and precious stones.

For a range of more unusual jewelry and accessories, try the **Swarovski Boutique**. Also of note is **Marie-Hélène de Taillac**, whose superbly elegant creations have a contemporary edge and are much coveted by fashionistas.

At a more affordable level, **Delphine Pariente** makes delicate gold- and silver-plated jewelry and recycles vintage pieces; while **Monsieur** – actually a woman, Nadia Azoug – creates fine handmade jewelry, each piece unique, in her Marais atelier-boutique. Over on the Canal St.-Martin, **Médecine Douce**'s delicate gold bracelets and necklaces have an understated elegance, while **Viveka Bergström** favors bold and striking designs made from raw materials such as glass. Also worth a visit is **Paulie and Me**, which describes itself as an "incubation store" for young designers; as well as innovative jewelry, you'll find one-off accessories and fashion for both men and women.

Shoes, Bags, and Belts

Fair Trade sneakers (made from organic cotton and natural Amazonian rubber) by Veja can be found in **Le Bon Marché**. Go to **Repetto** for cult pumps in a host of colors, or to **Sidonie Larizzi**, who will make up shoes from one of numerous leather swatches. Current favorites with the fashion set include **Michel Perry**, **Jérôme Dreyfuss**, and **Robert Clergerie**. **Christian Louboutin** and **Rodolphe Ménudier** are mainstays for sexy stilettos. **Carel** stocks smart basics, **Cosmo Paris** and **Vivaldi** sell trendy models, and **Jonak** is a must for good imitations of designer footwear. **Bowen** has a selection of traditional men's shoes, and **Berluti** is the last word in elegance for many Parisian men.

Beautifully made leather goods can be found at **Gucci**, **Longchamp**, and **Hermès**, who still make bespoke items in their Paris workshops. For purses, nothing beats **Chanel** or **Christian Dior** at the top end

of the scale, although **Goyard** comes close. Mid-range purses from the Italian brand **Furla** are a great compromise, as are the colorful designs from **Karine Dupont**. Fabric bags from **Jamin Puech**, **Vanessa Bruno**, or **Hervé Chapelier** feature in every chic Parisian's closet. **Lili Cabas** designs chic leather bags in a range of styles at prices that won't break the bank; the store in the 10th arrondissement also stocks accessories by other French designers, such as Ma Poésie wool scarves and Anne Thomas jewelry. For a great range of shoes, accessories, and bags at reasonable prices, **Lollipops** boutiques can be found across Paris.

Hats

One of Paris's favorite milliners is **Marie Mercié**, known for her glamorous and quirky straw, fur, and felt hats, while **Anthony Peto** creates a wonderful range of men's straw hats, fedoras, and trilbies in fabrics such as velour and fur. Around since 1875, **Grevi** makes beautiful hats for women and children.

Lingerie and Swimwear

For a delightful selection of beautiful, modern lingerie, go to **Fifi Chachnil**. **La Boîte à Bas** sells fine French stockings, **Princesse Tam Tam** offers trendy quality items at reasonable prices, and divine designer lingerie can be found at cult store **Sabbia Rosa**. The ultimate in magnificent Parisian lingerie can be bought off the peg or made to order at **Cadolle**, the store that invented the bra. **Aubade**, known for its sophisticated and sensual lingerie, is a trusted brand among French women. **Erès** is the place to shop for elegant swimwear.

Size Chart

For Australian sizes, follow the British and American conversions.

Children's clothing

French	2–3	4–5	6–7	8–9	10–11	12	14	14+ (years)	
British	2–3	4–5	6–7	8–9	10–11	12	14	14+ (years)	
American	2–3	4–5	6–6x	7–8	10–11	12	14	16 (size)	

Children's shoes

French	24	25½	27	28	29	30	32	33	34
British	7	8	9	10	11	12	13	1	2
American	7½	8½	9½	10½	11½	12½	13½	1½	2½

Women's dresses, coats and skirts

French	34	36	38	40	42	44	46
British	6	8	10	12	14	16	18
American	2	4	6	8	10	12	14

Women's blouses and sweaters

French	81	84	87	90	93	96	99 (cms)
British	31	32	34	36	38	40	42 (inches)
American	6	8	10	12	14	16	18 (size)

Women's shoes

French	36	37	38	39	40	41
British	3	4	5	6	7	8
American	5	6	7	8	9	10

Men's suits

French	44	46	48	50	52	54	56	58
British	34	36	38	40	42	44	46	48
American	34	36	38	40	42	44	46	48

Men's shirts

French	36	38	39	41	42	43	44	45
British	14	15	15½	16	16½	17	17½	18
American	14	15	15½	16	16½	17	17½	18

Men's shoes

French	39	40	41	42	43	44	45	46
British	6	7	7½	8	9	10	11	12
American	7	7½	8	8½	9½	10½	11	11½

DIRECTORY

Department and Concept Stores

BHV Marais
52–64 Rue de Rivoli
75004. **Map** 13 B3.
Tel 09 77 40 14 00.

Centre Commercial
2 Rue de Marseille
75010. **Map** 8 D4.
Tel 01 42 02 26 08.
W centrecommercial.cc

Colette
213 Rue St.-Honoré
75001. **Map** 12 D1.
Tel 01 55 35 33 90.
W colette.fr

L'Eclaireur
40 Rue de Sévigné
75003. **Map** 14 D3.
Tel 01 48 87 10 22.
leclaireur.com
One of several branches.

Galeries Lafayette
40 Blvd Haussmann
75009. **Map** 6 E4.
Tel 01 42 82 34 56.
One of two branches.

Merci
111 Blvd Beaumarchais
75003. **Map** 14 E2.
Tel 01 42 77 00 33.
W merci-merci.com

Printemps
64 Blvd Haussmann
75009. **Map** 6 D4.
Tel 01 42 82 50 00.

Spree
16 Rue de La Vieuville
75018. **Map** 6 F1.
Tel 01 42 23 41 40.
W spree.fr

Tati
174 Rue du Temple
75003. **Map** 14 D1.
01 42 71 41 77.
W tati.fr

Parisian Chic

Agnès B
6 Rue du Jour 75001.
Map 13 A1.
Tel 01 45 08 56 56.
W agnesb.com
One of several branches.

Anne Willi
13 Rue Keller 75011. **Map**
14 F4. **Tel** 01 48 06 74 06.
W annewilli.com

Antoine et Lili
95 Quai de Valmy
75010. **Map** 8 D4.
Tel 01 40 37 41 55.
W antoineetlili.com
One of several branches.

Autour du Monde
12 Rue des Francs
Bourgeois 75003.
Map 14 D3.
Tel 01 42 77 16 18.
W bensimon.com
One of several branches.

B&ash
21 Rue Etienne Marcel
75001. **Map** 13 A1.
Tel 01 42 33 77 92.
W ba-sh.com

Claudie Pierlot
1 Pl des Victoires 75002.
Map 12 F1.
Tel 01 44 82 55 38.
W claudiepierlot.com
One of several branches.

**Comptoir des
Cotonniers**
33 Rue des Francs
Bourgeois 75004.
Map 13 C3.
Tel 01 42 76 95 33.
W comptoirdes
cotonniers.com
One of several branches.

La Fausse Boutique
19 Rue des Ecouffes
75004. **Map** 13 C3.
Tel 06 62 17 59 02.
W lafausseboutique.
com

Gaëlle Barré
17 Rue Keller 75011.
Map 14 F4.
Tel 01 43 14 63 02.
W gaellebarre.com

Isabel Marant
16 Rue de Charonne
75011. **Map** 14 F4.
Tel 01 49 29 71 55.
W isabelmarant.com

Paul & Joe
64–66 Rue des Saints
Pères 75007.
Map 12 D4.
Tel 01 42 22 47 01.
W paulandjoe.com
One of several branches.

Sandro
42 Rue Etienne
Marcel 75002.
Map 12 F1.
Tel 01 44 82 58 87.
W sandro-paris.com
One of several branches.

Sessùn
34 Rue de Charonne
75011. **Map** 14 F4.
Tel 01 48 06 55 66.
W sessun.com

Swildens
16 Rue de Turenne
75004. **Map** 14 D3.
Tel 01 42 71 12 20.
W swildens.fr
One of several branches.

Vanessa Bruno
25 Rue St.-Sulpice
75006. **Map** 12 E4.
Tel 01 43 54 41 04.
W vanessabruno.com

**Yves Andrieux et
Vincent Jalbert**
55 Rue Charlot 75003.
Map 14 D1.
Tel 01 42 71 19 54.
W vincentjalbert.com

Zadig et Voltaire
3 Rue des Rosiers
75004. **Map** 13 C3.
Tel 01 44 59 39 06.
One of several branches.

Couture and High-End Designer Fashion

Barbara Bui
23 Rue Etienne-Marcel
75001. **Map** 13 A1.
Tel 01 40 26 43 65.
W barbarabui.com
One of several branches.

Chanel
42 & 51 Ave Montaigne
75008. **Map** 5 A5.
Tel 01 44 50 73 00.
W chanel.com
One of several branches.

Christian Dior
30 Ave Montaigne 75008.
Map 10 F1.
Tel 01 40 73 73 73.
W dior.com

Gianni Versace
45 Ave Montaigne 75008.
Map 10 F1.
Tel 01 47 42 88 02.
W versace.com

Givenchy
28 Rue du Faubourg-
St.-Honoré 75008.
Map 5 C5.
Tel 01 42 68 31 00.
W givenchy.com
One of several branches.

Hermès
24 Rue du Faubourg-
St.-Honoré 75008.
Map 5 C5.
Tel 01 40 17 46 00.
W hermes.com
One of several branches.

Jil Sander
56 Ave Montaigne
75008. **Map** 10 F1.
Tel 01 44 95 06 70.
W jilsander.com

Kabuki Femme
25 Rue Etienne Marcel
75001. **Map** 13 A1.
Tel 01 40 26 43 65.

Karl Lagerfeld
194 Blvd St.-Germain
75006. **Map** 12 D4.
Tel 01 42 22 74 99.
W karl.com

Kenzo
3 Pl des Victoires 75001.
Map 12 F1.
Tel 01 40 39 72 03.
W kenzo.com
One of several branches.

Lanvin
15 Rue du Faubourg-
St.-Honoré 75008.
Map 5 C5.
Tel 01 44 71 31 25.
W lanvin.com
One of several branches.

Nina Ricci
39 Ave Montaigne 75008.
Map 10 F1.
Tel 01 83 97 72 12.
W ninaricci.fr

Pierre Cardin
59 Rue du Faubourg-
St.-Honoré 75008.
Map 5 B5.
Tel 01 42 66 68 98.
W pierrecardin.com

Saint-Laurent
38 Rue du Faubourg-
St.-Honoré 75008.
Map 5 C5.
Tel 01 42 65 74 59.
W ysl.com
One of several branches.

DIRECTORY

Sonia Rykiel
175 Blvd St-Germain
75006. **Map** 12 D4.
Tel 01 49 54 60 60.
W soniarykiel.com
One of several branches.

Sonia by Sonia Rykiel
6 Rue de Grenelle 75006.
Map 11 B3.
Tel 01 49 54 61 10.
W soniaby.com

Menswear

APC
38 Rue Madame 75006.
Map 12 E5.
Tel 01 42 22 12 77.
W apc.fr
One of several branches.

Christophe Lemaire
28 Rue de Poitou 75003.
Map 14 D2.
Tel 01 44 78 00 09.
W lemaire.fr

French Trotters
128 Rue Vieille du
Temple 75003.
Map 13 C3.
Tel 01 44 61 00 14.
W frenchtrotters.fr

Giorgio Armani
18 Ave Montaigne 75008.
Map 10 F1.
Tel 01 42 61 55 09.
W armani.com

**Jean-Charles de
Castelbajac**
61 Rue des St.-Pères
75006.
Tel 09 64 48 48 54.
W jc-de-castelbajac.
com

Kenzo
3 Pl des Victoires 75001.
Map 12 F1.
Tel 01 40 39 72 03.
W kenzo.com
One of several branches.

Lanvin
(See p319).

Loft Design By
18 Ave Franklin
Roosevelt 75008.
Map 5 A5.
Tel 01 45 61 12 37.
One of several branches.

Michel Axel
44 Rue du Dragon 75006.
Map 12 D4.
Tel 01 42 84 13 86.
W michelaxel.com

Nodus
22 Rue Vieille du
Temple 75004.
Map 13 C3.
Tel 01 42 77 07 96.
W nodus.fr
One of several branches.

Paul Smith
22 Blvd Raspail 75007.
Map 12 D4.
Tel 01 53 63 08 74.

Pierre Cardin
(See p319).

Printemps Homme
64 Blvd Haussmann
75009. **Map** 5 A4.
Tel 01 42 82 50 00.

Saint-Laurent
6 Pl St.-Sulpice 75006.
Map 12 D4.
Tel 01 43 29 43 00.
W ysl.com

Sandro
30 Pl du Marché
St.- Honoré 75001.
Map 12 E1.
Tel 01 58 62 49 00.

Vintage, Secondhand and Discount Stores

Défilé de Marques
171 Rue de Grenelle
75007. **Map** 10 F3.
Tel 01 45 55 63 47.
W defiledemarques.
com

**Depôt-Vente de
Buci-Bourbon**
4 Rue de Bourbon-le-
Château 75006.
Map 12 E4.
Tel 01 46 34 28 28.

Didier Ludot
24 Galerie Montpensier
75001. **Map** 12 E1.
Tel 01 42 96 06 56.
W didierludot.fr

Free "P" Star
61 Rue de la Verrerie
75004. **Map** 13 B3.
Tel 01 42 78 00 76.
W freepstar.com
One of several branches.

Kiliwatch
64 Rue Tiquetonne 75002.
Map 13 A1.
Tel 01 42 21 17 37.
W spacekiliwatch.fr

Mamz'Elle Swing
35 Rue du Roi de Sicile
75004. **Map** 13 C3.
Tel 01 48 87 04 06.
W mamzelleswing.com

**Le Mouton à
Cinq Pattes**
8/18 Rue St.-Placide
75006. **Map** 11 C5.
Tel 01 45 48 86 26.
One of several branches.

Réciproque
89-92-95 & 101 Rue de
la Pompe 75016.
Map 9 A1.
Tel 01 47 04 30 28.

La Vallée
3 Cours de la Garonne,
77700 Seris.
Tel 01 60 42 35 01.
W lavalleevillage.com

Violette & Léonie
114 Rue de Turenne
75003. **Map** 14 D2.
Tel 01 44 59 87 35.
W violettetleonie.com

Children's Clothes

Bonpoint
320 Rue St.-Honoré
75001. **Map** 13 A2.
Tel 01 49 27 94 82.
W bonpoint.com
One of several branches.

Bonton
82 Rue de Grenelle
75007. **Map** 10 F3.
Tel 01 44 39 09 20.
W bonton.com
One of several branches.

Citadium
56 Rue de Caumartin
75009. **Map** 6 D4.
Tel 01 55 31 74 00.
W citadium.com

Du Pareil au Même
1 Rue St.-Denis 75001.
Map 13 B3.
Tel 01 42 36 07 57.
W dpam.fr
One of several branches.

Froment-Leroyer
7 Rue Vavin 75006.
Map 16 E1.
Tel 01 43 54 33 15.
W froment-leroyer.fr
One of several branches.

Jacadi
17 Rue Tronchet
75008. **Map** 5 C5.
Tel 01 42 65 84 98.
W jacadi.fr
One of several branches.

Petit Bateau
116 Ave des Champs-
Elysées 75008. **Map** 4 E4.
Tel 01 40 74 02 03.
W petit-bateau.com
One of several branches.

Six Pieds Trois Pouces
78 Ave de Wagram
75017. **Map** 4 E2.
Tel 01 46 22 81 64.
One of several branches.

Tartine et Chocolat
84 Rue du Faubourg-St.-
Honoré 75008. **Map** 5 B5.
Tel 01 45 62 44 04.
W tartine-et-
chocolat.fr

Jewelry

Boucheron
26 Pl Vendôme 75001.
Map 6 D5.
Tel 01 42 61 58 16.
W boucheron.com
One of several branches.

Cartier
13 Rue de la Paix 75002.
Map 6 D5.
Tel 01 58 18 23 00.
W cartier.fr
One of several branches.

Delphine Pariente
19 Rue de Turenne 75003.
Map 14 D3.
Tel 01 42 78 18 87.
W delphinepariente.fr

Dinh Van
16 Rue de la Paix 75002.
Map 6 D5.
Tel 01 42 61 74 49.
W dinhvan.com
One of several branches.

H Stern
Westin Hotel, 3 Rue
Castiglione 75001. **Map**
12 D1. **Tel** 01 42 60 22 27.
W hstern.net
One of several branches.

DIRECTORY

**Marie-Hélène
de Taillac**
8 Rue de Tournon 75006.
Map 12 E5.
Tel 01 44 27 07 07.
W mariehelenede
taillac.com

Mauboussin
20 Pl Vendôme 75001.
Map 6 D5.
Tel 01 44 55 10 00.
W mauboussin.fr

Médecine Douce
10 Rue de Marseille
75010. **Map** 8 D4.
Tel 01 82 83 11 53.
W bijouxmedecine
douce.com

Mikimoto
8 Pl Vendôme 75001.
Map 6 D5.
Tel 01 42 60 33 55.
W mikimoto.fr

Monsieur
53 Rue Charlot 75003.
Map 14 D2.
Tel 01 42 71 12 65.
W monsieur-paris.com

Paulie and Me
68 Rue Jean Jacques
Rousseau 75001.
Map 12 F2.
Tel 06 85 94 04 34.
W paulieandme.fr

Poiray
8 Rue de la Paix 75002.
Map 6 D5.
Tel 01 42 97 99 00.
W poiray.com

Swarovski Boutique
146 Ave des Champs-
Elysées 75008.
Map 4 E4.
Tel 01 45 61 13 80.
W swarovski.com

Viveka Bergström
23 Rue de la Grange
aux Belles 75010.
Map 8 D4.
Tel 01 40 03 04 92.
W viveka-bergstrom.
blogspot.co.uk

Shoes, Bags,
and Belts

Berluti
26 Rue Marbeuf 75008.
Map 4 F5.
Tel 01 53 93 97 97.
W berluti.com

Le Bon Marché
24 Rue de Sèvres 75007.
Map 11 C5.
Tel 01 44 39 80 00.

Bowen
12 Rue Marbeuf 75008.
Map 4 F5.
Tel 01 47 20 45 90.

Carel
2 Rue Tronchet 75008.
Map 6 D4.
Tel 01 43 66 21 58.
One of several branches.

Chanel
42 & 51 Ave Montaigne
75008. **Map** 5 A5.
Tel 01 44 50 73 00.
W chanel.com
One of several branches.

Christian Dior
30 Ave Montaigne 75008.
Map 10 F1.
Tel 01 40 73 73 73.
W dior.com

Christian Louboutin
38–40 Rue de Grenelle
75007. **Map** 10 F3.
Tel 0800 10 19 19 19.
One of two branches.

Cosmo Paris
25 Rue du Four 75006.
Map 12 E4.
Tel 01 56 24 15 49.

Furla
281 Rue St.-Honoré 75008.
Map 5 C5. **Tel** 01 42 97 50
47. W furla.com
One of several branches.

Goyard
233 Rue St.-Honoré
75001. **Map** 5 C5.
Tel 01 42 60 57 04.
W goyard.com

Gucci
350 Rue St.-Honoré
75001. **Map** 12 D1.
Tel 01 42 66 21 58.
W gucci.com

Hermès
(See p319).

Hervé Chapelier
1 bis Rue du Vieux-
Colombier 75006.
Map 12 D4.
Tel 01 44 07 06 50.

Jamin Puech
61 Rue de Hauteville
75010. **Map** 7 B4.
Tel 01 40 22 08 32.

Jérôme Dreyfuss
1 Rue Jacob 75006.
Map 12 E4.
Tel 01 43 54 70 93.

Jonak
70 Rue de Rennes
75006. **Map** 16 D1.
Tel 01 45 48 27 11.
One of several branches.

Karine Dupont
16 Rue du Cherche-Midi
75006. **Map** 12 D4.
Tel 01 42 74 20 20.

Lili Cabas
24 Rue des Petites
Ecuries 75010.
Map 7 B4.
Tel 09 54 40 00 16.
W lilicabas.com

Lollipops
326 Rue de Vaugirard
75015.
Tel 01 56 08 11 11.
W lollipopsparis.fr

Longchamp
21 Rue du Vieux
Colombier 75006.
Map 12 D4.
Tel 01 42 22 74 75.
W longchamp.com

Michel Perry
42 Rue de Grenelle
75007. **Map** 10 F3.
Tel 01 42 22 99 12.

Repetto
22 Rue de la Paix
75002. **Map** 6 D5.
Tel 01 44 71 83 12.
One of several branches.

Robert Clergerie
5 Rue du Cherche-Midi
75006. **Map** 12 D4.
Tel 01 45 48 75 47.

Rodolphe Ménudier
14 Rue de Castiglione
75001. **Map** 12 D1.
Tel 06 07 02 81 91.

Sidonie Larizzi
15 Rue Clément Marot
75008. **Map** 4 F5.
Tel 01 40 70 00 24.

Vanessa Bruno
(See p319).

Vivaldi
38 Rue de Rivoli 75001.
Map 13 A2.
Tel 01 44 54 08 56.

Hats

Anthony Peto
56 Rue Tiquetonne 75002.
Map 13 A1.
Tel 01 40 26 60 68.

Grevi
1 Pl Alphonse-
Deville 75006.
Map 14 D3.
Tel 01 42 22 05 69.
W grevi.com

Marie Mercié
23 Rue St.-Sulpice 75006.
Map 12 E4.
Tel 01 43 26 45 83.

Lingerie and
Swimwear

Aubade
22 Rue du Vieux
Colombier 75006.
Map 12 D4.
Tel 01 45 48 16 62.

La Boîte à Bas
27 Rue Boissy-d'Anglas
75008. **Map** 5 C5.
Tel 01 42 66 26 85.

Cadolle
4 Rue Cambon 75001.
Map 6 D5.
Tel 01 42 60 94 22.

Erès
2 Rue Tronchet 75008.
Map 5 C5.
Tel 01 47 42 28 82.
W eresparis.com
One of several branches.

Fifi Chachnil
68 Rue Jean-Jacques
Rousseau 75001.
Map 12 F2.
Tel 01 42 21 19 93.
W fifichachnil.com

Princesse Tam Tam
5 Rue Montmartre 75001.
Map 13 A1.
Tel 01 45 08 47 52.
One of several branches.

Sabbia Rosa
73 Rue des Sts-Pères
75006. **Map** 12 D4.
Tel 01 45 48 88 37.

Gifts and Souvenirs

Paris has a wealth of stylish gifts and typical souvenirs, from designer accessories and perfume to French foods and Eiffel Tower paperweights. Stores on the Rue de Rivoli and around major tourist attractions such as Notre-Dame or Sacré-Coeur offer a range of cheap holiday trinkets. Les Drapeaux de France sells historic uniformed and costumed figurines. For upscale mementos, try quality reproductions of artwork and jewelry in museum boutiques – the Musée du Louvre, Musée d'Orsay, Les Arts Décoratifs, or Musée Carnavalet.

Gifts

Printemps has excellent own-brand accessories, especially ladies' purses. The luxury floor is ideal for window-shopping or high-end purchases such as Tiffany jewelry or Cartier watches. It also stocks small, reasonably priced items.

For those wanting to take home gastronomic tasters, the famed food hall at **Le Bon Marché**, La Grande Epicerie, offers anything and everything you might need for a gourmet feast or quick snack.

Galeries Lafayette now boasts the world's biggest lingerie department.

Perfume and Cosmetics

Many stores advertise discounted perfume and cosmetics. Some, like **Buly 1803**, even offer duty-free perfume to shoppers from outside the EU, with discounts on the marked prices when you show your passport. The **Sephora** chain has a big selection, or try the department stores for a range of designers' perfumes. In particular, the beauty department at **Printemps** (see p313) is one of Europe's biggest, with one of the world's largest perfume selections. It stocks many beauty brands that are hard to find elsewhere.

If you fancy stepping back in time, **Detaille 1905** is the place for you. This old-fashioned perfumery filled to the brim with fragrant goodies personifies Belle Epoque style and charm. The store's own range of six main fragrances for women and for men is still made from original recipes.

Parfums Caron also has many scents created over 100 years ago, which are unavailable elsewhere, so this is the place to find exclusive presents that you will almost certainly decide to keep for yourself. Beautifully packaged perfumes made from natural essences are available from **Annick Goutal**. **Guerlain** has the ultimate in beauty care, while the elegant stores of **L'Artisan Parfumeur** specialize in exquisitely packaged scents that evoke specific memories. They have also reissued favorites from the past, including perfume made to exactly the same formula as one that was worn at the court of Versailles. Famed perfume-maker **Fragonard** sells an array of scents, soaps, and candles from the South of France. **Frédéric Malle** is another big name in top-of-the-range scent. Exclusive perfumes can also be found in the beautiful surroundings of the gardens of the Palais-Royal at **Serge Lutens**. Lutens, the company's creative director and a renowned parfumier, creates exquisite and exotic scents which can only be bought in this particular store.

Paris is also home to several *haute* cosmetics designers. One of the most renowned is Terry de Gunzberg, whose store **By Terry** stocks fantastic products. Personalize your gift by having a message inscribed on the sleek, silver packaging.

Household Goods

Though certain items are obviously rather delicate to carry home, it is difficult to ignore some of the world's most elegant tableware, found in Paris's chic stores. If you are wary of loading up your holdall with breakable pieces, many stores will arrange to ship crockery overseas. Luxury household goods can be found on the Rue Royale, where many of the best stores are located. They sell items such as rustic china and reproduction and modern silverware. **Lalique's** Art Nouveau and Art Deco glass sculptures are collected all over the world. Impeccable silverware, including fine photograph frames and even chopsticks, comes from **Christofle**.

For a great variety of porcelain and crystal, try **La Cristallerie Paradis**, which stocks Baccarat, Daum, and Limoges crystal, or go to **Baccarat** itself. Baccarat also has a boutique on the Place de la Madeleine. The interior designer **Pierre Frey** has a showroom displaying fabrics that have been made into a fabulous array of cushions, bedspreads, and tablecloths. Excellent quality bed linen can also be found at **Yves Delorme**.

Eiffel Tower cheese graters, porcelain doll umbrellas, and dog-shaped pie-cutters add just the right amount of kitsch to any gift from design store **Pylones**. **La Chaise Longue** has a selection of well-designed *objets*, along with fun gift ideas. **Sengtai** sells stylish, ethically and ecologically produced tableware and decorative items. **Storie Shop** and **Muskhane** stock hip and ethnic accessories for funky apartments. The extensive interior design store at **Galeries Lafayette** (see p313) has every-thing a proud homeowner could need, from fancy mops to cutting-edge living room sets. **Sentou** stores are full of chic designer pieces for Parisian living. Sentou Raspail, on the Left Bank, offers the store's complete range while Sentou Marais focuses on lighting and furniture.

Kitchen equipment which can't be beaten, including copper pans, comes from

E Dehillerin. A must-have item in many Parisian homes is a scented candle from **Diptyque**. *Figuier* is their most popular fragrance. The basement at **BHV** *(see p313)* is full of all sorts of tools and equipment for fixing up your house and sprucing up the garden.

Books, Magazines, and Newspapers

Many American and English publications can be found at large magazine stands or at some of the bookstores listed. If French is no obstacle, the weeklies *Pariscope*, *L'Officiel des Spectacles*, and *Télérama's* Paris supplement *Sortir* have the most comprehensive listings for the city.

The *International Herald Tribune*, an English-language daily newspaper, is published in Paris and contains good American news coverage. The *Paris Voice* webzine and the bi-weekly FUSAC (*France–USA Contacts* small ads magazine) are also published in English.

Some of the large department stores have a book section *(see Department Stores p313)*. There is a large branch of **WHSmith**, and **Galignani** was the first English bookstore to be established in Europe in 1801. The **San Francisco Book Company** offers English-language books at good prices and **Shakespeare & Co.** is a Left Bank legend facing Notre-

Dame. The **Abbey Bookshop** has a good selection of literary and academic secondhand books. **L'Emile** is a small children's bookstore stocking both French and English titles.

French-language bookstores include **Librarie La Hune**, specializing in art, design, architecture, photography, fashion, and cinema; **Gibert Joseph**, selling general and educational books; and **Le Divan**, which has social science, psychology, literature, and poetry sections. **I Love My Blender** on Rue du Temple is dedicated to English-language authors and sells wonderful gifts.

Flowers

Some Parisian florists, such as **Pascal Mutel**, are very well known, so be sure to buy one of their signature vases. **Monceau Fleurs** offers a good selection at reasonable prices; **Jacques Semer** is the place to go to in Montmartre. *(See also Specialty Stores, below.)* Stunning silk flowers can be found at **Sia**, a chic store that brims over with beautiful artifical blooms.

Specialty Stores

For cigars, **A La Civette** is perhaps Paris's most beautiful tobacconist. It is also probably the most devoted to its wares and has humidified store windows to keep its

merchandise in top condition. Go to **A L'Olivier** in the Rue de Rivoli for a wonderful selection of exotic oils and vinegar. Or, if honey is your favorite condiment, try **La Maison du Miel**, where you can buy all sorts of fine honeys, including varieties made from lavender and acacia flowers. You can also buy refreshing beeswax soap and a variety of candles here.

Mariage Frères has become a cult favorite for its 350 varieties of tea; it also sells teapots, and its tea shop serves up tempting treats *(see p310)*.

Couture fabrics can be purchased from a range at **Wolff et Descourtis**. For an unusual gift of traditional French card games or tarot cards, go to **Jeux Descartes**.

La Grande Recré is a chain of toystores, while the name **Armorial** is synonymous with high-quality stationery and paper products. **Calligrane** sells a tempting range of high-quality desk accessories and paper products.

Hidden away down an atmospheric passage, **Pep's** repairs all broken umbrellas and parasols in France's only brolly hospital.

Finally, for the ultimate in eccentric shopping, pay a visit to **Deyrolle**, Paris's famous taxidermist. Where else could you find the right gift for the person who has everything?

DIRECTORY

Souvenir and Museum Stores

Les Arts Décoratifs
107 Rue de Rivoli 75001.
Map 12 D1. **Tel** 01 42 60 64 64/64 95 (for books).

Les Drapeaux de France
1 Pl Colette 75001.
Map 12 E2.
Tel 01 40 20 00 11.

Musée Carnavalet
(See p97).

Musée du Louvre
(See p123).

Musée d'Orsay
(See p147).

Gifts

Le Bon Marché
24 Rue de Sèvres
75007.
Map 11 C5.
Tel 01 44 39 80 00.

Galeries Lafayette
40 Blvd Haussmann
75009.
Map 6 E4.
Tel 01 42 82 34 56.
One of two branches.

Printemps
64 Blvd Haussmann
75009. **Map** 6 D4.
Tel 01 42 82 50 00.

Perfume and Cosmetics

Annick Goutal
16 Rue de Bellechasse
75007. **Map** 11 C3.
Tel 01 45 51 36 13.
One of several branches.

L'Artisan Parfumeur
24 Blvd Raspail 75007.
Map 16 D1. **Tel** 01 42 22 23 32. Several branches.

Buly 1803
6 Rue Bonaparte
75006.
Map 12 E3.
Tel 01 43 29 02 50.

By Terry
36 Galerie Vérot-Dodat
75001.
Map 12 F2.
Tel 01 44 76 00 76.

Detaille 1905
10 Rue St.-Lazare
75009.
Map 6 D3.
Tel 01 48 78 68 50.

DIRECTORY

Fragonard
203 Rue St. Honoré
75001. **Map** 12 D1.
Tel 01 47 03 07 07.
W fragonard.com

Frédéric Malle
21 Rue du Mont Thabor
75001. **Map** 12 D1.
Tel 01 42 22 16 89.

Guerlain
68 Ave des Champs-
Elysées 75008. **Map** 4 F5.
Tel 01 45 62 52 57.
W guerlain.com
One of several branches.

Parfums Caron
34 Ave Montaigne
75008. **Map** 10 F1.
Tel 01 47 23 40 82.
W parfumscaron.com

Sephora
70–72 Ave des Champs-
Elysées 75008. **Map** 11 B1.
Tel 01 53 93 22 50.
W sephora.fr
One of several branches.

Serge Lutens
Palais-Royal, 142 Galerie
de Valois 75001.
Map 12 F1.
Tel 01 49 27 09 09
or 01 83 77 77 01.
W sergelutens.com

Household Goods

Baccarat
11 Pl des Etats-Unis 75116.
Map 4 D5. **Tel** 01 40 22 11
22. W baccarat.fr
(See also p204).

La Chaise Longue
30 Rue Croix-des-Petits-
Champs 75001. **Map** 12
F1. **Tel** 01 42 96 32 14.
One of several branches.

Christofle
24 Rue de la Paix 75002.
Map 6 D5. **Tel** 01 42 65 62
43. W christofle.com
One of several branches.

La Cristallerie Paradis
17 bis Rue de Paradis
75010. **Map** 7 B4.
Tel 01 47 70 20 54.

Diptyque
34 Blvd St.-Germain
75005. **Map** 13 B5.
Tel 01 43 26 77 44.
W diptyqueparis.com
One of several branches.

E Dehillerin
18-20 Rue Coquillière
75001. **Map** 12 F1.
Tel 01 42 36 53 13.
W e-dehillerin.fr

Lalique
11 Rue Royale 75008.
Map 5 C5.
Tel 01 53 05 12 81.
W lalique.com

Muskhane
3 Rue Pastourelle 75003.
Map 13 C2.
Tel 09 77 06 53 47.
W muskhane.com

Pierre Frey
1 & 2 Rue Furstenberg
75006. **Map** 12 E4.
Tel 01 46 33 73 00.
W pierrefrey.com

Pylones
57 Rue St. Louis en L'Ile
75004. **Map** 13 B4.
Tel 01 40 51 75 33.
W pylones.com
One of several branches.

Sengtai
6 Rue du Pont aux Choux,
75003. **Map** 14 D2.
Tel 09 82 38 43 58.

Sentou
26 Blvd Raspail 75007.
Map 12 D4.
Tel 01 45 49 00 05.
29 Rue François Miron
75004. **Map** 13 C3.
Tel 01 42 78 50 60.

Storie Shop
20 Rue Delambre 75014.
Map 16 D2.
Tel 01 83 56 01 98.
W storieshop.com

Yves Delorme
8 Rue Vavin 75006. **Map**
16 D1. **Tel** 01 44 07 23 14.
W yvesdelorme.com

Books, Magazines, and Newspapers

Abbey Bookshop
29 Rue de la
Parcheminerie 75005.
Map 13 A4.
Tel 01 46 33 16 24.

Le Divan
203 Rue de la Convention
75015. **Map** 12 E3.
Tel 01 53 68 90 68.
W librairie-ledivan.
com

L'Emile
136 Ave Emile Zola 75015.
Map 10 D5.
Tel 01 45 75 16 15.

Galignani
224 Rue de Rivoli 75001.
Map 13 A2.
Tel 01 42 60 76 07.
W galignani.com

Gibert Joseph
26–34 Blvd St.-Michel
75006. **Map** 12 F5.
Tel 01 44 41 88 88.
W gibertjoseph.com

I Love My Blender
36 Rue du Temple
75004. **Map** 13 C2.
Tel 01 42 77 50 32.

Librairie La Hune
16–18 Rue de l'Abbaye
75006. **Map** 12 E4.
Tel 01 45 48 35 85.

San Francisco Book Company
17 Rue M le Prince
75006. **Map** 12 F5.
Tel 01 43 29 15 70.

Shakespeare & Co.
37 Rue de la Bûcherie
75005. **Map** 13 A4.
Tel 01 43 25 40 93.
W shakespeareand
company.com

WHSmith
248 Rue de Rivoli 75001.
Map 11 C1. **Tel** 01 44 77
88 99. W whsmith.fr

Flowers

Jacques Semer
56 Rue Caulaincourt
75018. **Map** 2 E5.
Tel 01 42 23 53 04.
W jacquessemer.com

Monceau Fleurs
104 Rue Monge 75005.
Map 17 B2.
Tel 01 47 07 17 94.
One of several branches.
W monceaufleurs.com

Pascal Mutel
95 Rue de Courcelles
75017. **Map** 4 E2.
Tel 01 47 63 40 78.
W pascalmutel.com

Sia
3–5 Blvd Malesherbes
75008. **Map** 5 C5.
Tel 01 42 66 11 73.
W sia-homefashion.fr

Specialty Stores

Armorial
109 Blvd Haussmann
75008. **Map** 5 B4. **Tel** 01 42
60 20 08. W armorial.fr

Calligrane
6 Rue du Pont-Louis-
Philippe 75004. **Map** 13
B4. **Tel** 01 48 04 09 00.
W calligrane.fr

A La Civette
157 Rue St.-Honoré 75001.
Map 12 F2. **Tel** 01 42 96
04 99. W la-civette.fr

Deyrolle
46 Rue du Bac 75007.
Map 12 D3.
Tel 01 42 22 30 07.
W deyrolle.com

La Grande Recré
8–12 Rue d'Amsterdam
75009. **Map** 6 D3.
Tel 01 42 93 24 41.
W lagranderecre.fr
One of several branches.

Jeux Descartes
52 Rue des Ecoles 75005.
Map 13 A5.
Tel 01 43 26 79 83.
W jeux-descartes.fr

La Maison du Miel
24 Rue Vignon 75009.
Map 6 D5.
Tel 01 47 42 26 70.
W maisondumiel.fr

Mariage Frères
30 Rue du Bourg-Tibourg
75004. **Map** 13 C3.
Tel 01 42 72 28 11.
W mariagefreres.com
One of several branches.

A L'Olivier
23 Rue de Rivoli 75004.
Map 13 C3. **Tel** 01 48 04
86 59. W alolivier.com

Pep's
223 Rue St.-Martin 75003.
Map 8 E4. **Tel** 01 42 78 11
67. W peps-paris.com.fr

Wolff et Descourtis
18 Galerie Vivienne
75002. **Map** 12 F1.
Tel 01 42 61 80 84.

Food and Drink

Paris is as famous for food as it is for fashion. Gastronomic treats include *foie gras*, cold cuts from the *charcuterie*, cheese, and wine. Certain streets are so overflowing with food stores that you can put together a picnic for 20 in no time: try the Rue Montorgueil *(see p331)*. The Rue Rambuteau, running either side of the Pompidou Center, has a marvelous row of fishmongers, cheese delicatessens, and stores selling prepared foods. *(See also Bars, Tearooms, and Street Food pp309–11.)*

Bread and Cakes

There is a vast range of breads and pastries in France's capital. The *baguette* is often translated as "French bread"; a *bâtard* is similar but thicker, while a *ficelle* is thinner. A *fougasse* is a crusty, flat loaf made from *baguette* dough, often filled with onions, cheese, herbs, or spices. Since most French bread contains no fat, it goes stale quickly: the sooner you eat it, the better. The French would never eat day-old bread so be sure to be up in time to make it to the bakery for breakfast!

Croissants can be bought *ordinaire* or *au beurre* – the latter is flakier and more buttery. *Pain au chocolat* is a chocolate-filled pastry eaten for breakfast and *chausson aux pommes* is filled with apples. There are also pear, plum, and rhubarb variations. A *pain aux raisins* is a bread-like wheel filled with custard and raisins.

Poilâne sells perhaps the only bread in Paris known by the name of its baker (the late Lionel, brother of Max), and his hearty wholewheat bread is tremendously popular, with freshly baked loaves being jetted around the world to satisfy the cravings of certain movie stars. There are always long lines on the weekend and around 4pm when a fresh batch comes out of the oven.

Many think **Comptoir Gana** bakes the best bread in Paris. Thirty different kinds, including ingredients such as walnuts and fruit, are made in old-fashioned ovens.

Maison Kayser, a high-end chain bakery, produces a variety of artisan breads and baguettes including *pain au cèrèale* (multi-grain bread) and *pain d'amande* (almond bread), the owner's favorite.

It is very important to remember that every Parisian has a favorite neighborhood bakery, so when you are buying bread locally, simply choose the store with the longest lines.

Many of the Jewish delicatessens have the best ryes and the only pumpernickels in town. One of the best known is **Sacha Finkelsztajn**.

Le Moulin de la Vierge uses a wood fire to bake organic breads and rich pound cakes, while **Max Poilâne** in the Montparnasse area offers *pains classiques*, *baguettes*, *fougasses*, cakes, and pastries. **Pâtisserie Secco** sells a good selection of filled *baguettes*, salads, and excellent cakes. **Pierre Hermé** is to cakes what Chanel is to fashion, while the macaroons from **Ladurée** *(see p311)* are legendary. Guy Savoy has entered the *boulangerie* market to much acclaim with his **Goût de Brioche** store, specializing in the eponymous light sweet roll.

Chocolate

Like all food in France, chocolate is to be savored. **Christian Constant**'s low-sugar creations are made with pure cocoa and are known to connoisseurs. **Dalloyau** makes all types of chocolate and is not too expensive (it's also known for its pâtisserie and cold cuts). **Fauchon** is world famous for its luxury food products. Its chocolates are excellent, as is the pâtisserie.

Lenôtre makes classic truffles and pralines. Robert Linxe at **La Maison du Chocolat** is constantly inventing fresh, rich chocolates with mouth-watering exotic ingredients. **Richart** boasts beautifully presented and hugely expensive chocolates, which are usually coated with dark chocolate or liqueur-filled. **Debauve & Gallais** are best known for their wonderful and delicious glacé chestnut treats *(marron glacés)*.

Charcuterie and Foie Gras

Charcuteries often sell cheese, snails, truffles, smoked salmon, caviar, and wine as well as cold cuts. **Fauchon** has a good grocery, as does the department store **Le Bon Marché** *(see p323)*. **Hédiard** is a luxury store similar to Fauchon, and **Maison de la Truffe** sells *foie gras* and cured salami sausages as well as truffles. For Beluga caviar, Georgian tea, and Russian vodka, go to **Boutique Petrossian**.

Award-winning **Gilles Verot** is known for his *charcuterie*, which is also available in New York and London.

Maison Pou is a sparklingly clean and popular store selling *pâté en croute* (pâté baked in pastry), *boudins* (black and white puddings), Lyonnais sausages, ham, and *foie gras*. Just off the Champs-Elysées, **Vignon** has superb *foie gras* and Lyonnais sausages as well as popular prepared foods.

Together with truffles and caviar, *foie gras* is the ultimate in gourmet food, from cheaper *paté de foie gras* to the more expensive whole liver itself. Though most specialty food stores sell *foie gras*, you can be sure of quality at **Comtesse du Barry**, which has six outlets in Paris. **Divay** is relatively inexpensive and will ship overseas. **Comptoir de la Gastronomie** has a range of excellent *foie gras*.

Cheese

Although Camembert is undoubtedly a favorite, there is an overwhelming range of cheeses available.

A friendly *fromager* will help you choose. **Marie-Anne Cantin** is one of the leading figures in the fight to protect traditional production methods, and her fine cheeses are available at the store that she inherited from her father. Some say that **Alléosse** is the best cheese delicatessen in Paris. It is an Aladdin's cave of cheeses made according to traditional methods and matured in the store's own cellars. **Fromagerie Quatrehomme** sells farm-made cheeses, many of which are in danger of becoming extinct; these include a rare and delicious truffle Brie (when in season). **Le Jardin Fromager** is one of the best stores in Paris for all types of cheese – the *chèvre* (goat's cheese) is particularly good, and outside on the sidewalk, the daily specials are offered at remarkably reasonable prices. **Laurent Dubois**, a cheesemaker on the Boulevard St.-Germain, is known for his specialty, marinated goat cheese. **Androuet** is a Parisian institution with several branches across the city. Try a pungent Munster or a really ripe Brie. A charming cheese store on the bustling Rue Montorgueil market street, **La Fermette**, offers a dazzling array of dairy products, which the helpful and friendly staff will happily vacuum-pack for the journey home. This is imperative when bringing cheese through customs, so don't forget to ask your *fromager* to wrap it for you. Well-heeled locals line up in the street to buy oozing *livarot* and sharp *chèvre* from **La Fromagerie d'Auteuil**.

Wine

The chain store which has practically cornered the everyday tippling market is **Nicolas** – there's a branch in every neighborhood with a range of wines to suit all pockets. As a rule, the salespeople are knowledgeable and helpful. Try the charming **Legrand Filles et Fils** for a carefully chosen selection. **Caves Taillevent** on the Rue du Faubourg-St.-Honoré is worth a sightseeing tour. It is an enormous, overwhelming cellar with some of the most expensive wines. **Cave Péret** on the Rue Daguerre has a vast selection of wines and can offer personal advice. The beautiful **Ryst-Dupeyron**, in the St.-Germain quarter, displays whiskies, wines, ports, and Monsieur Ryst's own Armagnac. He will even personalize a bottle for that special occasion.

Other great wine stores include **La Cave des Papilles**, one of the best suppliers of organic wines in the capital. The salespeople in **Les Caves Augé** are also very knowledgeable and friendly.

Champagne

Fabulous fizz can be found at most wine stores, but some know their bubbles better than others. The **Nicolas** chain, mentioned above, frequently has great offers on well-known brands, so this is a good place to come and stock up on your favorite famous tipple. **La Cave de la Villette**, on Rue Eugène Jumin, is a friendly and well-stocked wine shop with charming staff to help you with your selection. The **De Verre en Vers**, on the Rue d'Auteuil, is a good place to go for hard-to-find vintages. The *sommelier* here is very knowledgeable and able to provide excellent alternative advice if your preferred brand is out of stock. **Legrand Filles et Fils**, on the Rue de la Banque, is one of the few stores in Paris to stock Salon, a rare high-end champagne. They also sell champagne by Jacques Selosse, which is little-known but well-loved by champagne connoisseurs. **Les Caves du Panthéon**, on the Rue St.-Jacques, is a small but lovely wine store that has a particularly interesting selection of champagnes. **Le Repaire de Bacchus** is a Parisian chain renowned for the quality of its wines, including champagnes, and its knowledgeable staff. The climate-controlled section of **Hédiard** at Place de la Madeleine is a good place to find rare, fine sparkling wines. The upscale **Cave de la Grande Epicerie** has a fine selection of champagnes. A stroll along the Boulevard St.-Germain can be enhanced with a visit to **La Maison des Millésimes**, a wonderful store carrying excellent vintages of household-name champagnes.

Oysters

The ultimate aphrodisiac for some, a slippery sea creature for others, there is no doubt that the once humble oyster can cause heated debate. In Paris, the argument tends to be over the best place to purchase the gourmet mollusc, with every seafood fan worth his platter claiming a favorite spot. It is, of course, important to get it right. A deciding factor for some is the grace with which your fishmonger will agree to open them for you. In general, a polite request will be honored, although sometimes you may have to wait a while before being presented with a platter perfect for a picnic. The fishmonger on the Rue Cler market street, **La Sablaise Poissonnerie**, has an excellent reputation, as does the **Poissonnerie du Dôme** in the city's 14th arrondissement. Over in the traditionally rough-and-ready area around the Rue Oberkampf, you can find excellent oysters at the **Poissonnerie Lacroix**. If you prefer to eat your oysters on the spot, then head to an *huitrerie* (oyster bar) such as **L'Ecume St.-Honoré** near chic Rue St.-Honoré, where you can tuck into your oysters and a wide range of other shellfish straight away at the few tables tucked into the corner of the store.

DIRECTORY

Bread and Cakes

Comptoir Gana
226 Rue des Pyrénées
75020.
Tel 01 43 58 42 62.

Goût de Brioche
54 Rue Mazarine 75006.
Map 12 F4.
Tel 01 40 46 91 67.

Maison Kayser
8 & 14 Rue Monge 75005.
Map 13 B5.
Tel 01 44 07 01 42.
[W] maison-kayser.com

Max Poilâne
87 Rue Brancion 75015.
Tel 01 48 28 45 90.

Le Moulin de la Vierge
105 Rue Vercingétorix
75014. **Map** 15 A4.
Tel 01 45 43 09 84.

Pâtisserie Secco
75 Blvd de Grenelle 75007.
Map 10 D5.
Tel 01 45 67 17 40.

Pierre Hermé
72 Rue Bonaparte 75006.
Map 12 E4.
Tel 01 43 54 47 77.

Poilâne
8 Rue du Cherche-Midi
75006. **Map** 12 D4.
Tel 01 45 48 42 59.

Sacha Finkelsztajn
27 Rue des Rosiers 75004.
Map 13 C3.
Tel 01 42 72 78 91.

Chocolate

Christian Constant
37 Rue d'Assas 75006.
Map 16 E1.
Tel 01 53 63 15 15.

Dalloyau
101 Rue du Faubourg-St.-
Honoré 75008. **Map** 5 B5.
Tel 01 42 99 90 00.

Debauve & Gallais
30 Rue des Sts.-Pères
75007. **Map** 12 D4.
Tel 01 45 48 54 67
One of two branches.

Fauchon
24–26 & 30 Pl de la
Madeleine 75008. **Map** 5
C5. **Tel** 01 70 39 38 00/02.
[W] fauchon.com

Lenôtre

36 Ave de la Motte
Picquet 75007. **Map** 10
F4. **Tel** 01 45 55 71 25.
[W] lenotre.com
One of several branches

**La Maison du
Chocolat**
225 Rue du Faubourg-St.-
Honoré 75008. **Map** 4 E3.
Tel 01 42 27 39 44.

Richart
258 Blvd St-Germain
75007. **Map** 11 C2.
Tel 01 45 55 66 00.

Charcuterie and Foie Gras

Boutique Petrossian
18 Blvd La Tour-Maubourg
75007. **Map** 11 A2.
Tel 01 44 11 32 22.

**Comptoir de la
Gastronomie**
34 Rue Montmartre
75001. **Map** 13 A1.
Tel 01 42 33 31 32.

Comtesse du Barry
1 Rue de Sèvres 75006.
Map 12 D4. **Tel** 01 45 48
32 04. [W] comtesse
dubarry.com
One of several branches.

Divay
4 Rue Bayen 75017. **Map**
4 D2. **Tel** 01 43 80 16 97.

Fauchon
26 Pl de la Madeleine
75008. **Map** 5 C5.
Tel 01 70 39 38 00.

Gilles Verot
7 Rue Lecourbe 75015.
Tel 01 47 34 01 03.
[W] verot-charcuterie.fr

Hédiard
21 Pl de la Madeleine
75008. **Map** 5 C5.
Tel 01 43 12 88 88.

Maison Pou
16 Ave des Ternes
75017. **Map** 4 D3.
Tel 01 43 80 19 24.

Maison de la Truffe
19 Pl de la Madeleine
75008. **Map** 5 C5.
Tel 01 42 65 53 22.

Vignon
13 Rue Clement Marot
75008. **Map** 4 F5.
Tel 01 47 20 10 01.

Cheese

Alléosse
13 Rue Poncelet 75017.
Map 4 E3.
Tel 01 46 22 50 45.

Androuet
134 Rue Mouffetard
75005. **Map** 17 B1.
Tel 01 45 87 85 05.
[W] androuet.com

La Fermette
86 Rue Montorgueil
75002. **Map** 13 A1.
Tel 01 42 36 70 96.

**La Fromagerie
d'Auteuil**
58 Rue d'Auteuil 75016.
Tel 01 45 25 07 10.

**Fromagerie
Quatrehomme**
62 Rue de Sèvres 75007.
Map 11 C5.
Tel 01 47 34 33 45.

Le Jardin Fromager
53 Rue Oberkampf
75011. **Map** 14 E1.
Tel 01 48 05 19 96.

Laurent Dubois
47 ter Blvd St-Germain
75005. **Map** 13 A5.
Tel 01 43 54 50 93.

Marie-Anne Cantin
12 Rue du Champ-de-
Mars 75007. **Map** 10 F3.
Tel 01 45 50 43 94.

Wine

La Cave des Papilles
5 Rue Daguerre 75014.
Map 16 D4.
Tel 01 43 20 05 74.

Cave Péret
6 Rue Daguerre 75014.
Map 16 D4.
Tel 01 43 22 57 05.

Les Caves Augé
116 Blvd Haussmann
75008. **Map** 5 C4.
Tel 01 45 22 16 97.

Caves Taillevent
228 Rue du Faubourg-
St.-Honoré 75008. **Map** 4
F3. **Tel** 01 45 61 14 09.

Legrand Filles et Fils
1 Rue de la Banque
75002. **Map** 12 F1.
Tel 01 42 60 07 12.

Nicolas

35 Blvd Malesherbes
75008. **Map** 5 C5.
Tel 01 42 65 00 85.

Ryst-Dupeyron
79 Rue du Bac 75007.
Map 12 D3.
Tel 09 54 39 72 78.

Champagne

**La Cave de la Grande
Epicerie**
38 Rue de Sèvres 75007.
Map 11 C5.
Tel 01 44 39 81 00.

La Cave de la Villette
21 Rue Eugène Jumin
75019. **Tel** 09 86 28 00 11.

**Les Caves du
Panthéon**
174 Rue St-Jacques
75005. **Map** 13 A5.
Tel 01 46 33 90 35.

De Verre en Vers
1 Rue de Joseph de
Maistre 75018.
Tel 01 46 06 80 84.

Hédiard
21 Pl de la Madeleine
75008. **Map** 5 C5.
Tel 01 43 12 88 88.

**La Maison des
Millésimes**
137 Blvd St-Germain
75006. **Map** 12 F4.
Tel 01 40 46 80 01.

Le Repaire de Bacchus
112 Rue de Mouffetard
75005. **Map** 17 B2.
Tel 01 47 07 39 40.
One of several branches.

Oysters

L'Ecume St-Honoré
6 Rue du Marché St.-
Honoré 75001. **Map** 12
D1. **Tel** 01 42 61 93 87.

Poissonnerie du Dôme
4 Rue Delambre 75014.
Map 16 D2.
Tel 01 43 35 23 95.

Poissonnerie Lacroix
44 Rue Oberkampf 75011.
Map 14 E1.
Tel 01 47 00 93 13.

La Sablaise
28 Rue Cler 75007. **Map**
10 F3. **Tel** 01 45 51 61 78.

Art and Antiques

In Paris, you can buy art and antiques either from shops and galleries with established reputations, or from flea markets and avant-garde galleries. Many of the prestigious antiques shops and galleries are located around the Rue du Faubourg-St.-Honoré and are worth a visit even if you can't afford to buy. On the Left Bank is Le Carré Rive Gauche, an organization of 30 antiques dealers. *Objets d'art* over 50 years old, worth more than a given amount (values vary for all categories of art object), will require a *Certificat pour un bien culturel* to be exported anywhere in the world (provided by the vendor), plus a *licence d'exportation* for non-EU countries. Seek professional advice from the large antiques shops.

Exporting

The Ministry of Culture designates *objets d'art*. Export licences are available from the **Comité National des Conseillers du Commerce Extérieur de la France**. The **Centre des Renseignements des Douanes** has a booklet, *Bulletin Officiel des Douanes*, with all the details.

Modern Crafts and Furniture

One of the best places for furniture and *objets d'art* is **Sentou** (*see pp322 and 324*), where you can find objects and textiles, as well as furniture by contemporary designers. Another essential venue is the showroom of the Italian designer **Giulio Cappellini**. **Le Viaduc des Arts** (*see pp274–5*) is a railroad viaduct, each arch of which has been transformed into a storefront and workshop space. It's a great place for contemporary metalwork, tapestry, sculpture, ceramics, and much more.

Antiques and Objets d'Art

If you wish to buy antiques, you might like to stroll around the areas that boast many galleries – in Le Carré Rive Gauche and Quai Malaquais, try **L'Arc en Seine** and **Anne-Sophie Duval** for Art Nouveau and Art Deco. Rue Jacob is still one of the best places to seek beautiful objects, antique or modern.

Close to the Louvre, the **Louvre des Antiquaires** (*see p130*) sells expensive, quality furniture. On Rue du Faubourg-St.-Honoré, you will find **Didier Aaron**, expert on furniture from the 17th and 18th centuries. **Village St.-Paul**, between the Quai des Célestins, the Rue St.-Paul, and the Rue Charlemagne, is the most charming group of antiques shops and is also open on Sundays.

Philippe de Beauvais focuses on antique lighting fixtures, especially chandeliers. **Le Village Suisse** in the south of the city also groups many art and antiques dealers. Located in Le Village Suisse, **Ghislaine Chaplier** carries an eclectic inventory of small antiques and rare glass objects.

Reproductions, Posters, and Prints

A beautiful, contemporary art gallery called **Artcurial** on the Rond Point des Champs-Elysées has one of the best selections of international art periodicals, books, and prints. On Rue St.-Sulpice, **J C Martinez** is a popular place for sketches, reproductions, prints and old engravings. The museum bookstores, especially those in the Palais de Tokyo (*see p205*), Louvre (*see p123*), Musée d'Orsay (*see p147*), and Pompidou Center (*see p111*) are good places to buy art books, posters, and postcards.

Galerie Documents on the Rue de Seine sells original antique posters. Or leaf through the secondhand book stands along the banks of the Seine.

Art Galleries

Established art galleries are located on or around the Avenue Montaigne.

Artcurial Gallery, located on the ground floor of the Hôtel Dassault, holds regular exhibitions and specializes in limited editions of contemporary sculpture, photography, prints, and multiples. **Galerie Lelong** is devoted to contemporary artists. The **Fondation Cartier** space is far from the crowds, in the 14th arrondissement. The garden surrounding the glass building adds an extra dimension to the gallery's mix of contemporary sculpture, urban art, and performing arts.

On the Left Bank, **Galerie Maeght** has a tremendous stock of paintings at prices to suit most budgets; it also publishes fine art books. **Galerie 1900–2000** specializes in works by Surrealist and Dada artists, and **Galerie Jeanne Bucher** represents postwar Abstraction with artists like Nicolas de Staël and Vieira da Silva. **Dina Vierny** is a bastion of Modernism, founded by sculptor Aristide Maillol's famous model of the same name. Rue Louise Weiss, in the east of Paris, is home to the **Air de Paris** gallery. In the Marais, try **Yvon Lambert**, **Galerie Daniel Templon** – specializing in American art, **Galerie Sit Down**, **Galerie Bernard Jordan**, and **Galerie du Jour Agnès B**. In the same area, **Galerie Florence Loewy** is a fashionable place to buy catalogues on new artists, if not their actual works.

Auctions and Auction Houses

The great Paris auction center, in operation since 1858, is **Drouot** (*see p220*). Bidding can be intimidating since most of it is done by dealers. Beware of the auctioneer's high-speed patter. *La Gazette de L'Hôtel Drouot* tells you what auctions are coming up.

Drouot has its own auction catalogue as well. The house only accepts cash and French checks, but there is an exchange desk on site. A 10–15 per cent commission to the house is charged, so bear this in mind and add it on to any price you hear. You may view from 11am to 6pm on the day before the sale, and from 11am to noon on the morning of the sale. Items considered not good enough for the main house are sold at Drouot Montmartre. Here, auctions take place from 9am to noon and viewing is just five minutes before the sales begin. Exhibits and events are held at their **12-Drouot** space.

The **Crédit Municipal** holds around 12 auctions a month, and almost all the items on sale are small objects and furs offloaded by rich Parisians. The rules follow those at Drouot. Information can also be found in *La Gazette de L'Hôtel Drouot*.

Service des Domaines sells all sorts of odds and ends, and here you can still find bargains. Many of the wares come from bailiffs and from Customs and Excise *(see p358)* confiscations. Viewing is from 10am to 11.30am on the day of the sale in St.-Maurice, southeast of the city.

DIRECTORY

Exporting

Centre des Renseignements des Douanes
Tel 08 11 20 44 44.
W douane.gouv.fr

Comité National des Conseillers du Commerce Extérieur de la France
22 Ave Franklin Roosevelt 75008. **Map** 5 A4.
Tel 01 53 83 92 92.
W cnccef.org

Modern Crafts and Furniture

Giulio Cappellini
242 Bis Blvd St.-Germain 75007. **Map** 12 D3.
Tel 01 42 84 03 78.
W cappellini.it

Sentou
26 Blvd Raspail 75007.
Map 12 D4.
Tel 01 45 49 00 05.
29 Rue François Miron 75004. **Map** 13 C3.
Tel 01 42 78 50 60.

Le Viaduc des Arts
1–129 Ave Daumesnil 75012. **Map** 14 F5.
Tel 01 71 18 75 68.
This comprises a series of shops on the Avenue.

Antiques and Objets d'Art

Anne-Sophie Duval
5 Quai Malaquais 75006.
Map 12 E3.
Tel 01 43 54 51 16.
W annesophie duval.com

L'Arc en Seine
31 Rue de Seine 75006.
Map 12 E3.
Tel 01 43 29 11 02.

Didier Aaron
152 Blvd Haussmann 75008. **Map** 5 B4.
Tel 01 47 42 47 34.
W didieraaron.com

Ghislaine Chaplin
Le Village Suisse, Gallery No. 65 Place de Zurich, 10 Ave de Champaubert 75015. **Map** 10 E5.
Tel 01 45 67 30 55 or 06 80 23 02 10.

Louvre des Antiquaires
2 Pl du Palais-Royal 75001.
Map 12 F2.
Tel 01 42 97 27 27.

Philippe de Beauvais
43–45 Ave Bosquet 75007. **Map** 10 F3.
Tel 01 47 63 20 72.

Village St-Paul
Between the Quai des Célestins, the Rue St.-Paul and the Rue Charlemagne 75004. **Map** 13 C4.

Le Village Suisse
54 Ave de la Motte-Picquet and 78 Ave de Suffren 75015. **Map** 10 E4.
Tel 01 73 79 15 41.
W levillagesuisseparis.com

Reproductions, Posters, & Prints

Artcurial Gallery
(See Art Galleries).

Galerie Documents
53 Rue de Seine 75006.
Map 12 E4.
Tel 01 43 54 50 68.

J C Martinez
21 Rue St.-Sulpice 75006.
Map 12 E4.
Tel 01 43 26 34 53.

Art Galleries

Air de Paris
32 Rue Louise Weiss 75013. **Map** 18 E4.
Tel 01 44 23 02 77.

Artcurial Gallery
7 Rond Point des Champs-Elysées 75008.
Map 5 A5.
Tel 01 42 99 20 20.

Dina Vierny
36 Rue Jacob 75006. **Map** 12 E3. **Tel** 01 42 60 23 18.

Fondation Cartier
261 Blvd Raspail 75014.
Map 16 E3.
Tel 01 42 18 56 50.

Galerie 1900–2000
8 Rue Bonaparte 75006.
Map 12 E3.
Tel 01 43 25 84 20.

Galerie Bernard Jordan
77 Rue Charlot 75003.
Map 14 D1. **Tel** 01 42 77 19 61.

Galerie Daniel Templon
30 Rue Beaubourg 75003.
Map 13 B1.
Tel 01 42 72 14 10.

Galerie Florence Loewy
9 Rue de Thorigny 75003.
Map 14 D2.
Tel 01 44 78 98 45.

Galerie Jeanne Bucher
53 Rue de Seine 75006.
Map 12 E4.
Tel 01 44 41 69 65.

Galerie du Jour Agnès B
44 Rue Quincampoix 75004. **Map** 13 B2.
Tel 01 44 54 55 90.

Galerie Lelong
13 Rue de Téhéran 75008. **Map** 5 A3.
Tel 01 45 63 13 19.

Galerie Maeght
42 Rue du Bac 75007. **Map** 12 D3. **Tel** 01 45 48 45 15.

Galerie Sit Down
4 Rue Sainte-Anastase 75003. **Map** 14 D2.
Tel 01 42 78 08 07.

Yvon Lambert
108 Rue Vieille du Temple 75003. **Map** 14 D2.
Tel 01 42 71 89 05.

Auction Houses

12-Drouot
12 Rue Drouot 75009.
Map 6 F4.
Tel 01 48 00 20 00.
W drouot.fr

Crédit Municipal
55 Rue des Francs-Bourgeois 75004.
Map 13 C3.
Tel 01 44 61 64 00/65 00.
W creditmunicipal.fr

Drouot
9 Rue Drouot 75009.
Map 6 F4.
Tel 01 48 00 20 20.
Montmartre:
64 Rue Doudeauville 75018.
Tel 01 48 00 20 99.

Service des Domaines
Tel 01 45 11 62 62.

Markets

For eye-catching displays of wonderful food and a lively atmosphere, there is no better place to shop than a Paris market. There are large covered food markets; markets where stands change regularly; and permanent street markets with a mixture of stores and stands that are open on a daily basis. Each has its own personality reflecting the area in which it is located. A list of some of the more famous markets, with approximate opening times, follows. For a complete list of markets, contact the Paris Office du Tourisme *(see p359)*. And while you're enjoying browsing round the stands, remember to keep an eye on your purse. Bargaining is not automatic, but you might be able to negotiate near closing time.

Fruit and Vegetable Markets

The French treat food with the kind of reverence usually reserved for religion. Many people still shop on a daily basis to be sure of buying the freshest produce possible, so food markets tend to be busy. The majority of fruit and vegetable markets are open from around 8am to 1pm and from 4pm to 7pm Tuesday to Saturday, and from 9am to 1pm on Sunday.

Buy produce loose rather than in boxes, but keep a close eye on what the vendor puts in your bag. Most outdoor vendors prefer to serve you rather than allow you to handle the produce yourself, but don't be afraid to point to the individual fruit and vegetables of your choice. Your connoisseurship will be respected. A little language is useful for specifying *pas trop mur* (not too ripe), or *pour manger ce soir* (to be eaten tonight). If you go to the same market every day, you'll become familiar to the vendors and will be less likely to be fobbed off with the occasional "reject" fruit or vegetable. You will also get to know the stands worth buying from and the produce that's worth buying. Seasonal fruit and vegetables are, of course, usually a good buy, tending to be fresher and cheaper than at other times of the year. Finally, it is best to shop at markets early in the day when the food is freshest and the lines are shortest.

Flea Markets

It's often said that you can no longer find bargains at the Paris flea markets. Though this may be true, it's still worth going to one for the sheer fun of browsing. And bear in mind that the price quoted is not the one that you are expected to pay – it is generally assumed that you will bargain. Most flea markets are located on the city's boundaries. Whether you pick up any real bargains has as much to do with luck as with judgement, and may depend on whether the seller knows the true value of their goods. The biggest, busiest, and most famous market, incorporating several smaller specialty ones, is the Marché aux Puces de St.-Ouen. Be sure to keep your eye on your wallet, as pickpockets frequent these markets.

Specialty Markets

Try the Marché aux Fleurs Madeleine, the Marché aux Fleurs Reine Elizabeth II *(see p87)*, or the Marché aux Fleurs Ternes in the Champs-Elysées district for fresh flowers. On the Ile de la Cité on Sundays, the Marché aux Oiseaux bird market replaces the flower market. Stamp collectors will enjoy the permanent Marché aux Timbres, where you can also buy old postcards. In Montmartre, the large Marché St.-Pierre, spread over six stories, is famous for inexpensive fabrics and is patronized by professional designers and dressmakers.

Marché d'Aligre

(See p237.)

Built in 1779, this lively covered market is one of the cheapest in the city. Here, traders hawk ingredients such as North African olives, groundnuts, and hot peppers and there are even a few halal butchers. The noise reaches a crescendo on weekends when the cries of the market boys mingle with those of militants of all political persuasions as the latter petition and protest in the Place d'Aligre. The stands on the square sell mostly secondhand clothes and bric-à-brac. This is a trendy, Bohemian area of town with few tourists and many Parisians.

Rue Cler

(See p192.)

This high-class, pedestrian-only food market is patronized mainly by the politicians and captains of industry who live and work in the vicinity, so it's good for people-spotting! The produce is excellent – there's a Breton delicatessen and some good *fromageries*.

Marché des Enfant Rouges

39 Rue de Bretagne 75003. **Map** *14 D2.* Ⓜ *Temple, Filles-du-Calvaire.* **Open** *8.30am–1pm, & 4–7.30pm Tue– Sat (to 8pm Fri, Sat); 8.30am–2pm Sun.*

This long-established, charming fruit and vegetable market on the Rue de Bretagne is part covered, part outdoors and dates from 1620. The produce is famous for its freshness, and there are cheap eateries too. On Sunday mornings, there are sometimes street performers and accordionists.

Marché aux Fleurs Madeleine

Pl de la Madeleine 75008. **Map** 5 C5. Ⓜ Madeleine. **Open** 8am–7.30pm Mon–Sat.

Marché aux Fleurs Ternes

Pl des Ternes 75017. **Map** 4 E3. Ⓜ Ternes. **Open** 8am–7.30pm Tue–Sun.

Marché St.-Pierre

Pl St.-Pierre 75018. **Map** 6 F1. Ⓜ Anvers. **Open** 10am–6.30pm Mon–Fri, 10am–7pm Sat.

Marché aux Timbres

Ave Marigny 75008. **Map** 5 B5. Ⓜ Champs-Elysées–Clemenceau. **Open** 9am–7pm Thu, Sat, Sun & public hols.

Marché Joinville

Corner of Rue Jomard and Rue de Joinville 75019. **M** *Crimée.* **Open** *7am–2.30pm Thu & Sun.*

This lively canalside market is known for its cheap fruit and vegetables. It is located on the Canal d'Ourcq, near the Parc de la Villette, and is always teeming with shoppers.

Marché St.-Germain

4–6 Rue Lobineau 75006. **Map** *12 E4.* **M** Mabillon. **Open** *8am–1pm & 4–8pm Tue–Fri; 8.30am–1.30pm & 3.30–8pm Sat; 8am–1.30pm Sun.*

St.-Germain is one of the few covered markets left in Paris and has been enhanced by renovation. Here, you can buy Italian, Mexican, Greek, Asian, and organic produce and other goods.

Rue de Lévis

75017. **Map** *5 B2.* **M** *Villiers.* **Open** *10am–7.30pm Tue–Sat, 10am–1pm Sun.*

Rue de Lévis is a bustling, popular food market near the Parc Monceau with an excellent choice of good pâtisseries, an excellent cheese delicatessen and a *charcuterie* which is known for its savory pies. The part of the street that leads to Rue Legendre sells haberdashery and fabrics. The stores on this pedestrian-only street also have stands outside selling their wares.

Rue Montorgueil

75001 & 75002. **Map** *13 A1.* **M** *Les Halles.* **Open** *10am–6pm Mon–Sat, am only Sun (subject to change).*

The Rue Montorgueil is what remains of the old Les Halles market. The street has been repaved and restored to its former glory. Here, you can buy expensive, exotic fruit and vegetables like green bananas and yams from the market gardeners' stands. You can also sample the delicious offerings from the delicatessens or from the Stohrer pastry shop.

Rue Mouffetard

(See p168.)

Rue Mouffetard is one of the oldest market streets in Paris. Although it has become touristy and somewhat overpriced, it's still a charming winding street full of quality food products and street musicians. There is also a lively African market down the nearby side street of Rue Daubenton, and a number of fashion boutiques and bars in the area.

Rue Poncelet

75017. **Map** *4 E3.* **M** *Ternes.* **Open** *8am–1pm & 3–7.30pm Tue–Sat, 8am–1pm Sun.*

The Rue Poncelet food market is located away from the main tourist areas of Paris but is worth visiting for its authentic French atmosphere. Choose from the many bakeries, pâtisseries, or *charcuteries* or enjoy authentic Auvergne specialties from Aux Fermes d'Auvergnes.

Marché aux Puces de la Porte de Vanves

Ave Georges-Lafenestre & Ave Marc-Sangnier 75014. **M** *Porte-de-Vanves.* **Open** *7am–2pm Sat & Sun.*

Porte de Vanves is a small market selling good-quality bric-à-brac and junk as well as some secondhand furniture. It's best to get to the market early on Saturday morning for the best choice of wares. Artists exhibit nearby in the Place des Artistes.

Marché Président-Wilson

Located on Ave du Président-Wilson, between Pl d'Iéna & Rue Debrousse 75016. **Map** *10 D1.* **M** *Alma-Marceau.* **Open** *7am–2.30pm Wed, 7am–3pm Sat.*

This very chic food market on Avenue Président-Wilson is close to the Musée d'Art Moderne and the Palais Galliera fashion museum. It has become important because there are no other food stores nearby. It is best for meat.

Marché aux Puces de Montreuil

Porte de Montreuil, 93 Montreuil 75020. **M** *Mairie de Montreuil.* **Open** *7am–7.30pm Mon, Sat & Sun.*

Go early to the Porte de Montreuil flea market, where you'll have a better chance of picking up a bargain. The substantial secondhand clothes section attracts many young people. There's also a wide variety of items including used bicycles, bric-à-brac, and an exotic spices stand.

Marché aux Puces de St.-Ouen

(See pp248–9.)

This is the best known, the most crowded, and the most expensive of all the flea markets, located on the northern outskirts of the city. Here, you'll find a range of markets, locals dealing from their car trunks, and a number of extremely large buildings packed with stands. Some of them are very upscale, others sell junk. The

flea market is a 10–15-minute walk from Clignancourt Metro – don't be put off by the somewhat sleazy Marché Malik, which you have to pass through on your way from the Metro. A *Guide des Puces* (guide to the flea markets) can be obtained from the information kiosk in the Marché Biron on the Rue des Rosiers. The more exclusive markets will take credit cards and arrange for goods to be shipped home. New stock arrives on Friday, when professionals come from all over the world to sweep up the best buys.

Among the markets here, the Marché Jules Vallès is good for turn-of-the-19th-century *objets d'art*. Marché Paul-Bert is more expensive, but charming. Items on sale include furniture, books, and prints. Both markets deal in secondhand goods rather than antiques.

In a different league, Marché Biron sells elegant, expensive antique furniture of very high quality. Marché Vernaison is the oldest and biggest market, good for collectables such as jewelry as well as lamps and clothes. No information about the Marché aux Puces is complete without mentioning Chez Louisette in the Vernaison market. This café is always full of locals enjoying the home cooking and the well-intentioned renditions of Edith Piaf songs. Marché Cambo is a fairly small market with beautifully displayed antique furniture. Marché Serpette is popular with the dealers: everything sold here is in mint condition.

Marché Raspail

Located on Blvd Raspail between Rue du Cherche-Midi & Rue de Rennes 75006. **Map** *12 D5.* **M** *Rennes.* **Open** *7am–2.30pm Tue, Fri, 9am–2pm Sun.*

The Raspail market sells typical French groceries as well as Portuguese produce on Tuesdays and Fridays. But Sunday is the day for which it's famous, when health-conscious Parisians turn up in droves for the organically grown produce. Marché Raspail is not a cheap market, but it is very good.

Rue de Seine and Rue de Buci

75006. **Map** *12 E4.* **M** *Odéon.* **Open** *8am–1pm & 4–7pm Tue–Sat, 9am–1pm Sun.*

The stands here are expensive and crowded, but sell quality fruit and vegetables. There are also a large florist's and two excellent pâtisseries.

ENTERTAINMENT IN PARIS

Whether you prefer classical drama or cabaret, showgirls or ballet, opera or jazz, movies or dancing the night away, Paris has it all. Free entertainment is aplenty as well, from the street performers outside the Pompidou Center to musicians in the Metro. Parisians themselves enjoy strolling along the boulevards or sitting at a pavement café, and nursing a drink. Of course, for the ultimate

"oh-la-la!" experience, showgirls await you at celebrated cabarets while bright young things pose in nightclubs. For fans of spectator sports, there is tennis, the Tour de France, horse racing, soccer, or rugby. Recreation centers and gyms cater to the more active, while the municipal swimming pools delight waterbabies. You can also catch a game of *boules* (or *pétanque*) in Paris's squares and parks.

Practical Information

For the visitor in Paris, there is no shortage of information about what's on offer.

The **Office du Tourisme**, near the Tuileries and Opéra, is the city's main tourism distribution point for leaflets and schedules of events. It has a recorded information telephone service giving details of free concerts and exhibitions along with information on transportation to the venues. Its website is also extremely useful. Your hotel reception desk or concierge should also be able to help you with any such information. They usually keep a wide range of brochures and leaflets for guests, and will generally be more than happy to make reservations for you.

Reserving Tickets

Depending on the event, tickets can be bought at the door, but for blockbuster concerts it is necessary to reserve well ahead. For most major events, including some classical music concerts and museum shows, tickets can be purchased online or at **FNAC** or **Carrefour** stores. For popular events reserve well ahead – Parisians can be very quick off the mark for hot tickets. However, for theater, opera, and dance performances, you can often buy inexpensive tickets at the last minute. If the tickets are marked *sans visibilité*, you will be able to see the stage only

Ballerina of the Ballet de l'Opéra

partially, or perhaps not at all. Often, obliging ushers will put you in a better seat, depending on availability, but don't forget to tip.

Theater box offices are open daily from approximately 11am until 7pm. Most box offices accept credit card reservations made by phone or in person, but you may have to arrive early to pick up your tickets if you booked by telephone, as they may be sold to someone else at the last minute. If you are really keen and can't get hold of tickets, you can always turn up at the box office just before the performance in case there are unclaimed or returned tickets.

Listings Magazines

Paris has several good listings magazines. Among them are *Pariscope* and *L'Officiel des Spectacles*. They are published every Wednesday. *Le Figaro* has a good listings section on Wednesdays. *Télerama*, France's leading culture and listings weekly, has a Paris supplement called *Sortir*. For English listings, see the webzine *Paris Voice* at www.parisvoice.com.

Ticket Touts

If you must have a ticket to a sold-out performance, do as the French do: stand at the entrance with a sign that says *cherche une place* (or *deux*, etc). Many people have an extra ticket to sell. Often the people selling the extra tickets are doing so because

Concert at the Opéra National de Paris Garnier *(see p340)*

The Odéon Théâtre de l'Europe, a major theater venue sometimes staging plays in English

a person in their party cannot come and they will simply sell the ticket on at face value. It is fine to buy these tickets, but do watch out for touts and be sure you don't buy a counterfeit or overpriced ticket.

Cut-Price Tickets

Half-price tickets to current plays are sold on the day of performance at **Kiosque Théâtre**. Credit cards are not accepted and a small commission is charged per ticket. There is a booth on the Place de la Madeleine *(see p218)*, on the Parvis de la Gare Montparnasse, and on Place des Ternes. All are open from 12.30 until 8pm Tuesday to Saturday and from 12.30 until 4pm on Sunday. The *kiosque* is a Parisian institution and often has tickets for the season's top shows.

Check the listings magazines for free concerts in parks and churches in summer

Disabled Visitors' Access

Where amenities do exist, they are very good. Many venues have wheelchair space, but always phone in advance to make sure or look

on en.parisinfo.com, which has a full list of theaters, movie theaters, and other venues that are accessible. As far as public transportation is concerned, much of the Metro, due to its long stairways and age, is not accessible to wheelchairs. However, the newer line 14, which runs from Olympiades to Gare Saint-Lazare and serves many prime sights such as the Opéra National de Paris Garnier, offers full accessibility to wheelchairs. All bus lines are equipped with ramps to make them wheelchair-accessible, but a few bus stops are not yet fully equipped: check with Infomobi *(see p360)* to find out which these are.

The Grand Rex movie theater *(see p346)*

DIRECTORY

Carrefour
Tel 08 9269 2492.
Ⓦ spectacles.carrefour.fr

FNAC
Forum des Halles, 1 Rue Pierre-Lescot 75001. **Map** 13 A2.
Tel 0825 020 020.
26 Ave des Ternes 75017.
Map 4 D3. **Tel** 0825 020 020.

G7 Taxis
Tel 36 07; 01 41 27 66 99 (English).

Kiosque Théâtre
Pl de la Madeleine/opposite Montparnasse station/Place des Ternes. Ⓦ kiosquetheatre.com

Office du Tourisme
25 Rue des Pyramides 75001.
Map 12 E1. Ⓦ parisinfo.com

Taxis Bleus
Tel 36 09 or 08 9170 1010.

Pétanque players

Theater

From the grandeur of the Comédie Française to slapstick farce and avant-garde drama, theater is flourishing in Paris and the suburbs – the training ground for the best young actors and directors. The city also has a long tradition of playing host to visiting companies, and it attracts many foreign productions, often in the original languages.

There are theaters scattered throughout the city and the theater season runs from September to July; national theaters close during August but many commercial ones stay open. For complete listings of what's on read *Pariscope* or *L'Officiel des Spectacles (see p332)*.

National Theaters

Founded in 1680 by royal decree, the **Comédie Française** *(see p130)*, with its strict conventions regarding the style of acting and interpretation, is the bastion of French theater. Its aim is to keep classical drama in the public eye and also to perform works by the best modern playwrights.

Inextricably linked in the national consciousness to Molière, the Comédie Française is the oldest national theater in the world and one of the few institutions of France's *ancien régime* to have survived the Revolution. It settled into its present home after players occupied the Palais-Royal during the Revolution. The traditionally styled red velvet auditorium has a vast stage equipped with the latest technology.

The majority of the repertoire is classical, dominated by Corneille, Racine and Molière, followed by second strings Marivaux, Alfred de Musset and Victor Hugo. The company also performs modern plays by French and foreign playwrights.

The **Odéon Théâtre de l'Europe**, also known as the Théâtre National de l'Odéon *(see p142)*, was at one time the second theater of the Comédie Française. It now has two sites and specializes in performing plays from other countries in their original languages. Next door, the **Petit Odéon** is a studio space specializing in new plays.

The **Théâtre National de Chaillot** is a huge underground auditorium in the Art Deco Palais de Chaillot *(see p202)*. It stages

experimental and contemporary theater, lively dance productions and, occasionally, musical revues.

The **Théâtre National de la Colline** has two performance spaces and specializes in contemporary dramas.

Farther Afield

A thriving multi-theater complex in the Bois de Vincennes, the **Cartoucherie** houses five separate avant-garde theaters, including the internationally famous **Théâtre du Soleil**.

Independent Theaters

Among the most important of the serious independents are the **Comédie des Champs-Elysées**, the **Théâtre Hébertot** and the **Théâtre de l'Atelier**, which aims to be experimental. Other notable venues include the **Théâtre Marigny**, for excellent modern French drama, the **Théâtre Montparnasse** and the **Théâtre Antoine**, which pioneered the use of realism on stage. The **Théâtre de la Madeleine** maintains consistently high standards and the **Théâtre de la Huchette** specializes in Ionesco plays. The British director Peter Brook has a loyal following at the **Théâtre des Bouffes du Nord**.

For over a hundred years, the **Théâtre du Palais-Royal** has been the temple of risqué farce. With fewer French Feydeau-style farce writers these days, translations of American and British sex comedies are filling the gap. Other notable

venues include the **Bouffes Parisiens**, **Théâtre La Bruyère**, the **Michel** and the **St.-Georges**. The **Théâtre du Gymnase** presents popular one-man comedy shows.

Café-Theaters and Chansonniers

There is a long tradition of entertainment in cafés, but the café-theaters of today have nothing in common with the "café-concerts" of the late 19th century. These modern entertainments have originated because young actors and new playwrights could not find work, while drama students were unable to pay to hire established theaters. Don't be surprised if there is an element of audience participation, or alternatively, in small venues, if the actors can sometimes seem a little too close for comfort. This form of theater is now so popular in Paris that one can often see posters advertising classes for café-theater or notices inviting people to join small troupes. Café-theaters rose to prominence during the 1960s and 70s, when unknowns such as Coluche, Gérard Depardieu and Miou-Miou made their debut at the **Café de la Gare** before going on to success on the screen, so who knows who you might see at your local café.

Good venues for seeing new talent include the **Théâtre d'Edgar** and **Le Point Virgule**, while **Cabaret Michou** is an old-fashioned spot that tends to specialize in broad caricature. Traditional *chansonniers* – cabarets where ballads, folk songs and humour abound – include **Au Lapin Agile** *(see p229)*, in Montmartre. Political satire is on offer at the **Caveau de la République** and the **Théâtre des 2 Anes**, also in Montmartre. Another form of café entertainment that often veers towards the theatrical is the *café-philosophique*. These are philosophical discussions or debates, held on topics such as justice, war and love, in which skilled orators take to the floor to declaim their positions. Audience participation is encouraged. Such events are held in many locations, including at **Les Editeurs**. Although debates take place in French, English language events also exist: play readings are a regular feature at the **Café de Flore** (see p141).

Children's Theater

Some Paris theaters, such as the **Théâtre du Gymnase**, the **Théâtre de la Porte St.-Martin** and the **Théâtre d'Edgar**, have children's matinées on Wednesdays and weekends. In the city parks, there are several tiny puppet theaters (marionnettes), which are sure to delight children and adults alike. The **Lido** also has an occasional children's season with shows at 2pm and 4pm (call for details).

Open-Air Theater

During the summer, weather permitting, open-air performances of Shakespeare and classic French plays are held in the Shakespeare Garden in the Bois de Boulogne. There are also occasional performances in the Tuileries and in Montmartre as part of Paris's summer festival; check listings magazines for these events.

English-Language Theater in Paris

The Improfessionals (improvised comedy) and Mondays @ 7 are Paris-based companies who perform in English (details in listings magazines). There are also several English-language poetry societies which host poetry and play readings, the best is the Live Poets Society. Kilometre Zero is an English-language arts collective that performs plays, publishes a magazine and hosts open-mike recital evenings. **La Java** puts on excellent stand-up comedy acts in English each month, courtesy of Anything Matters. Peter Brook occasionally puts on Shakespeare plays at the **Théâtre des Bouffes du Nord**.

A historic venue, it is much-loved by expatriates and plays host to some of the finest comic talent on the circuit at the moment. Some theaters now put on plays with illuminated surtitles in English above the stage. See theatreinparis.com for details of participating venues.

Street Theater

In summer, jugglers, fire-eaters, mime artists and musicians can be seen in tourist areas like the Pompidou Centre (see pp110–11), St.-Germain and Les Halles.

Cabaret

The music hall revue is the entertainment form most associated with late 19th-century Paris. It evokes images of Bohemian artists and absinthe-induced debauchery. Today, most of the women are likely to be non-French and the audience is made up mainly of foreign businessmen and tour groups.

When it comes to picking a cabaret, the rule of thumb is simple: the better-known places are the best. Lesser-known shows resemble nothing so much as Grade-B strip shows. All the cabarets listed here (see p336) guarantee topless women sporting outrageous feather and sequin-encrusted head-pieces, an assortment of vaudeville acts and, depending on your point of view, a spectacularly entertaining evening or an exercise in high kitsch.

The **Lido** is the most Las Vegas-like of the cabarets and stars the legendary Bluebell Girls. The **Folies Bergère** is renowned for lively entertainment. It is the oldest music hall in Paris and probably the most famous in the world.

The **Crazy Horse** features some of the more risqué performances, and dancers with names such as Betty Buttocks and Nouka Bazooka. It has been transformed from its Wild West bar-room into a jewel-box theater with a champagne bucket on each seat. Here, the lowly striptease of burlesque shows has been refined into a

vehicle for comedy sketches and international beauties. **Paradis Latin** is the most "French" of all the city's cabaret shows. It has variety acts with remarkable special effects and scenery in an old Left Bank theater partly designed by Gustave Eiffel.

The **Bobin'O** offers a commercial show that is inspired by all of Paris's cabarets. The **Moulin Rouge** (see p230), once the haunt of Toulouse-Lautrec, is the birthplace of the cancan. Today, the Moulin Rouge is less extravagant than the screen version portrayed in the famous movie, but cabaret fans can still be certain of an evening of glamour, glitz and good times. Outrageously camp, transvestite parodies of these showgirl reviews can be seen at **Cabaret Michou**.

Reserving Tickets

Tickets can be bought at the box office, by telephone or through theater agencies. Box offices are open daily 11am–7pm; some accept credit card payments by telephone or in person. Most tickets can also be bought online, via either theater websites or Internet ticket agencies like FNAC, Carrefour or Cultival.

Ticket Prices

Ticket prices generally range from €7 to €30 for the national theaters and €8 to €38 for the independents. Reduced-price tickets and student standbys are available in some theaters 15 minutes before curtain-up. For cabaret, expect to pay from €23 to €60; €68 to €105 with dinner.

The **Kiosque Théâtre** (see p333) offers half-price tickets on the day of performance; credit cards are not accepted and a small commission is charged for each ticket. There are booths in three locations.

Dress

These days, evening clothes are only worn to gala events at the Opéra National de Paris Garnier, the Comédie Française, or the premiere of an up-market play.

DIRECTORY

National Theaters

Comédie Française
Salle Richelieu,
1 Pl Colette 75001.
Map 12 E1.
Tel 08 25 10 16 80.
w comedie-francaise.fr

Odéon Théâtre de l'Europe
Ateliers Berthier,
1 Rue André Suares
75017. **Map** 12 F5.
Tel 01 44 85 40 40.
Théâtre de l'Odéon,
Pl de l'Odéon 75006.
Map 12 F5.
w theatre-odeon.eu

Théâtre National de Chaillot
1 Pl du Trocadéro 75016.
Map 9 C2.
Tel 01 53 65 30 00.
w theatre-chaillot.fr

Théâtre National de la Colline
15 Rue Malte-Brun 75020.
Tel 01 44 62 52 52.
w colline.fr

Farther Afield

Cartoucherie
Route du Champ-de-Manoeuvre 75012.
Tel 01 43 74 87 63.
w cartoucherie.fr

Théâtre de l'Aquarium
Tel 01 43 74 72 74/99 61.

Théâtre du Chaudron
Tel 01 43 28 97 04.

Théâtre de l'Epée de Bois
Tel 01 48 08 39 74.

Théâtre du Soleil
Tel 01 43 74 24 08.

Théâtre de la Tempête
Tel 01 43 28 36 36.

Independent Theaters

Bouffes Parisiens
4 Rue Monsigny 75002.
Map 6 E5.
Tel 01 42 96 92 42.
w bouffesparisiens.com

Comédie des Champs-Elysées
15 Ave Montaigne 75008.
Map 10 F1. **Tel** 01 53 23
99 19. w comediedes
champselysees.com

Théâtre Antoine
14 Blvd de Strasbourg
75010. **Map** 7 B5.
Tel 01 42 08 77 71.
w theatre-antoine.com

Théâtre de l'Atelier
1 Pl Charles Dullin 75018.
Map 6 F2.
Tel 01 46 06 49 24.
w theatre-atelier.com

Théâtre des Bouffes du Nord
37 bis Blvd de la Chapelle
75010. **Map** 7 C1.
Tel 01 46 07 34 50/01 46
07 33 00.
w bouffesdunord.
com/en

Théâtre La Bruyère
5 Rue La Bruyère 75009.
Map 6 E3. **Tel** 01 48 74
76 99. w theatre
labruyere.com

Théâtre du Gymnase
38 Blvd de Bonne-Nouvelle
75010. **Map** 7 A5.
Tel 01 42 46 79 79
w theatredu
gymnase.com

Théâtre Hébertot
78 bis Blvd des
Batignolles 75017. **Map** 5
B2. **Tel** 01 43 87 23 23
or 01 43 87 24 24 (info).
w theatrehebertot.com

Théâtre de la Huchette
23 Rue de la Huchette
75005. **Map** 13 A4.
Tel 01 43 26 38 99.
w theatre-
huchette.com

Théâtre de la Madeleine
19 Rue de Surène 75008.
Map 5 C5.
Tel 01 42 65 07 09.
w theatre-
madeleine.com

Théâtre Marigny
Carré Marigny 75008.
Map 5 A5.
Tel 01 53 96 70 30 or 08
92 22 33 33 (reservations).
w theatremarigny.fr

Théâtre Michel
38 Rue des Mathurins
75008. **Map** 5 C4.
Tel 01 42 65 35 02.
w theatre-michel.fr

Théâtre Montparnasse
31 Rue de la Gaîté 75014.
Map 15 C2.
Tel 01 43 22 77 74.
w theatre
montparnasse.com

Théâtre du Palais-Royal
38 Rue de Montpensier
75001. **Map** 12 E1.
Tel 01 42 97 59 76 or
01 42 97 40 00 (tickets).
w theatrepalaisroyal.
com

Théâtre de la Porte St.-Martin
18 Blvd St.-Martin 75010.
Map 7 C5.
Tel 01 42 08 00 32.
w portestmartin.com

Théâtre St-Georges
51 Rue St.-Georges 75009.
Map 6 E3.
Tel 01 48 78 63 47.
w theatre-saint-
georges.com

Café-Theaters and Chansonniers

Cabaret Michou
80 Rue des Martyrs 75018.
Map 6 F3.
Tel 01 46 06 16 04.
w michou.com

Café de la Gare
41 Rue du Temple
75004. **Map** 13 B2.
Tel 01 42 78 52 51.

Caveau de la République
1 Blvd St.-Martin/23 Pl de
la République 75003.
Map 8 D5.
Tel 01 42 78 44 45.

Les Editeurs
4 Carrefour de l'Odéon
75006. **Map** 12 F4.
Tel 01 43 26 67 76.

La Java
105 Rue du Faubourg du
Temple 75010. **Map** 8 E5.
Tel 01 42 02 20 52.
w la-java.fr

Au Lapin Agile
22 Rue des Saules 75018.
Map 2 F5.
Tel 01 46 06 85 87.
w au-lapin-agile.com

Le Point Virgule
7 Rue St.-Croix-de-la-
Bretonnerie 75004.
Map 13 C3.
Tel 01 42 78 67 03.
w lepointvirgule.com

Théâtre des 2 Anes
100 Blvd de Clichy 75018.
Map 6 D1.
Tel 01 46 06 10 26.
w 2anes.com

Théâtre d'Edgar
58 Blvd Edgar-Quinet
75014. **Map** 16 D2.
Tel 01 43 22 11 02/ 01 42
79 97 97. w theatre-
edgar.com

Cabaret

Bobin'O
14–20 Rue de la Gaîté
75014. **Map** 15 C2.
Tel 08 20 00 90 00
(tickets), 01 43 27 24 24
(general info).
w bobino.fr

Crazy Horse
12 Ave George V 75008.
Map 10 E1. **Tel** 01 47 23
32 32. w lecrazyhorse
paris.com

Folies Bergère
32 Rue Richer 75009.
Map 7 A4. **Tel** 08 92 68 16
50. w foliesbergere.com

Lido
116 bis Ave des Champs-
Elysées 75008.
Map 4 E4.
Tel 01 40 76 56 10
w lido.fr

Moulin Rouge
82 Blvd de Clichy 75018.
Map 6 E1.
Tel 01 53 09 82 82.
w moulinrouge.fr

Paradis Latin
28 Rue du Cardinal
Lemoine 75005. **Map** 13
B5. **Tel** 01 43 25 28 28.
w paradislatin.com

Classical Music

The music scene in Paris is busy and exciting, with many first-class venues offering an excellent range of opera, and classical and contemporary music productions. There are also numerous concerts in churches (some of which are free) and many music festivals, particularly during the summer months.

Information about what's on is listed in *Pariscope* and *L'Officiel des Spectacles*. A free monthly listing of musical events is given out at most concert halls. Also, try the Office du Tourisme in the Rue des Pyramides *(see pp332–3)* for details of many free and open-air classical music performances.

Opera

Opera lovers will find themselves well catered for, with many productions mounted at the Bastille, the main venue for opera, and also at the beautiful **Opéra National de Paris Garnier**. Opera is also an important part of the programming at the Théâtre du Châtelet, as well as being produced intermittently by a variety of small organizations, and there are occasional large-scale lavish productions at the **Palais Omnisports de Paris-Bercy** or POB *(see p342)*.

The Opéra de Paris's ultra-modern home is the **Opéra National de Paris Bastille** *(see p102)*, where performances make full use of the house's mind-boggling array of high-tech stage mechanisms. There are 2,700 seats, all with a good view of the stage, and the acoustics are excellent.

Productions feature classic and modern operas, and interpretations are often avant-garde: past examples include Philippe Mamoury's *K...*; Bob Wilson's production of *The Magic Flute*, done in the style of Japanese Noh; and Messiaen's *St. Francis of Assisi*, with video screens and neon added to bring the story up to date. On Thursday lunchtimes, they also offer free concerts, lectures and movies as part of an occasional programme known as *Casse-Croûte à l'Opéra*.

There are also occasional dance performances, when the Bastille plays host to the ballet company from the Opéra National de Paris Garnier *(see p219)*. The house includes two smaller spaces, the **Auditorium** (500 seats) and the **Studio** (200 seats) for smaller-scale events connected to the current productions on the main stages here and at the Opéra Garnier.

The **Opéra Comique** (also known as the Salle Favart), directed by Jérôme Deschamps, no longer has opera, but stages a wide range of eccentric, light-weight productions, including some popular music-hall-style work and operetta. It is reopening in January 2017 following major renovation.

North of the city centre, at St Denis, the **Stade de France** hosts occasional opera spectaculars. Past productions have included Verdi's *Aïda*, directed by Charles Roubaud, as well as Bizet's *Carmen* and *Nabucco* by Verdi.

Concerts

Paris is the home of three major symphony orchestras, and a good half-dozen other orchestras; it is also a major venue for touring European and American orchestras. Chamber music is also flourishing, either as part of the programming of the major venues, or in smaller halls and churches.

The **Salle Pleyel** is Paris's principal concert hall. After extensive renovation, it is now owned by the state-run Cité de la Musique and houses the Orchestre de Paris, directed by Christoph Eschenbach, as well as Radio France's Philharmonic Orchestra, led by Myung-Whun Chung. The Salle Pleyel has optimal acoustics for the classical and contemporary orchestra repertoire. In addition to running the Salle Pleyel, the Cité de la Musique also operates other venues at Parc de la Villette. These concert halls present a varied programme of music from all periods, genres and cultures.

The **Théâtre du Châtelet** has become one of the city's main venues for all kinds of concerts, opera and dance. The high-quality programme includes opera classics, from Mozart's *Così fan tutte* to Verdi's *La Traviata*, and more modern works, such as Boessman's *Contes d'Hiver*, and occasional concerts by international opera stars. Great attention is also devoted to 20th-century music here, and throughout the season, there are lunchtime concerts and recitals in the foyer.

The beautiful Art Deco **Théâtre des Champs-Elysées** is a celebrated classical music venue that also produces some opera and dance. Radio France is part-owner of the theater and its Orchestre National de France gives concerts here, as do many touring orchestras and soloists. The Orchestre des Champs-Elysées, directed by Philippe Herreweghe, is in residence here, and gives period-instrument performances.

Radio France is the biggest single concert organizer in Paris, with a musical force that includes two major symphony orchestras: the Orchestre National de France and the Orchestre Philharmonique. Many of its concerts are given in Paris's other concert halls, but the **Maison de Radio-France** has a large hall and several smaller studios that are used for concerts and broadcasts open to the public *(see p204, Maison de Radio-France)*.

The **Cité de la Musique** is a massive cultural centre devoted entirely to music – of all genres and from all eras. Classical music features heavily on its program, with lots of chamber music and recitals, as well as more ambitious orchestral concerts.

The **Auditorium du Louvre** was built as part of the Grand Louvre project (see pp122–9) and it is used mostly for chamber, piano and vocal recitals. The Musée d'Orsay's (see pp146–9) **Auditorium du Musée d'Orsay** is a medium-sized auditorium, with an active concert programme. Concerts are usually held once or twice a week, and prices vary.

Other museums often hold concerts as part of an exhibition theme – such as troubadours at the Musée National du Moyen Age (see pp154–7) – so do check the listings magazines.

Musique à la Sorbonne is a concert series in the **Grand Amphithéâtre de la Sorbonne** and the **Amphithéâtre Richelieu de la Sorbonne**. Productions have included a Slavonic music festival, featuring the works of East European composers.

Occasionally concerts are given in the **Conservatoire d'Art Dramatique**, where Beethoven was introduced to Paris audiences in 1828 and where Hector Berlioz's major work, *La Symphonie Fantastique*, was first performed. Otherwise, it's not usually open to public.

Contemporary Music

Contemporary music in Paris has a high profile and is definitely alive and kicking. Jonathan Nott now directs the experimental Ensemble InterContemporain, which is lavishly supported by the French state in its home at the Cité de la Musique (see pp238–9). **IRCAM** (see p114), founded and formerly directed by Pierre Boulez, a composer, conductor and writer who was a leading figure in the capital's contemporary music scene, is a major centre for groundbreaking new musical forms. It organizes a programme of new music performances, talks and an annual festival in June.

Other bright stars among the many talented composers include Pascal Dusapin, Philippe Fénelon, George Benjamin and

Philippe Manoury, as well as Georges Aperghis, who specializes in musical theater.

The fabulously designed **Cité de la Musique** complex at Parc de la Villette includes both a spectacularly domed *salle de concerts* surrounded by a glass-roofed arcade, and the Conservatoire National de Musique with its opera theater and two small concert halls. The Chamber Orchestra of Europe plays regularly here. Both venues are used for regular performances, including jazz, ethnic and contemporary music, as well as *chanson* and Early Music.

For details, either phone the venue concerned or consult the listings magazines. For those interested in contemporary music, the quarterly magazine *Résonance* is published by IRCAM at the Pompidou Centre.

Festivals

Some of the most important music festivals are the result of the work of the **Festival d'Automne à Paris**, which acts as a behind-the-scenes stimulator, commissioning new works, subsidizing others and in general enlivening the Parisian musical, dance and theatrical scene from September to December.

The Festival St.-Denis (see p65) running throughout June and July holds concerts, with an emphasis on choral works. Most performances are given in the Basilique St.-Denis.

Musique Baroque au Château de Versailles, from around the middle of March to the middle of June, is an offshoot of the **Centre de Musique Baroque de Versailles**, founded in 1988. Operas, concerts, recitals, chamber music, dance and theater are on offer in the fabulous surroundings of Versailles (see pp250–55).

Other interesting festivals include the **Festival Chopin**, held in the Orangerie in the Bois de Boulogne from mid-June to mid-July, and the **Quartier d'Eté Festival**, which hosts a series of outdoor

classical music concerts. For tickets, it is usually necessary to go to the theater box office or venue concerned, though some festivals may run an advance online or postal reservation service.

Churches

Music is everywhere in Paris's churches, in the form of classical concerts, organ recitals or religious services. The most outstanding churches which hold regular concerts include the **Eglise de la Madeleine** (see p218), **St.-Germain-des-Prés** (see p140), **St.-Julien-le-Pauvre** (see p158) and **St.-Roch** (see p131). Music is also performed in the **Eglise des Billettes**, **St.-Sulpice** (see p174), **St.-Gervais–St.-Protais** (see p103), **Notre-Dame** (see pp82–5), **St.-Louis-en-l'Ile** (see p91) and **Sainte-Chapelle** (see pp88–9).

A great proportion, but not all, of these concerts are free. If you have any difficulty contacting the church in question, try the Office du Tourisme for information (see pp332–3).

Early Music

A number of early-music ensembles have taken up residence in Paris. The Chapelle Royale gives a concert series at the **Théâtre des Champs-Elysées**, with programmes ranging from Renaissance vocal music to Mozart. Their enchanting sacred music concerts (look out for Bach cantatas) take place at **Notre-Dame-des-Blancs-Manteaux** (see p104).

Baroque opera is more the domain of Les Arts Florissants, founded and directed by American-born William Christie, who perform French and Italian operas from Rossi to Rameau, and Les Musiciens du Louvre, directed by Marc Minkowski. Both companies perform regularly at the Théâtre du Châtelet and the Opera National Garnier. The **Théâtre de la Ville** is also an excellent venue in which to hear Baroque chamber music, as is the pretty **Eglise St.-Germain l'Auxerrois**.

Reserving Tickets

For tickets, it's always best to deal directly with the relevant box office. Reserving tickets at the main venues is possible online or by post up to two months before the performance and by telephone two weeks to a month in advance. If you want a good seat, it's best to reserve in advance as tickets tend to sell quickly. Last-minute tickets may also be available at the box office, and certain venues, such as the Opéra National de Paris Bastille, keep some tickets

for the cheaper seats aside for the purpose. Ticket agents, notably in the **FNAC** stores (see p333), and a good hotel concierge can also help. These agencies accept credit cards– a useful service as not all venues are guaranteed to accept them.

Half-price tickets on the day of performance can be bought at one of three **Kiosque Théâtre** (see p333) locations at Place de la Madeleine, the Parvis de la Gare Montparnasse and Place des Ternes. However, these agencies usually only deal for

performances taking place at private theaters.

Note, however, that many theaters and concert halls may be closed during the vacation season in August, so enquire first to avoid disappointment.

Ticket Prices

Ticket prices can range from €8–€85 for the Opéra de Paris Bastille and the principal classical music venues, and from €5–€25 for the smaller halls and concerts in churches around the city, such as Sainte-Chapelle.

DIRECTORY

Classical Music Venues

Amphithéâtre Richelieu de la Sorbonne
17 Rue de la Sorbonne 75005. **Map** 12 F5.
Tel 01 40 46 20 19.

Auditorium
See Opéra National de Paris Bastille.

Auditorium du Louvre
Musée du Louvre, Rue de Rivoli 75001. **Map** 12 E2.
Tel 01 40 20 55 00/55.

Auditorium du Musée d'Orsay
102 Rue de Lille 75007.
Map 12 D2.
Tel 01 53 63 04 63.

Centre de Musique Baroque de Versailles
22 Ave de Paris, Versailles.
Tel 01 39 20 78 10.
w cmbv.fr

Cité de la Musique
Parc de La Villette, 221 Ave Jean-Jaurès 75019.
Tel 01 44 84 44 84.
w citedelamusique.fr

Conservatoire d'Art Dramatique
2 bis Rue du Conservatoire 75009. **Map** 7 A4.
Tel 01 42 46 12 91.
w cnsad.fr

Eglise des Billettes
24 Rue des Archives 75004. **Map** 13 C2.
Tel 06 62 45 91 29.

Eglise de la Madeleine
Pl de la Madeleine 75008.
Map 5 C5. **Tel** 01 44 51 69 00 (church); 01 42 50 96 18 (concerts).

Eglise St-Germain l'Auxerrois
2 Pl du Louvre 75001.
Map 12 F2.
Tel 01 42 60 13 96.

Festival d'Automne
156 Rue de Rivoli 75001.
Map 12 F2. **Tel** 01 53 45 17 00 or 01 53 45 17 17 (tickets). **w** festival-automne.com

Festival Chopin
Orangerie de Bagatelle Bois de Boulogne 75016.
Map 3 A4.
Tel 01 45 00 22 19 (info); 08 92 68 36 22 (tickets).

Grand Amphithéâtre de la Sorbonne
47 Rue des Ecoles 75005.
Map 13 A5. **Tel** 01 42 62 71 71/ 01 40 46 33 72.

IRCAM
1 Pl Igor Stravinsky 75004.
Map 13 B2. **Tel** 01 44 78 48 43 or 01 44 78 15 45.
w ircam.fr

Maison de Radio-France
116 Ave du Président-Kennedy 75016. **Map** 9 B4. **Tel** 01 56 40 22 22 or 01 56 40 15 16.
w maisondelaradio.fr

Notre-Dame
Pl du Parvis-Notre-Dame 75004. **Map** 13 A4.
Tel 01 44 41 49 99.

Notre-Dame-des-Blancs-Manteaux
12 Rue des Blancs-Manteaux 75004. **Map** 13 C3. **Tel** 01 42 72 09 37.

Opéra Comique
5 Rue Favart 75002. **Map** 6 F5. **Tel** 01 80 05 68 60.
w opera-comique.com

Opéra National de Paris Bastille
120 Rue de Lyon 75012.
Map 14 E4. **Tel** 08 92 89 90 90. **w** operadeparis.fr

Opéra National de Paris Garnier
Pl de l'Opéra 75009. **Map** 6 E4. **Tel** 08 92 89 90 90.
w operadeparis.fr

Quartier d'Eté Festival
Tel 01 44 94 98 00.
w quartierdete.com

Sainte-Chapelle
8 Blvd du Palais. **Map** 13 A3. **Tel** 01 53 40 60 80 or 01 44 07 12 38 (info).

St.-Germain-des-Prés
3 Pl St-Germain-des-Prés 75006. **Map** 12 E4.
Tel 01 55 42 81 10.

St.-Gervais–St-Protais
Pl St-Gervais 75004. **Map** 13 B3.
Tel 01 48 87 32 02.

St.-Julien-le-Pauvre
79 Rue Galande 75005.
Map 13 A4.
Tel 01 43 54 52 16.

St.-Louis-en-l'Ile
19 Rue St.-Louis-en-l'Ile 75004. **Map** 13 C4.
Tel 01 46 34 11 60.

St.-Roch
296 Rue St.-Honoré 75001. **Map** 12 E1.
Tel 01 42 44 13 20.

St.-Sulpice
2 Rue Palatine, Pl St-Sulpice 75006.
Map 12 E4.
Tel 01 42 34 59 98 or 01 43 25 03 10.

Salle Pleyel
252 Rue du Faubourg St-Honoré 75008. **Map** 4 E3. **Tel** 01 42 56 13 13.
w sallepleyel.fr

Stade de France
Rue Henri Delaunay, La Plaine St-Denis 93210.
Tel 08 92 70 09 00.
w stadefrance.com

Studio
See Opéra National de Paris Bastille.

Théâtre des Champs-Élysées
15 Ave Montaigne 75008.
Map 10 F1.
Tel 01 49 52 50 50.

Théâtre du Châtelet
2 Rue Edouard Colonne, Pl du Châtelet 75001.
Map 13 A3.
Tel 01 40 28 28 40.

Théâtre de la Ville
2 Pl du Châtelet 75004.
Map 13 A3.
Tel 01 42 74 22 77.
w theatredelaville.com

Dance

When it comes to dance, Paris is more a cultural crossroads than a cultural centre. Due to a deliberate government policy of decentralization, many of the top French dance companies are based in the provinces, although they frequently visit the capital. In addition, the greatest dance companies from all over the world perform here. Paris has a well-deserved reputation as a centre of excellence for modern and experimental dance, and has numerous workshops and places in which to learn its many forms.

Classical Ballet

The opulent **Opéra National de Paris Garnier** (see p219) is the home of the Ballet de l'Opéra de Paris which enjoys a reputation as one of the world's best classical dance companies.

Since the **Opéra National de Paris Bastille** opened in 1989, the Opéra National de Paris Garnier has been used for dance as well as for opera. Extensively restored both inside and out, it is one of the largest theaters in Europe, with performance space for 450 artists and a seating capacity of 2,200.

Modern dance companies such as the Martha Graham Company, Paul Taylor, Merce Cunningham, Alvin Ailey, Jerome Robbins and Roland Petit's Ballet de Marseille also regularly perform here. The Opéra National de Paris Garnier also shares operatic productions with the Opéra National de Paris Bastille.

Modern Dance

The **Théâtre de la Ville** (once run by Sarah Bernhardt) has become one of Paris's most important venues for modern dance. Through performances at the Théâtre de la Ville, modern choreographers such as Jean-Claude Gallotta, Regine Chopinot, Maguy Marin and Anne Teresa de Keersmaeker have gained international recognition. Here, you may also see troupes such as Pina Bausch's Wuppertal Dance Theatre, whose tormented, existential choreography may not be to everyone's taste, but is popular with Parisian audiences. Music performances also run throughout the season and

include chamber music, recitals, world music and jazz.

The **Maison des Arts et de la Culture de Créteil** presents some of the most interesting dance works in Paris. It is located in the modern, concrete, mid-20th-century Paris suburb of Créteil, southeast of the city. Under artistic director Didier Fusillier, dance at MAC is part of an ambitious programme of avant-garde theater, installations and performance as showcased at its annual festival EXIT, which is held in March. Acclaimed French choreographer Maguy Marin was MAC's resident dance guru for some years.

Set amid the opulent *couture* stores and embassies, the elegant Art Deco **Théâtre des Champs-Élysées** has 1,900 seats. It is frequented by an upscale audience who watch major international companies perform here. It was here that Nijinsky first danced Stravinsky's iconoclastic *The Rite of Spring*, which led to rioting among the audience.

The theater is more famous as a classical music venue, but visitors have included the Dance Theater of Harlem and London's Royal Ballet, plus a strong Russian presence, notably the St Petersburg Ballet Theatre.

The lovely old **Théâtre du Châtelet** is a renowned opera and classical music venue, but it is also host to international contemporary dance companies such as the Tokyo Ballet and the Birmingham Royal Ballet.

Experimental dance companies perform in the **Théâtre de la Bastille**, where innovative theater is also

staged. Many directors and companies start here, then go on to international fame.

The **Centre National de la Danse** in Pantin, a northeastern suburb of Paris, is France's national *conservatoire*. It hosts workshops, talks and performances, from classical ballet to experimental dance.

Events Listings

To find out what's on, read the inexpensive weekly entertainment guides *Pariscope* and *L'Officiel des Spectacles*. Posters advertising dance performances are widely displayed in the Metro and on the streets, especially on the green advertisement columns, the *colonnes Morris*.

Ticket Prices

Expect to pay €10–€195 for tickets to the ballet or opera at Opéra National de Paris Garnier, €6–€75 for the Théâtre des Champs-Élysées, and anything from €9 to €30 for other venues.

Dance Venues

Centre National de la Danse
1 Rue Victor Hugo 93507 Pantin.
Tel 01 41 83 98 98. 🔲 cnd.fr

Maison des Arts et de la Culture de Créteil
1 Pl Salvador Allende 94000 Créteil. **Tel** 01 45 13 19 19.
🔲 maccreteil.com

Opéra National de Paris Bastille
See p339.

Opéra National de Paris Garnier
See p339.

Théâtre de la Bastille
76 Rue de la Roquette 75011.
Map 14 F3. **Tel** 01 43 57 42 14.

Théâtre des Champs-Elysées
See p339.

Théâtre du Châtelet
See p339.

Théâtre de la Ville
See p339.

Rock, Jazz and World Music

Music lovers will find every imaginable form of music in Paris and its environs, from international pop stars in major venues to buskers of varying degrees of talent on the streets and in the Metro. There's a huge variety of styles on offer, with reggae, hip-hop, world music, blues, folk, rock and jazz – Paris is said to be second only to New York in the number of jazz clubs and jazz recordings made here, and there is always an excellent selection of bands and solo performers.

On the summer solstice (21 June) each year, the Fête de la Musique takes place. The whole city parties all night, with everything from huge outdoor stages and top bands to one-man buskers or accordionists playing traditional French songs invading Paris's streets, squares and cafés.

For complete listings of what's happening, buy *Pariscope* (published every Wednesday) at any kiosk. For jazz fans there's the monthly *Jazz* magazine for schedules and in-depth reviews.

Major Venues

The top international acts are often at the enormous arenas: **Palais Omnisports** at Bercy, **Stade de France** at St.-Denis or the **Zénith**. Other venues,such as the legendary *chanson* centre of the universe, the **Olympia**, or the **Grand Rex** (also a movie theater), offer a more traditional concert-hall atmosphere. They host everyone from bewigged and cosmetically enhanced iconic first ladies of country to acid jazz stars. (*See* Directories *p342 and p351*).

Rock and Pop

Until recently, Paris's indigenous rock groups (Les Négresses Vertes, the hit fusion band of the nineties and noughties, are probably the best-known) drew foreign attention precisely because they were French.

For too long, Paris pop meant Johnny Hallyday and insipid covers of US and UK hits, or Serge Gainsbourg and his distinctive, decadent style. Paris rock traditionally attracted (and deservedly) either patronizing praise or outright mockery.

That is no longer the case. The international success of the groups Daft Punk and Air, and the contribution to the music scene of producer,

songwriter and musician Bertrand Burgalat, led to a growth in confidence in the local music scene. The phrase "French Touch" often describes hip producers, writers or singers, now in demand all over the world. Banlieue-(suburb-) based rap, rai and reggae no longer sound like French versions of imported forms, instead they now have their own identity.

There is no shortage of gigs. The latest bands usually play at **Divan du Monde**, **Nouveau Casino** and **La Cigale** and its sister club, **La Boule Noire**. The **Rex Club** is the best place for R&B. The **Olympia** is the city's most famous rock venue, attracting top acts while the **Bataclan** has hosted some of Rock's edgiest names (the latter is closed for renovation – check the website for the latest details). Many nightclubs also double up as live music venues (*see pp343–5*).

Jazz

Paris is still jazz-crazy. Many American musicians have made the French capital their home because of its receptive atmosphere. All styles, from free-form to Dixieland and swing, and even hip-hop-jazz crossover, are on offer. Clubs

range from quasi-concert halls to piano bars and pub-like venues. One of the most popular places, though not the most comfortable, is the **New Morning**. It's hot and the table service can be a little erratic, but all the great jazz musicians continue to perform here, as they have in the past. Arrive early to ensure a good seat. **Le Duc des Lombards** is a lively jazz club in Les Halles, which also features salsa.

Many jazz clubs are also cafés, bars or restaurants. The latter includes the intimate **Autour de Midi... et Minuit** in Montmartre, with its vaulted "cave". Dining might not be a requirement, but it's always wise to check first.

Other hotspots are **Le Petit Journal Montparnasse** for modern jazz, **Le Petit Journal St.-Michel** for Dixieland. A trendy crowd is drawn to **La Bellevilloise**'s Sunday jazz brunches in Ménilmontant. **Caveau de la Huchette** looks like the archetypal jazz joint, but today, it favours swing and big-band music, and is popular with students. The **Caveau des Oubliettes** has a growing reputation for cutting-edge jazz.

For a change, try the local talent at small, friendly bars such as the less expensive **Bistrot d'Eustache** and super-cool **La Flèche d'Or**, set in an old railway station. The **Jazz Club Etoile** in the Méridien hotel is a well-respected venue which features Sunday jazz brunch. On the other side of town, the **Le Trabendo** has an intriguing mix of up-and-comers and down-and-outers. Although the **Sunset-Sunside** is primarily known for jazz, it also includes blues nights on its programme.

Paris has two international jazz festivals in summer: **Paris Jazz Festival** (*see p65*) and Jazz à la Villette in July. The former is the mainstay of the summer calendar, and Jazz à la Villette in the Parc de la Villette (*see pp238–9*) offers movies on jazz, debates and *boeufs* (jam sessions).

World Music

With its large populations from West Africa, the Maghreb, the Antilles and Latin America, Paris is a natural centre for world music. The **Chapelle des Lombards** has played host to top acts; it also has jazz, salsa and Brazilian music. **Aux Trois Mailletz** is a medieval cellar with everything from blues to tango and rock-and-roll covers, while **Kibélé** is a great place for North African sounds.

Many jazz clubs intersperse their programmes with ethnic music. These include **New Morning**, which also has shows with South American artists, and **Baiser Salé**, for popular acts including Makossa, Kassav, Malavoi and Manu Dibango.

World music in a stunning setting can be found at the **Institut du Monde Arabe** (see p166), which draws stars from the Arab music world to its concert hall.

Ticket Prices

Prices at jazz clubs can be steep, and there may be a cover charge of over €15 at the door, which usually includes the first drink. If there is no cover charge, the drinks will be expensive and at least one must be bought.

Tickets can be bought online on the FNAC website or from FNAC outlets (see p333), or directly from venue box offices and at the door of the clubs themselves.

DIRECTORY

Major Venues

Le Grand Rex
1 Blvd Poissonnière 75002. **Map** 7 A5.
Tel 01 45 08 93 89 or 08 92 68 05 96.
W legrandrex.com

Olympia
28 Blvd des Capucines 75009. **Map** 6 D5.
Tel 08 92 68 33 68.
W olympiahall.com

Palais Omnisports de Paris-Bercy
8 Blvd de Bercy 75012.
Map 18 F2.
Tel 08 92 39 04 90.
W bercy.fr

Stade de France
(See p339)

Zénith
211 Ave de Jean-Jaurès, Parc de la Villette 75019.
Tel 01 44 52 54 56 or 08 90 71 02 07.
W zenith-paris.com

Rock and Pop

Bataclan
50 Blvd Voltaire 75011.
Map 14 E1.
Tel 01 43 14 00 30.
W bataclan.fr

La Boule Noire
118 Blvd Rochechouart 75018. **Map** 6 F2.
Tel 01 49 25 81 75.
W laboule-noire.fr

La Cigale
120 Blvd Rochechouart 75018. **Map** 6 F2.
Tel 01 49 25 89 99.
W lacigale.fr

Divan du Monde
75 Rue des Martyrs 75018.
Map 6 F2.
Tel 01 40 05 06 99.
W divandumonde.com

Nouveau Casino
109 Rue Oberkampf 75011. **Map** 14 F1.
Tel 01 43 57 57 40.
W nouveaucasino.net

Rex Club
5 Blvd Poissonnière 75002. **Map** 7 A5.
Tel 01 42 36 10 96.
W rexclub.com

Jazz

Autour De Midi... et Minuit
11 Rue Lepic 75018.
Map 6 E1.
Tel 01 55 79 16 48.
W autourdemidi.fr

La Bellevilloise
19–21 Rue Boyer 75020.
Tel 01 46 36 07 07.
W labellevilloise.com

Bistrot d'Eustache
37 Rue Berger, Carré des Halles 75001.
Map 13 A2.
Tel 01 40 26 23 20.
W bistrotdeustache.fr

Caveau de la Huchette
5 Rue de la Huchette 75005. **Map** 13 A4.
Tel 01 43 26 65 05.
W caveaudela huchette.fr

Caveau des Oubliettes
52 Rue Galande 75005.
Map 13 A4.
Tel 01 46 34 23 09.

Le Duc des Lombards
42 Rue des Lombards 75001. **Map** 13 A2.
Tel 01 42 33 22 88.
W ducdeslombards.com

La Flèche d'Or
102 bis Rue de Bagnolet 75020. **Tel** 01 44 64 01 02.
W flechedor.fr

La Grande Halle de la Villette
211 Ave Jean-Jaurès, Galerie de la Villette 75019.
Map 8 F1.
Tel 01 40 03 75 75.
W villette.com

Jazz Club Etoile
Hôtel Méridien, 81 Blvd Gouvion-St-Cyr 75017.
Map 3 C3.
Tel 01 40 68 30 42.
W jazzclub-paris.com

New Morning
7–9 Rue des Petites-Écuries 75010.
Map 7 B4.
Tel 01 45 23 51 41.
W newmorning.com

Paris Jazz Festival
Parc Floral Bois de Vincennes 75012.
W parisjazzfestival.fr

Le Petit Journal Montparnasse
13 Rue du Commandant-Mouchotte 75014.
Map 15 C2.
Tel 01 43 21 56 70.
W petitjournal montparnasse.com

Le Petit Journal St-Michel
71 Blvd St-Michel 75005.
Map 16 F1. **Tel** 01 43 26 28 59. **W** petitjournal stmichel.fr

Sunset-Sunside
60 Rue des Lombards 75001. **Map** 13 A2.
Tel 01 40 26 46 60.
W sunset-sunside.com

Le Trabendo
211 Ave Jean-Jaurès, Parc de la Villette 75019.
Map 8 F1.
Tel 01 42 06 05 52.
W letrabendo.net

World Music

Baiser Salé
58 Rue des Lombards 75001. **Map** 13 A2.
Tel 01 42 33 37 71.
W lebaisersale.com

Chapelle des Lombards
19 Rue de Lappe 75011.
Map 14 F4.
Tel 01 43 57 24 24.
W la-chapelle-des-lombards.com

Institut du Monde Arabe
(See p166)

Kibélé
12 Rue de l'Echiquier 75010. **Map** 7 B5.
Tel 01 48 24 57 74.
W lekibele.fr

New Morning
(See Jazz)

Aux Trois Mailletz
56 Rue Galande 75005.
Map 13 A4.
Tel 01 43 25 96 86.
W lestroismailletz.fr

Nightclubs

Paris's nightlife is undergoing a revival, with a number of collectives breathing new life into the scene and bringing a more varied diet of music – not just techno, but hip hop, rock, pop, reggae, and electro-lounge – into the proceedings. These collectives aren't necessarily attached to one particular club, but they take over a venue for one-off events; the venues can be anything from traditional clubs, the best of which we've listed below, to warehouses in the suburbs. Many of the places listed here are not just clubs – they're bars, restaurants, live music venues, and clubs all rolled into one; live concerts usually take place from 7pm until midnight, then a DJ takes over until 2am or dawn. A number of bars also turn into clubs later on at the weekend; we've listed a few of the best below.

Mainstream Clubs

A great mainstay of the techno clubbing scene, the unpretentious **Rex Club** is popular with people of all ages. It has one of the best sound systems in the capital and attracts big-name French and international DJs.

Another stalwart is **La Java**, housed in a fabulous Art Deco building that has changed little since the 1930s, when the likes of Edith Piaf and Django Reinhardt performed here. Its music policy has become more adventurous of late, featuring garage rock, as well as electro.

Electronica dominates at **Zigzag Club**, in a glamorous location off the Champs-Elysées; it attracts big crowds with its large dance floor, top DJs and state-of-the-art Funktion One sound system.

The vast **La Machine du Moulin Rouge** has a more eclectic music policy – here, you'll dance to anything from electro to hip hop. There's also a concert space/downstairs dance floor, La Chaufferie (so named because it used to be the boiler room for the Moulin Rouge next door), and a bar upstairs.

Showcase is a hot venue on Paris's night scene. Boasting more than 32,000 sq ft (3,000 sq metres) of space below the Pont Alexandre III, it triples as a bar, nightclub and concert hall. Once rather exclusive, it has now become more mainstream, though you should still dress up to get in.

Under the same management, but on the other side of the bridge and with the Eiffel Tower as the backdrop to its terrace, is **Faust**, a stylish restaurant, bar, and club that is especially popular for its club nights of electro and house run by big-name DJs.

Exclusive Clubs

If you aren't rich, beautiful or, at least, super-hip (or an actual A-list celebrity), gaining entry to Paris's more exclusive clubs will be difficult. It's worth noting, however, that bouncers often treat foreign would-be entrants preferentially, so be sure to stand proud, ditch any attempts at French and speak English when you get near the door.

The hardest club to get into is probably **Le Montana**, in St.-Germain-des-Prés. This chic, intimate space is packed with celebrities and models quaffing champagne and expensive cocktails.

Equally exclusive is **Silencio**, opened by US director David Lynch and inspired by the club that appears in his movie *Mulholland Drive*. Lynch designed everything in this club – from the 1950s-style furniture to the gold-leaf walls.

Up until midnight it's members only, but after that, the doors open to the general public, though you still have to look the part to get in.

Also very selective is **Chez Raspoutine**, just off the Champs-Elysées, much favored by visiting foreign celebrities. The club used to be a Russian cabaret, and it has preserved its decadent red velvet decor, banquettes, and intimate corners.

Trendy Clubs

Clubs with cool riverside locations blossom in the capital, especially in the 13th arrondissement. One of the hottest spots is **Concrete**, on a boat on the Seine near the Gare de Lyon. It puts on all-day and all-night electro parties with some of the best DJs around and a state-of-the-art sound system. On the opposite side of the river is the enduring **Batofar**, the scarlet lighthouse ship moored on the Seine in front of the Bibliothèque Nationale. The music at this hybrid locale (restaurant, bar, live music venue, and club) varies from underground techno to reggae, depending on the night of the week, but the crowds are always friendly and relaxed. In the summer, try not to miss their wonderfully chilled-out afternoon sessions on the quayside, when they set out deckchairs and a barbecue for the Batofar Plage.

Nearby **Nüba**, on the top floor of the waterside Cité is also particularly appealing in the summer months, when you can enjoy a drink looking out at the Seine and listening to techno.

A firm fixture on the scene is **Le Social Club**, in *bobo*-chic Montorgueil, popular with a lively, unpretentious crowd who come to listen to an excellent line-up of live bands, followed by DJ sets, while knocking back the club's signature drink, mint vodka.

The **Nouveau Casino**, behind the ever trendy Café Charbon (see p311) in Oberkampf, pulls in an eclectic crowd for its live music and club nights, often run by cutting-edge collectives.

Creating a buzz in the Bastille area is **Badaboum**. Set in an old warehouse, it hosts live bands and club nights. It also has a cocktail and tapas bar, plus a secret room upstairs, complete with a bed, sofas, and a fridge.

Sporting a retro-industrial setting is **Yoyo**, a large club housed in the cavernous concrete basement of the Palais de Tokyo's contemporary art site. Its eclectic programming and renowned international DJs draw a young, glamorous crowd.

Out on the northeastern edge of the city, **Glazart** is a bit of a trek, but worth it for its slightly alternative vibe and wide range of music, including hip hop, drum 'n' bass and electro. As well as club nights, it puts on regular concerts, which, unusually, are mostly free. In summer, La Plage de Glazart creates a beach-party atmosphere: some 50 tonnes of sand are imported to create a mini-beach, where you can play boules and sit and enjoy open-air gigs.

On the city's eastern limits, old-timer **La Flèche d'Or**, set in a converted train station, also offers an eclectic array of concerts, DJ nights and concept evenings.

Though mostly a live music venue, it's worth checking what's on at **Le Cabaret Sauvage**, a swish locale in La Villette, shaped like a big-top tent, where collectives often stage electro and drum 'n' bass nights.

DJ Bars

Popular DJ bars – bars that turn into clubs on the weekend – include **Panic Room**, on happening Rue Amelot, with a bar on the ground floor and a dance floor in the basement; and **Glass**, a cocktail bar in the hip South Pigalle district.

Other good bets include **L'OPA**, an elegantly revamped New York-style loft that hosts free live bands and DJ sets late into the night; and **Carmen**, located in a ravishing Second Empire mansion, and drawing a select, good-looking crowd with its cutting-edge programing and experimental cocktails.

World Music

You can dance to more exotic sounds – Afro, Latin, Balkan, and tropical beats – at weekends at **La Dame de Canton**, a wonderful Chinese junk moored on the Seine in the 13th arrondissement, near Batofar. It also has a bar and restaurant. Another good option is **L'Alimentation Générale**, one of the most popular fixtures on the Oberkampf nightlife scene, where you can dance to live bands playing Afro and Balkan beats, samba and gypsy jazz; on weekend club nights, the music tends towards techno, hip hop, and funk. **La Bellevilloise**'s club nights often have a world-music slant.

For salsa, head to **Barrio Latino**. Occupying three floors of a building designed by Gustave Eiffel, it combines Latin music with great cocktails and tapas served from trolleys by roaming staff. Dancers can perfect their moves at the Sunday salsa classes. You can also take salsa lessons and then dance the night away at **La Pachanga**.

Gay and Lesbian Venues

Paris boasts a thriving LGBT scene. The traditional stronghold of the gay community is the Marais neighbourhood, which features many LGBT-friendly bars and clubs. One of the best known is **CUD (Classic Up and Down)**, with its ground-floor bar and vaulted basement dance floor. It pulls in people of all ages and gets jam-packed after 2am, since

it's one of the few places in the area that stays open till the early hours. The nearby **Le Free DJ** bar hosts popular weekend club nights.

The oldest gay club in Paris is **Le Club 18**, just behind the Palais-Royal. It's very small but friendly and attracts a good-looking young crowd.

Some mainstream clubs also host gay nights; one of the best is venerable **Bataclan**'s Nuit des Follivores/Crazyvores, where a young, relaxed crowd parties to 1980s pop music and house (Bataclan is closed for renovation at time of going to press – check the website for the latest information).

La Champmeslé, one of the most venerable fixtures on Paris's lesbian scene, also welcomes gay men and stages regular cabaret nights. In the Marais, **Le So What**'s club nights tend to attract thirty-something lesbians, who down mojitos inbetween DJ sets. Also with a strong lesbian following, though open to all, is **Rosa Bonheur**, hidden away in the Parc des Buttes-Chaumont. This is set in a former guinguette (an old-fashioned open-air café/dancehall) and is a lovely place to drink and dance, especially in summer.

Aimed at both gay and lesbians, **Le Tango** is a converted dance hall where you can spend the first half of the evening (till 12.30am) perfecting your tango, cha cha cha and other old-time dances, before letting your hair down to a traditional disco (techno is banned).

Admission Charges

Some clubs are strictly private, while others have a more open admission policy. Prices range from €10 to €30 or more and may be even higher after midnight and at weekends. Quite often, though, there are concessions for women.

In general, one drink (une consommation) tends to be included in the club's entry price; thereafter, it can become an expensive evening.

DIRECTORY

Mainstream Clubs

Faust
Beneath Pont Alexandre III,
Left Bank 75007.
Map 11 A2.
Tel 01 44 18 60 60.
ⓦ faustparis.fr

La Java
(See p336 – Cafe-Theaters and Chansonniers)

La Machine du Moulin Rouge
90 Blvd de Clichy
75018. **Map** 4 E4.
Tel 01 53 41 88 88.
ⓦ lamachinedu
moulinrouge.com

Rex Club
(See p342 – Rock and Pop)

Showcase
Under Alexander III
Bridge, Port des Champs-
Elysées 75008.
Map 11 A1.
Tel 01 45 61 25 43.
ⓦ showcase.fr

Zigzag Club
32 Rue Marbeuf 75008.
Map 4 F5.
Tel 06 35 25 03 61
ⓦ zigzagclub.fr

Exclusive Clubs

Chez Raspoutine
58 Rue de Bassano 75008.
Map 4 E5.
Tel 01 47 20 02 90.
ⓦ raspoutine.com

Le Montana
28 Rue St-Benoît 75006.
Map 12 E3.
Tel 01 44 39 71 00.

Silencio
142 Rue Montmartre
75002.
Map 13 A1.
Tel 01 40 13 12 33.
ⓦ silencio-club.com

Trendy Clubs

Badaboum
2 bis Rue des
Taillandiers 75011.
Map 14 F4.
ⓦ badaboum.paris

Batofar
Moored opposite
11 Quai François
Mauriac 75013.
Map 18 F4.
Tel 01 53 60 17 00.
ⓦ batofar.org

Le Cabaret Sauvage
211 Ave Jean Jaurès,
Parc de la Villette 75019.
Tel 01 42 09 03 09.
ⓦ cabaretsauvage.
com

Concrete
Port de la Rapée 75012.
Map 18 E2.
ⓦ Concreteparis.fr

La Flèche d'Or
(See p342 – Jazz)

Glazart
7–15 Ave de la Porte
de la Villette 75019.
Tel 01 40 36 55 65.
ⓦ glazart.com

Nouveau Casino
(See p342 – Rock and Pop)

Nüba
36 Quai d'Austerlitz
75013.
Map 18 E2.
Tel 01 76 77 34 85.
ⓦ lenuba.com

Le Social Club
142 Rue Montmartre
75002.
Map 13 A1.
Tel 01 40 28 05 45.
ⓦ parissocialclub.com

Yoyo
Palais de Tokyo,
13 Ave du President
Wilson 750016.
Map 10 E1.
ⓦ yoyo-paris.com

DJ Bars

Carmen
14 Rue Duperré 75009.
Map 6 E2.
Tel 01 45 26 50 00.
ⓦ le-carmen.fr

Glass
7 Rue Frochot 75009.
Map 6 E2.
Tel 09 80 72 98 83.
ⓦ glassparis.com

L'OPA
9 Rue Biscornet 75012.
Map 14 E5.
Tel 01 46 28 12 90.

Panic Room
101 Rue Amelot 75011.
Map 14 D1.
Tel 01 58 30 93 43.

World Music

L'Alimentation Générale
64 Rue Jean-Pierre
Timbaud 75011.
Map 14 F1.
Tel 01 43 55 42 50.
ⓦ alimentation-
generale.net

Barrio Latino
46–48 Rue du Faubourg
St-Antoine 75012.
Map 14 F4.
Tel 01 55 78 84 75.
ⓦ barrio-latino.com

La Bellevilloise
(See p342 – Jazz)

La Dame de Canton
Port de la Gare 75013.
Map 18 F4.
Tel 01 53 61 08 49.
ⓦ damedecanton.com

La Pachanga
8 Rue Vandamme 75014.
Map 15 C2.
Tel 01 56 80 11 40.

Gay and Lesbian Venues

Bataclan
(See p342 – Rock and Pop)

La Champmeslé
4 Rue Chabanais 75002.
Map 12 E1.
Tel 01 42 96 85 20.
ⓦ lachampmesle.com

Le Club 18
18 Rue de Beaujolais
75001.
Map 12 F1.
Tel 01 42 97 52 13.
ⓦ club18.fr

CUD
12 Rue des Haudriettes
75003.
Map 13 C2.
Tel 0142 71 56 60.

Le Free DJ
35 Rue Sainte-Croix
de la Bretonnerie 75003.
Map 13 C3.
Tel 01 48 04 95 14.
ⓦ reedj.fr

Rosa Bonheur
2 Allée de la Cascade
75019.
ⓦ rosabonheur.fr

Le So What
30 Rue du Roi de Sicile
75008.
Map 13 C3.
Tel 01 42 71 24 59.

Le Tango
13 Rue au Maire 75003.
Map 13 C1.
Tel 01 42 72 17 78.
ⓦ boite-a-frisson.fr

Film

Paris can justifiably claim to be one of the world's capitals of movie appreciation. More than 370 screens within the city limits, distributed among over 100 theaters and multiplexes, screen a fabulous cornucopia of movies, both brand-new and classic. American movies share the limelight with home-grown dramas and comedies, and virtually every moviemaking industry in the world has found a niche in the city's art houses. Theater programs change on Wednesdays. The cheapest practical guides to what's on are *Pariscope* and *L'Officiel des Spectacles (see p332)* with complete listings and timetables for some 300 movies. Those shown in subtitled original language versions are coded "VO" *(version originale)*; dubbed movies are coded "VF" *(version française)*. Most children's movies are shown in VF during the day. Paris's Film Festival is held for one week in late June/early July. The system is that you pay full price for one movie, after which a special card gives access to unlimited movies at just €3 a ticket, for the duration of the festival.

Movements in the Film Industry

Paris was the cradle of the cinematograph over 100 years ago, when Auguste and Louis Lumière invented the early film projector. Their screening of *L'Arrivée d'un Train en Gare de La Ciotat* (Arrival of a Train at la Ciotat Station) in Paris in 1895 is considered by many to mark the birth of the medium. The French reverence for film as a true art form is based on a theory of one of the world's first movie critics, Ricciotto Canudo, an Italian intellectual living in France, who dubbed cine-matography "the Seventh Art" in 1922. The title holds true even today. The city was of course also the incubator of that very Parisian vanguard movement, the New Wave, when directors such as Claude Chabrol, François Truffaut, Jean-Luc Godard and Eric Rohmer in the late 1950s and early 1960s revolutionized the way movies were made and perceived. The exploration of existential themes, the use of long tracking shots and the rejection of studios for outside locations are some of the characteristics of New Wave film. In 2001, the success of *Amélie Poulain* revitalized the Parisian movie-making scene; many of its locations are easy to spot as you walk around town.

The same is true of *The Da Vinci Code*, also featuring *Amélie* star Audrey Tautou.

Movie Theater Zones

Most Parisian movie theaters are concentrated in several areas of the city, which enjoy the added appeal of nearby restaurants and stores.

The Champs-Elysées remains the densest movie theater strip in town, where you can see the latest Hollywood smash hit or French *auteur* triumph, as well as some classic reissues, in subtitled original-language versions. Movie theaters in the Grands Boulevards, in the vicinity of the Opéra de Paris Garnier, show movies in both subtitled and dubbed versions. Boulevard de Clichy is home to two Pathé multiplexes with a total of 12 screens showing current dubbed, French and VO releases. A major hub of Right Bank movie theaters is in the Forum des Halles shopping mall.

The Left Bank, historically associated with the city's intel-lectual life, remains the center of the arthouse and repertory movie theaters. Yet, it has equally as many of the latest block-busters. Since the 1980s, many theaters in the Latin Quarter have closed down and the main center for Left Bank theaters is

the Odéon-St.-Germain-des-Prés area. The Rue Champollion is an exception. It has enjoyed a revival as a mini-district for arthouse and repertory movies.

Further to the south, Montparnasse remains a lively district for new movies in both dubbed and subtitled prints.

For specific movie theaters see the Directory on page 348.

Big Screens and Picture Palaces

Among surviving landmark movie theaters are two Grands Boulevards venues, the 2,800-seat **Le Grand Rex**, with its Baroque decor, and the **Max Linder Panorama**, which was refurbished by a group of independent film buffs in the 1980s for both popular and art film programing.

The massive 14-screen **MK2 Bibliothèque** theater (plus bar, stores and exhibition space) has opened up in the revitalized 13th arrondissement, and just across the river, the **UGC Ciné-Cité Bercy** theater complex is well worth a visit too.

In the Cité des Sciences et de l'Industrie at La Villette, scientific movies are shown at **La Géode** *(see p240)*. This has a hemispheric screen (once the world's largest) and an "omnimax" projector which uses 70-mm film shot horizontally to project an image which is nine times larger than the standard 35-mm print. Along the Canal St-Martin, **MK2**'s twin movie complexes – **Quai de la Loire** and **Quai de la Seine** – are linked by a canal boat.

Revival and Repertory Houses

Each week, more than 150 titles representing the best of world cinema can be seen. For old Hollywood movies, the independent **Grand Action** mini-chain can't be beaten. Other active and thoughtful repertory and reissue venues include the excellent **Reflets Médicis** screens in the Rue

Champollion and **La Pagode**. The latter is particularly striking; the Oriental pagoda was built in 1895. **Studio 28** in Montmartre is a lovely old movie house with lights in the theater designed by Jean Cocteau and a charming garden bar full of fairy lights and kitsch cut-outs of old movie stars. Opened in the 1920s, Studio 28 claims to be the first ever avant-garde movie theater and once played host to movie greats such as Luis Buñuel and Abel Gance. They screen everything from the latest releases through to Fellini festivals and documentary shows. There are at least ten movies screened here each week, including art-house classics and pre-releases. The theater also holds regular debates with well-known directors and actors. Another Parisian institution, **Cinema Studio Galande** has shown the *Rocky Horror Picture Show* to costumed movie-goers every Friday night for over 20 years.

Cinémathèque Française

The private "school" of the New Wave generation, this famous film archive and repertory movie theater was created by Henri Langlois in 1936 *(see p348)*. It has lost its monopoly on classic movie screenings, but it is still a must for cinephiles in search of that rare movie no longer in theatrical circulation or, perhaps, recently restored or rescued. The association is now housed at 51 Rue de Bercy in a wonderfully futuristic-looking building designed by Frank Gehry. The sail-like façade has given the building its nickname: "dancer revealing her tutu". The film library has more than 18,000 digitalized movies, and there are enough exhibitions, projections, lectures and work-stores to satisfy the appetite of any movie enthusiast. For those interested in the building's architecture, there are tours on the first Sunday of each month.

Non-Theatrical Venues

In addition to the Ciné-mathèque Française, film programs and festivals are integral parts of two highly popular Paris cultural institutions, the Musée d'Orsay *(see pp146–9)* and the Pompidou Centre *(see pp110–13)* with its two screening rooms. The Musée d'Orsay regularly schedules movie programs to complement current art exhibitions and is usually restricted to silent movies. The Pompidou Center organizes vast month-long retrospectives, devoted to national film industries and on occasion to some of the major companies.

Finally, the **Forum des Images** *(see p115)* in the heart of Les Halles is a hi-tech film and video library with a vast selection of movies and documentaries featuring the city of Paris from the late 19th century to the present day. The archives here are amazing and include news-reels and commercials featuring Paris alongside the feature films and documentaries. The Forum has three theaters, all of which run daily screenings of feature movies. One ticket allows the visitor access to both the video library and to the movie screenings. The screenings are frequently grouped according to theme or director, making it possible to spend several hours enjoying a mini-retrospective. See website for details.

Ticket Prices

Expect to pay around €10–12 at first-run venues or even more for movies of unusual length or special media attention. However, exhibitors practise a wide array of collective discount incentives, including cut-rate admissions for students, the unemployed, seniors, former soldiers and large families. Wednesday is discount day for everybody at some movie theaters – prices are slashed to as low as €4.

France's three exhibition giants, Gaumont, UGC and MK2, also sell special discount cards and accept credit card reservations for their flagship movie theaters, while repertory houses issue "fidelity" cards.

Movies Starring Paris

Historical Paris (studio-made)

An Italian Straw Hat
(René Clair, 1927)

Sous les toits de Paris
(René Clair, 1930)

Les Misérables
(Raymond Bernard, 1934)

Hôtel du Nord
(Marcel Carné, 1937)

Les Enfants du Paradis
(Marcel Carné, 1945)

Casque d'Or
(Jacques Becker, 1952)

La Traversée de Paris
(Claude Autant-Lara, 1956)

Playtime
(Jacques Tati, 1967)

New Wave Paris (location-made)

Breathless
(Jean-Luc Godard, 1959)

Les 400 coups
(François Truffaut, 1959)

Documentary Paris

Paris 1900
(Nicole Vedrès, 1948)

La Seine a rencontré Paris
(Joris Ivans, 1957)

Paris as Seen by Hollywood

Seventh Heaven
(Frank Borzage, 1927)

Camille
(George Cukor, 1936)

An American in Paris
(Vincente Minnelli, 1951)

Gigi
(Vincente Minnelli, 1958)

Irma La Douce
(Billy Wilder, 1963)

Paris when it Sizzles
(Richard Quine, 1964)

Frantic *(Roman Polanski, 1988)*

French Kiss
(Lawrence Kasdan, 1995)

The Ninth Gate
(Roman Polanski, 1999)

Moulin Rouge
(Baz Luhrmann, 2001)

The Bourne Identity
(Doug Liman, 2002)

Before Sunset
(Richard Linklater, 2004)

The Da Vinci Code
(Ron Howard, 2006)

Hugo *(Martin Scorsese, 2011)*

Midnight in Paris
(Woody Allen, 2011)

Film Festivals

Film festivals are a way of life for Parisian movie buffs. There are several major events each year and many small themed festivals at any given time around the city. The annual Paris Film Festival (Fête du Cinema), in late June/early July, may be dwarfed by its glitzier sister in Cannes, but the capital's version is a far friendlier event for the public to attend – and there are still more than enough opportunities to spot celebrities.

Open-Air Festivals

There are several outdoor film festivals throughout the summer, including the Festival Silhouette which shows short movies in the lovely Buttes Chaumont (see p236), the Cinéma au Clair de Lune festival which has projections of movies at Parisian sites which are relevant to the movie, and Le Cinéma en Plein Air which draws crowds to a lawn in La Villette (see pp238–9), where a giant inflatable screen shows old and contemporary classics. This is one of the summer's most popular events, so be sure to get there early and don't forget to take a hamper full of goodies to nibble on throughout the movie.

Indoor Festivals

During the annual Paris Film Festival, over 100 movies are shown at the **Gaumont Marignon** on the Champs-Elysées. The city's gay and lesbian film festival at the Forum des Images usually takes place in November. Paris Tout Court is an impressive short film festival held at the **Arlequin** in St.-Germain which also stages lectures and meetings with renowned directors and artists. Other film festivals include the L'Etrange festival, which shows weird and wonderful offbeat movies from around the world to enthusiastic audiences.

DIRECTORY

Movie Theaters

Arlequin
76 Rue de Rennes 75006.
Map 12 E4.
Tel 01 45 44 28 80.

Le Balzac
1 Rue Balzac 75008.
Map 4 E4.
Tel 01 45 61 10 60.
W **cinemabalzac.com**

Centre Pompidou
19 Rue Beaubourg 75004.
Map 13 B2.
Tel 01 44 78 12 33.

Le Champo
51 Rue des Ecoles 75005.
Map 13 A5.
Tel 01 43 54 51 60.

Christine 21
4 Rue Christine 75006.
Map 12 F4.

Cinémathèque Française
51 Rue de Bercy 75013.
Tel 01 71 19 33 33.
W **cinemateque.fr**

Cinema Studio Galande
42 Rue Galande 75005.
Map 13 A4.
Tel 01 43 54 72 71.

Le Desperado
23 Rue des Ecoles 75005.
Map 13 A5.
Tel 01 43 25 72 07.

La Filmothèque du Quartier Latin
9 Rue Champollion 75005. **Map** 12 F5.
Tel 01 43 26 70 38.
W **lafilmotheque.fr**

Forum des Images
(See p115)

Gaumont Marignan
27 Ave Champs-Elysées 75008.
Map 5 A5.
Tel 08 92 69 66 96.

La Géode
26 Ave Corentin-Cariou 75019.
Tel 08 92 70 08 40 or 08 92 68 45 40.
W **lageode.fr**

Grand Action
5 Rue des Ecoles 75005.
Map 13 B5.
Tel 01 43 54 47 62.

Le Grand Rex
(See p342 – Major Venues)

Lucernaire
53 Rue Notre-Dame-des-Champs 75006.
Map 16 E2.
Tel 01 45 44 57 34.
W **lucernaire.fr**

Luminor – Hotel de Ville
20 Rue du Temple 75004.
Map 13 C2.
Tel 01 42 78 47 86.

Majestic Bastille
2–4 Blvd Richard Lenoir 75011. **Map** 14 E4.
Tel 01 47 00 02 48.

Max Linder Panorama
24 Blvd Poissonnière 75009. **Map** 7 A5.
Tel 01 48 00 90 24.
W **maxlinder.com**

MK2
Beaubourg: 50 Rue Rambuteau 75003.
Map 13 A2.
Tel 08 92 69 84 84.
Bibliothèque: 128–162 Ave de France 75013.
Map 18 F4.
Tel 08 92 69 84 84.
Quai de la Seine/ Quai de la Loire: 7 Quai de la Seine; 14 Quai de la Loire 75019.
Map 8 F1.
Tel 08 92 69 84 84.
W **mk2.com**

Le Nouvel Odeon
6 Rue de l'Ecole de Médecine 75006.
Map 12 F4.
Tel 01 46 33 43 71.
W **nouvelodeon.com**

La Pagode
57 bis Rue de Babylone 75007. **Map** 11 C4.
Tel 01 45 55 48 48.

Reflets Médicis
3 Rue Champollion 75005. **Map** 12 F5.
Tel 01 43 54 42 34.

St-Andre des Arts
30 Rue St.-Andre des Arts (Salles 1&2) and 12 Rue Git-le-Coeur (Salle 3) 75006. **Map** 12 F4.
Tel 01 43 26 48 18.
W **cinesaintandre.fr**

Studio 28
10 Rue Tholozé 75018.
Map 6 E1.
Tel 01 46 06 36 07.
W **cinema-studio28.fr**

UGC Ciné-Cité Bercy
2 Cour St.-Emilion 75012.
Tel 08 25 12 12 02.

UGC Ciné-Cité Les Halles
7 Place de la Rotonde, Forum des Halles 75001.
Map 13 A2.
Tel 08 25 12 12 02.

Sport and Fitness

Paris offers plenty of opportunities to keep fit and exercise. The city has a superb range of sporting locations, from beautiful Art Deco swimming pools to state-of-the-art gyms and health clubs; the municipal website www.paris.fr and the town halls of each arrondissement are good sources of information. With its glorious backdrop of elegant streets, parks, and riverside, Paris is a great city for cycling and jogging. It's also the scene of some of France's most exciting spectator sports. The Roland Garros tennis tournament, for example, and the Tour de France bicycle race are national institutions. For details regarding all sporting events that take place in and around Paris, contact Paris's tourist office (see p359). The weekly entertainment guides L'Officiel des Spectacles, Pariscope and the Wednesday edition of Le Figaro also have good listings of the week's sporting events (see p332). For in-depth sports coverage, see the daily paper L'Equipe (www.lequipe.fr).

Bicycling

Riding a bicycle has become a much more attractive and viable means of getting around Paris. There are 700 km (435 miles) of bicycle lanes (pistes cyclables) in the capital, a figure that is set to double by 2020, and Parisian drivers are becoming more respectful of bicyclists as more people turn to traveling on two wheels. Take a copy of the free Paris à Vélo map from a tourist office or down- load it from paris.fr for details of all the city's bicycle lanes.

The nicest time to go for a bicycle ride is on Sundays and national holidays, when some of the quaysides next to the Seine and the Canal St.-Martin are closed to traffic. Otherwise, the most pleasant spots are the Bois de Vincennes and the Bois de Boulogne for a leisurely bike ride through the woods, or the 1.2-mile- (2-km) Berges de Seine.

The easiest way to hire a bicycle is to make use of the self-service **Vélib'** scheme. Bicycles can be hired at around 1,800 locations across the city. The first 30 minutes are free. Beyond the first half-hour, additional charges apply: €1 for the next 30 minutes, €2 for another 30 minutes, and thereafter €4 for every additional 30 minutes. You can also buy a one- or seven-day card (online). The service extends to children and is known as P'tit Vélib'.

If you'd prefer to take an organized bicycle tour through the city, there are several organizations that run fun trips. In spring and summer, **Fat Tire Bike Tours** organizes trips (from €32 per person) in which knowledgeable guides shepherd bicyclists around the streets of Paris while imparting interesting information on the city's landmarks. Its partner, **City Segway Tours**, offers guided tours on electric Segway scooters (over 12s only). **Paris à Vélo C'est Sympa!** operates multilingual tours to offbeat parts of the city (from €35).

Rollerblading

Rollerbladers can enjoy parades through Paris on Friday nights. The police close off boulevards around the city, allowing thousands of skate fans to join the fun every week. The 16.5-mile- (27-km-) circuit usually starts near the Tour Montparnasse at 10pm and lasts three hours, but you can join the route at any point if the whole circuit seems a little too much. In order to join in, you need to know how to brake and change direction. Contact www.pari-roller.com for details of the route and for rollerblade rental outlets. Another, more family-friendly, circuit starts from Place de la Bastille at 2.30pm on Sundays (see www.rollers-coquillages. org). As a safety precaution, the trip is canceled in wet weather.

Running and Climbing

Paris's parks are attractive places for jogging; among the most popular are the Jardin du Luxembourg, Parc Monceau, and the Jardin des Tuileries. The Berges de Seine is a nice short stretch, or you could do a longer circuit at the Bois de Boulogne and Bois de Vincennes. You can even combine running with sightseeing by hiring a guide to run with you, either individually or in small groups, with **Paris Running Tours**.

Just outside central Paris, in Pantin, is **MurMur**, one of the world's largest indoor climbing arenas. There are plenty of climbing walls, boulders, and a place to practice ice-climbing. MurMur has another branch in Issy-les-Moulineaux, set into the arches of a railway viaduct.

Swimming

There is a massive aquatic fun park, **Aquaboulevard**, in south Paris (see p355). In addition to an exotic artificial beach, swimming pools, water toboggans, and rapids, there are tennis and squash courts, golf, bowling, table tennis, billiards, a gym, bars, and stores.

Of the many municipal swimming pools, one of the best is the **Piscine Suzanne Berlioux**, in Place de la Rotonde, with an Olympic-sized pool in the underground shopping complex. For a handsome 1930s decor of mosaics, plus two levels of private changing cabins, a whirlpool, sauna, and water jets, go to the **Piscine Pontoise-Quartier Latin**. This complex also has a small gym overlooking the pool. Fitness fans can pump a little iron before taking a dip.

The **Piscine Henry de Montherlant** is part of a municipal sports complex that includes tennis courts and a gym.

The beautiful Art Nouveau **Piscine Butte-aux-Cailles** *(see pp276–7)* is a treat for serious swimmers and sunbathers. A decent-sized indoor pool is perfect for laps, while the two outdoor swimming areas are great for lounging. The villagey atmosphere of the surrounding area only serves to reinforce the feeling of relaxing on vacation, miles away from the city.

The **Piscine Joséphine Baker** floats on the Seine near the Bibliothèque François Mitterrand. In the summer, the rooftop terrace is a good spot for sunbathing.

Some of the more exclusive hotels and gyms also have their own swimming pools. It is possible to buy a day pass to the chic **Club Med Gym** in Rue Louis Armand and have access to their pool. Similarly, at the **Novotel Tour Eiffel**, non-guests are welcomed to their health club and pool, which has a retractable roof for swimming under the sun in spring and summer.

It is important to note that all municipal pools and some private ones insist that all bathers wear swimming caps and that male guests wear swimming trunks rather than baggy shorts.

Tennis and Squash

Tennis can be played at more than 40 municipal sites; you can reserve a slot online at www. tennis.paris.fr. The most central courts – and the ones with the nicest setting – are at **Tennis Luxembourg**, at the Jardin du Luxembourg. **Tennis La Faluère** in the Bois de Vincennes has the most courts (21), and because it has so many, you can often just turn up and find a court free. Squash can be played at the **Espace Sportif Pontoise**, which also has a swimming pool and gym. Other good clubs include the **Squash Montmartre** and the **Le Club du Jeu de Paume**.

Gyms

There are a number of gyms in Paris that you can use with a day pass. You can generally expect to pay €20 or more, depending on the amenities.

Club Med Gym is a well-equipped chain with over 20 gyms in Paris and the suburbs. The **Espace Sportif Pontoise**, in the Latin Quarter, offers a good-value (€11.10) weekday evening pass that allows you to use the gym, pool and sauna. More upscale is the sleek **L'Usine**, in the Opéra district, with a gym, hammam, and saunas. In theory, the **Ritz Health Club**, which has one of the finest indoor pools in Paris, is for guests or members only. However, if the hotel is not too full, you can buy a day pass. Note that some swimming pools also have gyms.

Skating

Ice-skating can be enjoyed year-round at the **Patinoire Sonja Henie de Bercy**; the DJ-led sessions on Friday and Saturday evenings are particularly lively. The city's other indoor rink is **Patinoire Pailleron**, in the 19th arrondissement. A winter-only rink operates outside the Hôtel de Ville and in the splendid setting of the Grand Palais.

Spectator Sports

The annual Tour de France bicycle race (www.letour.fr) finishes in July in Paris, with the French president awarding the coveted *maillot jaune* (yellow jersey) to the winner. For over 20 years now, the final stage of the tour has taken place over several laps of a circuit taking in the Louvre, the quays along the Seine, and the Champs-Elysées. Finding a spot to watch can be extremely tough, so it's best to hunt down your space several hours before the riders are expected. Other bicycling events, including time trials, are held at the **Vélodrome National**, in the suburbs at St-Quentin-en-Yvelines.

A day out at the races gives you a chance to see the rich and famous in all their finery.

The world-renowned Prix de l'Arc de Triomphe is held at the **Hippodrome de Longchamp**, in the Bois de Boulogne, on the first Sunday in October. More flat racing takes place at the **Hippodrome de St-Cloud** and **Hippodrome de Maisons-Laffitte**, which are a short drive west of Paris. For steeple-chasing, go to the **Hippodrome d'Auteuil**, in the Bois de Boulogne. The **Hippodrome de Vincennes** hosts the trotting races. For detailed information on all of these, consult France Galop (www.france-galop.com).

One of the best-known road races in the world is the 24-hour motor race at Le Mans, 115 miles (185 km) south-west of Paris. It takes place every year in mid-June. Contact the **Automobile Club de l'Ouest** for details.

A number of events, including the BNP Paribas Masters of tennis, world-class martial arts demon-strations, tournaments in every-thing from figure skating to handball, and rock concerts are held at the **AccorHotels Arena**.

The **Parc des Princes**, which can hold 50,000 people, is home to the main Paris soccer team, first-division Paris St-Germain.

The colossal **Stade de France** is a major venue for international soccer matches, the Six Nations rugby tournament and music concerts. Sports fans can go on a behind-the-scenes tour.

Famous for its international tennis tournament, the French Open, the **Stade Roland Garros** is located in Avenue Gordon-Bennett at the southern boundary of the Bois de Boulogne. From late May to mid-June, everyone lives and breathes tennis. Even business meetings are transferred from the conference room to the stadium. Apply for tickets several months ahead, and don't miss a trip to the stadium's excellent museum of tennis, featuring everything from prototype rackets to a Bjorn Bjorg headband. Also, be sure to reserve a table at one of the restaurants here, which are transformed into places to see and be seen.

DIRECTORY

Biycling

Fat Tire Bike Tours / City Segway Tours
24 Rue Edgar Faure 75015.
Map 10 D4.
Tel 01 82 88 80 96.
w paris.fattirebike
tours.com
w citysegwaytours.com

Paris à Vélo C'est Sympa!
22 Rue Alphonse Baudin 75011.
Map 14 E2.
Tel 01 48 87 60 01.
w parisvelosympa.com

Vélib'
Tel 01 30 79 79 30.
w velib.paris.fr

Running and Climbing

MurMur
55 Rue Cartier-Bresson, 93500 Pantin.
Tel 01 48 46 11 00.
w murmur.fr.
Also at: 1–6 Blvd Garibaldi, Issy-les-Moulineaux 92130.
Tel 01 58 88 00 22.

Paris Running Tours
Tel 06 02 11 52 10.
w parisrunningtour.com

Swimming

Aquaboulevard
4 Rue Louis-Armand 75015.
Tel 01 40 60 10 00.
w aquaboulevard.fr

Club Med Gym
26 Rue de Berri 75008.
Map 4 F4.
Tel 01 43 59 04 58.
149 Rue de Rennes 75006.
Map 15 C1.
Tel 01 45 44 24 35.
w cmgsportsclub.com

Novotel Tour Eiffel
61 Quai de Grenelle 75015.
Map 9 B5.
Tel 01 40 58 20 00.
w novotel.com

Piscine Butte-aux-Cailles
5 Pl Paul-Verlaine 75013.
Map 17 A5.
Tel 01 45 89 60 05.

Piscine Henry de Montherlant
30 Blvd Lannes 75016.
Tel 01 40 72 28 30.

Piscine Joséphine Baker
Quai François Mauriac 75013.
Tel 01 56 61 96 50.
w carilis.fr

Piscine Pontoise-Quartier Latin
19 Rue de Pontoise 75005.
Map 13 B5.
Tel 01 55 42 77 88.
w carilis.fr

Piscine Suzanne Berlioux
Forum des Halles, Niveau -3, access via Porte du Jour 75001.
Map 13 A2.
Tel 01 42 36 36 82.
w carilis.fr

Tennis and Squash

Le Club du Jeu de Paume
74b Rue Lauriston 75116.
Map 4 D4.
Tel 01 47 27 46 86.
w squashjeudepaume.com

Espace Sportif Pontoise
19 Rue de Pontoise 75005.
Map 13 B5.
Tel 01 55 42 77 88.
w carilis.fr

Squash Montmartre
14 Rue Achille-Martinet 75018.
Map 2 E4.
Tel 01 42 55 38 30.
w squashmontmartre-paris.com

Tennis La Faluère
113 Route de la Pyramide, Bois de Vincennes 75012.
Tel 01 43 74 40 93.

Tennis Luxembourg
Blvd St-Michel, Jardin du Luxembourg 75006.
Map 12 E5.
Tel 01 43 25 79 18.

Gyms

Club Med Gym
26 Rue de Berri 75008.
Map 4 F4.
Tel 01 43 59 04 58.
149 Rue de Rennes 75006. **Map** 15 C1.
Tel 01 45 44 24 35.
w cmgsportsclub.com

Espace Sportif Pontoise
19 Rue de Pontoise 75005.
Map 13 B5.
Tel 01 55 42 77 88.
w carilis.fr

Ritz Health Club
Ritz Hotel,
15 Pl Vendôme 75001.
Map 6 D5.
Tel 01 43 16 30 30.
w ritzparis.com

L'Usine
8 Rue de la Michodière 75008.
Tel 01 42 66 30 30.
w usineopera.com

Skating

Patinoire Pailleron
32 Rue Edouard Pailleron 75019.
Tel 01 40 40 27 70.
w pailleron19.com

Patinoire Sonja Henie de Bercy
222 Quai de Bercy 75012.
Tel 01 82 73 16 23.
w accorhotelsarena.com

Spectator Sports

AccorHotels Arena
8 Blvd de Bercy 75012.
Tel 01 75 44 04 00.
w accorhotelsarena.com

Automobile Club de l'Ouest
Tel 02 43 40 24 24.
w lemans.org

Hippodrome d'Auteuil
Route d'Auteuil aux Lacs, Bois de Boulogne 75016.
Tel 01 40 71 47 47.

Hippodrome de Longchamp
Route des Tribunes, Bois de Boulogne 75016.
Tel 01 44 30 75 00.

Hippodrome de Maisons-Laffitte
1 Ave de la Pelouse, Maisons-Laffitte 78600.
Tel 01 39 12 81 70.

Hippodrome de St-Cloud
1 Rue du Camp Canadien, St-Cloud 92210.
Tel 01 47 71 69 26.

Hippodrome de Vincennes
2 Route de la Ferme, Vincennes 75012.
Tel 01 49 77 17 17.

Parc des Princes
24 Rue du Commandant-Guilbaud 75016.
Tel 01 47 43 71 71.
w leparcdesprinces.fr

Stade de France
Rue Henri Delaunay, St.-Denis 93200.
Tel 08 92 70 09 00.
w stadedefrance.com

Stade Roland Garros
2 Ave Gordon-Bennett 75016.
Tel 01 47 43 48 00.
w rolandgarros.com

Vélodrome National
Place de la Paix Céleste, Montigny-le-Bretonneux 78180.
Tel 01 76 21 93 20.
w velodrome-national.com

CHILDREN'S PARIS

It's never too early to instil a lifelong taste for this magical city in your children. Activities such as scaling the dizzy heights of the Eiffel Tower *(see pp196–7)*, boating down the Seine *(see pp74–5)*, or visiting Notre-Dame *(see pp82–5)* are fun at any age, and having children in tow will allow you to see old haunts through new eyes. Many of the city's museums cater to younger visitors, with special trails or audioguides. And when your children need a break from all the stimulation, you can retire to one of the city's numerous parks and gardens, where playgrounds and sandpits abound.

A child engaging with the technology at La Cité des Enfants at La Villette

Practical Advice

Paris welcomes young families in hotels and most restaurants. Children under four travel free on public transportation, and four- to 11-year-olds travel at half price. Many sights and attractions offer child reductions, while infants under three or four enter free. Children under 18 are admitted free of charge to all state-run museums. Ask at the Office du Tourisme *(see p359)* for full details of child reductions, or check weekly entertainment guides such as *Pariscope, L'Officiel des Spectacles* and *Paris Mômes*.

A lot of children's activities are geared to end-of-school times, including Wednesday afternoons, when French children have time off. For information on museum workshops, contact the museums individually.

Babychou Services and **Kidizen** are specialty babysitting organizations in the city. They also offer a wide range of other services, including the rental of strollers and cribs.

Museums

Top of the museum list for children is the Cité des Enfants, a special section for children at the Cité des Sciences *(see pp240–41)*, in the Parc de la Villette. In 90-minute sessions, kids can play about with water, experiment with sound and light, and much more. The rest of the museum also has plenty of hands-on activities and changing exhibitions aimed at the young.

Museums such as the Louvre can be a bit daunting for anyone, let alone children. One way to engage young visitors is to follow a treasure hunt, like the ones run by **THATLou**, for example. Children follow a list of clues in order to find certain paintings. Hunts are organized around a theme, such as "Food and Wine" or "Angels and Wings." The same organization also runs treasure hunts around the Musée d'Orsay (**THATd'Or**) and the streets of the Latin Quarter (**THATRue**). The museums themselves also have art trails for children that can be downloaded in advance; in addition, the Musée d'Orsay has a variety of fun, interactive tours for children ages five to ten. Focusing on modern art, the Galerie des Enfants at the Pompidou Center *(see pp110–13)* mounts exhibitions and runs workshops for children. Similarly, the **Musée en Herbe**, dedicated entirely to children, finds fun ways to present art exhibitions, using jigsaws, costumes, and the like, and runs popular art workshops.

Other enjoyable museums for children include the Musée National de la Marine *(see p203)* and the Musée de la Musique *(see p238)*. The former illustrates the history of French maritime tradition with scale models of battleships, dreadnoughts, and submarines. The latter is a wonderful introduction to musical instruments, from Renaissance theorbos to Arabic ouds, helped along by audioguides specially aimed at children, free workshops, and concerts.

Parks, Zoos, and Adventure Playgrounds

The best children's park within Paris is the Jardin d'Acclimatation in the Bois de Boulogne *(see p247)*, with a children's puppet theater,

The Palais de Chaillot, housing the Musée National de la Marine

The Guignol marionettes

pony and camel rides, play-grounds, rides, a mini railroad, and boats.

The Parc Floral in the Bois de Vincennes *(see p249)* has some excellent adventure playgrounds and a treetop rope park (open Wed, weekends and holidays only). The *Bois* also hosts the largest funfair in France, open from Palm Sunday through to the end of May, and is the site of the city's main zoo, the Parc Zoologique, whose star attraction is its enormous tropical hothouse.

There's a smaller zoo in the Jardin des Plantes *(see p169)*, the beautiful botanical gardens. Also here are splendid hothouses and

some appealing museums *(see pp168–9)*, including the Galerie de l'Evolution, which has an impressive collection of stuffed animals and an interactive center for children on the first floor.

Children will also enjoy exploring the Berges de Seine, a pedestrian-only stretch of the riverbank with floating gardens, a climbing wall, children's bicycle rental (summer only), and cafés with board games.

Entertainment

Mime, dance, and puppet shows, with their emphasis on actions rather than words, are very accessible, especially to younger children. Most movies, however, will not have English subtitles.

Several theaters, including the **Théâtre Astral** in the Parc Floral and **Abricadabra** in a barge on the Canal de l'Ourcq, offer children's shows with mime, dance, or music. The most spectacular cinematic experience is in La Géode at the Cité des Sciences et de l'Industrie *(see p240)*. The **Chaplin Saint-Lambert** movie theater specializes in children's movies and comic strips in French.

Une Journée au Cirque offers a day's entertainment when children can meet the animals, put on clown make-up, or

Children playing in the traffic-free Berges de Seine

practice tightrope walking. Shows are in the afternoon, after lunch with the *artistes*.

The Guignol puppet shows are a great French tradition. Guignol himself is a far gentler character than the traditional English Mr Punch. Most of the main parks hold Guignol shows on Wednesday afternoons, on weekends, and daily during the holidays.

DIRECTORY

Abricadabra
Péniche Antipode, moored opposite 55 Quai de la Seine 75019. **Tel** 01 42 03 39 07.
W penicheantipode.fr

Babychou Services
Tel 01 43 13 33 23.
W babychou.com

Chaplin Saint-Lambert
6 Rue Péclet 75015. **Tel** 01 42 50 23 32. W lescinemaschaplin.fr

Kidizen
Tel 06 38 10 97 42.
W kidizen.fr

Musée en Herbe
21 Rue Hérold, 75001. **Tel** 01 40 67 97 66. W musee-en-herbe.com

Théâtre Astral
Parc Floral, Route de la Pyramide 75012. **Tel** 01 43 73 13 93.

THATLou, THATd'Or, THATRue
W thatlou.com

Une Journée au Cirque
115 Blvd Charles de Gaulle, Villeneuve-la-Garenne 92390.
Tel 01 47 99 40 40.
W journee-au-cirque.com

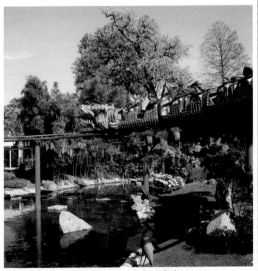

Le Dragon ride in the Jardin d'Acclimatation, in the Bois de Boulogne

Fireworks over Sleeping Beauty Castle, Disneyland® Paris

Theme Parks

The two parks of Disneyland® Paris (see pp256–9) are the biggest and most spectacular of the Paris theme parks, but it's also worth considering a visit to **Parc Astérix**, a theme park centered around the legendary world of Asterix the Gaul. Here, six themed areas feature gladiators, Roman slave auctions, and rides among the many attractions. The park is 24 miles (38 km) northeast of Paris. Take the RER line B to Charles de Gaulle Airport, then the shuttle bus to Parc Astérix.

Sports and Recreation

The giant **Aquaboulevard** waterpark is one of the best places to take energetic youngsters. The **Piscine Joséphine Baker**, which floats on the Seine, has a large paddling pool for children. Other recommended pools are listed on p351.

On Sundays and public holidays, many central streets, including those along the Seine (between Chatelêt and Bercy), are closed to traffic; cylists and rollerbladers descend en masse. The **Patinoire Pailleron** ice rink has family-friendly morning sessions during the holidays, while the winter-only **Patinoire de l'Hôtel de Ville** is a lovely, atmospheric venue with a smaller rink for children.

In summer, don't miss Paris Plages (see p65), when the riverbanks are transformed into a beach and host games such as boules and various children's activities. The Bassin de la Villette becomes a waterpark – you can hire pedaloes and kayaks and cross from one bank to the other on a zipline.

Traditional toys for sale in Pain d'Epices

Children's Stores

Children's stores abound in Paris. The department stores Le Bon Marché and Galeries Lafayette (see p313) have superb collections of clothes and toys. Two charming toy stores with very helpful staff can be found in the atmospheric, old-fashioned Passages – **Si Tu Veux** sells well-made traditional toys, craft kits, and dressing-up costumes, while the delightful **Pain d'Epices** stocks beautiful doll houses and all the furniture and accessories to go inside them. For children's fashions, see pp317 and 320.

Old-fashioned fairground carousels are locuated near Sacré-Coeur (see pp226–7) and in front of the Hôtel de Ville (see p104).

A fun way of inspiring interest in the city's history is a boat trip. Several companies compete from different departure points (see pp74–5), passing a host of riverside sights such as Notre-Dame, the Louvre, and the Musée d'Orsay.

In a tradition going back some 90 years, children can sail toy boats with a long pole around the pond in the Jardin du Luxembourg (see p174). You could also take the family boating on the lakes of the Bois de Boulogne (see p247) and the Bois de Vincennes (see p249).

A family boating on the Lac des Minimes, in the Bois de Vincennes

Street Life and Markets

Outside the Pompidou Center (see pp110–11), street entertainers draw the crowds on sunny afternoons. Musicians, magicians, fire-eaters, and artists of all kinds perform here. In Montmartre, there is a tradition of street-painting, predominantly in Place du Tertre (see p228), where someone is always willing to draw your child's portrait. It's also fun to take the funicular up the hill to Sacré-Coeur (see pp226–7), then walk down through the pretty streets.

Parisian markets are colorful and animated. Try taking the kids to the food markets on

Rue Mouffetard (see pp168 and 331), in the Jardin des Plantes Quarter, or Rue de Buci (see p331) in St.-Germain-des-Prés. The biggest flea market, the Marché aux Puces de St.-Ouen, takes place on weekends (see pp248–9 and 331).

Viewpoints and Sightseeing

Top of the sightseeing list for children is a trip up the Eiffel Tower (see pp196–7). On a clear day, spectacular views over Paris will enable you to point out a number of sights, and at night the city is magically lit up. If you are pushing a stroller, bear in mind that the ascent is in three stages, using two separate elevators.

Other interesting sights for children include Sacré-Coeur (see pp226–7), with its ovoid dome (the second-highest point in Paris after the Eiffel Tower), and Notre-Dame cathedral (see pp82–5), on the Ile de la Cité. Children will enjoy feeding the pigeons in the cathedral square, visiting the gargoyles on the West Front, and listening to you recount the story of the hunchback of Notre-Dame. There are incomparable views from the towers. Children and adults alike will appreciate the enchanting Sainte-Chapelle (see pp88–9), also on the Ile de la Cité.

Contrast ancient and modern Paris with a visit to the Pompidou Center (see pp110–13) and enjoy a ride on the caterpillar-like escalators outside, or go to the café on the roof terrace for the views.

A vintage-style carousel near the Sacré-Coeur basilica, in Montmartre

There is also the 59-story Montparnasse Tower (see p180), with shorter lines and, arguably, even better views than from the Eiffel Tower.

Other Interests

Children can be quick to see the funny side of unusual spectacles. Les Egouts (see p192), Paris's sewers, offer a short tour of the city's sewerage system, while the Catacombs (see p181) are a long series of quarry tunnels built in Roman times and lined with ancient skulls in the 18th century.

On the Ile de la Cité is the Conciergerie (see p87), a turreted prison where many hapless aristocrats spent their final days. The Musée Grévin (see p220), with its waxworks, is always a hit. The Revolution Rooms will especially appeal to older children, with gruesome scenes and grisly sound effects, demonstrating the reality of social upheaval.

Emergencies

Enfance et Partage is a free 24-hour child helpline (also for adults). One of Paris's largest children's hospitals is **Hôpital Necker**.

DIRECTORY

Aquaboulevard
4 Rue Louis Armand 75015.
Tel 01 40 60 10 00.
Open 9am–midnight Mon–Sat, 8am–11pm Sun & public hols.
W aquaboulevard.fr

Pain d'Epices
29 Passage Jouffroy 75009.
Map 6 F4.
Tel 01 47 70 08 68.
W paindepices.fr

Parc Astérix
BP8 Plailly 60128. **Tel** 08 26 46 66 26. **Open** mid-Apr–Oct: 10am– 6pm daily.
W parcasterix.fr

Patinoire de l'Hôtel de Ville
Place de l'Hôtel de Ville, 75004.
Open mid-Dec–Feb: 10am–10pm daily (from noon Mon & Thu, to midnight Fri & Sat).
W paris.fr

Patinoire Pailleron
32 Rue Edouard Pailleron, 75019.
Tel 01 40 40 27 70.
Open noon–1.30pm & 4.15–8.30pm Mon, Tue, Thu, Fri (to midnight Fri), 12.30pm–midnight Sat, 10am–noon & 2–6pm Sun (times vary during school vacations).
W pailleron19.com

Piscine Joséphine Baker
Quai François Mauriac 75013.
Tel 01 56 61 96 50.
Open 7am–8.30pm Mon–Fri, 11am–7pm Sat & Sun (times vary during school vacations).
W carilis.fr

Si Tu Veux
68 Galerie Vivienne 75002.
Map 12 F1.
Tel 01 42 60 59 97.
W situveuxjouer.com

Emergencies

Enfance et Partage
Tel 08 00 05 12 34.
W enfance-et-partage.org

Hôpital Necker
149 Rue de Sèvres 75015.
Map 15 B1. **Tel** 01 44 49 40 00.
W aphp.fr

Waxworks in an ornate room in the Musée Grevin

SURVIVAL GUIDE

PRACTICAL INFORMATION

Paris offers a wealth of things to see and do. A little advance planning can save time. Make use of tourist offices and call ahead to confirm that a sight is not closed for refurbishment or holidays. Guided tours are often the best way to see the essential sights while you get your bearings (see p375). A *Paris Pass* gives unlimited access to the city's many attractions, and cuts down on time spent in lines (see p359). If you're on a budget, note that entry prices may be lower at certain times of day, or on Sundays. Be aware that some stores and museums are closed all day on Monday. Card-carrying students and senior travelers can obtain discounts on some tickets (see p360). Purchase a *carnet* or travel pass to economize and simplify travel on the metro and buses (see pp374 and 376–9).

Visas and Passports

France is part of the Schengen common European border treaty, which means that travelers moving from one Schengen country to another are not subject to border controls. Schengen residents need only to show an identity card when entering France. Visitors from the UK, Ireland, the US, Canada, Australia, and New Zealand need to show a full passport. Tourists from these countries may stay in France without a visa for 90 days within a continuous 180-day period. For the latest information and visa requirements, visitors should consult the website of their embassy.

Tax-Free Goods and Customs Information

At stores displaying the Global Refund Tax-Free sign, visitors residing outside the EU can reclaim the sales tax (TVA) they pay on French goods as long as they spend more than €175 in the same shop in one day and take the goods out of France (see p312). Détaxe receipts can be issued on purchase to reclaim the tax paid (usually 12 per cent). The documents need to be endorsed at a *détaxe* office (located at airports) on exiting the EU within three months of purchase, then mailed in the envelope provided. Rebates cannot be claimed on some goods, including food and drink, medicines, tobacco, cars, and motorcycles. The **Centre des Renseignements des Douanes** provides full information about this.

In general, all personal goods, including cars and bicycles, may be imported to France if they are obviously for personal use and not for sale. There are no restrictions on the quantities of duty-paid and sales tax-paid goods that can be taken from one EU country to another, as long as they are for personal use.

The maximum value of currency that can be brought into or taken out of France is €10,000. Sums in excess of this must be declared to the customs authority.

Travel Safety Advice

Visitors can get up-to-date travel safety information from the **State Department** in the US, the **Foreign and Commonwealth Office** in the UK, and the **Department of Foreign Affairs and Trade** in Australia.

Tourist Information

The main tourist office in Paris, the **Office du Tourisme et des Congrès de Paris**, is near the Jardin des Tuileries (see p132). It will have maps, information, and brochures, and can provide comprehensive information about events in the city.

There are other tourist offices at Place du Tertre, at **Gare du Nord**, **Gare de l'Est**, and **Gare de Lyon**, at **Anvers** metro station, and at the **Paris Expo** exhibition center during trade fairs. There are also summer-only kiosks at sights such as Notre-Dame. **Paris Rendez-Vous** is an information point and store in the Hôtel de Ville.

Admission Charges

An admission fee is usually charged, or a donation expected, at museums.

Le Musée d'Orsay, where entry is free on the first Sunday of the month

◀ A busy platform next to the TGV Bullet train

The entrance fee to some national and municipal museums is waived on the first Sunday of each month for their permanent collections (for example, entrance to the Louvre is free on the first Sunday of each month from October through March). Visitors under 18 years of age and European Union passport holders 18–26 years old are usually admitted free to museums, and there are sometimes discounts for students and seniors who have ID showing their date of birth.

The *Paris Pass* gives the bearer unlimited access to over 60 of the city's attractions for 2, 4, or 6 days, without having to line up (temporary exhibitions are not included). It also offers unlimited travel on the metro, buses, and RER within central Paris, and a ticket for a hop-on hop-off bus tour. The pass must be bought in advance through the website (www.parispass. com) and is either mailed (allow time for delivery) or can be picked up in Paris (see website for details).

Opening Hours

Most of the city's museums and monuments open from 10am to 6 or 7pm. Municipal museums, such as those run by the city of Paris, are usually closed on Monday. The national museums are closed on Tuesday, except Versailles and the Musée d'Orsay, which are closed on Monday. Most ticket counters close 30–45 minutes before the official closing time. To avoid having to stand in line and visit packed museums, take advantage of the *nocturnes* (late-night opening) that many of the major museums offer, or visit on weekday mornings.

Most Paris stores and businesses are open from 9 or 9:30am to 7pm. Some close for lunch for an hour or two around 1pm. Smaller food stores tend to open earlier, around 7am, and take a longer midday break. Most businesses are

Kiosque Théâtre
ticket booth

closed on Sunday, but trading is allowed in tourist areas. Many stores close on Monday.

Listings and Tickets

The main listings magazines, available at all newsstands, are *Pariscope and L'Officiel des Spectacles (see p332)*. Each Wednesday they publish full information on the week's theater, movies, and exhibits, as well as on cabarets, dinner clubs, and some restaurants. FNAC ticket agencies take bookings for all entertainment venues, including temporary museum shows. There are FNAC branches throughout Paris. For further details, call one of their branches *(see p333)*.

For the theater only, the Kiosque Théâtre sells same-day tickets at a 50 per cent discount. There are kiosks at Place de la Madeleine, the Parvis de la Gare Montparnasse, and Place des Ternes *(see p333)*.

DIRECTORY

Customs Information

Centre des Renseigne-ments des Douanes
Tel 08 11 20 44 44
or 01 72 40 89 40.
Open 8.30am–6pm Mon–Fri. W douane.gouv.fr

Travel Safety Advice

Australia
Department of Foreign Affairs and Trade
W dfat.gov.au
W smarttraveller. gov.au

UK
Foreign and Commonwealth Office.
Tel 0207 0616 600.
W gov.uk/foreign-travel-advice

US
US Department of State
W travel.state.gov

Tourist Information

Office du Tourisme et des Congrès de Paris
25 Rue des Pyramides 75001. Map 12 E1. Tel 01 49 52 42 63. Open 10am–7pm daily (May–Oct to 9pm). W parisinfo.com

Anvers (Montmartre)
72 Blvd de Rochechouart 75018. Map 7 A2. Open 10am–6pm daily. Closed Jan 1, May 1, Dec 25.

Gare de l'Est
Opposite platforms 1 & 2, Pl du 11 Novembre 1918, 75010. Map 7 C3. Open 8am–7pm Mon–Sat. Closed Jan 1, May 1, Dec 25.

Gare de Lyon
Opposite platforms L & M, 20 Blvd Diderot 75012. Map 18 F1. Open 8am–6pm Mon–Sat. Closed Jan 1, May 1, Dec 25.

Gare du Nord
18 Rue de Dunkerque 75010. Map 7 B2. Open 8am–6pm daily. Closed Jan 1, May 1, Dec 25.

Paris Expo
1 Pl Porte de Versailles 75015. Tel 01 40 68 22 22 Open 11am–7pm during trade fairs.

Paris Rendez-Vous
29 Rue de Rivoli 75004. Map 13 B3. Open 10am–7pm Mon–Sat.

Embassies

Australia
4 Rue Jean Rey 75015. Map 10 D3. Tel 01 40 59 33 00. W france. embassy.gov.au

Canada
35 Ave Montaigne 75008. Map 10 F1. Tel 01 44 43 29 00. W canadainter national. gc.ca/france

Great Britain
35 Rue du Faubourg St-Honoré 75008.
Map 5 C5.
Tel 01 44 51 31 00.
W gov.uk/government/world/france.fr

Ireland
12 Ave Foch 75016.
Map 3 B4.
Tel 01 44 17 67 00.
W embassyofireland.fr

New Zealand
103 Rue de Grenelle 75007.
Map 11 B3.
Tel 01 45 01 43 43.
W nzembassy.com/france

US
2 Ave Gabriel 75008.
Map 5 B5.
Tel 01 43 12 22 22.
W france.usembassy. gov

Travelers with Special Needs

Services for people with special needs are improving in Paris. Most sidewalks are contoured to allow wheelchairs easier passage, and restaurants, hotels, and museums are adapting their amenities. There is, for example, wheelchair access to the first and second floor of the Eiffel Tower, at a reduced fee, while the Louvre and Musée d'Orsay are free to disabled visitors and their escorts.

Increasingly, sights are sporting the *Tourisme & Handicap* label denoting that they are accessible to people with physical, mental, hearing, and visual impediments. The Office du Tourisme et des Congrès *(see p359)* has a guide (*Les Sites Labellisés "Tourisme & Handicap" à Paris et en Île-de-France*) listing these. The association **J'accede** has details (in French and English) of accessible museums, hotels, bars, restaurants, and movie theaters in Paris and other French cities.

Metro stations and bus routes accessible to travelers with limited mobility are marked with a wheelchair symbol on their maps. The RATP's **Infomobi** website details all their accessible public transportation and stations. Paris's international train stations have elevators, ramps, courtesy wheelchairs, signs in Braille, and a magnetic loop at ticket counters for the

hearing impaired. **Accès Plus** is a free service to greet and accompany disabled travelers on their journey. **Les Compagnons du Voyage** will provide an escort for persons with limited mobility on any form of public transportation, for a fee.

Some Paris taxi companies (such as G7, *see p381*), have vehicles suited to travelers with limited mobility; taxis are required by law to assist disabled travelers.

For further up-to-date information on public amenities for the disabled, contact the **GIHP**.

Tourisme & Handicap sign

Student Travelers

Students with valid ID cards benefit from discounts of 25–50 per cent at theaters, museums, movie theaters, and many public monuments. An ISIC card (International Student ID card) may be bought from the main travel agencies and the **CIDJ**. The **BVJ** has two reasonably priced hostels in Paris *(see p283)*.

Senior Travelers

Some museums and monuments, theaters, and independent movie theaters offer reductions for visitors over 60. Théâtre du Chatelet *(see p339)*, for example, offers discounted tickets 15 minutes before showtime to over-65s. Expect to be asked for ID, such as a passport, to prove your date of birth. Canal tour operators **Canauxrama and Paris Canal** offer reduced fees. Over-60s are eligible for a 25 per cent discount from state railroad **SNCF** for off-peak travel. Check their website for details.

Etiquette and Smoking

Etiquette (*la politesse*) is everything to Parisians. On entering a store or cafe, you are expected to say *"bonjour, Madame"* or *"bonjour, Monsieur"* to staff, and when leaving to say *"au revoir."* Be sure to add *"s'il vous plaît"* (please) when ordering something, and *"pardon"* if you accidentally bump someone.

The French shake hands on meeting someone for the first time, and when greeting workmates or acquaintances. Friends and colleagues who know each other well usually greet each other with a kiss on each cheek. If you are unsure, wait to see if they proffer a hand or a cheek.

Smoking is prohibited in all public places, but is allowed on restaurant, café, and pub terraces, as long as they are not enclosed.

Public Restrooms

Automated, self-cleaning toilets can be found in restrooms across the city. They have been upgraded to be larger than previously, wheelchair-usable, and free. Children under ten are not allowed to use these toilets on their own because the automated cleaning function can be a danger to small children. There are also more than 30 free public restrooms in Paris; locations are listed on the **Mairie de Paris** website.

Paris Time

Paris is 1 hour ahead of Greenwich Mean Time (GMT) or British Summer Time (BST). New York is 6 hours behind Paris, Los Angeles is 9 hours behind, and Auckland is 11 hours ahead. France observes Daylight Saving in summer; clocks are set forward by 1 hour on the last weekend in March and put back by 1 hour on the last weekend in October. The French use the 24-hour clock.

The Eiffel Tower, a wheelchair-accessible attraction

Electrical Adapters

The voltage in France is 220 volts. Plugs have two small round pins; heavier-duty appliances have two large round pins. Better hotels offer built-in adapters for shavers only or will lend you an adapter. Adapters can also be bought at department stores, such as BHV *(see p313)*.

Conversion Chart

US to Metric
1 inch = 2.54 centimeters
1 foot = 30 centimeters
1 mile = 1.6 kilometers
1 ounce = 28 grams
1 pound = 454 grams
1 pint = 0.47 liter
1 gallon = 3.8 liters

Metric to US
1 millimeter = 0.04 inch
1 centimeter = 0.4 inch
1 meter = 3 feet 3 inches
1 kilometer = 0.6 mile
1 gram = 0.04 ounce
1 kilogram = 2.2 pounds
1 liter = 2.1 pints

Responsible Tourism

A green wave has been quietly rolling over Paris. Compost bins are appearing on apartment balconies, organic markets are thriving, recycling bins are popping up in mass transit stations, and hotels use eco-friendly products. Supermarkets usually charge a small fee for plastic bags for your purchases.

Paris has over 400 parks and gardens to help the city breathe, and sustainable development is a priority. "*Eco-quartiers*" are emerging, an example of which is the Rungis development in the 13th arrondissement, which has solar panels powering hot water and electricity and where 50 per cent of water on the roof is collected for gardens,

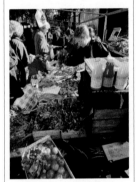
Fresh produce at one of Paris's organic markets

recycling is prevalent, and priority is given to pedestrians, cyclists, and mass transit. Even the Eiffel Tower is eco-aware – its power is 100 per cent renewable. Solar panels on some store roofs have further reduced energy consumption.

An increasing number of hotels, such as **Hotel Garvarni**, are sporting the European Ecolabel or the *Clef Verte* (Green Key), as a mark of their commitment to efficient energy and water consumption, waste separation, and reduction in chemical use.

Organic, or "*bio*," cafés and restaurants are flourishing, including **Le Bio d'Adam et Eve**, a deli serving fresh meals and sandwiches for eat-in or takeout, and **Le So**, an organic gourmet restaurant with a tiny *épicerie* at the back. **Le Petit Bazar** also sells fairtrade coffee and recycled toys.

There are weekly organic markets at Boulevard Raspail, Place Brancusi, and Boulevard Batignolles. Organic supermarkets, such as Naturalia and Biocoop, can be found across the city. **Canal Bio** is an independent store selling organic and fairtrade produce.

DIRECTORY

Travelers with Special Needs

Accès Plus (SNCF)
Tel 0 890 640 650, then press 1 (call 2 days ahead of planned travel).
w accessibilite.sncf.com

Groupement pour l'Insertion des Personnes Handicapées Physiques (GIHP)
61 Rue du Faubourg Poissoniere 75009.
Map 7 A4. Tel 01 43 95 66 36. w gihpnational.org

Infomobi
Tel 09 70 81 83 85.
w infomobi.com

J'accede
20 passage Turquetil 75011. Tel 01 43 71 98 10.
w jaccede.com

Les Compagnons du Voyage
34 Rue Campionnet 75018.
Tel 01 58 76 08 33 (emergencies: 06 62 24 72 91).
w compagnons.com

Student Travelers

BVJ
20 Rue Jean-Jacques Rousseau 75001.
Map 12 F2.
Tel 01 53 00 90 90.

44 Rue des Bernardins 75005.
Map 13 B5.
Tel 01 43 29 34 80.

CIDJ
101 Quai Branly 75015.
Map 10 E2.
Tel 01 44 49 12 00.
w cidj.com

International Student Identity Card (ISIC)
w isic.org

Senior Travelers

Canauxrama
13 Quai de la Loire 75019.
Map 8 F1. Tel 01 42 39 15 00. w canauxrama.fr

Paris Canal
21 Quai de la Loire 75019.
Map 8 F1.
Tel 01 42 40 96 97.
w pariscanal.com

SNCF
w sncf.com
w voyages-sncf.com

Public Conveniences

Mairie de Paris
Sanisettes Parisiennes.
w paris.fr

Responsible Tourism

Le Bio d'Adam et Eve
41 Rue St-Honoré 75001.
Map 13 A2. Tel 09 82 36 94 57/06 20 31 14 80.

Canal Bio
46 Quai de la Loire 75019. Map 8 F1.
Tel 01 42 06 44 44.
w canal-bio.net

Hotel Garvarni
5 Rue Gavarni 75116.
Map 9 B3. Tel 01 45 24 52 82. w gavarni.com

Le Petit Bazar
10 Rue Gramme 75015.
Tel 09 84 53 69 67.
w lepetitbazar.com

Le So
93 Rue Montmartre 75002. Map 13 A1.
Tel 01 40 28 02 83.

Personal Security and Health

Paris is as safe or as dangerous as other Western European capital cities. Common sense is usually sufficient to keep you out of trouble. If you get sick during your visit, pharmacists are an excellent source of advice. In France, pharmacists can diagnose many health problems and suggest appropriate treatment. For more serious medical help, someone at the emergency numbers in the box below will be able to deal with most issues. There are many specialty services available, including a general advice line for English-speakers in crisis and a hotline for psychiatric help.

French pharmacy sign

Emergency button at metro stations

DIRECTORY

Emergency Numbers

SAMU (ambulance)
Tel 15 or 112 (freecall).

Police
Tel 17 or 112 (freecall).

**Sapeurs-Pompiers
(fire department)**
Tel 18 or 112 (freecall).

SOS – all services
Tel 112 (freecall).

**SOS Médecins
(doctor, house calls)**
Tel 36 24 or 01 47 07 77 77.
W sosmedecins.fr

SOS Dentaire (dentist)
Tel 01 43 37 51 00.

Burn Specialists
Hôpital Cochin 75014.
Tel 01 5841 4141.

**SOS Help (English-
language crisis line)**
Tel 01 46 21 46 46.
W soshelpline.org

**SOS Psy Urgence (for
psychiatric help, in French)**
Tel 08 92 23 31 68
W sospsyurgence.fr

Police

Since Paris is one of the most visited capitals in the world, the police are no strangers to dealing with tourists. If you need assistance, look for bilingual officers sporting a badge identifying the languages they speak. Thefts, assaults, loss of property, and missing persons must be reported in person at the nearest police station; central police stations (*Commissariat de Police*) within the 20 arrondissements are open 24 hours a day, 7 days a week. Bilingual officers are usually available, but if not, there is a software program called SAVE (*Système d'Accueil des Victimes Etrangères*) available in 20 languages, which allows tourists to record their complaint in their own language. For lost or stolen passports, call your embassy or consulate (*see p359*).

What to Be Aware Of

Visitors should get up-to-date travel safety information from their relevant state department or foreign office (*see p359*).

Most visits to Paris are trouble-free. The center, in particular, experiences little violent crime. Muggings and brawls do occur, but they are rare compared to many world capitals. However, try to avoid poorly lit or isolated places. Beware of pickpockets, especially on the Metro and buses during rush hour and in major tourist areas. Keep all valuables securely concealed, and if you carry a purse or case, never let it out of your sight. Take only as much cash as you think you will need; most places accept credit cards. Travelers' checks are a safe method of carrying large sums of money.

When traveling late at night, avoid long transfers in Metro stations such as Châtelet-Les-

Parisian firefighter

Police officer

Police officer

Typical Paris police car

Paris fire engine

Paris ambulance

Halles and Montparnasse. Generally, areas around RER train stations tend to attract groups of youths from outlying areas who come to Paris for entertainment and may become unruly. The last RER trains to and from outlying areas should also be avoided.

Insure your possessions before arrival and do not carry valuables on sightseeing or entertainment trips. Never leave luggage unattended in Metro or train stations because it could cause a bomb scare.

In an Emergency

The emergency telephone number for the police is 17 and for an ambulance it is 15. In the event of an emergency in the Metro, call the station agent by using the yellow telephone marked *Chef de Station* on all Metro and RER platforms, or go to the ticket booth at the entrance. Most Metro stations have emergency buttons, and train cars have alarm pulls.

The RAPT has some 7,000 video cameras in stations and on trains, as well as 17,300 in the rail and bus network. Transit police patrol stations, and a small team of police officers survey the network electronically. Visitors should

be vigilant for pickpockets in heavy tourist areas and not let themselves be distracted. Caution should be exercised in the Les Halles area at night and on weekends.

In the case of a medical emergency, call **SAMU** (ambulance) or the **Sapeurs-Pompiers** (fire department). Fire department ambulances are often the fastest to arrive at an emergency. First-aid and emergency treatment is provided at all fire stations.

If you have been the victim of a physical assault, the police will ask that you undergo an examination at the medical-legal emergency unit near Notre-Dame.

Hospitals and Pharmacies

All EU nationals holding a European Health Insurance Card (EHIC) are entitled to use the French national health service. Patients must pay for all treatments and can then reclaim most of the cost from the health authorities. The process may be lengthy and travelers should therefore consider purchasing private travel insurance. Non-EU nationals must have full private medical insurance while in France and pay for services, claiming their costs back later from their insurance company.

Hospitals with emergency rooms are shown on the Street Finder maps *(see pp382–415)*. For English-speaking visitors, there are two private hospitals with bilingual staff and doctors: the **American Hospital of Paris** and the **Franco-Britannique Hospital**. The **Centre Médical Europe** is an inexpensive private clinic, which also has a dental practice.

There are many pharmacies throughout the city, and a short list is provided on this page. Pharmacies are indicated by a green cross on the store front.

DIRECTORY

Medical Centers

American Hospital of Paris
63 Blvd Victor-Hugo 92200, Neuilly-sur-Seine.
Map 1 A3.
Tel 01 46 41 25 25.
Private hospital. Inquire about insurance and costs.
W american-hospital.org

Centre Médical Europe
44 Rue d'Amsterdam 75009.
Map 6 D3.
Tel 01 42 81 93 33.
Open 8am–8pm Mon–Sat.
Private clinic. Appointments or walk-ins.

Franco-Britannique Hospital
4 Rue Kleber 92300, Levallois-Perret.
Tel 01 47 59 59 59.
Private hospital.
W ihfb.org

Pharmacies

British and American Pharmacy
1 Rue Auber 75009.
Map 6 D4.
Tel 01 42 65 88 29.
Open 9am–8pm Mon–Sat.

Pharmacie Anglo-Americaine
37 Ave Marceau 75016.
Map 10 E1.
Tel 01 47 20 57 37.
Open 8:30am–8:30pm Mon–Fri, 9am–8pm Sat.

Pharmacie Bader
10–12 Blvd St.-Michel 75006.
Map 12 F5.
Tel 01 43 26 92 66.
Open 8:30am–9pm daily.

Pharmacie Lafayette des Halles
10 Blvd Sebastopol 75004.
Map 13 A3.
Tel 01 42 72 03 23.
Open 9am–midnight Mon–Sat, 9am–10pm Sun.

Pharmacie Les Champs
84 Ave des Champs-Elysées 75008.
Map 4 F5.
Tel 01 45 62 02 41.
Open 24 hours daily.

Banking and Local Currency

Visitors to Paris will find that the banks usually offer them the best rates of exchange. Privately owned bureaux de change, on the other hand, have variable rates, and care should be taken to check small print details relating to commission and minimum charges before any transaction is completed.

Société Générale bank

Banks and Bureaux de Change

Most Parisian banks will exchange foreign currency and traveler's checks. Make sure you have some form of photographic ID with you. The main French banks are BNP Paribas, Société Générale, Crédit Agricole, and Crédit Mutuel (CIC). Banks generally offer the best exchange rates but the commission rates vary.

Private bureaux de change offer poorer exchange rates than banks. In central Paris, they are usually open Monday to Saturday, and can be found along the Champs-Elysées and near the main tourist attractions and monuments, as well as at airports, train stations, and some international hotels and stores.

Credit and Debit Cards

Major credit cards such as Visa and MasterCard, and debit cards such as Switch, Maestro, and Cirrus, are widely accepted by most businesses in Paris. Most banks have ATMs (outside or in an indoor area) which accept these cards. This is the quickest and most convenient way of obtaining money in the local currency, although a small charge for this service will be deducted from your account. Be aware that many French businesses do not accept American Express credit cards. French credit and debit cards operate on a chip-and-PIN system, so you will need to know your PIN *(code personnel)* for making purchases in stores. If you have a card that does not use chip-and-PIN technology, ask for your credit card to be swiped in the magnetic reader.

Be sure to notify your bank and credit card providers before you leave for France. Some banks forbid foreign transactions for security reasons unless they have been notified ahead of time.

Credit and debit card reader

Pre-Paid Currency Cards

Pre-paid currency cards are also widely accepted in Paris. You can use them to withdraw cash at an ATM, pay for purchases or make travel reservations. You can load up your card with credit ahead of the trip, and top it up online or by phone while you are abroad via such companies as **FairFX**.

Most credit card companies, including Visa, MasterCard, and American Express, also offer pre-paid cards. A charge is generally applied to top up your card.

Wiring Money and Bank Transfers

Bank transfers and money wires can also be arranged – either bank to bank or via companies such as Western Union and MoneyGram. **Banque Postale**, also known as La Poste, is an agent for Western Union and can facilitate bank transfers.

Often, the money is transferred to the main bank, then on to the relevant branch and can take 2–5 business days to arrive in the French account.

DIRECTORY

Foreign Banks

American Express
11 Rue Scribe 75009.
Map 6 D5.

Barclays
24 bis Ave de l'Opéra 75001.
Map 12 E1.

HSBC
103 Ave des Champs-Elysées
75008. **Map** 5 A5. **w** hsbc.fr

Bureaux de Change

Change Group
134 Blvd St.-Germain 75006.
Map 12 F4. **Tel** 09 64 08 24 70.

49 Ave de l'Opéra 75002.
Map 6 E5. **Tel** 09 63 26 25 42.

Travelex
125 Ave des Champs-Elysées
75008. **Map** 4 E4.
Tel 01 47 20 25 14.

Gare du Nord (opposite Eurostar arrivals), 18 Rue de Dunkerque.
Map 7 B2.

Pre-Paid Currency Cards

FairFX
Tel 020 7107 1206.
w fairfx.com

Visa
w usa.visa.com

Lost Cards and Travelers' Checks

American Express
Tel 08 00 83 28 20.

MasterCard
Tel 08 00 90 13 87.

Visa
Tel 08 00 90 11 79.

Wiring Money

**Banque Postale
(Western Union)**
111 Rue de Sèvres 75006. **Map** 15
B1. **w** labanquepostale.fr

The Euro

The euro (€) is the common currency of the European Union (EU). It went into general circulation on January 1 2002, initially for 12 participating countries, including France. EU members using the euro as sole official currency are known as the eurozone. Several EU members have opted out of joining this common currency. Euro bills are identical throughout the eurozone countries, each one including designs of fictional architectural structures and monuments. The coins, however, have one side identical (the value side), and one side with an image unique to each country. Both bills and coins are exchangeable in all of the participating eurozone countries.

Bills

Euro bills have seven denominations. The €5 bill (grey in color) is the smallest, followed by the €10 bill, €20 bill, €50 bill, €100 bill, €200 bill, and €500 bill.

€5 bill

€10 bill

€20 bill

€50 bill

€100 bill

€200 bill

€500 bill

€2 coin

€1 coin

50 cents

20 cents

10 cents

Coins

The euro has eight coin denominations: €1 and €2; 50 cents, 20 cents, 10 cents, 5 cents, 2 cents, and 1 cent. The €1 and €2 coins are both silver and gold in color. The 50-, 20- and 10-cent coins are gold. The 5-, 2-, and 1-cent coins are bronze.

5 cents

2 cents

1 cent

Communications and Media

The main French telecommunications agency is Orange (formerly France Télécom). The postal service is La Poste. Both work efficiently. Public telephones are located in most public places and usually require a phone card *(télécarte)*. Post offices have "hot stations" for customer information, and automatic vending machines for stamps and weighing packages. There are numerous post offices *(bureaux de poste)*, identified by the blue-on-yellow La Poste sign, scattered around the city. Foreign-language newspapers can be bought at newsstands throughout Paris, and some TV channels and radio stations broadcast foreign-language programs.

French Telephone Numbers

Telephone numbers in France have ten digits. The first two digits indicate the region: 01 and 09 are for Paris and the Ile de France; 02 is for northwest France; 03 is for the northeast; 04 is for the southeast; 05 is for the southwest. French cell phone numbers begin with 06 or 07; 08 indicates a special rate number. Toll-free numbers *(numéro vert)* begin with 0800. For useful telephone numbers and codes, please see the box below.

Public Telephones

Paris has a large number of public telephones. To use one, you need a phonecard *(télécarte)*, although some do accept credit cards. Sold in *tabacs*, post offices, France Télécom agencies, and some newsstands, there are two kinds of *télécartes* – smart cards, available in 50 or 120 telephone units, which you simply insert in the phone, and code cards for

which you dial in a code. For international calls, the International Telephone Card is a good deal. If using a credit card, you will receive credit for calls up to €15. When the limit is reached, the call is cut off. Most public telephones can also receive calls – the number will be displayed above the phone unit.

Cell Phones

In order to use your cell phone in France, it must be compatible with a minimum of GSM 900 or 1800 MHz frequencies. Contact your provider before leaving home to check your phone's compatibility.

Alert your network before traveling so that they can set your phone to allow roaming. If you don't do this, your phone may not work. Always check roaming charges with your service provider before traveling, since making and receiving calls can be very expensive. Some companies offer "packages" for foreign

calls that can work out to be much more economical.

If your phone is unlocked, you can insert a local SIM card into it. SIM cards can be obtained in Paris from one of the local providers, such as **Orange**, **Bouygues Télécom**, **SFR**, **Free** , or **La Poste Mobile** and topped off as required. This way you get a French phone number and pay normal, local cell rates.

Internet Access

Internet access is widely available in Paris. There are a huge number of Internet cafés. Public libraries also provide Internet access. There are many free Wi-Fi spots around the city, including in parks, gardens, and town halls. Thanks to the *Pass Paris-Wi-Fi*, a free wireless broadband service set up by the Paris City Council (Mairie de Paris), you can connect instantly to the Internet by selecting the option *"Paris wi-fi 2h"* within your device settings. The Mairie de Paris has a list of 260 free Wi-Fi sites *(Localisation des points Wi-Fi)* on their website (www.paris.fr), while www.cafes-wifi.com lists cafés with Wi-Fi Internet access. Many hotels offer Wi-Fi connections, but these are

Using the Internet in a library

Useful Telephone Numbers and Codes

- **To call the police**, dial 17; **for an ambulance**, 15.

- **Directory assistance**, dial 118 712.

- **International directory assistance**, for all countries, dial 118 700.

- **To make direct international calls**, dial 00 followed by the country code, area code (omit the initial 0) and the number.

- **To make a collect call (PCV)**, dial 0800 99 00 followed by the country code.

- Country telephone codes: **Australia**: 61; **Canada** and **US**: 1; **Ireland**: 353; **New Zealand**: 64; **UK**: 44.

- **Low-rate period**: 7pm–8am Mon–Fri, all day Sat, Sun, and public holidays.

- **To call France from your home country**, dial: from the US 011 33; from the UK 00 33; from Australia: 00 11 33. Omit the first 0 of the French area code.

rarely free. There are pay-for-service Internet kiosks and Wi-Fi hotspots at Charles de Gaulle and Orly airports. Wi-Fi cards are available from bookstores in the terminals or you can purchase a session ahead of time on the Paris airports site (www.adp.fr).

Postal Services

The postal service in France is fast and usually reliable. Postage stamps *(timbres)* can be bought at post offices and are sold individually or in *carnets* of ten. They can be bought either at a post office counter or vending machine. Post offices also have self-service machines on which you can weigh letters and parcels, both domestic and international, and then the machines dispense the appropriate stamps. There are eight different price zones for international mail. Alternatively, you can buy stamps online and print them at home, or they can be bought at *tabacs*. Post offices also sell phonecards, and will cash or send international money orders. They usually open 8am–7pm Mon–Fri and 9am–1pm Sat. Be prepared for long lines during peak times (early morning, lunchtime, and early evening).

Parisian mailbox

For *poste restante* (mail holding), the sender should write the recipient's name in block letters, then "Poste Restante," followed by the address of the Paris-Louvre post office *(see Directory)*.

Further information on all mail services is provided on the **La Poste** website.

Postal Codes

The first three digits of Paris postal codes (750 or 751) indicate Paris; the last two numbers indicate the arrondissement (district) number. Paris's arrondissements are numbered from 1 to 20 *(see p382)*. The postcode of the first arrondissement is 75001.

TV and Radio

The French TV channels are *TF1* and *France 2*, both with a lightweight mix; *France 3*, with documentaries, debate, and classic films; *5e ("La Cinquième")* with discussion programs; the Franco-German high-culture *ARTE*, specializing in arts, classical music, and movies; and *M6*, airing mainly music, reality TV shows, and commercial series. Cable and satellite channels include CNN, Sky, a variety of BBC channels, and the English- and French-language news channel *France 24*. *BBC Radio 4* can be picked up during the day, while *BBC World Service* broadcasts at night. *Radio France International* (738 AM), along with live broadcasting in French and English, gives daily news in English on their website (www.rfi.fr).

Newspapers and Magazines

British and other European newspapers can be bought on the day of publication at newsagents *(maisons de la presse)* or newsstands *(kiosques)* throughout the city. These include European or international editions, such as *Financial Times Europe*, the *Guardian International*, *The Weekly Telegraph*, *USA Today*, *The Economist*, and *The International Herald Tribune*.

The main French national dailies are – from right to left

A *kiosque* selling newspapers and magazines

on the political spectrum – *Le Figaro, Le Monde, Libération,* and *L'Humanité*. The weeklies include the satirical *Le Canard Enchaîné*, news magazines *Le Nouvel Observateur, Marianne,* and *L'Express*, as well as listings magazines *(see p332, 359)*.

DIRECTORY

Cell Phones

Bouygues Télécom
Tel 1034.
W bouyguestelecom.fr

Free
Tel 3244. **W** movile.free.fr

Orange
Tel 09 69 36 39 00 (English speaking). **W** orange.fr or orange-wifi.com

La Poste Mobile
Tel 08 05 30 50 09.
W lapostemobile.fr

SFR
Tel 1026. **W** sfr.fr

Internet Access

Luxembourg Micro
81 Blvd St.-Michel, 75005.
Map 16 F1. **Tel** 01 46 33 27 98.

Milk
5 Rue d'Odessa, 75014.
Map 15 C2. **Tel** 01 43 20 10 37.
31 Blvd Sebastopol, 75001.
Map 13 B2. **Tel** 01 42 33 68 17.
W milklub.com

Postal Services

La Poste
W laposte.fr

Paris-Forum des Halles
1 Rue Pierre Lescot, Forum des Halles, 75001. **Map** 13 A2. **Tel** 3631.

Paris-Louvre
52 Rue du Louvre 75001.
Map 12 F1. **Tel** 3631.

Paris St.-Lazare
7 Rue de la Pépinière 75008.
Map 5 C4. **Tel** 3631.

Delivery Services

Chronopost
Tel 08 25 80 18 01. **W** chronopost.fr

DHL
Tel 08 25 10 00 80 or
01 80 14 63 32. **W** dhl.fr

FedEx
Tel 08 20 12 38 00 **W** fedex.com.

GETTING TO PARIS

Paris is a major hub of European air, road, and rail travel. Direct flights from all over the world serve the French capital's two main international airports. Paris is also at the center of France's vast internal rail network and of Europe's high-speed train network, with regular, fast Eurostar services under the Channel from London, Thalys from Brussels, Amsterdam, and Cologne, and TGVs from Marseille and Geneva, as well as many other cities. Freeways (autoroutes) converge on Paris from all directions, including the UK via the Eurotunnel.

Arriving by Air

Paris is served by nearly all international airlines. It has two major airports, Charles de Gaulle (CDG) and Orly (ORY), and one secondary airport, Beauvais.

From the United States there are regular flights direct to Paris, mainly on **American Airlines**, **United**, **Delta**, and **Air France**. From Canada, **Air Canada** and Air France fly direct to Paris.

The main airlines with regular flights between the UK and Paris are **British Airways** and Air France, along with low-cost carriers **easyJet**, **Flybe**, and **Jet2**.

Qantas provides flights to Paris from Australia and New Zealand. **Air Austral** has flights from Australia via Réunion. **Emirates** and **Etihad Airways** fly from Australia via the Middle East, while **Cathay Pacific**, **Thai Airways**, and **Singapore Air** fly from Asia.

Ryanair flies from Dublin, Shannon, and Glasgow, and **Wizz Air** from parts of Eastern Europe to Beauvais airport.

For contact details of all these airlines, see page 369.

Tickets and Fares

The peak summer season in Paris is July through September. Airline fares are at their highest at this time. Different airlines may have slightly varying high summer season periods. Generally, airlines offer their lowest fares to passengers booking on the Internet via their websites. It often pays to book far in advance. However, last-minute deals are sometimes available. Addresses of some discount agencies in Paris are listed on page 371. These agencies offer flights to Paris at competitive prices. Internet travel reservation companies such as Expedia offer airline tickets at discounted prices.

Charles de Gaulle (CDG) Airport

Paris's main airport, Charles de Gaulle (also known as Roissy), lies 19 miles (30 km) north of the city. It has two main terminals, CDG1 and CDG2, and a charter flight terminal, T3. A free CDGVAL shuttle train connects the three terminals.

Charles de Gaulle airport train station

Buses, trains, and taxis all run to central Paris from Charles de Gaulle airport, but traffic is congested at rush hour, so leave plenty of time. **Air France Buses** operates two bus services from both CDG1 and CDG2: one goes to Porte Maillot and Charles de Gaulle–Etoile (running about every 12 minutes, with a travel time of about 40 minutes); the other runs to the Gare de Lyon and Montparnasse TGV train station every 30 minutes, with a travel time of about 50 minutes.

The **RATP Roissybus** serves all three terminals, and departs every 20 minutes from 6am until 11pm for L'Opéra, taking about 50 minutes.

Airport Shuttle provides a door-to-door private transfer service in a minibus between Charles de Gaulle, Orly, and Beauvais airports and individual hotels. It costs €40 per person, or €21–25 each for two or more people. Reserve at least 48 hours ahead, then call them after landing to confirm your ride. They also drop off at the Arc de Triomphe for €18 per person.

Disneyland® Paris runs the VEA shuttle bus service from 8:30am until 7:45pm daily (until 10pm Friday and 9:30pm Sunday) every 30–45 minutes from CDG1 and CDG2.

Access to central Paris by train is from **RER** stations (Line B) at CDG1 and CDG2. RER trains leave

Waiting area at Charles de Gaulle airport

every 5–15 minutes and take 25 minutes to Gare du Nord and 45 minutes to Châtelet-Les-Halles, and then continue to several other major stations including Luxembourg, St.-Michel, and Port Royal.

Taxis take 25–45 minutes to the center of Paris and cost €45–55. Lines for taxis can be long.

Orly Airport (ORY)

Paris's other main airport, Orly, is located 9 miles (15 km) south of the capital. It has two terminals, Orly Sud and Orly Ouest.

Travelers arriving at Orly can take a bus, train, or taxi to central Paris. The buses are run by **Air France Buses** and **RATP Orlybus**. Air France buses take about 30 minutes to reach the city center, stopping at Les Invalides and Gare de Montparnasse. The Orlybus runs every 12–20 minutes and takes about 25 minutes to reach the city center at Denfert-Rochereau.

Orlyval train leaving Orly Airport

The shuttle Jet Bus service takes travelers from the airport to Villejuif-Louis Aragon Metro station every 15–20 minutes.

A shuttle bus service (VEA) links the airport with Disneyland® Paris. It runs every 45 minutes between 8:30am and 7:30pm.

Orlyrail bus service links the airport with **RER** Line C at Pont de Rungis. Trains leave from here every 15 minutes (every 30 minutes after 9pm), taking 25 minutes to reach the Gare d'Austerlitz. An automatic train, Orlyval, links the airport with RER Line B at Antony station, from where trains leave every 4–8 minutes for Châtelet-Les-Halles.

Taxis to the city center take about 25–45 minutes and cost €25–30.

Beauvais Airport

Beauvais airport serves mainly budget airlines. It is 44 miles (70 km) from Paris. A shuttle bus service operates between Beauvais and Porte-Maillot – buses leave 20 minutes after a flight has landed. Tickets are available in the arrivals lounge, or at the sales points outside. Trains run from Beauvais station to Gare du Nord, but Beauvais station is a 15-minute taxi-ride from the airport, and the train trip takes 75 minutes into Paris. Taxis take 1–1½ hours and cost about €100–130.

DIRECTORY

Main Airlines Serving Paris

Air Austral
Tel 0825 013 012 (France).
🆆 air-austral.com

Air Canada
Tel 1 888 247 2262 (Canada), 0825 880 881 (France).
🆆 aircanada.com

Air France
Tel 36 54 (France).
🆆 airfrance.fr

American Airlines
Tel (800) 433 7300 (USA), 08 26 46 09 50 (France).
🆆 aa.com

British Airways
Tel 0844 493 0787 (UK), 0825 825 400 (France).
🆆 britishairways.com

Cathay Pacific
🆆 cathaypacific.com

Delta
Tel 01 800 221 1212 (USA), 08 92 70 26 09 (France).
🆆 delta.com

easyJet
Tel 0330 365 5000 (UK), 0820 420 315 (France).
🆆 easyjet.com

Emirates
Tel 01 57 32 49 99 (France).🆆 emirates.com

Etihad Airways
Tel 01 57 32 43 43 (France).🆆 etihad.com

Flybe
Tel 0371 700 2000 (UK), +44 1329 683152 (outside UK).
🆆 flybe.com

Jet2
Tel 0333 300 0404 (UK), 0821 230 203 (France).
🆆 jet2.com

Qantas
Tel 13 13 13 (Australia) 0845 7 747 767 (UK), 01 57 32 92 83 (France).
🆆 qantas.com

Ryanair
Tel 0871 246 0000 (UK), 0892 562 210 (France).
🆆 ryanair.com

Singapore Air
Tel 08 21 23 03 80 (France), +33 1 53 65 79 00 (from abroad).
🆆 singaporeair.com

Thai Airways
Tel 01 800 426 5204 (USA), 01 55 68 80 70 (France).
🆆 thaiairways.fr

United
Tel 01 800 864 8331 (USA), 01 71 23 03 35 (France).
🆆 united.com

Wizz Air
Tel 08 99 86 07 29 (France), 0911 752 2257 (UK).
🆆 wizzair.com

Airport Transfer Information

Air France Buses
🆆 cars-airfrance.com

Airport Shuttle
Tel 01 82 28 38 70.
🆆 parishuttle.com

RATP Roissybus/ Orlybus
Tel 3246 (information).
🆆 ratp.fr

RER Trains
Tel 3246.

CDG Airport Hotels

Holiday Inn
Tel 01 30 18 22 00.
🆆 holidayinn.com

Ibis
Tel 01 49 19 19 19.
🆆 ibishotel.com

Novotel
Tel 01 49 19 27 27.
🆆 novotel.com

Sheraton
Tel 01 49 19 70 70.
🆆 starwoodhotels.com

Orly Airport Hotels

Hilton Hotel
Tel 01 45 12 45 12.
🆆 hilton.com

Ibis
Tel 01 56 70 50 50.
🆆 ibishotel.com

Mercure
Tel 08 25 80 69 69.
🆆 mercure.com

Arriving by Rail

Eurostar trains travel directly from central London (St. Pancras) and Ashford and Ebbsfleet (both in Kent) to central Paris (Gare du Nord) in 2 hours and 15 minutes. There are up to 24 departures daily. Other high-speed services into Paris include Thalys trains from Brussels, Amsterdam, and Cologne, and **TGVs** from throughout France. Reservations are essential. **Rail Europe** offers a comprehensive information and reservation service for these and other trains throughout Europe.

As the rail hub of France and the Continent, Paris has six major international train stations operated by the French state railroad, known as **SNCF** (see p380). The Gare de Lyon (Map 18 F1) is the city's main station, serving southern France, the Alps, Italy, and Switzerland. The Gare de l'Est (Map 7 C3) serves eastern France, Austria, Switzerland, and Germany. Trains from Britain, Holland, Belgium, Scandinavia, and northeastern France arrive at the Gare du Nord (Map 7 B2). Trains from some Channel ports and Normandy arrive at the Gare St.-Lazare (Map 5 C3). The terminals for trains from Spain, as well as from the Brittany ports, are the Gare Montparnasse (Map 15 C2) and

Gare du Nord station concourse

Gare d'Austerlitz (Map 18 D2). Trains from southwestern France arrive at Gare d'Austerlitz. Other main stations are: Gare de Bercy; Massy-Palaiseau; Marne-la-Vallée for Disneyland® Resort Paris; and Aéroport Charles-de-Gaulle.

Accommodations can be reserved at the tourist office at the Gare de Lyon (see p359). All the train stations are served by city buses, the Metro, and RER trains, plus taxis. Directional signs show where to make connections.

Eurotunnel

Travelers coming to Paris from Britain by road will need to cross the English Channel. The simplest way to do so is on the vehicle-carrying train shuttles that travel through the Channel Tunnel. Operated by **Eurotunnel**, these trains run between the terminals at

Folkestone and Calais. The Tunnel terminal has direct freeway access on both the English and French side

Passengers are directed onto the trains and remain with their vehicle, though they may get out of their car and walk around inside the train during the trip.

The journey through the Tunnel takes about 30 minutes, plus waiting time for boarding the train. Trains depart every 15–30 minutes, depending on demand..

Arriving by Sea

Ship and catamaran car ferry companies operate across the Channel each day. On the short Dover–Calais route alone, there are up to 100 crossings per day, including those run by **Condor Ferries** and **P&O**, which offer fast, frequent services taking 90 minutes to cross the Channel. **DFDS Seaways** runs a route between Newhaven and Dieppe, that takes nearly 4 hours. **DFDS Seaways/LDlines** operates a 2-hour crossing between Dover and Dunkerque.

Three companies ply the longer western routes across the Channel. **Brittany Ferries** crossings from Plymouth to Roscoff take up to 8 hours, and from Poole to Cherbourg they take 4¼ hours. Condor

Main entrance of the Gare du Nord, one of the busiest train stations in Europe

A high-speed TGV train

The TGV

Trains à Grande Vitesse, or TGV high-speed trains, travel at speeds up to 186 mph (300 km/h). Paris is the nucleus for the TGV network, and it is possible to connect from the Eurostar to TGVs serving 150 destinations in France as well as Switzerland, Germany, and northern Europe. All of France's major cities can be reached by TGV, and the number of stations is growing all the time, making this an ever more convenient form of transportation *(see pp372–3)*.

Ferries run between Poole and St.-Malo, taking about 6 hours. From Portsmouth, Brittany Ferries take 6 hours to travel to Caen, and 11 hours overnight to St.-Malo. DFDS Seaways also runs ferries from Portsmouth to Le Havre in 5½ hours. Driving to Paris from Cherbourg takes 4–5 hours; from Dieppe or Le Havre, about 2½–3 hours; and from Calais, 2 hours.

Arriving by Road

The main long-distance bus operator to Paris is **Eurolines**, based at the Gare Routière Internationale above the Gallieni Metro station in eastern Paris. Its buses travel from Belgium, Holland, Ireland, Germany, Scandinavia, the UK, Italy, and Portugal. The Eurolines terminal in London is the centrally located Victoria Coach Station, from where there are between three and five departures for Paris each day, depending on the season. The journey from London to Paris takes 8 to 9 hours.

Paris is an oval-shaped city. It is surrounded by an outer beltway called the Boulevard Périphérique. All highways leading to the capital link in to the Périphérique, which separates the city from the suburbs. Each former city gate, called a *porte*, now corresponds to an exit from (or entrance to) the Périphérique. Arriving drivers should take time to check their destination address and consult a map of central Paris to find the closest corresponding *porte*. For example, a driver who wants to get to the Arc de Triomphe should exit at Porte Maillot.

For the uninitiated, driving to the center of Paris in heavy traffic and then parking can be a difficult experience *(see p381)*, which is why public transportation is a more appealing option *(see pp374–80)*.

A long-haul international Eurolines bus

DIRECTORY

Arriving by Rail

Eurostar
Tel 03448 224 777 (UK),
08 92 35 35 39 (France).
W eurostar.com

Rail Europe
W raileurope.com

SNCF & TGV
Tel 3635. W sncf.com or
voyages-sncf.com
(travel agency).

Arriving by Sea

Brittany Ferries
Tel 0871 244 0744 (UK).
W brittany-ferries.co.uk

Condor Ferries
Tel 0845 609 1024.
W condorferries.co.uk

DFDS Seaways
Tel 0871 574 7235 (UK).
W dfdsseaways.co.uk

P&O
Tel 0871 664 64 64 (UK).
W poferries.com

Arriving by Road

Eurolines
Galieni Metro Station,
Ave de Général de Gaulle,
93541 Bagnolet.
Tel 0892 899 091.

Victoria Coach Station,
London SW1.
Tel 0871 781 8178 (UK).
W eurolines.com

Eurotunnel
Tel 0844 33 35 35 (UK),
08 10 63 03 04 (France).
W eurotunnel.com

**Traffic Reports
around Paris**
W sytadin.fr

Discount Travel Agencies

Directours
Tel 01 45 62 62 62.
W directours.com

Havas Voyages
Tel 01 73 31 90 02.
W havas-voyages.fr

Jet Tours
Tel 08 20 83 08 80.
W jettours.com

Nouvelles Frontières
Tel 08 25 00 07 47.
W nouvelles-frontieres.fr

Arriving in Paris

This map depicts the bus and rail services between the two main airports and the city. It shows the ferry–rail links from the UK, the main railroad links from other parts of France and Europe, and the long-haul bus services from other European countries. It also shows the main city train and bus terminals, the airport shuttle connections, and the airport bus and train stops. The frequency of services and journey times from the airport are provided, as are the approximate times of train journeys from other cities. Metro and RER line connections to other parts of Paris are indicated at the terminals and route stops.

🚢 Calais
Ferry and Eurotunnel links with Dover and Folkestone. Eurostar train from London St. Pancras to Paris *Gare du Nord* (2 hrs 15 mins) passes through here. *SNCF* train to Gare du Nord (1 hr 30 mins–3 hrs 30 mins).

🚢 Le Havre
Ferry links with Portsmouth. *SNCF* train to *Gare St.-Lazare* (2 hrs 10 mins).

🚢 Dieppe
Ferry links with Newhaven (summer) *SNCF* train to *Gare St.-Lazare* (2 hrs 20 mins).

🚢 Caen
Ferry links with Portsmouth. *SNCF* train to *Gare St.-Lazare* (1 hr 50 mins).

🚢 Cherbourg
Ferry links with Portsmouth and Poole. *SNCF* train to *Gare St.-Lazare* (3 hrs).

Gare St.-Lazare
Rouen (1 hr 30 mins) .

Gare Montparnasse
Bordeaux (3 hrs 30 mins).
Brest (4 hrs 30 mins).
Lisbon (19 hrs 40 mins).
Madrid (12 hrs 25 mins).
Nantes (2 hrs 15 mins).
Rennes (2 hrs 15 mins).

Key

▬ SNCF *see pp370–71*
▬ Buses *see p371*
▬ Roissybus *see p368*
▬ Air France Bus *see pp368–9*
▬ RER *see p368*
▬ Orlyrail *see p369*
▬ Orlyval *see p369*
▬ Orlybus *see p369*
▬ Jet Bus *see p369*

For additional map symbols *see back flap*

Porte Maillot
Ⓜ ①
RER Ⓐ Ⓒ

Charles de Gaulle-Etoile
Ⓜ ① ② ⑥
RER Ⓐ

Champs-Elysées

Chaillot Quarter

Gare St-Laz
Ⓜ ③ ⑫ ⑬

Invalides
Ⓜ ⑧ ⑬
RER Ⓒ

Invalides and Eiffel Tower Quarter

Tui Qu

St-Ge des

Luxem Quar

Gare Montparnasse
④ ⑥ ⑫ ⑬ ⑭ Ⓜ

Montparn

Denfe Rochere
RER N
Ⓑ ⑥

Porte d'Orléans
Ⓜ ④

0 km   1
0 mile   1

Gare TGV de Massypalaiseau
Bordeaux (3 hrs 30 mins).
Lille (1 hr 50 mins).
London (4 hrs 15 mins).
Lyon (2 hrs 10 mins).
Nantes (2 hrs 30 mins).
Rennes (2 hrs 10 mins).

Antony
RER Ⓑ

Gare du Nord
Amsterdam (3 hrs 20 mins).
Bonn (4 hrs 30 mins–5 hrs).
Brussels (Thalys) (1 hr 25 mins).
Cologne (3 hrs 20 mins).
Lille (1 hr).
London (Eurostar) (2 hrs 15 mins).

M ⑫
Porte de la Chapelle

...nartre

...e du Nord
RER **M**
②④⑤

M ④⑤⑦
Gare de l'Est

Charles de Gaulle
Frequent bus and train services
to the city.
🚌 *Air France* to *Porte Maillot/
Etoile* (40 mins);
Gare de Lyon/ Montparnasse
(50 mins);
Orly (50 mins–1 hr 15 mins).
🚌 *Roissybus* to *Opéra*
(50 mins).
RER *Line B* to *Gare du Nord*
(25 mins).

Beaubourg
and Les
Halles

The Marais

Ile de la
Cité

*Ile
St-Louis*

Latin
Quarter

① ⑭ **M**
Ⓐ **RER**
Gare de Lyon

⑩ ⑤ **M**
Ⓒ **RER**
Gare d'Austerlitz

*Jardin des
Plantes*

...lejuif-
...uis Aragon
⑦

Pont de
Rungis

Ⓒ **RER**

**Gare TGV Aéroport Charles de
Gaulle**
Bordeaux (4 hrs 15 mins).
Brussels (1 hr 15 mins–2 hrs
5 mins).
Disneyland® Paris (10–15 mins).
Lille (50 mins).
Lyon (2 hrs 10 mins).
Marseille (3 hrs 50 mins–4hrs
30 mins).
Nantes (3 hrs).
Rennes (2 hrs 50 mins).

Gare de l'Est
Basel (3 hrs 40 mins–5hrs
50 mins).
Frankfurt (3 hrs 50 mins).
Luxembourg (2 hrs 10 mins).
Nancy (1hr 40 mins).
Strasbourg (2 hrs 20 mins).
Vienna (13 hrs 20 mins–14 hrs
20 mins).

O **M** ③
Galliéni

**Gare Internationale de
Paris-Gallieni**
All international bus services arrive
and depart from this station.

Gare de Lyon
Geneva (3 hrs 30 mins).
Lausanne (3 hrs 40 mins).
Lyon (2 hrs).
Marseille (3 hrs).
Milan (7 hrs 10 mins).
Rome (11 hrs 34 mins).
Zurich (6 hrs).

Gare TGV de Marne-la-Vallee
For Disneyland® Paris (40 mins).
Bordeaux (4 hrs).
Brussels (1 hr 30 mins–3 hrs
30 mins).
Lille (1 hr 5 mins).
London (3 hrs 30 mins).
Lyon (1 hr 50 mins).
Marseille (3 hr 50 mins).
Nantes (2 hrs 50 mins).

Orly
There are direct bus and train services
to the city every 12–15 minutes.
🚌 *Air France* to *Les Invalides*
(30 mins); *Montparnasse* (30 mins);
Charles de Gaulle (50 mins–1hr
15 mins).
🚌 *Orlybus* to *Denfert-Rochereau*
(25 mins).
RER *Orlyrail* to *Pont de Rungis* & *RER
Line C* to *Gare d'Austerlitz* (35 mins).
RER *Orlyval* to *Antony* & *RER Line B*
to *Châtelet* (35 mins).
🚌 *Jet Bus* to *VIllejuif* (15 mins).

Gare d'Austerlitz
Barcelona (11 hrs 50 mins).
Limoges (3 hrs 15 mins).
Madrid (13 hrs 30 mins).
Toulouse (6 hrs 30 mins).

GETTING AROUND PARIS

Central Paris is compact. The best way to get around is to walk. Cycling and rollerblading are also popular with Parisians and tourists alike. Public transportation is very efficient.The Metro, RER train, and bus system operated by the RATP makes getting around Paris cheap and easy, and the city government is working on green travel initiatives. The city is divided into five travel zones: zones 1 and 2 correspond to the center, and zones 3, 4, and 5 to the suburbs and Charles de Gaulle and Orly airports. Some suburbs are served by a streetcar. River boats are a scenic option. By contrast, driving downtown can be an unpleasant experience. Traffic is often heavy, there are many one-way streets, and parking is notoriously difficult and expensive.

Green Travel

Paris has one of the world's most efficient and dependable public transportation systems and the Mairie de Paris (Paris City Council) is eager to make the capital more environmentally friendly. Residents and visitors alike are encouraged to swap cars for bicycles, and to strap on rollerblades or walking shoes as busy thoroughfares shut down to traffic on weekends as part of the *Paris-Respire* (Paris Breathes) initiative. The Mairie is enlarging footpaths, declaring more streets pedestrian-only, increasing bike lanes, and planting trees in an effort to cut down on parking spaces and wean Parisians off cars. Around 55 per cent of city dwellers don't own a car.

In a bid to reduce carbon dioxide emissions by 22,000 tons a year and in order to improve traffic congestion, the Mairie is making 3,000 electric cars (Autolibs: www. autolib.eu) available for Parisians to pick up and drop off at rental stands throughout the city.

An eco-friendly Vélo taxi

The RATP is testing buses that run on second-generation bio-fuels and plans to gradually introduce vehicles equipped with hybrid electric-thermic engines in an effort to reduce fuel consumption along with noise and air pollution. The electric streetcar is punctual, silent, and super-green – and for every three trees that were removed during its constr-uction, four new ones were planted.

On the Paris Metro, the MF01 trains running on some lines have been designed to recover two-thirds of all energy lost during braking operations. In addition, a proportion of the water building up in the under-ground network is returned to nature instead of down city drains, and recycling bins have been placed in RER and a number of Metro stations.

Taxis G7 has introduced hybrid cars to their fleet and is putting drivers through eco-training courses, while Taxis Bleus is promoting the use of biofuels, hybrid engines, particle filters, and better driving techniques to reduce fuel consumption (see p381).

To estimate your carbon footprint, click onto the *ecocomparateur* on the SNCF website (see p371). This helps you work out how much carbon dioxide your trip produces according to your transportation method. Vélo taxis, popular with tourists, are electrically assisted tricycle rickshaws that are slower than traditional taxis, but adept at zipping in and out of traffic.

With 1,800 bicycle stations all over the city, the popular Vélib' self-service bicycle rental system is available 24 hours a day and has spawned a new generation of street-savvy cyclists.

Tickets and Travel Passes

Tickets can be purchased at all main Metro and RER stations, at the airports, and at several tourist offices. Individual tickets are relatively cheap, and you can buy a block of ten (*carnet*) for convenience. The *Paris Visite* pass for one, two, three, or five days includes discounted entry to some sights, but is comparatively expensive unless you intend to travel extensively.

To get a *Passe Navigo Découverte*, you do not need to be a resident of Paris, but you will need to provide a passport photo and pay €5. A *Passe Navigo* requires a Paris address. It has replaced all travel cards. Visitors can also buy a one-day Mobilis card, valid for travel on most public transportation.

Paris Visite pass

Mobilis card

Navigo travel card

Navigo Découverte pass

Walking In Paris

One of the best and easiest ways of getting around central Paris is to walk. Australian, British, Irish, and New Zealand visitors need to remember that cars drive on the right-hand side of the road. There are many two-stage road crossings where pedestrians wait on an island in the center of the road before proceeding. These are marked *piétons traversez en deux temps*.

Cycling in Paris

Paris is well equipped for cyclists. Except for Montmartre, it's reasonably flat, manageably small, and has many backstreets where car traffic is restricted as well as some 435 miles (700 km) of bicycle lanes *(pistes cyclables)*. Parisian drivers are increasingly respectful of cyclists as more and more of their fellow citizens turn to two wheels.

Vélib', a self-service bicycle rental program, offers both residents and visitors the cheapest way of getting around the city. Bicycle stands are located 330 yd (300 m) apart and payment is by credit card at the access terminals, which operate in eight different languages. See page 349 for rates.

Bicycles (aside from Vélibs) may be taken on SNCF trains, and suburban stations also rent bicycles. There are bicycle stores throughout Paris, and many also organize guided tours by bike.

Bicycles for rent by residents or tourists, at a Vélib' bicycle stand

Traveling by Boat

Paris's main riverboat shuttle service, the **Batobus**, runs every 20–45 minutes, depending on the time of year with more frequent services in the spring and summer months. It stops at seven of the city's most famous attractions – Eiffel Tower, Musée d'Orsay, St.-Germain des Près, Louvre, Hôtel de Ville, Champs Elysées, and Notre Dame. Tickets can be bought at Batobus stops, RATP, and tourist offices *(see pp74–5)*.

Paris Vision tour bus

Guided Tours

Double-decker bus tours with commentaries in English, Italian, Japanese, and German are organized by **France Tourisme**, which runs **Paris City Vision**. The tours begin from the city center and take about 2 hours. They pass the main sights but do not stop at all of them. **Big Bus Paris** runs bus tours stopping at many of the sights in Paris. Each ticket is valid for 2 days and allows you to hop on or off at any of the stops.

Bicycle tours are run by a number of companies. **Paris Charms and Secrets** runs 4-hour tours in English on electric bicycles departing from Place Vendôme. **Paris Bike Tour** departs from the Marais; **Paris à Vélo C'est Sympa!** leaves from near the Bastille, while **Bike About Tours** starts from close to the Hôtel de Ville.

Paris Walks conducts daily tours in English, including a "Chocolate Walk" and a "Fashion Walk." The **Comité Départemental de la Randonnée Pédestre de Paris** runs free themed walks in French.

More information on guided tours is available at the Office du Tourisme *(see p359)*.

DIRECTORY

River Boats

Batobus
Port de la Bourdonnais 75007.
Map 10 D2. **Tel** 08 25 05 0101.
W batobus.com

Bus Tour Operators

Big Bus Paris
17 Quai de Grenelle 75015.
Map 9 C4. **Tel** 01 53 95 39 53.
W eng.bigbustours.com

France Tourisme
33 Quai des Grands Augustins
75006. **Map** 12 F4.
Tel 01 53 10 35 35.
6–8 Rue de l'Amiral de Coligny
75001. **Map** 12 F2. **Tel** 01 53 10
35 35. W francetourisme.fr

Paris City Vision
2 Pl des Pyramides 75001.
Map 12 E1. **Tel** 01 44 55 61 00.
W pariscityvision.com

Bicycle Rental & Tours

Bike About Tours
4 Rue de Lobau 75004
(inside Vinci parking garage).
Map 13 B3. **Tel** 06 18 80 84 92.
W bikeabouttours.com

Fat Tire Bike Tours
See p351 – Outdoor Sports.

Paris à Vélo C'est Sympa!
22 Rue Alphonse Baudin 75011.
Map 14 E2. **Tel** 01 48 87 60 01.
W parisvelosympa.com

Paris Bike Tour
13 Rue Brantôme 75003.
Map 14 D2. **Tel** 01 42 74 22 14.
W parisbiketour.net

Paris Charms and Secrets
106 Rue Vielle du Temple, 75003
(meeting point: Place Vendôme).
Map 14 D2. **Tel** 01 40 29 00 00.
W parischarmssecrets.com

Vélib'
Tel 01 30 79 79 30.
W en.velib.paris.fr

Walking Tours

Comité Départemental de la Randonnée Pédestre de Paris
6 Rue Paul Enfert 75013.
Tel 01 46 36 95 70.
W rando-paris.org

Paris Walks
12 Passage Meunier 93200
St. Denis. **Map** 17 B5. **Tel** 01 48
09 21 40. W paris-walks.com

Traveling by Metro and RER

The RATP (Paris transit authority) operates 14 main Metro lines, referred to by their number and terminus names, which crisscross Paris and its suburbs. There are also two minor lines – 3b (Gambetta–Porte de Lilas) and 7b (Louis Blanc–Pré St. Gervais). The Metro is often the fastest and cheapest way to get across the capital, since there are hundreds of stations *(see map on inside back cover)*. Metro stations are easily identified by their logo, a large circled "M," and some by their Art Nouveau entrances. The metro and RER (Paris rail network) systems operate in much the same way. The trains run from 4:45am to between 12:40am and 1:30am (1 hour later on weekends).

Art Nouveau metro sign

Modern Metro sign

Reading the Metro Map

Metro and RER lines are shown in various colors on the Metro map. Metro lines are identified by a number, which is located on the map at either end of a line. Some Metro stations serve only one line, others serve more than one. There are stations sharing both Metro and RER lines, and some are linked to one another by interconnecting passages.

Metro and RER stations with interconnecting passage

RER and metro station serving the same lines

Metro line

Metro station serving one line

Metro station serving two lines

Metro line identification number

Using the RER

The RER is a system of commuter trains that travel underground in central Paris and above ground in outlying areas. Metro tickets and passes are valid on it. There are five lines, known by their letters: A, B, C, D, and E. Each line forks. For example, Line C has six forks, labeled C1, C2, etc. All RER trains bear names (for example, ALEX or VERA) to make it easier to read RER timetables in the station halls and on platforms. Digital panels on all RER platforms indicate train name, direction of travel (terminal), and upcoming stations. RER stations are identified by a large circled logo. The main city stations are: Charles de Gaulle-Etoile, Châtelet-Les-Halles, Gare de Lyon, Nation, St.-Michel-Notre-Dame, Auber-Haussmann St.-Lazare, and the Gare du Nord–Magenta.

The RER and Metro systems overlap in central Paris. It is

often quicker to take an RER train to a station served by both, as in the case of La Défense and Nation. However, getting into the RER stations, which are often linked to the Metro by a maze of corridors, can be very time-consuming.

The RER is particularly useful for getting to Paris airports and to many of the outlying towns and tourist attractions. Line B serves Charles de Gaulle airport and Orly airport; Line A goes to Disneyland® Paris; and Line C runs to Versailles and Orly airport.

RER logo

Buying a Ticket

Ordinary Metro and RER tickets can be bought either singly or as a *carnet* of ten, from ticket booths or ticket machines in the station halls (carry some euro coins). The useful Paris Visite bus, Metro, and RER pass *(see p374)* is widely available, and you can also buy it in advance at certain travel agencies and rail ticket agents abroad (e.g., Rail Europe in London). There is also the Passe Navigo Découverte *(see p374)*, which requires a passport photo. One Metro ticket entitles you to travel anywhere on the Metro, and on RER trains in central Paris. RER trips outside the center (such as to airports) require special tickets. Fares to suburbs and nearby towns vary. Consult the fare charts posted in RER stations. You must retain your ticket during the trip, since regular inspections are made and you can be fined for not having a ticket or having the wrong ticket.

Traveling by Metro

1 To determine which Metro line to take, travelers should first find their destination on a Metro map. (Maps can be found inside stations and also on the inside back cover of this book.) Trace the Metro line by following the color coding and the number of the line. At the end of the line you will see the number of the terminal – remember this, since it will help you to find the correct train.

2 Metro tickets are sold at all stations, which are equipped with coin-operated automatic machines. One Metro ticket allows the bearer travel for one trip, including any transfers on the metro system, and on RER trains in central Paris.

Insert the train ticket in the first slot.

Remove the ticket from the second slot.

3 To enter the platform area, insert the metro ticket, with the magnetic strip facing down, into the first barrier slot. Remove the ticket from the second slot, then walk through. Alternatively, swipe your *Passe Navigo Découverte* over the reader in the barrier.

← DIRECTION
Ⓜ① CHÂTEAU DE VINCENNES

GARE DE LYON
REUILLY-DIDEROT
NATION
PORTE DE VINCENNES
SAINT-MANDÉ-TOURELLE
BÉRAULT
CHÂTEAU DE VINCENNES

4 At the entrance to each station platform, and in the station corridors, there are lists of upcoming stations corresponding to a given terminal. Terminal names are also indicated on the platform and should be checked before boarding the train.

DIRECTION
Ⓜ①
CHÂTEAU DE VINCENNES

7 To change lines, get off at the appropriate transfer station and follow the *correspondance* (connections) signs on the platform indicating the appropriate direction.

5 There is a release button that you press to open the metro doors. Before the doors open and close, a single tone will sound.

6 Inside the trains are charts of the line being served by the train. The station stops are plotted on the chart, so travelers can track their journeys.

8 The "Sortie" sign indicates the way out. At all metro exits there are neighborhood maps.

← SORTIE

Traveling by Bus

The bus is an excellent way to see the great sights of Paris. The bus system is run by the RATP, which also runs the Metro, so you can use the same tickets for both. There are more than 350 bus lines in greater Paris and over 4,300 buses in daily circulation during rush hour. Buses can be the fastest way to travel short distances, especially now that there are more bus-only lanes. However, during peak hours buses may get caught in heavy traffic and are often crowded. Visitors should check the times for the first and last buses as they vary widely, depending on the line. Night buses run throughout the night.

Ticket-validating machine

Bus Stop Signs

Signs at Parisian bus stops display the numbers of the routes stopping there and count down the minutes until the arrival of the next bus.

Bus stop

Tickets and Passes

A single bus ticket entitles the bearer to a single journey on a single line. If you want to make a change, you'll need another ticket. (Exceptions to this rule are the buses Balabus,

Noctambus, Orlybus, and Roissybus, and lines 221, 297, 299, 350, and 351.) Children under four travel for free, and those aged between four and ten may travel at half price.

Although a Metro/RER ticket is valid, bus-only tickets can be purchased from the bus driver and must be validated on board. To do this, insert the ticket into the validating machine inside the bus. Hold on to your ticket until the end of the journey; inspectors make random checks and can levy on-the-spot fines if you cannot produce a validated ticket for your journey.

You can also purchase a *carnet* of ten tickets, each of

Validating a Bus Ticket

Insert the ticket into the machine in the direction of the arrow, then withdraw it.

them valid for a single bus, Metro, or RER journey. However, a *carnet* cannot be purchased on buses, and can only be bought at Metro stations.

Travel passes are a good idea if you are planning a number of journeys during your stay. For a set fee, you can enjoy unlimited travel on Paris buses with a *Paris Visite* pass *(see p374)*. Never validate these as it will render them invalid. They should be shown to the bus driver whenever you board a bus, and to a ticket inspector on request. If you have a *Passe Navigo Découverte* *(see p374)*, swipe it across the card-reading machine as you board the bus.

Paris's Buses

Passengers can identify the route and destination of a bus from the information on the panels at the front. It's possible to enter some buses from the middle door; there's a button on the exterior of the bus.

Bus route number

Bus destination

Passengers enter the bus at the front door

Bus front displaying information

Using the Buses

Bus stops and shelters are identified by the number shields of the buses that stop at them, and by the distinctive RATP logo. Route maps at bus stops indicate transfers and nearby Metro and RER stops. Bus stops also display timetables, and show first and last buses. Neighborhood maps are also displayed at most bus shelters.

Most buses must be flagged down. Some models have multiple doors which must be opened by pressing a red button inside the bus to exit, or outside the bus to enter. All buses have buttons and bells to signal for a stop. Some buses do not go all the way to their terminal, in which case there will be a slash through the name of the destination on the front panel.

All of central Paris's 60 bus routes are equipped to allow wheelchair access; this means that at least 70 per cent of stops on the route are accessible; suitable stops are designated by a wheelchair symbol on the bus route sign. All buses have some seats reserved for disabled and elderly persons. These seats are identified by a sign and must be given up on request.

Night and Summer Buses

There are 31 night bus lines, called Noctilien, serving Paris and its suburbs (from 12:30am–5:30am Monday to Thursday and 1am–5.30am Friday and Saturday). The network is laid out around the five major transfer stations of Gare de Lyon, Gare de l'Est, St-Lazare, Montparnasse, and Châtelet. The terminal for most lines is Châtelet, at Avenue Victoria or Rue St.-Martin. Noctilien stops are identified by a letter "N" set in a white circle on a blue background. Noctilien buses must be flagged down. Travel passes are valid, as are normal Metro tickets, which must be validated on board. Travelers may buy tickets on board the bus. See www.noctilien.fr for more details.

In summer, the RATP also operates buses in the Bois de Vincennes and Bois de Boulogne, and the Balabus, which stops at major tourist sites. **RATP Information** has useful details about these and the best ways to get around.

RATP Information
54 Quai de la Rapée 75012.
Tel 32 46. **w** ratp.fr

Streetcars

There are three RATP streetcar routes operating in Paris – T1 (Gare de St.-Denis–Noisy le Sec), T2 (La Défense–Porte de Versailles), and T3 (Pont du Garigliano–Porte d'Ivry), and the network is expected to grow. T3, dubbed the *Tramway des Maréchaux* as it follows the wide boulevards named after military marshals, is handy for exploring the outer reaches of the 13th, 14th, and 15th arrondissements.

The T4 (Aulnay-sous-Bois–Bondy) is run by SNCF and is a streetcar-train line.

RATP Metro and public bus tickets are valid for use on streetcars.

Passengers embarking at an RATP streetcar stop

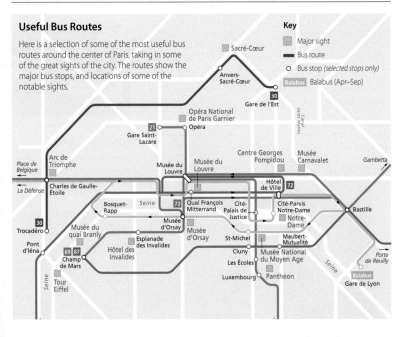

Useful Bus Routes

Here is a selection of some of the most useful bus routes around the center of Paris, taking in some of the great sights of the city. The routes show the major bus stops, and locations of some of the notable sights.

Key

- Major sight
- ▬ Bus route
- O Bus stop *(selected stops only)*
- Balabus Balabus (Apr–Sep)

Sacré-Cœur
Anvers-Sacré-Cœur
30
Gare de l'Est
Opéra National de Paris Garnier
21 Opéra
Gare Saint-Lazare
Place de Belgique
Arc de Triomphe
Centre Georges Pompidou
Musée Carnavalet
Gambetta
La Défense
Charles de Gaulle-Étoile
Musée du Louvre
Musée du Louvre
Hôtel de Ville **72**
Bosquet-Rapp
Seine
73 Quai François Mitterrand
Cité-Palais de Justice
Cité-Parvis Notre-Dame
Bastille
30
Trocadéro
Musée du quai Branly
Musée d'Orsay
Musée d'Orsay
St-Michel
Notre-Dame
Maubert-Mutualité
Porte de Reuilly
Pont d'Iéna
69 87
Champ de Mars
Hôtel des Invalides
Esplanade des Invalides
Cluny
Les Écoles
Musée National du Moyen Age
Seine
Balabus
Gare de Lyon
Tour Eiffel
Seine
Luxembourg
Panthéon

Using SNCF Trains

The French state railroad, Société Nationale des Chemins de Fer (SNCF), has two services in Paris: the *Banlieue* suburban service and the *Grandes Lignes*, or long-distance service. The suburban services all operate within the five-zone network *(see p374)*. The long-distance services operate throughout France. These services allow visitors to travel to parts of France close to Paris in a one-day round trip. The TGV high-speed service is particularly useful for such trips, since it is capable of traveling about twice as fast as standard trains *(see pp370–71)*.

Gare de l'Est train station in 1920

Train Stations

France has always been known for the punctuality of its trains, and has maintained a high level of investment in the state-owned rail system, SNCF.

As the rail hub of France, Paris boasts six major international train stations operated by the SNCF: the Gare du Nord, Gare de l'Est, Gare de Lyon, Gare d'Austerlitz, Gare St.-Lazare, and Gare Montparnasse *(see p370)*.

All the main train stations have long-distance and suburban destinations. Some of the main suburban locations, such as Versailles and Chantilly, are served by both long-distance and suburban trains.

Stations have departures and arrivals boards showing the train number, departure and arrival times, delay, platform number, place of departure, and main stops en route. For those with heavy luggage, there are carts, requiring a €1 coin (refunded when the cart is returned). See the SNCF website for further information *(see p371)*.

Tickets

Tickets to suburban destinations can be purchased at automatic machines located inside station halls (the machines give change; most also take credit cards). You can also buy tickets at the ticket counters. These are marked with panels indicating the kind of tickets *(billets)* sold: *Banlieue* for suburban tickets, *Grandes Lignes* for mainline tickets, and *Internationale* for international tickets. Fare rates vary according to the type of train.

For all trains that can be reserved online through the SNCF or Rail Europe websites, there are two or three basic fare rates for each class. The cheapest tickets are called *PREMs*, and they are advance-purchase fares that cannot be altered after payment; weekend and last-minute specials are also offered as *PREMs*. On some trains, fares are cheaper at off-peak times *(périodes bleus)*. Peak times *(périodes blanches)* are from 5am until 10am on Monday and from 3pm until 8pm on Friday and Sunday.

Compositeur Machine

The compositeur *machines are located in station halls and at the head of each platform. Tickets and reservations must be inserted face up.*

A time-punched ticket

SNCF sells several travel cards that give fare reductions of around 50 per cent, including the *Carte 12–25* for young people, *Carte Senior* for people over 60 years of age, *Carte Escapades* for frequent travelers, and *Carte Enfant +* for parents with small children. Further details of fares are available on the SNCF website *(see p371)*.

Before boarding a train, travelers must remember to time-punch *(composter)* their tickets and reservations at a *composteur* machine. Be aware that inspectors do check travelers' tickets, and anyone who fails to time-punch their ticket can be fined.

A double-decker Banlieue train

Suburban Trains

Suburban lines are found at all main Paris train stations and are clearly marked *Banlieue*. Tickets for city transportation cannot be used on *Banlieue* trains, with the exception of some RER tickets to stations with both SNCF and RER lines. Several tourist destinations are served by *Banlieue* trains, including Chantilly, Chartres, Giverny, and Versailles *(see pp250–55)*. For further destinations, look at the SNCF website *(see p371)*.

Traveling by Car

Although driving and parking can be difficult in central Paris, a rental car might be useful for visiting outlying areas. Taxis are a more expensive way of getting around than trains or buses, but can be an advantage late at night when the Metro has stopped running. There are about 800 taxi stands *(stations de taxis)* throughout Paris.

Driving

To rent a car, a valid driver's license, passport, and proof of insurance are required (most firms also require one major credit card). International driver's licenses are not needed for short-term visitors (up to 90 days) from the EU, North America, Australia, and New Zealand.

Cars drive on the right-hand side and must yield to traffic merging from the right, even on thoroughfares, unless marked by a *priorité* sign, which indicates right of way. Cars on a traffic circle usually have right of way, though the Arc de Triomphe is a hair-raising exception as cars yield to traffic on the right.

Parking

Parking in Paris is difficult and expensive. Never park where there are *Parking (Stationnement) Interdit* signs or yellow painted lines on the road and curb. Park only in areas with a large "P" or a *Payant* sign on the sidewalk or road, and pay at the *horodateur* (parking meter). Buy a *carte de stationnement* or Paris Carte (€15 or €40 from a *tabac*) to use in the meter, and place the parking ticket so that it is clearly visible through the windshield. Parking meters operate from 9am until 7pm Monday to Saturday. Unless otherwise indicated, parking is free on Sunday, and public holidays.

Illuminated sign on a taxi

Taxis

There are over 15,000 taxis operating in central Paris, yet there never seem to be enough to meet demand, particularly during rush hours and on Friday and Saturday nights. The wider city is thought to have more than 19,000 taxis.

Taxis can be hailed on the street, but not within 55 yards (50 m) of a taxi stand. Since stands always take priority over street stops, the easiest way to get a cab is to find a stand and get in line. Stands are located at many busy intersections, main Metro and RER stations, hospitals, train stations, and airports. An illuminated light on the taxi roof shows that it is available. A small light lit below means that the taxi is occupied. If the white light is covered, the taxi is off duty. Taxis on their last run can refuse to take passengers.

The meter should have a specified initial amount showing at the stand, or when it is hailed. If you order a taxi, the meter will show the charge from where the driver started his journey to pick you up. Initial charges for radio taxis vary widely, depending on the distance the taxi covers to arrive at the pickup point. Payment by check is not accepted but many vehicles take credit cards.

Rates vary according to the city area and the time of day. Rate A, in the city center, is charged per kilometer. The higher rate B applies in the city center on Sundays, holidays, and at night (7pm–7am), or daytime in the suburbs or airports. The highest rate, C, applies to the suburbs and airports at night. Taxis charge for each piece of luggage, and for a fourth passenger. Drivers expect fares to be rounded up.

No entry sign

INTERDIT
SUR TOUTE LA LONGUEUR
DE LA VOIE

Parking Interdit (no parking)

AXE
ROUGE

ARRÊT GÊNANT

Tow-away zone

30

Speed limit sign in km

DIRECTORY

Car Rental Agencies

Here is a list of major firms with agencies at Charles de Gaulle and Orly airports, main train stations, and city center locations.

Avis
Tel 0821 230 760.
🆆 avis.com or avis.fr.

Budget
Tel 0825 003 564. 🆆 budget.com

Enterprise
Tel 01 49 75 36 38 (Orly); 01 48 62 65 81 (CDG). 🆆 enterprise.fr

Europcar
Tel 0825 358 358.
🆆 europcar.com or europcar.fr

Hertz
Tel 08 25 88 92 55 (Orly), 08 25 88 97 55 (CDG). 🆆 hertz.com

Sixt
Tel 0820 007 498 (France), 01 44 38 35 55 (from abroad).

Taxis and Car Services

Citybird
Tel 0826 100 100. Motorbike taxis and chauffeur-driven cars.
🆆 city-bird.com
(Reservations can be made online.)

Les Taxis Bleus
Tel 3609. 🆆 taxis-bleus.com
(Reservations can be made online.)

Taxis G7
Tel 01 41 27 66 99, 01 47 39 00 91 (special needs). 🆆 taxisg7.com
(Reservations can be made online.)

Urban Driver
Tel 0825 625 100. Motorcycle taxi service. 🆆 urban-driver.com
(Reservations can be made online.)

STREET FINDER

The map references given with all sights, hotels, restaurants, stores, and entertainment venues described in this book refer to the maps in this section (see How the Map References Work *opposite*). A complete index of street names and all the places of interest marked on the maps can be found on the following pages. The key map shows the area of Paris covered by the *Street Finder*, with the arrondissement numbers for each district. The maps include not only the sightseeing areas (which are color-coded), but the whole of central Paris with all the districts important for hotels, restaurants, shopping, and entertainment venues. The symbols used to represent sights and features on the *Street Finder* maps are listed opposite.

Paris is divided into 20 arrondissements, numbered on this map.

Key

- - Arrondissement boundary

How the Map References Work

The first figure tells you which *Street Finder* map to turn to.

⓭ Hotel de Ville

4 Pl de l'Hôtel-de-Ville 75004.
Map 13 B3. **Tel** 01 42 76 50 49.
Ⓜ Hotel de Ville. **Open** groups: by arrangement. **Closed** public hols, official functions Ⓐ Ⓒ

The letter and number give the grid reference. Letters go across the map's top and bottom; figures on its sides.

The map continues on page 17 of the *Street Finder*.

Key to Street Finder

- ▨ Major sight
- ▨ Other sight
- ▨ Other building
- Ⓜ Metro station
- 🆁🅴🆁 RER station
- 🚆 Train station
- 🚌 Main bus stop
- ⛴ Boat service boarding point
- ⛴ Batobus boarding point
- 𝒊 Tourist information office
- ✚ Hospital with emergency room
- 🚔 Police station
- ✝ Church
- ✡ Synagogue
- ▰ Autoroute
- ▱ Railroad track
- ▭ Pedestrian-only street
- ◄21 House number (main street)

Scale of Map Pages

0 meters	200	
0 yards	200	1:11,000

Street Finder Index

Each place name is followed by its arrondissement number and then by its Street Finder reference

Each place name is followed by its arrondissement number and then by its Street Finder reference

Each place name is followed by its arrondissement number and then by its Street Finder reference

Each place name is followed by its arrondissement number and then by its Street Finder reference

Each place name is followed by its arrondissement number and then by its Street Finder reference

Each place name is followed by its arrondissement number and then by its Street Finder reference

General Index

Acknowledgments

Dorling Kindersley would like to thank the many people whose help and assistance contributed to the preparation of this book.

Main Contributor
Alan Tillier has lived in all the main areas of Paris for 25 years, during which time he has been Paris correspondent for several journals including *Newsweek, The Times,* and the *International Herald Tribune.* He is the author of several *Herald Tribune* guides for business travelers to Europe.

Contributors
Lenny Borger, Karen Burshtein, Thomas Quinn Curtiss, David Downie, Fiona Dunlop, Heidi Ellison, Leonie Glass, Alexandre Lazareff, Robert Noah, Nick Rider, Andrew Sanger, Martha Rose Shulman, David Stevens, Ian Williams, Jude Welton.

Dorling Kindersley wishes to thank the following editors and researchers at Websters International Publishers: Sandy Carr, Siobhan Bremner, Valeria Fabbri, Gemma Hancock, Sara Harper, Annie Hubert, Celia Woolfrey.

Additional Photography
Marta Bescos, Anna Brooke, Andy Crawford, Michael Crockett, Lucy Davies, Mike Dunning, Philip Gatward, Steve Gorton, Alison Harris, Andrew Holligan, Chas Howson, Britta Jaschinski, Dave King, Ranald MacKechnie, Oliver Knight, Michael Lin, Eric Meacher, Neil Mersh, Ian O'Leary, Stephen Oliver, Poppy, Susannah Price, Tim Ridley, Rough Guides/Lydia Evans, Rough Guides/James McConnachie, Philippe Sebert, Jules Selmes, Sheillee Shah, Steve Shott, Valerio Vincenzo, Peter Wilson, Steven Wooster.

Additional Illustrations
John Fox, Nick Gibbard, David Harris, Kevin Jones Associates, John Woodcock.

Cartography
Jasneet Arora, Mohammad Hassan, Andrew Heritage, James Mills-Hicks, Suresh Kumar, Alok Pathak, John Plumer, Chez Picthall (DK Cartography). Advanced Illustration (Cheshire), Contour Publishing (Derby), Euromap Limited (Berkshire). Street Finder maps: ERA-Maptec Ltd (Dublin) adapted with permission from original survey and mapping by Shobunsha (Japan).

Cartographic Research
Roger Bullen, Tony Chambers, Paul Dempsey, Ruth Duxbury, Ailsa Heritage, Margeret Hynes, Jayne Parsons, Donna Rispoli, Andrew Thompson.

Design and Editorial
Managing Editor Douglas Amrine
Managing Art Editor Geoff Manders
Senior Editor Georgina Matthews
Series Design Consultant Peter Luff
Editorial Director David Lamb
Art Director Anne-Marie Bulat
Production Controller Hilary Stephens

Picture Research Naomi Peck
Production Controller Hilary Stephens
Proofreaders Stewart Wild, Kathryn Glendenning
Indexer Helen Peters
DTP Designer Andy Wilkinson

Revisions Team
Janet Abbott, Emma Ainsworth, Michelle Arness Frederic, Shruti Bahl, Claire Baranowski, Vandana Bhagra, Sonal Bhatt, Hilary Bird, Anna Brooke, Vanessa Courtier, Maggie Crowley, Lisa Davidson, Simon Davis, Guy Dimond, Neha Dinghra, Nicola Erdpresser, Elizabeth Eyre, Simon Farbrother, Fay Franklin, Michelle Arness Frederic, Anna Freiberger, Rhiannon Furber, Eric Gibory, Lydia Halliday, Amy Harrison, Kaberi Hazarika, Lilly Heise, Paul Hines, Fiona Holman, Gail Jones, Laura Jones, Nancy Jones, Bharti Karakoti, Sumita Khatwani, Stephen Knowlden, Rahul Kumar, Kim Laidlaw Adrey, Maite Lantaron, Chris Lascelles, Delphine Lawrance, Jude Ledger, Darren Longley, Carly Madden, Hayley Maher, Nicola Malone, Alison McGill, Sam Merrell, Rebecca Milner, Fiona Morgan, Rakesh Kurma Pal, Lyn Parry, Shirin Patel, Susie Peachey, Penny Phenix, Khushboo Priya, Pure Content, Rada Radojicic, Pamposh Raina, Ruth Reisenberger, Lucy Richards, Philippa Richmond, Louise Rogers, Ellen Root, Philippe Rouin, Shreya Sarkar, Azeem Siddiqui, Sands Publishing Solutions, Beverly Smart, Meredith Smith, Andrew Szudek, Alka Thakur, Roseen Teare, Ajay Verma, Richa Verma, Nikhil Verma, Dora Whitaker.

Special Assistance
Miranda Dewer at Bridgeman Art Library, Editions Gallimard, Lindsay Hunt, Emma Hutton at Cooling Brown, Janet Todd at DACS.

Photographic Reference
Musée Carnavalet, Thomas d'Hoste.

Photography Permissions
Dorling Kindersley would like to thank the following for their kind permission to photograph at their establishments: Aéroports de Paris, Basilique du Sacré-Coeur de Montmartre, Beauvilliers, Benoit, Bibliothèque Historique de la Ville de Paris, Bibliothèque Polonaise, Bofinger, Brasserie Lipp, Café de Flore, Caisse Nationale des Monuments Historiques et des Sites, Les Catacombes, Centre National d'Art et de Culture Georges Pompidou, Chartier, Chiberta, La Cité des Sciences et de l'Industrie and L'EPPV, La Coupole, Les Deux Magots, Fondation Cousteau, Le Grand Colbert, Hôtel Atala, Hôtel Liberal Bruand, Hôtel Meurice, Hôtel Relais Christine, Kenzo, Lucas-Carton, La Madeleine, Mariage Frères, Memorial de la Shoah, Thierry Mugler, Musée Armenien de France, Musée de l'Art Juif, Musée Bourdelle, Musée du Cabinet des Medailles, Musée Carnavalet, Musée Cernuschi: Ville de Paris, Musée du Cinema Henri Langlois, Musée Cognacq-Jay, Musée de Cristal de Baccarat, Musée d'Ennery, Musée Grévin, Musée Jacquemart-André, Musée de la Musique Méchanique, Musée National des Châteaux de Malmaison et Bois-Préau, Collections du Musée National de la Légion d'Honneur, Musée de

Notre-Dame de Paris, Musée de l'Opéra, Musée de l'Ordre de la Libération, Musée d'Orsay, Musée de la Préfecture de la Police, Musée de Radio France, Musée Ro-din, Musée des Transports Urbains, Musée Zadkine, Notre-Dame du Travail, A l'Olivier, Palais de la Découverte, Palais de Luxembourg, Pharamond, Pied de Cochon, Lionel Poilaêne, St. Germain-des-Prés, St. Louis en l'Ile, St. Médard, St. Merry, St. Paul–St.-Louis, St.-Roch, St.-Sulpice, La Société Nouvelle d'Exploitation de La Tour Eiffel, La Tour Montparnasse, Unesco, and all the other museums, churches, hotels, restaurants, stores, galleries, and sights too numerous to thank individually.

Picture Credits

a-above.; b-below/bottom; c-centre; f-far; l-left; r-right; t-top. Works of art have been reproduced with the permission of the following copyright holders:
© ADAGP/SPADEM, Paris and DACS, London 2011: 46c; © ADAGP, Paris and DACS, London 2011: 63tr, 63br, 109br, 111tc, 111crb, 112bl, 112cla, 112br, 113bl, 113br, 115br, 182br, 183crb; © DACS 2011: 47c, 52br, 57cr, 59tl, 100t, 100br, 100clb, 100cl, 100cra, 101t, 101crb, 101bl, 109t, 113c, 139tl, 224bc.

Christo–The Pont Neuf wrapped, Paris, 1975-85: 42cl; © Christo 1985, by kind permission of the artist. Photos achieved with the assistance of the Courtesy of l'Etablissement Public du Musee et du Domaine National de Versailles 250–255; EPPV and the CSI pp 238-241; Courtesy of Erben Otto Dix: 110bl; Fondation Le Corbusier: 61t, 247tr; Courtesy of The Estate of Joan Mitchell: 113t; © Henry Moore Foundation 1993: 193br. Reproduced by kind permission of the Henry Moore Foundation; Courtesy of the Maison Victor Hugo, Ville de Paris: 99cl; Musée Carnavalet: 216br; Musée de L'Orangerie: 133bl; Musée du Louvre: 125br, 128c; Musée de La Poupée 116tl; Musée National des Châteaux de Malmaison et Bois-Préau: 248cr; Musée Marmottan: 60c, 60cb, 61c; Musée de la Mode et du Costume Palais Galliera: 59br; Musée de Montmartre, Paris: 225t; Musée des Monuments Français: 201tc, 202cr; Musée National de la Légion d'Honneur: 34bc, 145bl; Courtesy of Musée National du Moyen-Age Thermes de Cluny 154 -7; Musée de la Ville de Paris: Musée du Petit Palais: 56cl, 209crb; Courtesy of the Musée du Vin, Paris 203bc.

The Publishers are grateful to the following individuals, companies and picture libraries for permission to reproduce their photographs:

Les Abeilles: 276br; **Académie de la Grande Chaumiére:** 179tc; **Aeroports De Paris:** 369tc; **Agence Républic:** 374bc, 374br; **Alain Ducasse Entreprise:** 297tl, Matt Aletti 303tl, C. Sarramon 290cra; **Alamy:** Martin Bache 214; Tibor Bognar 117tr; Christel Broque 203cra; Bertrand Collet 273cl; CW Images 355tc; Directphoto.org 299tl, 364tl; Garden Photo World 296br; Franck Guizou/hemis.fr 103bc; Glenn Harper 216tr, 354cr; Hemis 81cr, 307t, 354bl; hemis.fr / Jean-Claude Amiel 288cl, 302bc; hemis.fr / René Mattes 92; Louise Heusinkveld 193tl; Image State 274br; Brian Jannsen 116br; John Kellerman 136; Lautaro 83cr; A la Poste 367c; GA Rousseau 221br; RosalreneBetancourt 6 353tr Sylvain Sonnet/ hemis.fr 105cr; Jack Sullivan 363cla; Travel Pictures 222; Justin Kase Zfivez 363tl; worldimages 300tl; **Allsport UK:** Sean Botterill 43bl; **The Ancient Art and Architecture Collection:** 24clb.

Banque de France: 135t; Bateaux Parisiens: 74crb; **Brasserie Bofinger:** 290tl; **Gérard Boullay:** 84tr, 84bl, 84br, 85 all; **Bridgeman Art Library, London:** 23br, 24cr, 25cl, 32cr–33cl, (detail) 37br; British Library, London (detail) 20br, (detail) 25bl, B N, Paris 21bl, (detail) 25tr, (detail) 25cr; Château de Versailles, France 21ftr, 21bc, (detail) 21br, (detail) 32br, (detail) 155b; Christie's, London (detail) 26cb, 36cla, 46cla; Delomosne, London 34clb; Giraudon 18, 27cra, (detail) 28bl, (detail) 28clb, (detail) 29br, (detail) 32bl, (detail) 32cla, (detail) 33bl, 35cb, 60br, (detail) 62bl, 62cra, 62cb; Lauros– Giraudon 25tc; Louvre, Paris 27cb, 58b, 62br, 63clb, 63tl; Roy Miles Gallery 29tr; Musée de L'Armée, Paris (detail) 83bc; Musée Condé, Chantilly (detail) 4tr, 20bl, 21tc, (detail) 21tr, (detail) 21cb, (detail) 28bc; Musée Crozatier, Le Puy en Velay, France (detail) 27bl; Musée Gustave Moreau, Paris 58tr, 235bc; Musee National d'Art Moderne, Centre Pompidou, Paris 111ca; National Gallery (detail) 31tl, (detail) 46bl, Musée de la Ville de Paris, Musée Carnavalet (detail) 33br, (detail) 33tr, 33crb, 97cb. CineAqua: 202bl. Collection Painton Cowen 42cl; Palais du Tokyo, Paris 61b; Temples Newsham House, Leeds 27cr; Uffizi Gallery, Florence (detail) 26br; **© British Museum:** 32ca.

Cité des Sciences et de l'Industrie: EPPDCSI P. Sorin - A. Robin 241crb; Sophie Chivet 241bc; NASA/ESA 240bc; Sylvain Sonnet 240ca; **Cliché Photothèque des Musées de la Ville de Paris - © DACS 2011:** 23ca, 23crb, 30cr–31cl, 97tl; **Collections du Mobilier National-Cliché du Mobilier National:** 169br; **Corbis:** The Art Archive/Alfredo Dagli Ort 8–9; Bettmann 243tl; Godong / Fred de Noyelle 235tc/ robertharding 245b; Jose Fuste Raga 368bl; Hemis/René Mattes 298bl; Hemis/ Arnaud Chicurel 246t, 247bl,/ Sylvain Sonnet 150, 304br; JAI/David Bank 291bl; Jasper Juinen 65cra; Ray Juno 10bl; Richard List 11cl; Robert Harding World Imagery/Richard Nebesky 198; Ocean 12tl, Christine Osborne 12cr; Sylvain Saustier 272b; **Tom Craig:** 275tr, 277tl, 277br. **Les Degrés de Notre-Dame:** 280cr; **Disneyland ® Paris:** 256tr, 257bl, 257cr, 318t, 354tl. The characters, architectural works and trademarks are the property of The Walt Disney Company. All rights reserved; **Dreamstime.com:** Andersastphoto 221tl; Aoo3771 98b; Michal Bednarek 72tc; Christian Bertrand 313bl; Dan Breckwoldt 45cr; Dennis Dolkens 106; Roberto Giovannini 206; Rostislav Glinsky 74cla; Ixuskmitl 248tr; Jdanne 236bl; Jianqing Gu 45clb; Jmffotos 16cl; Julia161 138tr; Aliaksandr Kazlou 228tl; Kemaltaner 219tc; Ladiras81 90b; Laraslk 76-7; James Mackenzie 118; Maisicon 132bl; Minacarson 315cr; Nightman1965 278–9; Anna Pakutina 248br; Photogolfer 217tl; Tatiana Savvateeva 73bl; Sborisov 68; Jozef Sedmak 44; Lee Snider 236tr; Nigel Spiers 230tl; Tupungato 162; VanderWolf Images 16bl; Lestouquoy Véronique 232; Vvoevale 94clb; Roman Zaremba 184; Adrian Zenz 87br.

Espace Montmartre: 224cb; Eurolines: 371crb; **Mary Evans Picture Library:** 40bl, 89tl, 143cl, 197crb, 213b, 227tl, 181bc, 253t, 254bl, 380tr.
Four Seasons Hotel George V: 281bl; Michelle Arness Frederic: 378cl.
Getty Images: AFP/Pierre Verdy 108clb; Fred Dufour 194clb; Boris Horvat 180; Miguel Medina 294tr; Craig Pershouse 156tl; FilmMagic/Marc Piasecki 301br; Gamma-Rapho/ Maurice ROUGEMONT 300tr, 305br; Yvan Travert 83tl;

Giraudon: (detail) 24bl, (detail) 25crb; Lauros–Giraudon (detail) 35bl; Sami Sarkis 13br; **Le Grand Véfour:** 289tr, 299br.

Roland Halbe: 194tr; La Halle Saint Pierre 229bc;

Robert Harding Picture Library: 24br, 31ca, 31br, 38cla, 43tl, 67br, 243br, 373cr; B M 29cra; B N 193tr, 212bc; Biblioteco Reale, Turin 127t; Bulloz 212cb; P Craven 372b; Stuart Dee 170; Directphoto 356-7; Neil Emmerson 78; R Francis 82br; H Josse 212br; Musée National des Châteaux de Malmaison et Bois-Préau 35tc; Musée de Versailles 28cl; P Tetrel 253crb; Explorer 14bl; F. Chazot 333b; Girard 67cr; P Gleizes 64bl; J Moatti 340bl, 332c, 332bl; Roy Rainford 2-3; Walter Rawlings 45bc; A Wolf 123br, 123tl; **Alison Harris:** Le Village Royale 134tl; **Hôtel d'Aubusson:** 280bl; **Hotel Le Bristol/Oetker Collection:** Eric Deniset 285tr; **Hôtel Duc de Saint Simon:** 286tl; **Hotel Caron De Beaumarchais:** 284bc; **Hotel Lancaster/PRCo France:** 281tr; **Hotels Paris Rive Gauche/Hôtel des Grands Hommes:** 280br; **Hulton Getty:** 101cr, 183tc, ; Charles Hewitt 42clb; Lancaster 183tc.

© IGN Paris 1990 Authorisation N° 90–2067: 15b; **Institut du Monde Arabe:** Georges Fessey 167tl.

The Kobal Collection: 142b; Columbia Pictures 183br; Société Générale de Films 40ca.

Leonardo Media Ltd.: 281tl. **Magnum:** Bruno Barbey 66b; **Le Meurice:** Peter Hebeisen 280tl; **Ministère de L'Economie et des Finances:** 365c; **Ministère de L'Intérieur SGAP de Paris:** 362b; **© photo Musée de L'Armée, Paris:** 189cr; **Musée des Arts Décoratifs, Paris:** L Sully Jaulmes 56t, Cabinet (1922-1923) Jacques-Emile Ruhlmann 59tr; **Musée Cantonal des Beaux-Arts, Lausanne:** 117br; **Musée Carnavalet:** Dac Karin Maucotel 96tr; **Musée D'Orsay:** Jim Purcell 147crb; **Musée Grevin:** Stanislas Liban 355bl; **Musée National de L'Histoire Naturelle:** D Serrette 169cl; **© Musée de L'Homme, Paris:** D Ponsard 203c; **© Photo Musée de la Marine, Paris:** 34bl, 200cl; **Musée National d'Art Moderne – Centre Georges Pompidou, Paris:** 63tr, 110br, 110bl, 111t, 111crb, 112cla, 112bl, 112br, 113t, 113c, 113bl, 113br; **Musée des Plans-Reliefs, Paris:** 190cra; **Musée du Quai Branly:** 194cla, 195cb, 195br; Patrick Gries/Bruno Descoings 56cb, 194br.

The Odéon-Théâtre de L'Europe: 333t.

Paris Convention & Visitors Bureau: Marc Bertrand 224br, 375bl; Fabian Charaffi 367bc; Amélie Dupont 57tr,164cl, 315bl, 374ca; David Lefranc 358br, 360bl; Alain Potigon 361c, 366crb; **© Paris Tourist Office:** Catherine Balet 274cla; David Lefranc 272c, 273t, 273br, 274tr, 275cr, 276cl, 276cb; **Paris Vision & Cityrama:** 375ca; Le Petit Moulin/ MangoPR 287br; **Photolibrary:** F1 Online/Widmann Widmann 364c; Photononstop/Jean-Marc Romain 363cl;

Philharmonie de Paris: by the architect Jean Nouvel 239b; **Philippe Perdereau:** 135b; Le Pre Verre: 288cr; **PunchStock:** Thinkstock/Ron Chapple 82cla. **Qui Plume La Lune/ PimliCom:** 290bc.

Paul Raferty: 244bl; **Rapho: R Doisneau:** 145tl.RATP: 374crb, 377ca, 377cb, 379cr; Redferns: W Gottlieb 40cb; **© Photo Réunion des Musées Nationaux:** Grand Trianon 28crb; Musée Guimet 204cr; Musée du Louvre 29cb, (detail) 34cr–35cl, 57tl, 124t, 124bl, 125t, 125c, 126cl, 126bl, 126br, 127b, 128tr, 128br, 129tr, 129cl; Musée Picasso 57cr, 100t, 100cra, 100cl, 100clb, 100br, 101bl, 101crb, 101t; **Restaurant de La Tour d'Argent:** 305tl; **Roger-Viollet:** (detail) 26clb, (detail) 41bl, (detail) 196c, (detail) 213tl; **Philippe Ruault:** Fondation Cartier 31bc; **Photo Scala, Florence:** Musée du Quai Branly/Patrick Gries/Valérie Torre 195tl, 195cr; **Sipapress:** 228c; **SNCF – Service Presse Voyages France Europe:** 5tl, 380bl; CAV/Christophe Recoura 370b; CAV/Jean-Marc Fabbro 370tc; /French railways 368cra; **Frank Spooner Pictures:** F Reglain 66cra; P Renault 66cr; **SuperStock:** Hemis.fr 13ca, 115t; Nordic Photos 258, Photononstop 176; **Sygma:** 37crb, 242c; Keystone 42br, 243cra; Keler 43crb; J Van Hasselt 43tr; P. Habans 64cra; P Vauthey 67bl; Y Forestier 188tr; Sunset Blvd 243bc.

Tallandier: 27bc, 27tl, 30cl, 30clb, 30bl, 31bl, 33cr, 33tl, 34cb, 34br, 40cla, 41ca, 41br, 54cla; B N 30br, 34crb, 40bc; Brigaud 41crb; Brimeur 36bl; Charmet 38clb; Dubout 19b, 26ca, 28br, 32cb, 35crb, 35tr, 36br, 37bl, 38cb, 38bl, 38br, 39bl, 39br, 39cb, 39tl, 40br; Josse 22 all, 23tl, 38bc; Joubert 40clb; Tildier 39ca; Vigne 36clb; **Tourisme & Handicaps:** 360tr; Le Train Bleu: 291t.

Vedettes de Paris: 74clb; **Agence Vu:** Didier Lefèvre 332cr.

Front Endpaper

Alamy Images: BonkersAboutTravel Rbr, hemis.fr/René Mattes Rcrb, John Kellerman Lbc, Iain Masterton Rcra, Travel Pictures Rtr; **Corbis:** Hemis/Sylvain Sonnet Rbc, Robert Harding World Imagery/Richard Nebesky Lfclb, Sygma/ Bernard Annebicque Rfbr, Sygma/Nathalie Darbellay Rtc; **Dreamstime.com:** James Mackenzie Lclb, Tomas Marek Ltr, Roman Zaremba Lbl; **SuperStock:** Hemis.fr Rbl, Photononstop Lbr; Back endpaper: RATP CML Agence Cartographique.

Map Cover

Getty Images: Pawel Libera

Cover

Front, Main and Spine t – **Getty Images:** Pawel Libera

Special Editions of DK Travel Guides

DK Travel Guides can be purchased in bulk quantities at discounted prices for use in promotions or as premiums. We are also able to offer special editions and personalized jackets, corporate imprints, and excerpts from all of our books, tailored specifically to meet your own needs.

To find out more, please contact:

in the United States **specialsales@dk.com**

in the UK **travelguides@uk.dk.com**

in Canada DK Special Sales at **specialmarkets@ dk.com**

in Australia **penguincorporatesales@ penguinrandomhouse.com.au**

Phrase Book

In Emergency

Help!	**Au secours!**	*oh sekoor*
Stop!	**Arrêtez!**	*aret-ay*
Call a doctor!	**Appelez un médecin!**	*apuh-lay uñ medsañ*
Call an ambulance!	**Appelez une ambulance!**	*apuh-lay oon oñboo-loñs*
Call the police!	**Appelez la police!**	*apuh-lay lah poh-lees*
Call the fire department!	**Appelez les pompiers!**	*apuh-lay leh poñ-peevay*
Where is the nearest telephone?	**Où est le téléphone le plus proche?**	*oo ay luh tehlehfon luh ploo prosh*
Where is the nearest hospital?	**Où est l'hôpital le plus proche?**	*oo ay lopeetal luh ploo prosh*

Communication Essentials

Yes	**Oui**	*wee*
No	**Non**	*noñ*
Please	**S'il vous plaît**	*seel voo play*
Thank you	**Merci**	*mer-see*
Excuse me	**Excusez-moi**	*exkoo-zay mwah*
Hello	**Bonjour**	*boñzhoor*
Goodbye	**Au revoir**	*oh ruh-vwar*
Good night	**Bonsoir**	*boñ-swar*
Morning	**Le matin**	*matañ*
Afternoon	**L'après-midi**	*l'apreh-meedee*
Evening	**Le soir**	*swar*
Yesterday	**Hier**	*eeyehr*
Today	**Aujourd'hui**	*oh-zhoor-dwee*
Tomorrow	**Demain**	*duhmañ*
Here	**Ici**	*ee-see*
There	**Là**	*lah*
What?	**Quoi, quel, quelle?**	*kwah, kel, kel*
When?	**Quand?**	*koñ*
Why?	**Pourquoi?**	*poor-kwah*
Where?	**Où?**	*oo*

Useful Phrases

How are you?	**Comment allez-vous?**	*kom-moñ talay voo*
Very well, thank you.	**Très bien, merci.**	*treh byañ, mer-see*
Pleased to meet you.	**Enchanté de faire votre connaissance.**	*oñshoñ-tay duh fehr votr kon-ay-sans*
See you soon.	**A bientôt.**	*byañ-toh*
That's fine	**C'est bon**	*say bon*
Where is/are...?	**Où est/sont...?**	*ooay/soñ*
How far is it to...?	**Combien de kilometres d'ici à...?**	*kom-byañ duh keelo-metr d'ee-see ah*
Which way to...?	**Quelle est la direction pour...?**	*kel ay lah deer-ek-syoñ poor*
Do you speak English?	**Parlez-vous anglais?**	*par-lay voo oñg-lay*
I don't understand.	**Je ne comprends pas.**	*zhuh nuh kom-proñ pah*
Could you speak slowly please?	**Pouvez-vous parler moins vite s'il vous plaît?**	*poo-vay voo par-lay mwañ veet seel voo play*
I'm sorry.	**Excusez-moi.**	*exkoo-zay mwah*

Useful Words

big	**grand**	*groñ*
small	**petit**	*puh-tee*
hot	**chaud**	*show*
cold	**froid**	*frwah*
good	**bon/bien**	*boñ/byañ*
bad	**mauvais**	*moh-veh*
enough	**assez**	*assay*
well	**bien**	*byañ*
open	**ouvert**	*oo-ver*
closed	**fermé**	*fer-meh*
left	**gauche**	*gohsh*
right	**droite**	*drwaht*
straight ahead	**tout droite**	*too drwaht*
near	**près**	*preh*
far	**loin**	*lwañ*
up	**en haut**	*oñ oh*
down	**en bas**	*oñ bah*
early	**de bonne heure**	*duh bon urr*
late	**en retard**	*oñ ruh-tar*
entrance	**l'entrée**	*l'on-tray*
exit	**la sortie**	*sor-tee*
restroom	**les toilettes, le WC**	*twah-let, vay-see*
free, unoccupied	**libre**	*leebr*
free, no charge	**gratuit**	*grah-twee*

Making a Telephone Call

I'd like to make a long-distance call.	**Je voudrais faire un appel á l'étranger.**	*zhuh voo-dreh fehr uñ apel a laytroñ-zhay*
I'd like to make a collect call.	**Je voudrais faire une communication en PCV.**	*zhuh voo-dreh fehr oon komoonikah-syoñ oñ peh-seh-veh*
I'll try again later.	**Je rappelerai plus tard.**	*zhuh rapel-eray ploo tar*
Can I leave a message?	**Est-ce que je peux laisser un message?**	*es-keh zhuh puh leh-say uñ mehsazh*
Hold on.	**Ne quittez pas, s'il vous plaît.**	*nuh kee-tay pah seel voo play*
Could you speak up a little, please?	**Pouvez-vous parler un peu plus fort?**	*poo-vay voo par-lay uñ puh ploo for*
local call	**la communication locale**	*komoonikah-syoñ low-kal*

Shopping

How much does this cost?	**C'est combien s'il vous plaît?**	*say kom-byañ seel voo play*
I would like ...	**Je voudrais...**	*zhuh voo-dray*
Do you have?	**Est-ce que vous avez**	*es-kuh voo zavay*
I'm just looking.	**Je regarde seulement.**	*zhuh ruhgar. suhlmoñ*
Do you take credit cards?	**Est-ce que vous acceptez les cartes de crédit?**	*es-kuh voo zaksept-ay leh kart duh kreh-dee*
Do you take traveler's checks?	**Est-ce que vous acceptez les cheques de voyages?**	*es-kuh voo zaksept-ay leh shek duh vwayazh*
What time do you open?	**A quelle heure vous êtes ouvert?**	*ah kel urr voo zet oo-ver*
What time do you close?	**A quelle heure vous êtes fermé?**	*ah kel urr voo zet fer-may*
This one.	**Celui-ci**	*suhl-wee-see*
That one.	**Celui-là**	*suhl-wee-lah*
expensive	**cher**	*shehr*
cheap	**pas cher, bon marché**	*pah shehr, boñ mar-shay*
size, clothes	**la taille**	*tye*
size, shoes	**la pointure**	*pwañ-tur*
white	**blanc**	*bloñ*
black	**noir**	*nwahr*
red	**rouge**	*roozh*
yellow	**jaune**	*zhohwn*
green	**vert**	*vehr*
blue	**bleu**	*bluh*

Types of Shops

antiques shop	**le magasin d'antiquités**	*maga-zañ d'oñteekee-tay*
bakery	**la boulangerie**	*booloñ-zhuree*
bank	**la banque**	*boñk*
bookstore	**la librairie**	*lee-brehree*
butcher store	**la boucherie**	*boo-shehree*
cake store	**la pâtisserie**	*patee-sree*
cheese store	**la fromagerie**	*fromazh-ree*
dairy	**la crémerie**	*krem-ree*
department store	**le grand magasin**	*groñ maga-zañ*
delicatessen	**la charcuterie**	*sharkoot-ree*
drugstore	**la pharmacie**	*farmah-see*
fishmonger	**la poissonnerie**	*pwasson-ree*
gift shop	**le magasin de cadeaux**	*maga-zañ duh kadoh*
greengrocer	**le marchand de légumes**	*mar-shoñ duh lay-goom*
grocery	**l'alimentation**	*alee-moñta-syoñ*
hair salon	**le coiffeur**	*kwafuhr*
market	**le marché**	*marsh-ay*
newsstand	**le magasin de journaux**	*maga-zañ duh zhoor-no*
post office	**la poste, le bureau de poste, le PTT**	*pohst, booroh duh pohst, peh-teh-teh*
shoe store	**le magasin de chaussures**	*maga-zañ duh show-soor*
supermarket	**le supermarché**	*soo pehr-marshay*
tobacconist	**le tabac**	*tabah*
travel agent	**l'agence de voyages**	*l'azhoñs duh vwayazh*

Sightseeing

abbey	**l'abbaye**	*l'abay-ee*
art gallery	**la galerie d'art**	*galer-ree dart*
bus station	**la gare routière**	*gahr roo-tee-yehr*

cathedral	la cathédrale	katay-dral
church	l'église	l'aygleez
garden	le jardin	zhar-dañ
library	la bibliothèque	beebleeo-tek
museum	le musée	moo-zay
tourist information office	les renseignements touristiques, le syndicat d'initiative	roñsayn-moñ toorees-teek, sandee-ka d'eenee-syateev
town hall	l'hôtel de ville	l'ohtel duh veel
train station	la gare (SNCF)	gahr (es-en-say-ef)
closed for public holiday	fermeture jour férié	fehrmeh-tur zhoor fehree-ay

Staying in a Hotel

Do you have a vacant room?	Est-ce que vous avez une chambre?	es-kuh voo-zavay oon shambr
double room, with double bed	la chambre à deux personnes, avec un grand lit	shambr ah duh pehr-son avek un gronñ lee
twin room	la chambre à deux lits	shambr ah. dûh lee
single room	la chambre à une personne	shambr ah oon pehr-son
room with a bath, shower	la chambre avec salle de bains, une douche	shambr avek sal duh bañ, oon doosh
porter, bell hop	le garçon	gar-soñ
key	la clef	klay
I have a reservation.	J'ai fait une réservation.	zhay fay oon rayzehrva-syoñ

Eating Out

Do you have a table?	Avez-vous une table de libre?	avay-voo oon tahbl duh leebr
I want to reserve a table.	Je voudrais réserver une table.	zhuh voo-dray rayzehr-vay oon tahbl
The check, please.	L'addition s'il vous plaît.	l'adee-syoñ seel voo play
I am a vegetarian.	Je suis végétarien.	zhuh swee vezhay-tehryañ
waitress/ waiter	Madame, Mademoiselle/ Monsieur	mah-dam, mah-demwahzel/ muh-syuh
menu	le menu, la carte	men-oo, kart
fixed-price menu	le menu à prix fixe	men-oo ah pree feeks
cover charge	le couvert	koo-vehr
wine list	la carte des vins	kart-deh vañ
glass	le verre	vehr
bottle	la bouteille	boo-tay
knife	le couteau	koo-toh
fork	la fourchette	for-shet
spoon	la cuillère	kwee-yehr
breakfast	le petit déjeuner	puh-tee deh-zhuh-nay
lunch	le déjeuner	deh-zhuh-nay
dinner	le dîner	dee-nay
entrée	le plat principal	plah prañsee-pal
appetizer, first course	l'entrée, le hors d'oeuvre	l'oñ-tray, or-duhvr
dish of the day	le plat du jour	plah doo zhoor
wine bar	le bar à vin	bar ah vañ
café	le café	ka-fay
rare	saignant	say-noñ
medium	à point	ah pwañ
well done	bien cuit	byañ kwee

Menu Decoder

apple	la pomme	pom
baked	cuit au four	kweet oh foor
banana	la banane	banan
beef	le boeuf	buhf
beer, draft beer	la bière, bière à la pression	bee-yehr, bee-yehr ah lah pres-syoñ
boiled	bouilli	boo-yee
bread	le pain	pan
butter	le beurre	burr
cake	le gâteau	gah-toh
cheese	le fromage	from-azh
chicken	le poulet	poo-lay
chocolate	le chocolat	shoko-lah
cocktail	le cocktail	cocktail
coffee	le café	kah-fay
dessert	le dessert	deh-ser
dry	sec	sek
duck	le canard	kanar
egg	l'oeuf	l'uf
fish	le poisson	pwah-ssoñ

fresh fruit	le fruit frais	frwee freh
fries	les frites	freet
garlic	l'ail	l'eye
grilled	grillé	gree-yay
ham	le jambon	zhoñ-boñ
ice, ice cream	la glace	glas
lamb	l'agneau	l'anyoh
lemon	le citron	see-troñ
lobster	le homard	omahr
meat	la viande	vee-yand
milk	le lait	leh
mineral water	l'eau minérale	l'oh meeney-ral
mustard	la moutarde	moo-tard
oil	l'huile	l'weel
olives	les olives	leh zoleev
onions	les oignons	leh zonyoñ
orange	l'orange	l'oroñzh
fresh orange juice	l'orange pressée	l'oroñzh press-eh
fresh lemon juice	le citron pressé	see-troñ press-eh
pepper	le poivre	pwavr
poached	poché	posh-ay
pork	le porc	por
potatoes	les pommes de terre	pom-duh tehr
rice	le riz	ree
roast	rôti	row-tee
roll	le petit pain	puh-tee pañ
salt	le sel	sel
sauce	la sauce	sohs
sausage, fresh	la saucisse	sohsees
seafood	les fruits de mer	frwee duh mer
shellfish	les crustaces	kroos-tas
shrimp	les crevettes	kruh-vet
snails	les escargots	leh zes-kar-goh
soup	la soupe, le potage	soop, poh-tazh
steak	le bifteck, le steack	beef-tek, stek
sugar	le sucre	sookr
tea	le thé	tay
toast	pain grillé	pan greeyay
vegetables	les légumes	lay-goom
vinegar	le vinaigre	veenaygr
water	l'eau	l'oh
red wine	le vin rouge	vañ roozh
white wine	le vin blanc	vañ bloñ

Numbers

0	zéro	zeh-roh
1	un, une	uñ, oon
2	deux	duh
3	trois	trwah
4	quatre	katr
5	cinq	sañk
6	six	sees
7	sept	set
8	huit	weet
9	neuf	nerf
10	dix	dees
11	onze	oñz
12	douze	dooz
13	treize	trehz
14	quatorze	katorz
15	quinze	kañz
16	seize	sehz
17	dix-sept	dees-set
18	dix-huit	dees-weet
19	dix-neuf	dees-nerf
20	vingt	vañ
30	trente	tront
40	quarante	karoñt
50	cinquante	sañkoñt
60	soixante	swasoñt
70	soixante-dix	swasoñt-dees
80	quatre-vingts	katr-vañ
90	quatre-vingt-dix	katr-vañ-dees
100	cent	soñ
1,000	mille	meel

Time

one minute	une minute	oon mee-noot
one hour	une heure	oon urr
half an hour	une demi-heure	oon duh-mee urr
Monday	lundi	luñ-dee
Tuesday	mardi	mar-dee
Wednesday	mercredi	mehrkruh-dee
Thursday	jeudi	zhuh-dee
Friday	vendredi	voñdruh-dee
Saturday	samedi	sam-dee
Sunday	dimanche	dee-moñsh

Paris Metro and Regional Express Railway (RER)